A

M/

SLEEP-TALKING:
Psychology and Psychophysiology

SLEEP-TALKING:
Psychology and Psychophysiology

ARTHUR M. ARKIN, M. D.
Department of Psychology
City College of the City
University of New York

Department of Psychiatry
Mt. Sinai School of Medicine,
New York

LEA LAWRENCE ERLBAUM ASSOCIATES, PUBLISHERS
1981   Hillsdale, New Jersey

Lawrence Erlbaum Associates, Inc., Publishers
365 Broadway
Hillsdale, New Jersey 07642

Library of Congress Cataloging in Publication Data

Arkin, Arthur M.
  Sleep-talking.

  Bibliography: p.
  Includes indexes.
  1. Sleeptalking.   I. Title.   [DNLM: 1. Sleep dis-
orders. 2. Sleep disorders—Psychology. 3. Speech.
WM 188 A721s]
BF1073.S58A74   154.6   81-3300
ISBN 0-89859-031-0   AACR2

Printed in the United States of America

Contents

Foreword

This book contains, to the best of my knowledge, virtually everything that is publicly known about sleep-talking, with the greatest amount and most important of this information coming from the author's own research. The work is thorough, careful, and thoughtful. It is that rare product that says just about all that can be said on a subject. In short, it is now the "authoritative work" on sleep talking, and it is likely to remain such for many years.

To all of this, one impulsive response might be a resounding "So what?". To the potential reader who has seen man leave his planet for the first time and who is bombarded daily with claims of unsurpassed excellence, the announcement of "the authoritative work on sleep-talking" could produce visions of "sleep reading." Afterall, as the data of this book show, sleep talking does not occur very frequently; it rarely reveals the sleeper's deepest secrets, and it has not received very much clinical or theoretical attention. Is the book much ado about an insignificant anomaly that is useful mostly for newpaper fillers on oddities or for cocktail party chatter? Our answer is a resounding "No."

It turns out that the core of both popular and scientific interest in sleep talking is that it happens when "it isn't supposed to," or, more pedantically; it is a behavior which occurs during sleep although it involves a complexity of psychomotor coordination which is almost excluded from sleep by definition. Sleep and the absence of complex psychomotor activity have become *disassociated*. It is in the nature of disassociations that they are anomalies. However, fine minds have always been drawn to disassociations. They are exceptions to the rule which demand a better rule. They are invitations to elevate generalizations to higher or more accurate levels. It is with this kind of broad perspective that Dr. Arkin deals with sleep-talking. His main interest is not in how quaint, comical, revealing, or unusual sleep utterances may be. He is interested in how our concepts of sleep, speech, and psychophysiological integration may account for the phenomena of sleep-talking and how they may have to change to do so. The challenge to sleep scientists is to explain the differential effects of sleep on motor activity, cognition, memory, and perception which make it possible for them to function at different times, in different ways, and in different combinations. Obviously, sleep is not a simple matter of all our faculties declining in unison. For psychology and psycholinguistics, the challenge is to evaluate how the generalizations based on the data of wakefulness square with the data of sleep talking. Which generalizations are applicable to all language, and which reflect the unique contribution of the waking brain?

Dr. Arkin would be the last to claim final answers to such questions. He is too true to his phenomenon to permit its violation by speculative excess or other inaccuracies. However, he has used every reasonable perspective in pursuit of the answers. He has appealed to the data and concepts of psychology, psychiatry, neurology, neurophysiology, psycholinguistics, and others for keys to understanding. The other side of that coin is that the phenomena of sleep-talking may have insights to offer each of these fields. Until now, anyone interested in sleep-talking had no single place to turn for comprehensive data, review, and conceptual analyses. Now we have this fine book.

Allan Rechtschaffen, Ph.D
Professor
Psychiatry and Behavioral Science
Director, Sleep Laboratory
University of Chicago

Preface

Sleep-talking is a fascinating and enigmatic phenomenon. It has intrigued ancient and modern observers alike and has become endowed with the cachet of the mysterious, the significant, the portentous, and sometimes of the comic. It has been mentioned by physicians, psychiatrists, psychologists, philosophers, writers of fiction, and everyday people.

As described in detail later, spontaneous sleep-talking is much more widespread than has been hitherto realized, and it is now capable of experimental stimulation and modification in the laboratory. Such availability of subject-produced signals closely associated with ongoing sleep and laden with psychological, linguistic, and affective content clearly indicates that detailed study of sleep-talking possesses important potential for new areas of research in sleep mentation, sleep psychophysiology, cognitive and clinical psychology, psycholinguistics, and neuropsychology.

Such assertions do not seem unreasonable. Yet, interestingly, sleep-talking has never received systematic treatment in the scientific literature. Accordingly, this book is the first scholarly, comprehensive treatise dealing with sleep-talking and related phenomena.

The reader will possess in one volume (1) a detailed description of all known laboratory studies and findings on spontaneous and experimentally produced sleep-speech; (2) all known clinical reports and anecdotal observations on sleep-utterance made by intelligent, conscientious individuals; (3) review essays concerning psychoanalytic and cognitive psychological perspectives on sleep-utterance; (4) comprehensive presentations of clinical psychiatric aspects of sleep-utterance including possible therapeutic uses (an area in its barest infancy); and (5) a unique extended appendix 2 that reproduces verbatim *all* sleep-speeches (approximately 600) ever recorded in the several laboratories in which studies were carried out.[1] In addition, in all but a small proportion, for each sleep-speech so reproduced, the reader is supplied with the sleep-stage with which it was associated, and information specifying whether it was uttered less than 3 hours after sleep-onset. Finally, in close to 200 instances, the verbatim contents of mentation reports, elicited from subjects awakened shortly after each utterance, are reproduced. This appendix may be extremely useful, therefore, as raw data on which the reader may carry out systematic study in whatever manner he deems useful.

This book is intended primarily for scholars and scientists working in the field of sleep-mentation, but it should be of equal interest to psychophysiologists, cognitive and clinical psychologists, psychiatrists, neuroscientists, psycholinguists, and philosophers concerned with mind–brain relationships. In addition, the intelligent lay public appears to have a lively interest in the subject.

It is my hope that readers will be encouraged to carry forward with new research in sleep utterance.

As shown in this book, experimental techniques are now available capable of significantly influencing or provoking sleep-speech. New techniques should certainly be possible to develop. I believe that our knowledge of sleep-cognition and sleep-psycholinguistics could be greatly enhanced by a systematic multivariate study of the following categories of data collected concomitantly:

1. Specific experimental sleep-utterance-provoking stimuli and techniques applied prior to and/or during various sleep stages and times of night.
2. Specific content and patterns of the sleep-utterances themselves.
3. Specific content and patterns of mentation reports elicited upon awakening subjects immediately after sleep-speeches.
4. Specific content and patterns of an array of free associations elicited after the completion of each such mentation report.
5. Psychological evaluation by clinical tests and interviews of the subjects employed (both chronic, spontaneous sleep-talkers and those without a history of sleep-talking).
6. Psychophysiological indices.

Arthur M. Arkin, M.D.

---

[1] In a sense, this appendix is, therefore, the result of a cooperative effort made possible by the generosity of the various investigators cited.

ACKNOWLEDGMENTS

My deep thanks to Jane Woolman, Phyllis Gross, Agnes Salinger, Gerry Levin, and Bruna Ciceran for their indefatigable industry, patience, and good humor in the course of getting this book together—secretaries non pareil!

I am gratefully indebted to Irma Farrington for translations of scientific literature in German and French and to Robert Dempsey for the translation from the Russian of case material in Chapter 20. The author is deeply grateful to the entire library staff of the New York Academy of Medicine for their cheerful, patient assistance but especially wishes to thank Ada Gams, Denis Gaffney, Barbara Hull, and Cherl Silver for their help.

Finally, I wish to thank Ruth Anne Reinsel for her conscientious and creative proofreading, and Sondra Guideman and the entire staff of Lawrence Erlbaum Associates for their devoted and patient attention.

To my mother
Rose Taubenblatt Arkin Schwartz

1 Introduction

We must not act and speak like sleepers, for in our sleep too we act and speak.

The waking have one world in common, but the sleeping turn aside each into a world of his own.

—Heraclitus of Ephesus (500 B.C.)

A scientist told me that while lying beside her soundly sleeping husband, also a scientist, the following dialogue took place:

> *He:* Boy—do I have an idea!
> *She* (after a brief pause): What idea, dear—tell me about it.
> *He:* The workers in the east, and the workers in the west—they don't know about it.
> *She:* Tell me, honey—what is it?
> *He* (after a pregnant pause): Why should I tell *you?*

He had no recall of any of this when questioned by her after awakening. This was the first of many anecdotes related to me by conscientious, intelligent observers, anecdotes that kindled my interest in somniloquy (talking while asleep)—a phenomenon known and described by the ancients. Somniloquy is much more prevalent than people realize. Seemingly, out of the depths of sleep, fragments of verbal information bubble up to the surface. Might they be parts of an ongoing dream? A reflection of some inner, secret torment? Or meaningless linguistic detritus discharged by some unruly, rogue neurons? Can we learn anything from such occurrences having relevance and general significance for psychology?

1

The content of sleep-speech is as close as investigators can get at present to "hot-off-the-griddle," "eyewitness," or "brief bulletins" of the ongoing content of the mind while asleep, without interference from factors associated with attempts at wakeful retrospective recall. Such interference is the usual case in varying degree when sleeping subjects are awakened in the laboratory by an experimenter who asks them to relate what had been passing through their minds prior to the awakening signal. By contrast, if we regard any specific verbal output as an indicator of some feature or component of cognitive "structures" and processes, then sleep-speech may be considered to be *spontaneous, subject-emitted, direct* expressions or derivatives of ongoing mentation associated with sleep.[1] Surely, if we desire to understand dreaming, imagery, cognition, and language function during sleep, opportunities to glimpse the phenomena nearly "naked," or to eavesdrop on them, would be occasions *par excellence* for observation from a novel perspective.

In addition to the advantage of immediacy to the mental life of sleep, somniloquy possesses many important features by which researchers may acquire new knowledge of sleep psychology and psychophysiology. As we see later, evaluation of the degree of concordance between sleep-speech and associated wakeful mentation reports also provides material to study short-term memory function in sleep. Also, each utterance is susceptible to examination by whatever psycholinguistic measures and conceptualizations have proven useful elsewhere when applied to wakeful fragmentary outputs. Sleep-speech data may ultimately be found important for general psycholinguistic theory that has been developed thus far mostly on the basis of observations of language function during wakefulness. Our observations have enabled us to formulate and discuss sleep-utterance as manifestations of dissociated cognitive subsystems in accordance with Hilgard's Neo-Dissociationist Theory (Hilgard, 1973, 1977) and thus have extended this theory's investigative domain and validity. Attempts to experimentally stimulate somniloquy have not only yielded encouraging preliminary results but have provided additional data by which we can understand the phenomenon. Finally, on one or two rare occasions, sleep-talking has been used adjunctively in psychotherapy, and it is hoped that recounting them will encourage further utilization of such opportunities when available and appropriate.

To the best of my knowledge, there has been no previous attempt to treat somniloquy exhaustively in the published scientific literature. For this reason, I believe it worthwhile to provide not only a detailed account of contemporary research and observation relating to this topic but to review

---

[1]Mentation is not an easy word to rigorously define. It is used here in the widest possible sense to denote the set of all items in awareness, psychologically meaningful actual and potential behavior sequences that are not present in awareness (as well as their precursors), rudimentary constituents, and neuropsychological correlates.

older material as well. I have also included many published and unpublished anecdotal descriptions and beliefs, provided that I was convinced of the intelligence and integrity of the sources. Although some may consider this out of place in scientific writing, the most influential documents in the history of psychology are case histories and thoughtful essays, many of which may be considered a special sort of extended anecdotal writing. Anecdotal observations are frequently the stimulus to controlled research, and in view of the youth of our field, they are valuable to record in selective fashion. Inasmuch as phenomena observed under naturalistic conditions are often differently manifested under controlled laboratory conditions, anecdotal description may sometimes complement experimental observation.

I hope to include, under one cover, as much potentially valuable accumulated information on somniloquy as possible, because until now material has been available only in a scattered manner in scientific and scholarly writing. Where appropriate, each chapter is developed by initially reviewing whatever relevant historical, clinical, anecdotal, or systematic material I was able to find. This is then followed in each case by a detailed presentation of all laboratory work known to me dealing with sleep-talking and relevant selected findings from related areas, such as somnambulism and night terrors. Separate treatment is given to two topics: somniloquy in relation to psychoanalysis, and attempts to experimentally stimulate and influence sleep-talking. In a later section, I endeavor to conceptualize somniloquy in theoretical terms and explore areas of contact with cognitive psychology and psycholinguistics.

ORIENTING REMARKS
ON ELECTROGRAPHIC FEATURES
OF THE SLEEP CYCLE

For the sake of completeness, I have included a concise description of features of the sleep cycle. It has become standard laboratory procedure in sleep research to continually measure at least three electrographic parameters: the EEG, EOG, and chin EMG (Rechtschaffen & Kales, 1968).

The EEG is usually recorded from sites C3 or C4 as defined by the Ten Twenty Electrode System of the International Federation for Electroencephalography and Clinical Neurophysiology. The EOG is usually recorded from both eyes with electrodes applied to a site slightly lateral to and above the outer canthi. In both EEG and EOG, reference electrodes are attached to the contralateral and homolateral earlobe (or mastoid process) respectively. The EMG is recorded bilaterally from the muscle areas on and beneath the chin and it is often termed the mental or submental EMG.

We now continue with the essential features and changes registered by these electrographic indicators during the course of a night's sleep of "normal" young adults (see figures at end of section).

When the subject is lying quietly in a darkened bedroom immediately after receiving permission to go to sleep, the EEG is likely to show prolonged intervals of more or less sustained alpha rhythm (8–13 Hz; 25–100µv in amplitude), often with varying admixtures of low-voltage mixed frequencies (LVM); the EOG may contain REMs and eyelid blinks, and the tonic chin EMG is relatively high. This condition is termed Stage W.

Presently, as the subject becomes progressively drowsy, there is gradual fragmentation of the sustained epochs of alpha frequencies giving way to shorter intervals of alpha, interspersed with LVM, and finally more or less complete disappearance of alpha and replacement by LVM with 2–7 Hz activity prominent. Vertex sharp waves may appear. REMs and blinks disappear from the EOG and are replaced by slow rolling eye movements (SEMs) or minimal or no eye-movement activity. The tonic EMG is generally below that of the preceding Stage W. This condition is termed Stage 1 NREM or Sleep Onset Stage 1.

After 5–10 min of Stage 1 NREM elapse, sleep spindles and K complexes appear. The former consist of recurrent groups of sinusoidal waves 12–14 Hz in frequency and at least 0.5 sec in duration. The latter are biphasic EEG forms exceeding 0.5 sec with initial negative sharp wave and succeeding positive components. EOG activity is minimal or absent, and the EMG continues at a level lower than relaxed Stage W. Such an electrographic picture defines Stage 2.

After a varying interval, high-voltage, slow waves occur. These occupy a range in excess of 75 up to 200µV and are 2 Hz or less in frequency. At first they appear sporadically but gradually increase and come to dominate the EEG.

When such slow waves comprise 20–50% of the EEG, the sleep stage is termed Stage 3; and when in excess of 50%, it is termed Stage 4. The EOG and EMG continue more or less as before in both stages (sometimes called slow-wave sleep, or SWS, collectively). Stages 1 through 4 are also grouped as NREM or nonrapid eye-movement sleep.

Finally, sometime during the second hour of sleep, polygraphic changes occur that indicate the presence of REM sleep. The EEG consists of relatively low-voltage mixed frequencies with occasional bursts of lower-than-waking-frequency alpha and "saw-toothed" waves (averaging about 3 Hz). This configuration is correlated with intense central nervous system (CNS) activation. The EOG in striking contrast to NREM sleep, contains repeated clusters of one or more conjugate rapid eye movements. Finally, the EMG is at its lowest tonic level of the night. The latter corresponds to massive inhibition of muscular activity. Occasionally, brief episodes of increased EMG activity are interspersed with this general background.

These intervals of REM sleep are termed REM periods or REMP(s). The first REMP of the night is usually the shortest, tends to contain the smallest number of REMs, is occasionally omitted entirely, and compared to the subsequent REMPs of the night, is likely to be associated with less mentation and less dream-like mentation. REMPs may last from a few minutes to times well in excess of a half hour. REMPs reappear at intervals on the average of 90 min throughout the night. With the passage of time, they tend to become longer and the intervals between them shorter. Healthy young adults have 3–5 REMPs per night (7–8 hrs of sleep).

Following the termination of the REMP, Stage 1 NREM typically reappears briefly and is followed by Stage 2. In the first half of the night, Stages 3 and 4 succeed Stage 2 as before; but in the second half, slow-wave sleep is usually insignificant in amount.

The events from Sleep-Onset Stage 1 NREM to the end of the first REMP comprise the first sleep cycle; subsequent components of the sleep cycle are bounded by events from the end of one REMP to the end of the next, regardless of whether in the last half of the night slow-wave sleep occurs in between. Thus, the typical night of a healthy young adult is characterized by recurrent sleep cycles as described.

TABLE 1.1
Sleep-Cycle Stages

Stage W or wakefulness (see Figs. 1.1, 1.2)
    EEG: more or less sustained alpha activity, and/or LVM
    EOG: various amounts of REMs and blinks
    EMG: relatively high tonic level
Stage NREM
  Stage 1 (Fig. 1.2)
    EEG: LVM, vertex sharp waves
    EOG: SEMs or no EM activity
    EMG: lower than Stage W
  Stage 2 (Fig. 1.3)
    EEG: sleep spindles and K-complexes with a background of LVM
    EOG: absence of significant EM activity
    EMG: lower than Stage W
  Stage 3 (Fig. 1.4)
    EEG: moderate amounts of high amplitude, slow wave activity comprising
    20–50% of the epoch
    EOG: as in Stage 2
    EMG: as in Stage 2
  Stage 4 (Fig. 1.5)
    EEG: large amounts of high amplitude slow wave activity comprising
    more than 50% of the epoch
    EOG: as in Stage 2
    EMG: as in Stage 2
  Stage REM (Figs. 1.6, 1.7)
    EEG: LVM, saw-toothed waves, alpha bursts at slightly lower than Stage W
    frequency
    EOG: recurrent episodes of the conjugate REMs
    EMG: lowest tonic EMG of the night

The following series of tracings are all from the same night with a 25-year-old normal male college student as subject. The specimens were recorded on a Grass Model IV-C electroencephalograph. The paper speed was 15 mm per sec. The time constant for the EEG and EOG was 0.3 sec, and the calibration was 1 cm = 50 μV. The time constant for the EMG was 0.03 sec, and the calibration was 1 cm = 10 μV.

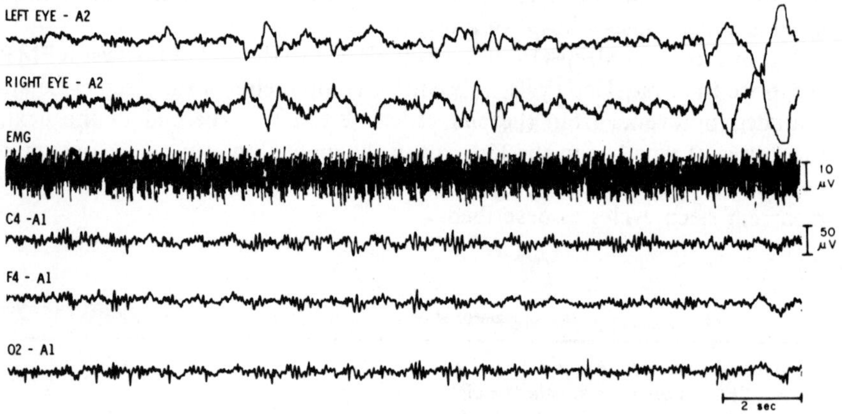

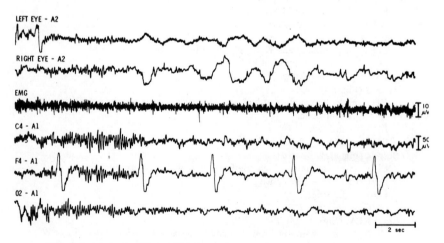

FIG. 1.1.   A tracing illustrating unambiguous stage W. Note high EMG, sustained alpha and REM [(from Rechtschaffen & Kales, 1968).]

FIG. 1.2.   A tracing illustrating the transition between Stage W and Stage 1 NREM. Note low-voltage activity replacing alpha, high EMG, and slow eye movements (from Rechtschaffen & Kales, 1968).

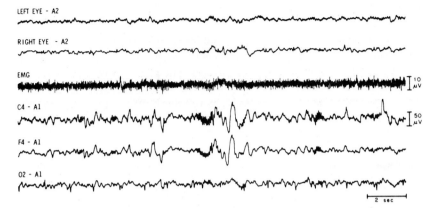

FIG. 1.3.   A tracing of unambiguous Stage 2. Note spindles and K-complexes (from Rechtschaffen & Kales, 1968).

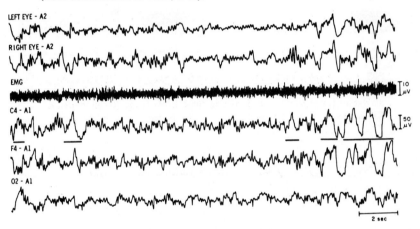

FIG. 1.4.   A tracing of Stage 3. Note approximately 28% high-amplitude slow-wave activity (from Rechtschaffen & Kales, 1968).

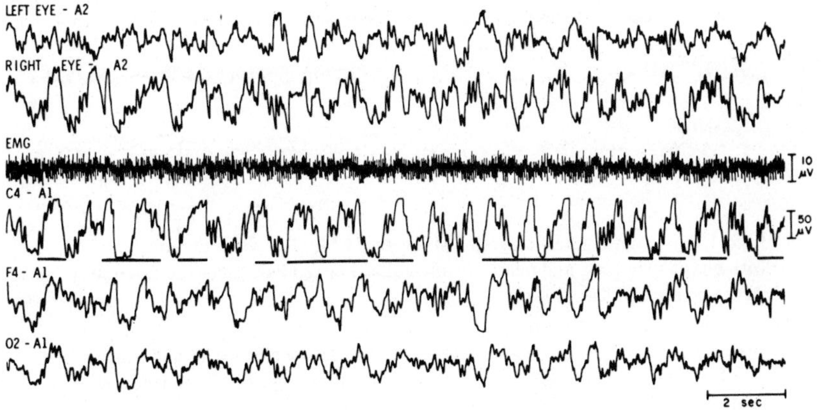

FIG. 1.5.   A tracing of unambiguous Stage 4. Note predominance of high-amplitude slow-wave activity (from Rechtschaffen & Kales, 1968).

7

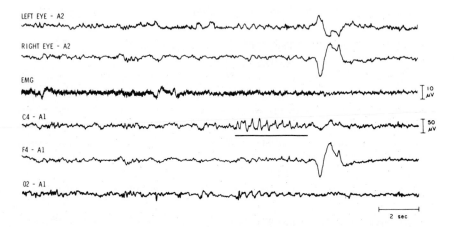

FIG. 1.6. A tracing illustrating transition from Stage 2 to Stage REM. Note REMs, relatively low-voltage mixed frequencies, saw-toothed waves in C4-A1 derivation (underlined), and decreased tonic EMG (from Rechtschaffen & Kales, 1968).

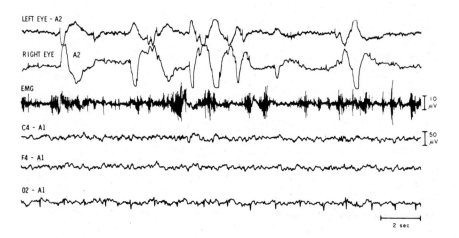

FIG. 1.7. Unambiguous stage REM. Note REMs, low-voltage tonic EMG with phasic twitching, and relatively low-voltage mixed EEG frequencies (from Rechtschaffen & Kales, 1968).

Readers are referred to Arkin, Antrobus, and Ellman (1978) for a comprehensive introduction to the psychology and psychophysiology of sleep mentation.

NOTES ON THE USAGE OF
TERMS IN THIS BOOK

In accordance with the recommendations of Rechtschaffen and Kales (1968), we have employed the terms Stage REM or REM sleep. The recurrent intervals occupied by such sleep are called REM periods and are often abbreviated as REMPs. Correspondingly, NREM or NREMP are also used. Finally, in an effort to avoid the hydraulic implications of "REM pressure," we use instead the term REM deficit or deprivation.

In transcribing sleep speeches, the following conventions were employed:

1. A question mark in parentheses indicates that the preceding word was not enunciated or recorded with crystal clarity but was nevertheless intelligible. Sometimes the question mark is preceded by more than one word, and the entire group is contained in a larger set of parentheses. This indicates that the entire larger enclosed group was "fuzzy" but still intelligible. Thus, in the speech "(that was (?)) really beautiful," the two words "that was" were intelligible though not sharply enunciated.

2. A question mark *not* contained within parentheses indicates, as in standard prose, an interrogative expression.

3. "Mbl" denotes speech that is mumbled and hence completely unintelligible.

4. [p] indicates a long pause; —indicates a short pause.

5. Italics in a verbal expression in the sleep-speech and/or mentation report column denote a special feature to which the reader's attention is drawn, such as the words on which a concordance categorization was based in the event that such basis was not obvious, or clang associations, repetitions, etc. By contrast, material spelled out entirely in capital letters denotes an occasion of the subject's inflectional emphasis in the expression. In the event that a special feature receives such inflectional emphasis, it is both spelled in capitals and italicized as well.

Throughout the book, reference is made to various speech numbers, as in (speech numbers 43, 421, 503). These denote the specific identifying speech numbers in Appendix 2. Table A.2.

2 Definitions of Sleep-Utterance

Sleep-utterance is a general term denoting vocalization in association with sleep, including somniloquy.

Somniloquy (sleep-talking, sleep-speech) is the utterance of *speech* or other psychologically meaningful sound in association with sleep without subjective simultaneous, critical awareness of the event in its real environmental context, or how it might appear to a wakeful observer. Thus, somniloquy includes: (1) utterances consisting of one or more clearly enunciated words and/or mumbled words that although unintelligible, clearly convey the impression of attempts at speech; and/or (2) affectively tinged sounds other than speech that appear to possess some psychologically meaningful quality, such as laughter, weeping, humming, or whimpering.

Sleep-utterances also include *nonlinguistic vocalizations* that often seem devoid of psychological significance, such as isolated monosyllabic grunts, brief moans, groans, and sighs frequently occasioned by or associated with a change in body position.

QUALIFYING TERMS IN THE DEFINITIONS

First, *in association with sleep* is more appropriate than *during sleep*. Although some electrographic records obtained precisely coincident with sleep-utterance episodes have been those of unambiguous, typical sleep, the majority of them possess varying degrees of muscle tension and/or movement artifact that do not permit definite classification under standard terminology

(Rechtschaffen & Kales, 1968). What is beyond equivocation, however, is the close temporal *association* of vocalizations with clear electrographic sleep, and that subjects, without exception, either say or give typical behavioral indications that they had been asleep just prior to experimental awakenings immediately after episodes of sleep speech.

Second, the defining feature of lack of simultaneity between critical awareness and sleep-speech episode was included to cover the few occurrences of chiefly REM-sleep–associated somniloquy in which subjects, in the course of vocally responding to people or events in a dream, awakened themselves and stated their hunch that they might have been talking in their sleep. This was a *retrospective,* after-the-fact realization, however, rather than one of simultaneity. During the moment of such sleep-speech, the subject had been responding to events imagined in sleep and was apparently unaware of the real environmental context, i.e., that he had been in bed and asleep. These considerations are discussed more fully later.

After taking pains to carefully delineate the set and subsets of sleep-utterances, I now ask the reader's indulgence for not following this classification rigorously throughout. There are, after all, only about five terms capable of denoting the phenomena with which we are concerned: *sleep-talking, sleep-speech, somniloquy, sleep-utterance,* and *sleep-vocalization.* In general, sleep-talking, sleep-speech, and somniloquy are synonymous as verbs. Sleep-speech is also used as a noun to refer to the product of sleep-speech as a process; sleep-utterance and sleep-vocalization are also synonymous as the most inclusive set and may indicate process or product of the process.

Confronted with the choice between plodding consistency and an easier-to-read, looser variegated usage, I opted for the latter. It is important at the outset to differentiate among the sleep-utterances as indicated previously, and I trust the reader experiences little difficulty in discerning from the context the sense in which the term is used in the momentary situation.

3 Clinical Classifications of Sleep-Utterance Syndromes

From a nosological viewpoint, two useful questions regarding sleep-utterance are:

1. May sleep-vocalization occur in psychologically "normal" people? And with what pathological conditions has sleep-utterance been observed?
2. How might sleep-utterance phenomena be classified so that clinical and laboratory observations, as well as psychological theoretical considerations, can be related in an intelligible manner?

In attempting to answer the first question, a survey of the clinical literature was made from the first half of the 19th century until the present, and note was made of each reference to sleep-talking with regard to concurrent clinical conditions specifically designated as varieties of morbidity *or* of good health. The results gave rise to the following classification:

A. *Primary idiopathic sleep-talking: sleep-talking unaccompanied by other sleep disorders, significant psychopathology, or an organic disease* (see Andriani, 1892; Arkin, 1966; Bañuelos, 1940; Bleuler, 1923; Bregman, 1910; Gastaut, 1967; Goode, 1962; Kleitman, 1963; Kraepelin, 1906; Landauer, 1918; Massarotti, 1950; Moll, 1889; Oswald, 1962; Pinkerton, 1839; Schilder & Kauders, 1956; Skinner, 1957; Thomas & Pederson, 1963; Trömner, 1911*a, b;* Vogl, 1964).

B. *Sleep-talking accompanying and/or reflecting serious psychic conflict, environmental stress, and/or classical psychiatric conditions but occurring in the absence of other sleep-disorder syndromes* (see Andriani, 1892; Arkin, 1966; Bañuelos, 1940; Bleuler, 1923; Bregman, 1910; Cameron, 1952; Clardy

& Hill, 1949; DeBartolo, 1977; DeSanctis, 1899; Esquirol, 1892; Hammond, 1883; Janet, 1925; Neufeld, 1951; Popoviciú, 1977; Popoviciú & Szabó, 1973; Rice & Fischer, 1976; Salmon, 1910; Vaschide & Pieron, 1902; Vogl, 1964; West, 1967).

Much of this literature does not take pains to clearly specify the nosological category of the condition in which sleep-talking was observed. Rather, reference is made to "neurotic or nervous manifestations," hysteria, dementia, "neuropathic disposition," and the like. However, the symptomatology and the case-history material strongly suggest that, in effect, sleep-talking has been observed by one or more of the foregoing authors in what we would currently classify as schizophrenia, transitory anxiety states related to situational stress, anxiety neuroses, hysterical dissociation syndromes, certain pathological personality disorders, etc. It should be recalled that a good deal of the material cited antedated modern nosology and was of pre-Kraepelinian vintage.

C. *Sleep-talking accompanying other sleep-disorder syndromes* (see Andriani, 1892; Bleuler, 1923; Bregman, 1910; Carpenter, 1849, 1886; Ellis, 1926; Fischer, 1839; Marburg, 1929; Maury, 1878; Moreau, 1820; Pinkerton, 1839; Salmon, 1910; Tissie, 1898; Trömner, 1911a,b; Vaschide & Pieron, 1902).

1. Somnambulism (Abe & Shimakawa, 1966; Broughton, 1968, 1973; Edmond, 1967; Gastaut, 1967; Gastaut & Broughton, 1965; Jacobson & Kales, 1967; Kales & Jacobson, 1967; Kales, Kales, Humphrey, Kuhn, Tan, & Soldatos, 1977; Kales, Humphrey, Martin, Russek, Kuhn, Pelicci, & Kales, 1978b; Sadger, 1920; Sours, Frumkin & Indermill, 1963; Teplitz, 1958, Trömner, 1911a, b; Tuke, 1892).

2. *Pavor nocturnus* (Bregman, 1910; Broughton, 1968; Fischer, Kahn, Edwards, & Davis, 1973a, 1974; Gastaut & Broughton, 1965; Höche, 1928; Massarotti, 1950; Sperling, 1958; Teplitz, 1958; Vogl, 1964; Waelder, 1935).

3. Enuresis (Berdie & Wallen, 1945; Pierce, Lipcon, McLary, & Noble, 1956).

4. Narcolepsy (Brock & Wiesel, 1941; Passouant, 1967; Sours, Frumkin, & Indermill, 1963).

5. Sleep paralysis (Goode, 1962).

6. Rhythmical nocturnal rocking syndromes— crooning, humming, moaning—(Oswald, 1969; Evans, 1961).

7. Sleep apnea (Zorick, Roth, Kramer, & Flessa, 1977).

D. *Sleep-talking occurring with post-traumatic states* (see Crile & Mot, cited by Walsh, 1920b; Janis, Mahl, Kagan, & Holt, 1968; Pai, 1946; Wile, 1934).

E. *Sleep-talking with headache syndromes* (Mick, 1974).

F. *Sleep-talking related to seizure phenomena* (see Aird, Venturini, & Spielman, 1967; Andriani, 1892; Banuelos, 1940; Bleuler, 1923; Dement, Karacan, Ware, & Williams, 1978; Gowers, 1907; Guilleminault, Pedley, & Dement, 1977; Gutheil, 1960; Wallis, 1956).

G. *Sleep-talking with organic disease or abnormality.*
1. Organic brain disease and brain damage (Hammond, 1883).
2. Toxic and drug states including deliria (Gross, Goodenough, Tobin, Halpert, Lepore, Perlstein, Sirota, Dibianco, Fuller & Kishner, 1966; Johnson, Burdick & Smith, 1970; Kay, 1975; Tachibana, Tanaka, Hishikawa, & Kaneko, 1976).
3. Helminthiasis (Salmon, 1910).
4. Febrile states (Salmon, 1910; Vaschide & Pieron, 1902).
5. Mental Retardation (Clardy & Hill, 1949; Walsh, 1920).
6. Drug Withdrawal States (Oswald, 1969; Tachibana *et al.,* 1976).
7. Brain Tumor (Barros-Ferreira, Chodkiewicz, Lairy, & Salzarulo, 1975).

In the references just cited, gross differences exist in the accounts of various observers of the characteristics of sleep-utterance. This is quite in accord with the laboratory findings described later. It is probable, however, that the clinical reports reflected additional factors leading to intersubject variability, although these would be difficult to specify. For example, without electrographic recording, it is uncertain whether subjects who were described behaviorally as talking in their sleep were in fact awake but "groggy", in some kind of trancelike state, or in stage REM or NREM sleep. Furthermore, the older clinical literature often contained no clear indication as to whether reports were based on first-hand observation. These considerations should be kept in mind regarding the following reviews of the bulk of the available clinical literature dealing with sleep-utterance.

To reiterate, the classification just set forth indicates only the clinical conditions in which somniloquy has been observed by one or more authors. It is clear that sleep-utterance is associated with a large variety of conditions, which may differ from one another in many respects. It seems reasonable, therefore, to hypothesize that among the individual differences that prevail across subjects, there is a "psychosomatic compliance" factor held in common that lowers thresholds for sleep-utterance. The synergistic or additive interaction between this compliance factor and whatever etiological factors are peculiar to each syndrome would then result in sleep-utterance. It seems necessary to postulate such a compliance factor because the syndromes listed, for the most part, are certainly capable of occurrence without sleep vocalization.

Let us turn now to the second question—that of the classification of sleep-utterance phenomena in accordance with electrographic and psychological observation. Detailed consideration is given to these matters in Chapters 7 and 17, in which it is proposed that sleep-utterance episodes are best viewed as heterogeneous psychological and psychophysiological dissociated states (Hilgard, 1973; 1977) of varying qualities and durations.

In an excellent clinical essay, West (1967) distinguished between "normally occurring sleep-talking, or gross bodily movements during sleep, and dissociated states that appear similar to them [p. 896]." Normally occurring sleep-talking is described as mainly unintelligible mumbling with an occasional comprehensible word or phrase, as a slow-wave sleep phenomenon, and as unrelated to dreaming. The dissociated state, on the other hand, is deemed to be a variety of somnambulistic trance state, so-called because it is "profound, self-limited, and nocturnal [p. 896]." Subjects prone to such episodes are thought by West to actually awaken initially and then enter into a dissociated trance. Although classified as somnambulistic, the subject may merely "lie in bed and carry on elaborate conversations for which they have no memory but which otherwise display all the characteristics of communication under hypnosis [p. 896]." West suggests that between the extremes of "normal sleep-talking and bodily movements" and "clear-cut trance behavior or dissociated somnambulism," there are gradations of varieties of sleep-walking and -talking that "exist as dissociative phenomena related to sleep in ways not yet fully understood [p. 897]."

The extensive laboratory observations presented in this book are essentially consistent with West's formulation, differing only in certain details. Contrary to West's assertion, however, much sleep-utterance occurs in NREM Stages 1 and 2 as well as in slow-wave sleep (Stages 3 and 4), and at least 15–20% of occurrences were observed in association with REM sleep. Furthermore, many mentation reports elicited immediately after both NREM and REM sleep-speeches are spontaneously described as dreams by the subject and are clearly concordant with the sleep-speech content.

The issues involved here are discussed at length, especially in Chapter 7 and 17 of this book. The perspective from which sleep-utterances are here viewed involves the central notion that they are forms of psychic dissociative episodes that occur within a context of sleep, and that may be arranged along a continuum. At one extreme, *microdissociation,* is a type that signifies minimal alteration or perturbation of psychological, behavioral, and physiological aspects of sleep; and at another extreme, *macrodissociation,* is a form in which behavioral and electrographic criteria of Stage W appear to be fulfilled, but the subject is nevertheless "psychologically asleep." The token of the latter state component is that the subject has an experience that he labels as having "come awake" upon the termination of such episodes.

Between these two extremes of the continuum lies a spectrum of psychological behavioral and physiological occurrences that are comprised of components of either extreme in varying patterns and proportions, *intermediate dissociation.*

Such gradations may well correspond to similar wakeful normal experiences of momentary distraction, brief nonreality-related mentation episodes, and prolonged, self-absorbed daydreaming. In wakeful dissociative episodes, however, the dissociated mentation is probably more accessible to retrospective recall than in sleep mentation, unless severe psychopathology is present.

As is emphasized again later, this classification into micro-, intermediate-, and macro-dissociative episodes serves primarily a descriptive purpose. No claim is made that these dissociations are basically similar as to qualitative components and differ only along quantitative dimensions, although such a possibility is not excluded; only future research will clarify the issue.

4 Demography of Sleep-Talking

Valid estimation of the prevalence of sleep-utterance in the general population is difficult, because as a rule subjects do not remember, or are not aware of, their sleep-talking, and roommates, spouses, siblings, parents, or lovers are themselves usually asleep during occurrences. For the same reason, uncertainty exists about the age of onset in any particular instance, because yet earlier occurrences may have escaped notice. The ideal study would involve obtaining a random subject sample properly selected from various age groups and both sexes, and without their knowledge, installing home bedroom microphones leading to continuously operating tape recorders throughout a series of nights. For ethical and practical reasons, such studies are not likely to ever be carried out, and we shall have to make what we can out of less than methodologically perfect sources.

REPORTS OF CLINICIANS AND AUTHORITATIVE OBSERVERS

Most observers state or imply that sleep-talking is a frequent occurrence in the general "normal" population, and especially so in children, adolescents, and young adults (Bleuler, 1923; Brown, 1910; Kanner, 1957; Kleitman, 1963; Oswald, 1962; Trömner, 1911 a&b,). Inasmuch as older observers are usually still awake while the young are asleep, the former have greater opportunity to witness episodes, and so the opinion about its greater prevalence in the young may be partly artifactual. Cameron (1952) observed that sleep-talking was ubiquitous among the barracks of U.S. troops in the Persian Gulf command in World War II—a setting with unusually severe stress. Oswald (1962) believes that any spouse or anyone who has slept in a college dormitory or military barracks is certain to have heard sleep-talking frequently. Also, B. F. Skinner (1957) stated that "most people speak occasionally while asleep (p. 388)." These opinions accord well with my own observations and those of many colleagues.

QUESTIONNAIRE AND DEMOGRAPHIC SURVEYS

I was able to locate seven questionnaire and demographic surveys of the incidence of sleep-talking. Four yielded a high estimate ranging from 31–75% of the adult population reporting a history of sleep-talking; and three yielded a considerably lower estimate ranging from 10–15%.

Child (1892), on the basis of replies from 178 American college-educated respondents of both sexes, ranging from 20 to 30 years of age, reported that 40% volunteered that they talked in their sleep. The incidence was much higher in subjects under 25. The proportion of males was said to be slightly higher than females (41 vs. 37%). The questions asked were:

1. Do you talk in your sleep?
2. If you do, answer from your family report:
   a. Are you able (if accosted when so talking) to answer intelligently questions put to you?
   If yes, then (b) do you answer any questions, or only questions on the subject that you are talking about [p. 462]?

It should be mentioned that these questions were the last of a series of eight similar ones designed to elicit data on "unconscious cerebration," and included items dealing with aspects of recall of known but momentarily difficult-to-retrieve information, ability to self-awaken from sleep at a preselected time, problem solving during sleep and states of distraction, creative flashes, déjà vu, and nocturnal dreaming.

Gahagan (1936) asked 228 male and 331 female American college psychology students (median age 19 years) to fill out a questionnaire on 23 items pertaining to their sleep characteristics, dreams, and so forth including sleep-talking. The results were that 65.0% of the females and 56.6% of the males reported a history of sleep-talking (average = 60.8%). Of those so reporting, 176 (51.2% or 31.5% of the total sample of 559 students) stated that their sleep-talking had persisted until the time of the report. In commenting on his results, Gahagan stated that:

> Our values are undoubtedly less than the true proportion of sleep-talkers in the group because one will give a history of sleep-talking as a rule only if he has been

informed of his behavior by some other person. These results indicate that a history of sleep-talking should be considered normative, i.e., modal [p. 234].

Gahagan provided no description of the specific question regarding sleep-talking as asked in the questionnaire.

In a more recent paper, Goode (1962) reported data on the general incidence of sleep paralysis, an episodic sleep disorder. He circulated a questionnaire to four separate populations. The questionnaire began: "In a study of sleep and its mechanisms I am surveying several 'normal' population groups to determine the rough incidence of certain symptoms associated with variations from normal sleep." The last of a total of six items, dealing with various sleep behaviors such as dreaming, sleep-walking, daytime sleep attacks, etc., was the question, "Have you ever experienced talking in your sleep?" [p. 229].

The populations were:

Group I.   The entire student body of Duke Medical School, consisting of 287 persons in residence: 163 (56%) responded.

Group II. A group of 68 University of Oklahoma Medical School junior and senior students who were present at a lecture.

Group III. A group of 53 Duke University School of Nursing sophomore students attending a lecture.

Group IV. A group of 75 Duke Hospital private inpatients (medicine 67, open-ward psychiatry 8) available for questioning one day.

The incidence of sleep-talking obtained in this fashion was reported as:

Group I.   53.1%
Group II. 58.5%
Group III. 72.2%
Group IV. 69.2%

The total population was 359 (females 109, males 250), with a total number reporting sleep-talking of 194 (54%).

A very high estimate of the incidence of somniloquy was reported by Evans (1969) on the basis of a self-selected population of about 25,000 readers of the *London Sunday Times,* who were invited to respond to a sleep-behavior questionnaire.

Among them were 15,373 women and 8,856 men. In both sexes, peak responses occurred within the age ranges of 22–31. A second peak was observed in the 17–21-year-old subset. In the female population alone, there was a bias toward middle-aged women. As a whole, the population was derived from the better educated classes, and only those interested in dreams in the first place were willing to take the trouble to reply. They were queried about the incidence of a large number of sleep behaviors and experiences, such as frequency of dreaming and varieties of dreams, sleep-walking, disturbed sleep, and many others including sleep-talking. The exact question dealing with sleep-talking was not specified; Evans merely stated that "Talking in one's sleep was, as one might expect, exceedingly common (70.9% of men and 74.9% of women)."

Of the three surveys yielding a lower estimate of sleep-talking prevalence, the earliest was a study of enuretics in the U.S. Marines carried out by Berdie and Wallen (1945). Data were collected during personal interviews with Marine recruits recently arrived at the training base. Fifty-five enuretics were compared to 135 nonenuretics randomly selected from the same population. An interview schedule was employed containing over 23 topics, one of which was sleep-talking. The criterion for classification as a sleep-talker was self-report of any sleep-talking episodes during the prior three months. By this standard, 10.5% of the normal controls were categorized as sleep-talkers.

Although Thomas and Pederson (1963) employed a subject population of freshman medical students, similar to that used by Goode (1962), they obtained a much lower incidence of sleep-talking: Their subject pool was comprised of 1027 males and 89 females with a median age of 22 years. As in the previous surveys, data were collected by means of self-description of "sleep habits" (21 items) and a variety of sleep-related occurrences. The specific question asked was "Are you subject to talking or walking in your sleep?" The results were that "Fewer men than women noted... talking in their sleep (men 11.4%; women 15.7%; average = 13.6%) [p. 1101]. The difference between males and females regarding the overall incidence of somniloquy was significant at the .02 level—a result opposite to that reported by Child (1892), but consistent with Gahagan (1936).

In the Aird, Venturini, and Spielman (1967) study on nocturnal phenomena in temporal-lobe epileptics, "The past histories of 164 'normal' individuals (patients, doctors, nurses, students, secretaries, and technicians), who had no known disease of the CNS, were obtained as a control to evaluate the significance of the data obtained in the patient group" (i.e., the epileptics [p. 68]. The manner of eliciting these past histories was not specified. No mention was made of a structured questionnaire. The authors based their results throughout on close scrutiny and analysis of case history material. The results were that the "normal" control group, who provide the data of interest at this point, gave past histories of which 20 (12%) were positive for sleep-talking.

What are we to make of these widely disparate results? There seems to be no clear and easy way to reconcile them. What sorts of factors would be conducive to erroneous estimates grossly different from the "true" population incidence?

First, there is the issue of *whether responses were derived from a self-selected sample versus a "captive" sample* upon whom was brought to bear some degree of pressure to respond. The highest incidence of sleep-talking was produced by Evans' *London Times* survey (1969), which utilized a self-selected, volunteer, well-educated population. They were presumably especially interested in sleep-related occurrences; otherwise, they would not have gone to the trouble to respond without appreciable reward, and their enthusiasm doubtless favored a high estimate. By contrast, all of the other investigations must have entailed imponderable amounts of suasion or pressure to respond. The extreme case is exemplified by Berdie and Wallen's (1945) interview data-gathering approach to a sample of U.S. Marine recruits. It is likely that the latter felt they had no choice but to respond. Intermediate between these extremes were surveys using students and institutional personnel who might anticipate some discomfort and disapproval if they stubbornly refused to answer a few questions "for the sake of science."

This issue of self-selected versus experimenter-selected subjects has a direct bearing on the second source of error, viz. *reluctance to admit to sleep-talking out of resentment of enforced compliance and for fear of stigmatization.* Clearly, this was not true of Evans' *London Times* subjects. But it very likely played a role in reducing the recorded incidence of sleep-talking in the Berdie and Wallen (1945) survey. U.S. Marines are a highly select group of men, proud to begin with and further trained to greater pride in stereotyped "masculinity," efficiency, and freedom from tokens of human frailty. Furthermore, under the military conditions prevailing in 1945, they could not feel certain that their confidentiality was sacrosanct. Their names at the very least, were known, to the medical authorities. We can only surmise that in groups where possessing some "mental quirk" like sleep-talking made one suspect, incentives must have abounded to conceal positive histories out of shame, fear of stigmatization, and resentment at having thrust upon them the obligation to respond. To a lesser degree, this may well have been true with the other experimenter-selected subject populations. In support of such a hunch are comments of Goode (1962) that 124 subjects in his total population of 483 did not hand in their questionnaires. Such social psychological factors also seem likely to have been influential among the permanent hospital staff population in the work of Aird et al. (1967).

A third source of error is *omission of positive histories out of honest lack of awareness of the existence of sleep-talking in oneself.* We have already touched on this point. Unless so informed by an external observer, chronic sleep-talkers are rarely aware of their proclivities.

Fourth, one must give thought to lack of uniformity in results due to *intrinsic differences in subject populations.* Clearly, U.S. Marine recruits in 1945 were different from the bulk of the other subjects by way of age, education, and social psychological factors. In addition, U.S. Marines probably achieved a higher standard of physical health than the others. The populations in the other surveys were certainly less dissimilar from one another. It is therefore interesting and puzzling that similar populations like those of Goode (1962) and Thomas and Pederson (1963) (both largely medical students) produced high and low estimates respectively (54.0 vs. 13.6%). This discrepancy could be partly accounted for by the next source of variance.

Differences in the nature of the questions put to subjects doubtless affected results. Some questions clearly imply that the investigator is interested in whether the subject is a currently active sleep-talker without regard to earlier tendencies. Thus, the questions "Do you talk in your sleep?" (Child, 1892) and "Are you subject to talking in your sleep?" (Thomas and Pederson, 1863) connote present or recent activity. And "Have you ever experienced talking in your sleep?" (Goode, 1962) connotes all-inclusive past combined with present occasions (i.e., a cumulative history). Although Gahagan (1936) did not specify his question, he clearly tallied separately past from present activity; and the criterion of Berdie and Wallen (1945) was one of unambiguous current activity (any episode during the prior 3 months).

A final source of discrepancies in incidence figures might be the indirect result of differences in the average level of interest in dreams among the various populations studied.

Is there anything in the literature to suggest that psychological interest in dreams and sleep-talking frequency could be associated? The answer is yes.

That personal interest in dreams is a factor in good dream recall has been indicated by several studies (see Goodenough [1978] for an excellent review). And MacNeilage, Cohen, and MacNeilage (1972) have demonstrated a significant association between subjects' estimates of dream recall and alleged sleep-talking propensities. It is thus reasonable to suppose that the subjects used by Gahagan (1936), Child (1892), and the *London Times* (Evans, 1969) tended to have an unusually intense interest in dreams, greater dream recall and, in accordance with the findings of MacNeilage et al. (1972), a greater tendency for somniloquy. This factor could also partly explain the differences in results between Gahagan's subjects and those of the three low-incidence reports—all utilized investigator-selected subjects, but Gahagan's subjects were also psychology students who might be presumed to have possessed a comparatively more intense personal interest in dreams and sleep cognition.

It is noteworthy that with the possible exception of the report of Child, none of the studies mentioned thus far described any attempt to corroborate the claims of subjects that they talked in their sleep. Child is a little indefinite on this point, indicating that if his subjects volunteered a positive history of sleep-talking, they were asked to respond to additional related questions based on their "family report." However, allowing for even gross errors, it would be difficult to account for such large numbers of people claiming to be sleep-talkers if it had not been brought to their attention in some convincing way. Thus, the results cited to date enable us to conclude that sleep-talking is far more common than most people suspect, despite our being unable to specify a more or less precise quantitative incidence figure for the general population. But the issue of corroboration makes the next topic important.

SLEEP-TALKING INCIDENCE STUDIES
EMPLOYING OBSERVER CORROBORATION
OF OCCURRENCES

The questionnaire surveys reviewed earlier provided estimates of the incidence of sleep-talking based on the self-report of the respondents. By contrast, in this section I present material from four studies that specified in varying degree attempts to corroborate actual sleep-talking occurrences by reports of a wakeful external observer. Unfortunately, the indices employed by each investigator differed, making cross-comparison difficult. Still, they are the only publications I could locate carrying data on the topic.

One such indication of the prevalence of somniloquy is a serendipitous result of a study on the therapeutic effects of relaxation training in the U.S. Navy during World War II (Neufeld, 1951). Among other outcome items observed (injuries, absenteeism, athletic achievement, anxiety, and tension) was the sleep behavior of 190 Naval cadets as recorded by trained observer officers. Each observer was assigned four to eight cadets to whom he had ready access, and he was obliged to keep individual record tallies on an hourly basis throughout the night. The cadets slept in dimly lighted rooms to facilitate observation. Talking and mumbling episodes from taps to reveille were included in the inventory of sleep behaviors. An average of 2.7 such incidents per night was counted. An additional group of 140 similar cadets received training in muscular relaxation (Jacobson, 1938) and with the same technique of observation, a nightly average of 1.2 vocalization episodes was detected. In both groups, the greatest amount of vocalization was heard 2–3 hours after retiring. Of course, the study has severe limitations for the purposes of estimation of sleep-utterance prevalence. First, the sleep was not monitored polygraphically, so we do not know whether episodes fulfill electrographic criteria for sleep-utterance (see Chapter 7). Second, although the population consisted of healthy young men, they were living under conditions of real stress. This probably increased the tendency toward vocalization (see Chapter 9) above its "natural" baseline. That relaxation training was associated with a 56% lower average occurrence per night supports this conjecture. Finally, the results reported as group averages preclude our learning about the prevalence of sleep-vocalization in terms of the proportion of individual sleep-talkers in their subject population.

Abe and Shimakawa (1966a,b) have carried out an extensive survey on the incidence of sleep-talking, bruxism, and somnambulism in two generations of

Japanese urban subjects. I present this work in greater detail later on when considering the possible role of hereditary factors in sleep-talking. For our purposes at the moment, it suffices to mention that of a sample of 310 3-year-old children receiving a "physical and psychiatric checkup" in 1965, satisfactory information regarding the incidence of sleep-talking in these children *and* their parents was obtained. The parent population was 620. Corroboration of the presence or absence of sleep-talking in the children was obtained from their mothers. In addition, corroboration of sleep-talking tendencies of the fathers was obtained from the paternal grandmothers and from the spouse (the children's mothers); the somniloquy of the mothers was also verified by the maternal grandmothers but not by their husbands (the children's fathers). All information was obtained by means of a detailed questionnaire requiring that all respondents be literate and in good health.

The results were that 14.5% of the children ($n = 45$) and 16.1% of the parents ($n = 100$) were reported as active sleep-talkers. Of this latter group, 17 had talked in their sleep as children and continued to do so as adults; and 29 began their sleep-talking as adults, not being known to do so as children. Finally, 54 parents had talked in their sleep as children but did not continue in adult life. Thus, the findings are in accord with a conservative estimate of somniloquy incidence and with the belief that it is more prevalent in childhood.

Although I did not attempt to study the incidence of sleep-talking in the general population, my own experience is consistent with the results of those reporting a higher rather than lower incidence range of somniloquy. In the course of attempting to determine whether personal histories and psychological characteristics of people with a history of sleep-talking were different from those without a known history, it was difficult to obtain a sample of New York City college students who claimed that to the best of their recall, they had *never* been told by someone that they had talked in their sleep on at least one occasion.

SLEEP-TALKING INCIDENCE STUDIES EMPLOYING OBSERVER CORROBORATION INCLUDING LABORATORY FINDINGS

Detailed presentation of work on the frequency of sleep-speech in the laboratory observed among self-professed volunteer *chronic sleep-talkers* with a previously verified history appears in Chapter 6. However, some laboratory evidence is available that bears on the issue of the incidence of sleep-talking in the general population. In two studies on the effects of REM deprivation on sleep mentation (Arkin, Antrobus, & Ellman, 1978), healthy college-age paid volunteer males were selected on the basis of having good dream recall and being light sleepers. This selection was carried out *without* reference to or inquiry after any sleep-talking history. In one study, 14 of 36 subjects (39%) spending a total of 206 laboratory nights were heard by the technician to have talked in their sleep at least once. The mean number of speeches per subject was 1.5; and the mean number of speeches per night was 0.4. In a second study, 20 similar subjects all (100%) emitted sleep-speech at least once during a 12-night protocol. Results calculated for 12 subjects upon whom reliable data were collected showed that 332 speeches were uttered during 144 subject nights, yielding a mean nightly frequency of speeches and mean number of speeches per subject of 2.3 for both items.

Because there is evidence that experimental sleep interruption stimulates sleep-speech production, it is doubtful whether the foregoing figures are indicative of the "true baseline" sleep-speech incidence of these subjects. The results do demonstrate, however, that sleep-speech occurs frequently in a population of subjects not selected for sleep-talking propensities, even if the circumstances are unusual.

A similar demonstration is provided by the data of Batson, Arkin, and Ellman (1978) on a population of tobacco addicts who smoked at least 20 cigarettes daily and were between 18 and 40 years of age. A single night was used to obtain baseline measurements as part of a study on the effects of tobacco or food deprivation on sleep mentation. During this baseline, the sole experimental intervention consisted of a schedule of experimental awakenings for mentation reports. Of the first nine subjects tested, six talked in their sleep, producing a total of 24 speeches (mean per subject = 2.7). It is to be noted that these subjects were not selected with regard to a history of sleep-talking but rather on the basis of a dependency upon tobacco, good dream recall and sound sleep propensities, absence of specific sleep disorders, and the presence of interest in their own dreams. They were all psychologically "normal." Naturally, the same cautionary note mentioned earlier applies here as well; the experimental awakenings do not permit one to conclude that the date reflects "true" baseline sleep-speech incidence in this population.

The best incidence study available involving self-report, corroboration from external observers, and laboratory data is that of MacNeilage (1971), who administered a questionnaire to 218 undergraduates taking an introductory psychology class at the University of Texas. The unique asset of this study is the refinement of responses into six ordinally arranged categories; all other investigations employed a dichotomous response scheme. The subjects' ages ranged from 18–25, and the population was comprised of 114 females and 104 males. Besides inquiry about sleep-talking, the questionnaire covered estimates of the frequency and vividness of dream recall, average sleep duration, ease of falling asleep, difficulty in being "fully awake" in the morning, and sleep-walking.

The specific questionnaire items dealing with sleep-talking and the responses are tabulated as follows:

TABLE 4.1
"Within the past year or so, have you talked in your
sleep?"[a]

Frequency	No. Students	
a. Every night or about every night	3	(1.4%)
b. At least every other night	1	(0.5%)
c. Frequently	7	(3.4%)
d. Occasionally	67	(32.2%)
e. Hardly ever	59	(28.4%)
f. Never	71	(34.1%)
Total	208	(100%)

[a]From MacNeilage, 1971.

The results reflect the current and partly cumulative sleep-talking incidence of the population sampled. It seems reasonable and conservative to surmise that 5.3% are currently active sleep-talkers—the sum of the first three categories, including students who list themselves as sleep-talking at least "frequently." When the next category is added, the total proportion of students who list themselves with corroboration as having talked in their sleep at least "occasionally" increases to 37.5%; and when all students who admit to sleep-talking are included, the total proportion climbs to 65.9% who have been heard by a roommate or some other wakeful observer to have talked at least once during the time interval specified as "the past year or so." Of the remaining 34.1% who report themselves as "silent sleepers" to the best of their knowledge, one must expect that an imponderable proportion have talked in their sleep at least once during the same period but were undetected. It is of great interest that when five of these students, who dreamed frequently and reported themselves as talking in their sleep only "occasionally," were subsequently studied in the laboratory, four talked in their sleep at least once over a 6-night schedule—i.e., in actuality, more than just occasionally. In short, MacNeilage's (1971) results clearly support Gahagan's (1936) contention that a "history of sleep-talking should be considered normative, i.e., modal," especially if one is willing to accept at least a single externally corroborated incident as a criterion for qualifying as a "history of sleep-talking." Pragmatic considerations are certainly involved. A single headache might not be a suitable criterion for categorizing someone as having a "history of headache"—one might well require recurrent headaches for such a purpose. On the other hand, it would be imprudent to dismiss a single episode of a grand mal seizure, gross melena, or hematuria.

In conclusion, we can only repeat that sleep-talking is an extremely frequent occurrence in the general "normal" population, and its approximate "true" incidence is difficult to establish. Taking all studies together, conservative estimates range from 7–15%. Liberal estimates range from 31–75%. Finally, the prevalence of sleep-talking appears to be greater among children and tends to disappear with the advent of adult life, although a sizable proportion of people begin to sleep-talk *de novo* as adults.

INCIDENCE OF SLEEP-TALKING IN PATHOLOGIC POPULATIONS

As indicated in the clinical classification of sleep-utterance syndromes (Chapter 3), sleep vocalization episodes have been observed to occur in association with a variety of other sleep-associated disorders such as somnambulism, enuresis, and night-terrors. In addition, they have been noted in posttraumatic and febrile states, seizure disorders, headache syndromes, acute and chronic organic brain disease, toxic psychoses, functional psychoses, pathological personalities, psychoneuroses, and environmental stress-induced tension states. In most of the publications cited in Chapter 3, such associations were remarked upon rather than presented with quantitative estimates. The following paragraphs contain what little numerical data I have been able to glean:

Enuresis. Of 55 young adult enuretics in the U.S. Marines, 26 gave a concurrent history of sleep-talking, whereas the control group of 135 contained only 14 such cases. That is, 47% of the enuretics and 10% of the controls were active sleep-talkers (Berdie & Wallen, 1945).

Temporal-Lobe Epilepsy. Aird et al. (1967) carried out a study in which the prevalence of nocturnal phenomena in 156 patients with temporal-lobe epilepsy was compared to that in a control group of 164 "normal" individuals (other patients, doctors, nurses, students, secretaries, and technicians, without known CNS disease), whose past history was elicited. The relevant statistics for the epileptic group as opposed to the controls are listed in Table 4.2.

It is of interest that the epileptic group exceeded the control in prevalence of all varieties of pathological nocturnal behavior with the sole exception of sleep-talking, in which category the reverse was true.

Somnambulism. Sours *et al.* (1963) reported that five of 14 U.S. Navy men (36%) diagnosed as *bona fide* somnambulists also talked in their sleep.

Abe and Shimakawa (1966b) have examined correlations between sleep-walking and somniloquy in a population of 611 Japanese children given a routine health examination within 10 days of their third birthday. The results are listed in Table 4.3.

TABLE 4.2
Prevalence of Nocturnal Phenomena[a]

	Epileptics (%)	Controls (%)
Enuresis	23	12
Seizures	22	0
Nightmares	17	11
Sleep-walking	16	7
Sleep-talking	7	12
Other (miscellaneous)	17	8

[a]From Aird et al., 1967. Copyright 1967, American Medical Association.

TABLE 4.3
Association of Sleep-Walking With Sleep-Talking[a]

	Sleep-Walking		
	+	–	Total
Sleep-talking	+ 15	65	80
	– 13	518	531
Total	28	583	611

Thus, there was a significant association between the two behaviors (χ^2 = 42.7, $p < .001$). The authors concluded that they tend to occur in combination rather than by themselves, suggesting that they could be "different manifestations of a similar neurophysiological deviation (p. 307)." The data certainly indicate that in the population studied, a 3-year-old somnambulist is likely to be a somniloquist as well, but that a 3-year-old somniloquist is much less likely to also be a somnambulist. That is, sleep-talking alone is much more common than sleep-talking in combination with sleep-walking.

More recently, Kales, Humphrey, Kuhn, Tan, and Soldatos (1977) reported on sleep questionnaire data obtained from 26 adult males and females with a current or past history of sleep-walking; 54% offered a history of sleep-talking as well.

Narcolepsy. Sours et al. (1963) reported that of 75 patients diagnosed as ill with primary idiopathic narcolepsy, four (5.3%) were also sleep-talkers. It is of interest that Sours describes these patients as having "complained" of somnambulism and somniloquism. It is extemely rare for patients to seek treatment for sleep-talking per se, and possibly Sours used "complained" merely as an indicator of the presence of the symptom rather than of genuine suffering and inconvenience, or rather that the patients complained solely of sleep-walking. In any case, the wording suggests that these patients were current active sleep-talkers at the time of the data collection.

Sleep Paralysis. Goode (1962) found that of 17 patients afflicted with attacks of sleep paralysis, 11 (64.7%) volunteered a history of sleep-talking. Perhaps the main reason for the difference in the proportion of sleep-talkers in this population as compared to that of Sours' cases of narcolepsy (a closely related syndrome) is the nature of Goode's question eliciting the incidence of sleep-talking. As remarked earlier, "Have you ever experienced talking in your sleep?" logically includes past as well as current occasions and might well have been a factor in yielding the high proportion of sleep-talkers in this special population. Actually, this percentage is similar to that recorded by Goode for his normal control population.

Psychological Disorders. Popoviciú and Szabó (1973) report that of 25 sleep-talkers of unspecified age and sex, 68% were classified as possessing neurotic disturbances. Taken together with the absence of EEG alterations, such somniloquy was deemed as psychogenic in origin. The remaining 32% were associated with other sleep disorders (particularly with somnambulism), which at times were considered to be of epileptic etiology.

Finally, about one-fourth of children hospitalized at Rockland State Hospital for delinquency and/or feeble-mindedness were habitual sleep-talkers (Clardy & Hill, 1949).

In conclusion, it is clear that sleep-talking is a frequent accompaniment of many other neurological, psychological, and more specific sleep disorder syndromes, occurring more usually, however, as an isolated manifestation. In this respect, it is like headache—a common symptom with many forms and that may occur without discernible structural or organic pathology, or be an accompaniment or manifestation of it.

ADDENDUM

The following information relating to the incidence of sleep-talking was received too late to have been easily incorporated in the chapter and is, therefore, detailed in this addendum: Bixler, Kales, Soldatas, Kales and Healey (1979) surveyed a stratified representative population of adults (18 and over: N = 1006) derived from the Los Angeles, California area. The focus of interest was the prevalence of various sleep disorders. The method involved use of an extensive questionnaire designed to elicit information about sleep difficulties. Each individual was asked whether a particular sleep "problem" currently existed, how long such difficulty had lasted, and whether the

TABLE 4.4

Incidence of Sleep-Talking: Questionnaire Surveys

Investigators	Subject Population	Question Asked: Current vs. Cumulative History	Proportion Subjects Positive for Sleep-Talking
Child (1892)	178 college-educated Americans: both sexes, 20–30 years old	"Do you talk in your sleep?" Responses apparently corroborated by family member.	Apparently currently active: males = 41%, females = 37%.
Gahagan (1936)	559 American college students	Actual question not specified but separate tallies made for current vs. cumulative history.	Currently active = 31.5%. Cumulative history: females = 65.0% males = 56.6%
Goode (1962)	284 American medical and nursing students; 75 private in-patients. Total = 359.	"Have you ever experienced talking in your sleep?"	Cumulative history: 54%.
Evans (1969)	15,373 female, 8,856 male British, well-educated readers of the *London Times*: age range 17–middle age, all subjects self-selected volunteers	Actual question not specified; although wording of report implies currently active cases, ambiguity remains.	Males = 70.9%, females = 74.9%.

Study	Sample	Method	Results
Berdie and Wallen (1945)	135 American non-enuretic U.S. Marine recruits	Data obtained from structured interview. Criterion: one or more self-reported sleep-talking episodes during prior 3 months.	Currently active = 10.4%.
Thomas and Pederson (1963)	1116 American medical students: 1027 males, 89 females.	"Are you subject to talking or walking in your sleep?"	Males = 11.4%, females = 15.7%.
Aird et al. (1967)	164 "normal" adult hospital staff members	Question not specified; cumulative history implied.	12%
Abe and Shimakawa (1966)	310 Japanese 3-year-old children.	Question not specified; cumulative history implied; history given by family member.	14.5%
MacNeilage (1971)	208 college students	"Within the past year or so, have you talked in your sleep?" (See text for the ordinal scale used.)	18–25 years old: 114 females, 104 males. Currently active = 5.3% Cumulative history over previous 1–2 years: at least one occurrence = 65.9%, occasionally or more often = 37.5%.

specific difficulty had existed in the past. Thus, this investigation encompassed both current and past history items. Among the many questions were those pertaining to sleep-talking.

Results. Fifty-three subjects (5.3%) "complained of either a current or past problem with sleep-talking [p. 1259]." Twenty-four were currently active sleep-talkers and all dated the onset of their problem prior to age 40. Of the currently active group, 7 (29% of the total of 24) indicated the time of onset prior to age 10. Most of the 24 subjects (92%, N = 24) had had the problem for over 1 year. Although there were more women than men in the group, the difference was not statistically significant. On the other hand, the prevalence among the younger subjects (age 18–30) was significantly higher.

Discussion. The findings warrant the inclusion of this study among those providing a very low estimate of the incidence of sleep-talking. However, one should note that the figures were derived from self-responders without apparent attempt at external verification, positive or negative. Furthermore, the wording of the questions suggests that a possible condition for description of oneself as a "sleep-talker" required that one had to perceive the sleep-talking as a "problem" [p. 1258]; that is, the wording of the question may have biased an imponderable number of actual sleep-talkers to exclude themselves because their sleep-talking may not have been viewed as a source of difficulty by the responders. Similarly, wakeful observers may have failed to inform the subjects of their proclivities, because it presented no "problem." Thus, a neutral, independent inquiry of family members or roommates without regard to an assessment of problematic status of the sleep-talking might well have disclosed a higher prevalence figure. The results must be taken, therefore, as a biased, unduly low estimate of actual prevalence of sleep-talking in the general population.

Summary. In summary, then, assessing the true prevalence of sleep-talking is fraught with difficulty; the investigator is attempting to zero in on an elusive phenomenon. A parallel model is the assessment of the prevalence of penile erections in sleep. If one were to ask the general male population how often they experience penile erections during sleep, one now knows in advance that whatever figure obtained would be invalidly low. The same principle holds true with questionnaire assessments of sleep-talking prevalence. That is, if one were to ask a population sample, as did Bixler et al. (1979), "Have erections during sleep ever been a problem?", one would very likely obtain, accordingly, a great preponderance of negative answers leading to a falsely low estimate.

5 Psychopathological Significance of Somniloquy

Do occasions of sleep-talking, particularly *if recurrent,* inevitably signify psychopathology? And, if so, is sleep-talking correlated with any psychiatric syndrome already described in the literature?

LITERATURE DESCRIPTIONS

Evidently, Andriani (1892) had observed sleep vocalization in so many people who seemed otherwise "normal" that he deemed it valid to call this subspecies "common" sleep-talking. By clear implication, this precedent is consistent with comments of many other authors (Abe & Shimakawa, 1966a; Bañuelos, 1940; Bleuler, 1923; Bregman, 1910; Gastaut, 1967; Kanner, 1957; Kleitman, 1963; Landauer, 1918; Oswald, 1962; Pinkerton, 1839; Schilder & Kauders, 1956; Skinner, 1957; Trömner, 1911a, 1911b; Vogl, 1964; West, 1967). In addition, Andriani (1892) indicated that sleep-talking might occur in normal people possessing a "nervous temperament"; and Moll (1889) noted an association between sleep-talking and normals with a "sanguine temperament." Kleitman (1963) stated that "talking during sleep, or somniloquy, can hardly be called an abnormality except when it is associated with other parasomnias [p. 281]."

In a somewhat different vein, a number of authors have considered sleep-talking in normals to be a precursor or transitional form of somnambulism (Bleuler, 1923; Brown, 1910; Carpenter, 1849; Ellis, 1926; Fischer, 1839; Moreau, 1820; Pinkerton, 1839). Finally, one writer believed that somniloquy is a sign of an hysterical or degenerative constitution (Ziehen, 1926).

INVESTIGATIONS OF PSYCHOPATHOLOGY
OF SLEEP-TALKERS

In the course of my own work, I have had an opportunity to interview about 70 subjects offering a history of sleep-talking at some time in their lives. Most of them (males and females of college age) volunteered in response to advertisements for sleep-talkers posted at placement bureaus of several colleges in New York City, and they were paid a small fee. Other individuals in the sample were friends, relatives, acquaintances, and a few psychiatric patients. The age range of the entire group was from 9 to over 50. My clinical impression is that, in and of itself, sleep-vocalization is not pathognomonic of any specific syndrome or of serious psychiatric illness. The symptom has occurred in a heterogeneous set of personalities: people who would be classified as having borderline and fully developed schizophrenia, character neuroses, psychoneuroses of various types, overt homosexuals, and lastly those with insignificant or no easily detectable psychopathology.

To check further, I attempted to compare a college population of subjects with a history of sleep-talking (even if somniloquy was sparse) to a control nonsleep-talker group. Actually, sleep-talking is so prevalent that it was difficult to locate individuals who had never been told by someone at least once that they had talked in their sleep. The control group consisted of similar paid volunteers from the same colleges who responded to an advertisement for participants in a "psychological survey." There were 32 subjects in the sleep-talker group and 20 nonsleep-talker controls. The latter approximately matched the sleep-talking group, except that they did not have a history of sleep-talking at any time in their lives, as far as they, their roommates, or relatives knew or remembered.

Each subject was required to prepare an autobiography in accordance with the outline employed in a study of Murray et al. (1938). This was expanded to include the menstrual histories of females and a comprehensive inventory of sleep behavior and other developmental details not included in the original source. In addition, each subject received at least one clinical interview. A close examination of the results failed to disclose any striking, obvious psychological pattern of a descriptive, dynamic, or developmental nature as typical and distinctive of the sleep-talking group. In addition, two independent blind judges using the biographical protocols described earlier were instructed to discriminate between the two groups. They were likewise completely unable to make any systematic distinctions between them.

These results were more or less consistent with the findings of Bone, Hopkins, Buttermore, Belcher, McIntyre, Calef, and Cowling (1973), who administered the Sixteen Personality Factor Questionnaire (16 PF) to 66 sleep-talker college students (27 male and 39 female) and 31 nonsleep-talkers from the same school population (12 males and 19 females). Differences were revealed for only two factors: Female sleep-talkers scored higher on Radicalism ($t = 2.95$, $p < .01$) and male sleep-talkers scored lower on Superego Strength ($t = 2.08$, $p < .05$). Thus, the two groups were much more similar than different.

These findings leave open the possibility that although sleep-talking tendencies need not be inevitably associated with psychopathology, they might nevertheless be associated with certain psychological *characteristics*. Such a notion is supported by the previously cited results of MacNeilage, Cohen, and MacNeilage (1972), who found a significant association on questionnaire responses between subjects' estimates of their sleep-talking propensities and their estimates of their dream recall. Specifically, whereas subjects with high recall of dreams may or may not sleep-talk, subjects who recall few dreams are much less likely to be sleep-talkers. This admittedly preliminary finding requires confirmation in a prospective laboratory study with appropriate controls. Both the Bone et al. (1973) and MacNeilage et al. (1972) reports suggest nevertheless that with further investigation, subtle psychological differences between sleep-talkers and "silent sleepers" may yet be revealed.

Popoviciú (1977) reported exploratory findings on "frontier states between sleep incidents and nocturnal epileptic attacks [p. 65]." Of a population of 900 subjects complaining of various nocturnal episodic manifestations (NEM), such as assorted somnambulisms, enuresis, night terrors, bruxism, and myocloniae, 89 were selected for close study who had tendencies to produce "nocturnal verbal automatisms [p. 74]" (NVA). No indication was provided as to the principles guiding selection of cases from the parent population; i.e., it was not specifically stated whether cases were selected on a random basis, greatest severity, or whatever. The NVA subcategory was further divided into "simple NVA (sleep-talking) [p. 74]"—25 cases (28.1%); and "NVA associated with other NEM [p. 74]"—64 cases (71.9%). Over 150 EEG recordings were made, and 25 subjects were polygraphically studied in the sleep laboratory.

Daytime EEG examination produced the following results:

1. Simple NVA (sleep-talking): $N = 25$
    a. 17 cases (68%) with normal tracings
    b. 8 cases (32%) with:
       a. nonspecific diffuse anomalies (especially slow dysrhythmias): $N = 6$ (24%)
       b. hemispheric asymmetries: $N = 2$ (8%)
       c. epileptic discharges on all derivations: 0
       d. temporal foci: 0
2. NVA associated with other NEM: $N = 64$
    a. 16 cases (25%) with normal tracings

    b. 48 cases (75%) with:

        (1) nonspecific diffuse anomalies (especially slow dysrhythmias): $N = 30$ (46.9%)

        (2) hemispheric asymmetries: $N = 5$ (7.8%)

        (3) epileptic discharges on all derivations: $N = 5$ (7.8%)

        (4) temporal foci: $N = 8$ (12.5%)

Sleep studies revealed that all episodes were associated with slow-wave sleep.

Popoviciú (1977) concluded that the results "bring an important support in the favor of the psychogenous origin of the majority of cases (Diatkine, 1963; Gastaut, Dongier, Broughton, & Tassinari, 1963; Passouant, 1974). Thus, in the simple NVA, there were not found critical or intercritical epileptic anomalies, but only diffuse and nonspecific ones. In turn, in those cases in which somniloquy is associated with other NEM, we noticed the frequency of certain alterations of an epileptic type (12.5% temporal foci and 7.8% generalized epileptic discharges [p. 74]." No statistical analyses were reported.

It is appropriate to foreshadow a theme of the next chapter by stating that although sleep-talkers as a group possess little by way of distinctive psychological features, there is some evidence that a hereditary factor plays a role in a significant proportion of cases.

In summary, recurrent sleep-talking is compatible with psychological health and does not necessarily reflect psychiatric morbidity. In addition, sleep-talking is a common accompaniment of many functional and organic psychiatric syndromes but shows no predilection for any specific nosological subgroup. Also, heredity may play a role, albeit an indefinite one. One weakness of my own unpublished study based upon interview and biographical inventory data (as described on page 34) is that the sleep-talker population pooled somniloquists of all degrees of severity, from mild to severe. It is possible that positive findings would have been obtained if we had employed only the most severe, currently active somniloquists to compare with the "silent" controls.

In over 25 years of clinical practice (both my own and that of colleagues), there have generally been no instances in which sleep-talking has been a chief or important complaint. Only recently, however, I was consulted by someone on behalf of a relative who vocalized profusely in sleep, but even here, what actually provoked the request was recurrent night terrors with concomitant sleep-speech. Similarly, Wile (1934) reported on the therapy of 25 sleep-vocalizing children who suffered primarily from nightmares; and more recently, Rice and Fisher (1976) have reported on sleep-talking during nocturnal fugue episodes. Usually, however, sleep-talking does not cause distress beyond occasional embarrassment, nor does it impair adaptation or fulfillment of any sociocultural role. Recently, however, LeBoeuf (1979) described the successful behavior therapy of a 27-year-old Navy officer, who intensely discommoded his woman friend with sleep-speech. It is likely that a great many cases develop initially out of psychic conflict, and several subjects known to the author date the time of onset of their sleep-talking to a childhood psychological crisis; e.g., one subject believed that his parents' quarrels ultimately leading to their divorce was a possible cause of his sleep-talking. A second subject came with both parents to the United States at the age of 10 from a foreign country—all spoke only their native tongue. The subject began his sleep-talking shortly after this time, speaking only in English. A third began consciously to feign sleep-walking with talking at about the age of 10, allegedly to get her parents' attention and to intimidate her half-sister by a display of the uncanny. She was living in a large household with many full, half-, and foster siblings. With the passage of time, both the somnambulism and somniloquy became involuntary and have remained so. A fourth subject was a sporadic bed-wetter from age 5 to 9 years and had her menarche at 9 years of age. She dates the onset of sleep-talking from the age of 8 or 9 years. Thus, in those cases where sleep-talking clearly originates in the context of psychic conflict, it may continue in "automatic" fashion even after the crisis subsides.

In conclusion, it seems reasonable to regard "common" or primary idiopathic somniloquy as a psychomotor abnormality of sleep that is usually benign but may reflect deeper disturbance. Perhaps the capacity to talk during sleep is a special idiosyncrasy of the same order as absolute pitch, eidetic imagery, and mirror or automatic writing.

PROGNOSIS AND THERAPY

Sleep-talking, unaccompanied by other major psychopathology or organic disease, apparently tends to occur less often after the age of 25. Of those individuals in whom the onset of sleep-talking occurred in childhood, a large proportion somniloquize progressively less often after the age of 25, with final disappearance. Another large proportion continue to talk in their sleep; and a third sizable group without a known prior history begin sleep-talking in adult life de novo. Where somniloquy is secondary to some other process, pathological or otherwise, it is likely that its course will reflect the vicissitudes of that process. This is especially true of the voluminous sleep-talking frequently observed in military barracks and occasioned by emotional tension in time of war. That is, one might well expect subsidence of these manifestations when the environmental stress is removed.

As noted previously, some authors believe somniloquy has a tendency to progress to somnambulism, but the evidence for this is not convincing. Usually, treatment is not required for sleep-talking. However, as mentioned earlier, LeBoeuf (1979) administered an aversive event contingent upon sleep-utterance to a loquacious somniloquist. The patient had a 6-year prior history of active sleep-utterance (as often as about 17 nightly episodes). The stimulus was a 1000-Hz tone of 5 seconds duration with an intensity of 100 dB that awakened the subject after each utterance. It was activated by a small throat microphone. Sleep utterance was virtually eliminated rapidly with no recurrence reported at the time of a 9-month follow-up. No adverse effects were mentioned.

6 Somniloquy, Other Episodic Sleep Disorders and the Question of Hereditary Predisposition

As previously stated, clinical observation indicates that certain major sleep disorders—somnambulism, nocturnal enuresis, and night terrors—are often concurrent. Epilepsy, various EEG abnormalities, CNS infection and trauma, familial tendencies, and psychopathology are commonly part of the background of each of these conditions. (See Williams, Karacan, & Hursch, 1974, for a discussion and extensive bibliography pertaining to this issue.) Sleep-walking, enuresis, and night terrors tend to occur predominantly (but by no means exclusively) in association with the first third of the night's sleep, and because they are concommitant with arousal processes from slow-wave sleep, Broughton (1968) has grouped them together as "Disorders of Arousal."

Despite the difficulties in arriving at valid figures for the incidence of these "classical" sleep disorders in the general population, the consensus suggested by study of the available literature and clinical experience is that sleep-talking occurs more frequently than any other single disorder of this group and very likely even exceeds the sum of their total combined frequencies, especially in adults. (See Williams & Karacan, 1975.) But sleep-talking is also frequently associated with each of these syndromes, as we have seen (Chapter 3). If somniloquy was rarely or never observed in their absence, it would be reasonable to uniformly classify sleep-speech as a component of a larger diathesis that becomes manifest in varying modes and degrees—sometimes minimal (as mere nonspecific sleep-vocalization) and at other times fully developed (somnambulism, nocturnal enuresis, and night terrors and sleep-speech combined). Such a view would be strengthened by evidence of a hereditary predisposition for this entire group of disorders.

On the other hand, if a significant proportion of chronic sleep-talkers were found to possess no other significant sleep anomaly and no apparent familial tendency, then one might validly subdivide sleep-talkers and sleep-vocalization episodes into two classes: those presenting as part of a larger sleep disorder syndrome complex and those existing independently— "primary idiopathic somniloquy," which, perhaps, would be comprised overwhelmingly of microdissociative sleep-utterances.

FAMILIAL TENDENCIES

Several observers have noted instances in which familial tendencies to talk while sleeping were striking, so that even entire families were heard to chatter away at night by wakeful observers—the family members would joke about it by day (Arkin, 1966; Burrell, 1904; Trömner, 1911a,b). Mick (1974) noted instances of familial tendencies of sleep-walking, severe and frequent headaches, and sleep-talking.

The most extensive systematic study I know is that of Abe and Shimakawa (1966a). The children in the Abeno district, Osaka, Japan, were routinely examined within 10 days of their third birthday at the Osaka Medical School Clinic. Before the checkup, a health questionnaire comprised of 30 items was sent to both the paternal and maternal grandmother of each child. It was their task to provide information about the childhood behavior of the *parents* of the children currently being evaluated. Among the items in the questionnaire were those inquiring after sleep-walking, sleep-speech, teeth grinding, and convulsions. Only the responses of healthy, literate grandmothers were used. In addition, each child's mother provided information regarding the current relevant sleep habits of the child, her husband, and herself. The results are found in Table 6.1.

The data indicate that a similar proportion of children and parents have childhood histories of somniloquy. Two additional analyses were carried out by Abe and Shimakawa (1966a), comparing the incidence of sleep-talking among children and parents, and are presented in the following Tables 6.2 and 6.3.

The second analysis appears to say that parents whose sleep-talking begins in childhood and persists into adult life are more likely than any other group of parents to show an association with their 3-year-old children who talk in their sleep. One is tempted to conclude that sleep-talking tendencies of early onset and stubborn persistence into adult life betoken potent positive genetic loading.

Thus, the data collected by Abe and Shimakawa (1966a) indicate that:

1. A hereditary factor increases the likelihood of sleep-talking in the children of sleep-talking parents.

TABLE 6.1
Familial Sleep Histories[a]

Children		
Sleep-talkers	45	(14.5%)
Nonsleep-talkers	265	(85.5%)
Total	310	

Parents manifested sleep-talking		
During childhood and later	17	
		71 (11.5%)
In childhood only	54	
		100 (16.1%)
Exclusively after childhood	29 (4.6%)	
No sleep-talking at any time		520 (83.9%)
Total		620

[a]From Abe and Shimakawa, 1966a. Copyright 1966, Acta Paedopsychiatrica, Basel, Schwabe & Co. AG.

TABLE 6.2
Sleep-Talking in 3-Year-Old Children and Their Parents[a]

	Number of Children		
Sleep-Talking Was Present in:	*With Sleep-Talking*	*Without Sleep-Talking*	*Total*
One or both parents	71	20	91
Neither parent	194	25	219
Total	265	45	310

[a]($\chi^2 = 5.50$, df = 1, $p < .02$).
Note: From Abe and Shimakawa, 1966a. Copyright 1966, Acta Paedopsychiatrica, Basel, Schwabe, & Co. AG.

TABLE 6.3
Incidence of Sleep-Talking in Children of Parents with Sleep-Talking During Childhood Persisting into Adulthood, Versus Those of Parents Who Never Had Sleep-Talking[a]

Sleep-Talking Was Present in:	*Children With Sleep-Talking*	*Children Without Sleep-Talking*	*Total*
One of the parents from childhood into adulthood	9	8	17
Neither of the parents	25	194	219
Total	34	202	236

[a]($\chi^2 = 22.1$, $P = < .001$).
Note: From Abe and Shimakawa, 1966a. Copyright 1966, Acta Paedopsychiatrica, Basel, Schwabe & Co. AG.

2. Sleep-talking can occur in children even when neither parent is a sleep-talker, although such children are in the minority.
3. A sizable proportion of parents begin to sleep-talk as adults without a known previous childhood history.

In my own work, I obtained dependable, relevant questionnaire data on 23 "corroborated" sleep-talkers and controls matched for age, sex, and education who have never talked in their sleep to the best of their knowledge. Of the sleep-talkers, 52% (12) mentioned that at least one additional family member had been heard to sleep-talk, whereas 48% (11) specifically answered no to this question. By contrast, 40% (8) of the controls offered a positive family history and 60% (12) a negative one.

In an independent study at Duke University, Sewitch (1976) studied seven female college students (18–24 years old), each with a history of sleep-talking previously verified by wakeful observers. Of these five claimed a negative and two a positive family history of sleep-talking. A single control subject who described herself as a nonsleep-talker also had a positive family history. If we pool the data of Sewitch and my own, we have a total of 30 sleep-talkers of whom 14 (46.7%) had a positive family history, and 21 "silent sleepers" of whom 9 (42.9%) also had a positive family history.[1]

Thus, in this population, self-professed, external-observer–corroborated, chronic sleep-talkers do *not* differ significantly from a similar sample of self-professed nonsleep-talkers with regard to family history of sleep-talking.

These numbers are small compared to those available to Abe and Shimakawa (1966a) and are at best merely consistent with the direction of their findings. Both the results of the former and those just cited (Sewitch, 1976) are compatible with a familial and possibly hereditary tendency; but all indicate that a sizable, but somewhat smaller, proportion of the general population may be sleep-talkers *without* a positive family history, although such a group would be in the minority.

Further, before accepting the results of Abe and Shimakawa as valid reflections of the influence of hereditary factors, it is well to keep the following two reservations in mind. First, as indicated by the pseudo-"nonsleep-talker" in Sewitch's sample, we have no means of knowing what proportion of subjects employed in other incidence studies using this criterion would turn out to sleep-talk as this subject was observed to do, with adequate methods of detection. Actually, as mentioned in Chapter 4, we have observed a great many episodes of sleep-talking in the laboratory among subjects who

---

[1] It is interesting that the subject professing not to be a sleep-talker was actually observed to talk in her sleep on five separate subsequent occasions over 28 nights at home by means of a tape recorder in continuous operation. For the purpose of the discussion at hand, however, she would still be categorized as a "nonsleep-talker" by the *self-professed* criterion—that criterion used in the majority of the incidence studies cited.

were selected on the basis of being good dream recallers and light sleepers without reference to or knowledge of sleep-talking histories. So we must take seriously the possibility that this source of significant systematic error artifactually diminished the reported "true" incidence of sleep-talking in the general population, based on family testimony alone; and that if this unknown moiety could be estimated in some way, the true incidence could only be higher.

Second, I have the distinct impression from my conversations with chronic sleep-talkers that their proclivities are frequent occasions for much family discussion, anecdote, and other commentary. This often sensitizes the family to the topic of sleep behaviors and alerts them to the possibility of *other* family members talking in their sleep as well. I draw this to your attention because the presence of one sleep-talker may well increase the likelihood of the detection of others in the family who might otherwise have escaped notice. Conversely, a family in which none of the members have observed sleep-talking in the household may well tend to be less alert to its occurrence in others.

In this way, families may actually harbor some decorous, soft-spoken sleep-talkers who escape detection, leading to such families being tabulated among those with negative sleep-talking histories. And by contrast, a family with one sleep "chatterbox" might be more likely to have their members achieve tabulation as among those with positive family histories. The total effect would be enhancement of the recorded incidence of false negatives and true positives in the tabulations.[2]

That an impressive moiety of the sleep-talking population have negative family histories makes it instructive to compare the most prevalent episodic sleep disorders with regard to their similarities, differences, and association with sleep-talking. Table 6.4 reveals that several factors are held in common, and a certain degree of confluence exists—i.e., a single person often harbors several such syndromes or related components; but it is also true that each syndrome has unique, distinctive features and that an impressive proportion of patients are afflicted with one and only one syndrome in isolation. This argues for the validity of reserving a subcategory of each as a phenomenon capable of independent origins and manifestation in "pure culture." It suggests further that the variegated clinical pictures are the outcomes of interacting constitutional, developmental, and environmental factors in accordance with Freud's (1917) conception of the complemental series as a useful perspective in assessment of etiologies.

---

[2]That frequent *sotto voce* sleep-talking may escape detection is illustrated by Sewitch's (1976) "control nonsleep-talker" subject. Even with the alerting presence of her sleep-talking father, her own sleep-talking, verified by all-night tape recording in the laboratory, eluded notice in her family.

TABLE 6.4

Comparison of Chief Episodic Sleep Disorders in the General Population

	Somnambulism	Enuresis	Night Terrors	Nightmares	Bruxism	Microdissociative Primary Somniloquy
Overall prevalence	1–6%; less in adults (Kales & Kales, 1974	10–15% of children; 1–3% adults (Kales & Kales, 1974)	1–3% of children, less in adults (Fisher et al., 1975; Jacobson et al., 1969)	Common	5–15% less in adults (Reding et al, 1966)	10–75% of adults (see Table 4.4)
Association with other sleep disorders	Common	Common	Common	Common	Not reported	Common
Association with sleep stages	4	3–4	3–4 typically	REM	Occurs in all sleep stages. Stage 2 preponderance	Occurs in all sleep stages. NREM preponderance, 2, 3, & 4 about equal (see Table 7.1)
Time of night	First one-third	First one-third	First one-third	Second two-thirds	Second two-thirds	Equally throughout night
Severe psychopathology	Common	Common	Common in adults	Common in frequent nightmares	Not characteristic	Not characteristic

EEG abnormality	Common	Common	Reported but not typical	Not reported	Absent	Typically absent
Salient psychological features of episodes	Tense, dysphoric affect; postarousal confusion. Poor mentation recall in laboratory: better at home.	Affect not remarkable; poor mentation recall.	Extreme terror, postarousal confusion. Moderate-to-maximum motoric activity. Poor mentation recall in children; better in adults.	Moderate–intense anxiety. Good dream recall; minimal motoric activity.	Affect not remarkable; poor mentation recall. Minimal motoric activity.	Broad range of affect: blandness, humor, to dysphoria. Fair–good mentation recall (see Table 10.1). Minimal motoric activity.
Vocalization	Common	Not typical	Typical	Common	Not reported	Always—by definition
Motoric and autonomic effects during episodes	Maximal motoric activity. Autonomic activity variable	Marked autonomic. Minimal motoric activity.	Extreme autonomic and marked motoric activity.	Variable: minimal to moderate autonomic and minimal motoric activity.	Variable: both autonomic and motoric activity minimal to moderate.	Variable: motor activity minimal; increased autonomic activity observed but not systematically studied.
Familial tendency	Marked	Marked	Not reported	Not reported	Common	Common among both sleep-talkers and "silent sleepers"

Perhaps the most striking demonstration of independent specific components is provided by a comparison between primary idiopathic somniloquy and bruxism. Both are similar in that they may occur in any sleep stage and throughout the night, may be associated with momentary arousal from sleep and need not be associated with psychopathology, may have familial tendencies, show minimal to moderate motoric activity, be accompanied by bland affect, possess no typical EEG abnormality, and even become manifest by means of overlapping muscle groups partly held in common. That is, with regard to the latter, both talking and teeth-grinding make use of the jaw muscles. It seems reasonable to expect that activation of neural circuits involved in one would produce "cross-talk" in the other condition, and therefore one would imagine that it would be difficult to be a bruxist and not be a somniloquist concurrently. After all, sleep-talking has been observed with vastly different episodic sleep disorders such as enuresis and somnambulism; why then should it not appear in an apparently "closer relative" such as bruxism? Two separate, careful laboratory studies with elaborate electrographic recording fail to mention concomitant sleep-talking: Reding, Zepelin, Robinson, Zimmerman, and Smith (1968), and Satoh and Harada (1971). An additional laboratory investigation by Tani, Yoshu, Yoshino, and Kobayashi (1966) reports findings on bruxists, enuretics, and somniloquists. Although bruxism was seen concurrently with enuresis in this work, somniloquy was associated with neither and occurred independently. Finally, two demographic studies of bruxism fail to mention sleep-talking as an associated finding (Abe & Shimakawa, 1966b; Reding, Rubright, & Zimmerman, 1966).

When one compares microdissociative primary sleep-talking with night-terrors, one is impressed by the striking differences between them despite their sharing sleep-associated vocalization. Night terrors, particularly in adults, are rare and tend to occur typically in association with Stage 3–4 sleep and in the first third of the night. They are usually accompanied by agitated panic and intense autonomic and motoric activity usually leading to final awakening; they also tend to be associated with severe psychopathology. By contrast, microdissociative primary sleep-talking is common, and episodes may occur in Stages 2, 1 NREM, and REM, as well as 3–4. They may be equally distributed throughout the night, be accompanied by a broad variety of affects (including blandness, humor, euphoric excitement, as well as anxiety and sadness), and show minimal to moderate autonomic and motoric activity; they are also shorter in duration, do not tend to terminate in wakefulness, and need not be associated with psychopathology.

In short, these two comparisons lend weight to the contention that although sleep-talking is often concurrent with somnambulism, night terrors, and enuresis, it is capable of independent origin and manifestation justifying the clinical and psychophysiological concept of microdissociative primary idiopathic somniloquy.

7

Laboratory Studies on Normative and Electrographic Features of Sleep-Talking

The scientific literature contains a large number of observations on sleep-utterance in the laboratory. Perhaps the majority of them were based on subjects who were selected without regard for a history of sleep-talking but rather for research projects with broader goals, such as the assessment of sleep mentation (Kamiya, 1961; Rechtschaffen, Goodenough, & Shapiro, 1962), or episodic sleep disorders in general (Gastaut & Broughton, 1965; Popoviciú & Szabó, 1973; Szabó & Waitsuk, 1971), and therefore were subjects who fortuitously produced one or more sleep-utterances in the laboratory. With the accumulation of sufficient quantities of such episodes, it became possible to acquire data suitable for scientific study. I know of only four investigations, however, that specifically employed self-professed, chronic sleep-talkers *prospectively* and that included one or more undisturbed baseline nights in the laboratory schedule: Tani, Yoshu, Yoshino, and Kobayashi (1966), Arkin, Toth, Baker, and Hastey (1970a), MacNeilage (1971) and Sewitch (1976). The others cited may also have had some baseline nights, but this was not made clear in the published report. That is, in pursuit of other goals, they used such procedures as mentation report awakenings or even indwelling catheters with enuretic patients. The resulting statistics were calculated on the basis of heterogeneously pooled observations. I therefore turn initially to those reports with one or more baseline nights using subjects with a self-professed, externally corroborated history of sleep-talking.

BASELINE FREQUENCY
OF SLEEP-UTTERANCE AMONG
SELF-PROFESSED CHRONIC SLEEP-TALKERS

Included in the report of Tani et al. (1966) were data on three male chronic sleep-talkers (ages 52, 50, and 23), each of whom spent one night in the laboratory. The two older subjects uttered three speeches each, and the youngest produced two speeches (2.7 speeches per subject per night). There is a slight ambiguity in the description of methods that Tani (1966) used.

> Twenty persons were studied in this experiment. They had complained of frequent sleep-talking, enuresis or tooth-grinding, but had no neurological signs of disorders, psychotic diseases, and were not mentally retarded. Subjects who did not display the sleep behavior were excluded from this report [p. 241].

Thus, it is not known for certain whether the three subjects mentioned comprised the entire subset of self-professed sleep-talkers in the entire population of 20 subjects or whether a number of subjects professing sleep-talking remained silent in the laboratory and were excluded from the analysis. The information in the paper does not provide one with a means of deciding this point. If self-professed sleep-talkers were indeed observed in the laboratory and did not vocalize, then inclusion of this unknown number would drastically reduce the tabulations which indicate that 100% of subjects somniloquized at least once.

In my own work (Arkin et al., 1970a), it was usually an easy matter to obtain paid experimental subjects volunteering a history of sleep-talking. With a few exceptions, they had responded to advertisements placed on college bulletin boards in the New York City area. The notices made specific mention of sleep-talking as a requirement, and the subjects were accepted on the basis of their word that roommates and/or relatives had overheard them talk in their sleep recently. None were aware of their own sleep-talking other than being so informed by such witnesses. As a group, they did not seem to differ in any obvious way from a comparable "normal" population. None were psychotic.

Our basic pool of sleep-talkers on whom we drew for a variety of studies described in this book consisted of 43 subjects (17 females and 26 males). Two were high-school students, one was a medical technician, and one was a professional subject in the teaching of medical hypnosis; the remaining 39 were college students or recent graduates.

Fifty-three baseline experiments consisting of one or more nights of monitored but otherwise undisturbed sleep were performed with 13 subjects who were part of this basic pool. Each subject slept in the laboratory in a private room equipped with a bed, a microphone leading to a continuously running tape recorder, and an intercommunication system enabling the experimenter to hear and note down on the polygraph record all sounds emitted by the subject at the moment of occurrence. The subject was connected by a set of electrical leads to a polygraph in continuous operation that monitored his electroencephalogram (EEG) and electrooculogram (EOG) in accordance with the technique of Dement and Kleitman (1957). In many instances, the chin EMG and heart rate were also recorded.

Results

A total of 206 speeches was uttered during the 53 nights. Ten subjects spoke one or more words at least once; one merely moaned, groaned, and emitted other types of sounds, and the remainder failed to vocalize in any significant manner. Briefly:

1. Total number of subjects = 13.
2. Total number of laboratory nights = 53.
3. Number of baseline nights per subject = 4.1 (range 1–5).
4. Total number of speeches = 206.
5. Number of sleep-speeches per subject per night (13 subjects) = 3.9 (weighted mean).
6. Number of subjects uttering at least one speech = 10 (76.9%).
7. Number of sleep-speeches per subject per night among those 10 subjects who actually talked in the laboratory = 5.3 (weighted mean).
8. Median of individual mean nightly frequencies of sleep-speech by subjects (10 subjects) = 1.3.

In independent work, MacNeilage (1971) studied five male college students who reported both recall of dreams "almost every morning" and sleep-talking at least "occasionally." The first part of the study consisted of three laboratory nights of baseline uninterrupted sleep with a unique addition of two EMG needle electrodes inserted into the tongue muscles (genioglossus), seeking to precisely observe concurrent activity of speech musculature. The results were:

1. Total number of subjects = 5.
2. Total number of baseline nights = 15.
3. Number of baseline nights per subject = 3.
4. Total number of speeches = 13.
5. Number of speeches per subject night (5 subjects) = 0.9 (weighted mean).
6. Number of subjects uttering at least one speech = 3 (60%).

7. Number of speeches per subject per night among those who actually talked in the laboratory (3 subjects) = 1.3 (median of individual means = 1).

Finally, Sewitch (1976) selected two female undergraduate subjects (each 21 years old) for all-night observation in a college dormitory, rather than in a laboratory setting. One subject was a self-professed chronic sleep-talker and the other a control who claimed she was not a sleep-talker. Both occupied the same room. Vocalization was monitored by means of a tape recorder operating continuously throughout the night; two microphones, each close to the respective subject's head, picked up the output, which was separately recorded on two different tracks. A unique feature of this work was the large number of mostly *consecutive* observation nights. The results were:

1. Number of subjects = 2 (one of whom had claimed she was not a sleep-talker).
2. Number of nights recorded: 38 for the sleep-talker, 28 for the "control."
3. Total number of speeches = 48 (both subjects).
4. Total number of speeches uttered by the sleep-talker = 37.
5. Total number of speeches uttered by the control = 11.
6. Number of speeches per observation night: for the sleep-talker subject = 1.3, for the control = 0.6.

It is of interest that the "control" nonsleep-talker actually somniloquized on an impressive number of occasions. As noted earlier, such an observation lends support to the contention that any incidence study of sleep-talking relying on self-report is likely to underestimate the true incidence.

The overall results of the four studies are presented in Table 7.1 and establish that:

1. Among a population of self-professed chronic sleep-talkers, one can expect that the *majority* can be relied upon to talk in their sleep at some time under laboratory observation conditions over five nights or less. This information might be useful to any investigator who is interested in somniloquy but is concerned about whether he will have sufficient data for analysis.
2. A *minority* of subjects claiming to be active sleep-talkers cannot be depended upon to vocalize in the laboratory, unless perhaps the investigator can afford to have such subjects under observation for an indefinite number of nights.
3. One cannot accept at face value a subject's claim to be a *non*sleep-talker, inasmuch as such subjects may be observed to talk in their sleep under laboratory conditions.

TABLE 7.1
Incidence of Sleep-Utterance Among Self-Professed Chronic Sleep-Talkers Under Baseline Laboratory Conditions

Investigation	Total No. Subjects	Total No. Laboratory Nights	No. Baseline Nights per Subject	Total No. Speeches	No. Sleep-Speeches per Subject per Night	No. Subjects Actually Emitting One or More Sleep-Speeches	No. Sleep-Speeches per Subject per Night (Laboratory Sleep-Talkers Only)
Tani et al. (1966)	3	3	1	8	2.7	3 (100%)	2.7
Arkin et al. (1970c)[a]	13	53	4.1 (range 1–5)	206	3.9 (weighted mean) median = 0.8	13 (76.9%)	5.3 (weighted mean) median = 1.3
MacNeilage (1971)	5	15	3	12	0.9 (weighted mean) median = 1.0	3 (60%)	1.3 median = 1.0
Sewitch (1976)	1 sleep-talker	38	38	37	0.97	2 (100%)	0.97
	1 control "non-sleep-talker"	28	28	11	0.49		0.4

[a]The data reported in this study (1970c) are the same as those tabulated here but included neither the median nor the weighted mean.

4. There is enormous variability in sleep-utterance output from one subject to the next. This was particularly striking in my own subject population (Arkin, 1970a). Although the mean number of speeches per subject per night in the subgroup of 10 who somniloquized in the laboratory was 5.3, the range was 0.25–20.2 speeches per subject per night, and the standard deviation was 6.5. The median was 1.3.

5. There is also enormous variability within subjects in the amount and number of episodes of sleep-utterance from one laboratory night to the next. Nights of reticence and nights of loquacity were often observable in the same subject. Such within-subject variability could well account for a number of occasions in which self-professed, externally corroborated chronic somniloquists were silent in the laboratory; they may have been going through a "dry spell."

What can one say about the incidence of sleep-speech in the laboratory among subjects who offer a history of chronic sleep-talking? The mean frequencies are discrepant across studies. Arkin et al. (1970a) reported a weighted mean of 3.9 speeches per night, in contrast to the figures of MacNeilage (1971) and Sewitch (1976), which closely agree at about one speech per subject per night. There was considerable skewing in the data of Arkin et al. (1970a), however, and the results of these three studies are brought into agreement when the median of the Arkin et al. (1970a) data is used, inasmuch as it is, in this case, a more appropriate measure of central tendency. With this measure, the average number of sleep-speeches per subject per night among subjects professing to be chronic sleep-talkers is 0.8–1.0, and similar agreement is obtained when the median is used for data on subjects who somniloquized at least once in the laboratory: 0.97–1.3. The results of Tani et al. (1966) were not included in this discussion because they were obtained over only one laboratory night per subject.

In conclusion, the definitive study on the "natural" baseline frequency of sleep-talking among self-professed chronic sleep-talkers in the laboratory has yet to be carried out. A larger, more truly representative population should be observed for an extended series of nights in order to arrive at an authentic estimate.

RELATIONSHIPS BETWEEN
SLEEP-UTTERANCE EPISODES
AND SLEEP STAGES

General agreement prevails among reports providing data on a relatively large heterogeneous pool of subjects that most sleep-talking occurs in association with NREM sleep (Arkin et al. 1970a; Gastaut & Broughton,

1965; Kamiya, 1961; MacNeilage, 1971; Popoviciú, 1977; Popoviciú, Asgian, Corfariu, & Szabó, 1973; Popoviciú & Szabó, 1973; Rechtschaffen et al., 1962; Szabó & Waitsuk, 1971). There is, nevertheless, a definite, albeit smaller, proportion of episodes that occur in intimate association with ongoing Stage REM (Arkin et al., 1970c; Kamiya, 1961; MacNeilage, 1971; Rechtschaffen et al., 1962; Tani et al., 1966). As we see later, some REMP-associated utterances occur at REMP onset, the bulk sandwiched within immediately preceding and following REMP sleep, and a final set at REMP termination (Arkin et al., 1970a; MacNeilage, 1971; Tani et al., 1966), and Oswald (1964) and MacNeilage have each independently observed occasions of REMP-associated sleep speech accompanied by *sustained* alpha frequencies but preceded and followed by typical REMP sleep. Arkin et al. (1970a) have found that similar episodes may occur at REMP termination as well. Finally, although most NREM sleep-utterance is associated with Stages 2, 3, and 4, a small share occurs in connection with Stage 1 NREM, even at sleep onset as well (Arkin et al., 1970a; Gastaut & Broughton, 1965).

In reviewing the following literature containing relevant findings, we report results or entire studies, where possible, on the basis of whether data were obtained on nights of uninterrupted baseline sleep, as opposed to nights during which experimental awakenings were carried out. The reason for this separation is that experimental awakenings have been shown to be capable of altering spontaneous baseline frequencies of sleep-utterance in association with the different sleep stages (Arkin, Farber, Antrobus, Ellman, & Nelson, 1973; Farber, Arkin, Ellman, Antrobus, & Nelson, 1973).

Findings Derived From Uninterrupted Baseline Nights

Tani et al. (1966) reported on three self-professed male chronic sleep-talkers whose average age was 42 (52, 50, and 23), and therefore, they were somewhat older than those in the study of Arkin et al. (1970c) and MacNeilage (1971). Between them, eight speeches were uttered over one subject night each, all in association with REM sleep—none in NREM.

MacNeilage (1971) reported that of 13 utterances from three subjects, 8% were REMP-associated and 92% NREM-associated (by sleep stages, 1 = 8%; 2 = 76%; 3 = 8%; and 4 = 0).

Arkin et al. (1970c) found that of 206 speeches uttered in the laboratory by 10 self-professed chronic sleep-talkers (see Table 7.4), 48% were REMP-associated and 52% were NREM-associated (by sleep stage, 1 = 4%; 2 = 24%; 3 = 9%; and 4 = 15%).[1] As mentioned in the footnote of Table 7.4, these

---

[1]The present figures are correct and differ somewhat from those published earlier (Arkin et al., 1970c), which are incorrect. The differences, however, are of no apparent practical or scientific importance and do not affect the essential nature of the findings.

figures are skewed somewhat by the contribution of our most voluble sleep-talker who vocalized mainly in association with REM sleep. If her speeches are removed from the tally, we arrive at a total of 105 speeches uttered by nine subjects, 19% of which were REMP-associated and 81% NREM-associated (by sleep stage, 1 = 1%; 2 = 36%; 3 = 17%; and 4 = 27%). Table 7.2 presents the 206 sleep-speeches uttered by the same 10 subjects in accordance with the sleep stage with which they were associated.

It will be noticed that five subjects spoke entirely in association with NREM sleep, four in association with both REM and NREM sleep, and one solely with Stage REM. Once more, this should dispel the widely but not universally held notion that sleep-talking is exclusively a NREM phenomenon; and again attention is drawn to the marked between-subject and between-sleep-stage variability.

Subjects normally spend unequal amounts of time in the various sleep stages. Is the high total number of Stage 2 sleep-speeches merely a reflection of the greater natural abundance of Stage 2, or does each sleep stage contain a different potential for sleep-speech production? If each sleep stage were equally conducive to sleep-speech occurrences, the distribution of sleep-speeches in each sleep stage would directly parallel the amount of time spent in that sleep stage by each subject.

TABLE 7.2
Baseline Sleep-Speech in Relation to Associated Sleep Stage[a]

| | Total of 206 Sleep-Speeches by Sleep Stage | | | | | |
| | NREM | | | | | |
Subjects (N = 10)	1	2	3	4	REM	Number of Nights
S.R.	0	2	1	1	0	5
O.A.	1	25	11	13	13	5
M.R.	0	0	1	0	0	4
L.H.	0	6	1	10	0	2
K.W.	0	0	0	0	4	4
B.H.	0	0	0	1	0	2
H.E.	0	4	3	1	1	5
D.C.	7	12	0	3	79	5
W.G.	0	1	0	0	2	5
N.D.	0	0	1	2	0	2
Totals and percent	8(3.9%)	50(24.3%)	18(8.7%)	31(15.0%)	99(48.1%)	39
Mean	0.8	5	1.8	3.1	9.9	3.9
Median	0	1.5	1	1	0.5	4.5

[a]N = 10: Data collected by Arkin et al. (1970c).

Accordingly, Dr. John Antrobus suggested to me that it would be useful to have an indication of the number of sleep-speeches uttered per unit time spent in each sleep stage. This would provide a rough measure of the "sleep-speech production potential" differentially possessed by each sleep stage.

The following determinations were based on 31 available experimental flow charts prepared from the original electrographic records of nine subjects.[2] The rate of sleep-speech production per unit time spent in each sleep stage was obtained by dividing the total number of speeches uttered by each subject in each sleep stage, during all nights included in the calculations, by the total number of hours spent by that subject in each sleep stage. This enabled us to arrive at the number of sleep-speeches uttered in each sleep stage per average hour spent in each sleep stage. The results are presented in Table 7.3.

The greater figure for the mean number of sleep-speeches per hour spent in Stages 1 NREM and REM in comparison to Stages 2 and 3–4 do not adequately reflect the respective central tendencies because of wide scatter and high scores on the extremities of the distribution. The median is a much more faithful reflection of these central tendencies, therefore, and they indicate that Stages 2 and 3–4 are associated with the highest number of sleep-speeches per hour of sleep: Stage 2 = 0.10; 3–4 = 0.34; Stages 1 NREM and REM = 0.0. When the median number of sleep-speeches per hour of sleep stage per subject is divided by the median number of hours of each sleep stage across all nine subjects, the results are: Stage 2 = 0.025; Stage 3–4 = 0.17; Stages 1 NREM and REM = 0. This suggests that Stage 3–4 is maximally conducive to sleep-speech emission.

The findings may be considered in the light of at least three mutually compatible hypotheses:

1. Psycholinguistic ideational activity tendencies are relatively greater in Stages 2 and particularly 3–4 than during Stages REM or 1 NREM.

2. Speech emission thresholds are lower in Stages 2 and 3–4 than during Stages REM and 1 NREM.

3. Psychoneural mechanisms involved in the conversion of psycholinguistic ideational activity into overt speech are more available or are more efficient in Stages 2 and 3–4 than during the other sleep stages.

In view of the high frequency of speech activity recalled in REM mentation reports (Cipolli, Dubois, & Salzarulo, 1974; Salzarulo & Cipolli, 1974; Snyder, 1970), the hypothesis of diminished linguistic ideational activity

---

[2]As stated earlier, most of our original stored electrographic records had been inadvertently discarded by the janitorial department of our institution. Thus, these data are lacking the contribution of subject W. G. (Table 7.2), who produced one Stage 2 and two Stage-REM speeches; also lacking are data from three other nights distributed one each across three subjects.

TABLE 7.3
The Number of Sleep-Speeches per Hour of Sleep Stage

Subject (N = 9)	No. of Nights	No. Sleep-Speeches per Total No. Hours Sleep Stage			
		NREM Sleep Stages			
		1	2	3 & 4	Stage REM
S.R.	5	0	0.10	0.17	0
O.A.	5	2.13	1.26	2.04	2.38
M.R.	3	0	0	0.16	0
L.H.	2	0	0.63	3.24	0
K.W.	3	0	0	0	.69
B.H.	2	0	0	0.34	0
H.E.	4	0	0.25	0.39	0.13
D.C.	5	8.43	0.68	0.25	8.49
N.D.	2	0	0	0.92	0
Mean	3.4	1.17	0.33	0.83	1.30
Median	3	0	0.10	0.34	0
Average hours spent in each sleep stage (all 9 subjects)	Means	0.39	4.17	2.02	1.62
	Median	0.26	3.96	2.08	1.60
Median sleep speeches per hour per subject divided by median hours sleep stage Σ 9 subjects	—	0	$\frac{0.10}{3.96} = 0.025$	$\frac{0.34}{2.08} = 0.17$	0

seems an unlikely candidate for a partial accounting of the relatively low incidence of REM and 1 NREM sleep-speech. REM mentation possesses abundant speech content.

The finding of a massive tonic motor inhibition during REM sleep (Rechtschaffen & Kales, 1968) is compatible with the relatively low frequency of REM sleep-speech that requires the availability of somatic linguistic musculature. However, this does not jibe with the even lower frequency of 1 NREM sleep-speech in the absence of tonic motor inhibition; nor does it accord easily with the fairly common occurrence of phasic gross body movement in REM sleep that is unaccompanied by vocalization of any sort. Nevertheless, it seems reasonable to assume that the tonic motor inhibition of REM sleep is one effective factor in accounting for the relatively low frequency of sleep-speech in REM sleep.

What evidence suggests that motor output thresholds are relatively lower in Stages 3–4 and 2? MacNeilage (1971) found that frequent, brief, aperiodic EMG activity episodes occurred in speech-related muscle components throughout the night in five subjects who gave a currently active history of sleep-talking. Both the amplitude and duration of such episodes were greatest in Stage 3–4 with Stage 2 following. Second, Stage 3–4 is known to be correlated with somnambulism and enuresis—pathological motor anomalies of sleep (Broughton, 1968; Gastaut & Broughton, 1965; Kales, Jacobson, Paulson, Kales & Walter, 1966). However, a comprehensive review of motor activity in sleep indicates that relationships between sleep stage and motor activity are complex (Gardner & Grossman, 1976). For example, NREM large-scale motor episodes decrease with the approach of slow-wave sleep, are lowest while slow-wave sleep prevails, and increase with the approach of REM periods. Halász, Rajna, Pál, Kundra, Vargha, Balogh, & Kemény (1977) report a similar pattern for "micro-arousals," a related phenomenon. Also, MacNeilage (1971) found that although the amplitude and duration of speech-related EMG was greatest in Stage 3–4, the rate of motor-episode emission was paradoxically greatest in Stages 1 NREM and REM. This lack of uniformity in parameters of motor output activity in relation to sleep stage, therefore, makes it unlikely that a simple relationship between sleep-speech frequency and motor emission thresholds will be found.

Finally, one must consider the contribution of the psychoneural mechanisms responsible for the conversion of linguistic ideation and/or information into speech. Activation of linguistic ideation sequences without succeeding execution of linguistic program articulation (inner speech) occurs ubiquitously during wakefulness and sleep as indicated by mentation reports. That Stage 3–4 is the condition most conducive to overt sleep-speech suggests that availability of articulation programs to ideational sequences is greatest at such times in comparison to other sleep stages. This constitutes a tentative conclusion regarding the status of an important component of psycholinguistic functioning during sleep and provides an interesting contrast to the status of other types of cognition and psychophysiological patterns occurring both in Stage 3–4 and in other sleep stages.

Specifically, certain subcomponents of linguistic articulatory programs are *maximally* available during those sleep stages peculiarly characterized by a relative *paucity* of recalled mentation—mentation with visual imagery, hallucinated dramatic sequences, and so forth. The expression "certain subcomponents" of articulatory programs was selected advisedly because, as we see later, although articulatory programs seem more available for speech emission in Stages 3–4, overall efficiency tends to be impaired then. That is, Stage 3–4, more than any other sleep stage, is more likely to be associated with speeches with varying degrees of linguistic disorganization. A type of sleep-speech bearing striking resemblances to severe aphasia in the wakeful speech of the brain damaged shows a special predilection for occurrence in Stage 3–4 in comparison to Stages 2 and REM. Naturally, it is difficult to differentiate whether this observation reflects time-of-night effects as opposed to sleep-stage effects, inasmuch as most Stage 3–4 occurs in the first half of the night.

Findings Derived from Heterogeneous Subjects Sleeping in the Laboratory Under Heterogeneous Conditions Usually Entailing Sleep Interruption for Mentation Reports

Kamiya (1961) reported that of 98 episodes uttered by an unspecified number of subjects, 12% were REMP- and 88% NREM-associated.

Rechtschaffen et al. (1962) found that of 84 speeches produced by 28 subjects, 8% were REMP- and 92% NREM-associated (by sleep stage, 1 = 0; 2 = 63%; and 3–4 = 29%). Gastaut and Broughton (1965) reported that 8% of speeches recorded by them were REMP- and 92% NREM-associated (by sleep stage, 1 = 33%; 2 = 33%; 3 = 17%; and 4 = 9%). Neither the number of subjects nor the total number of speeches were specified in this article, but clearly both came to a sizable total.

Arkin et al. (1970c) found that of 258 speeches produced by 40 self-professed chronic sleep-talkers, 14% were REMP- and 86% NREM-associated (by sleep stage, 1 = 3%; 2 = 54%; 3 = 12%; and 4 = 17%).

MacNeilage (1971) reported that four self-professed chronic sleep-talkers produced 14 sleep-speeches over three nights each in the laboratory. Of this total, 43% were REMP- and 57% NREM-associated (all Stage 2).

Finally, Szabó and Waitsuk (1971) with 10 subjects, and Popoviciú et al. (1973; Popoviciú and Szabó, 1973) with 25 subjects, found that 100% of sleep-speeches were associated with NREM sleep. The total number of speeches was unspecified, although apparently considerable in number. They were said to occur mostly in relation to "light slow-wave sleep."

Both Rechtschaffen et al. (1962) and Arkin et al. (1970c) attempted to assess the central tendencies of their data to minimize bias arising from aberrant subjects. (These results were not included in Table 7.4.) To do this, Rechtschaffen et al. (1962) recalculated their results on the basis of one incident selected at random from each subject. Such calculation reduced the number of sleep-talking incidents to 28, of which four (14%) were in REM periods, 12 (43%) were in Stage 2, and 12 (43%) were in Stages 3 and 4. (Total NREM = 86%; total Stage REM = 14%.)

In attempting to arrive at a comparable value of the central tendencies of the data from our own subjects (Arkin et al., 1970c), we determined the mean percentage (across 40 subjects) of sleep-speech episodes in each sleep stage. The results were as follows: NREM Stage 1 (.9%), 2 (21.5%), and 3 (21.5%), and 4 (28.5%). Total NREM = 72.3%; Stage REM = 27.7%. Omitting the exceptionally prolific Stage-REM sleep-talker mentioned earlier yielded NREM Stages 1 (0.1%), 2 (22.5%), 3 (23.9%), and 4 (31.4%). Total NREM = 77.9%. Stage REM = (22.1%). These findings are similar to those of Rechtschaffen et al. (1962) mainly in that the preponderance of sleep-speech in both studies appears to be associated with NREM sleep, with the smaller share occurring with Stage REM. Otherwise, the intragroup proportions are distinctly different.

Commentary

The variability of results across studies is almost bewildering. First, the difference in incidence of REMP- versus NREM-associated speeches is striking. Inspection of Table 7.4 indicates that in one study (Tani et al., 1966) 100% of speeches were REMP-associated, whereas in others (Szabó et al., 1971, and Popoviciú et al., 1973), 100% of speeches were NREM-associated, with results of the others falling at various points between these two extremes.

Second, there are marked differences in the incidence of Stage 1-NREM speeches. Gastaut and Broughton (1965) indicate that fully one-third of their entire population of episodes occurred in association with Stage 1-NREM ("phases Ia and especially Ib"; these phases are defined by slowing and diffusion of alpha rhythm in the former, and loss of alpha in the latter, both in the context of sleep-onset). By contrast, Kamiya (1961) did not mention a single instance of sleep-onset 1–NREM sleep-utterance. Rechtschaffen et al. (1962), although aware of the existence of such phenomena, specifically excluded them from their population sample because the phenomena were considered as arising from transitional states between sleep and wakefulness rather than being associated with prior definitive sleep. MacNeilage (1971) mentions observing one Stage 1-NREM speech out of a total of 28 episodes. In our laboratory (Arkin et al., 1970c), we saw eight speech occurrences (4% of our baseline population) in association with a Stage 1-NREM electrographic picture either at sleep-onset or later during the night.

Third, Table 7.4 presents group results only. It is important to reiterate that individual differences were striking. That is, some subjects spoke little, others much. Some spoke entirely in association with NREM, some in association with both NREM and REM sleep, and our most prolific sleep-talker (Arkin et al., 1970c) spoke *mostly* in association with stage REM. Rechtschaffen et al. (1962), Oswald (1964), and MacNeilage (1971) have likewise noted the REM sleep episodes could be emitted by subjects who also produced NREM incidents.

TABLE 7.4
Somniloquy in Association with Sleep Stages

Study	Number Subjects	Total Number Episodes	% of Sleep Stage (rounded off) NREM	% of Sleep Stage (rounded off) REM
Chronic sleep-talker subjects: baseline conditions of uninterrupted sleep				
Tani et al. (1966)	3	8	0	100%
MacNeilage (1971)	3	13	92% (by sleep stages) 1 = 8% 2 = 76% 3 = 8%	8%
Arkin et al. (1970c)—1[a]	10	206	52% 1 = 4% 2 = 24% 3 = 9% 4 = 15%	48%
Arkin et al. (1970c)—2[a]	9	105	81% 1 = 1% 2 = 36% 3 = 17% 4 = 27%	19%

60

Heterogeneous subjects and/or heterogeneous conditions (usually interrupted sleep for mentation reports)	Study	Subjects	Number	%	Stage breakdown	
	Kamiya (1961)	Not specified	98	88%		12%
	Rechtschaffen et al. (1962)	28	84	92%	1 = 0% 2 = 63% 3–4 = 29%	8%
	Gastaut & Broughton (1965)	Not specified	Not specified	92%	1 = 33% 2 = 33% 3 = 17% 4 = 9%	8%
	Arkin et al. (1970c)	40 Chronic sleep-talkers	258	86%	1 = 3% 2 = 54% 3 = 12% 4 = 17%	14%
	MacNeilage (1971)	4 chronic sleep-talkers	14	57%	1 = 0% 2 = 57% 3–4 = 0%	43%
	Szabó et al. (1971)	10	Not specified	100%		0
	Popoviciú et al. (1973)	25	Not specified	100% (mostly "light slow-wave sleep")		0

[a]The first tabular entry with 10 subjects contains an unrepresentative high percentage of REMP-associated sleep-speech. This "disproportion" is the result of our most voluble sleep-talker who contributed 101 speeches to our total sample collected under conditions of baseline undisturbed sleep. As mentioned, she spoke mostly in association with Stage REM and uttered 79 of our 99 stage REM speeches. The second entry with nine subjects omits the contribution of this unusual subject and the results more closely resemble those of the other studies.

I must confess that besides ascribing the differences across studies to sampling variability, I am at a loss to account for them in any simple way. Several of the studies were carried out prior to 1968, at which time the standard sleep-stage scoring manual appeared (Rechtschaffen & Kales, 1968). It is possible that employment of nonuniform scoring systems may have contributed to the differences under discussion, but this doesn't seem to provide a convincing explanation for more than a small proportion of the variation in outcomes.

INCIDENCE OF SLEEP-UTTERANCE
IN RELATION TO THE TIME OF NIGHT

Rechtschaffen et al. (1962) concluded that "the chance sleep-talking would occur during any one particular hour of sleep was about as great as the chance that it would occur during any other hour [p. 421]" and that "NREM sleep-talking never initiated REM periods [p. 421]." In attempting to evaluate our observations with regard to the same question for the entire nightly sleep period, each REM period and NREM period of the night were divided into tenths, and the occurrences of all sleep-speech in each such time interval were tabulated for each baseline record for all subjects on whom baseline sleep was recorded (Arkin et al., 1970c). This procedure failed to disclose any well-marked tendencies and these results were, therefore, consistent with those of Rechtschaffen et al. (1962). There was a suggestion, however, of slight increases in frequency during the second tenth and the eighth tenth of the entire sleep period and also during the last tenth of each NREM and REM period, i.e., during intervals of sleep-stage transition. Moreover, we observed 16 instances of sleep-speech and 12 additional nonspeech vocalizations in NREM sleep just preceding Stage-REM sleep, many of them occurring at or immediately before REMP onset. Thus, although one cannot say that the NREM speech "initiated" the REMP in any causal sense, it is clear that the aforementioned temporal sequence is observable repeatedly.

Sewitch (1976) studied sleep-utterance incidence in relation to time of night in two sets of self-professed, chronic sleep-talking subjects, all of whom slept without interruption in their usual home-like setting with no laboratory equipment except tape-recording devices. With the first set, a sampling technique rather than continuous recording was utilized, resulting in a disappointingly low yield of sleep-utterance. The second set was comprised of one self-professed, chronic sleep-talker and a control self-professed "nonsleep-talker." With continuous, all-night tape recording for 38 nights with the former and 28 for the latter subject, a total of 37 and 11 sleep-utterance episodes were detected, respectively. Analysis of the data revealed (1) that temporal onsets of sleep-talking episodes do not differ significantly from a random, normal curve distribution; (2) that there is a slight tendency for episode clustering during the second to fifth hours after retiring for the night; and (3) that there is a slight tendency for sleep-utterance to cluster in several nights over an extended series of nights.

The results of all three reports are in agreement that sleep-utterance episodes are distributed more or less randomly throughout the night. This is true, apparently, regardless of whether subjects are selected for self-professed, chronic sleep-talking tendencies, whether they are observed in laboratory or "naturalistic" settings, or whether they are permitted uninterrupted versus experimentally interrupted sleep. Further, the Arkin et al. (1970c) and Sewitch (1976) data both agree on a slight tendency for increased frequency of sleep-utterance during the approximate middle third of the night.

The lack of any tendency of sleep-speech episodes to cluster in some specific portion of the night provides an interesting contrast with "night terrors," which do indeed tend to occur more frequently during the first two hours of sleep (Fisher, Kahn, Edwards, & Davis, 1973a). Thus, two syndromes both characterized by sleep-associated utterances nevertheless display different temporal patterning.

It would be of great interest to extend Sewitch's (1976) observation of a tendency for sleep-utterance episodes to cluster in several nightly groupings during a series of consecutive nights. If this finding were borne out with a larger subject sample, it would suggest an infradian biological rhythmic factor in sleep-utterance production. Rechtschaffen et al. (1962) specifically state that they observed no such clustering tendencies across a series of nights, but one gains an impression that none of their series was carried on for as long as those of Sewitch (1976).

ELECTROGRAPHIC CONCOMITANTS
OF SLEEP-UTTERANCE

As indicated in Chapter 3, I intend to treat sleep-utterance as varieties of psychic dissociative episodes (Hilgard, 1973; 1977). Such an approach enables one to usefully relate laboratory and clinical observation to a more general theory and to broader realms of psychology.

Experience with somniloquy quickly persuades one that it is by no means a unitary phenomenon with uniform significance and causation, any more than headaches are always the same, both as subjective states or physiological occurrences. A definitive scheme of classification of somniloquy would seemingly require factor analytic approaches that take into account sleep stages, time of night, number of words, affective qualities, linguistic organization, and mental content analyses, together with relationships to associated mentation reports and recent daytime events, all in relation to the sleep-speeches concerned. At the present time, the data necessary for such a program are not available.

The territory to be mapped is swampy and difficult to formulate with even a pretense at rigor. However, psychophysiology finally progresses in defining "states of consciousness" and "sleep" versus "wakefulness." I am trying to deal here with the following considerations.

Some sleep-speeches, at one extreme, impress one essentially as a momentary interruption of silent sleep with more or less rapid resumption of sleep afterward, whereas others at a different extreme seem to accompany or be part of a "somnambulistic trance" state (West, 1967) of varying degrees of departure from a sleep-based state of consciousness, and of varying durations from brief to quite long. In between these extremes fall imponderably large numbers of occurrences possessing admixtural features of both.

To adequately characterize sleep-utterance episodes, one must take into consideration the subject's reported experience, behavior, electrographic concomitants, and durations of each. As yet, we have no standard composite index useful for the accomplishment of such a task. As stated in Chapter 3, to the extent that a sleep-speech and its accompanying change in consciousness and physiology represent a *minimal* perturbation of ongoing sleep, it is referred to as a *microdissociative* episode; and to the extent that it signifies a *major* departure from behavioral and physiological sleep, it is categorized as a *macrodissociative* episode. In the latter case, the subject may nevertheless experience and self-define his state as one of "sleep." To cover the spectrum of instances between these extremes, the term *intermediate dissociative* episode is used. These categories may be happily dispensed with or modified at some future time with continuing progress in psychophysiology.

I begin with the microdissociative episodes that comprise by far the most frequent, and therefore, the most typical sleep-utterances. After completion of the detailed presentation of their electrographic features, I attempt to relate the findings to possible psychophysiological factors.

The Microdissociations

The electrographic characteristics of most sleep-utterance episodes are consistent with Rechtschaffen and Kales' criteria (1968) for "movement arousal" (MA) episodes (Arkin, Toth, & Esrachi, 1970b). These are defined by Rechtschaffen and Kales (1968) as:

> Any increase in EMG on any channel, which is accompanied by a change in pattern on any additional channel. For EMG channels, the change in pattern may consist of either an increase in amplitude of the EMG signal or an amplifier blocking artifact. For EOG channels, the change . . . may consist of . . . occurrence of EMG activity, amplifier blocking artifacts, or blink artifacts. For EEG

channels, the change... may consist of... a decrease in amplitude, an increase in alpha activity, a paroxysmal burst of high voltage activity, or amplifier blocking artifacts [pp. 4–5].

These criteria for movement arousal episodes associated with sleep-speech hold regardless of sleep stage. The actual vocalization occurs shortly after the onset of the movement arousal, the electrographic signs of which generally persist for varying durations following the utterance.

Rechtschaffen et al. (1962) and MacNeilage (1971) report that muscle tension as recorded electrographically is greater in amplitude and duration than for comparable episodes of wakeful speech, and that, furthermore, such tension tends to appear in *all* channels with sleep-utterance rather than selectively as in wakeful speech. These observations suggested to them that sleep-speech is associated with generalized body muscular tension, whereas wakeful speech is confined to speech-producing muscles. In a general way, our own results conform to this description (Arkin et al., 1970b), but despite this apparent agreement across laboratories, it is well to accept the report with caution. In our own work, we compared the muscle tension associated with sleep and wakeful utterances utilizing the following four conditions during wakefulness as controls:

1. speech at low conversational intensity while head and eyes were both kept motionless.
2. similar speech while moving the eyes, but with the head remaining as motionless as possible.
3. similar speech while moving the head, but with the eyes motionless.
4. similar speech while gently moving both head and eyes.

The results were that, especially in Condition 4, and to a lesser extent Condition 3, muscle tension and movement artifacts appeared in *all* channels in a manner indistinguishable from that associated with sleep-speech. Therefore, it seems necessary to employ controls which would permit assessment of the contribution of these possible confounding factors before finally concluding that there is indeed something distinctive about the pattern of intrinsic muscular activation during sleep-utterance. It is to be noted, however, that MacNeilage (1971), in addition to standard electrode placements, employed elaborate measures to obtain speech musculature activity records; therefore, her work is described in greater detail later in this volume.

Electrographic concomitants of sleep-utterance episodes possess great variability, both within and across subjects. Because of this variability, meaningful quantitative comparison is difficult, and most commentary in the literature, with a few exceptions (Cohen et al., 1965; Tani et al., 1966;

MacNeilage, 1971), describes what seemed typical to the author on the basis of inspection of large numbers of records, rather than the central tendencies of precise measurements. Thus, the available information is best presented here as a composite of the published reports giving descriptions, albeit in varying detail, of electrographic features prior to, during, and following sleep-speech (Arkin et al., 1970b; Cohen, Shapiro, Goodenough, & Saunders, 1965; Kamiya, 1961; MacNeilage, 1971; Oswald, 1964; Rechtschaffen et al., 1962; Schwartz, 1960; Szabó & Waitsuk, 1971; Tani et al., 1966). The main and significant electrographic features of sleep utterances are presented in Table 7.5.

Events Prior to Utterance

NREM-Associated Episodes (2, 3, and 4).   These are most often heralded by a sudden eruption of muscle tension and/or amplifier blocking in all leads. Although by no means invariably present, the duration of this muscle tension may range from 1–30 sec. According to MacNeilage (1971), the mean duration of 19 Stage 2 episodes uttered by four sleep-talkers was 10.4 sec. The peak amplitude of the muscle tension may likewise range from minimal or barely noticeable changes from previous levels to major or gross increases. In my own experimental records, tension was much less likely to be manifested if the utterance was low in volume, brief in duration, and consisted of unclearly spoken speech or sounds which, though affectively tinged, were not clearly spoken words, or else were brief words such as "un-huh" or "oh" (spoken with an intonation usually used when someone communicates something like "Oh, now I understand"). As a rule, however, even if the utterances were brief and of low volume, some artifact from minimal to major would occur in association with clearly spoken words, in contrast to those without clarity.

An additional common occurrence is the appearance in the EEG of paroxysmal flurries of high-voltage slow waves and/or K-complexes, often interlaced with bursts of higher frequencies up to 10 Hz or more. Such formations may last from 1–10 sec prior to the actual sleep-utterance and are particularly demonstrable with Stage 2 or 3 sleep-associated somniloquy. Szabó and Waitsuk (1971) describe these paroxysmal discharges as synchronous, bilateral, and symmetrical, considering them as indicators of activation of "certain synchronizing subcortical structures [p. 522]." Such high-voltage waves frequently precede by several seconds the moment of onset of the muscle tension.

Heart-Rate Findings.   We take up in detail later the question of whether a proportion of sleep-utterance represents the continuation of a stream of ongoing prior sleep mentation that attains vocal expression episodically versus the possibility that sleep-associated utterance is exclusively derived from the state temporally encompassed by the boundaries of the movement-arousal episode and is therefore essentially unrelated to previous sleep. Detection of cardioacceleration just before a sleep-utterance would be consistent with the notion that prior sleep mentation may find momentary expression as sleep speech, at least in a significant proportion of occurrences, and so I devote to it what may strike the reader as an otherwise disproportionate amount of space.

Unfortunately, in my own earlier work, we did not routinely monitor heart rate because of needs to limit the number of channels used as a way of economizing on polygraph paper. However, on a number of occasions, heart rate was monitored and measured. We took as a point of departure the precise moment of increased EMG level, EEG artifact, or sustained alpha frequencies and measured the heart rate beat-by-beat in a reverse direction for 30 beats. The results with two subjects suggested a tendency toward increased heart rate prior to sleep-utterance episodes, particularly in the five beats preceding the onset of the movement arousal. In Fig. 7.3, the average heart rate is 88.8 beats per minute (BPM) for the five beats previous to the onset of huge deflections of the pen indicating EMG levels. By contrast, the average heart rate for preceding groups of five beats in reverse order are 82.9, 84.5, 79.6, 81.6 and 82.0, i.e., a difference of 4.3–9.6 BPM; and the difference between the average heart rate for the five beats just prior to the markedly heightened EMG and the average of the previous overall averages of five beats each is 6.7 BPM. In Fig. 7.2, the average heart rate is 94.4 BPM for the five beats previous to the amplifier-blocking artifact in the EEG channel, whereas the average heart rate for preceding groups of five beats in reverse order are 87.3, 78.4, 75.9, 78.5, 75.7, 75.9 and 77.7, i.e., a difference of 7.1–18.7 BPM. The difference between the average heart rate just prior to the amplifier blocking and the average of the previous averages of five beats each is 15.9. (In both figures, we did not have space enough to display the earlier groups of five beats each.)

More recently, Arkin, Batson, and Ellman (1978) had a serendipitous opportunity to assess heart-rate changes preceding Stage 2 movement arousals with and without associated sleep-speech. The subjects were tobacco addicts participating in a Batson, Arkin, & Ellman (1978) study dealing with the effects of tobacco and food deprivation on sleep mentation. They were selected *without* inquiry after a history of sleep-talking but rather on the basis of being good dream-recallers and sound sleepers. Beat-by-beat measurements of heart rate were carried out for 30 beats going backward in time from movement arousal (MA) onset with and without accompanying sleep-speech. Each such episode pairs were selected from Stage 2, as close as possible in time from the same subject and same night. Ten pairs of episodes were selected from baseline nights and 10 pairs from deprivation nights. Ten subjects contributed unequal amounts of pairs to the total of 20. Following the procedure of Muzet and Michel (1977), the group average heart rate of beats 20 through 11 beats prior to MA onset was determined and subtracted from the group average heart rate of the beat immediately preceding the MA onset. The difference was taken as an index of heart-rate change preceding MA.

The results show that heart rate undergoes an increase just before MA onset, regardless of association with sleep-speech, and ranging from about 4–8 BPM (see Table 7.5). The magnitude of the change is modest in comparison to those reported by Townsend et al. (1975) and Muzet and Michel (1977), but in the same direction.

Townsend et al. (1975) studied heart-rate changes preceding body movements and in a "pseudomovement" control condition during sleep in five normal adult males. Instead of determining mean heart-rate levels over relatively long epochs (Broughton, 1968; Fisher, Kahn, Edwards, & Davis, 1975), they based their findings on beat-by-beat measurements for 20 prebody-movement onset beats. The group beat-by-beat heart rate averages were calculated for measurements preceding spontaneous Stage 2 and REM body movements using the average responses for each subject. They found that spontaneous movements in Stage 2 and REM were preceded by significant heart-rate increases (35.3% in Stage 2) beginning approximately 8 sec (beats 20 through 15) before the onset of the movement. The results were interpreted as supporting the hypothesis that the heart-rate acceleration before spontaneous movements in sleep may be triggered by internal arousal stimuli which, like body movements, have sleep-stage-specific rates of occurrence.

In a study on heart rate preceding short activation phases in sleep, Muzet and Michel (1977) likewise used a beat-by-beat method of heart-rate determination preceding short activation phases in both Stage 2 and REM sleep. They subdivided transient arousal episodes into those accompanied and those unaccompanied by actual movement. These seem equivalent, more or less, to MA with and without actual movement.

TABLE 7.5
Heart Rate Preceding Movement Arousals (MA)

Condition	Average Heart Beats 20–11	S. D.	Average HR—Last Beat Prior to MA	Change
With sleep-speech:				
Baseline	56.3	0.92	60.6	+4.3 BPM (7.6%)
Deprivation	60.2	0.16	68.4	+8.2 (13.6%)
Without sleep-speech:				
Baseline	56.8	1.3	61.2	+4.4 (7.7%)
Deprivation	69.4	4.3	68.1	+8.7 (14.6%)

Employing 10 young adult male subjects, it was found that preactivation phases in Stages 2 and REM produced heart-rate increases (17.7% in Stage 2), beginning about 7–8 beats prior to the instant of onset, regardless of whether it was accompanied by actual movement. Like Townsend, Johnson, Naitoh, and Muzet (1975), Muzet and Michel (1977) concluded that activation phases during sleep are preceded by heart-rate increases possibly due to an internal, spontaneous trigger and may be independent of whether an actual body movement is associated. In partial accord with these results are the earlier findings of Jackson (1942), who observed a sleep cardioacceleration 30 seconds prior to body movements throughout the night in one intensively studied subject.

What observations have been published regarding the close cousins of somniloquy—bruxism, somnambulism, night-terrors, and enuresis—all of which occur episodically in association with NREM sleep?

Bruxism.   Reding, Rubright, Robinson, Zimmerman, and Smith (1968) report that statistically significant mean heart-rate increases of 16.2 BPM were observed with approximately the fourth heart beat just prior to the onset of a tooth-grinding episode. Twenty-five subjects with chronic nocturnal bruxism participated in the study and, although the preponderance of episodes occurred in association with Stage 2, they were observable repeatedly in all four sleep stages (including REM).

In a study employing eight subjects, Satoh and Harada (1971) always observed tachycardia in association with episodes, with an unspecified proportion occurring prior to the onset of the masseter contractions and another proportion postonset.

Enuresis and Somnambulism.   Gastaut and Broughton (1965) have indicated that increases in heart rate often occur prior to the onset of EMG increases in both enuresis and somnambulism. Proportions of incidents in which this was observed before the episode onset as opposed to afterward were not specified, nor was the duration of such preceding intervals.

Stage 4 Night-Terrors.   Fisher et al. (1975), in a large-scale study of night-terror episodes, report the uniform absence of heart-rate increases just prior to episode onsets. However, their method of evaluating heart-rate changes as described in their published work was based upon the mean heart rate for the 2½-min interval prior to the night-terror onset. Use of the average heart rate over a relatively long interval rather than a narrowly focused beat-by-beat determination (as in the work of Muzet & Michel, 1977; Reding et al., 1968, and Townsend et al., 1975) favors the likelihood that actual but short-lived changes prior to arousal would remain undetected. That is, such changes might be overshadowed and "canceled out" by fluctuations in the much larger

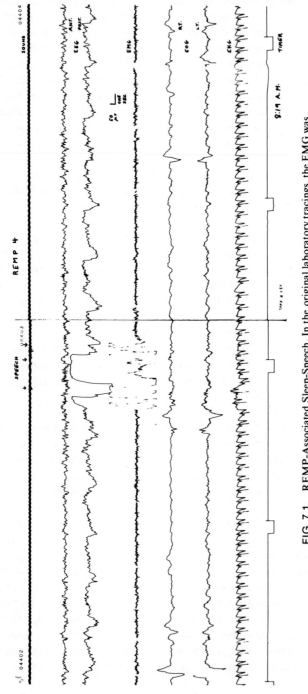

FIG. 7.1. REMP-Associated Sleep-Speech. In the original laboratory tracings, the EMG was recorded lightly due to a slight mechanical impairment of ink flow. What looks like a gap in the reproduction of the tracing of the EMG in Fig. 7.1 results from limitations of the reproduction process involved preparing the figure for publication; in the original, one may see the EMG, albeit faintly, and it was of markedly elevated amplitude blended with some electrode movement artifact.

What seem to be apparent gaps in the tracings of other figures are similarly the effects of faint ink writing in the originals.

tally of heart beats recorded over the 2½-min pre-arousal interval used by Fisher et al. (1975).

This possibility must be taken seriously in view of two independent published observations of increased heart rate just prior to the onset of night-terror episodes. The first is contained in a paper of Gastaut and Broughton (1965, Fig. 10A, pp. 214–215) and the second in a paper by Guilleminault and Brusset (1973). The issue has been presented to Fisher (Arkin, 1978), who argued that these instances were atypical, and well they may be. In addition, Fisher (1978) stated that in Fisher et al.'s (1975) work, beat-by-beat analysis had been carried out similar to those of Townsend et al. (1975) and Muzet and Michel (1977), but with negative results; i.e., no pre-arousal cardiac acceleration was observed. Unfortunately, neither these data nor the detailed analyses have been published, and so critical evaluation of the statistical processing methods is not yet possible. This is all-important inasmuch as Gambi, Torrioli, Stafanini, Torre, and Santalucia (1977) presented results on heart rate preceding night-terrors in five children, age 6–12 years. Statistically significant increases in heart rate were found in the 20-sec interval preceding night terror onset, in comparison to three earlier consecutive 20-sec intervals ($p < .05$).

In conclusion, with the evidence at hand, it appears that heart-rate increases are regularly observable during the seconds preceding spontaneous arousal episodes during sleep. Such increases have been found most often in Stages 2 and REM, with and without sleep-utterance; furthermore, there is reason to expect that fine-grained, brief-interval heart-rate measurements may indicate that such increases are to be found in spontaneous arousals in Stages 3 and 4, both in normal sleep and in night-terror episodes.

Electrical Skin Resistance Findings. Verdone (cited in Rechtschaffen et al., 1962) observed that of 11 NREM sleep-utterance episodes, five were accompanied by sudden diminutions of skin resistance atypical for intervals of sleep selected at random. The six instances in which this result did not occur were not necessarily considered to mean that no arousal was involved, because occasionally full awakenings from sleep are not associated with skin resistance decreases.

REMP-Associated Utterances. These are almost always preceded by temporary cessation of rapid eye movements. On occasion, however (Fig. 7.1), they may persist up until the moment immediately before the speech. In addition, there may be brief discharges of increased EMG amplitude and/or amplifier blocking and short emissions of alpha frequencies. Tani et al. (1966) report on the EEG frequency analysis of eight REMP speeches produced by three subjects. Employing 23 band-pass filters ranging from 1–30 Hz, they found suppression of wave components 5–6–7 and 10–11 Hz prior to utterances. In addition, heart rate and respiration either increased or became more unstable during the same interval.

Events During Utterance

NREM Utterance.   Usually the EEG accompanying NREM-associated-utterances is marked by muscle tension artifact and/or amplifier blocking. It is to be emphasized, however, that this tends to be intermittent and in varying degree. As in the pre-utterance interval, such interferences are less likely to be present or obscure the record if the utterances are brief, low in volume, and enunciated with diminished clarity in the case of speech. When the previous sleep stage is 3 or 4, high-voltage slow waves commonly persist singly and in groups in portions of record devoid of artifact. Another common finding during the speech is that slow waves not obliterated by artifact undergo voltage reduction while still remaining in the delta frequency range. When the previous sleep stage is 2, such slow waves are less common and likely to be of lower voltage. Often, relatively low-voltage mixed frequencies and bursts of 8–10 Hz are observable in portions of readable records. In addition, regardless of previous sleep stage, sharp spike-like signals appear, the origin of which cannot be ascertained.

In Fig. 7.3, the Stage 4 sleep-utterance is accompanied by sustained high-voltage slow waves, which contain either small amounts of artifact or else are totally free of it. Rudimentary signs of superimposed faster frequencies are visible in several areas in the vicinity of the utterance. The slow wave cephalic activity appears to invade the EOG with significant evidence of muscle tension artifact and amplifier blocking in the right EOG only. The EMG displays markedly increased activity throughout. The utterance is also associated with cardioacceleration.

In Fig. 7.2, the EEG concomitant with the Stage-2 associated speech is difficult to evaluate. At the precise moment of the shout, amplifier blocking and muscle tension artifact completely obscure the EEG and EOG, making interpretation impossible. About 2 sec later, unclear words are uttered, the last portion of which is concomitant with the beginning of the resolution of the EEG and is closely followed by clear delta waves of medium amplitude with superimposed higher frequencies. After about 3 sec of silence, the subject emits moans that an independent observer described as "resigned" in affective quality. This ends about 4 sec later and is accompanied by clear delta waves. The EMG remains high in amplitude during the shout and words, but begins to diminish with the last part of the moan. During the shout and words, the EOG and EKG are not interpretable, but during the moans, a cardioacceleration is discernible and the EOG contains slow waves of presumably cephalic origin.

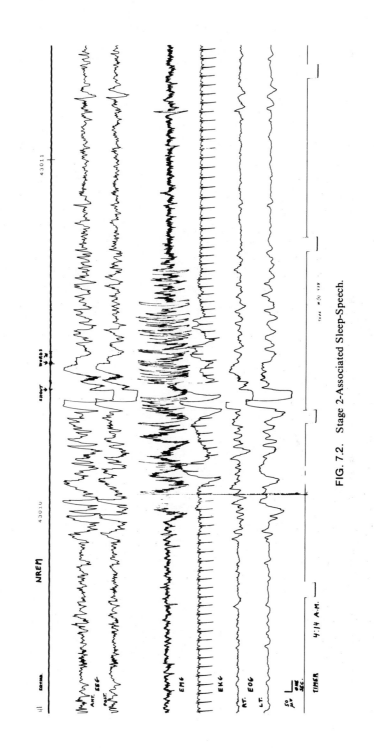

FIG. 7.2. Stage 2-Associated Sleep-Speech.

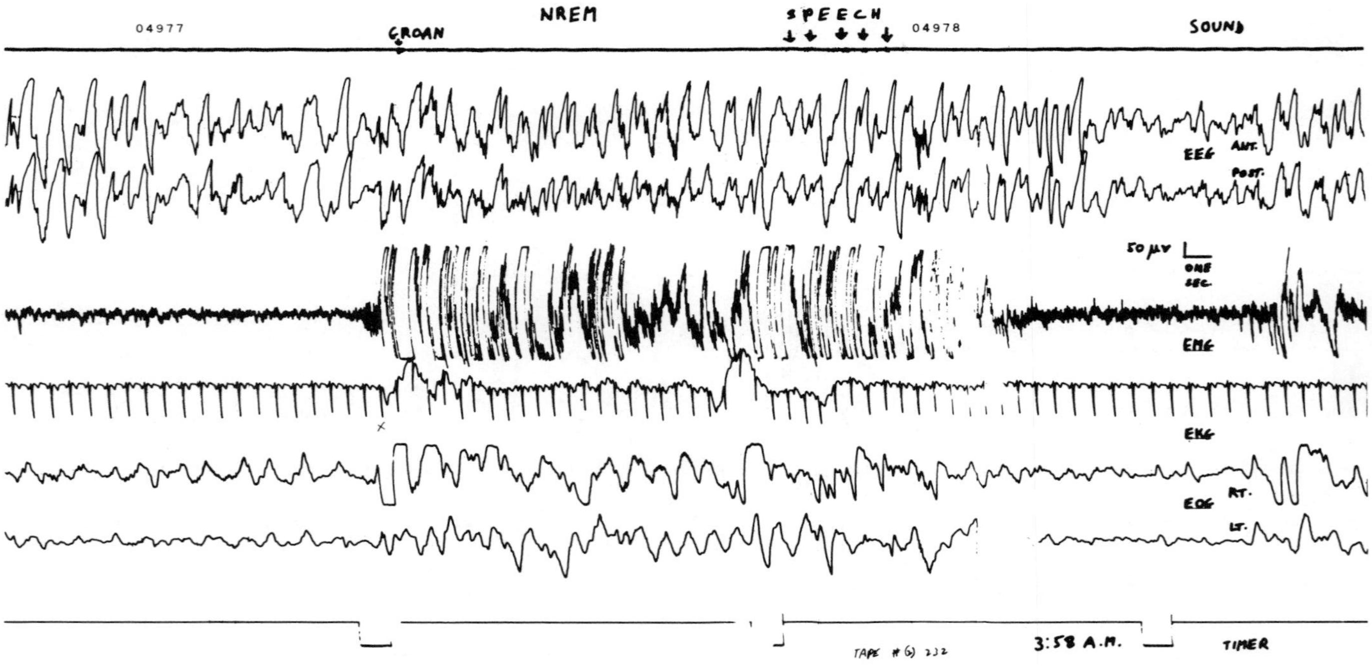

FIG. 7.3. Stage 4-Associated Sleep-Speech.

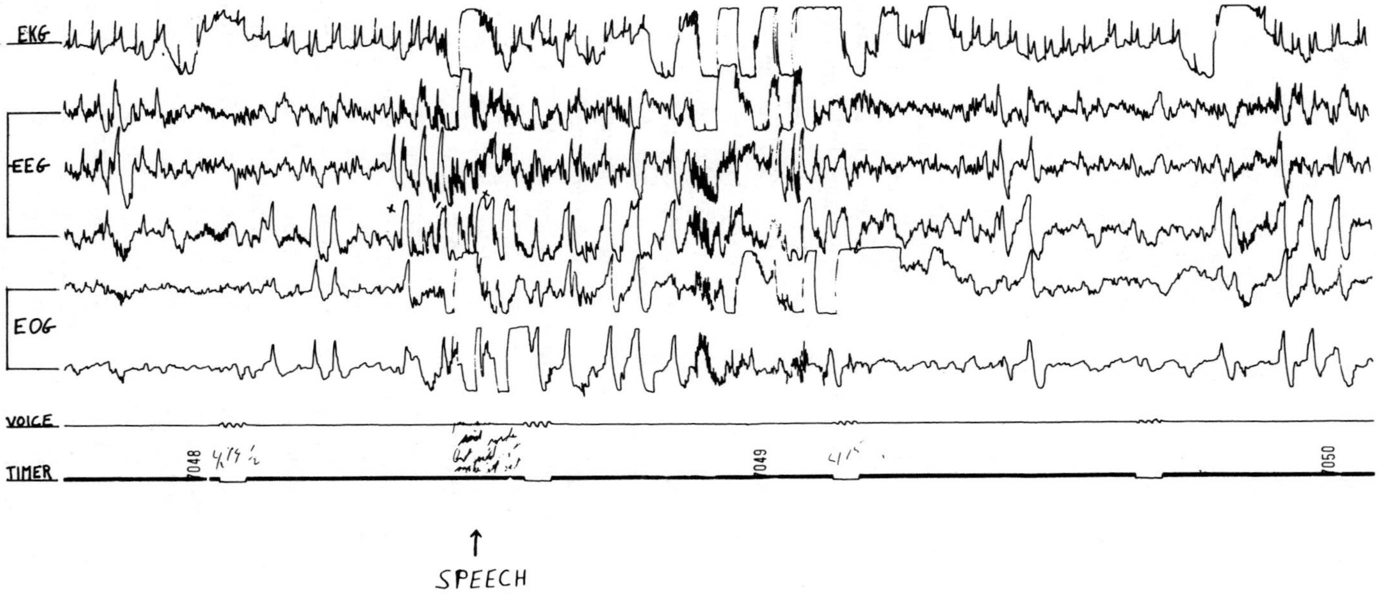

FIG. 7.4. Stage 3–4 Associated Sleep-Speech.

75

REMP Utterance.   REMP-associated utterances usually display minimal or absent muscle tension, although many exceptions exist. Amplifier blocking in some degree is the most common barrier to observing readable portions of the EEG. When sufficiently clear, theta and alpha volleys of a few seconds' duration are often observed. Alpha is more likely to be prominent and sustained if the speeches are longer, louder, and more clearly enunciated. When records are interpretable, REMs are absent during the speech interval itself. Tani et al. (1966), on the other hand, report persistence of REMs during the utterance, but inasmuch as they employed only one EOG channel, these results must be accepted with caution.

Events Following Sleep-Utterance

NREM Utterance.   NREM utterance episodes (Stages 2–4) are characterized by persistence of intermittent muscle tension and/or amplifier blocking, again with extreme variability. This interval usually lasts 10–20 sec but may range from 1–60 sec or more. MacNeilage (1971) reports that the mean duration of muscle activity in association with Stage 2 utterances is about 20 sec. (Her measurements cover the interval from the *onset* of the speech until the final subsidence of the muscle tension. Thus, this figure should be shortened by a brief interval occupied by the speech itself to give a truer picture of the mean duration of post-speech muscle tension.) In intervening artifact-free portions of the record, clusters of the high- and low-voltage delta waves and K-complexes are common. The general finding is that the postspeech record contains the same or *lower* concentrations of high voltage slow waves in comparison to the prespeech epoch. That is, if the pre-utterance stage is 3 or 4, the post utterance stage might quickly return to the same electrographic picture or to one with fewer delta waves, Stage 2 or 1 NREM. If, however, the pre-utterance sleep stage is 2 or 1 NREM, the postutterance sleep stage never contains a high concentration of the slow waves; i.e., they were never followed by Stage 3–4. Commonly, postutterance paroxysmal clusters of high-voltage slow waves and K-complexes, as in the pre-utterance interval, were observed. Less often, pre-utterance Stages 2 or 3–4 are followed immediately after utterance by REMP onset or Stage 2.

In Fig. 7.3, the high-voltage slow waves persist for about 7 sec free of tension artifact with the exception of the brief burst about 1 sec after the end of the utterance. These high-voltage slow waves give way to 7 sec of low-amplitude slow waves with superimposed faster frequencies, after which high-voltage slow waves appear marking resumption of Stage 4.

Following termination of the utterance, the high-amplitude EMG activity continues for about 4 sec and then undergoes an abrupt diminution, though it is still somewhat higher than its preutterance epoch level. With the resumption of the Stage 4 EEG, new bursts of high EMG activity recur but this time without vocalization. The EOG remains artifact-free and reflects the concomitant EEG. The pulse rate displays some instability in that it becomes slower after the EMG activity is reduced and slightly more rapid toward the end of the tracing when the EMG activity increases once more.

In Fig. 7.2, following cessation of the words, the EEG displays diminished-amplitude slow waves succeeded by low-voltage mixed frequencies. After about 13 sec of this type of EEG, an unambiguous K-complex and spindle occurs, marking resumption of the pre-utterance Stage 2 sleep. With the cessation of vocalization, the EMG activity becomes sharply reduced, remaining at a higher level, however, than that of the pre-utterance epoch. Notable is persistence of spiking. The EOG remains clear and devoid of signs of eye movement. The pulse rate abruptly slows during this postutterance interval but increases following a large EMG spike and concurrently with the K-complex and spindle.

REMP Utterance. REMP-associated utterance episodes are character-ized by continuation of the REMP with minimal change, such as longer intervals of alpha, or no change from a clear typical REMP tracing. REMs may resume in as little as a few seconds after speech or be delayed by one or more minutes. SEMs are not uncommon, occurring singly or in groups. However, other frequent sequellae are a brief interposed interval of Stage W or 1 NREM, followed by REMP resumption; or a brief interval of "phases intermédiaires" (Goldsteinas, Guennoc, & Vidal, 1966); or REMP termination with W or 1 NREM. Tani et al. (1966) report persistence of increased and/or unstable heart rate and respiration for an unspecified interval.

In Fig. 7.1, immediately following the utterance, the EEG gave rise to two brief bursts of intermittent alpha frequency and then reverted to the typical Stage REM EEG. The EMG likewise quickly reverted to a low-amplitude tracing. The EOG contained suggestions of SEMs, but true conjugate REMs did not reappear until about 16 sec after the utterance. The EKG revealed a transitory postutterance bradycardia followed by a resumption of pre-utterance heart rate. The electrographic characteristics of microdissociative sleep-utterance are summarized in Table 7.6.

The Special Case of Stage 1 NREM-Associated Utterance

Gastaut and Broughton (1965) do not comment specifically on whether muscle tension artifact is associated with their Stage 1 NREM episodes. However, in our laboratory, we have observed several episodes of 1 NREM speeches without muscle tension in the EEG. These observations are worth mentioning because contrary to reasonable expectation, in the stage of sleep that has the lowest auditory arousal threshold (1 NREM), partial or complete

TABLE 7.6

Electrographic Characteristics of Microdissociative Sleep-Utterance

Nature of Sleep	Before Utterance	During Utterance	Following Utterance
REM	1. REMs usually cease.	1. Mostly minimal or no muscle tension artifact in EEG but many exceptions observable. Uncommon for EEG to show absolutely no change —amplifier blocking in some degree most common change in recording. 2. REMs absent. EOG usually not readable. 3. Alpha bursts not uncommon.	1. EEG continues with minimal (longer intervals of alpha) or no change from a clear typical REMP tracing. However, other common sequellae are: a brief interposed interval or Stage W or 1 NREM; or REMP termination with 1 NREM of W. 2. REMs may resume as little as a few sec after speech or be delayed by minutes. 3. One or more SEMs not uncommon.

NREM stages 2 and 3-4	1. Sudden eruption of muscle tension and/or amplifier blocking in all leads almost always but to varying degree from minimal to major. 2. Commonly preceded by a 1–10 sec flurry of high-voltage waves and/or K-complexes often interlaced with bursts of higher frequencies up to 10 Hz.

1. Muscle tention and/or amplifier blocking almost always present but tends to be intermittent in varying degrees.

2. When the previous sleep stage is 3–4, slow high-voltage waves commonly appear singly and in groups in portions of record devoid of artifact. When the previous sleep stage is 2, such high-voltage slow waves are less common. Often, relatively low-voltage mixed frequencies and bursts of 8–10 Hz are to be observed in portions of readable records. Also to be commonly seen regardless of previous sleep stage were sharp spikelike signals of uncertain origin.

1. Tension artifact and/or amplifier blocking almost always present and may persist for one or a few sec or continue intermittently for as much as 60 sec or more.

2. In the artifact-free portions of record or record following cessation of artifact, the general but not invariable finding is that the postspeech record contains the same or a lower concentration of high-voltage slow waves characteristic of Stage 3–4. Thus, the following are among the most common sequences:

Stage 3-4 → speech → Stage 3-4
Stage 3-4 → speech → 1 NREM → 3-4
Stage 3-4 → speech → 1 NREM → 2 → 3-4
Stage 3-4 → speech → 2 → 3-4
Stage 2 → speech → 1 NREM → 2

Less often, NREM utterance (2 or 3-4) → W or REMP onset. In addition, flurries of high-voltage waves and K-complexes as in prespeech interval are common.

amnesia for the sleep-speech was nevertheless observed in some of the mentation reports obtained immediately afterward. This has relevance for the dissociation hypothesis of sleep-utterance episodes to be discussed more fully later on.

MacNeilage's Study (1971)

This work is described in some detail because of its unique technological features, enabling collection of some of the most precise electromyographic data on sleep-talking currently available. MacNeilage was interested in studying evidence of subvocal EMG activity during sleep, its possible association with verbal sleep mentation, and sleep-talking in relation to both. The work received its stimulus from a preliminary report of McGuigan and Tanner (1970), describing covert oral behavior during conversational as opposed to visual REM dreams. Five young adult subjects were selected who were good dream recallers and who had claimed that they talked in their sleep at least occasionally. The data to be described were obtained from the second and third baseline nights of a six-night protocol. Besides the standard placements, surface electrodes were attached to the lips, chin, and on the skin over the thyroid cartilage for the recording of laryngeal muscle potentials. In addition, delicate wire electrodes were inserted in to the belly of the genioglossus muscles of the tongue, but the output of this electrode was excluded from the data analysis because technical difficulties prevented satisfactory recordings. The criterion for subvocal verbal activity was that the pattern of the EMG activity be analogous to that observable during overt wakeful speech but of diminished amplitude. In order to be included in the data analysis, such episodes of EMG activity had to exceed 1 sec in duration and appear simultaneously on *all* EMG channels. Typically, in wakeful speech, continuous moderate levels of activity occur with rapid fluctuations, which are generally not in phase, within and across channels. MacNeilage also remarked that wakeful speech produces very little muscle tension artifact in the EEG and EOG; however, as mentioned at the beginning of this section, we found in our own work that this was true only if the head was kept motionless (Arkin et al., 1974a). The results follow.

"Silent" (Nonvocal) EMG Activity Episodes.   Subjects spent an average total of about 19 min of an average of 7 hours of sleep per night in episodes of *simultaneous* activity in all EMG channels. The average number of episodes was 96 and comprised about 4.5% of total sleep time. The mean rate of occurrence of episode activity throughout sleep was once every 4.5 min. In descending order, the highest rate of linguistic muscle activity was in Stage 1 NREM, alpha (apparently roughly equivalent to *phases intermédiares* as in Goldsteinas et al., 1966, or ambiguous REM, as in Cartright, Monroe, &

Palmer, 1967), REM phasic, REM tonic, Stages 2, 3, and 4. It was further noted that the rates for Stages 2, 3, and 4 were much lower than that to be expected if muscle activity occurred randomly during the various sleep stages.

The average duration of these EMG activity episodes was 12 sec. Such durations were shortest in association with REM phasic sleep and increased in the following order: Stage 1 NREM, REM tonic, Stages 2, 3, and 4.

The peak EMG amplitudes were highest during Stages 2 and 4, least during REM sleep, and intermediate in Stages 1 NREM and 2. Peak amplitudes of 87% of sleep EMG activity episodes were at least 67% as high as those recorded during wakeful speech and about 41% of sleep episodes were equal to or greater than wakeful speech. These tendencies were manifested most markedly in the EEG channel.

Qualitatively, the typical pattern of presumably subvocal EMG episodes consisted of intermittent bursts of high-voltage activity, synchronous on all channels with concomitant large EMG bursts in the EEG channels. This was in special contrast to waking EMG speech patterns, that consisted of continuous, varible, medium amplitude activity mostly of an asynchronous nature across channels and with little concomitant EMG activity recorded from EEG electrode placements. MacNeilage (1971) found that very few instances of linguistic muscular activity episodes met her predetermined criteria for covert, subvocal activity during sleep. However, rather than conclude that little sleep subvocal activity occurs, she recommended revision of subvocal activity criteria appropriate for sleep. Indeed, she remarked that her initial criteria were based on observations of wakeful speech in which subjects remain motionless except for talking or performing cognitive tasks; and inasmuch as during sleep, subjects were not under such constraints, the possibility exists that "vocalization-related innervation may occur concurrently with other innervation of the same musculature, some of which may also be a part of more general body movements [p. 89]." This comment is in accord with our findings mentioned earlier that electrographic tracings of sleep-speech are indistinguishable on inspection from those of presleep wakeful talking with concurrent movement of head and eyes.

Electrographic Concomitants of Sleep-Talking Episodes.   As mentioned earlier, MacNeilage (1971) recorded 28 sleep-speech episodes, of which 19 occurred in association with Stage 2, and seven with REM sleep (three with REM-tonic, two with REM-phasic, and two with Stage "alpha" accompanying REM period interruption). The average duration of EMG activity related to sleep-speech was 19.7 sec. This was about 66% greater than the corresponding time intervals of speech musculature activity in general, and such greater duration was observed regardless of the associated sleep stage. Sleep-talking occurrences were preceded by an average of 10 sec and followed by an average of 8 sec of EMG activity, with an average of 2 sec occupied by the sleep-speech itself sandwiched in between. This latter phenomenon, in which utterances are preceded and followed by EMG activity, was rarely observed in wakeful speech. It was of interest that the only two occasions in which sleep-utterances were neither preceded nor followed by EMG activity were during the REM sleep-associated "alpha" episodes.

In addition, 54 incidents of nonlinguistic vocalization occurred that were also preceded and followed by EMG activity similar to this.

Individual Differences in Relation to Sleep Volubility of Subjects.   In the first section of this chapter, it was mentioned that although all five subjects provided a corroborated history of sleep-talking, all but one of the 28 speech episodes were produced by three of the five subjects. Accordingly, MacNeilage designated the three relatively voluble subjects as the "sleep-talkers" and the two taciturn ones as the "nonsleep-talkers," and between these two subsets, certain differences were observed. The sleep-talkers produced an average of 113 nonvocal EMG activity episodes per night, in comparison to an average of 70 per night for the nonsleep-talkers. That is, the sleep-talkers produced about 60% more EMG activity incidents per night. In addition, the average duration of such incidents among sleep-talkers was 1.6 sec greater than that of the nonsleep-talkers. Curiously, the average amplitudes of EMG activity were lower for the nonsleep-talkers during REM sleep and higher in Stages 2, 3, and 4.

How does MacNeilage's (1971) report of greater nocturnal EMG activity among sleep-talkers relate to the findings of other investigators? Consistent with her observations is the report of Jovanovíc (1976) that muscle activity is abnormally great in the sleep of patients with tendencies to sleep-walk—a syndrome with increased tendencies to nightly motor behavior. However, it is well to view her conclusion with caution.

First, the mean total sleep time for her three sleep-talker subjects was 443.5 min, whereas that of her two nonsleep-talkers was 406.5 min, a difference of 37 min. This longer duration of sleep in the former permitted a greater total of EMG incidents to accumulate. That is, if the total sleep time had been equal, there might have been less striking differences between the two groups.

Second, it is instructive to relate MacNeilage's figures to comparable data in other published reports on the incidence of movement arousal (MA) episodes. Lichter and Muir (1975) found a nightly average total of 68.9 MAs in 420 min of sleep, with 10 adult subjects (half female, half male). Sassin and Johnson (1968) found in five adult males on two consecutive nights with a total sleep time (TST) of 360–480 min, a range of 38–99 MAs per night. It is of interest that subjects were individually consistent across nights. Naitoh et al. (1973) reported on the incidence of MAs in 14 adult male subjects during their second and third baseline laboratory nights. An average of 73.5 occurred during an average total sleep time of 452.5 min. The range was 40–109, and it is of particular interest to note that two subjects with total sleep times of 459 and 469 min had 103 and 109 MAs respectively. Thus, with subjects who were described as normal adults (and presumably nonchronic sleep-talkers), the incidence of MAs was not much different from that reported by MacNeilage for her sleep-talkers. It is, therefore, premature to conclude that sleep-talkers as a group possess greater than normal tendencies to general nocturnal MA episodes.

Psychophysiological Comments on Microdissociation Episodes

Although the review of electrographic findings relating to micro-dissociative sleep-utterance clearly bears out the contention that most occurrences fulfill the criteria of "movement arousal" episodes, the two conditions are not identical. First, only a small proportion of MAs are accompanied by utterance.

Second, a small but definite minority of sleep-utterance occurs without electrographic criteria of MA. This typically occurs when utterances are brief, nonverbal, and of low intensity.

Third, Gardner and Grossman (1976), in reviewing motor patterns in human sleep, summarize the evidence that movement arousal is *not* distributed randomly throughout sleep. For example, large body movements tend to appear before REM periods and to be sparse during slow-wave sleep. By contrast, the evidence from several studies presented earlier indicates that sleep-utterance episodes are distributed more or less randomly throughout the night (although in my own work, as mentioned, there was a tendency for the frequency to peak slightly during the second and eighth 10th of the entire sleep period of the night and during the last 10th of each NREM and REM period).

Fourth, as we shall see later, many mentation reports from all stages of sleep contain scenes with sleep-imagined dialogue and vocalization without concomitant overt utterance. Along similar lines Hobson, Goldfrank, and Snyder (1965), in their investigation on respiration and mental activity in REM and NREM sleep, found that their highest psychophysical correlations were between apneic pauses and respiration-related mental content such as sleep-imagined utterance, laughter, choking, and crying. No mention was made of concomitant overt sleep-speech, providing further independent evidence that sleep-imagined utterance need not become manifest despite indications of activated psycho-physiological tendencies in such directions.

The evidence suggests, therefore, the microdissociative sleep-utterance is most likely to occur when a suitable combination of at least three factors is present: specifically, an endogenous activated tendency to produce linguistic outputs, an activation or lowered threshold for activation of the linguistic apparatus, and the functional availability of articulatory programs.

The notion of increased activation *occurring* prior to the first electrographic signs of the instant of onset of MA episodes is crucial to the formulation just outlined; and data from studies with indwelling electrodes provide a partial basis for believing in its physiological reality.

Freemon, McNew, and Adey (1969) observed the neural activity from cortical and subcortical areas by means of implanted depth electrodes in five unrestrained chimpanzees. They found that arousal from NREM sleep usually entailed a sequence of initial flattening of activity in the hippocampus for about 2–6 sec, succeeded by cortical flattening. This tendency was most clearly observable for Stage 4. Freemon and Walter (1970) made similar observations in eight humans, six of whom were ill with temporal-lobe epilepsy and two with schizophrenia. Again it was found that Stage 4 arousals involved flattening of activity recorded from hippocampal leads prior to cortical activity flattening.

A futher observational detail (Freemon and Walter, 1970) of considerable importance in the human studies is that in Stage 4 arousals, the "hippocampal complex would flatten a few seconds before the appearance of increased EMG activity, which itself preceded cortical disappearance of HVS [high-voltage slow] activity. Often the cortical delta would continue until obliterated by movement artifact [p. 549]." The preponderating low-voltage frequencies (LVF) in Stages 2 and REM were said to prevent similar observations from being made at such times. The reason for stressing this detail of sequence is its possible relevance to the question of the existence of mentation and physiological change immediately *prior* to sleep arousals in general. That is, Freemon and Walter's data are consistent with the hypothesis that typically a CNS change *precedes* MA onset by several sec and that such changes are tokens of potential affect-arousing ideation interwoven with and participating in the events prior to MA onset, and hence concurrent sleep-utterance episodes.

The Intermediate Dissociations

Utterances Occurring Within a NREM Sleep Context

On many occasions in association with NREM sleep, somniloquy of unusually long duration (30–60 sec) and word count has been observed. (Speech numbers 302, 464, and 551 are good examples.) When the EEG is not obscured by muscle tension artifact, the pattern is generally one of low-voltage mixed frequencies suggestive of either Stage 1 NREM or else aroused wakefulness. During a few such occasions, brief interchanges between the sleeper and the experimenter have been possible. (See Chapter 12 for examples). Total and partial amnesias for the speech and associated mentation are common or else an apparently unrelated sequence of mentation is elicted upon awakening the subject.

Jacobson, Kales, Lehmann, and Zweizig (1965) and Gastaut and Broughton (1965) have shown that a high-voltage, slow-wave EEG record is compatible for similarly sustained intervals with ongoing somnambulistic episodes in children, and that brief verbal interchanges are likewise possible at such times without definitive awakening. It seems reasonable, therefore, to consider occurrences of this sort as varieties of intermediate dissociations.

Utterances Occurring Within a Stage REM Context

I have observed that a small group of utterance episodes occur within a "context" of REM sleep but less intensely immersed within it or less proximate to REMP termination than the bulk of those previously designated as REMP-associated utterances. That is, REM sleep ceases and is replaced by sustained alpha frequencies in the EEG. Oswald has published an electrographic tracing of one such event (1964, p. 118). These occurrences may then be followed quickly by resumption of the REM period or else proceed to NREM sleep, in which case it may be inferred that the utterance episode had coincided with REMP termination. Against this background of alpha frequencies, the utterance occurs during a state which is sleep-like behaviorally. Also, muscle tension artifact is minimal.

The content of the speeches appears to be related to an ongoing dream-like hallucinated experience, and there need not be discernible concordance between the speech and recalled mentation (MacNeilage, 1971). Along similar lines, Popoviciù et al. (1973) report that certain episodes of somniloquy were observable during some atypical intervals of REM sleep— the so-called "intermediate phases." It seems likely that the "*phases intermédiaires*" of Goldsteinas et al. (1966), the ambiguous REM of Cartwright et al. (1967), the phenomena mentioned by Popoviciù et al. (1973), and these transitory alpha states sandwiched in between intervals of REM sleep or at REMP termination (Arkin, this book; MacNeilage, 1971) all share many electrographic features in common. To my knowledge, there has been no attempt to examine the records obtained in the laboratories of each of these workers to ascertain whether differential features are detectable—it is possible that the same electrographic phenomenon has been observed with or without sleep-utterance and given a different label by each investigator.

The Macrodissociations

Macrodissociative sleep-utterance episodes are uncommon events characterized by extensive, elaborate, florid speech lasting one or more minutes. Descriptive details of their content are furnished in Chapter 8.

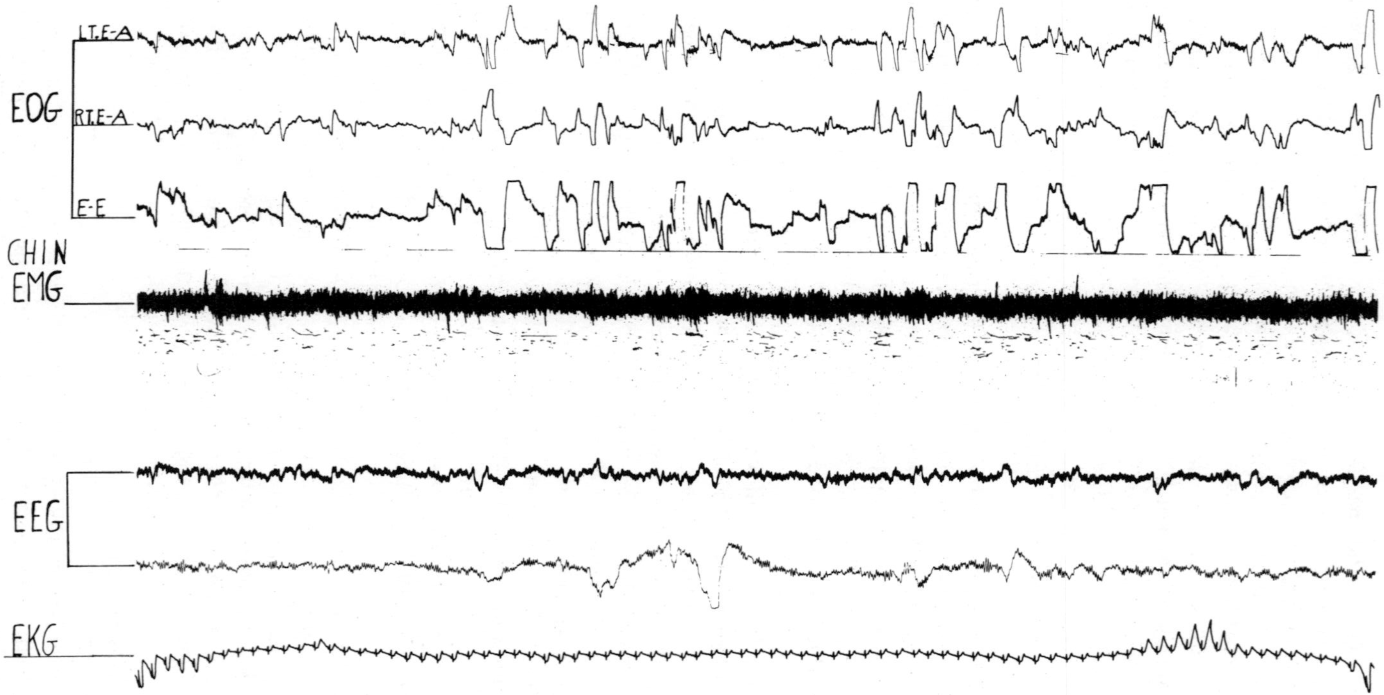

FIG. 7.5. Macro-Dissociative Sleep-Speech Preceded by Stage 2 Sleep (note sustained alpha rhythm and REMS).

In the laboratory, macrodissociations have been observed both as spontaneous occurrences and as immediate sequellae of experimenter interventions, or following experimental, presleep priming procedures, such as posthypnotic suggestion. In addition, closely related phenomena like sleep-walking with sporadic speech and night-terrors with abundant speech have been monitored both as spontaneous occurrences and as a result of experimenter intervention (Fisher, Kahn, Edwards, Davis, & Fine, 1974; Gastaut & Broughton, 1965; Jacobson et al. 1965; Kales & Jacobson, 1967).

Several reports and vignettes have been published that describe occurrences fulfilling clinical criteria of macrodissociation in relation to sleep (Burrell, 1904; Cook, 1937; Engel, 1959; Goddard, 1926; Hadamard, 1954; Janis, Mahl, Kagan & Holt, 1969; Krippner & Stoller, 1973; West, 1967). The relevant material of the Krippner and Stoller article (1973) is presented in Chapter 14, and case material of my own dealing with sleep-talking and automatic writing is included in Chapter 20. The tape recordings of McGregor's sleep-speeches (1964) are spectacular examples.

Spontaneous Occurrences Observed in the Laboratory.

Typically, the electrographic background of macrodissociations has been characterized by sustained alpha rhythm, with admixtures of LVM frequencies. REMs, SEMs, and possibly eye-blinks may be sparsely or abundantly present. The same is true of muscle-tension artifact, which may be surprisingly minimal or else so dense as to obscure most of the record. Figure 7.5 contains a typical part of a lengthy macrodissociation (Batson, 1977), which succeeded prolonged Stage 2 sleep at 3:09 a.m. during the baseline study of a "normal" male tobacco addict. The specific mental content may be found in the appendix (speech number 572). Spontaneous macrodissociation has been observed immediately preceded by REM sleep (appendix-speech number 192) and during wakeful predormescence in a patient subject to fugue states (Rice & Fisher, 1976).

Macrodissociation Following Experimental Interventions

Arkin, Hastey, and Reiser (1966a) have reported on the results of attempts to produce dialogue between sleep-talkers and experimenters. This material is described at length in Chapter 12. It is sufficient at this point to note that the electrographic picture during such attempts, when apparently effective to some degree, most closely resembles Stage 1 NREM.

Presleep posthypnotic suggestion to talk in one's sleep is an effective priming stimulus, with susceptible subjects, in increasing the amount of sleep-talking (Arkin, Hastey, & Reiser, 1966b). This work is presented in detail in

Chapter 11. Subject number 3, as the reader will see, produced several macrodissociative episodes in the laboratory.

Rice and Fisher (1976) were able to evoke two episodes of macrodissociative sleep-speech in a patient ill with fugue tendencies. These came about following the sounding of a buzzer during REM sleep. The electrographic picture, like that of the posthypnotic subject just mentioned, consisted of sustained alpha rhythm and sporadic eye movements but with somewhat more muscle tension.

Fisher et al. (1974) have similarly evoked night-terror episodes by a buzzer stimulus administered during Stage 4. The electrographic picture appeared to be indistinguishable from spontaneous occurrences.

Broughton (1968) and Kales et al. (1966) were able to produce sleep-walking episodes in children prone to spontaneous episodes. These were brought about by physically bringing the children to an erect standing posture immediately preceding Stage 4 sleep. Broughton (1968) describes the accompanying EEG as showing "diffuse and rather high-amplitude alpha rhythm which reacted poorly or not at all to intense light stimuli, or else showed patterns of low voltage delta and beta activity, lacking spindles [p. 1074]."

In grouping such diverse phenomena as extended sleep-speech in "normals," hysterical subjects, nocturnal fugue episodes, Stage 4 night-terrors, and sleep-walking, it is emphasized that no claim is made that the basic psychological and physiological factors are identical. Far from it. They are categorized as macrodissociative phenomena insofar as they are all examples of dissociation of relatively long duration in terms of Hilgard's theory (1973, 1977).

8 Structural and Physical Aspects of Sleep-Utterance

Does sleep-speech tend to be coherent? Correct grammatically? Well-enunciated and intelligible rather than mumbled? Loud rather than soft? Short rather than long in duration and in word count? That is, what are the characteristics of sleep-utterance from a structural and physical perspective, as opposed to one of mental content? And how do sleep-utterance episodes strike an external observer?

CLINICAL AND ANECDOTAL LITERATURE

According to MacNish (1838), sleep-speech is at one time "rational and coherent and at other times full of absurdity. The voice is seldom the same as in the waking state. This I would attribute to the organs of hearing being mostly dormant, and unable to guide the modulations of sound [p. 181]." It is interesting that this notion foreshadows more recent developments and scholarly thought on the monitoring function of hearing one's own voice (Holzman & Rousey, 1970; Klein, 1965; Kraepelin, 1906; Mahl, 1972; Skinner, 1957).

In essential agreement, Carpenter (1886) remarks that:

> Among sleep-talkers there are some who merely utter meaningless sequences of words or strangely jumbled phrases, and are utterly incapable of being influenced by suggested ideas [ideas suggested aloud to the sleeper by an awake observer, but uttered below waking threshold intensity] whilst there are others who give utterance to a coherent train of thought, still without any receptivity of external suggestion; and others again obviously hear what is said to them, and attend to it or not according to the impression it makes on them (and still remain "asleep") [p. 591].

Andriani (1892), in the only extended paper known to me from the old literature dealing with the subject, stated that unlike speech of normal wakefulness, somniloquy rarely consists of long speeches. In general, the "lighter the sleep," the clearer is its articulation and orderliness. In some instances of "diseases of the brain," the speech is disconnected, confused, and mostly unintelligible. In common sleep-talking and in cases of "dementia," sentences or clauses tend to be short, more or less complete, and not very well connected to each other. In the majority of occasions, utterances consist mainly of simple words, interjections, exclamations, shouts and groans, and intensely emotional sounds that often awaken the sleeper. At other times, one might observe only mumblings, whispers, or simply lip movements. In another part of the paper, however, he remarked that if one compares sleep-talking to "normal language," the basic difference is not as clear as it first appears, and the transition from one to the other is not by leaps but by slow degrees—from incoherent fragments at one end of the scale to sleep-speeches at the other and which are "far from lacking in logic."

According to Trömner (1911a,b), sleep-talking is usually unclear, indistinct, uttered at low volume, and difficult to understand. Single words, brief sentences, and emotional sounds prevail. On the other hand, Trömner cites specific instances of loud remonstrative commands, exclamations and scoldings, all in short declarative sentence form.

Bañuelos (1940) claims that sleep-speeches tend to be uttered in a "very loud" voice. Kraepelin (1906) and Bleuler (1923) concur that enunciation is seriously impaired. In addition, Bleuler states that sleep-speeches sometimes make sense and at other times seem senseless. Furthermore, suggestions have appeared comparing speech in dreams (Kraepelin, 1906) and sleep-speech (Trömner, 1911a; Pötzl, 1929a,b) to forms of motor aphasia and sensory aphasia (Marburg, 1929).

Walsh (1920a) reported that the sleep-speech of mentally defective subjects in most instances was "intelligible." Generally, a few words were uttered at any given time which might be followed in a few moments by more words. One young girl would continue sleep-talking for 30 min or more.

Reports of the behavior of the linguistic apparatus during sleep-speech are rare. Thus, according to Lechner (1909) and Bregman (1910), the language is mostly indistinct and difficult to understand because the coordination of the muscles is disturbed—the lungs do not "participate," the mouth does not open, and the teeth are frequently pressed together. In addition, Bregman noted that utterances tend to consist of single words, sentences, and more rarely monologues and conversations. In addition, sometimes orders and abusive words are spoken, and questions are asked and answered in the stream of utterances emitted by the sleeper.

In contrast to those observers who stress the formal defects of sleep-utterance, however, Elder (1927) stated that sleep-speech may show little or no fault either in pronunciation, grammar, or ideas. Perhaps the most recent extended description of the formal characteristics of sleep-speech, which also provides some notion of the flavor of the phenomenon, is that of Cameron (1952). The personal observations on which his brief paper was based were made on sleeping soldiers in 1944 in the Persian Gulf command. The most impressive fact was:

> The incidence and quality of sleep-talking. The writer had served as an enlisted man for a year and a half at that time and had had plenty of opportunity to observe men talking in their sleep, so that this was not in itself a new phenomenon. In most cases of sleep-talking, the talk is usually erratic, jumbled and varies in volume, mostly at a rather low level, and it is difficult for an observer to understand. In Bandar Shapur, however, the speech of the sleepers was virtually normal in volume, enunciation, and general flow of content, being clearly audible, distinct and easy to follow. In fact, it was so "normal" that it was two weeks before the writer and his replacement buddy realized that it was sleep-talking. At first they simply assumed that two men were holding a conversation and that one was speaking so softly that only one side of the discussion was heard. The impact of this discovery was hardly lessened when some time later the writer cautiously informed his buddy that *he* was also beginning to talk that way, only to be told, "If you think that's news, so are *you*!" [p. 95].

Several detailed case reports have been published of somniloquists who possess accompanying psychopathology (Burrell, 1904; Cook, 1937). These contain unusual examples of abundant, elaborate sleep-talking with much clearly enunciated, structurally coherent speech and evidence of relatively high-level cognitive functioning. More recently, the sleep-speeches of a lyric writer were tape-recorded by his roomates, allegedly unbeknownst to him, and with his subsequent permission edited for publication (McGregor, 1964). An unique feature of this book is an accompanying LP phonograph record with many complete actual reproductions of his somniloquy. They are more or less uninterrupted speeches up to several minutes in duration. (See succeeding text for further comment on McGregor.)

In general, a prevalent attitude in the old literature has been that utterances of "common sleep-talkers" are likely to be brief, infrequent, and devoid of signs of emotional distress. In those cases where sleep-talking reflects psychic tension in adult life, however, somniloquy may occur once or more nightly and utterances are usually longer. Under such circumstances, they are often infused with dysphoric emotional qualities—anger and/or anxiety (Bregman, 1910; Trömner, 1911a,b). The tension need not be primarily of intrapsychic origin but may result from environmental stress (Cameron, 1952; De Sanctis, 1899; Pai, 1946).

In summary, the older nonlaboratory literature indicates that the structural and physical characteristics of sleep-utterance possess great variability with regard to:

1. degree of clarity (mumbles to clear enunciation);
2. linguistic coherence (chaotic, incoherent groups of words or phrases suggestive of motor and sensory aphasia, to sustained segments of more or less linguistically correct speech);
3. number of linguistic units and duration of segments (solitary interjections of words or emotional sounds to chains of words and sounds, and even harangues lasting several minutes or more);
4. grammatical form (utterances in the forms of questions, assertions and declarations, interjections, verbal and nonverbal expressions of affect, imperative orders, as well as unclassifiable examples); and
5. volume (whispers to shouts).

Seen from the point of the dissociation continuum, perhaps the main reason for this extreme variability has been that the clinical–anecdotal literature lumped all sleep-utterance together indiscriminately. In the light of the laboratory data presented, it seems reasonable to categorize some of the old clinical papers in accordance with our basic organizing scheme as possibly exemplifying:

1. microdissociation episodes (Andriani, 1892; Bleuler, 1923; Carpenter, 1886; Bregman, 1910; Kraepelin, 1906; Lechner, 1909; some of MacNish, 1938; some of Trömner, 1911a,b; some of Walsh, 1920b);
2. macrodissociation episodes (Burrell, 1904; some of Cameron, 1952; Cook, 1937; MacGregor, 1964); or
3. intermediate dissociation episodes: the clinical comments are too sparse to enable confident categorization under this heading. However, the information provided suggests that some of the observations of Cameron (1952), Carpenter (1886), Elder (1927), MacNish (1838), Walsh (1920) and Andriani (1892) may have included examples of intermediate dissociations.

LABORATORY DATA ON STRUCTURAL AND PHYSICAL CHARACTERISTICS

There is almost as much variability in sleep-speech as there is in wakeful speech and one cannot provide, therefore, a concise description of the "typical" sleep-speech. But perhaps the most straightforward item is that of the average number of words per speech.

The material to follow consists, in part, of attempts to determine the central tendencies of the number of intelligible words per sleep-speech, and, in part, of comments based on careful observation of well over 700 sleep-utterances recorded in the laboratory. The latter contained a large proportion of apparently nonspecific vocalizations with ambiguous verbal or communicative content.

Word-Count per Sleep-Speech

The population of sleep-speeches employed in this determination was drawn from 468 spontaneous episodes containing at least one intelligible word uttered by 31 chronic sleep-talkers, all of which were tape-recorded in the laboratory, and for which the associated sleep stage had been classified by the senior author (Arkin & Toth, 1970). These sleep-speeches occurred during either undisturbed baseline nights or else on nights with multiple mentation report awakenings. As mentioned earlier (Chapters 1 and 7), the participating subjects spent unequal numbers of nights in the laboratory and contributed unequal numbers of sleep-speeches to the population studied. The results are therefore presented in terms of the *weighted* mean word count per speech (to proportionately reflect the differential contributions of each subject), the medians of the separate mean word counts determined for each subject (Table 8.1), and the modal word counts of the speeches (Fig. 8.1).

Results

1. Weighted mean word counts per speech in relation to sleep stage (Table 8.1):

   a. Stage 2—8.2 words per speech (n = 157 speeches)
   b. Stage 3-4 = 10.5 words per speech (n = 128 speeches)
   c. Stage 1 NREM = 12.6 words per speech (n = 16 speeches)
   d. Stage REM = 11.3 words per speech (n = 167 speeches)

2. Medians of separate mean word counts per speech for each subject (Table 8.1):

TABLE 8.1
Central Tendencies of Word Counts per Sleep-Speech

Sleep Stage	2	3-4	1 NREM	REM
Weighted mean word count per speech	8.2 (n = 157)	10.5 (n = 128)	12.6 (n = 16)	11.3 (n = 167)
Median of separate mean word counts per speech for each subject	7.2	6.3	13.5	7.4

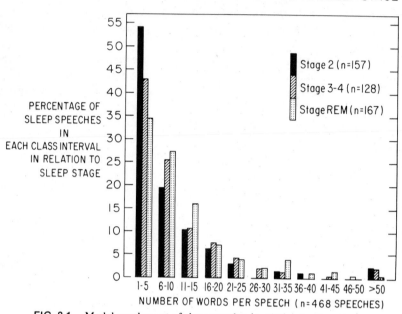

FIG. 8.1.   Modal word count of sleep-speeches in relation to sleep stage.

a. Stage 2 = 7.2 words per speech
b. Stage 3–4 = 6.3 words per speech
c. Stage 1 NREM = 13.5 words per speech
d. Stage REM = 7.4 words per speech

Modal Word Counts of Speeches.   In *all* sleep stages except 1 NREM, the greatest number of sleep-speeches by far fell into the 1–5 words per speech category. The total number of 1 NREM speeches was too small to permit definite conclusions. In Stages 2 and 3–4, the percentage of speeches in class intervals 6–10 and over fell away sharply, and the rate of such falling off in the Stage REM speech population was a little less so. That is, although the bulk of REM speeches were 1–5 words in length, an impressive proportion were in the 6–10 word range in comparison to that of Stage 2, and in the 11–15 word range in comparison to those of both Stages 2 and 3–4 (Fig. 8.1).

Discussion.   These results are consistent with the ad hoc classification of sleep-utterances as examples of micro, intermediate, and macrodissociation episodes. That is, the great bulk of occurrences were microdissociative, with a progressively decreasing proportion of intermediate and macrodissociations. The data presented in Table 8.1 and Fig. 8.1 are consistent with the mean word count of 5.1 words per Stage 2 sleep-speech (*n* = 12 speeches) as calculated from data reported by MacNeilage (1971).

In the main, the laboratory findings bear out the contention of those clinicians mentioned earlier that most sleep-speech is brief and consists of a few words rather than extended remarks. Lest this lead one to adopt a demeaning attitude toward sleep-speech in regard to the central tendencies of word counts per speech, however, it is well to be reminded that wakeful speech need not be drastically different. Thus, Goldman-Eisler (1964) states, "Half of our speech time seems to issue in phrases not longer than three words, and three-quarters in less than five words at the utmost [p. 98]"—a number per wakeful speech comparable to that of sleep-speech. And although Deese (1978) does not provide word-count data on similar types of wakeful speech, the *duration* of speeches was used as a measure; it was found that over 90% of 20,000 spontaneously uttered sentences were less than 10 sec long, and 50% lasted 3–4 sec or less.

An important item, not to be overshadowed by the typical brevity of sleep-speech, is the unusual but definitely observable occasions of longer speeches in excess of 50–100 words. Witness the macrodissociative utterance of over 300 words uttered by a subject previously asleep in Stage 2, in Appendix 2, Speech #572; (Batson, 1977).

Behavioral Observations on Sleep-Utterance Episodes

We were able to make no systematic eyewitness observations of behavioral features of somniloquy. What follows for the most part, therefore, are reconstructions based on the electrographic record and what could be heard on tape recordings.

Regarding microdissociative occurrences, the most typical sequence was:

1. a prior interval of silent sleep accompanied by more or less regular breath sounds and bodily quiescence;
2. a spectrum of sound changes beginning with the least departure from the immediately preceding state of affairs:
   a. vocalization with or without words;
   b. change in respiratory rate, depth and rhythm, and frequency succeeded by vocalization—sometimes there was a cough, throat clearing, or sighing;
   c. change in respiratory parameters accompanied by or followed by rustling of sheets, head movement sounds on pillow, and in one subject (D.C.), frequent self-scratching, all succeeded by vocalization. (These sounds suggested fairly gross displacement of the body or one or more of its parts. Occasionally, a percussive sound was heard apparently resulting from a limb or head striking the microphone.)

Any element of these sequences might be repeated and finally followed by sleep resumption or sustained Stage W.

In brief, one observes events that may be construed as behavioral expressions of movement-arousal episodes of varying duration and complexity. Intermediate and macrodissociative episodes may approach small-scale somnambulistic occurrences in overall dimensions.

Duration and Clarity of Sleep-Speeches

Although most sleep-speeches contain at least a few words, many consist of only one, such as "good," "now," "yes," "O.K.," "mm-hm," "uh-huh," "mm," and the like. It has always been an intriguing experience for me to hear a sleeper suddenly utter such expressions seemingly out of the blue and then continue sleeping in silence. It reminds one of a seal swimming under water, surfacing for a cordial, peremptory, or meditative bark and deftly resubmerging.

Most sleep-utterances are short and occur over 1–2 sec or less, but longer ones may last a minute or longer. In the latter case, the duration is estimated from the first to the last vocalization within the episode, including brief silent pauses, and does not refer to the total accumulated time occupied by vocalization proper.

Similarly, the range of clarity extends from unintelligible mumbles, mixtures of mumbles and intelligible syllables, and mumbles with intelligible words, phrases, and clauses, to sustained sequences of crystal-clear words. The belief is widespread that most sleep-speech is indistinct. I have been repeatedly surprised, however, by utterances that, unclear when heard over the laboratory intercommunication system, turned out to contain some clear *sotto voce* or whispered speech on the tape recording. The most likely explanation for this discrepancy is that the microphone leading to the tape recorder was of high quality and positioned close to the subject's head, in contrast to the microphone serving the intercom. The same consideration applies to sleep-speech outside the laboratory, when the wakeful observer is likely to be at some distance from the sleeper.

Structural Features of Sleep-Utterance

Comments on the structural features of spontaneous sleep-speech are based perforce on naturally occurring fragments of sequences that are of varying linguistic completeness. The overwhelming bulk of speeches were of phrase-, clause-, or sentence-like word sequences. The most common finding was that in such short strings of words, syntax resembled that of usual wakeful speech of similar length. However, whenever the sleep-speech became more extensive, degrees of disorganization and departures from normal wakeful syntax appeared.

Once again, lest we hastily declare sleep-speech to be uniformly inferior to wakeful speech in regard to syntax, Goldman-Eisler (1964) reminds us, "The sentences which I submitted to transitional analysis had to be grammatically correct sentences and these are very difficult to find in spontaneous speech. I went through heaps of recorded speech uttered by highly educated academic people and I found only seven such sentences! [p. 113]"

Correct syntax and inflection of sleep-speech seemed somewhat more likely to occur in REM than in NREM speech. If one were to arrange REM and NREM speeches along a continuum from no or mild structural-inflectional disturbance at one end and severe disturbance at the other, NREM speeches would reach the furthest extremity of the severest abnormality characterized by sheer gibberish, clang associations, and perseverated morphemes, words, and phrases. Under such circumstances, "neologisms" were occasionally observed. Episodes of such severely disorganized speeches were especially prone to occur in association with Stages 3 and 4, in the first half of the night, and often possessed an explosive quality with rapid rates of emission of words. Many such speeches bear striking resemblances to aphasic utterances and, in a sense, may provide a physiological model of aphasia (Arkin and Brown, 1972; Brown, 1972). An interesting example is the following Stage 4 speech:

> Mm—uh—duh—she shad hero sher uh sher sheril S-H-A-W (spelled out by subject) takes part—loses but lost—uh invincible is u as usual—mbl.

Abundant additional specimens are provided in Tables 18.2 and 18.3 in Chapter 18.

In Chapter 18, the topic of sleep-speech, aphasic speech, schizophrenic, and drowsy speech receives fuller treatment, along with other structural features of sleep-speech.

Often longer speeches consist of small groups of words, each with more or less usual wakeful syntax and each separated by silent pauses. The overall effect suggests sleep dialogues with hallucinated partners, sometimes resembling one half of a telephone conversation.

Examples of a microdissociative type of intraepisode sleep dialogue are:

> [Stage 2]   Mbl—oh yeah—I didn't think you were—so?—mm.
> [NREM]   Mbls—it's strange—to describe (?) that—oh—come on guys—you embarrass me—mbl.
> [Stage 3]   How come you say—I'm sorry—my mistake.
> [Stage 4]   Mbl—oh, come on now—boy!—Jesus Christ!—you guys are special—mbl—voting.
> [Stage 4]   Mbl—what do you want to travel for—how much does he want to sell them for—and as much as you can get—[groan] exASPERATING—mbl.
> [Stage 4]   It's following me—it's following you—not bad [laughter].
> [Stage REM]   Mm—hm—mother—you gotta get some eggs 'cause seeing all these people all know that I like eggs too, so get a dozen eggs. Please put this in a soft bag, thank you.

Another frequent occurrence is sudden interruption of a clear sequence of speech in the middle, followed by an apparently meaningless sustained silence or else mumbled petering out. The hearer is left with the impression of a thought which has been truncated, fragmented, or left incomplete overtly but possibly continued implicitly. Sometimes a series of such sequences comprised a single utterance.

Examples of an intermediate dissociative type are:

[Stage REM]   Oh yeah—there was something else I was s'posed to talk about [p]—hey, doctor, aren't you mbl—[giggles].

[Stage REM]   [giggles]—touched your face—[giggle]—no, mother, I'm just kidding [p] - well—[sings]—we—mbl.

[Stage 2]   Mm—hm—mm—hm—mm—oh Jesus Christ feeling great— ooh huh huh mm mm tch!—oh just great—[sigh]—[sigh]— [sigh]—tch!—uh—hm—yeah—uh—oh—ooh damn—tch!— gotta see the proof of the play, you know—[sigh] uh such a major thing—we should should always say that proofs are— mbl—actually mbl—pending we decide what we want to do based on that. But anyway it's a twenty-four hour thing and uh.

[Stage 2]   Mike—Mike[p]—from the window—[p]I don't want to get up. I don't want to.

As previously indicated, the three-category classification of sleep-speeches into degrees of dissociation was presented partly as an organizing perspective and partly as an attempt to delineate and capture real differences between types of sleep-utterance episodes. The dividing lines between them are far from precise, and it is somewhat arbitrary of me to classify the foregoing examples as intermediate dissociative episodes. The reason for so doing, however, is that the psychophysiological tendencies resulting in sleep-speech were not "exhausted" in a single isolated utterance but rather manifested themselves as interrupted segments in a series.

The reader is invited to examine the appendix for a comprehensive collection of sleep-speeches from other investigators' material as well as my own.

It may be concluded that the results of laboratory observation of sleep-speech and clinical-anecdotal observation are mutually compatible. The most frequent findings are brief speeches both in word-count and duration with varying degrees of disorganization from none to maximal. However, florid, extensive sleep-speeches, although less common, or even rare, have been repeatedly observed in the laboratory. (See Appendix 2, speech numbers 7, 8, 9, 10, 11, 12, 13, 14, 67, 80, 183, 572, and others.)

9 Psychological Content of Somniloquy

CLINICAL AND ANECDOTAL LITERATURE

What sorts of things are said during sleep-talking episodes? Judging from the nonlaboratory literature under review, once again there is at least as much variability here as during wakeful speech.

In the most elaborate older paper on sleep-talking available, Andriani (1892) stated that:

> The co..ent of sleep-speech is often emotional, and reveals a desire, an unsatisfied wish, an awaited pleasure, a regret, or more often a state of fear, anxiety, anguish or terror. The terrifying ideas of ghosts, goblins and ogres in children, persecution ideas of the demented, the unconscious reproduction of dreadful events, a terrible remorse manifesting itself in an hypnagogic hallucination [sic], scenes of imminent peril or tenderness, the unconscious memory of many moral and physical sufferings, the thousand struggles of the mind, varied, intertwined and exaggerated by a dream—these are the common subjects of sleep-talking [p. 305].

Among the specimens quoted by Andriani (1892) were those of two 13-year-old boys. One was given to experiencing terrifying dreams about the devil during which the sleeper took two parts. On the one hand, the sleeper cried out "We caught you, we caught you." Concomitantly, he could smell the odor of sulphur and tar and shouted, "It is not I; it is not I; I didn't do anything!" The other boy was overhead to say, "Again! Again! I'm afraid! I don't want to!" [p. 307–308].

Trömner (1911a,b) reports that an observer may hear sleepers emit utterances of quarrels, angry words, commands, expressions of fear, references to recent days' events and, in children, talking to playmates as if in games. Generally, they are said to be expressions of "after-sensations" of daytime experiences. Similar to the examples of Andriani, Trömner cites the speeches of children sounding as if they were addressing their playmates, "Let me go! What are you doing this for? You old donkey!" and the like. In addition, he mentioned a personal friend 45 years of age who was devoted to sailing and would often issue nautical commands in his sleep. Walsh's findings (1920a) and also those of Vogl (1964), both dealing with emotionally disturbed children, are in agreement with those of Trömner (1911a,b). Walsh (1920a), studying 100 mentally defective subjects (age range 6–40), states that sleep-speeches dealt almost entirely with daily incidents and only rarely in remotely occurring events. A quarrel during the day or near bed-time seemed to provide a potent stimulus and subject matter for sleep-utterance. Vogl (1964), in discussing the sleep-utterances of children, refers to "clear pearl-like laughter in the midst of sleep, bright shouts as if the child were at play [p. 128]," as well as intense dysphoric vocalizations and speeches. And in adults, she observed that "heated discussion during the day may in the following night's sleep take the form either of an intelligible or unintelligible oral repetition or reappear merely as a series of groans [p. 128]." In any case, the content of the sleep-utterances is deemed to be a nocturnal continuation and expression of intense affect-infused daytime experience containing vocal components. Parallel observations were made by Wile (1934) on his juvenile patients.

Pai (1946) in a similar vein confirms the widely held idea (Mot & Crile, cited in Walsh 1920b) that soldiers with combat neuroses tend to relive battle scenes in sleep—orders are shouted and other psychomotor accompaniments of fighting occur. The same episodes, words, and phrases are observable almost every night. And, accordingly, as we shall see later, many sleep-utterances occurring in the laboratory contain references to the experimental situation (Arkin 1966; Farber, Arkin, Ellman, Antrobus, & Nelson, 1973; Rechtschaffen, Goodenough, & Shapiro, 1962), just as do many dreams elicited under the same conditions.

Sadger (1920) reports a case of a woman somnambulist who talked in her sleep frequently as a child. The content consisted of references to sermons, memorized poems, songs, and to the previous day's play.

Burrell's case (1904) is one of a 38-year-old farmer with a family history of somniloquy, who in adult life developed a florid psychosis on two occasions (not easily classified, but suggestive of a macrodissociative reaction). The patient spoke spontaneously and also conversed in sleep with an observer; he had total amnesia for all this sleep-speech when in the waking state. His speech was frequently punctuated and interrupted by snores. Its general flavor resembled the childish wit, suspiciousness, petulance, oratory, and yarn-spinning of an alcoholic in his cups. The following were observed repeatedly: speaking as if conducting a prayer meeting, with quotations from scriptures, singing, exhortation and prayer; correctly performing complicated arithmetic computations, telling humorous anecdotes, uttering self-reproaches, and dialogues between the patient and real companions. On one occasion, personally observed by Burrell, the patient slept in the same room with a visiting brother who was also a sleep-talker. The two reportedly conversed in their sleep between snores and laughter. Neither recalled any of this in the morning.

Reil, quoted by Radestock (1879), described two additional such cases; and I have myself interviewed a healthy young college woman who gave a similar history of sleep conversations with siblings who were likewise asleep and talking.

McGregor (1964), cited earlier, was 38 at the time of the publication of his book. He was a professional writer of lyrics and a somniloquist since the age of four. He kindly consented to be personally interviewed by me and he impressed me as a sensitive, shy, honest, unconventional man with an artistic temperament, and certainly not psychotic. His sleep speeches, typical examples of macrodissociation, were tape-recorded by roommates, initially without his knowledge, and later recorded and published with his consent and cooperation. They were of considerable length (up to several minutes) and more or less continuous. They sounded for the most part as if the subject was talking to one or more imaginary companions who apparently made replies to him, for there are appropriate silent pauses. Sometimes they were perorations on various subjects. There was usually a unifying or coherent subject running through the entire length of an otherwise digression-filled, childlike, gossipy monologue, which contained much slapstick and phrases reminiscent of "sick jokes." Often there was silliness, repetitiveness, word play, bathos, righteous indignation, shouting, sarcasm, and philosophizing. The speeches frequently started at a low affective level and gathered momentum until, at the end, there was commonly climactic shouting, screaming, and incoherent vocalizations at a rapid rate, ususally ending in awakening. The material covered a wide range: movie stars, artists and models, social criticism, a Ouija board seance, a mustard-throwing battle, major surgery, and the like. The following is a full quotation of a short speech in the McGregor (1964) collection:

Run call mommy, run call mommy. Umm umm umm. Time to eat. Time to eat. That's the last story...no, I'm not gonna tell you any more stories. You have had it in the story department. No more stories little soldier uh huh. Run call mommy, run call mommy. That's right.

Hey, Claire? What time—what—what's holding up the dinner? Oh! You've *squashed* the squabs! Aaaahhh, what a graceless cook, graceless! Squashed squab, humph! I don't care, it sounds mouthwatering. Why in a good restaurant you'd pay plenty for squashed squab, yes you would. Just bring it on that way...I don't care...with smashed potatoes—ah hahhah hah hah—strained peas, yes...ummmm, a delicacy, it's a delicacy. Is everybody ready? Let's go...ummmm, why it's delicious, it's delicious! Ohhh! Mmmmm mmmm! Do you know we didn't say grace. We attacked our squashed squab without grace. No grace, no squab. Put it up, put it up, put it up, put it up. But just you remember the next time. Do you know that's so delicious, the next time you have it—squash it! Ummmm mmmm. All the little bones are lovely. I thought they'd be brittle; they're not brittle at all. Ummmm, no, the *peanut* is brittle—peanut brittle? Ahh hah hah hah...boo! Well...

Knock—oh—there's a knock at the door. Ohh! Hands up everybody. Hands up everybody. Ohh! Put your hands up, put your hands up, they'll shoot us! Put your hands up! Put your—Claire, put your hands up. Little Soldier, put your hand up. Ahh, he only has one hand. Oh, whaddya think? That little soldier was in a...a grave situation, lost his hand, can only put one up!

Oh Claire, the squashed squab's getting cold. Look at that and we got our hands in the air. I want to eat the *squab.*

Oh ya devils! Take what you want and hurry. We're in the middle of our dinner. Oh look at that—g'w'on, g'w'on, we want our dinner. Look at that—you won't find anything in this house. You will not find—Noo! Nooo! Nooo! Claire, he's taking the squashed squab. He's taking the squashed squab! *He's taking the squashed squabbbbbb!*

Sleep-Talking and the Revelation of Secrets

Episodes of sleep-speech have often been used by creative writers. Usually, its content is employed to present some fateful, dramatic truth. Lady MacBeth betrays herself and her husband by her anguished somnambulic soliloquy; Othello feels constrained to take seriously Iago's innuendos regarding Desdemona when the former relates to him the content of Cassio's alleged sleep-talking depicting an amorous interlude with Desdemona; the audience reacts with awe to the portentous sleep-speech of Calpurnia, "Help, ho! They murder Caesar!" Thus, a sleep-speech endows a key factor in the dramatic narrative with the cachet of genuine truth—one cannot disbelieve it or dismiss it lightly.

This attitude is entirely in accord with much popular belief. Many anecdotes jokingly refer to sleep-talking as an occasion of involuntary self-betrayal. Patients have been known to lead tortured lives and suffer from severe insomnia because of their morbid apprehensions of unwitting disclosure of forbidden sex. I have been approached by an anxious college student who wanted treatment lest she reveal the name of one lover to another in the course of somniloquy.

One instance known to me of imminent revelation of a secret in naturalistic home conditions was provided by a patient who was living with a jealous lover. The subject reported that on the night previous to the therapeutic session, there occurred a vivid subjective experience of talking to someone after retiring while awaiting sleep. The person to whom the speech was addressed was not recalled nor was the content remembered on the following morning except that it contained a reference to a former sweetheart. The subject was startled when awakened by the current lover of whose presence awareness had been lost. Anxiety was felt and a verbal self-admonition was given about having to "Watch myself about this shit"; Awkwardly enough, the subject had been aware of many recent vivid nocturnal dreams about the former old flame. The current lover then volunteered having heard a great deal of sleep-speech lately that didn't make sense.

In another instance, a patient had lived in dread for many years lest she reveal a political secret through sleep-utterance, and suffered marked, concomitant sleep disruption.

Many observers (Andriani, 1892; Carpenter, 1849; Cook, 1937; Elder, 1927; Esquirol, cited by Andriani, 1892; Lindner, 1945; Lucretius, 1951; MacNish, 1838; Moll, 1889; Vaschide & Pieron, 1902; Winterstein, 1953) claim that preciously guarded secrets have been unwittingly betrayed in spontaneous sleep-talking or were wheedled out of a somniloquist by an observer who was in a rapport with the subject. These include references to such matters as illicit sexual relations, peccadilloes of schoolmates, and possibly, in one case, the confession of a crime (Lindner, 1945). Cook (1937) presented anecdotal records of the voluble sleep-talking of a young girl who revealed in her sleep, to an audience of three roommates, the events of the previous day. Among other things, there were detailed accounts of love scenes with her fiance, which she had steadfastly kept secret in her waking state. One sleep-talking episode lasted for 2½ hrs. The next morning, the subject had a total amnesia for this occurrence, felt "like a wreck," and was "unaccountably hoarse." Finally, not too long ago, a news item in the *London Times* (September 22, 1970) read: "Theft discovered after man talked about it in his sleep."

Freud (1962), in a dissenting opinion, stated that secrets are never betrayed in sleep-talking. His view is supported by case material of Burrell (1904) and Sadger (1920). Burrell's patient in particular seemed like a very cagey individual who, though quite voluble, never let down his guard.

In summary, the clinical and anecdotal literature on sleep-utterance indicates that there is:

1. enormous variability in the mental and affective content categories of sleep-speech approaching that of wakefulness in scope;
2. rare or uncommon, direct, overt, unambiguous disclosure of personal secrets, contrary to popular belief and expectation;
3. commonly a tendency to allude to, or reproduce, in sleep-utterance certain experiences of daily life, especially those accompanied by intense wakeful affect;

4. commonly a tendency to emit utterances infused with negative affect that is often of greater intensity than that produced during wakefulness (as in night terrors). On the other hand, sleep-speeches with positive affect usually have less intensity than corresponding positive wakeful experiences.

LABORATORY DATA ON THE
PSYCHOLOGICAL CONTENT OF SOMNILOQUY

In accordance with previous indications, the mental content of somniloquy is as variable as that of wakeful speech. References to trivial gossip, school matters, newspaper items, everyday occurrences, entertainment, art, science, the laboratory situation itself, food, philosophical discussion, slapstick inanity, fearful and dramatic events, remorse, visual scenes, opinions about all sorts of things, and the like were common. Curiously, overt references to sexual matters or related topics, though observed were rather rare. The reader is invited to examine Appendix 2, which contains hundreds of sleep-speeches, to gain his own impression.

In addition, as previously indicated in an earlier chapter, a large number of speeches consisted merely of short expressions of assent or negation. In the case of assent, one-word utterances such as "yes," "O.K.," "good," or equivalent forms such as "mm-hm" or "uh-huh," were common. And in the case of negation, one often heard speeches like "no!" or "no! no! stop! don't! [etc.]," often in a frenzied manner.

Laboratory Observations on
Revelation of Secrets in Somniloquy

Sleep-talking in the laboratory has rarely resulted in the disclosure of secrets, and then only indirectly. First, it is difficult to define a "secret" operationally. What would strike one person as a secret revealed would simply impress another as a neutral, forthright, candid expression of everyday thoughts. Perhaps the best we can do is to say that if a subject is permitted to hear a playback of a tape-recorded sleep-speech and displays unambiguous visible signs of shame or guilt or else a blend of amusement and mild embarrassment, then we may say that the sleep-speech revealed a secret. Even here, however, the judgment of signs of shame would be a subjective decision of the experimenter. Be that as it may, the following are the only two occurrences we observed which seemed to fit this criterion.

1. A young male college student said in his sleep, "Am I queer or something?" On hearing the playback of this speech in the following morning, the subject chuckled with apparent mild shame.

2. A similar subject, in the course of a sleep-speech, used the abbreviation "C.P.W." On hearing it, I initially thought it stood for "Central Park West"; but when the subject heard the tape recording in the following morning, he burst out into loud uncontrollable laughter and his face flushed. He explained that a close friend married a short time before the laboratory session and that his wife had plans to guarantee his submission to her by threatening him with her "Cosmic Pussy Whip" if he stepped out of line. The couple affectionately referred to this implement by the abbreviating initial letters. The subject appeared intensely embarrassed to have revealed this in his sleep.

In addition to the foregoing, several subjects (four males and one female) said words like "shit" and "fuck" in their sleep on rare occasions but appeared cool as clams when permitted to learn of the content of their somniloquy.

Thus, the consensus of both the clinical literature and laboratory observation is that secrets are rarely disclosed in sleep-speech, although several reputable clinical students of the phenomenon take exception. In addition, some authorities also believe that a clever, intuitive, and empathic wakeful observer is able, with suitable subjects and technique, to coax secrets from sleep-talkers. (See Chapter 12 for further discussion.)

We are faced with an interesting puzzle. At least some sleep-speeches reflect an organized, temporary, hallucinatory state that arises spontaneously; its components may be interactive in meaningful ways with external interventions, for which there is lack of simultaneous critical awareness of reality on the part of the subject, and for which a strong amnestic tendency exists. One would expect, along with the poets and dramatists, that sleep-talkers could not help but reveal all manner of secrets and strangenesses; and who does not have at least one secret? Yet the opposite is true. This suggests that some kind of intrapsychic censorship is unflaggingly vigilant in sleep (as Freud asserted) or, perhaps, that the same mechanisms that result in sleep-utterances simultaneously alert and intensify censorship tendencies just prior to sleep-vocalization. Actually, it is not unlikely that more "secrets" are revealed or betrayed in wakeful than in sleep-speech.

Broughton (1978) describes a case of a male somnambulist, whose assaultive violent behavior during sleep was enacted with total amnesia afterward. In the laboratory, these were found, as usual, to be associated with Stage 4 sleep. Germane to our present topic, however, the patient had in real life participated in a violent robbery and subsequently began to talk in his sleep about the robbery and about bringing a brother, dead from suicide, back to life.

Affective Qualities of Somniloquy

Not infrequently, sleep-speeches involve tense, anxious, and dramatic fragments. Doubtless many of these are examples of what might be considered to be mild arousal NREM night terrors and REMP nightmares (Fisher, Kahn, Edwards, & Davis, 1974). The most common affect, however, is one of conversational blandness appropriate in quality to the content of the speech but of somewhat diminished intensity. However, the range is broad. Subjects chuckled, laughed, sang, whimpered; sounded petulant, sulky, childish, irritable, sarcastic; displayed intense anger with shouting, anxiety of all degrees, sobbing with both fear and remorse; and sometimes evinced an inchoate, nonspecific high intensity affect accompanying the discharge of the outburstlike utterances just mentioned with clang associations and recurrent utterances. (See Appendix 2 for examples.)

Finally, another group of sleep-talking phenomena resembles words and sounds one utters in solitude while awake. Exclamatory words, phrases, one-syllable sounds of surprise, curiosity, pleasure, and/or agreement are common. In addition, one encounters utterances resembling wakeful vocal self-priming or self-stimulation reminiscent of someone following a recipe or other stepwise task and wondering aloud what to do next.

In summary, the psychological content of somniloquy observed in the laboratory is on the whole similar to that reported in clinical–anecdotal literature. It is possible, of course, that a fine-grained content analysis would reveal subtle differences, but subject-sampling as well as other methodological problems would most likely make such a complicated enterprise unprofitable.

10 Sleep-Utterance and Associated Mentation Recalled during Subsequent Wakefulness

CLINICAL AND ANECDOTAL LITERATURE

Is there a discernible relationship between the content of sleep-speech and mentation reports obtained subsequently? Views on this matter, like so much else in the literature surveyed, show considerable disparity. Some authors maintain that there is no correspondence whatsoever between somniloquy content and that of associated wakeful mentation, whether the latter is recalled on being awakened immediately after the speech (Carpenter, 1849; Ellis, 1926; Maury, 1878; Moreau, 1820; Trömner, 1911a,b), or on awakening the following morning (Bregman, 1910; Burrell, 1904; Cook, 1937; Elder, 1927; Landauer, 1918; Schilder & Kauders, 1956). In either condition, there is said to be complete amnesia for the sleep-speech and its associated mentation. On the other hand, many other authorities contend that a definite relationship between sleep-speech and recalled wakeful mentation is demonstrable at least some of the time, as examined in this section.

Several categories of such relationship may be discerned in comments in the literature concerning sleep-speech content and proximate sleep mentation. In all instances, the author states or implies that the subject unwittingly emitted an overt utterance during behavioral sleep and was queried immediately, or else sometime afterward while awake, as to what had been passing through his mind. The subject may then recall one or more of the following four sorts of *sleep-imagined events:*

First-Order Concordance

Events in which one or more words were uttered in a "dream" and in which words were unambiguously expressed in the sleep-speech, represent first-order concordance. (See Andriani, 1892; Baudry, 1974; Crile and Mot both cited by Walsh, 1920b; Fischer, 1839; Fosgate, 1850; Pai, 1946; Pinkerton, 1839; Walsh, 1920b).

Beyond asserting that such relationships are indeed observable, the older literature contains no clear-cut illustrative examples. The following citations are of instances that come closest to fitting in this category.

Pai confirms the widely held idea (Crile and Mot cited in Walsh, 1920b) that soldiers with combat neuroses tend to relive battle scenes in sleep mentation—orders are shouted and other psychomotor accompaniments of fighting occur. The same episodes, words, and phrases are uttered almost every night. In the morning on awakening, subjects recount battle dreams of the night before. Although such observations support the validity of the relationship category in question (i.e., first-order concordance), the possibility nevertheless remains that the battle dreams and battle speeches could have occurred at separate times (much as an actual enuretic episode and a dream about accumulating moisture or water are now known to occur at two different times of the same night. See Gastaut & Broughton, 1965).

Walsh (1920b) contends, without presenting evidence, that a sleep-talker speaks aloud only those words which "in the dream" he experiences as his own. On the whole, whereas laboratory evidence, as we later see, is consistent with this assertion, I have personally observed at least one exception outside the laboratory and have recorded it in writing shortly afterward (see pages 382-383).

Wile (1934) described a sample of 25 children, ranging in age from 6–14 years, who talked and cried out in their sleep about matters related to recent disturbing and frightening real events, and whose recall of dreams on the following morning was said to reflect these events in an unambiguous manner.

And recently, Baudry (1974) described an unequivocal instance of a patient who awakened her husband by shouting "No! No!" in her sleep. Her immediate recall included a dream in which she shouted these same words when seeing her baby fall out of bed.

Second-Order Concordance

Events in which words or sounds were uttered, although not identical to any of the actual words of the overt sleep-speech, but which nevertheless belonged to the same conceptual topic reflected in the somniloquy, represent second-order concordance.

Ferenczi (1916) reported on an episode of loud overt laughter while asleep; following this, the subject was immediately awakened and related a dream in which he was laughing at something that had struck him funny.

Dement (1972) described an amusing instance of sleep-speech uttered by his little daughter who was under 2 years of age at the time. Dr. Dement had entered her room one morning before she had awakened and observed eye-movements. Suddenly she said, "Pick me! Pick me!" He awakened her immediately whereupon she said, "Oh, Daddy, I was a flower [p. 53]."

A special variety of second-order concordance may be found in instances where sleep mentation events are infused with strong affects, but *implicit* vocalization in the sleep-imagined occurrences is absent or inhibited. Despite this lack of vocalization in the sleep-imagined events, wakeful observers hear actual words or sounds that clearly express concordant affects. Thus, Henning (1914) reports on a fascinating subject who was given to recurrent nightmares in which he tried in vain to cry out for help—in the dream he remained mute and strangulated. In reality his utterances would echo throughout the house. In one recurrent nightmare, in which thieves broke into the house, he tried to no avail with all of his force to yell repeatedly, "Burglars!" Instead what he actually called out was "Mama!" six times, at which point his brother wakened him. If one did not arouse him on other occasions, he would awaken spontaneously after the 10th or 12th cry. In other instances, in trying to yell "Fire!," he would only succeed in making howling sounds. At no times were these vocalizations registered in awareness as actual sensory experience during the dreams. Such observations are of interest because they illustrate the possibility of activity of the linguistic apparatus in sleep somewhat independently of specific concomitant mentation content, nevertheless reflecting the momentarily prevailing affect—a phenomenon in clear accord with the concept of sleep-speech as a dissociation-process-derived event. That is, the affect involved in the sleep mentation may be concordant with the somniloquy without recall of vocalization events in the "dream."

Third-Order Concordance

Events that contain references to vocalization but without other available specific concordant content represent, third-order concordance.

As previously cited, Cameron (1952) remarked that during his military service in the Persian Gulf, "his own dream content, and apparently that of most other men in the area, was greatly elaborated in detail, to the point that the writer must confess that he had difficulty numerous times in being certain whether or not he was dreaming" and "sleeping behavior [in this case, talking] became more and more like the normal waking behavior [p. 95]."

Along similar lines, McGregor (1964) commented to me in a personal interview that he sometimes feels that his sleep-talking had occurred while partly awake, but he never recalls any specifics of what he had said aloud.

No Discernible Concordance

Events that bear no discernible relationship to the overt sleep-speech content, represent no discernible concordance.

Maury (1878) provides a clear account of this relational category. "I have several times aroused persons abruptly from their sleep, who had just, while sleeping, pronounced words; they never remembered them. What they had said was completely gone out of their mind, and the dreams which they reported to me, now and then, had no connection at all with the words uttered by them [p. 209]." And Henning (1914) similarly states that the "dreamer is ignorant of what he says aloud. When one tells him afterward what he has said, he specifically denies having thus expressed himself. Although he can quite exactly recall his dream, everything is missing which would be related to the words spoken. When I heard a dreamer speak whole sentences in his sleep, I would not get the slightest explanatory association after his awakening [pp. 19–22]."

In summary, examination of the comments and observations of the clinical, psychological, and serious anecdotal literature on somniloquy permits one to formulate a series of categories expressing degrees of concordance between sleep-speech and associated mentation content. At one extreme, concordance is unambiguous, and at the other there is either no discernible concordance or total lack of recall of sleep mentation; and in between, there are several intermediate categories of concordance that are convincing but indirect. Later on, in the course of presenting laboratory studies of this problem, we provide more systematic observations in electrographic contexts. For the present, it is sufficient to remark that the portion of the literature just reviewed contains implications for related areas of psychology dealing with dissociation of cognitive subsystems, short-term memory function in sleep, and psycholinguistic mechanisms, as well as central questions pertaining to sleep mentation. All of these topics are discussed further in subsequent chapters.

Recall in Relation to Exceptional Conditions of Wakeful and Sleep Consciousness

Is it possible that recall of sleep mentation concordant with sleep-speech is more likely in one state of consciousness rather than another?

Fosgate (1850), Pinkerton (1839), and Fischer (1839) independently distinguished between two types of sleep-talking, one occurring during "dreaming" sleep and the other during "torpor" or "somnambulic sleep." All three agree that awakening subjects after somniloquy in dreaming sleep allows for recall of dreams that correspond to the sleep-speech. But when the subject is awakened after uttering a sleep-speech during torpor, it is usually impossible to elicit recall of concordant mentation. All three investigators described the arousal threshold during torpor as being markedly increased compared to dreaming sleep, with the "faculties" returning less quickly to normal after being awakened. (These three observers were possibly the first to note the existence of what we now recognize as REM and NREM sleep.)

Four authors report instances indicating the possibility of recall, under special conditions, of the content of mentation accompanying sleep-talking. Moll (1889) comments on an episode of sleep-speech that was heard by a bedfellow of the subject. On awakening, the subject was unable to recall a dream; but when subsequently hypnotized, a dream was remembered that matched the content of the speech as described by the hearer. (Additional laboratory experience of my own bearing on this point is described in Chapter 11.) Burrell's case (1904) was unable to recall in his conscious waking state any mentation that corresponded with his sleep-speeches. However, he was able to recount memories of previous sleep-speeches in episodes of subsequent sleep conversation with friendly observers. Tuke (1884), Miller (1889), and Maury (1878) report similar findings.

These comments are consistent with the recent demonstration of Evans, Gustafson, O'Connell, Orne, and Shor (1970) of the possibility of verbal induction of Stage-REM-dependent responses during sleep with intervening waking amnesia for both the perception of the stimuli and the execution of the behavioral response. Thus, the old reports cited earlier seem a trifle more credible when a modern controlled experiment shows that state-dependent learning, perception, and memory is possible during sleep.

Turning now to comments on additional aspects of wakeful recall of sleep-speech-associated mentation, McGregor, in a personal communication, stated that on hearing tape recordings of his own sleep-speeches, he has *déjà vu* experiences, i.e., he feels that he has "heard it before, or has been there before." Furthermore, he can sometimes recall "other lines of people in the dream that were unspoken"—(the other half of the "dream" conversation to which he listened and responded by his overt sleep-speech).

In an account of recall after somnambulism that is at variance with recent laboratory findings (Kales & Jacobson, 1967), as well as many of the older clinical descriptions, Tuke (1884) mentions cases of somnambulism with speech and singing in which, following waking, the subjects can "recall accurately the particular dream and connect it with the deed performed in sleep." A recent clinical experience of my own has made me cautious about dismissing such reports as aberrant and unreliable. An intelligent, nonpsychotic patient in his late thirties reported the following occurrence of the night before during a psychotherapy session:

In my dream I was standing in long-sleeved, winter pajamas at the side of my bed talking to someone whom I can't remember now except I believe it was to a male friend. I said to this person that the place we were in and the whole atmosphere was very pleasant and that I desired to remain. I commented that I thought the whole apartment was very nice and that I was very fond of the people in it and wanted to live with them. In the dream my wife was sleeping in the bed while I was talking, but the children that I mentioned to the other person were not in the room, in the dream, but were in their own rooms. I told the person that I was going to get into bed next to the sleeping woman (my wife) and stay at this place and that I couldn't think of a more pleasant place to live and I was happy with her (my wife). At this point either I said to the person or the person said to me (I can't remember or distinguish now) that it most certainly was as nice as I was describing but there was only one problem and to be careful about it. The problem was that your money disappears in this house and you had to keep an eye on where you put it. At this point I got out of bed or moved from the bed in the dream and went into our closet. The other person I was talking to left as soon as the comment about being careful of the money was exchanged and shut the door (in my dream) to the bedroom.

In the closet (and in my dream) I started to look for my wallet. Suddenly in my dream I found the wallet and it had been emptied and I was upset as I had no other money with me and I was concerned that I would have no money if I *had* to leave the place.

As I opened the wallet in my dream I "woke up" or came out of the dream. I realized I was in my closet. My wife (whom I recognized fully, was sleeping)—it was my apartment and bedroom; I was in *summer*[1] pajamas and I knew I was sleep-walking. As I woke up standing in my closet I laughed and returned to bed aware of my actions fully. However, I stopped at my dresser and found my wallet where it always is—unopened, of course, and I laughed at the dream. I am unaware of going into the closet; I woke up in the closet and as I woke up I knew I was sleep-walking and that the wallet was in the dresser, not the closet where I went in the dream (though I don't remember heading for the closet—only for the the wallet). I am unsure if I was fully awake when I went to the dresser on the way back to bed. I may not have been fully awake then, but I know by the time I opened the dresser and saw the actual wallet I was fully awake. Also, though I had awakened in the closet I don't really remember picking the closet as the place to look first. I only remember going to look for the wallet, groping in the closet for something, though it has an automatic light that went on, and then awakening. When I first went into the closet I did not recognize it as my closet though I was aware of having gotten out of bed in my dream.

This patient previously had had many such experiences, dating back to childhood, that were also accompanied by vivid dreams. Observations of this sort point up the importance of the possibility of individual differences among subjects. Such factors are entirely in accord with more recent findings in sleep research disclosing the role of individual differences (see Arkin, Antrobus, & Ellman, 1978; Cartwright, 1977).

Finally, turning to other factors affecting the likelihood of mentation recall in association with sleep-utterance, three observers report that recall of dreams accompanying somniloquy is less if body movements occur concomitantly (Darwin, 1800; Maury, 1878; Moreau, 1820).

In summary, according to most reports in the clinical–anecdotal literature, mentation associated with sleep-utterance is less accessible to wakeful recall when vocalization occurs under the conditions of:

---

[1]Author's italics to denote contrast with *winter pajamas* in the dream.

1. high-arousal-threshold sleep;
2. body movement episodes;
3. somnambulistic episodes. (However, exceptions to this rule have been reported by more than one observer.)

Contrariwise, concordance between sleep-utterance and wakeful recall is greater when vocalizations issue from "dreaming sleep." As we see later, these older clinical and anecdotal reports are surprisingly consistent with results obtained in the laboratory; i.e., conditions associated with less concordance and recall appear to be related to what we now know as features of NREM sleep, and the opposite with REM sleep.

The anecdotal literature also indicates the possibility that state-dependent memory mechanisms may reveal themselves under suitable circumstances and, once more, laboratory findings (Evans, Gustafson, O'Connell, Orne, & Shor, 1970) suggest that such notions should not be summarily rejected.

Finally, the clinical–anecdotal literature contains many examples of macrodissociative episodes (e.g., Burrell, 1904; Cameron, 1952; McGregor, 1964; Tuke, 1884). The detailed account of the inner experience of my own somnambulist patient is a vivid example of macrodissociation.

LABORATORY FINDINGS

The literature relevant to relationships between sleep-utterance and mentation recalled in subsequent wakefulness is best presented chronologically.

Kamiya (1961) reported that a comparison of sleep-speech content and mentation elicited on waking the subject afterward failed to disclose any obvious relationship. However, the data were too meager to support definite conclusions.

Rechtschaffen, Goodenough, & Shapiro (1962), in a more extensive publication, mentioned that of two awakenings following REMP speech, the content of one mentation report bore an unambiguous relationship to the sleep-speech (which would be classified as first-order concordance). In addition, nine of 12 (75%) awakenings following NREM speech resulted in the recall of at least some cognitive content that the subject believed had occurred just prior to the awakening. In seven of these nine NREM awakenings (58.3% of the total), a relationship between the content of the mentation report and the sleep-speech could be inferred (presumably classifiable as either first- or second-order concordance). The remaining two sleep-speech-mentation report pairs (16.7%) seemed devoid of concordance.

In their study of episodic phenomena during sleep, Gastaut and Broughton (1965) agreed with Rechtschaffen et al. (1962) that the content of several of their observed REMP speeches "related to dreaming [p. 208]." By contrast, however, NREM speeches were associated with a "lack of recalled dreaming [p. 208]" and it was concluded that the speeches were "not exteriorized symptoms of true oneiric activity [p. 208]." Furthermore, they expressed a belief that NREM sleep-speech is either "liberated from low level continuous mental life during sleep" or else stems from "simple perceptual confusion during abrupt awakening [p. 208]."

Neither Kamiya nor Gastaut and Broughton mentioned the number of sleep-speech mentation report pairs on which they based their conclusions.

Arkin (1968) and Arkin, Toth, Baker, and Hastey (1970a) have published findings based on 166 sleep-speech mentation report pairs uttered by 28 paid chronic sleep-talking subjects in the laboratory. They constituted a subset of the subject pool mentioned in Chapter 7 dealing with the frequency of sleep-talking. This study will be described in some detail. Of the total sample of 166 pairs, a subsample of 32 was obtained on recovery nights following two previous consecutive nights at home, after ingestion of a 15-mg spansule of amphetamine sulphate in combination with 100 mg of sodium pentobarbital prior to retiring. Analysis will be presented for the entire sample and also separately for the recovery-night subsample alone. (This latter aspect of the work was part of a pilot project on the effects of REMP deprivation on sleep-utterance and NREM mentation, Arkin, Antrobus, Toth, & Baker, 1968.)

Experimental Procedure.   Subjects slept the entire night in the laboratory with continuous monitoring of EEG, EOG, and vocalization. An experimenter was in constant attendance in an adjacent room, which contained an intercommunicating device. This permitted him to hear all vocalizations emitted by the subject and communicate with the subject freely when necessary.

Vocalizations were tape-recorded by a continuously operating machine. A transducer operated an event marker on the polygraph record so that the exact moment of vocalization in relationship to other electrographic tracings could be determined. Before retiring, each subject was told that he would be awakened a number of times during the night and, on all of these occasions, he was to relate aloud everything that had been going through his mind just prior to awakening. He was told to report these contents regardless of whether they were dreams, thoughts, or images. Subjects were awakened up to 11 times each night, sometimes immediately after sleep-utterances and at other times after a 45-min or longer interval of "silent sleep" (unassociated with utterance), when a mentation report was similarly elicited. Initially, subjects were awakened by sounding a loud buzzer but later, as the work progressed, we found it preferable to awaken them by calling their first names through the intercom. There was a certain amount of inevitable variability of the time between the end of the utterance and the awakening signal because one could never be sure when the sleeper had finished "having his say." Thus, this interval ranged between 5 sec or less to a typical maximum of about 40 sec. In addition, on some occasions, the subject was encouraged by nonleading questions to attempt further recall, or else asked directly whether some distinctive word, phrase, or sound in his sleep-utterance (as heard by the experimenter) meant anything to him. Finally, in a few instances, we included results of a "dialogue" between the subject and experimenter (Arkin, Hastey, & Reiser, 1966a; Arkin et al., 1970a) which, although departing from the usual method of eliciting mentation reports, nevertheless appeared to demonstrate close concordance between sleep-speech and mentation report. On these latter occasions, the subject always spoke first "in his sleep" and the experimenter responded.

Data Processing

In accordance with the category scheme presented earlier in the clinical–anecdotal literature review, the content of each sleep-speech was compared to its associated wakeful mentation report with regard to similarities and differences in manifest content alone. Each such associated pair was scored as showing:

1. *First-order concordance* when they possessed in common one or more words, phrases, or other clearly identifying features. *Example:* REMP sleep speech, "telling her how I can tell—that really likes"; associated mentation report, "I was thinking *how I can tell* philosopher better than the other—how much more I *liked* them."

2. *Second-order concordance* when they possessed in common some specific feature of mental content or subject matter but did not share identical words, phrases, etc. *Example:* Stage 3 sleep-speech, "No good as a dry dock"; associated mentation report, "This—one passage where it says—the hull of a ship, single mast, single boom for a cutway sail."

3. *Third-order concordance*[2] includes a group of instances in which the *only* element of concordance between the sleep-speech and mentation report was the latter's reference to someone (usually the subject) vocalizing. Thus a postutterance mentation report describing someone as "talking," "saying," "asking," etc., was scored separately as third-order concordance because recall of a sleep event involved vocalization, and criteria for second- or first-

---

[2]In our preliminary report (Arkin, 1968), third-order concordance as described here was included in the second-order concordance group, and a third-order concordance category was reserved for concordance discernible by psychoanalytic interpretation. In the Arkin 1970a paper and the present chapter, because of the somewhat subjective nature of such psychoanalytic interpretations, the latter were not separately categorized but included instead in the "no discernible concordance" group.

order concordances were not fulfilled. *Example:* Stage 2 sleep-speech, "um—yeah(?)"; associated mentation report, "Oh, I had something to do with—er—I don't know—I don't remember except it just had something—like they were waiting for my opinion and I had—gave, I gave it to them in about a word."

4. *No discernible concordance* when concordance was not discernible on the basis of the manifest content of both speech and the recalled mentation.

5. *No mentation recalled.* If no mentation whatsoever was recalled on awakening, the associated pair was placed in this category.

Four ambiguous instances of concordance were excluded from the analysis.

In addition to the above, separate categorizations and counts were made of instances in which we attempted to stimulate the subject's recall with words taken from the sleep-speech, and in other instances by responding to him directly in the spirit of the sleep-speech (dialogue method—see procedure subsection).

With the former method, the subject was awakened shortly after the sleep-speech and asked to report his mentation. This gave rise to two subsets of pairs: a first in which the initial attempt to elicit recall failed (no content), and a second in which the initial attempt yielded *some* content but was incomplete (partial content). An example of "no content" is as follows, with *E* representing the experimenter and *S* the subject:

NREM sleep speech: Uh—excuse me—mbl.
E: Charlotte!
S [awake]: Yes. Yes?
E: Can you remember anything that was going through your mind?
S: No.
E: Do the words, "Excuse me" mean anything?
S: No. Nothing more than just excuse me.
E: O.K. Go back to sleep.

This was categorized as "no recall."

An example of "partial content" is as follows:

NREM sleep speech: Uh—yes—fro—yes, was crossing yes it was crossing we were crossing an intersection; it was one which I'd mbl many times before crossing the intersection, I expressed some doubts that I did ordinarily when I was driving, it goes drench [sic] more about Ronnie and Charlie than I thought that I thought—.
E: Jane!
S [awake]: Yes?
E: What was going through your mind?
S: Just now?
E: Yes.

S: Oh—uh....

E: Can you remember anything?

S: Um—I remember—uh—we went to some place which was, er, I don't know, had more names in it anyway. I mean it had more names in its own name— that's all I remember its name about [sic], but now I can't remember it.

E: Can you remember anything else?

S: No I can't remember anything.

E: Would there by any reason for talking about crossing an intersection as you had done many times before?

S: I can't think of any reason.

E: O.K.—then, go back to sleep.

This was likewise categorized as no additional recall because even though concordant material was *intially* elicited by the *conventional* method (e.g., the "names" and "went to some place"), the presentation of the stimulus words "crossing an intersection," etc. elicited no *additional* recall.

The reason for separately categorizing these outcomes is that, in the case of the "no content" report, the short-term memory mechanisms may be nonfunctional and prevent any retrieval of mentation that may have attained even fleeting consciousness. On the other hand, the recall of some content (partial content) demonstrates that short-term memory mechanisms were functioning at least to some degree and results might vary accordingly, thus providing a useful index of the degree of integrity of these mechanisms.

An example of the dialogue between subject and experimenter method is as follows:

NREM sleep-speech: Yeah—yeah—obviously.

E: Obviously what?

[awake]: Uh—someone—uh—someone had come up with—it was a saying which followed directly from a title or something, you know—they started—they started to say it and I said 'Obviously'—you know, it followed.

The advantage of the dialogue method is the immediacy between sleep-speech and the experimental intervention.

Thus, the pairs grouped under the rubric *"stimulated recall"* are classified as: initial no content; initial partial content; and dialogue. These pairs in turn are categorized according to the same concordance scheme as the pairs first described, i.e., first-order concordance, second-order, etc.

Degree of Concordance and Sleep Stage

The following analysis of the degree of concordance, as related to sleep stage in association with which speech occurred, is based on 166 sleep-speech-associated mentation report pairs.

1. Of 24 REMP speech report pairs:
   First-order concordance was shown by eight (33.3%).
   Second-order concordance was shown by five (20.8%).
   Third-order concordance was shown by six (25.0%).
   Combined concordance was shown by 19 (79.2%).
   No discernible concordance was shown by four (16.7%).
   No recall was available for one (4.2%).
2. Of 85 Stage 2 speech-report pairs:
   First-order concordance was shown by 15 (17.6%).
   Second-order concordance was shown by seven (8.2%).
   Third-order concordance was shown by 17 (20.0%).
   Combined concordance was shown by 39 (45.8%).
   No discernible concordance was shown by 28 (32.9%).
   No recall was available for 18 (21.2%).
3. Of 52 Stage 3–4 speech-report pairs:
   First-order concordance was shown by five (9.6.%).
   Second-order concordance was shown by four (7.7%).
   Third-order concordance was shown by two (3.8%).
   Combined concordance was shown by 11 (21.1%).
   No discernible concordance was shown by 21 (40.4%).
   No recall was available for 20 (38.5%).
4. Of five Stage 1 NREM speech-report pairs:
   First-order concordance was shown by three (60%).
   Second-order concordance was shown by one (20%).
   No recall was available for one (20%).

It is clear that, with the possible exception of Stage 1 NREM pairs, concordance is much more likely to occur with REMP-associated pairs than with NREM and that concordance is much more likely with Stage 2 pairs than with those of Stage 3–4.

Degree of Concordance with
Stimulated Recall Techniques

Only four REMP speech-stimulated recall pairs were available. Of these, three—as a result of the dialogue method—showed first-order concordance and one partial-content pair was categorized as no recall.

The following analysis is based on 36 NREM sleep-speech stimulated recall pairs obtained from 12 subjects.

1. Of seven initial no-content pairs (four subjects), *100% were scored as no recall;* i.e., additional mentation was *not* retrieved by use of the stimulus words and concordance was not demonstrable.

2. Of 16 initial partial-content pairs (seven subjects):
   First-order concordance was shown by three (18.6%).
   Second- and/or third-order concordance was shown by one (6.3%).
   Combined concordance was shown by four (24.9%).
   No concordance was shown by two (12.5%).
   No additional recall was shown by 10 (62.5%).
3. Of 13 "dialogue" pairs (five subjects):
   First-order concordance was shown by nine (69.2%).
   Second- and/or third-order concordance was shown by three (23.1%).
   Combined concordance was shown by 12 (92.3%).
   No concordance was shown by none (0%).
   No recall was shown by one (7.7%).

The "dialogue" method clearly yielded a significantly greater number of concordant pairs.

Pairs Obtained on Drug Recovery Nights

The following analysis is based on 32 sleep-speech–mentation-report pairs. These were originally included in our main analyses on 166 pairs reported earlier but are described here separately for comparison.

1. Of three REMP pairs obtained on drug recovery nights:
   First-order concordance was shown by none.
   Second-order concordance was shown by one (33%).
   Third-order concordance was shown by one (33%).
2. Of 25 Stage 2 pairs obtained on drug recovery nights:
   First-order concordance was shown by two (8%).
   Second-order concordance was shown by one (4%).
   Third-order concordance was shown by three (12%).
   Combined concordance was shown by six (24%).
   No discernible concordance was shown by 13 (52%).
   No recall was available for six (24%).
3. Of 4 Stage 3–4 pairs obtained on drug recovery nights:
   Concordance of any order was not demonstrable.
   Two pairs showed no concordance.
   Two pairs were categorized as no recall.

These results suggest that pairs obtained on drug recovery nights are less likely to show concordance than those obtained on baseline nights. The inclusion of this subset in our main sample of 166 pairs, therefore, biased the main analysis in the direction of pairs showing *less* concordance than would a sample of similar size all drawn from baseline nights.

TABLE 10.1
Sleep–Speech–Mentation–Report Concordance in Relation to Associated Sleep Stage

	Concordance	*REMP (N = 24)*	*NREM Stages*		
			2 (N = 85)	*3–4 (N = 52)*	*1 NREM (N = 5)*
Initial recall following experimental awakening	First-order	33.3%	17.6%	9.6%	60.0%
	Second-order	20.8	8.2	7.7	20.0
	Third-order	25.0	20.0	3.8	0.0
	Combined conc.	79.2	45.8	21.1	80.0
	No disc. conc.	16.7	32.9	40.4	0.0
	No recall	4.2	21.2	38.5	20.0
	Concordance	*N = 0*	*Combined NREM (N = 16)*		
Stimulated recall— partial content	First-order	—	18.6%		
	second- and third order combined	—	6.3		
	no additional		24.9		
	recall	—	62.5		
	No disc. conc.	—	12.5		
	Concordance	*N = 0*	*Combined NREM (N = 7)*		
Stimulated recall— no initial content	No additional recall	—	100%		
	Concordance	*N = 4*	*Combined NREM (N = 13)*		
Stimulated recall— dialogue method	First-order	75%	69.2%		
	second- and third-order	—	23.1		
	combined	75%	92.3		
	No disc. conc.	—	0		
	No recall	25%	7.7		

Relation to Proximity to REM Periods

For analysis of the degree of concordance with Stage 2 pairs in relation to proximity to REM periods, only first- and second-order concordance pairs were pooled.

Of 51 Stage 2 pairs occurring more than 15 min from the nearest REMP, 23 (45%) showed some concordance; of 29 Stage 2 pairs occurring 15 min or less from the nearest REMP, 12 (41%) showed some concordance. Thus, proximity to REMPs seemed unrelated to concordance.

Relation to Time of Night

For analysis of the degree of concordance in relation to time of night, NREM speeches (Stages 2, 3, and 4) were pooled.

Of 77 NREM speeches occurring after the first 3 hrs of sleep, 43% showed some concordance (combined first- and second-order); of 45 NREM speech occurring during the first 3 hrs, 22% showed some concordance ($p = .04$, two-tailed test). Therefore, concordance is more likely after the first 3 hrs of sleep.

Special Types of Concordance

Concordance Based on Transformations

An interesting feature of concordance in certain instances can be noted when the mentation report contains material that seems to be the result of transformations of components of the speech. Consider the following Stage 2 speech:

> Together with the usual number of parts, joints that is, where bones fit together—. [And the immediately subsequent mentation report:] Mm—um— not very clear at all. [p] all my thoughts are fragmented—which is not usually the case but I'm very tired—um—I was thinking in *part*, about my roommate and his girl friend, and she's always over at the *apart*—at the *apartment*, she's always there, so much so that he doesn't even have time to do his work—mm.

In this case, the sleep-speech word "parts" appears three times in the mentation report as a transformation based on assonance, viz. "in part," "apart," and the "apartment." Furthermore, the *concept* of "parts" is represented in the mentation report as "my thoughts are fragmented" and by the phrase "in part."

Concordance Based on Psychoanalytic Interpretation

As mentioned in the data-processing section, we included pairs that seemed to be concordant *solely* as a result of psychoanalytic interpretation, no matter how plausible, in the category *"no* concordance discernible." This step was taken because of the large subjective element in such interpretations. Nevertheless, one illustration among many possible is worth providing.

> *REMP sleep-speech:* Tar(?)—smells sort of like Cassius Clay's armpit and old Pryne's snatch.
> *Mentation report:* Oh boy—yeah—I was going through a turnstile in a subway and put 35 cents in for a hamburger—well it was kinda silly of me but I didn't realize you couldn't get a hamburger from a turnstile so I went to the lady in the booth who I told my problem and she said I'd have to sign a whole bunch of papers and I'd get my 15 or 20 cents back in the mail—big deal—so I watched them come through—then someone else popped into my group—an age difference—sort of funny—2 years, 12 years, 1 month, no years, 26 days.

The most obvious psychoanalytic consideration is the symbolization of the subject's cloaca fantasy by means of the "subway" and the woman in the booth in the dream as recalled. This is interpreted as relating to the explicit mention of the female genital in the sleep-speech.

Discussion of Sleep-Speech in Association with Hallucinatory States

We attribute to a psychic state the quality of being hallucinatory when, during this stage, the subject has experiences that feel real to him at the moment and that do not correspond, during the same interval, to the actual specific ongoing reality, such reality being defined by a convergence of data from experimental recording devices and the consensus of observations of experimenters. Psychic states may vary along dimensions of duration (long vs. short), sense modality with the greatest intensity (e.g., visual vs. nonvisual), and degree of correspondence with reality at the moment, and still be hallucinatory in nature.

By this definition, if concordance is discernible between the content of a sleep-speech and its associated mentation report and this content fails to correspond in some degree to the specific experimental reality of the moment, we may presume that the sleep-speech refers to a hallucinatory state. Actually, many subjects volunteered (in concordant mentation reports), *without* having been specifically asked, that the immediately previous experience had been a dream (examples 195 and 558, Appendix 2). Once more, this was so with NREM as well as REMP speeches.

It is evident from the data that significant concordance between both REMP- and NREM-associated speech and related wakeful mentation report is a common occurrence; and in whatever way the psychophysiological concomitants of sleep-speech are ultimately clarified and defined, one may also say that both REMP- and NREM-associated sleep-speeches commonly occur in association with a hallucinatory state.

The data do not permit us to assert, however, that sleep-speech *invariably* occurs in this manner; but in view of the evanescence of sleep mentation, one is tempted to assume that *more* instances of concordance could be demonstrated if only recall of sleep mentation were more efficient. This is supported by the finding that occasionally subjects are reminded of an additional associated concordant "sleep event" after an initial partial amnesia, when queried by the experimenter as to whether a specific striking word from the sleep-speech "means anything" to him. This is well illustrated in the folowing example of a first-order concordance *between* a Stage 2 sleep-speech and the stimulated recall:

Sleep-Speech: Uh—[sighs] chicken her other ones—oh—all other ones—chickens.

E: Charlotte.

S: Yes?

E: What were you thinking?

S: Um—oh—let's see—oh—first of all I was thinking about the Julia (?) books, and how they were outside getting them—um—and then—

E: Yes? and then?

S: Then they had, had a guy in green sweater, he kept disappearing after he comes to ours—.

E: Do you remember anything else?

S: Um—.

E: Do you remember anything else, Charlotte?

S: Um. No.

E: Do you remember about chickens?

S: Yes. Yes. In the first part, er, they was all about chickens—red chickens and then—yellow chickens and all kind of mesu—mezuzah(?) and chickens and chickens—.

Further support for the assumption that the incidence of concordance would be greater if memory functions were more efficient is provided by two additional findings; First, the dialogue method of stimulation of sleep recall results in a significantly greater frequency of concordance, i.e., when the relationship between the stimulus and the sleep-speech is at its most intimate and immediate, concordance is more likely (see results under "Stimulated Recall' and examples 448, 502, and 309 in Appendix 2). Second, concordance is much more common in connection with REMP speeches as opposed to NREM and, in general, as we later see, REMP mentation also is better remembered than NREM (see Chapter 18).

Equally fascinating as the results on concordance are instances of mentation reports in which concordance with sleep-speech is not discerned. It often produces a feeling of uncanniness in the listener to hear a subject say something in sleep that is quite clear and lively and then to elicit a mentation report immediately afterward with which it is at complete variance (see example 53, Appendix 2).

At least four hypotheses may account for a *portion* of the data:

Hypothesis 1.   As previously stated, the discordance between the content of sleep-speech and mentation report is merely an effect of the difficulty in recall; i.e., no sooner has the subject uttered a speech then he forgets its content although he was aware of it briefly, and his recall is of other mentation, perhaps occurring subsequent to the speech. In support of this are the following considerations;

1. The subject often reports his feeling that mentation has "slipped his mind" and indicates that more was going through his mind than he is able to retrieve.
2. Presenting a key word to a partially amnestic subject has occasionally stimulated concordant recall (see aforementioned).
3. The dialogue method with its greatest immediacy to the sleep-speech yields a strikingly greater frequency of first-order concordance in NREM pairs than that arising from any other method of obtaining mentation reports.

Hypothesis 2.   Some sleep-speeches are mediated by a special psychoneural organization which produces speech through channels not involving awareness—a variety of psychic dissociation as previously discussed. Such a possibility is supported by occurrences in which the subject was awakened as little as 5 sec after a sleep-speech and recalled no concordant mentation. Here are some examples:

Stage 4 sleep-speech: Mbls—a—mi—be—better—seems that six books home and I haven't even got them yet—i—ea—where—i—ea—what?—mbl—a rag in a rags bed, rag! I don't even have a rag—mm—bag—mm—baggette—okay.
S's mentation report: Um—flowers and a boat—.
E: Can you be more specific? What about the flowers and the boat?
S: Th'—th'—th'—the boat was receding and I um—under a bridge and boat and flowers in opposite direction and that—that direction's away from me—

Subsequent attempts to stimulate further recall by asking the subject if anything was remembered about a "rag and a bag" elicited no further recall.

Stage 4 sleep-speech: Yep—mm—it's high enough—yeah, its not (tied to that thing(?)) mbl—right.
Subject's mentation report [elicited 5 sec later]:   No—no it's still—actually I was thinking about having the subject sleep—that's—getting uh, getting the subject to sleep.
E: Anything else?
S: No.

The foregoing observations suggest that these two subjects were emitting overt speech without awareness of it as such and experiencing concurrent but nonconcordant mentation. An even more striking demonstration is an instance in which even the dialogue method failed to recover any clearly concordant mentation:

> *Stage 2 sleep-speech:* Mm—mm—hey—wait a minute, will ya? I'm not even
> there yet—mbl—people—mbl—wait a minute—mm?
> *E:* Who did you want to wait, Al?
> *S:* Mm?—excuse me?
> *E:* Who do you want to wait a minute?
> *S:* I can't—I don't understand.
> *E:* Could you tell me what you were thinking about just now?
> *S:* Uh—yes—let me see—it's uh—I was not—I was not sleeping at the same time—I was not, you know—I was on the verge of falling asleep—wh—it seemed as if several ideas going through my head sort of—you know—one—one tangled up with the other ones—I can't really pinpoint any—any one specific—a specific one—that's about all I can tell off-hand—unless I can remember anything else [sic].

Both the inefficiency of recall mechanisms and dissociation hypotheses could also explain the many instances of no-content reports following sleep-speeches.

Hypothesis 3.   A number of occasions have been observed in which the sleep-speech and mentation report display no concordance on the basis of our classification scheme and yet psychological interpretation suggests the existence of subtle concordance (see special types of concordance p. 121–122). It is possible in such cases that both the sleep-speech and recalled mentation are derived from a *common source* that itself is not directly manifested.

Hypothesis 4.   The subject's own utterance may be perceived by him and constitute a stimulus influencing immediately succeeding mental processes. The mentation report would then represent primary-process-like transformations of the content of the immediately preceding speech.

On the basis of these latter two hypotheses, I would predict that additional and subtle concordances would have revealed themselves if we had allowed the subject a period of wakeful free association after the sleep-speech. In line with these considerations. Berger (1963) has shown that primary-processlike transformations may be produced when personal names are uttered by an external source and impinge on the sleeping subject. Lasaga and Lasaga (1973) have reported on similar effects with verbal stimuli other than personal names. There seems to be no reason in principle to believe that auditory stimuli provided by one's own verbal utterance could not influence one's own subsequent mentation accordingly, but such a hypothesis does not lend itself to an easy test.

Differences Between REMP and
NREM Pair Concordance

It is clear that concordance is more discernible following REMP than NREM speeches.[3] Several factors could be involved in explaining this difference.

First, during Stage REM, more mentation may occur than during NREM stages. Such a surmise is supported by the finding that REMP mentation reports have higher word counts than those from NREM. This factor alone could increase the probability of concordance in REMP pairs.

Second, during Stage REM, recall mechanisms may function more efficiently than during NREM sleep, resulting in greater likelihood of retrieval of concordant mentation. The sleep-speech–mentation-recall evidence to support this hypothesis is presented in Chapter 18 on memory process and sleep-utterance phenomena; also, this explanation is consistent with the dream recall model of Goodenough (1978) and Koulack and Goodenough (1976).

Third, the greater central nervous system activation during REMP states as opposed to NREM may account for both the greater production of mentation and improved efficiency of recall mechanisms during the former. However, it is unlikely that activation is the only factor. If efficiency of recall went hand-in-hand with activation, then good recall on other occasions of high activation should be present. Yet during the course of our work, there were many instances in which the subject cried out and spoke with intense emotion in association with NREM sleep and yet could recall little or nothing on being awakened. This has been reported by others (Dement, 1965; Fisher, Kahn, Edwards, David, & Fine, 1974; Gastaut & Broughton, 1965).

Concordance in Relation to Time of Night

Although the sample sizes are different, the data indicate that NREM sleep-speeches are less likely to show concordance with mentation reports if they occur within the first 3 hrs of sleep rather than afterward. This is consistent with other observations that suggest that sleep mentation is generally recalled in greater abundance during the later hours of sleep than the earlier (Foulkes, 1966; Pivik & Foulkes, 1968; Verdone, 1965).

---

[3]This discussion excludes Stage 1 NREM pairs from consideration because of their small total in our sample. The results that we do have suggest the possibility, however, that the combined concordance rates of Stage 1 NREM and REMP could be similar (80.0% vs. 79.2% respectively). If the trend of a larger sample of Stage 1 NREM pairs supported this, it could have significant implications for the special psychophysiology of Stage 1 NREM in relation to the recall and mentational processes prevailing during this state. Such a thought is consistent with the report of Vogel, Barrowclough, and Giesler (1972) that emphasizes the many qualities possessed in common by sleep-onset Stage 1 NREM and Stage REM mentation.

Shapiro (1962) has presented data that support the hypothesis that the NREM–REMP sleep cycle is superimposed on an underlying biological cycle with a longer period. This latter cycle is related to the "time of night" effects that presumably reflect the operation of restorative processes during the early hours of sleep. Thus, one might expect that during the first 3 hrs of sleep, recall processes and/or mentation are depressed. This would favor a reduction in concordance in pairs obtained during this interval.

Summary

Twenty-eight chronic sleep talkers were awakened in the laboratory following sleep-speeches, and reports of sleep mentation were then elicited. The mentation reports and sleep-speeches were categorized in terms of closeness of concordance.The most significant results were as follows:

1. Of 24 REMP-speech–mentation-report pairs, concordance could be discerned in 79.2%; no concordance could be discerned in 16.7%.
2. Of 85 Stage 2 mentation-report pairs concordance could be discerned in 45.8%; no concordance could be discerned in 32.9%.
3. Of 52 Stage 3–4 mentation-report pairs, concordance could be discerned in 21.1%; no concordance could be discerned in 40.4%.
4. No recall was available for 3.7% of REMP pairs, 21.1% of Stage 2 pairs, and 38.5% of Stage 3–4 pairs.

What Have Been the Findings of Other Investigators?

Comparison of our results with those reported by Rechtschaffen et al. (1962) shows that in our data a somewhat smaller proportion of concordance and a higher proportion of no recall were found overall in NREM pairs. It should be noted, however, that only 12 NREM awakenings were performed by Rechtschaffen et al. (1962), and the discrepancies could be related to differences in size of sample. Also, although their findings on REMP speech are consistent with ours, their sample contained only two REMP pairs. The REMP speech findings reported by Gastaut and Broughton (1965) are likewise consistent with ours, but they did not mention the number of speech-report pairs in their paper.

With regard to the speech associated with night-terrors arising in association with Stage 4, Gastaut and Broughton were impressed by the nearly complete tendency for amnesia during full wakefulness for the mental content associated with the episode. However, some instances were described that might possibly be included in our categories of first- and second-order concordance, but no differential proportions were mentioned. By contrast, our data contain a sizable number of instances of recall as well as concordance. This may be explained on the basis that our sample contained many instances of Stage 4 associated sleep-speeches which were bland in quality and apparently not infused with anxiety—a sort of nocturnal episode that is quite different from a night-terror. This indicates the importance, once more, of stressing that sleep-speech is not an unitary phenomenon but rather one in which important differences exist both within and between subjects.

On the one hand, in contrast to the findings of Gastaut and Broughton, Fisher et al. (1974) reported that 58% of their night-terror arousals (12 subjects) resulted in recall of mentation occurring during the immediately prior attack. Regardless of whether awakenings were made in association with night-terrors accompanied by heart rates less or greater than 108 beats per minute, the percentage of *no* recall was 35–37% and vague recall 6–7%. In addition, many striking instances of unambiguous first- and second-order concordances were observed between "night-terror speech" and following mentation reports, as well as examples of no discernible concordance. Fisher et al. (1974) were impressed, as were we, by the great variability of the sleep-associated utterance phenomena concomitant with night-terrors and presented evidence that at least some night-terror episodes had been triggered or preceded by ongoing prior NREM mentation. In the latter case, the "examples of pre-arousal content during Stage 4 are nontraumatic in nature and are not associated with autonomic increase [p. 184]." That is, in some instances, the night-terror "scenario" was preceded by a brief sequence of bland mentation. Finally, it was observed that concordance was more frequent and more striking and that sleep-talking itself was more abundant, in association with milder arousals (with less autonomic activity), than with the severe ones that were accompanied by heart rates in excess of 108 beats per minute.

In reviewing the findings of MacNeilage (1971), it is important to remind the reader than a unique feature of her study was the care with which muscle activity of the speech apparatus was specifically monitored along with the standard measures. Three of her five subjects provided 16 sleep-speech–mentation-report pairs, most of which occurred in association with Stage 2. "Verbal content" in the mentation reports was found in 43.8% of this sample. In addition, there was only one instance of first-order concordance, and this occurred in a pair associated with Stage "alpha" considered by MacNeilage to be a transitional state between sleep and wakefulness associated with spontaneous REMP interruption. Also specifically described was an occasion of no recall following a Stage "alpha" speech and another of no discernible concordance following a Stage 2 speech. MacNeilage stated, in effect, that concordance might have been observed more often if technical limitations had not interfered. That is, some episodes were unintentionally recorded at very low levels and with noise levels that sometimes made useful transcription impossible even if the speech had been inherently intelligible.

One of the most important findings of MacNeilage, however, was the high proportion of verbal content mentation reports (40.9%), following muscle activity of the speech apparatus without overt vocalization. This is only slightly less than that after sleep-speech. In contrast, verbal content was present in only 23.1% of control reports elicited from a control interval devoid of both muscle activity and vocalization. This outcome complements the report of McGuigan and Tanner (1970), which indicated the occurrence of covert oral behavior in "conversational dreams" during Stage REM. Taken together, their results suggest that verbal components of sleep mentation are related to motor activity of the speech musculature even in the absence of utterance. This finding, if validated by independent study on a larger population, could provide an electrographic signal correlated with implicit verbal activity during sleep and aid in the study of psycholinguistic function during this elusive one-third of our lives.

In conclusion, laboratory results are consistent with the variegated clinical–anecdotal reports that assert both the frequent occurrence of concordance between sleep-speech and subsequent mentation, on the one hand, and either no discernible concordance or no recall on the other.

11 Experimental Manipulation of Sleep-Talking

Following my first acquaintance with electrographic techniques of sleep research, I became intrigued by the possibility of acquiring a measure of control over sleep-talking with the object of obtaining first-hand, eyewitness accounts of ongoing sleep mentation, much as a radio reporter describes ongoing events to a listening audience. I hoped in this fashion to gain glimpses of dreams in progress, influenced as little as possible by cognitive distortion during wakeful recall and by factors associated with the nature of awakening procedures. Over the subsequent course of time, additional technical approaches to this problem were developed in several laboratories, including my own. The results have been of interest not only in their own right, but also for their implications regarding cognition during sleep and wakefulness. The studies are, therefore, related in detail.

STUDIES EMPLOYING
POSTHYPNOTIC SUGGESTION

In 1960, (Arkin, 1960) exploratory pilot experiments were conducted to determine the feasibility of posthypnotically induced sleep-talking as a means of sampling sleep ideation. I should like to emphasize that the choice of posthypnotic rather than some other method of control was made on the basis of expediency rather than attempting to demonstrate the effective potency of posthypnotic suggestion per se. I would have selected any technique that gave promise of capabilities of stimulating sleep-speech with minimal disruption of the subject's sleep by external stimuli introduced during the night. As it turned out eventually, presleep *non*hypnotic instructions to sleep-talkers to talk in their sleep while dreaming may be just as effective as posthypnotic suggestion in accomplishing this task (see later on), and other techniques not involving presleep suggestion or instruction also have potential for stimulating sleep-speech.

Initial observations with posthypnotic suggestion were encouraging and led to a more extensive investigative program. The results of work with our best subject were published (Arkin et al., 1966a,b) and are presented next, following which other findings are described.

The subject, a former paratrooper 25 years of age, had been a college student majoring in English and motion-picture making. He was without significant psychopathology, in good physical health, and had a history of sporadic sleep-talking of many years' duration. No specific content of previous sleep-speech was available for comparison, but he was not especially aware of any colorful or sensational episodes.

In the laboratory, the subject slept for the entire night in a separate, dark, sound-attenuated room, containing a bed, a microphone leading to the adjacent instrument room containing a tape recorder, and an automatic device to note the occurrence of sleep-talking on the polygraph record. A set of electrical leads connected the subject to the EEG and EOG that, together with the tape recorder, were in continuous operation throughout the night. Finally, through an intercom, a technician in constant attendance could hear the subject's speech and movements and make appropriate notes on the experimental record.

The experimental procedure, a variant of an A–B–A design, was organized in a stepwise fashion in order to gauge effects of additional variables as they were introduced and also to enable the subject to learn adequately the complicated tasks imposed upon him. The work was carried out in accordance with the following plan:

One Adaptation Night. The subject spent one initial night in the laboratory with electrodes applied. The results were not included in this data analysis. No somniloquy occurred.

Procedure A

First Baseline Series. Subsequently, the subject slept once weekly in the laboratory for four uninterrupted nights, while his "baseline" sleep-talking and nocturnal sleep were continuously monitored without the introduction of any specific experimental variable.

On awakening in the following morning, he was asked to write down all he remembered of his dreams of the previous experimental night and then to fill out a routine sleep log. After this was completed, he was allowed to listen to any recorded sleep-utterances and assist in "deciphering" obscure parts.

Hypnosis Series. This phase consisted of a series of steps in which hypnosis was induced and resolved prior to applying the electrodes and retiring for the night. Each hypnosis session lasted about 15–25 min. In addition, there were practice hypnotic sessions (one or two per week) that occurred in the daytime but not always on the same day as the experiment.

In the practice sessions and in all other hypnotic sessions, two types of posthypnotic suggestions (PHS) were employed, which were specifically *not* programmed to become active during sleep. The first type was a simple short-term PHS, which was triggered a few minutes after trance termination. The purpose of this was to provide the subject with repeated experience of posthypnotic signals and training in carrying them out. *With this response well established, the next step was to label a spontaneous nocturnal dream occurring during sleep as a posthypnotic signal "like any other", which would oblige the subject to talk in his sleep in response to it.*

The second type was a long-term PHS, which was to be acted on the day after experiments had been completed. The subject was told that he was to telephone me on the following day "just to say hello" and not realize why he had done so. The purpose of this was to demonstrate that PHS given to the subject prior to sleep were capable of preserving their potency undiminished by a night's slumber and, therefore, could well have been the effective variable in determining results. For if the subject would not carry out a long-term PHS, we would have a less substantial case in contending that the PHS did indeed stimulate somniloquy. Actually, the subject uniformly carried out both such short- and long-term PHS.

Starting from a hypnosis baseline, PHS were gradually introduced in a manner as described hereafter. This enabled us to observe the effects first of a presleep hypnotic session alone without PHS on subsequent sleep-talking and sleep patterns and then the effects of progressively more elaborate PHS.

Hypnosis Baseline—Procedure B—Five Nights

One hour before retiring for the night, the subject was hypnotized and allowed to remain in that state undisturbed for 10 min at the deepest level, before termination. No PHS was given at this time. The hypnosis was then terminated, and the experiment allowed to continue as described under Procedure A. In all, therefore, there were nine baseline nights, four without and five with presleep hypnotic sessions, but without PHS.

Posthypnotic Suggestion to Increase Sleep-Talking—
Procedure C—Six Nights

One hour before retiring for the night, the subject was hypnotized and given the following PHS: "Tonight, you will sleep normally and naturally and *talk in your sleep in the same manner as you do at home, but more abundantly.*"

This PHS, as with all subsequent PHS, was reinforced by various similes and metaphors (such as, "you will feel like a steam boiler under high pressure that will be temporarily relieved by talking in your sleep, only to build up pressure again that will also be relieved by more sleep-talking"). In addition, the subject was required to repeat the PHS aloud, using the first person singular. The hypnotic trance was then terminated and the experiment allowed to continue as described under Procedure A.

Posthypnotic Suggestion to Talk in Sleep While Dreaming— Procedure D—Seven Nights

One hour before retiring, the subject was given this PHS: "Tonight you will sleep normally and naturally and dream normally and naturally, just as you do at home, but whenever you do have such a normal, natural dream, you will *talk in your sleep without awakening, while the dream is going on."* The experiment then continued as indicated under Procedure A.

Posthypnotic Suggestion to Talk in Sleep and Describe the Dream Aloud Without Awakening— Procedure E—Ten Nights.

One hour before retiring the subject was given the followingPHS: "Tonight you will sleep normally and naturally, and dream normally and naturally just as you do at home, but whenever you do have such a normal dream, you will *talk in your sleep without awakening and describe the dream in detail while the dream is going on."* The experiment was then continued as described under Procedure A.

Waking up the Subject for Mentation Reports Occurring on Nights Employing PHS to Describe Aloud Ongoing Dreams Without Awakening— Procedure F—Eleven Nights.

This was identical with Procedure E, except that the subject was awakened three to nine times during the course of the night. The times of awakening were selected so that some occurred shortly after, and some at times remote from, sleep-speech. The subject was given prior instructions (incorporated in the PHS) that when he was awakened, he was to relate *all* that had been passing through his mind for the previous 10–15 min. In this fashion, we obtained mentation reports immediately following REM, and NREM utterance, as well as from silent sleep. We were naturally interested in the degree of concordance between posthypnotically stimulated sleep-utterances and the associated mentation reports.

Terminal Baseline—Procedure G-Six Nights

Throughout this series, the subject was *not* hypnotized before retiring, nor was he experimentally awakened during the night. Dream recall in the morning was elicited. It was essentially a repetition of Procedure A. However, in Procedures B through E, an additional hypnotic trance was induced in the morning and attempts were made to elicit further dream recall. This was always done *after* the recall procedure in the conscious waking state (after arising) was concluded; and this was likewise carried out in Procedure G.

Procedure H—Three Experimental Sessions

Phenomenological and electrographic comparison of wakeful hypnotic trance dreams and nocturnal sleep dreams during nights with PHS made up Procedure H—three experimental sessions carried out in each of three successive mornings of the last portion of Procedure G. That is, during the last three experiments of Procedure G, an additional procedure was added in the morning, after all of the originally sought-for data had been collected. The subject was hypnotized with the tape recorder, EEG, and EOG still recording from the previous night, and was told, "You are now very deeply asleep, exactly like your normal natural sleep; in a moment, you will have a dream, just as you do at night when you sleep naturally; when this dream is underway, it will be a hypnotic signal to you to talk in your 'sleep' and describe your dream in detail while it is going on, just as you did in previous experiments. Begin now."

The reason for Procedure H was to attempt to control for the possibility that when the subject talked in his sleep in response to a PHS, he might "awaken," go back into hypnosis momentarily, have a *hypnotic dream,* describe it, and then return to normal sleep, thus revealing nothing of the content of his natural dream. We hoped that comparing the electrographic results with those of Procedure E would help in evaluation of this possibility.

Summary

In summary, then, our procedures enabled us first to describe and compare the temporal relationship between somniloquy, dreams, and EEG and EOG patterns as they occurred during natural sleep observed throughout the night, under the following five experimental conditions:

1. sleep without preceding hypnosis;
2. sleep preceded only by a brief hypnotic trance induced and terminated prior to retiring, and without any posthypnotic suggestion (PHS);
3. sleep preceded by a PHS to "talk in your sleep just as you do at home but more abundantly";

4. sleep preceded by PHS to "talk in your sleep whenever you are having a natural dream"; and

5. sleep preceded by PHS to "talk in your sleep whenever you are having a natural dream, describing it in detail while it is going on."

This was done initially in a series without mentation report awakenings and followed by a series in which mentation reports were obtained.

Additional experimental conditions included a terminal baseline series without a presleep hypnotic trance, and a morning, postarising hypnotic trance dream series.

Second, our procedure enabled us to assess and compare the ideational content of dreams and/or sleep mentation occurring under the conditions just mentioned as inferred from:

1. the subject's recall of his dreams in the morning after termination of the night's sleep: first, as elicited in the conscious waking state very shortly after arising; second, as elicited in a morning hypnotic session induced after completion of recall in the conscious waking state; and third, as further elicited in the same hypnotic state when the subject heard the tape recordings of his own sleep-speeches of the previous night;

2. the content of the experimental night's sleep-speeches, as recorded by a continuously running tape recorder;

3. the content of the subject's recall of his sleep mentation on being awakened during the night in comparison to the content of the sleep-speeches themselves; and

4. the content and subjective phenomenology of dreams induced during wakeful hypnotic trances.

Method of Hypnosis

The method of hypnosis used was that formulated by Pascal and Salzberg (1959), with minor modifications. The subject was able to experience positive hallucinations and anesthesia to pin-prick, to tolerate logical absurdities, to carry out PHS, to perform simple acts (both immediately after and 24 hrs after termination of the hypnosis), to spontaneously develop selective amnesia for certain trance events, and to remain in hypnosis with his eyes open and sitting up. He was unable to resist a suggestion that his arm was rigid—he could not bend it though commanded to try; nor could he likewise resist commanded automatic rotation of an arm, though challenged to try.

Data Processing

Quantitative Aspects. For each experiment, a detailed graph was prepared, the ordinate consisting of the EEG stages of sleep, and the abscissa denoting the passage of time. Beneath the abscissa, depending on the times of occurrence, additional data were represented: time of onset, duration and termination of REM periods, body movements, and sleep-speeches. The temporal relationships between these were determined and tabulated according to the various experimental conditions. Speeches occurring 15 min or less before or after REMPs were categorized as REMP-proximate; those occurring more than 15 min on either side of a REMP were termed REMP-distal.

Qualitative Aspects.   These aspects of data were given special emphasis. Comparisons were made between the following groups of data in order to assess their degrees of concordance: (1) content of sleep-speeches; (2) content of dreams recalled in the morning (Procedures A–E and G); and (3) content of mentation elicited following awakenings during nights (Procedure F).

The sleep-speeches in relation to the dreams and/or sleep mentation were scored as showing *first order concordance*[1] when a sleep-speech and a recalled dream or night-waking mentation report possessed in common a *clearly identifying noun or phrase,* e.g., "Claudette Colbert," appearing in both sleep-speech and night-waking report of a dream. Only the manifest content of the dream and sleep-speeches was considered.

Results

Quantitative and Topographic Features

These are best described under the following headings, summarized in Table 11.1.

Changes in the Mean Frequency of Sleep-Speeches (Chosen as a way of Assessing the Effectiveness of a PHS in Stimulating Sleep-Talking).   The mean frequency of somniloquy in the baseline groups of experiments (Procedures A and B) was relatively low (.78 speeches per night) in comparison to the great increase observed in all subsequent experimental groups utilizing PHS (10.0 speeches per night). The mean frequency of the terminal group, Procedure G (7.8 speeches per night) was slightly lower than the combined mean frequency of the experiments using PHS (10.0 speeches per night). A total of 47 speeches occurred during all of the experiments comprising Procedure G. Twenty-one of these 47 speeches occurred on the third night of the series. If the mean total frequency is recalculated, omitting the results of this aberrant night, the mean for five nights drops to 5.3 (indicated in the parentheses in Table 11.1).

---

[1]In the original publication (Arkin et al., 1966b) this category was termed *direct correspondence.*

TABLE 11.1

Quantitative and Temporal Aspects of Experimental Results

Exp. Cond.	# Exper. Nights[1]	Total # Episodes[2]	Mean # Epis./Night[3]	% 1st Half[4]	% 2nd Half[5]	% Intra-REMP[6]	% REMP Margin[7]	% REMP Prox.[8]	Total % REMP Assoc.[9]	% REMP Distal[10]
Baseline										
PROC. A	4	4	1.0	100.	0	0	0	50	50	50
PROC. B	5	3	0.6	100.	0	0	0	0	0	100.
Total baseline		7	0.78	100.	0	0	0	28.6	28.6	71.4
PROC. C	6	49	8.2	4.0	96.0	45.0	4.0	12.0	61.0	39.0
PROC. D	7	92	13.1	24.0	76.0	33.0	3.0	34.0	70.0	30.0
PROC. E	10	89	8.9	43.0	57.0	33.0	5.0	22.0	60.0	40.0
TOTAL PHS	23	230	10.0	26.9	73.1	35.2	3.9	24.8	63.9	36.1
Proc. G— without hyp.	6	47 (26)*	7.8 (5.3)*	78.7 (73.1)*	21.3 (19.1)*	10.6 (19.2)*	0.0	31.9 (12.0)*	42.5 (31.2)*	57.4 (68.8)*

[1] *# Exper. Nights* = Total number of nights in which the specified procedure was used.

[2] *Total # Episodes* = Total number of occurrences of sleep-speech.

[3] *Mean # Epis/Night* = Total number of occurrences of sleep-speech observed when utilizing a specific experimental procedure divided by the total number of nights in which this procedure was used.

[4] *% 1st Half* = The percentage of the total number of speeches observed which occurred in the 1st half of the total sleep period during a specific group of experiments.

[5] *% 2nd Half* = As above in 4 except that the 2nd half of the sleep period is the interval concerned.

[6] *% Intra-REMP* = Percent of total number of sleep-speeches occurring after the onset and before the end of a REMP.

[7] *% REMP Margin* = Percent of total number of sleep-speeches occurring during an interval $\leqq$ 1 min before the onset or after the end of a REMP.

[8] *% REMP - Prox.* = Percent of the total number of sleep-speeches occurring during an interval $\leqq$ 15 minutes but > 1 min before the onset or after the end of a REMP.

[9] *Total % REMP Assoc.* = Percent of total number of speeches of intra-REMP + REMP margin + REMP prox. occurrences.

[10] *% REMP Distal* = Percent of total number of speeches occurring in an interval > 15 min before or after a REMP.

* *Procedure G*, omitting results of 3rd night of series, which contributed an aberrantly high proportion of total # episodes—21 out of 47; see paragraph VIIIA of paper for discussion.

137

Changes in Portion of Night in Which Sleep-Speeches Occurred.   The changes observed in this section are striking. During baseline conditions (Procedures A and B), 100% of the speeches occurred during the first half of the night. During PHS groups, the bulk of the speeches (73%) occurred during the *second* half. During the terminal phase without hypnosis (Procedure G), the bulk of the speeches (78%) occurred once more in the *first* half of the night. Inasmuch as the subject was not awakened in the morning until some time after the end of his last REMP, total sleep times varied somewhat. In order to control for the aforementioned results inordinately reflecting unequal sleep times, the speeches for each night were separately counted for the first 4 hr and the second 4 hr after sleep onset, and the percentages determined accordingly.

The results were: During baseline conditions (Procedures A and B), 100% of the speeches occurred in the first 4 hr; during the PHS groups (Procedures C–E), 15.0% occurred in the first 4 hr, 64.7% in the second 4 hr, and 20.2% after the eighth hour of sleep; during the terminal phase (Procedure G), 69.6% occurred in the first 4 hr, 26.0% in the second 4 hr, and 4.4% after the eighth hour of sleep.

Location of Speeches with Respect to REMP.   In the baseline groups, only a minority (about 29%) of the speeches fell into the REMP-proximate category.[2] The speeches in this portion were not *closely* associated with the REMP, however. By contrast, with the introduction of PHS, a significant number of speeches occurred *during* a REMP (intraREMP, 35%) and at the margin of the REMP (REMP-margin, 4%). If the speeches occurring in the REMP-proximate group[3] (about 25%) are added to the preceding, the bulk of the PHS speeches appear to be associated with REMP (about 64% REMP-associated).

In the terminal phase (Procedure G), although the total frequency is only slightly lower than with the PHS groups, the percentage of REMP-associated speeches dropped from about 64 to 43. Furthermore, the sector of the greatest drop occurred within the intraREMP and REMP-margin group (35% to 11%, and 4% to 0% respectively).

Of possible interest is the fact that of the REMP-proximate speeches observed, more than half occurred in the 15-min interval *before* the onset of a REMP.

EEG and EOG Characteristics.   In the baseline records, there was no evidence of any qualitative anomaly of the EEG or EOG record, or pathologic

---

[2]The selection of category was not completely arbitrary, however. The 15-min interval was chosen because of a report by J. Kamiya (1961) that about 15 min before the onset of a REMP, there is a tendency for irregularity in respiration and heart rate to begin and persist throughout the REMP.

[3]See legend of Table 11.1 for detailed explanation of these terms.

wave forms. The sleep cycles and REMP times were likewise within normal limits.

The following comments are based on general impressions of the records throughout the study and detailed analyses of 20 representative sleep-speech episodes selected from Procedures C–E (10 associated with REM sleep and 10 with NREM). Each sleep-speech episode, arbitrarily divisible into three parts, was ushered in by phase of "onset" and ended by a terminal phase, leading ultimately to a continuation of sleep. Between the two, the speech was uttered.

NREM sleep-talking occurred in all NREM stages of sleep, perhaps more commonly in Stages 2 and 3. The onset phase usually began with muscle-tension artifact, although occasionally even before this, a shower of high-voltage slow waves appeared (delta waves and K-complexes). The average interval between the onset of muscle tension and onset of speech was about 10 sec, with a range of 1–26 sec. The terminal phase, lasting from the end of the speech until the return of spindling, averaged 23 sec, with a range of 7–39 sec. The average length of the speech was 6 sec, with a range of less than 1–15 sec. Throughout the entire episode, including the speech itself, muscle-tension artifact was usually intermittent. Portions of record, free of artifact and of variable length, frequently occurred between the muscle potentials and revealed an EEG with a variety of waves—mostly trains of alpha and low-voltage mixed frequencies (LVM), but spindle frequencies and delta were often visible. It was not always possible to definitely differentiate these delta waves from nonspecific artifacts, however, which commonly accompany body movements. Following cessation of muscle-tension artifact, low-voltage rhythms were followed by sleep spindles and K-complexes.

The electrographic morphology of NREM sleep-speech episodes during baseline procedure (A and B) was similar to the foregoing, but the baseline sleep-speeches themselves were generally much shorter in duration and word count.

In Procedures C–G, there were often clusters of these episodes resulting in a chain of intermittent sections of muscle tension, speech, and various mixtures of EEG frequencies. Between sections, there was commonly a variable brief period of LVM with alpha bursts, or NREM sleep, with K-complexes and spindles predominating. Usually, NREM sleep would finally persist, and sleep-talking activity would then cease for the time being. However, in many instances, a REMP began in 5 min or less following the cessation of NREM sleep. NREM speeches varied in length from less than 1 sec to 15 sec or more in any one episode in the chain, as just described.

REMP sleep-speech occurred during Procedures C–G only. In comparison to NREM episodes, there was more variability. The onset phase seemed to begin with a cessation of REMs, following which a variety of courses were observable: often, a section of LVM occurred, sometimes with one or more SEMs. More commonly, muscle-tension artifact followed the cessation of REMs and persisted for a brief time before speech began. During the onset phase and the speech itself, muscle tension was somewhat less evident than

TABLE 11.2
Electrographic Features of Sleep-Speech Episodes

Type of Sleep Speech	Mean Duration Onset Phase (sec)	Mean Duration of Actual Speech (sec)	Mean Duration of Terminal Phase (sec)	Onset Phase	Sleep Speech	Terminal Phase
REMP	30	16	108	REMS cease, LVM with or without muscle tension and alpha (SEMs less common)	Same	Same with or without saw-toothed waves; more SEMs
NREM	10	7	23	Muscle tension artifact with or without LVM, alpha, spindles (Ks and delta less often)	Same	Same, but more spindles, Ks, and delta

with NREM speech; often it was minimal or absent. When the EEG was clear, it was generally LVM with or without alpha.

The EEG concomitants of the termination were similar to both preceding phases (alpha trains with LVM, and occasional SEMs with and without muscle tension), *but in addition, about half the time, saw-toothed waves were clearly present.*

The onset phase, timed from the end of the last REM preceding the speech until the onset of the speech itself, averaged 30 sec with a range of 3–59 sec. The speech itself averaged 16 sec with a range of 1–62 sec. The terminal phase averaged 108 sec with a range of 12–290 sec. In nine out of the 10 REMP speeches analyzed in detail, the end of the terminal phase coincided with the continuation of the REMP. In the one exception, it ended with a sleep spindle, and an NREM phase of the sleep cycle began.

The results of the detailed analysis are presented in Table 11.2.

Comparison of these results with the available normative data described in Chapter 7 indicates that the electrographic features of posthypnotically induced sleep-utterances produced by this subject are largely indistinguishable from sleep-utterances occurring during the baseline normal sleep of other sleep-talkers producing both REMP and NREM sleep-utterance. When the results of these experiments were first published (Arkin et al., 1966a,b), it was remarked that the tracings of experimental REMP utterances often contained more than usual alpha frequency activity. With accumulated observation of REMP speeches produced by other subjects, however, this must be retracted; the alpha activity associated with such speeches is not inordinate. Attention is invited to a published tracing of a natural REMP speech with alpha and muscle tension equaling those of our speeches which were most abundantly laden with similar alpha and tension (Oswald 1964).

Figure 11.1 A-C shows an episode of "nonREM sleep-speech" from Procedure E. Figure 11.2 A-C shows two episodes of "intra-REMP sleep-speech" from Procedure E.

The paper speed employed throughout this study was 10 mm per sec, making accurate assessment of alpha frequencies difficult. Visual inspection

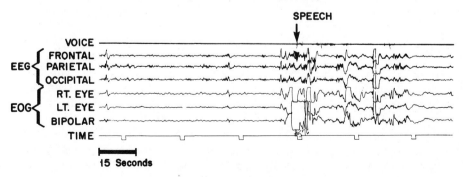

FIG. 11.1-A. Non-REM Speech (continuous record).

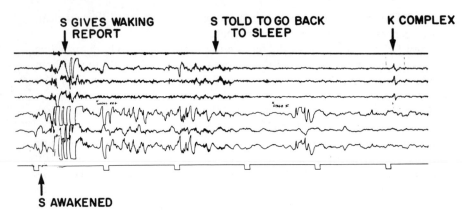

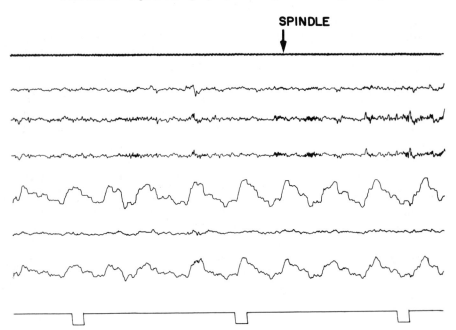

FIG. 11.1-B.   S gives waking report; S told to go back to sleep; K complex.

FIG. 11.1-C.   Spindle.

of suitable records suggested that they tend to be of slightly slower frequency than the waking alpha of this subject and only slightly higher than the frequency of the "natural" alpha bursts occurring in the same REMP before the onset of the sleep speech—but this is a most tentative impression.

The nature of ocular activity concomitant with sleep-speech is also difficult to evaluate, regardless of whether the utterance is associated with REM or NREM sleep. Not unexpectedly, this stems from the muscle-tension artifact,

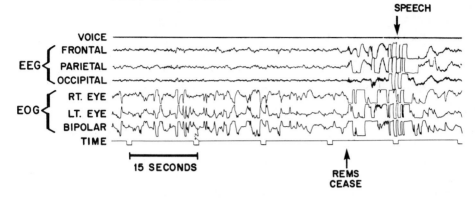

INTRA- REMP SPEECH

SPEECH

VOICE
EEG { FRONTAL
PARIETAL
OCCIPITAL
EOG { RT. EYE
LT. EYE
BIPOLAR
TIME

15 SECONDS

REMS
CEASE

FIG. 11.2-A. Intra-REMP speech.

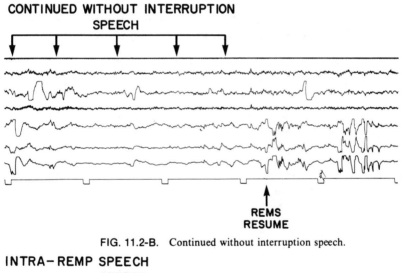

CONTINUED WITHOUT INTERRUPTION

SPEECH

REMS
RESUME

FIG. 11.2-B. Continued without interruption speech.

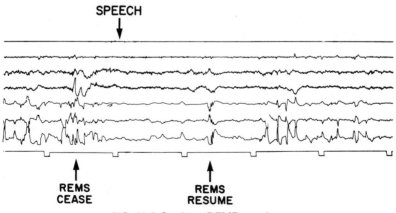

INTRA− REMP SPEECH

SPEECH

REMS
CEASE

REMS
RESUME

FIG. 11.2-C. Intra-REMP speech.

usually involved in speaking and facial movements, which obscures or distorts the eye movement record. Prior to almost every experiment, the subject, while still awake, was asked to move his eyes. In this preliminary testing phase, the conjugate eye movements without speech, made on request, were clearly recorded as such. Then the subject was asked to talk and hold his eyes in a fixed position. Under these conditions, the EOG showed chiefly muscle tension and what appeared electrographically to be uncoordinated eye movements although they were behaviorally still. Our sleep-speech EOG records for the most part resembled the latter. On a few occasions, it seemed as though conjugate eye movements were clearly recorded during the actual sleep-talking. The more usual occurrence was that some eye movements were present, but lacked the typical sharpness of rapid eye movements and were not often electrographically conjugate. Two experiments were performed with ocular strain gauges. These indicated abundant ocular activity during sleep-speech, but strain gauges do not provide reliable information as to whether eye movements are conjugate.

Aspects of Subject's Inner Experience During Procedures C–E

Memory Disturbances. Prior to the research and the use of PHS, the subject was able to remember vividly, spontaneously, and easily his nocturnal dreams after waking in the morning at home and in the laboratory. Following the first few hypnotic trances, his memory for trance events was likewise good. As time went on, however, even though amnesia for dreams or trance events was not suggested during hypnosis, the subject's ability to recall *both* markedly diminished. Amnesia for dreams then occurred for *dreams at home,* as well as in the laboratory. The subject *spontaneously* complained about his loss of dream recall, as he used to derive stimulation from dream events in creative endeavors.

Alertness Disturbances. During the first few experiments using PHS, the subject would come out of the hypnotic trance and awaken in the morning with a "feeling of absolute fatigue," and he would usually "be forced by such feelings to go to bed for at least two and as many as six or eight hours" in order to regain his energy—this in the morning at home, after 8 to 9 hr of monitored laboratory sleep the night before. As time passed, both the posthypnotic and morning fatigue disappeared, and aside from not being able to remember his dreams easily, he felt well and refreshed in the morning and stated that these two effects paralleled one another. There were two interruptions of several weeks or more in the work and, during these, a reversal of the aforementioned occurred each time—ability to spontaneously recall dreams at home and in the laboratory returned, and the subject noted temporary morning fatigue following the resumption of experiments. After the experiments were over, the ability to recall his dreams returned to the former preresearch level (Table

TABLE 11.3
Changes in Memory and Alertness Accompanying Experimental Procedures

	Pre-research	*Initial Experiments Using PHS*	*Subsequent Experiments Using PHS*	*After Termination of Research*
Ability to re-call dreams	Good	Good	Poor	Good
Ability to re-call trance events	—	Good	Poor	—
Posthypnotic fatigue	—	Marked	Little or none	—
Morning fa-tigue	Ab-sent	Marked	Little or none	Ab-sent

11.3.) These observations are consistent with new hypnosis research findings to the effect that carrying out dissociated posthypnotic suggestions entails the expenditure of cognitive effort capable of significantly taxing cognitive capacity (Coe, Basden, Basden, & Graham, 1976; Hilgard, 1977; Stevenson, 1976).

Somniloquy–Sleep-Mentation Concordance

The material to follow is based on sleep-speeches containing at least one distinct word as heard in the playback of the tape recording. This sample comprised a subset of the totals in Table 11.1, which included all speeches regardless of whether they contained a distinctly heard word; and the speeches in all of the following cases were those heard on nights when only Procedures E and F were used (see Table 11.4).

In Procedure E, the content of the sleep-speeches was compared to the content of dreams as recalled by the subject in his following morning conscious waking state and in an immediately subsequent hypnotic state. There were 36 instances of intraREMP or REMP-adjacent speech (out of a total of 60) that were available for comparison. Ten of these 36 speeches (28%) showed first-order concordance with recalled dreams. Only one NREM speech (4%) showed first-order concordance.

In Procedure F, the subject was awakened during the night by a buzzer 3 to 4.5 *min* after episodes of REMP speech; and 30 *sec* or less after episodes of NREM speech. The striking finding with respect to awakenings adjacent to REMP speech was the high frequency of first-order concordance between the content of the speech and the associated recalled mentation (87.5%). On filling out the sleep log the following morning, this same corresponding REMP mentation was usually *spontaneously* recalled and described as a dream.

TABLE 11.4
Somniloquy–Sleep-Mentation Concordance: Results from Morning Recall and Night
Awakenings Compared

Experimental Procedure	Total No. Episodes of Sleep-Talking (1)	Total No. First-Order Concordance (2)	% of First-Order Concordances: (2)/(1) × 100
Procedure E			
Total	60	11	18
Recall of dreams in morning:			
REMP and REMP-adjacent speech	36	10	28
NREM speech	24	1	4
Procedure F			
Total	43	14	32.5
Recall on awakening during night adjacent to sleep speech			
Adjacent to REMP speech	8	7	87.5
Immediately adjacent to NREM speech	35	7	20

By contrast, first-order concordance between immediately following waking recollection and NREM speech was evident in only 20% of the awakenings. When a first-order concordance between sleep-speech and adjacent waking recall *did* occur within this 20%, it was usually striking and convincing. The following morning, the sleep log showed only one instance of such corresponding NREM mentation spontaneously recalled as a dream. In view of the fact that REMP awakenings occurred 3–4½ *min* after the sleep-speech was uttered and that NREM awakenings occurred from 5–30 *sec* afterward, the difference in first-order concordance scores in the two conditions is even more striking. The proportion of first-order concordance

TABLE 11.5
First-Order Concordance

Total morning recall (Procedure E) versus	$t = 1.67$
total post-speech night awakenings (Procedure F)	(n.s.)
REMP speeches morning recall	$t = 2.13$
(Procedure E) versus post-REMP speech night awakenings (Procedure F)	$p < .036$
NREM speeches morning recall	$t = 2.04$
(Procedure E) versus post-NREM speech night awakenings (Procedure F)	$p < .045$

was significantly greater for both REMP ($p < .036$) and NREM ($p < .045$) speeches in Procedure F in comparison to Procedure E.

A number of examples of first-order concordance between sleep-speech and waking mentation from Procedure F are given in detail in a later section.

Results of Procedure H: The Hypnotic Dream

The latency between the experimenter's signal to begin having the dream and the first utterance describing the dream was 50–90 sec in range. (By contrast, the latency between momentary cessation of typical REMs and the onset of sleep-speech during Procedures E and F was rarely over 50 sec.)

The EEG was a mixture of low-voltage mixed frequencies and long trains of alpha.

There were no REMS observed at *any* time during or after the "dream," despite the fact that the "dream" often involved much activity. Actually, ocular movements of any sort seemed to be at a minimum.

The dream report itself was not grossly differentiable from that of a morning recollection of a natural dream or that following night awakenings.

In the first two experiments, the subject was not successful in carrying out the suggestion. He said, somewhat apologetically, that he could have only "images." He was a little more successful with the third attempt in that he was able to experience something resembling a "nap dream." It was not until the sixth attempt that he could experience something that he said approached a dream such as he had had on experimental nights in Procedures A–G. Even here, he experienced differences—the command to dream and the experimenter as expectant audience were constantly in his awareness during the hypnotic dream but absent in night dreams. The "deepest" hypnotic dream also seemed less "deep" than the night dreams he had had in Procedures A–G. Thus, comparison of the hypnotic dream with nocturnal dreams reveals crucial differences with regard to the concomitant EEG, EOG, and related subjective experiential qualities.

Sleep-Speeches and Waking Reports
Showing First-Order Concordance

Table 11.6 presents some transcriptions of actual sleep-speeches and the waking reports elicited immediately following their utterance (Procedure F). The subject was awakened 30 sec or less following NREM speeches, and 3–4½ min after REMP speeches. Only examples of clear-cut first-order concordances were reproduced in the table.

The frequent references to movies and photography are less puzzling when it is borne in mind that the subject had been taking special courses in film-making and planned to make film-direction his career.

TABLE 11.6
Sleep-Speeches (NREM and REMP) as Compared with Waking Reports

Sleep-Speeches (NREM)	Waking Reports
Hi buddy–how ya been? [Spoken as if in actual conversation with someone real. It is immediately followed by a more detached tone and manner as if giving a report about an observed event instead of participating in it.] Having a party or some-thing—I just recognized a boy from Columbia—David is his name—I think he's a Beta—it's sure a boring party.	I was in the course of thinking about a party—something—and there was somebody from Columbia I know—kind of an ass—I think his name was David Z—he's a Beta—he nodded to me from across the room and I thought, "Oh, oh-it's going to be a bad party."
Yes—a little man in subway station coming out of a subway track with pistol and brandishing it and shouting and people all standing—he's firing the pistol up into the air and they're still doing every thing they normally do.	Guy coming out of the subway well—like the one at 5th Avenue stop on the D line—where near the Museum of Modern Art—shooting a gun and nobody noticing him—that's about all.

Mm—mmm—how about this hat (?) from India— how about—how about—hat from India where— where it was made by camel driver—damn thing [pause] pretty little bugger.

Now viewing a film of past experiences in gallery for small admission charge.

This—uh—group photography always makes me think of all the trouble you have to go through since you make a good movie—and I DO have some record which I made—and from when I was all messed up from those weirdo films—of which some imagination can be applied—so that things come out in a synchronization—it's so much better when you have a synchronized movie—even (?) Da Vinci said so—but anyway you can do that without it—is to make it on inferior (?) grade film.

Uh—uhm—uh—gee—I—something about—yeah —a hat—belonging to you know—one of those old sheep herder hats—I don't remember what it was all about though.

Uh—[pause]—there's a theater that you pay admission charge and they run films of your life— that's all I remember except that I was in one of those theaters a minute ago.

Well—this time I had sort of a filmic fantasy— it was sort of filmic fighting—a sort of filmic Pied Piper leading myself—which is sort of one more glorifying version of Pied Piper where everyone turns out to be the same guy—like citizenship—I used to think about it taking away and they had thought about giving it—each (?) country—it's a funny feeling—I don't know—it would take a good deal of consideration, a good deal more than I know how—that's about all. E then said, "You can go back to sleep now" and S responded "I practically am anyway".

(continued)

TABLE 11.6 (continued)

Sleep-Speeches REMP	Waking Reports
Mbl—in brown shirts—suede—then—mbl—mbl—very tragic.	There's a bund of people who wear brown suede leather—tan—in a kind of a quasi—Fascist organization—there's a girl in there, named Madeleine, I think, who's not going to marry the leader—maybe she will, maybe she won't—I'm not certain—anyway—it's not too cool because he's not a very good guy, either I can't remember any more of that—I think there's a war—I can't recall any more.
Claudette Colbert is trying to seduce me into a dream and I think she's HORRIBLE but has a friend —a BEAUTIFUL girl from the University of California and—.	Mbl noot (?)—Claudette Colbert—trying to put the make on me conversationally and she was so ugly—but she brought her daughter from U. C. and we were hitting it off and joking around Claudette and we were getting in elevators and things and we would come out and there would be Claudette—and other kinds of illusions—elusive methods—going through tunnels—that's about all I can remember.
I heard it (?) said all film—all music is cosmopolitan—I don't know—he's wrong.	Umh—talking about music—this professor Scharff—and he said that all music was cosmopolitan and I disagreed with him—that's all there was to it—that's all.

Doctor Arkin will telephone a buddy of mine—and telegraph a cake—his birthday—it's on Good Friday—the buddy is Doctor Straw—and do this for birthday and All Saints Day.

Lex Barker is dying in the Bronx—in a swimming pool—he's at the bottom of the pool and—his life gurgling away—and people are talking about guys they knew who died and saying, "Well—he's a nice guy—but it's just the way it goes,"—and the other one saying, "I know such a guy—and it (?) was such a body—my uncle in the Bronx—he could press him with either hand," and the other said, "It's a pity—with all the—uh—uh—.

It's OK Daddy, I'll (use the seat (?)) behind you.

Uh—Doctor Arkin sent a gift to—a birthday gift to a buddy of mine on his birthday—he was very happy to receive it and it was a very timely gift—it was something he could use very much and he was overjoyed to get—there was something else—I can't think of it at the moment.

Uh—dreamed about Lex Barker—the actor drowning in a swimming pool—people standing over him making all kinds of comments—I don't think I remember any but they were strikingly careless, tasteless, and uninvolved like, "Chee—ya know once—I had a brudder like that—that kind of thing—but he isn't drowning at the bottom of the pool,"—it went on like that with all those comments til the man drowned—it's about all.

Uh—my dad and I were going to the circus—but not the circus—it's Coney Island—more like a penny arcade kind of thing—you know—only in Coney Island and went to Pat's (?) for dinner and the Queen Theatre where they had 99 different kinds of movies and then we were running around after a bus and subway combination and I was getting on the subway and he was getting on bus so he got off the bus and I got off the subway so we could find each other—that kind of thing—I was in the middle of it when the buzzer rang.

Needless to say, the best results fell far short of the goal of a sustained verbal account of an ongoing dream. On the other hand, the results, such as they are, were unusual and remarkable.

Discussion

Quantitative and Topographical Features

The increase in the mean frequency of sleep-speeches after the employment of PHS is striking. It is noteworthy that this increase remained even when specific suggestions to talk more abundantly were discontinued. There is some evidence to indicate that a previously given PHS retained some of its force beyond the period of action originally specified; e.g., the subject indicated his surmise that Procedure G was introduced because we were attempting to test whether a PHS would retain its force over a long period of time. It is also likely that merely sleeping in the laboratory took on qualities of a conditioning stimulus that became paired with a previous PHS to sleep-talk more abundantly. (The subject would spontaneously announce with good humor that as soon as he set foot in the lab, he would feel intense sleepiness.)

Another noteworthy finding is the shifts in location of speeches with respect to REMPs and time of night. The data indicate that following PHS, the bulk of sleep-speeches occurred in the second half of the night, as opposed to the first half during the baseline periods, and that the bulk of the speeches following PHS became associated with REMPs. It is possible that both of these findings are related to the fact that most of the REMP time occurs in the second half of the night.

The findings are only partially consistent with the specific nature of the PHS given; e.g., the mean frequency of speeches should have been greatest following the PHS to "talk more abundantly" (Procedure C). Instead, the mean frequency of sleep-speeches in Procedures D and E was greater. Perhaps the PHS only induces a nonspecific excitement, which in turn stimulates sleep-speech, rather than there being a specific relationship between the exact content of the PHS and its outcome.

The changes in location (intraREMP, REMP-association, first and second halves of night) and mean frequencies of speeches observed in the PHS group compared to those of the procedures in which PHS were not employed suggest that the PHSs were indeed effective in stimulating speeches that were related to or reflected the psychophysiological conditions of the REMP.

It is noteworthy that the bulk of the speeches in Procedure G occurred once more during the first half of the night, just as during the initial baselines (Procedures A and B), and that the degree of REMP association and intraREMP speech diminished.

During the baseline period, there were no occurrences of a sleep-speech during or on the margin of the first REMP. During all of the experiments using PHS, only one instance of sleep-speech occurred at the "posterior" margin of the *first* REMP and none in the interior. (This is consistent with indications from other studies that the first REMP is different from its successors. The first REMP is often "absent" or relatively short [Dement & Kleitman 1957a]. Also, reports of dreams following awakening from the first REMP are less frequent than reports derived from succeeding REMPs [Dement & Kleitman, 1957b; Goodenough, Lewis, Shapiro, & Sleser, 1965]). On several occasions during the repeat baseline series (Procedure G), the first REMP did not appear in its usual place, and abundant streams of sleep-speech were uttered during NREM sleep instead.

Electrographic Characteristics

A question arises: Is there any electrographic evidence to support the hypothesis that the subject, in producing sleep-speech following PHS, merely awakened transitorily from sleep, entered a brief posthypnotic state obligingly, had a "hypnotic dream," and reported verbally on that experience rather than his physiological dream? After all, many students of hypnosis have claimed that when one carries out a PHS, one momentarily reverts to the hypnotic state during the process (Schiff, Bunney, Jr., & Freedman, 1961; and Kratochvíl and MacDonald (1972) have maintained that "hypnosis can continue after periods of sleep which occur during hypnosis [p. 29]."

The bulk of the evidence is inconsistent with this hypothesis and none of the data supports it. As indicated earlier, the electrographic concomitants of sleep-speech following PHS were indistinguishable from those accompanying natural sleep-utterance. Further, the frequent presence of saw-tooth waves virtually unique to REM sleep and the associated bursts of conjugate REMs themselves clearly set these occurrences apart from the electrographic picture of this subject's hypnotic dreams elicited during Procedure H. The reader is reminded that the EEG of the latter was one of sustained wakefulness, and both REMs and saw-tooth waves were absent. The contention that the psychophysiological state during sleep-speech following PHS is essentially unrelated to the hypnotic state itself, or to hypnotic dreams, derives further support from review of observations pertaining to the subject's psychic state during sleep-speech episodes following PHS. This will be discussed further.

Correspondence Between Somniloquy and Waking Recall

That close correspondence between the content of sleep-speech and sleep mentation occurred often under the experimental conditions is unmistakable.

This was most obvious when the subject was awakened shortly after REMP speeches and asked to recount what had been passing through his mind

(Procedure F). In almost all such cases, this recalled mentation was spontaneously remembered as a dream, which by our criteria also directly corresponded to the sleep-speech (first-order concordance). The single REMP speech not included in this first-order concordance category was nevertheless associated with closely related dream material—the sleep-speech dealt with making a movie film; the waking recall was of a dream about a film. This was not scored as first-order concordance because the speech and recalled dream did not possess a clearly "identifying" noun or phrase in common, despite their obvious close relationship; rather, a categorization of second-order concordance would have been appropriate. Waking the subject very shortly after NREM sleep was much less productive in eliciting instances of first-order concordance (20%). Here the recalled mentation was spontaneously described only once as a dream. Furthermore, the vividness and quantity of recall was generally much less with NREM speech than with REMP speech. There was a high frequency of "no recall" on waking after NREM speech; on one striking occasion, the subject was awakened during a NREM speech and said, "Bang—you awakened me in the middle of a comment," but he was unable to remember anything about what he had been saying. There was never any instance of "no recall" on waking after REMP speech.

The findings closely parallel those reported by others to the effect that REM mentation is typically more abundant, more likely to be available for recall (Rechtschaffen, Verdone, & Wheaton, 1963a), and that evidence suggests that qualities of REM versus NREM sleep persist into immediately subsequent wakefulness and influence mentation produced at that time (Fiss, Klein, & Bokert, 1966). In other words, the regularities observed in our REMP versus NREM speeches of associated mentation reports, both following PHS, correspond to the analogous regularities observed with REMP and NREM reports elicited from nonsleep-talking subjects. This, therefore, constitutes added evidence that the sleep-speeches following PHS truly reflect sleep mentation rather than a wakeful or returned hypnotic state.

The Psychic State During
Sleep-Utterance Following PHS

In our original publication (Arkin et al., 1966b), we suggested that the psychic state during sleep-talking following PHS might be best described as a composite between "natural sleep and dreaming with sleep-talking" and posthypnotic state. This was a conservative statement made to take into account what seemed to us to be on many occasions unusually large amounts of alpha and muscle tension occurring in association with such sleep-vocalization. As mentioned earlier, however, accumulated observation has shown repeatedly that such phenomena are observable with natural, spontaneous sleep-talking and silent movement arousal episodes. We, therefore, take this opportunity to withdraw this suggestion and state instead that we are unable, with the data on hand, to reliably distinguish between sleep-talking with and without PHS.

In addition to the considerations set forth in previous sections, we wish to add the following:

1. The subject said that, with rare exceptions, he was unable to discern differences between his dreaming in the laboratory, with or without PHS, and his dreaming at home.

2. It is generally believed that phenomena experienced in a hypnotic state are easily available to recall in subsequent hypnotic states. In our experiments, the contents of the bulk of our speeches, REMP as well as NREM (in Procedures C–E), were *not* available to recall during the hypnosis of the following morning. This was the case even in those instances when the subject was given an additional PHS *prior* to retiring for the night—that he would be able to remember all of his dreams easily on the following morning—during hypnosis. Most important, our data on recall in Procedures E and F are quite consistent with findings in other studies on "natural" REMP and NREM recall (Foulkes, 1966; Goodenough, 1968; Rechtschaffen et al., 1963a) not only with respect to frequency of recall, but also to qualities (vividness, mentation labeled as dream, length and elaboration of report).

3. The data on hypnotic dreams (Procedure H) indicate, first of all, that the subject had to *learn* to have dreams during the hypnotic state. He could only have "images" until the third trial, and it was not until the sixth trial that he was able to experience something that approached in quality the dreams he had had in Procedure E; even this was not the same experience. Such a finding would be difficult to explain with the hypothesis that during the previous year of experimentation, he had been waking from sleep, then regularly having hypnotic dreams on which he would give verbal reports, instead of giving reports on natural dreams. If this were the case, he would have required no learning period in Procedure H.

4. The latency between the command to dream during the hypnotic trance and onset of the subject's concurrent description aloud was much longer than the latency between momentary cessation of REMs and the onset of sleep-speech in Procedures E and F. In the former case, it ranged from 50–90 sec, whereas in the latter, it was rarely over 50 sec. This difference is again consistent with the hypothesis that the sleep-speech following PHS intimately reflected prior and/or concurrent sleep mentation, rather than arising from a temporary posthypnotic state.

Interim Conclusions

1. It appears possible with PHS to stimulate a subject to "talk in his sleep" at times that tend to be associated with REMPs, and often in the midst of an

ongoing REMP. These sleep-speeches, when occurring adjacent to, or in the midst of, a REMP, tend directly and unmistakably to correspond to the subject's recalled associated mentation (87.5% of awakenings), and to the subsequent memory of his dreams spontaneously labeled as a dream by the subject in the morning.

2. It is possible with PHS to induce the subject to "talk during NREM sleep" and sometimes these sleep-speeches directly and unmistakably correspond to the subject's recalled associated mentation (20% of awakenings), and only rarely to the subsequent memory of a dream spontaneously labeled by the subject as a dream in the morning.

3. It seems to be possible to influence certain temporal characteristics of somniloquy by means of hypnosis, such as producing a shift in the time of night during which the bulk of sleep-talking occurs, and enhancing the closeness of its association with REMPs.

4. It is possible by means of PHS to stimulate an increase in the frequency of sleep-speech.

Additional Research Utilizing PHS to Stimulate Sleep-Talking

I was pleased to learn that C. T. Tart (1974) had independently confirmed the essential findings published in the just mentioned experimental case study (Arkin et al., 1966b), and his comments deserve full quotation:

> Basically, a group of about eight well-trained hypnotic subjects who had been participants in other experiments in affecting dream content by post-hypnotic suggestion spent several nights each sleeping in the lab with suggestions to talk during their sleep. Seven of the eight were non-sleep-talkers; judging by their previous nights in the lab, you hardly even heard any sound out of them. I would say four or five words a night.
>
> The post-hypnotic suggestion was to talk almost continously about the content of ongoing dreams.
>
> The result was an approximate eight-fold increase in the verbal output of all subjects. What that meant was that those who essentially never said anything would grunt six [to] ten times a night or mutter a single word ... while the one who ordinarily talked a few words each night showed an eight-fold increase with phrases and sentences.

The data on distribution of these utterances in REM and NREM sleep were unfortunately not available, and this study was not pursued further.

In view of this independent confirmation, it seems worthwhile to present here in some detail further work of my own that has never been published. One who is familiar with sleep research knows how arduous it can be, and my hope is to stimulate others, particularly indefatigable ones, to explore the potentialities of PHS and other types of training methods in experimentally influencing sleep-utterance.

The next subject was an intelligent, imaginative 28-year-old college graduate who was working in motion picture public relations and responded to advertisements for sleep-research subjects out of intellectual interest. It turned out by happenstance that he was a chronic sleep-talker, and he enthusiastically participated in the work.

At the outset, the experimental schedule was similar to that employed for the previous subject, with the sole exception that after the first baseline series was completed and before going on to the hypnosis baseline experiments, a set of baseline wake-up nights was interpolated. This was done in order to obtain a sample of baseline mentation reports uninfluenced by subsequent presleep hypnosis. In all other respects, the procedure was similar until unforeseen problems forced an innovation on us, which we describe presently.

Thus, after one adaptation night, as with the subject presented earlier, there were five once-a-week initial baseline nights during which the subject's sleep and vocalizations were continuously monitored during experimentally uninterrupted sleep (Procedure A).

This was followed by a baseline wake-up series of four nights, during which the subject was repeatedly awakened for mentation reports, both following sleep-utterances and from silent sleep (Procedure A plus wake-ups).

At this point, after hypnosis practice by day was begun, the subject spent four baseline hypnosis nights identical to the first baseline series with the sole exception that a hypnotic trance was induced and resolved 1 hr prior to sleep. As before, no experimental sleep interruption was carried out (Procedure B).

The next steps involved the introduction of presleep posthypnotic suggestions to talk in sleep as at home, but more abundantly (Procedure C), and talk in sleep as at home whenever dreams occur (Procedure D). Flushed with optimism arising from results with the first subject, I was unprepared for the disconcerting outcome. In Procedure A and B, only one sleep-speech was uttered in nine laboratory nights, which was fine; but Procedure C netted no sleep-speech whatsoever in three nights, and Procedure D produced only four speeches distributed over five nights.

During a concurrent daytime hypnosis practice session, I had asked the subject while he was in trance to think about why he had not carried out the PHS to talk in his sleep and that I would ask him about this during the forthcoming presleep hypnosis in the laboratory. His response that night while under hypnosis was that I had asked him to talk in his sleep like he does at home, and he couldn't do this because he didn't *know* how he talked in his sleep—he had never heard himself.

I tried to deal with this in the following manner: In subsequent daytime practice hypnotic sessions, I gave him within-trance hypnotic suggestions to dream, and then to talk aloud during his dreaming, without interrupting it. He quickly became quite adept at carrying out this task—talking sporadically during vivid hypnotic dreaming. I had hoped that such experience would generalize to the laboratory nocturnal dreaming situation, but results were unchanged—still no appreciable sleep-speech.

I then decided to wake the subject during a REM period and elicited a vivid dream report. Next, I confronted the subject with, "If you were dreaming, why do you suppose you didn't talk in your sleep?"; whereupon he replied that he hadn't realized he was dreaming—his experience felt real. This was, after all, in accord with Havelock Ellis' well-known remark, "Dreams feel real while they are going on; may we say more of life?"

The experiments were temporarily interrupted and the subject was requested to sleep with a tape recorder at his bedside at home and without any artifice, "Find some way, I can't say just how, to alert yourself to the occurrence of a dream while in progress, wake yourself up, and dictate it into the tape recorder." With practice, he reported that he had become skilled at this stunt, had decided to dispense with the tape recorder and to simply continue "in training" as a self-alerter to dream experience during sleep without talking aloud afterward; i.e., he had learned to some extent to detect when he was dreaming. The possibility of acquiring such a skill has been independently demonstrated by Antrobus, Antrobus, & Fisher (1965).

After some weeks, he was tested in the laboratory again in two experiments employing posthypnotic suggestions to talk during sleep whenever he dreamed (Procedure D) and to talk during sleep and describe the dream aloud while it was going on without interrupting the dream (Procedure E). In combination with the previously learned dream occurrence self-alerting skill, the sleep-utterance frequency underwent a prompt six-fold increase over that of the baseline. But was this effect due to PHS specifically or could it be produced just as well without PHS, with the self-alerting skill being the chief effective agent?

To settle this question, a new series of experiments was conducted over the ensuing months, consisting of a series of baseline nights, PHS nights, and non-PHS self-alerting instruction nights in interspersed, roughly alternating order. Unfortunately, due to undetected equipment failure, many tape recordings came out defective. Thus, the following data analyses are based in part on the ongoing separate manual records kept by the technicians who monitored the experiments throughout the night; these records are certainly adequate for drawing preliminary conclusions. The records were made by them as they listened for sleep-vocalization over the intercom connected with the subject's bedroom.

We will be comparing the frequencies of sleep-vocalizations that could be conservatively classified as sleep-utterances containing at least one clear word, or else that impressed the actively listening experimenter as unclear but unmistakably speech-like. The results are presented in Table 11.7.

Comparing all baseline night sleep-speech frequency to that of the PHS or presleep instruction night series resulted in a clear-cut significantly greater

TABLE 11.7

Frequencies of Sleep-Speech or Speech-Like Vocalizations for Second Subject

			Experimental Conditions			
	All BL	*First BL Procedure A*	*Hypnosis BL Procedure B*	*Middle & Terminal BL*	*PHS nights*	*Instruction nights*
Number of nights	19	5	4	10	10	10
Mean frequency of sleep-speech	1.0	0	0.25	1.8	4.6	4.2
t-test comparisons	—	—	—	—	PHS vs. all BL $t = 3.87$ $p < .01$	Instruction vs. all BL $t = 3.05$ $p < .01$
					PHS vs. middle & terminal BL $t = 2.198$ $p < .05$	Instruction vs. middle & terminal BL $t = 1.67$ $p < .10$ (n.s.)

amount of sleep-speech on either of the latter two experimental night series. The mean baseline frequency was 1.0 speech per night in contrast to 4.6 and 4.2 per night for the PHS and Instruction conditions respectively ($p < .01$ for both analyses).

Inasmuch as several series of awakening nights were interposed between the initial baseline (Procedure A) and subsequent series during the subject's tenure in the laboratory, we carried out a separate comparison between the sleep-speech frequency of the combined middle and terminal baseline series versus that of nights with PHS and Instruction separately. This seemed wise because evidence had arisen that the mere process of repeated awakenings for mentation reports had a stimulating effect on sleep-speech production. Even though the baseline wake-up series (Procedure A plus wake-ups) had not resulted in significantly more sleep-speech in the subsequent baseline hypnosis series (Procedure B), it was nevertheless possible that a cumulative effect might be demonstrable; i.e., many awakening nights could ultimately prime the subject to increased sleep-utterance. In effect, we were asking whether the striking difference between sleep-speech frequency for all baseline nights versus experimental nights in the first data analysis could have merely reflected the virtual absence of sleep-speech during the initial baseline series (Procedures A and B); and whether the increase of sleep-speech following PHS and Instruction may have resulted from accumulated previous nights with experimental awakenings having conditioned stimulating effects that carried over to them, rather than being experimental variable effects. By contrast to Procedures A and B, the middle and terminal baseline series had been performed after the subject had had much prior experience with laboratory awakenings and thus would provide a more valid baseline for evaluation of PHS and presleep Instruction effects.

This second analysis revealed that the sleep-speech frequency produced by PHS was still significantly greater than that under middle and terminal baseline conditions, albeit to a lesser extent than when all baseline nights were used in the analysis ($p < .05$). Thus, PHS seems to be effective in stimulating sleep-speech. The mean frequency of sleep-speech with PHS was 4.6 per night, as opposed to 1.8 for the combined groups of middle and terminal baseline nights.

The same analysis comparing the effects of presleep instruction, however, disclosed only a trend in the same direction. The mean frequency of sleep-speech in the latter series was 4.2 per night ($p < .1$).

What do these results indicate overall regarding this specific subject? First, PHS appears to be capable of increasing sleep-speech.

Second, presleep Instruction is almost as effective as PHS, just barely missing statistical significance. Thus, it is by no means a foregone conclusion that the effective specific variable was posthypnotic suggestion. A greater number of experimental nights may eliminate the superiority of PHS.

Third, previous experience with laboratory awakenings alone may have been an active variable in producing a proportion of the increased amounts of sleep-speech observed on experimental nights (see p. 202–208 for further experimental studies bearing on this point.)

As with our first subject, the sleep-speeches and associated mentation reports showed considerable variability as to word count, content, style (detached reporting versus "lived-in" experience reflected by the sleep-speech), and degrees of concordance. Table 11.8 provides typical illustrations of various relevant features. It cannot be concluded from these samples, however, that the lived-in type of speech was correlated with the PHS "talk whenever you dream" and that the detached reporting type was correlated with the PHS "talk and describe your dream while it is going on." Many exceptions were observed.

The third subject to be presented was in reality the first with whom the initial exploratory experiments were carried out (Arkin, 1960). I apologize in advance for the lack of completeness in polygraphic recording and for the lack of controls and methodological refinement. I nevertheless feel that the observations are most interesting and, as previously mentioned, my hope is to stimulate others to perform similar work. Many readers will doubtless feel that the material to follow is presented in burdensome detail. The justification for this is given in the discussion section. However, for those who lack a special interest in this phase of the topic, it may be skipped without loss.

The subject was a 32-year-old married woman of Hispanic origin. She had six children and was a devout member of the Pentecostal church. She had a brother of 19 and an adoptive sister of 27. When she was 4 years old, a sister (age 5) died from some acute process involving her face, neck, and a hemorrhage. The subject remembers the sister being placed in a coffin and "everybody crying." A younger sister also had died. The subject's mother considered the subject to be a cranky child; she had always been shy, sensitive and somewhat anxious. She liked to read novels and mysteries but did not care for TV or the movies. She finished secondary school. The subject recently had had a post-partum depression of moderate severity. After giving birth to a son, she felt that nobody paid any attention to her. At about this time she required some oral surgery and was terrified of "needles." Hypnotic analgesia was used with such great success that she has participated in hypnosis teaching demonstrations ever since.

The subject had a vivid, dramatic dream life. This observation was based on self-report and samples of dreams provided by her prior to the first laboratory sessions. The dreams were filled with urgency, physical and sexual attack, missing body parts, mutilation, rescue themes, healing of mutilation, fire, and the like. The subject's husband reported that she had walked and talked in her sleep in a dramatic manner for many years. The episodes were frequent and she remembered little or nothing after awakening. This was certainly

TABLE 11.8

Sleep-Speech and Mentation Reports Following PHS—Second Subject

Experimental Condition	Sleep Stage and Time of Night	Sleep—Speech and Style	Mentation Report[a]	Concordance Category and Concordance Features
PHS: "Talk whenever you dream."	REMP (?) 5:20 a.m.	Uh—uugh— beast—um not any more" [lived-in style]	"Um—that—producing independent films—and a friend is with Filmways was *telling me* that they're going to be producing *more* independent films in the future, but also, that they're going to be producing independent films and distributing themselves, and he *told me* earlier that—where there was low grass it would be southern grass— when there was *more* southern grass, it would be knee-high grass 'cause it's very executive and I'm very aggressive, but, uh —that's good news—.	Third-order concordance based on "telling me." In addition, "not any more" in the sleep-speech suggests ideas relating past and future. This may be reflected in the future plans of Filmways. "More" appears once in the speech and twice in the mentation report. "Beast" appears in the speech and may be related to "aggressive" in the mentation report.
PHS: "Talk whenever you dream.	REMP 6:23 a.m.	"Dumb blonde— dumb brunette — [lived in]	"Uh huh, yeah, we were going down to the lake to get the, to get something for this *dumb blo*—oh, we're going down to the lake to get the registers we were borrowing from this handyman, and *we started talking* about	First-order concordance based on clearly identifying words held in common by both sleep-speech and mentation report.

PHS	NREM		
PHS: "Talk whenever you dream."	NREM 2:22 a.m. "Mm—mm— checking in— uh, huh—uh, huh." [lived-in]	this *dumb blonde*, she was a *dumb brunette*, but she acted like a dumb blonde and, uh—while *we're talking to her*, we're at MGM yesterday, having a very important meeting and this *dumb blonde* or *brunette* came in and announced not only to the people at MGM and our visitors that henceforth we would no longer have secretaries in the afternoon because she thought it was a waste of time and they should come out and help her, so it's just as well she's leaving—". "That—there was this trip that was very important. I wasn't quite sure when it was and—it was about—somewhere in Europe but all of a sudden, it came into focus—with a photograph of a plane that it was Europe and that I was to photograph the plane and to—uh—mbi—but it was no photograph, it was all about Yugoslavia and about Bulgravia—that we must get to Yugoslavia—and then there was—I kept thinking, my God, we've got to get this stuff right now—because if it's 1970, that's, you know, that's here, that's now, then we've got to decide that it's a—about everybody and make all the arrangements and get half the people here, and that was it."	Of further interest is the last part of the mentation report suggesting that the subject drifted into rendering an account of real events of the previous day related to the dream. Second-order concordance based on the relationship between "checking in" and plane travel arrangements with some momentous sense of urgency. In real life, the subject was due to leave for Europe by plane within two days and was quite excited about the prospect.

(continued)

TABLE 11.8 (continued)

Experimental Condition	Sleep Stage and Time of Night	Sleep—Speech and Style	Mentation Report[a]	Concordance Category and Concordance Features
PHS: "Talk in your sleep and describe the dream as if it is going on without waking up or interrupting the dream."	Sleep stage not ascertainable 5:26 a.m.	"Mm—mm—at the airport mbl —a girl I used to be at work— we were very good friends. I'm just about to take the 6:25 TWA plane to Cairo and she was coming off a plane from Louisiana, hold- ing a folded (?) jacket and it was very good to see her, had- n't seen her for 10 years or so —." [detached re- porting]	"Hm?—I was at the airport—I was in the army, I think and I was getting ready to go overseas—to—to Cairo, but I saw this girl that I'd known—and—it was very good to see her—she was wearing a forge club jacket, or carrying a forge club jacket—that's it."	First-order concordance based on details of airport, Cairo, girl etc. Note the presence of certain details in the sleep-speech omitted from the mentation re- port (6:25 TWA plane, Louisiana, girl he used to work with, etc.) and vice versa of details in the report omitted in the sleep-speech ("I was in the army").

PHS: "Talk in your sleep and describe the dream as if it is going on without waking up or interrupting the dream."

Sleep stage not ascertainable 5:32 a.m.

"Uh huh— she's walking down the family room, Melanie, she just took off her pan— um—oh, by the way, mbl, cleaned up, her room—she's eating the dog's bone, the dog doesn't care —and peep with the parakeet boss— mbl."

[detached reporting]

"Huh? —I was in New York driving and —and—and—an uptown street and I—Iwas going to wash my car because it was just filthy, and it's brand new and —I mbl weren't so good mbl wash it my- self—so I drove it off to wash it and there was very mbl traffic on the road—and we had a blue car, a maroon car—and Melanie's diaper off—she was all soggy, and someone else had a cream car— Mustang—"."

First-order concordance based on Melanie, the subject's infant daughter, appearing in both sleep-speech and report in need of some hygienic care. Note once more the various sleep mentation report discrepancies.

ªItalics denote special features, not inflectional emphasis; see Appendix 1 for key.

consistent with laboratory observation of her somniloquy, for which a strong amnestic tendency existed when recall was tested in wakeful normal consciousness. For example, while apologizing one laboratory night for not being able to remember much of any dream preceding a post-somniloquy spontaneous awakening, she said that all she could remember was a sense of having been "running and the minute I sit up in bed, it kind of snaps out of my head, I try and I try; if I tell about it before I sit up—like when I'm in the house, I tell my husband, I usually remember parts of it." Clinically, she was clearly not psychotic but possessed tendencies to become anxious, depressed, and undergo nocturnal macrodissociative episodes in association with sleep. The subject was paid for her participation and fully informed about the purposes of our research program.

During the first four experiments, she slept the entire night in a private room in the laboratory. By her bedside was: (1) a microphone leading to a tape recorder that operated for the entire night in an adjacent room; and (2) an intercom through which I could listen for any vocalization. There was no polygraphic recording during the first four exploratory experiments.

About 45 min prior to retiring for the night, she was deeply hypnotized and given the following posthypnotic suggestion:

> Tonight, when you sleep in the lab, you may or may not—just exactly as you like—have natural dreams during your sleep. In the event that you *do* dream, you are to continue to sleep naturally, but you are to describe all of your dreams in detail as they are occurring, in clearly spoken words; in short, to talk in your sleep for the purpose of describing whatever dreams you may have. Do not dream more or less than you would normally. If you have a nightmare, you may awaken from it, should you so desire, as long as you describe it aloud while it is occurring.

She was then aroused from the trance and returned to the normal conscious waking state. She retired at her usual bedtime in her otherwise normal, natural manner. At no time was any amnesia suggested to her for events of the trance, including the content of the posthypnotic suggestion. She did spontaneously, apparently, have an amnesia for trance events, although the extent of this was never systematically tested.

Attempts were made after natural awakening in the morning to elicit as much of her dreams as she could remember during her conscious waking state and during a second immediately subsequent period of hypnosis, also in the morning. Comparisons of material so obtained were made with the actually recorded vocalizations of the night.

Results of the First Experiments
Considered as a Group

The subject talked in her sleep for varying periods at least once during each night. In each case, the content of the sleep-speech bore some obvious relationship to the content of a dream recalled in the morning. With one exception, that of Experiment I, the most complete information was, generally, the dream as recalled during the morning hypnotic state. Every item of content of the sleep-speech was also usually present in the content of a dream as recalled in hypnosis. This was equally true for every item of dream content as recalled in morning wakeful consciousness. The reverse is not true, however. There were items appearing in the dreams as recalled in hypnosis that were not present either in the sleep-speeches or in the dream as recalled in morning wakefulness prior to the morning trance induction. Thus, the most complete recall of sleep mentation (with the exception of Experiment I) occurred during the morning-after hypnosis.

The results of each experiment are now described in detail.

Experiment I.   Approximately 50 min after retiring (11:00–11:15 p.m.), the subject began to sob and weep dramatically, and a few words were spoken. She eventually awakened and asked for permission to urinate. She mentioned spontaneously that she had had a nightmare in which she had been talking to her husband about her fear of entering the hospital on the following day to undergo abdominal surgery. (This was based on reality. She was, in fact, due to enter the hospital on the day following the first experiment for an elective abdominal surgical procedure.) After urination, she returned to sleep. On awakening at 5:00 a.m., she said that she had "slept like a log" for the remainder of the night and that such a sound sleep was most unusual for her.

She recalled one dream *in normal wakefulness,* which she described as follows:

> I had a nightmare. I went to bed and it seemed like I was so sleepy. I said, "Yes, I want to sleep," and I started dreaming I was with my husband and me. I was going into the hospital and I was afraid they were going to open me up. I was crying and telling him I was afraid of the operation and then he was kind of asking me how I felt and I told him I thought I was coming down with a head cold or a sore throat or something like that. And then he was trying to calm me down, you know? That's about it; I woke up.

This was recounted in a slightly somber but controlled manner. No other dreams were recalled.

The subject recalled the following dream *during morning hypnosis:*

I was going—I dreamed I was going to the hospital and, oh, and I was so scared of it. I didn't want to go in, I didn't want to go into the hospital. [Begins to sob and is out of control; after about 30 sec and being told to relax, she was able to continue.] I was going into the hospital and afraid of my operation. My husband—he was with me. I was so scared. He was trying to calm me down. I was crying.

No other dreams were recalled. The recognizable tape-recorded fragments of somniloquy (besides much sobbing) were, "Operated on (?)—tengo frio—cuber." "Tengo frio" (I am cold) was especially clear.

Experiment II.   At approximately 1:50 a.m., about 3 hr after retiring, a few words were spoken and after 2–3 min of silence, an additional few words were added. Following 5–7 min, the silence was broken by rustling of bed clothes and a little coughing. No further words were recorded for the remainder of the night. She awakened at 5:30 a.m., complained of a headache, and wanted to put cold water on her head to relieve the ache. She remarked spontaneously that she did not dream at all during the night. In normal wakefulness, she was asked if she remembered some fragment or feeling having to do with a dream. She replied:

All I remember is that feeling. I woke up about the middle of the night, I would say, and I had a feeling like as if I had been arguing or trying to settle a fight or something with someone. I couldn't place it or I couldn't remember with who and—ah—I felt kind of uneasy, you know, and I went back to sleep and this morning when I woke up I had the feeling I, either my sister or my brother or me were crying and—ah—I was trying to quiet them down. Some mixed up feeling, you know, like when there is an accident either happened or is going to happen, a kind of funny feeling you get and a terrific headache.

The recorded content of the somniloquy was as follows: 1. Uh—uh—but uh—why do I have to do that: What if I don't want to? Uh—oh well—O.K.—just—uh—[a few unclear words]—OK then. 2. [A few minutes later] No no, don't let her jump—no, no, she's gonna fall—yes, yes—she's going to fall into the water [Some Spanish words among which was *Chica*].

In her conscious waking state, she was then allowed to hear the record of the sleep-talking. She spontaneously remarked that *Chiquita* is the name of her sister. No further recollection of the dream was stimulated nor was any new thought. She seemed surprised that she had talked in her sleep at all.

She was then hypnotized and asked to recall her dreams. In this state, accounts of two dreams were elicited:

I had that feeling when I went to bed last night that I was going to make a lot of noise as soon as I went to sleep and ah—somehow I was trying to—praying to God that I wouldn't make too much noise and scare you and wake you up. I don't know why I make a lot of noise when I dream sometimes and—ah—I felt kind of embarrassed.

I was dreaming that I—I was dreaming that I was with you. [brief pause] Yes, I remember now. You were ordering me to dream and—ah—I was asking you why—why must I dream? Then you told me because you wanted me to dream—then I was trying to figure out why must I dream instead of just going to sleep then—then I remember about—uh—you walking out of the room being mad at me and I went to sleep; and then I remember my kid sister, she was running toward the bridge and she was going to jump into the water and I was telling my mother and brother to stop her—don't let her jump into the water, but she did jump—my brother got her out of there—she was crying—and she was crying she was sorry she had jumped into the water.

E: Is there any other detail that you remember?

S: They were all crying because she didn't jump — no, because she *was saved* and my brother got her out of the water. We were all crying with happiness.

E: Is there any other detail that you remember?

S: No, I don't.

Next, her sleep-talking was played back. Her facial expression was one of recognition of something familiar—interest, a slight smile and knowing nodding of her head. She was asked what thoughts hearing her sleep-talking provoked, and the following was elicited:

S: It reminds me of when [a few unintelligible words] of me dreaming—[a few unintelligible words]—you had some fight with me." [Pause during which time she had difficulty finding words]—I feel like I am having this fight all over again with you.

E: Do you feel it unpleasant to dream?

S: Yes.

E: Why? Can you tell?

S: Yes, because I have no reason why I should feel this way about you and I dreamed (?) funny. I have this fight with you and this argument and your walking out of the room and being mad at me. [She sounded contrite and embarrassed.]

Her responses to her hearing the second part of her sleep-talking were as follows: "My sister was going to jump into the water and—uh—she did jump—my brother—she almost drowned—but I guess she didn't. [Pause during which she became visibly agitated during this phase of her account.] We're all very happy that she didn't drown and my mother and my brother and me—".

She was asked if she had any idea why she had just then started to cry and she replied, "I feel like it was just happening this very moment, and I still feel like it's happening all over again [weeps more freely]."

It is of interest that on the previous evening prior to the beginning of the experiment and while she was being chauffered to the laboratory, she remarked spontaneously that her younger adopted sister was to be married in the near future. She expressed extreme disapproval especially because the groom was too young and had no ambition. Was her sister "taking the plunge" against advice?

Experiment III. At 5:17 a.m., 6¾ hr after retiring, spoken words were heard through the intercom. At 6:20, she awakened spontaneously, ending her night's sleep. In normal wakefulness, she gave the following account of her dreams:

> I was telling you about some trouble I had with Dr. M. I didn't explain to you. I thought you knew about it. As far as I remember, I was telling you that I never expected such a thing from him, and then you said, "Oh, the rat," referring to him. Then I walked into that office next door. You started writing some papers at the desk. I stood here sitting with a man and after a while you called me, "Carmen! Carmen!, where did you get the middle name from?" It sounded funny to me that you asked me such a question—it seemed like none of your business. I thought you should know that my middle name was French. Then you asked me, "Come, tell me where you got your middle name from?"—and then the man sitting with me answered you. He said, "She got her middle name from France," and then I was repeating my name to myself in my thoughts. It was my great grandmother's name.

She recalled no other dream fragment and denied awareness of sleep-talking. In her morning hypnosis, her dream recall was:

> I was with my children—I was with my daughter in the house. Somebody rang the bell. I told her to see who it was and it was my two boys coming from school. I was downstairs in the basement and as I came I saw my Junior, my second son—he was all dirty and his books from school were all full of dirt. I asked him what happened to him. He told me another boy pushed him into a hole where they tore down the school. I asked his brother John if he knew who the boy was. I turned around to Junior and said, "You shouldn't come that way—you should come the other way so those boys wouldn't push you into those holes," and then I told him, "Look at yourself—all dirty—books all dirty." I can't remember any more.

I inquired as to whether she remembered any other dream. At first she said she couldn't remember. When I repeated the question, however, she replied, "Yes, but not too clear," and proceeded to recount:

I was sitting here with a man. I was telling this man that I've given you complaint about Dr. M. Something had to be done. The man asked me what you had to say about it. I said that you said Dr. M. was a rat and you were going to send him a letter telling him so. You walked into your office and started writing down what must have been that letter and then you called me by my first name, "Carmen! Carmen!, where did you get your middle name from?" I didn't answer you. I thought it was none of your business, but the man sitting with me answered you, saying, "She got her middle name from France." After he said that, it came to my mind that it's true—my name was French, and then I started to say my name. Then you finished your letter, but I never saw it. That's all.

Because of a breakdown in the tape-recorder playback mechanism on this particular morning, it was impossible for the subject to hear her somniloquy at that time. This was arranged 10 days following the experiment. It turned out that the sleep-speech was in Spanish and consisted of a group of comments that resembled one end of a telephone conversation, not only in content but also in style (with pauses for replies, etc.) and tone of voice. She translated these tape-recorded comments literally as follows during normal wakefulness:

Rosa, Rosa [her daughter's first name]—Kid—go and open the door. Hurry up—caramba—it sounds like somebody is knocking. [pause] Make sure you close the door. Junior, Junior—oh my God, what happened to you? Look at your clothes—they're dirty. [pause] John, didn't you see who pushed him? Caramba—look at how he dirtied the books. [pause] look, tomorrow when you quit school, don't pass that way. Chico, you don't realize that somebody might push you again. [slight pause] Yes—(like somebody giving me excuses)—don't pass by there any more. Go the other way and you, John—yes mm.—hm— [slight pause] well—well—anyway [these latter three words were spoken in English in the original] you go with your brother and be watching the kid—then nothing happens to him on the way because he is so dumb.

The dream that corresponded to this somniloquy had not been recalled during normal wakefulness, being elicited only during the morning hypnosis. During the session 10 days later in which she heard and translated her sleep-speech during normal wakefulness, she was also subsequently apprised of the content of the corresponding dream, and she likewise did not remember the dream. Evidently, there was something about this dream which was not easily compatible with wakeful recall. It is not immediately clear why it was barred from recall.

Experiment IV. During the hypnosis, which was induced prior to retiring on this particular occasion, the subject was reminded of the previous experiment. Inquiry was made as to the reasons for talking with one dream and not the other. She replied in essence that in the dream about her middle name she did not speak *words;* she only had thoughts. Although this seemed like a clever excuse rather than an explanation, in view of the reasonable clarity of the posthypnotic suggestion, the point was not pressed. It is possible, however, that like the second subject previously presented, this was an example of the literalness so commonly seen with hypnotic subjects. Accordingly, she was then instructed to try to describe *everything* she dreamed aloud—her thoughts, the events, what she and others say, etc., just like a new reporter might do on TV.

At 2:35 a.m., 3 hr and 50 min after retiring, the longest sleep-speech of the series thus far was recorded. At 2:58 a.m. she awoke announcing a need to urinate. She was in good humor and said spontaneously, "I've been sleeping like a log." There was no spontaneous mention of a dream. I asked if she had dreamt or said anything in sleep. She replied, "No, nothing tonight so far." She was not apprised of the sleep-speech heard 25 min earlier. At 6:00 a.m., she awoke spontaneously, recalling no content of her dreams. She denied even having the feeling that she had dreamed at all.

The sleep-speech was once more in Spanish. She was allowed to hear the playback and translated it literally.[4] She was asked if it reminded her of anything she had dreamed. She replied, "No, nothing. It reminds me of something from 10 years ago—the Pastor in Sunday School [the subject was a member of the Pentecostal Church]—something from the Bible—my daughter was still a baby. But it doesn't remind me of any dream."

The translation was as follows:

I go through a pathway—there is many, many stones like with fire—then I go crying, I go crying and asking, asking that somebody get me out of there. I find myself going up a pathway, up, up, up, like in the top of the mountain—it is Him—there He is—dressed in white and He is offering me His hands—He takes me to the top of the mountain—He shows me two ways and He says to me, "Which way do you want to choose—this way that has many flowers or this way that has many thorns?" And there I think I do not know what to decide—that the flowers are so pretty but on the other side of the flowers I see fire and I see sulfur and the flowers were wilting. Nevertheless, on the other side, the way that the thorns are at the end, I see many white flowers and I see many people who are very happy—and then He turns to me and says, "If you choose the way that is to the left, you will live happy here—then at the end what will be is eternal death, but nevertheless if you choose this way you will suffer here but at the end you will have eternal life and live very happy."

At 8:05 a.m., she was hypnotized and asked to recall her dreams of the previous night. Her response was as follows:

---

[4]Although not fluent in Spanish, I have sufficient familiarity with it to corroborate the general accuracy of the subject's translation.

I dreamed that I was going through a pathway and there was many many stones underneath my feet—like with fire, and I'm walking through that pathway and then I'm going up, up to a hill and I see a man standing at top, at the top of a hill—just like—like Jesus—and He's all dressed in white and He's offering me His hands and I go up to Him and we go up to the top of a—it's like a big mountain. He shows me two ways—one way to the left and another one to the right—and then He asks me which way I do choose—like which way do I choose—which way do I want to go through—if I want the one on the right [pauses and thinks]—Yes—if I want the one on the *right*—He says to me I will have happiness. I will live happy but then I will have eternal death. I look at the ways and I see a beautiful way—so many red roses—so pretty that way but like on the other side—on the other side of the flowers—I see something like—something like—something like sulfur or fire burning—I saw the flowers were starting to wilt. I don't know which way I should decide—the beautiful way or the way with the thorns—which He already showed me. He says to me, "If you choose this way, this one on the left—it would be—your life is going to be all sufferings but at the end you are going to live happy—but if you choose *this* way you're going to be happy here but then it's nothing but death at the end"—I feel like I been crying, but then all of a sudden I don't feel like crying any more.

No other dream was recalled.

Further Experiments

At this point in the research (1960), it was decided to present the results of these experiments to Dr. William Dement and Dr. Charles Fisher, then both at Mount Sinai Hospital in New York City. It seemed to us that the next logical step was repetition of the previous experiments with the addition of the new monitoring techniques involving observation of REMs and EEG.

The next four experiments were performed using this method in the sleep laboratory of Dr. William Dement, who carried out the electrographic procedures and interpretation of the findings.

Experiment V. This experiment was performed without hypnosis in order to have available at least one baseline night for comparison. The record was judged to be completely normal. There were three REM periods and the REM time percent was 18.4. There was no spontaneous somniloquy. There had been a lapse of about 6 weeks between Experiment IV and Experiment V. During this time, the subject announced spontaneously that she had ceased talking in her sleep completely at home, according to her husband's report. She had the feeling that she might "give something away."

Between Experiment V and Experiment VI, there was an additional lapse of about 3 months. On the night of Experiment VI, she said that her husband reported that she had resumed sleep-talking at home but only in mumbles.

Experiment VI. This experiment repeated the method of Experiments I–IV but included the EEG and EOG monitoring technique. Six and one quarter hours after retiring, the subject talked in her sleep. Thirty-six minutes later, she awakened spontaneously, completing her night's sleep. In her conscious waking state, she said that she believed she dreamed but recalled no content. She stated that she did not think that she had talked in her sleep. She was asked what gave her that feeling and she replied:

> When I talk a lot in my dreams, in the morning my head feels something like a little lighter. I don't know—it is a funny feeling around in my head.
> *E:* And how does your head feel now?
> *S:* Not this morning.

She was then asked to describe this "funny feeling" a little further. Her remarks were not clear, but the general sense of them was that she compared this "funny feeling" to that which is in one's head when one tries to remember something difficult to recall.

In the hypnotic state immediately following, she recounted the following dream:

> I remember I was going some place with my babe and I was to meet you and another doctor in a big office and then when I was walking, holding my babe; the baby started to cry and I looked down and he had something like a bite on his stomach and I left him and I walked toward your place where I was supposed to meet you. I didn't see you at all in your place and I then thought you had changed your mind—you didn't go there to meet me. And then I remembered dreaming I was in my house and then I went to the front of the house and then I saw a man and a moving van stop in front of the house and I called my husband. I asked him to come and see, somebody was moving from that bad (?) building. I remember telling him it must be a woman that lives up there—who's moving out—and uh—I noticed they brought down a big package from the people they were moving out—and that's all.

The subject said that the just-cited passage was two separate dreams. She also said that she could recall no other dreams but believed nevertheless she dreamed more than the foregoing account.

Immediately after recounting her dreams, while still in hypnosis, she was allowed to hear the playback of her own somniloquy and literally translated it thus:

> Listen—look Papi [nickname for her husband]—that is the people of the moving van, from across the street, yes, look. Listen to me, look, upstairs went that man, the one from the moving van. Must be the woman from the second floor. Looks like she is moving out. Must be that blonde one who is moving out.

Look, listen, they are taking down a package of something. I wonder what is in it.

The sleep-speech and 2nd dream show clear 1st order order concordance.

The EEG concomitants of the foregoing episode were as follows: The third and last REM period of the night, after 27.5 min of progress, suddenly ceased coincident with a small body movement in the form of a single jerk. Hard on its heels followed a cough and a clearing of the throat (not uncommon in sleep-talkers) and the onset of somniloquy in Spanish. The EEG muscle-tension artifact lasted about 10 sec and was followed by 10 min of sustained alpha rhythm in all leads and *no* body movements. For the first seven of these 10 min, particularly at the beginning, there were observed eye movements that were slightly atypical in that they were more regular and smaller than those of the typical REM period. This segment was brought to a close by a second body movement, and within 3–4 min, the subject was in Stage 2 sleep. REM time percent was 17.1, TST was 5½ hr, and TSP was 6 hr 50 min.

Experiment VII.   It was decided that in this experiment an attempt would be made to compare the EEG findings observed in Experiment VI to those accompanying "natural" sleep-talking. Unfortunately, we had no guarantee that she would spontaneously talk in her sleep on any particular night. In order to save time, she was given a posthypnotic suggestion, prior to retiring, to "talk in your sleep just like you used to do at home before we started any experiments."[5] There was an additional variable in the procedure—her hypnosis was induced on this night in the presence of a virtual stranger (Dr. Fisher), who was visiting.

The results of this experiment were negative—sleep-talking was not heard. The dreams recalled in the morning were replete with reference to the stranger–observer, who was distorted into an unwanted and feared monster. During the morning hypnosis, she spoke of her resentment of his presence with petulance—he was an intruder and she would "never talk in her sleep while he was there." The REM time percent was 28.2, the TST, 7 hr 35 min, and the TSP, 8 hr 25 min.

Experiment VIII.   It was decided to repeat the previous experiment (VII) without the presence of people new to the subject; i.e., the PHS once more was to "talk in your sleep just as you used to do at home before the experiments started."

At 3:56 a.m., about 4 hr 20 min after retiring, she talked in her sleep in English. At 7:20, she awakened spontaneously, completing her night's slumber.

---

[5]I am indebted to Dr. Charles Fisher for the wording of this suggestion.

During her conscious waking state, she related the following; she felt she had two dreams the previous night but could only recall one.

> I remember talking to my daughter—like I was angry (?) with her on account of her school work. She was telling me it wasn't her fault, it was the teacher's fault and that she did her homework all the time—and I was mad at her—I was telling her we were going to punish her. I had spoken to—I believe, it must have been the teacher, I had spoken about her [pause] and, uh, I was telling her I was gonna check her homework and see all the work she did in school and if she didn't I was going to get her out from school—I was mad at her—my goodness! That's all.

The subject felt that she had talked in her sleep but remembered none of it. She was at a loss to explain how she knew she talked in her sleep—she again referred to "that feeling in her head" and then said, "I really can't explain it." During her morning hypnosis, she recalled the following dreams:

> I was going with my husband to school in the evening and I was talking to my daughter's teacher about her work in school and the teacher was telling me that my daughter was not doing the work she should do and that she acts like she's not interested in the school and that she *can* do better than she is doing—and I tell her I'm sorry to hear that but I didn't know she was doing so bad in school since she does so much homework in the house and she's always looking at books and suppose might be making believe that she is doing homework and maybe she doesn't do it. But they even tell me that she doesn't bring in the homework sometimes, in school—and then they tell me if she continues this way she's gonna fail and she's had very poor marks, even in the tests they give her. And I'm tellin' her maybe I should take her out from school—and let her stay home if she's not gonna do the work she's supposed to do in school.
>
> And then I dreamed about a telephone call I made to a friend of mine in the hospital—and I was supposed to bring in my son. I called up to find out if I could bring him in—and my friend told me that he'll have to speak to the doctor first about it because they didn't have any beds available now in the hospital. And I was telling him about my son's condition—he had a bad cold and I had to have that operation—soon. He said he would find out for me and let me know—that's all.

She recalled no other dreams.

She was allowed to hear her somniloquy that consisted of the following tape-recorded speech in English:

> Come on—yes—hurry—I don't want to be late. We are almost there. That's the teacher. Good evening. We are Rosa's parents.—Yes, I understand that she has been doing very poor school work. OK I tell you the truth. I help her as much as I can. She always is doing her homework. I don't know what I'm going to do with that kid. All she can do is doing her hair and changing her dress and fooling

around. I don't know what I'm going to do with that kid. I tell you what I'll do. I am going to talk to her and I am going to check her homework every single night. And then we'll see. If this goes on she might as well stay home.

After hearing her "sleep-speech" played back, while still in deep hypnosis, she said that it did not come as a surprise; i.e., there was nothing said that she did not remember; and that it seemed as though she had been "half awake and half asleep" at the time of the episode—a state described as feeling different from that of the ongoing hypnosis of the moment. Thus, the two were phenomenologically distinguishable, though overlapping.

The EEG and EOG concomitants of this episode of sleep-talking were as follows: At 3:35 a.m., the subject was awake by EEG criteria and remained so until 3:38, at which time she returned to Stage 1 NREM sleep. This was followed, beginning at 3:41, by a long period of waking EEG lasting until about 4:12, at which time she drifted back into Stage 1 NREM for about 4 to 5 min. By about 4:20, she was behaviorally awake. At 3:50, against this waking EEG background, there was observed an isolated eye movement, which was followed by eye movements of increasing frequency. They were of the slightly atypical variety that had been observed in Experiment VI. At 3:45, she "spoke in her sleep." Body movements were insignificant throughout this entire episode—much less than usually observed in a person who is awakening. The total number of REM periods was four; TSP was 7:27; TST was 6:13; and TRT was 1:55; REM time was 30.8. (The episode of somniloquy was not included in the REM time calculations.) The sleep-utterance occurred about 1 hr following the end of the second REM period and ended about ¾ hr before the beginning of the third REM period.

Experiment IX. This experiment occurred 3 years after the preceding one. The subject arrived at the laboratory in a tearful, agitated state out of worry over her daughter Rosa, who was in the hospital psychiatrically ill. Customary electrographic technique was utilized, and prior to retiring, she was hypnotized and given the posthypnotic suggestion as in previous experiments to talk in her sleep and describe her natural dreams whenever she had them, without awakening out of sleep (Procedure E). The subject had earlier expressed doubts about her ability to comply with the PHS because of her emotional agitation concerning her daughter.

The results were as follows: While in her first NREM sleep of the night, about 1 hr after retiring, Stage 3 was interrupted by a small body movement and precipitately succeeded by sustained alpha rhythm in the EEG and occasional REMs. After 5 min in this state, she began to talk emotionally for about 100 sec and fell silent for about 350 sec. Without significant electrographic change, the subject having remained in sustained alpha all the while, she resumed speaking. At first, it dealt with a quiet, contemplative scene of looking with interest at some young girl, but then escalated to an agitated, angry crescendo. This second speech lasted for about 248 sec; and 136 sec later she spontaneously called my name announcing that she was awake, felt ill, had a headache, wished to urinate, and desired some water. After returning from the bathroom, she seemed more composed, the headache had disappeared suddenly, and she seemed a little surprised that there were no tears on her face, as she had the impression that she had been weeping. She had little specific recall of her mentation prior to her spontaneous awakening. The verbatim transcript (slightly edited) follows, including the two sleep-speeches, the post-sleep mentation report following the spontaneous awakening, and the morning recall of her previous night's experiences as elicited first in normal wakeful consciousness and then under hypnosis.

The subject's first sleep-speech (depressed sounding—low volume) follows:

Oh—ooh—oh—I mbl it caramba—oh—she has me so nervous—you know, sometime—mbl when she was away—you know, doctor—mbl—I was mbl when she was away Doctor Arkin but what to do? tsk—oh my goodness, you know somethin?—I don't know, I thought I was going to die [weeps audibly]. I thought she was going to be sick mbls like last time. I dunno know what to do [sobs, moans and cries—25 sec] OK—OK I shouldn't be crying right now, I shouldn't be crying—mbls to live (?) (I can't help it (?)) [more moaning—35 sec] that poor kid, I'm so sorry for her—I'm so sorry for her, Doctor [moans 10 sec] oh please mbl. (Don't be talking to me (?)) to me anymore about it—mbls [moans]. That poor kid, she's been so sick [moans—10 sec]

I really don't want to talk about it—I didn' want to mention it anymore [p] OK—OK, Thank you very much Doctor—G'Bye, now—

I don't think I'll ever want to speak to—anybody about it, not even (a doctor (?)), I don't want to—I want to forget about it maybe, mbl forget about it—mbls [moans 45 sec—rhythmically at first and then slowly tapering off].

The second sleep-speech was recorded as follows:

I'm standing on a big hill—mbls (this girl (?))—she has long hair or she's a boy— and she's stood (?) looking on me—I'm trying to see her face, but (?) she's not my daughter—she's somebody else, and then [p] oh, I see her chest oh boy, she has—she has a bad lung—oh—mbl—I can see the x-rays of her du-chest—oh, she has a bad lung—it's black all over on one side—like if she has TB—I know she's lookin' at me but I—I don't know who she is at all—it seems like I know her but I didn'—I've never seen her before—I'm calling her—I think she doesn't want to listen to me—she's running away from me now—she's going down the hill, I'm trying to catch up with her—I call her but she doesn't want to listen to me [louder and "lived-in"] come on! Stop! Stop, come! I want to talk to you! Come! (tsk) [louder and angry] Hey! Don't be afraid of me! Come on! [Shouts!] COME *ON!* [Screams] COME *ON!* I'M *CALLING* YOU! *HEY,* YOU LITTLE JERK, COME *HERE!'*—HEY-Y—Y [p] [softer] Come on! [softly whimpers] Oh! Oh, I did it—It's all right—she'll come back—she'll come back—I hope she comes back, anyway—mbl she looks like just (?) such a beautiful girl but I can't see—I don't, uh—I have never seen her before—somehow she looks familiar but—she has long hair—and then—all of a sudden she's a boy, aah?—I don't quite know who she is at all—(tsk) poor kid, and she has such a bad lung—she doesn't even know about it (tsk)—well—(tsk) mmmm—I suppose they'll probably let her know, you know—but maybe they'll let her know—that she has a bad lung [p] oh—(tsk) [silence 30 sec] I know I'm only talking to myself, I shouldn' be doing it—(tsk) yeah—aah, it's kinda foolish but I can't help it, I feel sorry for that kid—(tsk). I feel sorry for her—(tsk) aah! if only she knew she's so sick from de chest—aah!—um—mbl 'll happen I just worry over everybody, I dunno, mm [silence about 130 sec].

With the subject awake, the following post-speech mentation report was obtained:

(S): Um, mm, mbl. Dr. Arkin! Hello! I'm awake! Oh boy, I have a headache. I have a headache. I have a headache doctor, could you come in and give me some water, please.

[E enters]: Mbl—my headache.

E: Do you want to go to the bathroom?

S: Mm—hm (?).

E: Did you have a dream?

S: I dunno know.

E: Hah?

S: Mbl - a nightmare or something.

E: A nightmare about what?

S: I can't remember it.

E: Nothing at all?

S: Mbls No—mbls.

E: Try to think of what the nightmare was about.

S: Mm—I have a feeling I was running [laughs]—I have a funny feeling I was running.

E: You don't remember any dream at all?

S: Mbl—as if I was running.

E: As if you were running?

S: Mm—mm that the (?) girl was running.

E: As if you were running?

S: Mm—hm.

E: That's all you remember about the dream?

S: Mm [silent pause].

E: Can't remember anymore?

S: [long pause] Mbl—talking to somebody [pause] mbls—I feel sorry [apologetically].

The subject returned to sleep in a few mintues.

The subject reported the following morning recall of her previous night's experiences in normal wakeful consciousness.

E: I'd like to have you tell whatever you remember of your dreams of last night—*every* detail you can remember.

S: Um—I don't know—I really don't remember much—when I—uh—woke up last night, I felt like I—I didn't—feeling like I had been—running and I had a—terrific headache—I *thought* I had one—when I called you—you know, and uh—by the time I got to the bathroom, the headache disappeared—I forget about it—and uh—I don't really remember—having dreams but, I had the feeling like that when I—like when I'm in the house and I have a nightmare or something like that, and my husband wakes me up and uh, like if—that night and it felt like if I had been running after something—or like wanting to catch a person, it wasn't an animal, it was a person, whether it was a girl or a boy, I really didn't—don't remember—and then—that was the kind of feeling I had when I woke up. And remembering like if I had been dreaming. I don't know the minute I sat up in bed, it kind of snaps out of my head—I try to remember and I try and I try, if, if I uh tell about it before I sit up like when I'm in the house I tell my husband I usually remember—parts of it.

E: Well, now—did this—what happened last night, did this feel like anything that goes on at home—ever?

S: No, no. It feels, it uh—it—part of it, I think part of it, it's something I am very familiar with. As like uh—my daughter—one of my kids.

E: No—I mean—.

S: But uh, when I woke up, dat wasn't the feeling, it was a feeling like if I had been [p] you know—uh, like reading somebody else's ideas.

E: Like what?

S: Like reading somebody else's ideas.

E: Reading somebody else's ideas?

S: Uh huh.

E: That you've been—.

S: Like if I had been reading somebody else's idea—Uh either from a book or I don't know dat's just, just—.

E: Now what, in other words, what went on last night, was that *like* one of these nightmares you have at home?—or was it different?

S: It was a little bit different, it was a little bit different. Uh I never really felt so—upset about it. 'Cause, I was, I didn't have a headache when I got to the bathroom, I didn't have a headache and, when I woke up my head shh uh oh.

E: Did you feel more upset here than at home, or less upset?

S: Well, I was a little, little bit upset here, not that I wanted to, it's just that when I went to the ladies room and I saw this man[6] uh uh it got a little bit of the, of the relaxation which I could have you know. For, I don't know why cause, it's just foolishness, I guess.

---

[6]The subject encountered a member of the janitorial staff, apparently, while on her way to using the conveniences.

E: But, uh, you see what I want to know is that experience you had last night with the waking up, what did that *feel* like? You say that didn't feel like the kind of dream you had at home ever or nightmare?

S: No. No. No, no.

E: You never had anything like this at home?

S: I *do* get—but not—I usually I don't, I don't wake up to go to the bathroom, I don't like to go to the bathroom.

E: What does happen at home?

S: Well, my husband wakes me up and he makes me sit up and he maybe says something?

E: What does he say?

S: Aaah—you are going crazy.

E: Why does he say that?

S: Oh, he says I talk a lot of nonsense.

E: He says that you said that, that you have been talking a lot of nonsense.

S: Um, that I have been carrying on like as if I was a child and I make things look so big, my gracious—so he says.

E: But yet that feels different to you than—.

S: Well, in my house, I um, my husband wakes me up and the minute he holds me, I know it's not true.—because somehow I have the feeling that it's true what I am dreaming and well it's been going on for so many years he's getting used to it.

E: Yeh.

S: And, well, I am getting used to it too. And uh, when he wakes me up I know it's not true and I try to forget it.

E: But here?—

S: Well, here, I forgot it—but—I been trying to think of what it was it—that gave me that feeling, so miserable feeling when I woke up.

E: Well, what would you say?—.

S: I went to sleep—trying to recollect in my mind what happened—.

E: Would you say that you had a dream—was that a dream when you woke up or was it something else?

S: It was it was uh a little—it was a dream, but it was—I think like—I was tossing from one side to the other, in bed and—I had the feeling I tried to talk or something last night.

E: Tried to what?

S: To talk.

The subject was then hypnotized, and the remainder of the interview occurred during this hypnosis.

E: Now think as hard as you can and try to remember everything you dreamt last night and tell me. Try as hard as you can, try to tell me everything of every dream you had last night.

S: I was—I was taking my daughter, some place like, uh, it looks like—like a to visit a friend. You know my daughter's room—.

E: Mm.

S: And then after she is in that place, I am talking to—a friend, and it's about her on a telephone—and I am explaining that she has been very sick, she has been very sick but I never thought that really she was—so—so sick like I— like she really is—and then—my friend is trying to tell me to—take it easy and to try to forget that it really isn't true, that it really isn't so bad—and I'm crying for a little while there, and I am trying to—take it easy—but uh—it keeps coming back to my mind every time I think about it. I, I get very— worried about her. And then I decide to forget it. Better to forget it. And I think the other person was listening; hung up the telephone or somethin'— and then I remember, I remember—being up in a place—in a place very— very high like a oh, like a—like a little uh—like a little, like a small mountain,—and I was standing on top of it and I see—I see this girl. And she's a very young girl about 18 or 20 years old. She has, uh, oh she has very long hair, but she is dressed in—in slacks, er, somehow she resembles a boy. I see—I see her chest—I look at her and I can see through her clothes, she has some kind of uh—some kind of disease in her uh—her uh an her chest like in the lungs. Uh, she turns—she turns to me but I don't see her—I don't—I only see her from here down, from the shoulders down, I don't see her face, I don't see her face, uh I am trying to see if I can see her face but I can't. I can't, she turns around and she is running—I'm trying to tell her to uh—stop and let me tell her that she is sick she needs something—she needs to see a doctor or something; uh, now I see her—both her lungs, I see now—it is just like, like I was looking at an x-ray film. You know? Have you seen them?"

E: Uh hum.

S: And then, she has one uh of her lungs is all black,—one of them is all black from the—disease or something she must have but she is running from me, I want to tell her, and I am running to try to catch her but I couldn't catch her at all. Like uh, it is no use, she disappear running. [p] Now I remember how dis, dis uh uh commanding myself to be quiet uh uh to rest and to sleep and to stop talking and to stop all this—And I am having a hard time to to to convince myself to go to sleep. [p] I don't remember anything else.

E: You remember no other detail, or any other dream?

S: I, I was—oh I had this small dream, I had this small dream, I was, I was walking you know, I was walking in, in a—like in a pathway like dis, straight not a pathway like this, like in an open field—and somebody grabbed me like this—.

E: Uh, hum.

S: Really, I have been trying, I have been trying to talk and I have been trying to say something and—and I don't know what really got me if it was a hand (?) something, something really got me. I been trying to fight it and take it off my mouth and I could never do it, it was something, really, very, very strong— Now I, I don't really know, I don't remember—.

E: You don't remember anything else?

S: No, I don't remember anything else.

E: Now is there any way, is there any difference between the dream you told me about the girl with the diseased lungs and these other dreams?

S: Which other dreams?

E: The dream about talking with a friend, about Rosa and the dream about this hand over your mouth.

S: Oh *yes,* dis, dis, a dis last dream was kind of frighten, dis—somebody holdin, tried to grab me, holdin me like this and dis, and dis one idea, the girl with the lungs, this is horrifyin'. Ugh!

E: But do they both feel like the same kind of dream? I mean would you call them all dreams or would you call some dreams and the others something different?

S: Oh, the last one is a dream. Dis one is a dream. It has been like a, uh, it it feels like a a dream.

E: But the first—?

S: The first one, I would call it a nightmare, I think I would call it a nightmare—just a—

E: Which would you call?—

S: Just like a nightmare, and dis, this one with dis other girl—I would like to give her a name—It's worse than a nightmare. It's, you know, it's like a, like a revelation, dat's dat's what it looks like, like a, a, I am seeing things that are going to happen soon or what happenin'—dat's the way I think I would call this dream, about this girl, like a revelation—like a—something that should be looked into—make sure it's true or false—Dat's the way it feels, I feel about this dream about this girl, or this, uh, uh, trouble in her chest or something, the disease.

E: That's the dream that feels like a revelation.

S: Uh, hum.

E: And uh you know [persisting] would you call all of them dreams? Would you call all of them dreams? or would you call one a dream and one something else?

S: I would call them, one a dream, one a dream, and the others—*nightmares* [despairingly].

E: What's the difference between a dream and nightmare?

S: It well, in a dream, uh nothing much happens, it's like a a like, it feels like when you are under a drug, or—a—like when you are under a drug, one of these uh, one of these anaesthetics that they use in the hospitals, and in a nightmare, it's a, its a, it's a strong feeling, a very strong feeling, that—it's different, it's different completely—it's different completely, in a dream you feel relaxed, and in a nightmare you feel awful. You feel—ugh! Tense and sick and everything. It's kind of a like there was a battle going on in the head and in the body. It's not a good feeling at all.

E: Which would you call a nightmare last night?

S: I think I would call, I'd call nightmare the first two I had. Those I would call nightmares.

E: The first two being which?

S: About me walking with my daughter going to this place and then when I was speaking about her I would call that a nightmare.

E: And the other?

S: And this other one, and dis dis girl that was a nightmare, ita, ita, ita, it has some kind of a, a some kind of a a uh, it has some kind of a—influence on me, I suppose, on me. Thata, I call it a nightmare.

E: The one about the girl with the diseased lungs?
S: Yes.

Discussion: Subject #3

The paucity of experiments with electrographic recording and the variety of experimental conditions makes interpretation of the results of this subject hazardous or impossible. To this consideration must be added the lack of adequate baseline nights without PHS on which to base comparisons. Why then were the observations reported at such length and in such detail? There were several reasons:

1. The phenomenological and several electrographic findings are similar in most respects to the relatively rare occurrences of spontaneous macrodissociative sleep-speech episodes in the laboratory. Thus far, we have at least the following laboratory observations on events fulfilling criteria for sleep-related macrodissociative somniloquy:
   a. Batson's report of a spontaneous, extensive sleep-speech against a background of sustained alpha (Fig. 7.5 and Speech #572 in Appendix 2);
   b. Sleep-speech numbers 7–15 (Appendix 2) emitted by PHS subject number 1 as described earlier in this chapter, during his terminal baseline series;
   c. Rice and Fisher's report (1976) of a fascinating case study of a patient with fugue states occurring in association with both sleep and wakefulness, together with extensive spontaneous speech uttered in both conditions; and
   d. Fisher, Kahn, Edwards, & Davis' report (1975) of sleep-speech in association with Stage 4 night-terrors, as well as those of Gastaut and Broughton (1965).

Because laboratory observation of these sorts of events are difficult to come by, it seems worthwhile to describe such findings in detail when obtained so that material is available for a review of the topic in the future, when a sufficient number of similar phenomena have been reported on. After all, it is not likely that any one investigator would have an opportunity to collect a large series of such cases in order to carry out a detailed comparison of similarities and differences between the various types of macrodissociative occurrences. Along these lines it is interesting that some of the sleep-speeches of our female PHS subject occurring within the earlier part of the night suggest a resemblance between the phenomena observed and the Stage 4 night-terrors described by Gastaut and Broughton (1965) and Fisher *et al.* (1974). We have no way of deciding the case definitely with the first tumultuous episode recorded without electrographic monitoring in Experiment I; but a resemblance is suggested by the two electrographically monitored agitated speeches of Experiment IX occurring about 1 hr after bedtime.

At least two points run counter to the notion, however, that the PHS phenomena in this subject and those of Stage 4 night-terrors are basically similar. The affective tone of the episodes following PHS seem to fall short of the intensity and strident terror of those reported by Fisher et al. (1975) and Gastaut and Broughton (1965). And in the typical Stage 4 night-terror, the subject on entering the arousal episode from Stage 4 does not temporize with a preliminary silent interval in sustained alpha frequencies but rather suddenly begins to vocalize agitato et fortissimo, whereas the female PHS subject spent an initial 5 min in sustained alpha prior to uttering a sound.

2. For the most part, the results of the experiments are in conformity *phenomenologically* with the PHS. That is, the subject did in fact talk in association with behavioral and subjective if not electrographic sleep, and the accompanying mentation was clearly concordant with experiences spontaneously designated as dreams or nightmares by her. We have no way of knowing, however, whether the subject *acted* on the PHS or whether she reproduced in the laboratory a type of macrodissociation episode she had been prone to producing at home for many years. Perhaps the PHS, in some instances, served to merely activate more or less prior-formed mechanisms of such dissociations. In any case, detailed descriptions of such events are rare and deserve full presentation.

3. The phenomena of psychic dissociation are intrinsically interesting to students of cognition because of what they imply about the potentialities of mental processes. Specifically, the findings demonstrate the possibility that under conditions where brain function is neither altered by drugs nor by other physical intervention, it is possible for a subject to elaborate complex, hallucinatory, dramatic mentation; respond to it; and "live in it" in the presence of sustained alpha rhythm in the EEG. This is succeeded by almost total wakeful amnesia immediately afterward. Furthermore, this amnesia is capable of removal many hours later when the subject is deeply hypnotized, at which time the unavailable information is retrievable.

Negative Results with Presleep PHS

Attempts were made to employ presleep PHS on five additional chronic sleep-talkers, all of whom were poor, resistant hypnotic subjects. They were either consciously fearful of it or hostile or refractory to hypnotic suggestions. These experiments, interestingly enough, resulted in *diminution* of sleep-talking frequency following PHS. One of the subjects spontaneously expressed anger and goadings toward himself for not producing sleep-speech because he desperately needed the money he earned by his participation. He amply somniloquized during baseline experiments but was clearly resentful of attempts to hypnotize him.

It is possible that if we had given these subjects nonhypnotic presleep instructions and training rather than attempts at PHS, they would have felt more congenial toward the procedure, less threatened, and would have produced positive results. Unfortunately, such experiments were not carried out.

General Discussion and Conclusions

The Two Male Subjects

The experiments with these subjects have shown that it is possible to experimentally induce two subjects by suggestion techniques (PHS as well as waking suggestion) to talk aloud in association with both REM and NREM sleep and provide samples of ideation reflecting ongoing sleep mentation. Although the data at hand indicate that presleep PHS has the edge over wakeful presleep instruction in capability of producing this effect, it is premature to regard this as a foregone conclusion.

It is of great interest that some of these sleep-speeches seem to reflect direct participation in elaborate, concurrent, real-to-the-subject, "lived-in" sleep experience, whereas others have a somewhat detached quality of reportage as if describing events at a distance. First-order concordance between REMP-speech–mentation-report pairs occurred in the overwhelming majority of those available for study. Further, the associated sleep mentation was frequently spontaneously described by the subjects as dreams. Also, concordance was often observed with dreams retrieved in wakeful consciousness during the following morning.

By contrast, the incidence of first-order concordance between NREM-speech–mentation-report pairs was far less, the degree of amnesia much greater, the subjects' spontaneous labeling of the preawakening mentation as a dream occurred rarely, and the concordance with morning dream recall was virtually absent.

The mentation reports associated with REMP speeches, and many of the speeches themselves, contained abundant visual, auditory, and kinesthetic imagery; whereas those reports associated with NREM speeches tended to be less vivid and skimpier in the sheer quantity of mentation.

The differences between REMP and NREM conditions closely parallel those found in spontaneous sleep-speech characteristics and in the concordance trends with their associated mentation reports. Furthermore, the qualitative and quantitative differences between REMP and NREM mentation elicited in postspeech awakenings conform quite well with those found in mentation reports elicited from REMP and NREM sleep of nonsleep-talkers. (Rechtschaffen et al. (1963a).

Moreover, the electrographic concomitants of the experimentally produced sleep-speeches were those of typical movement-arousal episodes and were indistinguishable from those typically observed in spontaneous sleep-talkers uninfluenced by experimental stimuli.

The previous findings taken together strongly suggest that the two male subjects responded positively to the PHS and/or presleep instructions and produced sleep-speeches which closely reflected ongoing sleep mentation. To what extent the subjects were "really asleep" when they somniloquized is a natural question, and this entire issue is taken up in a later chapter in relation to sleep-speech in general.

The Female Subject

Phenomenologically, our female subject yielded similar results in that she also somniloquized, the contents of which were subsequently recalled as a dream, but only under special conditions. The tendency toward amnesia for these dreams was striking, and equally impressive was the uniformity with which the amnesia could be lifted during morning hypnosis, at which time recovery of such first-order concordant material was regularly retrieved.

Electrographically, her behavior was considerably different from that of the two male subjects. All speeches occurred against a background of sustained alpha frequencies lasting for minutes rather than seconds. On no occasion was the sleep-speech "sandwiched in" between immediately preceding and following unambiguous sleep, as was the usual case with the two male subjects. In Experiment VI, a REMP came to an end with a small body movement and a sudden transition into sustained alpha rhythm, after a few seconds of which the somniloquy began. This electrographic state continued for several minutes after the sleep-speech ended, and curiously, muscle-tension activity was absent throughout. In Experiment IX, Stage 3 also came to an end with a muscle twitch and emergence of sustained alpha; but the latter continued for 5 min prior to the onset of the first sleep-speech, remained unchanged until and throughout the second speech, and outlasted the speech until spontaneous behavioral awakening about 2 min afterward. Sporadic REMs were present with each of the experimental sleep-speeches in experiments VI, VIII, and IX. And in Experiment VIII, she drifted in and out of Stages 1 NREM and W until succeeded by an interval of 1 NREM with following sustained alpha; she then produced a long sleep-speech. During the hypnosis of the morning afterward, this latter speech was remembered as part of a dream that occurred in a state intermediate between sleep and wakefulness. Thus, in all cases of somniloquy observed with this subject, the electrographic background was one of sustained alpha rhythm normally associated with relaxed wakefulness—a finding that seems difficult to reconcile with the dreamlike hallucinatory quality of the concomitant experience for which she tended to have amnesia.

The electrographic picture in Experiments VI, VIII, and IX is consistent with phenomena described by Schiff et al. (1961), in which allusion was made to an unpublished experiment indicating that the performance of all posthypnotically suggested acts (whether motor acts or dreams) that were to occur during a natural nocturnal sleep was accompanied by a return of the subject to his trance state, as defined by his EEG pattern (one of sustained alpha rhythm). As we have seen with the first two male subjects, however, this finding does not hold uniformly, for with them alpha was often absent, minimal, or not more extensive than in many naturally occurring sleep speeches.

In pondering over the electrographic results of our female subject, I was gratified to read Rice and Fisher's paper (1976) on sleep-laboratory findings in a patient with marked dissociative tendencies in wakefulness and sleep. The patient was a 46-year-old male with fugue states both by day and by night, upon whom electrographic studies revealed striking resemblances to those of our female subject. Like the latter, he had a long history of frequent screaming in his sleep, to which his spouse attested. His syndrome developed following the death of his father, to whom he was closely attached and his preoccupation with his need to deny the bereavement, was obvious and dramatic. At home, as in the laboratory, many of his fugue states arose out of sleep. The content of his "wakeful" fugue states and those observed in the laboratory, and a home nocturnal dream occurring just prior to laboratory studies, were all related to concerns about his father. Also similar to our subject was the dramatic, affect-laden quality of the utterances.

The spontaneous predormescent and two post-REMP speeches occurred during one of the laboratory nights, and a Stage 2 speech occurred shortly after the first REMP, on another night. The post-REMP speeches immediately followed an experimental awakening stimulus. All were accompanied by sustained EEG alpha frequencies. All speeches, particularly those post-REMP, reflected intense, elaborate, ongoing "lived-in," hallucinatory experience. They are worth quoting in full:

Episode A.   Predormescent; 1 min, 15 sec in duration.

Patient: He's in the hospital today. That's right. I have to wait for my father to come home. Yes, I'm going to wait for my father. No, he's not dead. He can't be dead. He's home. Yes, he's home; yes, he's home.

Episode B.   Predormescent; 3 min in duration.

Patient: I wish I knew myself or—my father mbls [sighs]. I wish my father were still here. Uh, I'll wait for him. Yes, I will wait for him. I will wait for him. [p] [Sighs] I did everything I could to keep him alive. I couldn't do any more. I spent every penny I had on nurses and doctors. I just couldn't. Well [sigh], he'll be back—one day. There's nobody really that can help me, maybe, except myself. My father, I wish he were here to help me. I wish my father was here to help me

[Sighs] Oh, well,—it's just not so mbls—. What's the—anything going on. I don't know any more. It's just terrible, terrible, it's just terrible.

Episode C.   Immediately following REMP 2; 5 min, 45 sec in duration.

Patient: [buzzer sounds] Mbls—Well, I think I see—[shouting]. What's my father doing here? My father. Hello. Here's my father, my father wants me now. My father wants me. Yes, I'm waiting for my father. Yes, I'm waiting for my father—Do you hear that noise?. That's the ambulance bringing my father home. I guess he fooled me. Everybody keeps telling me my father is dead. Do you hear that noise? That's the ambulance bringing my father home. I guess he fooled me. Everybody keeps telling me my father is dead. Do you hear that noise? That's the ambulance—it says whoop—whoop [he imitates the ambulance's sound]. Help me. I guess it's not true, it's not true. I'm going to wait right here, I know. Don't take me to the doctors anymore. Don't take me to the doctors. They can't help me. They can't help me. Nobody can help me anymore. Nobody. No, I'm going to wait here for my father. Wait here for my father— they—everybody keeps saying that he's dead and I know he *isn't* dead. He's the only one that can help me. The doctors don't seem to know. Nobody, nobody, nobody. [pause] How I wish I were dead again. Oh, well—no, no—oh—[pause] I can't stand it anymore. [pause] Oh, I can't stand it. I can't stand life anymore. There's nobody anymore. Nobody. Nobody. [Sobbing, he bangs the bed, then, more softly, slaps his body.]

Episode D.   Immediately following REMP 3; 1 min, 45 sec in duration.

E calls patient by name.
Patient: What the—who's calling him—what—[buzzer sounds]. Yeah—well, yeah, who's making that noise, who's making that noise?
E: What was going through your mind just now?
Patient: Well, uh, I don't know what you mean. Who? Who's that? I don't know. Who's talking? I'm going to sit right here [with increasing crescendo and banging] because I want my father home. [He resumes in a more normal voice.] He's not dead, I tell you. He's home—yes, I need him. What? What is it Huh? Oh [sighs], what's going on—oh, God.

Rice and Fisher (1976) state that amnesia was present for all fugal episodes, implying that this was equally true of the laboratory episodes as well. When apprised of the content of his dissociated productions during subsequent normal wakefulness, he was embarrassed and frightened. Noteworthy is the evidence of incorporation of the buzzer into the REMP dream (Episode C) and its transformation into an ambulance siren. This supports the notion of continuity between some of the mentation occurring during immediately preceding REM sleep and the subsequent speech accompanied by sustained alpha rhythm.

As previously indicated, these findings bear the following resemblances to those of our female PHS subject and Batson's "normal" subject (1977), who spontaneously produced a macrodissociative speech in the laboratory. (Fig. 7.5 and Speech #512 in Appendix 2).

Electrographic.
1. All speeches were accompanied by sustained alpha lasting minutes, rather than seconds, with all three subjects.
2. Both subjects were capable of elaborating such episodes immediately after both preceding REM sleep and predormescence, although the predormescent epoch of our female subject occurred following a prolonged spell of wakefulness in the middle of the night. The macrodissociative speech of Batson's subject (1977) was preceded by prolonged Stage 2 in the middle of the night.
3. REMs were observable during episodes of all three subjects.

Phenomenologic.
1. Amnestic tendencies for the dissociated episodes were clearly evident in all three subjects when efforts were made to induce recall. My female subject spoke openly of "wanting to forget" and Rice and Fisher's patient evinced fear and embarrassment when informed of the content of his sleep-speeches. Batson's subject was apparently unaware of having talked aloud and evinced surprise on being so informed. Amnestic tendencies were also marked with other clinically observed cases of a probably similar nature, characterized by prolonged somniloquy. Examples are to be found in the automatic-writing patient described in Chapter 19, as well as the cases of Burrell (1904) and Dion McGregor (1964). However, the unavailable events related to the nocturnal speech episodes were fully retrieved in the morning hypnosis of our female subject. It would have been most interesting to have had carried out hypnotic recall procedures with Rice and Fisher's patient.
2. The speeches of Rice and Fisher's patient, most of those uttered by my female subject, and that of Batson's subject possessed a dramatic, "lived-in," affect-laden, hallucinatory quality strongly suggestive of an imagined audience of one or more persons to whom the speeches were directed.

Because of the lack of adequate controls, we have no way of knowing definitely whether the PHS given to the female subject was specifically effective in influencing the nature of the outcome. According to her husband, she had been subject to such episodes frequently at home for an indefinitely prior interval. Perhaps she merely reproduced in the laboratory what she did at home, or perhaps the PHS merely triggered a number of these episodes in a nonspecific manner. Certainly several of them seemed to conform to the "spirit" of the PHS when they seemed to possess a component of detached reportage.

These considerations by no means rule out the possibility that the phenomena observed with the three subjects in the laboratory (Arkin & Toth, 1970; Batson, 1977; Rice & Fisher, 1976) are intimately related to sleep mentation. Rice and Fisher (1976) conclude that their data suggests continuity and interrelatedness between the psychological states involved in wakefulness, dissociated states, REM and NREM sleep, and associated sleep-speech—a point of view with which I am in partial agreement (Arkin, 1966; Arkin et al., 1972a). By "partial," I mean that such interrelatedness is indeed striking over one extremity of a continuum of psychological contents and phenomena, but it is difficult to discern at the other extremity; and there is an intermediate range between, characterized by convincing evidence of interrelatedness but with varying degrees of ambiguity.

The Persistence of Effects of Presleep Psychological Interventions During Sleep

It is of theoretical interest that experimental procedures carried out before sleep and aimed at influencing subsequent sleep behavior are capable of demonstrable effect. Such effects have been demonstrated by others. The topic has received a general review by Williams (1973), who concluded that during human sleep, analyzer mechanisms may carry on functioning so that information can be processed, encoded, categorized, and stored. Discriminated physiological and motor responses acquired prior to retiring may persist during sleep, and in certain sleep stages, it may be demonstrable that instructions and items of information received during wakefulness can persist and be effective throughout the night. This indicates that during sleep, analyzer systems have functional relations with long-term memory. Contradictory evidence was cited as to whether specific learned behavioral responses could occur without associated EEG signs of arousal. Stimulus preprocessing and encoding phases were deemed capable of occurrence during sleep without prior awakening. The experimental studies referred to were those in which the persistence of effects of presleep learning or intrasleep learning (Evans, 1969; Evans, Gustafson, O'Connell, Orne, & Shor, 1970) was demonstrated by application of stimuli externally introduced from time to time by the experimenter. Williams (1973) did not describe work in which *internally produced* biological signals were the immediately effective stimuli. Our studies described earlier involving presleep PHS and instructions are examples of the latter experimental approach; i.e., the task of the subject was to talk aloud in response to his naturally occurring dreaming—an internally produced signal. A similar experiment that further shows that such feats might be accomplished by sleepers is that of Antrobus et al. (1965), in which subjects were shown capable of spontaneously signaling with a finger switch preferentially during REM sleep, and that most of such signals indicated dreaming, although discrimination between "dreaming and nondreaming sleep" was not demonstrable; and more recently, with a similar microswitch technique, Brown and Cartwright (1977) have shown the same feat with eight subjects, and NREM ongoing dream experience.

Actually, the mere process of alerting oneself to internally produced stimuli may, in itself, have a tendency to stimulate sleep speech. Orr et al. (1968) gave seven high school students (14–18 years of age) presleep instructions to awaken themselves at arbitrarily experimenter-specified times. Four of the seven did so within 16 min of the prearranged time. "At 4:54 a.m. [one] subject woke saying to herself, "Vi, I suggest you do." It was not specified whether this was implicit or overt sleep speech, but it was a self-awakening out of REM sleep. A second subject who failed to awaken at the appointed time said at 2:30 a.m. during Stage 3 sleep "to try to wake up at 4:30." The latter figure was the correct designated time at which he should have self-awakened. And a third subject who reported no dreams also talked during Stage 3 sleep, saying, "Yes, Mamma." It is notable that all subjects who were successful in self-awakening at designated times reported dreams showing anticipation and apprehension. Such overt anxiety was observed by the experimenters at no other time. The content of the sleep speeches all seems consistent with the experimental task imposed. This study provides an interesting footnote to the technique of self-alerting required of our second male PHS subject, who was asked to find some way to induce awareness of the fact of dreaming while it was in progress. That is, Orr et al. (1968) provide independent suggestive confirmation of the feasibility of such a method and also an indication that it may play a role in itself in experimental sleep-speech production.

In conclusion, it seems to be possible for some subjects to learn to remain alert to internally produced spontaneous signs of dreaming, emit verbal or motor tokens, indicate evidence or fragments of such dreaming, carry out the production of such dreams, and participate in the experience of it all at the same time. One might object to this conclusion on the grounds that to the extent that subjects may do all of these things simultaneously, they are not "truly asleep' nor are they "truly dreaming." This point is discussed more fully later on.

STUDIES EMPLOYING
SLEEP-INFLUENCING DRUGS

Inasmuch as a variety of drugs have been shown capable of influencing sleep and specific sleep stages (Arkin & Steiner 1978), it is reasonable to expect that administration of such drugs might have effects on sleep-speech production, particularly among chronic sleep-talkers. Clinical descriptions of drug reactions, addictive drug withdrawal states, febrile conditions, and toxic psychoses commonly mention associated emotion-laden bursts of vocalization and speech. Presumably, pathological biochemical and psychoneural factors interact to produce such effects.

The Effects of Recovery from a Presleep Dextroamphetamine–Pentobarbital Combination on Sleep Utterance

In 1968, we carried out pilot studies on the effects of REM deprivation on NREM mentation, using chronic sleep-talkers as subjects (Arkin, Antrobus, Toth, & Baker, 1968). Because most sleep-utterance is associated with NREM sleep, we anticipated that sleep-speech content would provide, in addition to routine NREM mentation reports, a useful complementary source of information, especially because NREM mentation tends to be relatively difficult to retrieve following laboratory awakenings. We initially used a pharmacological method of REM deprivation to minimize subject fatigue and mental disruption occasioned by mechanical REM deprivation.

Seven male and five female paid subjects were drawn from our basic subject pool. They all spent at least three nonconsecutive nights in the laboratory: night 1 for adaptation, 2 for a prebaseline, 3 for REM recovery (REM deficit condition), and 4 for a postbaseline. (One subject had 4 baseline nights followed by his recovery night.) For all laboratory nights, the technicians were given flexible instructions to awaken subjects from seven to nine times nightly to obtain mentation reports. If the subject made no utterance whatsoever, he was to be awakened regardless every 45 min. Inasmuch as two of our technicians were inexperienced in reading sleep records, no special attempt was made to focus on particular sleep stages. If the subject *did* vocalize, he was to be awakened immediately afterward for a mentation report to a maximum of five such awakenings per night; and the remainder of the awakenings made from silent sleep were to adhere as far as possible to the 45-min schedule, taking the last postspeech awakening as a starting point. These constituted our pre- and postbaseline nights—2 and 4. Night 3 was a recovery night following 2 consecutive nights at home, during which time the subjects were REM-deprived by taking pentobarbital (100 mg) and dextroamphetamine (15 mg spansule) just before retiring on both nights. Subjects were required to avoid daytime napping and received the same awakening schedule on night 3 as on the pre- and postbaseline nights.

Results

The mean frequencies of sleep-speech episodes alone and sleep-speech plus other vocalizations were significantly greater on the recovery night (night 3) as compared to either baseline night (2 or 4). (See Table 11.9.) Specifically, the mean frequency of sleep-speech episodes alone was 1.7 and 1.9 for the pre-

TABLE 11.9
Mean Frequencies of Sleep Speech and Other Vocalizations

	Prebaseline Nights		Drug Recovery Nights		Postbaseline Nights		Comparison	
	Total Episodes	Mean	Total Episodes	Mean	Total Episodes	Mean	Prebase vs. Recovery	Postbase vs. Recovery
Sleep-speech alone	19	1.7	47	4.3	21	1.9	$p < .05^a$	$p < .05^a$
Sleep speech + other vocalizations	21	1.9	57	5.2	24	2.2	$p < .02^a$	$p < .01^a$

[a]Two-tailed t-tests.

and postbaseline nights respectively, and that of the drug recovery night was 4.3 ($p < .05$). Similarly, the mean frequency of sleep-speech plus other vocalizations was 1.9 and 2.2 for the pre- and postbaseline nights respectively, and that of the drug recovery night was 5.2 ($p < .02$). The differences were assessed by two-tailed t-tests.

Discussion

Recovery processes following two successive nights on the d-amphetamine–pentobarbital combination appear to stimulate vocalization and sleep-speech in subjects with an active history of sleep-talking. It is tempting to ascribe this result to the effects of enhanced REM sleep deficit with its consequent REM rebound on the recovery night. We did not measure REM indices because the experimental awakenings done to obtain mentation reports would have rendered such determination invalid. The surmise that a REM rebound played a direct role is based on prior demonstration that d-amphetamine–pentobarbital combinations produce marked REM suppression and subsequent rebound on recovery nights (Baekeland, 1967; Rechtschaffen & Maron, 1964). Two factors dictate caution in accepting this conclusion. First, d-amphetamine–pentobarbital combinations are capable of affecting other sleep parameters besides that of REM (Baekeland, 1967). For example, the combination of the two produces more Stage W and Stage 2, and less Stages 3 and 4, than does pentobarbital alone. The latter produces less Stage W and has no significant effect on Stages 2,3, and 4. Second, both drugs have differential effects on indices of intrasleep restlessness (motor discharges) during administration and withdrawal nights (Oswald, 1973; 1974). We have no way of knowing the nature of the interaction patterns between all of these variables. Inasmuch as sleep-utterance is correlated with movement-arousal episodes, which in turn are indicators of intrasleep restlessness, it seems equally plausible that our experimental effects were reflections of such increased motor discharge tendencies rather than direct rebound of REM phasic events displaced into NREM sleep.

Incidental observations of the effects of drugs on sleep utterance have been reported by others. The most detailed have been those of Gross, Goodenough, Tobin, Halpert, Lepore, Perlstein, Sirota, Dibianco, Fuller, and Kishner (1966) on sleep disturbances of four male patients with acute alcoholic psychoses. The general observation was that Stage REM sleep was much increased in duration and intensity, during which time frequent and elaborate episodes of sleep-utterance with speech were observable. On two occasions, mentation reports showed first-order concordance with the immediately preceding sleep-speeches. One such speech was "Hell of an express," which was associated with a dream about taking the subway from one borough of New York City to another.

Tachibana, Tanaka, Hishikawa, and Kaneko (1976), reporting on patients with delirium tremens, alcoholic hallucinosis, and meprobamate-associated delirium, likewise mention the frequent occurrence of sleep-talking. This tended to occur in a special sleep state classified by the authors as Stage 1-REM with tonic EMG as opposed to typical Stage REM. The former was characterized by: (1) relatively high tonic EMG rather than minimal EMG levels; (2) absence of "sawtooth" waves; (3) occurrence as part of sleep onset processes rather than the typical REM cycle; (4) presence of low-voltage, mixed frequency EEG activity; and (5) REM bursts. Contrary to observers reporting strikingly high proportions of Stage REM in alcoholic psychotic deliria (Gross et al., 1966; Greenberg & Pearlman, 1967), Tachibana et al. (1976) contend that it is this special Stage 1-REM rather than typical Stage REM (Rechtschaffen & Kales, 1968) that is increased. They argue against interpretation of drug deliria as the simple outcome of REM rebound factors. This viewpoint is in accord with more recent developments concerning relationships between REM sleep suppression, compensation, and deliria. (See Arkin & Steiner, 1978, for a review of drugs and dreams.)

That REM rebound may more directly stimulate sleep-utterance on occasion is suggested by observations made during a monoamine oxidase (MAO) inhibitor withdrawal syndrome. Oswald (1969) mentions that he and Le Gassicke observed shrieking in association with REM nightmares following withdrawal of long-term tranylcypromine ingestion.

Scharf, Moskovitz, Lupton, and Klawans (1978) reported that 6 of 88 (6.8%) patients on long-term levodopa therapy for Parkinsonism developed night-terrors. The patients would scream, cry out, and move frantically while sleeping. On awakening they were uniformly amnesic; however, extremely vivid dreams (often emotionally neutral) occurred even more commonly (22.7%), and nightmares less often (5.7%). The authors considered their findings difficult to interpret but suggested that a pharmacologically altered REM cycle resulted in either distorted REM phenomena, REM experience temporally displaced into NREM sleep or waking activity, or distinct NREM dreams. No electrographic studies were carried out.

Regarding opioids, Kay (1974, 1975) mentions that six subjects (post addicts) produced "noises, words, and phrases" in 30% of their REMPs *during* methadone administration, whereas it was not observed during either a prolonged premethadone control or a postmethadone abstinence condition. Nocturnal sleep was said not to be markedly altered by chronic methadone administration, although during abstinence, REM and delta sleep, morning reports of dreaming, and restless, poor sleep were all observed. The latter result is contrary to what we might have predicted from the hypothesis suggested earlier—that perhaps increased sleep-utterance during *d*-amphetamine–pentobarbital withdrawal was due to increased secondary intrasleep restlessness rather than direct REM rebound factors. Martin, Jasinski, Haertzen, Kay, Jones, Mansky, and Carpenter (1973) also found increased vocalization during REMPs when methadone was being administered.

In conclusion, it seems reasonable to conclude that sleep-speech may be stimulated by withdrawal of previously adminstered sleep-influencing drugs such as *d*-amphetamine with pentobarbital, MAO inhibitors, alcohol, and meprobamate. In addition, it appears that drugs like 1-dopa- or methadone stimulate sleep-vocalization. The mechanisms by which such stimulation is brought about do not lend themselves to simple formulation. Any explanation should include reference to drug-produced changes in cognitive controls, increased motor discharge tendencies and CNS arousal leading to intrasleep restlessness, and possible more direct effects of REM rebound factors in those situations involving administration and withdrawal of REM suppressant drugs.

STUDIES INVOLVING LEARNING MECHANISMS

Biofeedback research has demonstrated the far-reaching capabilities of humans to learn control of a large variety of autonomic processes and behavior patterns (Miller, 1969). Operant conditioning of simple motor responses during sleep without obligatory evocation of EEG change and/or awakening has been reported by several investigators (Gradess, Stone, Steiner, & Ellman, 1971; Granda & Hammack, 1961; Williams, Morlock, & Morlock, 1966). Such work makes it reasonable to attempt to gain control over sleep-utterance by utilization of learning paradigms.

Accordingly, Aarons (1969, 1970) has reported preliminary findings on efforts to condition sleep-vocalization by escape-avoidance techniques. Using three paid male students (ages 21–23), who were apparently in good mental and physical health and without a history of sleep-talking or other sleep disturbance, the EEG, EOG, submental EMG, respiration, and voice were monitored for a total of three control adaptation and eight experimental nights. The basic strategy was that of shaping and developing operant responses in avoidance behavior. The termination of various combinations of noxious light and sound stimuli applied during sleep were first made contingent on *any* vocalization and by gradual steps changed to requiring increasing overt verbalization as the desired operant response. The goal of this shaping procedure was the elicitation of speech of sufficient duration, intensity, and clarity to be easily comprehensible, but without awakening the subject. For a variety of reasons, the procedure was not strictly uniform. In general, most of the experimental nights were carried out without informing the subjects of the desired goal, but in the latter part of the series, they were explicitly told that the purpose of the experiment was to produce sleep-talking and that if they spoke, the unpleasant stimuli would cease. Vocal responses during sleep were counted as sleep-talking incidents if they fulfilled the following criteria:

1. Vocalization regardless of clarity or intensity, including mumbling and phonemic interjections.
2. Verbalization had to be without any reference to the subject's awareness of being awake or dreaming.
3. Speech that occurred during or up to 1 min after stimulation trials, regardless of pauses, was counted as one response.
4. The EEG preceding stimulation had to be unambiguous with regard to sleep stage.

The data analyses were limited to responses of two subjects, A and B; data for subject C were limited to one session and analyzed separately to illustrate a technique amenable to response measurement as a rate function.

Results

No subject vocalized during the control nights, whereas each vocalized during the experimental nights. The total responses per session were obtained from 28–100% of the stimulation trials, with 57% classified as transient awakenings. Excluding such awakenings, responses in weighted percent by sample size, accompanied by alterations in EEG stage but devoid of alpha evidence of awakening, were distributed by sleep stage as shown in Table 11.10.

In general, the responsiveness of Subject A increased over three nights, and that of Subject B decreased over four nights.

The EEG of Subject A had alpha only during escape responses, whereas alpha for Subject B was about equal during avoidance and escape. Avoidance responses decreased from Stages 1 through 4 and then increased during REM for both subjects, in which case the proportion of escape and avoidance responses were about equal.

The performance of Subject C when graphed produced curves the shapes of which were rate functions inversely proportional to the amount of verbalization.

TABLE 11.10
Results of Conditioned Sleep Vocalization Method[a]

Stage	%	Sample Size
1 NREM	62	(n = 4)
2	88	(n = 5)
3	70	(n = 27)
4	96	(n = 22)
REM	40	(n = 10)

[a]From Aarons, 1969, 1970.

TABLE 11.11
Sample of Conditioned Sleep Vocalizations[a]

EEG Stage Without Signs of Awakening	Subject A	Subject B
1 NREM	"Ah, ah, ah." "No, not again." "Mbl"—[snoring]	"Yes, there we go, that's a boy." "Excellent." "Oh, that's good."
2	"Ha—mbl."	"Kindly stop—good." "Hi, Jake." "Uh, huh." "Humbug." "Interesting."
3	[sigh]—"Oo." [groaning]	'Dr. Aarons, I will murder you— probably" "My gracious sakes." "Light—lovely."
4	"Okay."—[snoring]	"Yes, yes, yes, now try again. My, my, my." "Hello." "Silence, a little silence, let's start right now."
REM	"Mbl"—[sigh]	"Good morning."

[a]From Aarons, 1970. Copyright 1970 by *Perceptual and Motor Skills*. Reprinted by permission.

Aarons (1969, 1970) concluded that the results demonstrated the feasibility of conditioning techniques for experimental stimulation of sleep-talking.

Qualitatively, the somniloquy did not appear to differ among sleep stages. A wide variety of responses were emitted, including groans, sighs, unintelligible mumbling, and clearly enunciated, coherent words, phrases, and sentences. The utterances showed similar broad variation in affective tone, relation to the experimental situation versus lack of such relation, and stereotyping versus richness in content. Table 11.11 presents a sample of vocalizations uttered in association with different sleep stages.

Unfortunately, much of the output of Subject A was of low intensity and masked by air-conditioner noise on the tape recording. Nevertheless, coherent and elaborated speeches in all sleep stages ranging from 5–40 sec were detectable, though the content was lost. Curiously, the responses of Subject C were stereotyped, consisting of repetitions of the word "Stop." Subject C reported one dream, but A and B never reported dreaming, either when awakened during the night or on the following morning; and neither was the content or the act of sleep-talking remembered, but only that they had been awakened several times during the night.

Aarons (1970) is aware of the limitations of his study and is cautious about generalizing. Dement (1972) has expressed his opinion that the "technique seems to be lacking in respect to obtaining any ongoing description of dreaming, because the intelligible responses seem to be geared more toward the external stimuli than toward any internal dream experience" (p. 52). Nevertheless, with specially selected and carefully shaped subjects, it is possible that this could be circumvented in some way. For example, selection of chronic sleep-talker subjects rather than the nonsleep-talkers selected by Aarons (1969, 1970) might yield more striking results. Also, the employment of a positive reinforcement paradigm may be more likely to produce success in such an undertaking, inasmuch as evidence exists suggesting that aversive experience such as sensed pain is incompatible with dreaming experience (Arkin et al., 1975). For example, *pre*sleep conditioning with operant verbal behavior with positive reinforcement such as food or small amounts of money and introduction of the discriminative stimulus during sleep might be usefully attempted. The obtaining of ongoing dream mentation is certainly not the only use to which conditioned utterance in sleep may be put; much useful information about psycholinguistics and other cognitive functioning in wakefulness and sleep could be provided by such a technique.

More recently, Bertini *et al.* (1972a,b; 1974a,b) attempted to train subjects to emit dreamlike speech out of REM sleep in response to a signal learned during wakefulness. Eleven subjects were individually trained during 11 daytime sessions to free-associate aloud in response to a white noise (WN). Then, in counterbalanced order, the subjects slept for three nights in the laboratory under the following experimental conditions: (1) Routine REM and NREM awakenings to obtain mentation reports; (2) REM sleep with WN; and (3) NREM sleep with WN. That is, during REM and NREM sleep, the subjects were exposed to the WN stimulus.

Polygraphic records were scored "blind" with conservative criteria based on the EEG, EOG, and EMG. Every 30-sec epoch was scored as: awake with REM (WREM); awake (W); awake with slow eye movement (WS); Stages 1, 2, 3, 4; and REM. A special rating of the degree of sleepiness and degree of recognition of any tape-recorded verbalizations was carried out by the subject himself during a long, in-depth morning interview, and content analyses of the material were performed. The subject was required to listen to his tape and rate each sentence on degree of comprehensibility, temporal remoteness of reported events, presence of color, and degree of sleepiness.

Independent blind judges carried out systematic analyses along "customary" dimensions of dreamlike versus thoughtlike mentation with appropriate scales. Subsequently, all ratings and polygraphic records were correlated.

Results of Bertini et al. (1972a,b; 1974a,b)

First, the feasibility of the technique was demonstrated; that is, an unspecified number of subjects were found capable of fulfilling the task.

Second, while the subjects were talking, unambiguous Stage REM was not present; however, the authors neglected to comment on the nature of the electrographic recording ambiguity.

Third, the following positive findings were obtained:

1. The level of vigilance in both REM and NREM WN conditions during verbalization was significantly lower than in the daytime reverie sessions or in the standard mentation report awakening procedures ($p < .001$).

2. Sleep resumption latency was significantly shorter after the WN procedure than after standard mentation report awakenings. The mean latency for REM WN is 12 min 10 sec, and after NREM, WN mean latency is 8 min; whereas after standard awakenings, the latencies were about 24 min ($p < .01$).

3. Subjects recognized the verbalizations of both REM and NREM WN conditions to a significantly lesser degree than those of the daytime reverie or standard awakening procedures ($p < .001$).

4. A preliminary content analysis made by ranking the WN verbalizations of each subject under the three experimental conditions from the most to the least dreamlike gave significant results in favor of the REM WN condition, the NREM WN condition being second.

The authors concluded that the REM and NREM WN verbalizations were not simply "free associations" or "hypnopompic phantasies," but rather reflections of specific underlying psychobiological states. In two separate abstracts, full quotations are given of REM WN verbalizations that were uttered in the present tense and appear to arise out of and accompany a dramatic, dreamlike, hallucinatory macrodissociative kind of experience. One such quotation is the following:

There is a heap of rubbish [p] I've got here a can—no—rubbish there is as somebody who picks it up—all over Italy—she goes all—around Italy. [p] doesn't want me, [p] doesn't want me [p] she is self-confident—is rather young [p] I pick it up [p] is not fit—mine—then I throw it away—she carries on without hesitation [p] and then there are—those things to collect garbage [p] in this one [words not understandable].—

Where goes? she walks like Mrs. Bianchi [p] because she treated me this way [p] my mother [p] we were at the table [p] I have the feeling—that starting tomorrow she will go on a diet [p] Marco—the record—must bring [p] don't know to whom [p] Mother eats salami with salad [p] Mother—no—that's not her [p] why she leaves me alone [p] doesn't want me [p] I run, she is wearing a long dress like in the fifties [p] she is slim [p] goes around the corner [p] there was the thrash [p] then a small hill [p] with grass [p] a can stuck in there no—how do you say it [p] Mother [p] how come? [long pause] goes away [p] somebody looks out of [p] a window [p] No—it's not daddy [p] no—no [p] why does he go away [p] doesn't want me [p] Who is at the window? I can't see—I can't see well [p] it is daytime [p] I am sitting—next to this rubbish—She goes away at—I feel like crying. No—but why [p] nooo—[sighing and moaning]—Mother—[is about to cry] [is crying] I'm scared [keeps moaning] then there is a man [p] he draws near—he is higher up—yes—Stephen—and—he doesn't do anything—he cannot do anything [p. 398].

Hauri (1972) attempted to replicate this work with four male college students and failed to produce sleep-talking during REMPs. His subjects often reported that they "heard the white noise in their dreams, but when they realized that they were now supposed to talk, they 'lost' their dream experience and free-associated instead [p. 61]." Hauri did report, however, that *spontaneous* sleep-talking increased during the experiment, especially in Stages 2 and 3. As mentioned earlier, Bertini et al. (1974a,b) reported that the mean sleep resumption latency following WN stimulation was much decreased in comparison to that following standard awakenings (REM = about 12 min; NREM = 8 min). Hauri (1972) also found that sleep resumption latency was shortened after WN but, by contrast, the magnitude of the decrease was striking—his subjects resumed sleep from 10–15 sec after the stimulus condition terminated. This finding persuaded Hauri to train two further subjects during wakefulness to report whatever had been passing through their minds *just before* the onset of the white noise. Subsequently, using this as a conditioned stimulus, the subjects could be awakened as much as 10–15 times nightly for mentation reports without experiencing undue stress. Such conditioned reporting was evidently much less arousing than the standard procedure. The students fell alseep again in a matter of seconds after the report and rarely remembered having been awakened when asked about it on the following morning. In attempting to explain the discrepancy between the findings of Bertini et al. (1972a,b), Hauri invoked such factors as differences between the personality dynamics of their respective subject populations, between the qualities of subject-experimenter rapport, and nuances of experimental design not precisely replicated in his study.

The final set of reports on experimental stimulation of sleep-utterance deals with the positive effects of frequent awakenings from sleep, and obtaining mentation reports. It has been included in this section on experimental sleep-utterance involving learning mechanisms because it seems likely that learning factors played a role. Yet, as we later discuss, there is good reason to consider additional variables in explaining the experimental results.

Initially, in the course of earlier research, it was noticed that the frequency of sleep-utterance of chronic somniloquists in the laboratory increased on nights when they were awakened for mentation reports (Arkin, Farber, Antrobus, Ellman, & Nelson, 1973). It was surmised that this was possibly the outcome of the awakenings themselves. Briefly, from our basic subject pool, a subset of seven subjects were available (two female, five male), with the following characteristics: They had each spent at least two nights of undisturbed baseline sleep in the laboratory, and at least two subsequent nights in which their sleep had been interrupted throughout the night to obtain mentation reports, both during silent sleep and after sleep-utterances. Inasmuch as the number of nights per subject in each condition was not uniform, the central tendencies of results were calculated on the basis of weighted means that compensate for inequalities so introduced. Under baseline conditions, the weighted mean number of sleep-speeches per night per subject (total of 30 nights) was 4.4; whereas, on mentation report awakening nights (22 nights), the mean number of sleep-speeches per night per subject was 7.5. This noticeably greater amount of sleep-speech on awakening nights is at best a suggestive result because of the small sample and nonuniform number of nights per subject.

The next two occasions enabling us to note the effects of mentation report awakenings on sleep-utterance frequencies came about serendipitously in connection with two large-scale studies on the effects of REM deprivation on NREM mentation (Arkin et al., 1978a); and in both studies, the subjects were selected not on the basis of sleep-talking histories, which were not inquired after, but on the basis of their being light sleepers and good dream recallers.

In the first study, (Arkin et al., 1970c), 36 subjects spent a total of 206 nights in the laboratory and were awakened frequently to accomplish REM and NREM control deprivation. The mean number of nights per subject was 5.7. On the occasion of each deprivation awakening, subjects were required to twice squeeze a resistant dynamometer apparatus in order to terminate an awakening bell. In addition, approximately eight mentation reports were obtained each night. The unexpected finding was that 14 subjects (39%) talked in their sleep at least once. The mean number of speeches per subject for the six nights was 1.5 and the mean number of speeches per night was .4. Unfortunately, our design for the REM deprivation project did not require baseline studies and so the foregoing results were again at best suggestive.

By contrast, the subsequent study (Farber, Arkin, Ellman, Antrobus, & Nelson, 1973) provided for adequate baseline procedures, enabling us to draw comparisons between experimental and baseline night results. Our population was similar to that described earlier—20 paid adult "normal" male college students selected without regard to sleep-talking propensities, but who were light sleepers and good dream recallers. A consecutive nightly laboratory schedule was employed, as indicated in Table 11.12.

TABLE 11.12
Sleep-Talking Production—Forced Awakenings
Method[a]

Nights	Purpose
1 2 3	Adaptation

*Nights with Eight Mentation-Report Awakenings
(REM and Stage 2) Throughout*

4 5	First baseline (B)
6 7 8	Sleep-stage deprivation (REMP [RD] or NREM [NRD]) in counterbalanced order with nights 12–14
9	First recovery (REC-1)
Rest at home, 3–8 nights	
10 11	Middle baseline (MB)
12 13 14	Sleep-stage deprivation (as in nights 6–8)
15	Second recovery (REC-2)
16 17	Terminal baseline (TB)

[a]From study by Farber, Arkin, Ellman, Autrobus, and Nelson (1973).

That is, there were three adaptation nights without sleep interruption (nights 1–3), a first baseline (nights 4–5), sleep-stage deprivation (REMP or control NREM) in counterbalanced order (nights 6–8), first recovery, rest period at home, middle baseline (nights 10–11), sleep-stage deprivation (as before, nights 12–14), second recovery (night 15), and a terminal baseline (nights 16–17). The first group of 10 subjects underwent REMP deprivation

(RD) in the first half of the sequence and NREM deprivation (NRD) in the second half; this order was counterbalanced for the second group of 10.

The deprivation procedure entailed awakening subjects at a moment fulfilling predetermined criteria and then keeping them awake on each occasion for at least 2 min by requiring them to calculate *aloud* the product of two-digit by two-digit numbers. It is important to note that the technique of sleep-stage deprivation in the present study differed in a major way from that of the foregoing study describing similar but less dramatic effects. That is, the present technique required a great deal of verbalization aloud on the occasion of *each* deprivation awakening, whereas the earlier study required of the subject only that he silently squeeze a resistant hand dynamometer grip to enforce the requisite wakefulness and accomplish the deprivation. Inasmuch as the number of required deprivation awakenings per night often exceeded 30, it is clear that a great deal more enforced talking aloud was required in the present study compared to that described earlier (Arkin et al., 1970c). This is emphasized because it probably accounts for the greater amounts of sleep-utterance produced in the work of Farber et al. (1973).

Results of Deprivation by Farber et al. (1973)

All 20 subjects were heard through the intercom to talk in their sleep at some time as the nightly series progressed. It wasn't until this effect seemed to recur typically, however, that careful notation of each sleep-talking incident was made on the polygraph records of the remaining subjects. Thus, the following statistical findings are based on the results with 12 carefully monitored subjects, six in each deprivation procedure counter-balanced group (see Table 11.13).

1. The frequency of sleep-speech across the three sets of baseline nights showed no significant differences ($\chi^2 \geq 5.87$ for df = 3, $.30 > p > .20$).

2. The data of the first two baseline nights and the first middle baseline night were combined (because they were undisturbed nights with little or no carryover effects from previous deprivation nights) for comparison with the equally numbered RD and NRD nights.

The comparisons between conditions were made by means of the Wilcoxon matched pairs signed ranks test. The frequency of sleep-speech was significantly greater on:

    a. NRD nights (BL, BL_2, & MBL, versus NRD_1, NRD_2, & NRD_3, $T = 3.5$, $N = 10$, $p < .02$)

    b. RD nights (BL_1, BL_2, & MBL_1 versus RD_1, RD_2, & RD_3, $T = 9.5$, $N = 11$, $p < .05$)

    c. REC nights, both RD and NRD (BL_1 & BL_2 versus REC_1 & REC_2, $T = 3.5$, $N = 10$, $p < .02$)

TABLE 11.13

Effects of a Repeated Sleep Interruption–Deprivation and Concomitant Forced-Verbalization Procedure on Sleep-Speech Frequency[a]

Nights	BL_1	BL_2	NRD_1	NRD_2	NRD_3	REC_1	MBL_1	MBL_2	RD_1	RD_2	RD_3	REC_2
Total	7	13	23	52	41	51	18	18	13	31	35	30
Mean	0.58	1.08	1.92	4.33	3.42	4.25	1.50	1.50	1.08	2.58	2.92	2.50

[a]BL_1, BL_2, MBL, vs. NRD_1, NRD_2, NRD_3: $p < .02$
BL_1, BL_2, MBL, vs. RD_1, RD_2, RD_3: $p < .05$
BL_1, BL_2, vs. REC_1, REC_2: $p < .02$
REC_1, (NRD), vs. REC_2 (RD): $p < .01$

that delta-sleep compensation typically occurs following its deprivation. Thus, sleep-utterance has occurred frequently on recovery nights subsequent to two different techniques of sleep-stage deprivation. Whether this means that nonspecific recovery night processes, regardless of specific sleep-stage deprivation, plays an important role, only further experiments will tell.

It is likely that the effects of the deprivation awakening procedure (Farber et al., 1973) are the outcome of several factors. First, a learning mechanism is suggested by the fact that increases of sleep-speech begin to occur on the second night of the deprivation–interruption procedures and carry over into the recovery night. Conditions for learning were indeed established. Continuous positive reinforcement resulted from permission to resume sleep following each repeated awakening with forced verbalization. That is, the sequence was experimental awakening → forced verbalization → positive reinforcement (permission to return to sleep). One hypothetical learning mechanism, therefore, could be that stimulus characteristics of these experimental wakeful situations (e.g., increased activation) may have sufficient factors in common with those present in association with ubiquitous endogenous movement-arousal episodes occurring in sleep. The response of talking aloud in wakefulness could then generalize to spontaneous movement-arousal episodes in sleep (typically associated with sleep-utterance) and thus result in "talking aloud in sleep." Specifically, a sudden spontaneous increment of activation during sleep could be established as a discriminative stimulus to emit speech as an operant response, aimed at obtaining the positive reinforcement initially afforded by permission to resume sleep after experimental awakenings. This hypothesis is consistent with the large number of sleep-speech episodes that sound as if the subject was immersed in a dream about the experimental situation and "giving mentation reports" in such dreams, or else dreaming about carrying out the verbal computational tasks required of them following deprivation awakenings. This proposed mechanism does not directly involve escape–avoidance learning as in the experimental paradigm of Aarons (1969, 1970). In the latter situation, sleep-utterance occurred as an escape–avoidance operant response to an externally applied stimulus, whereas the present hypothesis suggests that the sleep-utterance occurs in response to spontaneous, internally produced increments of activation that have become endowed with discriminative stimulus properties—properties developed on the basis that sudden states of increased activation in sleep may bear sufficient similarity to the state of activation existing during experimental awakenings, with attendant verbalization receiving positive reinforcement by subsequent permission to resume sleep.

A second possible factor contributing to the experimental results may stem from affective arousal. That is, repeated awakenings of subjects is aversive and usually produces accumulations of anger and anxiety. These, in turn, may find direct expression in vocalization or else produce a higher frequency of movement-arousal episodes. The latter might then stimulate sleep-speech in accordance with the same learning mechansims just outlined.

Third, as previously mentioned, sleep-speech frequencies were greatest on nights associated with, or in recovery from, Stage 2 rather than REMP deprivation–interruption procedures. This suggests that factors associated with recovery from Stage 2 disruption contributed to the observed effects.

Finally, additional explanatory factors are suggested by the work of Horowitz and Becker on poststress intrusive imagery (Horowitz, 1978). In their theoretical terms, it seems appropriate to classify our experimental awakenings and required tasks as external stress events that lead to initiation of internal stress events. The latter, in turn, tend to stimulate programmatic cognitive sequences that are involved in assimilation of these stress events. Such processes, Horowitz and Becker suggested, possess the potential for acquisition of awareness frequently in the form of intrusive event-repetitive, and/or unusually vivid or intense mental representations. It seems likely, in view of our results, that the latter occur during the course of sleep mentation and lead to mental representations of the experimental situation as well as of additional psychologically related material derived from other sources. With such occurrences, it may seem to the subject that the context of these mental representations, which feel real at the time, calls for verbalization, and sleep-talking is the frequent outcome.

Plans are under way to test these hypotheses in our laboratory. Thus, the learning hypothesis would predict differential effects in accordance with the experimental tasks that are required of the subject during experimental awakenings and that receive sleep-resumption reinforcement. For example, silently squeezing a hand-grip during awakenings should produce increased hand movements in sleep; whispering versus shouting verbalization tasks should produce more sleep-whispering or sleep-shouting, respectively. Similarly, the affect-arousal hypothesis predicts that abrupt sudden awakenings should produce more intense, higher amounts of sustained anger and anxiety than an equal number of gentle awakenings and thus be reflected accordingly in sleep-speech frequency. Finally, NREM awakenings could be confined to Stage 3–4 instead of 2, in order to test the Stage 2 specificity-factor hypothesis.

If the techniques described earlier prove generally applicable and the mechanisms of experimental sleep-speech become better understood, I imagine that a powerful experimental tool could be developed for the further exploration of psycholinguistic processes in sleep and wakefulness. Although we comment further on this later, it suffices to draw attention now to the possibilities of observing the effects of alteration of verbal tasks during experimental awakenings on the verbal output in sleep-speech. For example, in what way might sleep-speech resemble and differ from forced experimental-awakening verbal tasks involving recitation of poetry, nursery rhymes, the Pledge of Allegiance, number sequences, mental arithmetic, and affect-laden passages involving sex, anxiety, depression, self-reproach, self-praise, etc.? Are typical patterns of relationship or lack of relationship or transformation discernible between experimental task and sleep-speech? Do such patterns, if observable, tend to show sleep stage or time-of-night effects? Do they relate to silent mentation reports from both REM and NREM sleep?

In conclusion, it has been shown that sleep-speech can be experimentally influenced by a variety of methods including posthypnotic suggestion, presleep instruction, drug effects, and experimental awakenings with forced verbalization. It seems likely that a rich area of research may be opened by a controlled experimental program dealing with attempts to control sleep-utterance.

12 Dialogue Between Sleep-Talkers and Wakeful Observers

Discussion of this topic will be facilitated by drawing a preliminary distinction between sleep-speech as a component of internal dialogue with fantasied people imagined during sleep mentation, and sleep-speech as a component of overt dialogue between an actual external wakeful observer and a sleep-talking subject.

CLINICAL AND ANECDOTAL OBSERVATIONS

Regarding internal dialogue, many observers have noted that much somniloquy sounds like half of a conversation or attempts to verbally interact with another person, often with pauses during which the "other" replies or else replies are awaited (Burrell, 1904; Cameron, 1952; Cook, 1937; Trömner 1911a,b; Walsh, 1920a; Winterstein, 1953). For the most striking occurrences, the reader should examine the transcriptions of McGregor's somniloquy (1964), one of which has been quoted at length earlier (p. 101–102 this volume). In addition, McGregor himself, in a personal interview with me, related his impression of active dialogue when hearing playbacks of his sleep-speeches; i.e., his hearing them brought to mind the commentary and rejoinders of the hallucinated cast in his sleep-imagined scenario, which were not spoken aloud but apparently heard internally. Actually, of course, the subject creates the entire scenario and dialogue, gives part of it to "dream characters" to speak implicitly, and then responds to their utterances with his sleep-speech spoken aloud.

Turning now to the phenomenon of dialogue between sleep-talkers and wakeful observers, it is striking that a large number of observers—including Aristotle—describe this as genuine (Aristotle, in Hutchins, 1952, pp. 99 and 706; Bañuelos, 1940; Bossard, 1951; Burrell, 1904; Carpenter, 1849; Fosgate, 1850; Griesinger, 1867; Guthrie, 1938; Hammond, 1883; Landauer, 1918; Lindner, 1945; Löwenfeld, 1907; MacNish, 1838; Massarotti, 1950; Maury, 1857, 1878; Moll, 1889/1958; Pinkerton, 1839; Radestock, 1879; Schilder & Kauders, 1956; Seashore, 1916; Symonds, 1851; Trömner, 1911a,b; Vogl, 1964; Winterstein, 1953).

Fischer (1839) states that when a waking observer speaks to a subject talking in "dreaming sleep," the responses are likely to be irrelevant and irrational, whereas speaking with someone talking in "somnambulic sleep" tends to elicit relevant and rational responses.

Carpenter (1849) comments that "in most cases, the sleep-talker hears and comprehends what is said to him provided that this harmonizes with what is going on within and will answer rationally so as to sustain a conversation"[p. 691]. Others (Fischer, 1839; Fosgate, 1850; Lowenfeld, 1907; Moll, 1889; Pinkerton, 1839; Radestock, 1879; Symonds, 1851) have likewise commented on the necessity of the question harmonizing with the inner psychic state and fulfilling other conditions in order to elicit this phenomenon. Thus, if the questioning is "adroit," if the interrogator is "en rapport" with the sleeper, or if the observer "insinuates himself" into the consciousness of the sleeper, then sleep-talkers can be induced to talk of many things. Often, the sleeper will not respond to some interrogators and will to others; e.g., Moll(1889) mentions a female subject who would respond to her husband if he spoke as "X," but would apparently ignore him if he spoke as himself. Radestock (1879) describes a subject with whom sleep conversation could be sustained if the observer spoke in the same manner and tone as the subject, whereas the subject would not respond or else he awakened if there was a difference.

Landauer (1918) states that a wakeful observer can often provoke sleep-speech by subwaking-threshold questions and comments. Sleep-talking thus produced is described as usually scanty in amount, uttered at low volume, and frequently "meaningful." However, if the sleep-speech responses are not related to the observer's question, they are mostly connected with current wakeful strivings or with a concurrent dream. Confirmation of the latter is obtainable on awakening the subject.

On the other hand, Winterstein (1953) claims that some sleepers may answer questions and converse with *no* recall on awakening.

I know of only one reference in the scientific literature that provides results of a group survey on the capabilities of sleep-talkers to engage in dialogue with wakeful observers. Based on information obtained from college-educated subjects' families (n = 178), Child (1892) stated that if sleep-talkers are interrogated while they are talking in their sleep:

1. The proportion of women who "intelligently" answer questions put to them is greater than that of men.
2. Males who do answer during the sleep-talking are likely to answer only those questions related to the subject matter of the sleep-talking of the moment.
3. Females are more likely to answer queries on *any* subject, even if unrelated to the concurrent sleep-talking.
4. The proportion of sleep conversationists is much higher in those younger than 25 years.

Maury (1857), a sensitive observer with a gift for introspection and vivid dream recall, provides an intriguing anecdote from his own experience that conveys the details of his state of mind during a provoked sleep speech.

> I had dozed off during a lecture; the lecturer asked me a question about a passage which she had read; I answered: "There is no tobacco in this place"; this was totally unrelated, totally without sense, with regard to the words addressed to me. My response caused loud laughter and suddenly my drowsiness vanished; I had only a vague awareness of what I have answered, but my memory retained some mental images which had passed before my imagination; I remembered that the idea of tobacco had presented itself among a pageant of ill-assorted words and ideas linked illogically. Thus, I had answered to my dream, not to the question [p. 166].

In this example, an external event was correctly perceived as a linguistic stimulus specifically addressed to the subject, but subsequent processing was inefficient and evoked a response more appropriate to his hallucinated experience rather than the externally derived input.

Several anecdotal occurrences suggest that a characteristic dialogue pattern is not uncommon. In one case, the sleeper may say something spontaneously and the wakeful observer tries to "draw the sleeper out." This may be feasible for the initial exchanges, but eventually results in evasive replies, unequivocal rebuffs, or lapses into silence. The interchanges, though capable of possessing more or less syntactic correctness, are sort of nonsensical. And in other cases, the same sequence is observable, except that the experimenter provokes the first sleep-speech rather than responding to it.

Thus, according to Landauer (1918), Lipps (1909) described the following procedure: One establishes contact with the sleeper by asking him an innocuous question. If the subject does not awaken and the subject is compliant, an answer is promptly given. A further question, or something the questioned person is reticent to talk about while awake, is answered by an evasive answer. In Landauer's self-observation, the answer may be "Nothing"; often, the answer is direct, as with Lipps' account of himself consisting of "I'm asleep," but mostly the questioned sleeper becomes silent.

Then, a third question, again innocuous, results in an answer from which the inference was drawn that communication with the sleeper was maintained.

Burrell's (1904) case of a habitual, florid sleep-talker likewise illustrates the phenomenon of a sleeper engaged in conversation with a wakeful observer and sporadically becoming suspicious and close-mouthed during dialogues.

Finally, two interesting anecdotes illustrating the same pattern were described by a wakeful spouse in interchange with a sleeping one. The first was quoted in the introduction to this book on page 1; the second was published in the *New Yorker* magazine (1974).

> A friend of ours, the wife of a psychiatrist, reports that her husband, who recently gave up cigarettes, has taken to talking in his sleep. The other midnight, he announced, "It's not just interesting, it's beautiful!" Reading alongside him, his wife laid down her book. "What is beautiful?" she inquired. "The world," he answered. "And why is the world beautiful?" Her mate smiled beatifically. "Eight thousand years of civilizations, and all of them overlapping," he said. "That is beautiful," she agreed. "But tell me some more of what you mean." No luck. Suddenly stern, the psychiatrist said, "Look, I've given you the facts. You take it from there."

Detailed descriptions of this sort have been given to me by reliable, intelligent observers on numerous occasions. There is no doubt that they are common occurrences. It seems likely that the capacity of sleep-talkers to engage in such dialogues is more widespread than is generally known and thus holds promise for a fruitful line of investigation. To begin with, for example, it would be interesting to collect a series of home or natural-setting dialogues with sleep-talkers to determine whether any patterns are recurrent or typical. If so, it would provide useful information pertaining to the qualities of sleep-related states of consciousness. Thus, during sleep, how is externally derived linguistic input perceived, how subsequently processed, and how subsequently encoded in outputs? What is the moment-to-moment status of psychological defense (guardedness) during such states? How does the subject's sense of conviction regarding the reality of the experience in progress relate to the above questions? And how do these relate to what is recalled during immediately subsequent awakening? In the next section, I describe some laboratory observations that further highlight these questions but unfortunately do not begin to answer them.

LABORATORY EXPERIENCE RELATING TO SLEEP-UTTERANCE AND DIALOGUE

In one sense, the observations to be described are analogous to those in which somnambulistic (Broughton, 1968; Kales, Jacobson, Paulson, Kales, & Walter, 1966) or night-terror episodes were experimentally produced (Fisher et al., 1975). With the former, sleep-walking followed when the experimenter aroused subjects and stood them up on their feet; and with the latter, typical night-terrors often followed the sounding of a buzzer. The opportunities made available by experimental dialogues with sleep-talkers may provide unique advantages with respect to the study of perception, information-processing, linguistic output, and self–object relations during sleep and related states.

Examples Sounding Like Half a Conversation

Laboratory observation has provided abundant examples of sleep-speech sounding like half of a conversation. These may belong to:

1. *REM sleep-speech:* Mm-hm—mother—you gotta get some eggs 'cause seeing all these people all know that I like eggs too, so get a dozen eggs. Please put this in a soft bag, thank you.
2. *Stage 4 sleep-speech:* What do you mean it's wrong—it's confidence, confidence—ah, cut it out—mbl.

Many more examples may be found in Appendix 2. These observations are entirely consistent with Snyder's findings (1970) that dream mentation almost always involves interpersonal interaction and characters talking. Calkins' (1893) results are in agreement.

Contemporary Observations

Contemporary observations have also been made on attempts to engage sleep-talkers in dialogue with wakeful observers.

Guided by published anecdotal observations and those of friends who have been able to engage their spouses, children, parents, or lovers in a sleep conversation, exploratory attempts were made accordingly. Knowing of my interest in sleep-talking, at least seven intelligent, conscientious couples in recent years have volunteered that they can regularly engage their respective partners in prolonged sleep-conversation, with complete amnesia in the morning on the part of the sleep-talker. Attempts to observe this phenomenon in the laboratory have met with only partial success (Arkin, Hastey, & Reiser, 1966b). The reason for this qualified comment is that thus far the dialogues recorded do not seem as sustained as those that have been described in the anecdotal reports of the just-mentioned reliable persons. Is it possible that the laboratory, its equipment, and an experimenter who is not an intimate of the subject has an inhibiting effect? This is a plausible surmise.

There are two techniques that may be useful—the "answering method" and the "provocation method." Using the former, the experimenter waits patiently for the subject to talk in his sleep, and when he does, attempts to answer him audibly in the same spirit, intensity, and on the same topic as if he were conversing empathically with a wakeful partner. In so doing, the experimenter should strive to "feel his way" into the experiential world of the subject at the moment and respond accordingly for as many interchanges as possible. With the latter (provocation) technique, the experimenter softly speaks to the at-the-moment "silent" sleeper, using the subject's or another's name, word, or topic that the experimenter knows is of interest to the subject. When sleep-talking is thus initiated, the experimenter continues as with the answering method.

Examples

The first dialogue occurred with a female college student in association with REMP sleep at 6:30 a.m. and employed the answering method. The experimenter was seated at her bedside.

S: Oh, I don't know. [A spontaneous sleep-speech]
E: What don't you know?
S: Oh, it's so funny.
E: What's so funny?
S: [Short p] That man.
E: That what?
S: [30-sec p] [Mayuhn] [sic] [said rather coyly]
E: [105-sec p] Tell me more.
S: Huh?
E: Tell me more about what's so funny.
S: It's just that that man is so obvious.
E: What's the man's name? [This was said hoping to assist evaluation of whether the subject had awakened and was in fact saying in wakeful consciousness that the experimenter was "funny" and "obvious" because of his clumsy attempts to engage the subject in a sleep dialogue.]
S: I don't know.
E: [p] What's he been doing?
S: Talking.
E: What's he been saying?
S: Oh—asking questions. [consistent with the above hunch]
E: What question did he ask?
S: Well—[105-sec p]
E: He was asking you questions?
S: I'm sort of like awake maybe.
E: You sort of like awake now?
S: Mm.
E: Before, too?
S: I've been becoming more awake.

E: Remember telling me, remember talking to me a few minutes ago?

S: Yeah, but I don't know what, but I remember you asking me something now, about what somebody said or something.

E: You were telling me that a man was so obvious.

S: Mm.

E: Do you know who that man was?

S: UNH, unh, just a minute, I may be able to remember. [long p] I think it was some man who's a teacher, I don't know. [The experimenter was known to the subject as a psychiatrist who was interested in sleep research, rather than a teacher.]

E: You also said, "It's so funny."

S: UH, oh. What's so funny?

E: That's what *you* said before.

S: Oh.

Then the subject remembered that she had been in the midst of a long, involved dream about a school building, lunch with an old friend, and finally a continuously smiling old man who was trying to date her girl friend in an apparently *obvious* way. She recognized him as the man who owned the typewriter repair shop she actually visited on the day before the dream.

During the early part of this REMP-associated dialogue, the EEG contained admixtures of muscle-tension artifact, low-voltage mixed frequencies, short bursts of 6–8 Hz waves about ½-sec in duration, some SEMs, and an occasional K-complex. Toward the latter part, more bursts of 8 Hz appeared. However, this subject was a poor alpha producer, making evaluation of the EEG concomitants of the dialogue difficult.

Several observations suggest that the subject had a definite amnesia for at least the first part of the dialogue and that the dialogue was related to a previous dream. That is, when she was reminded toward the end that she had said, "It's so funny," she reacted with a surprised "UH, oh. What's so funny?"; appeared to be puzzled; and recognized neither the words nor the general content of this portion of the interchange. And in her imagained experience, she was conversing with a "teacher" rather than, say, a doctor or directly with the experimenter as himself. Finally, her preceding dream about the *obvious* smiling old man clearly matches with a part of the earlier section of the dialogue. These three items indicate that for at least the first part of the sequence, the experimenter was able to establish or avail himself of conditions in which his voice and words could be momentarily incorporated into her illusory "real world" of the moment and misperceived so as to suit the requirements of the ongoing scenario.

A second example occurred with a male college student in association with Stage 4 sleep at 2:15 a.m. and resulted from the provocation method. The following might better be termed an instance of experimentally stimulated sleep-speech than a "dialogue," however.

E: Al [p]. Al [p]. Al. [The experimenter spoke through the intercom.]

S: Hm? (It's my (?)) book (?), look—no, it's my wallet (?).

E: Al.

S: Hm? Oh, oh, YOURS. Jesus (?) Oh, no, I was looking at mine. I was looking at your, ha, ha, ha, hah! Oh, Jesus, Christ (?), okay, I'm sorry—mbl, mm.

E: Al?

S: Hm?

E: Could you tell me what was going through your mind just now? Dreaming about anything? Thinking about anything?

S: [Now unambiguously awake] Yes, I was dreaming I was with some—actually it WAS my aunt and also my, someone else that I know, that I used to know from the neighborhood that used to know Turkish and uh—we had put an ad for people answering for Urdish—you know answering—answering ads that were in Turkish and my aunt was among them and also this other—friend and—uh—they were in a—they both of them were in a—ad is—[yawns and voice begins to trail off and become unclear] mbl—ad is (add it (?)) [p] Mmph [p].

E: Anything else, Al?

S: Yes both of them—are—well—both of them were in a place where, you know, they were in a place where they were free—nobody was after them—uh, so that—I just remember where, you know, this one incident(?) where someone was after—was after this friend of mine and I guess these are two people that were involved. That's all I can remember.

The concomitant electrographic changes were as follows: Initially, with the first three calls of the subject's name, the amplitude of the delta waves diminished. The speech before the definitive awakening occupied 35 sec and was accompanied by 3-Hz waves, alpha bursts, low-voltage mixed frequencies, muscle tension, and an occasional conjugate REM. Accompanying the actual mentation report were intervals of sustained alpha, low-voltage mixed frequencies, muscle tension, and a few low-amplitude conjugate REMs. About 3½ min after the conclusion of the mentation report, the subject was in Stage 3 sleep.

With regard to the second dialogue quoted, the experimenter employed the subject's name as a stimulus with the provocation technique. The discrepancy between the content of the subject's sleep-utterance and the stimulus is striking. Furthermore, the following mentation report seems to possess either no discernible, or possibly third-order concordance if very liberal criteria are used. That is, the mentation report contained verbal and linguistic references.

It is striking that recall of mentation was by no means sparse nor lacking in specific items, e.g., the subject's aunt, advertisements, Turkish, Urdish, etc. Yet, there was no unambiguous concordance. Such phenomena are consistent with the hypothesis that at least some sleep-speeches are emitted in varying degrees of dissociation from concomitant sleep mentation.

In both of the two examples described, the electrographic concomitants are best described as a transitional state from previous unambiguous Stages REM and 4 sleep, respectively. The pattern fulfills the criteria for Stage 1 NREM. This corresponds to the contention of Cohen, Shapiro, Goodenough, & Saunders (1965) that sleep-talking episodes occur within an evanescent Stage 1 NREM context.

A third subject, an adult female former psychiatric inpatient, participated in the following dialogue through the intercom, with a female technician. The time was 4:32 a.m., and the spontaneous sleep-speech occurred in association with Stage 2. (Unfortunately, the experimental record was among those inadvertently discarded as waste by our janitorial staff and so detailed descriptions of electrographic concomitants are not available.)

S: Mike—Mike [p] from the window [p] I don't want to get up, I don't want to.
E: Why don't you want to get up?
S: I don't want to face them.
E: What don't you want to face?
S: I don't want to face another day.
E: Why?
S: I'm tired.
E: What are you tired of?
S: I'm tired of having—having the same problems, never achieving anything.

The subject was then definitively awakened by a repeating tape loop calling her name; she responded at the fifth repetition, giving the following mentation report categorized by her as an extremely clear dream and spoken with a sense of exhaustion:

S: Yes, I, uh, was in the doctor's office and he wanted me to leave and, uh, I didn't want to leave [p] and, um [p] and, huh, uh, it was morning—and I didn't want to get up [p], uh, I kept telling the doctor that I didn't want the same kind of problems that I have all the time. [The technician (E) was female.]
E: Anything else?
S: I seem to be walking up a hill 'n, 'n I was very tired and I didn't want to go on—and people were urging me to—come up. There was a whole group of people climbing—it was a hill—and they kept urging me to go on and I didn't want to, I wanted to stop and sit down—. [sigh] I was tired.

In this last instance, the answering method had been employed, and the feature of greatest interest is that our female technician was addressed as if she were the subject's male psychotherapist (who was in no way related to the institution in which our work had been carried out). The mentation report item, "I kept telling the doctor that I didn't want the same kind of problems that I have all the time," suggests that the state of consciousness during which the previous experimental dialogue had occurred was a hallucinatory one. Furthermore, requiring five repetitions of the awakening stimulus before she was aroused sufficiently to respond with a mentation report suggests that she was at least behaviorally asleep to a significant extent during the dialogue.

A fourth example is worth relating, because it is typical of a common recurrent phenomenon with many subjects, in which following an awakening stimulus to elicit mentation reports from silent NREM sleep, the subject produces an utterance indistinguishable from many spontaneous sleep-utterances, instead of an unambiguous mentation report. Often, such utterances are identical in form to wakeful aphasic speeches (see Chapter 19). They are included here because they follow a verbal awakening stimulus and therefore could be considered as examples of sleep-speech produced by the provocation method, or else alternatively, simply as resulting from a nonspecific experimental stimulus analogous to experimenter-produced night-terror episodes (Fisher, Kahn, Edwards, & Davis, 1975). During NREM sleep at 3:17 a.m., the following occurred:

E: David. [the subject's name]
S: David—I Day David that *you*—*you*—that's *you*—that's *you* that Day— Dated—Day—Dravid Dave Dravid about 25 or 30 noked naked day dreams—the second dream tie it all up—you kept bouncing them—you kept bouncing them on and on as if you had a regular meter—and as if you had a regular dream in—look on and on as if you were continuing on to the next paragraph—then you knew it at last—.
E: Anything else, David?
S: That's all.

The perseveration, disorganization, clang associations, and lack of easily discernible meaning are striking. It is reasonable to surmise in this case that the stimulus of his name, "David," was perceived during sleep and played a determining role in the ensuing perseveration on the name; and that the references to dreams and "daydreams" in the remaining context suggests that the subject may have been interweaving "sleep-speech" and attempts at rendition of a mentation report.

In all, we have made at least 15 planned attempts at producing dialogue between many sleep-talkers and three different experimenters, using both answering and provocation methods. Most have utilized the intercom, and this artificiality may have negatively influenced our results; but on at least three occasions, the experimenter was at the subject's bedside. The just-described examples are our best and, as the reader can see, the results, though intriguing, are by no means clear-cut. It is difficult to assess during the episodes the extent to which the subject is momentarily at the sleep extremity of the continuum versus the wakeful extremity, i.e., at what point in the continuum a specific occurrence should be located. This is, of course, a common problem in sleep research. But certainly, our laboratory results are pallid compared to those of the florid, dramatic accounts in the anecdotal and clinical literature. In any case, however, it seems clear that these dialogues may be classified as intermediate or macrodissociative episodes.

But what may we say by way of amplification about the phenomena with the observations we have at hand, both from the laboratory and elsewhere?

The findings of Berger (1963) in his experiments on modification of dream content by meaningful verbal stimuli should have an important bearing. Subjects in REM sleep were exposed to subawakening-threshold tape recordings of proper names and awakened shortly afterward for mentation reports. Compelling evidence was obtained that the stimuli were often selectively perceived by the sleeper and incorporated into the ongoing dream experience, usually, but not always, in some transformed manner. The types of such transformations were categorized as follows in order of decreasing frequency:

Assonance (n = 31).   The relationship between stimulus name and dream content item was based on their possessing some phonic feature in common; e.g., "Jenny" appeared in the dream as "Jemmy" and "Robert" as "Rabbitt."

Direct (n = 8).   The stimulus was directly incorporated into the dream as an externalized or internalized voice. In five of the eight occasions, the stimulus appeared as a background voice repeating the stimulus name or a distorted form of it without any discernible effect on the dream sequence. Once, the stimulus name appeared in the form of the thought "Eileen," the subject's girl friend, which he believed he may have shouted out in his dream. On the remaining two occasions, the subjects dreamed of the actual experimental situation—that a name or names were being sounded while they were asleep.

Association (n = 6).   The relationship between the dream and stimulus name was not apparent on direct comparison between the two and only came to light when spontaneous associations of the subject, as he listened on a later date to the playback of his dream report, provided relatively unambiguous associative links.

Representation (n = 3).   This category included occurrences in which the person bearing a stimulus name appeared in the dream either directly or in some transformed manner.

Of the overall total of 89 dreams in the data pool, 48 (54%) were scored positive for incorporation of the external stimulus. Similar qualitative results have been obtained in experiments employing verbal stimuli during NREM sleep (Castaldo & Shevrin, 1970; Lasaga & Lasaga, 1973), and electrographic correlates of perception of specific verbal stimuli have been demonstrated for NREM sleep (McDonald, Schicht, Frazier, Shallenberger, & Edwards, 1975; and Oswald, Taylor, & Treisman, 1960) for REM sleep (McDonald et al., 1975).

In general, the overall results show that it is a commonplace occurrence for sleeping subjects to selectively perceive and incorporate into ongoing dream experience externally derived verbal stimuli; and that although the manner of such incorporation tends to be one in which the stimulus enters sleep awareness transformed in some way, it is nevertheless possible for direct, relatively undisguised incorporations to occur as well. For our purposes, it is important to note further details reported by Berger (1963).

First, when a stimulus name had been incorporated into a dream, it was frequently associated with a sense of anomalous experience; e.g., subjects often preceded their description of the incorporated dream element by "something that seems strange...," "I don't know why...," "I remember suddenly thinking...," or "I had a vivid sort of picture," and sometimes, following the description of the incorporated element, the subject might add, "It was a funny thing that...rather odd [p. 732]." In other words, the perception and incorporation of an externally derived or influenced dream element was often accompanied by a sense of strangeness, vividness, or incongruity and was capable of perturbing sleep awareness momentarily like a pebble thrown into a slowly moving stream.

Second, it was the rule that the subject was unaware of the fact of having incorporated an externally perceived stimulus as such and having blended it with his ongoing dream. As far as the dreamer's psychological reality was concerned, his awareness was comprised of what he experienced as a dreamed event, even when the stimulus name was directly incorporated.

These observations of Berger, taken together with both the anecdotal and laboratory findings on sleep-talker–experimenter dialogues related earlier, suggest the following tentative categories of phenomena:

1. *A verbal stimulus from the experimenter is selectively perceived by the sleep-talker, following which overt speech is produced.* This may result from the stimulus' activation of predisposed or primed, but hitherto quiescent or inhibited linguistic speech units, or it may result from incorporation of the verbal stimulus into a sequence of ongoing sleep mentation. The stimulus may operate in a nonspecific manner, serving only to increase arousal levels which in turn result in a breach of utterance thresholds; or it may operate in a specific manner by virtue of the verbal stimulus' meaning activating a particular psycholinguistic organization whose responsivity is biased toward it. In any case, the stimulus is perceived but the reaction is mostly elaborated in terms of the internal variables prevailing at the moment.

Examples of this category are the results of the provocation method described earlier (the "Al" and "David" instances) and also the anecdotal account of Maury (1857) when questioned during sleep. As previously stated, Maury correctly perceived that the lecturer had specifically questioned him, but reacted not in terms of the question, but in terms of his dream. The laboratory dream of "Al" is similar.

2. *A verbal response from the experimenter is directly incorporated into the ongoing dream of the subject and responded to accordingly.* In this case, the experimenter's response is perceived as if it were a component of an ongoing dream and interwoven with it such that, at least for the moment, the two are not distinguished as to origin. The voice and words of the experimenter appear to be capable of substituting momentarily for those of the subject-created, sleep-imagined characters. The words of the experimenter are experienced as such by the sleeper and are psychologically perceived and located as being within the matrix of a dream rather than having arisen from the outside. Actually, these observations fit well with some of the anecdotal descriptions of the possibility of "entering into the sleep-talker's world" (Moll, 1889 (1958); Radestock, 1879), and are exemplified to some degree by our two descriptions of the answering method in the laboratory.

Have occurrences similar to features of the phenomena described been described elsewhere?

Gross, Goodenough, Tobin, Halpert, Lepore, Perlstein, Sirota, Dibianco, Fuller, & Kishner (1966) have studied by electrographic methods patients with alcoholic deliria. During pathologically prolonged and intensified "Stage REM sleep," some subjects spoke spontaneously and the experimenter answered in terms of the apparent intrapsychic experience reflected by the patient's speech. This led to several interchanges that were directly related to mentation recalled as dreams after immediate definitive awakening.

Gastaut and Broughton (1965) describe instances of appropriate one-word verbal responses to questioning during Stage 2 sleep in children who are prone to "sleep drunkeness" syndromes. During such moments of simple response, one observes brief electrographically defined awakening reactions occurring against a sustained background of Stage 2 and 3 sleep patterns.

The Perky phenomenon provides an example in which wakeful subjects are unable to distinguish between self-produced imagery and an actual image mechanically projected on a screen (Segal, 1971). The subject is asked to imagine an image projected on a screen while the experimenter covertly illuminates the screen with an actual slide of that image. The subject could often not say whether the image was his own projection or whether his own projected image actually prevented his being able to detect an image as externally produced.

Estabrooks (1957) and Cook (1937) believed that subjects answering questions in sleep are really in a state of hypnosis. This seems to be a gratuitous assumption that further presupposes general acceptance of the meaning of the expression that someone is "really in hypnosis."

In recent years, the concept of state-dependent learning has received a great deal of research interest and critical discussion (Overton, 1964, 1972; 1973). Evans, Gustafson, O'Connell, Orne, and Shor (1970) have also published experiments that demonstrate the possibility of state-dependent learning during sleep. It would be fascinating to attempt to engage a sleep-talker in a dialogue and impart a specific item of information to him that was irretrievable during wakefulness or some other sleep stage, but possible of retrieval in a subsequent sleep dialogue associated with a sleep stage and time of night similar to that of the initial learning experience.

What would be needed ideally to carry forward with research on dialogue between sleep-talkers and wakeful observers is, above all, subjects who have been shown capable of such dialogues repeatedly with the same wakeful observers. Second, experiments should be carried out in the home setting initially, with the same wakeful observer and portable electrographic equipment. Third, when the sleep-talker is thoroughly "trained" and performs more or less predictably, the experiments may, if desired, be transferred to the laboratory. One might try to parlay dialogues into fairly extensive conversations, following which subjects would be definitively awakened and mentation reports obtained. Tests of recall and recognition might be carried out. On other occasions, an interval of free association could be requested to observe whether indirect derivatives of the sleep conversations persist. If possible, inspection of EEG records should be supplemented by spectral analyses and hemispheric difference fluctuations to determine degrees of similarity and difference between the electrographic concomitants of "sleep conversations," other sleep stages, the hypnagogic state, and wakefulness. It might thus be possible to more definitively characterize the state of consciousness associated with sleep dialogue. It would be of great interest to correlate these variables with whether the external input would be merely detected but reacted to in terms of ongoing, self-produced mentation (as in Maury's 1857 anecdote), or whether the input would have acquired a further degree of incorporation and penetration and actually became a line of inner dialogue. In the latter case, the wakeful observer's specific words would be perceived by the sleeper as the same utterance but as if occurring within the matrix of a dream. Such findings would have bearing on the issue of self–object differentiation in sleep mentation (Schwartz, 1976). Clearly, experimental observations on dialogue between sleep-talkers and wakeful observers have great significance for the study of psycholinguistic functions during sleep, as well as for the study of psychic dissociation. These topics receive further discussion later in this volume.

13

Comparison of Mentation Associated with NREM Sleep-Speech and NREM Silent Sleep

Rather than being a valid reflection of sleep mentation, is it possible that microdissociative sleep-talking merely indicates the mental content of the movement-arousal episode (as defined by the standard criteria, Rechtschaffen & Kales, 1968) and is essentially unrelated to sleep mentation as such? The results of studies in several different laboratories have a bearing on this question.

First, with regard to REMP-associated sleep-talking, the high proportion of concordance between sleep-speech content and the usual relatively elaborate REMP mentation reports described as dreams by the subject provides convincing evidence that REMP-associated sleep-speech arises out of and reflects previous ongoing REMP mentation. On the other hand, the same conclusion with regard to NREM-associated utterances cannot be drawn quite so easily. This caution is required by the lack of well-established electrographic correlates of NREM sleep mentation, in contrast to those of REMPs. That is, in the latter instance, electrographic signs of Stage REM permit a reasonably valid inference that dreamlike mentation was in progress immediately prior to the actual onset of the sleep-utterance and continuous with it, whereas this is not yet the case with NREM sleep.

An effort was made by us (Arkin, Antrobus, Toth, Baker, and Jackler, 1972a) to approach this problem by comparing NREM mentation reports elicited immediately after NREM-associated sleep-utterance to reports elicited during NREM "silent sleep." It is to be emphasized that the empirical study in this chapter involves microdissociative NREM sleep-utterance episodes only. We sought to evaluate the following hypothesis: Many (not all) NREM-associated utterances are the outgrowths of previous streams of ongoing NREM mentation that, from time to time, find expression in overt vocalization of the subject. Evidence that this could indeed occur would be important because we would then possess a spontaneous, subject-emitted, objective indicator of the presence and content of some NREM mentation. Support for this hypothesis would require the following three findings:

1. An analysis of the *general* content of mentation reports elicited immediately after NREM-associated utterance would reveal *no* significant differences from reports elicited from NREM "silent" sleep, i.e., sleep without proximate sleep-vocalization.

2. There would be *no* significant differences in the total word counts of the mentation reports elicited from these two conditions and also no significant difference in proportion of reports categorized by judges as lacking in content altogether. That is, there would be no differences in the amount or efficiency of recall of sleep mentation in the two conditions because such differences, if indeed found, could confound results.

3. By contrast, on awakening the subject after NREM sleep-utterance, the frequency with which he recalls an imagined occurrence in which he *himself* was vocalizing would be *greater* than after an interval of NREM silent sleep. Examples of such occurrences would be those in which the subject reports, "I was (or we were) talking, discussing, teaching, arguing, conversing, etc." in an imagined incident prior to being awakened.

If these hypotheses were borne out, they would be consistent with the assertion that *a portion* of the population of NREM utterances occur as a short-lived "surfacing" of segments of sequences of NREM mentation in which the subject is hallucinating or vividly imagining an event in which he has been vocalizing something, and that sleep-utterances and associated mentation reports need not reflect merely the mental content of transitory arousal states *unrelated* to previous sleep mentation. In effect, I am contending that a NREM mentation report after sleep-utterance may be a valid sample of the NREM mentation of the moment differing from silent-sleep NREM mentation in one respect only, namely whether the subject had been vocalizing in an imaginary sleep experience. It would then follow that the content of the actual utterance itself would likewise be a true sample of the NREM mentation at the time.

These hypotheses were supported by preliminary findings (Arkin, Toth, & Baker, 1969) and subsequently in a publication (Arkin et al., 1972a). However, the latter study had been criticized by Hauri (1973) as follows:

While the paper shows very careful data gathering and statistical analysis, an important flaw lies in the relatively low interjudge reliability reported for dream content rating. The findings of no significant differences in NREM mentation after sleep-talking and after silent sleep seems questionable because true differences might have been obscured by the large error variance in content scoring. A more intensive training of the scorers would have yielded higher interscorer reliabilities and therefore would have made these findings more convincing.

In response to this comment, I repeated the study with the same data but used considerably improved content analysis scales and two new "blind" judges who had training in scoring sufficient for them to acquire higher interjudge reliability. Accordingly, this replication study is presented in detail here for the first time and compared with the previous results (Arkin et al., 1972a) where appropriate.

For those readers who do not have a taste for suspense, the final outcomes differed only in small details, and hence, the work described here confirms the earlier conclusions (Arkin et al., 1972a).

THE DATA POOL

The data were obtained from the sleep-speeches and mentation reports of 23 of those 28 subjects who participated in the study on the degree of concordance between sleep-utterance and associated wakeful mentation. (See Chapter 10 and also Arkin, Toth, Baker, & Hastey, 1970a.) Inasmuch as this phase of the work concerned NREM mentation and sleep-speech only, all REMP-associated utterances and reports were excluded from the data pool of present work. In addition, NREM data obtained during recovery nights following REM-depriving drugs were also excluded. (This part of the research was described in Chapter 11.) Thus, the data pool was drawn exclusively from three nonconsecutive nights per subject during which the only experimental intervention was awakening subjects for mentation reports.

We were not able to make advance predictions as to just when the subject would vocalize in his sleep. Accordingly, to insure a sample of mentation reports in close proximity to sleep-utterance episodes as well as more remote from them, the technicians had been instructed to awaken the subjects throughout the night immediately after sleep-vocalization, and at other times at least 45 min after the last previous vocalization, regardless of sleep stage, for the silent sleep awakenings. After some of the latter occurrences, the subject vocalized a short time after resuming sleep and would be awakened once more for another postsleep-utterance report.

This procedure provided us with a pool of mentation reports with the following characteristics:

1. Some were elicited immediately after sleep-vocalization and others after an interval of silent sleep.
2. The time interval between postutterance and silent-sleep report elicitations ranged from 8 to 194 min (mean = 54.1 min).
3. Awakenings were carried out in all NREM sleep stages.

From this pool of NREM reports, pairs were set up such that each pair consisted of one report associated with sleep-utterance and one associated with silent sleep. Both members of a given pair came from the same subject, the same night and were so chosen as to minimize the time difference between the two reports comprising each pair. This procedure yielded a total of 74 report pairs for initial data processing. The number of report pairs in relation to the number of subjects emitting them were as follows:

```
4 subjects yielded 1 pair(s) each = ( 4)
7 subjects yielded 2 pair(s) each = (14)
4 subjects yielded 3 pair(s) each = (12)
3 subjects yielded 4 pair(s) each = (12)
4 subjects yielded 6 pair(s) each = (24)
1 subject yielded 8 pair(s)        = ( 8)
                                     ─────
                                     74 (total)
```

AROUSAL THRESHOLD AND MENTAL CONTENT-ELICITING QUESTIONS

The awakening procedure was not strictly uniform on a particular night; e.g., differences in the ease of arousal and subject readiness to respond at different times of the night, and in different stages of sleep, inevitably produced variability in the number of stimuli necessary to awaken them, and in the number and manner of questions put to the subject in order to elicit reports. Did these differences unwittingly introduce a systematic bias into our procedure? In order to assess this issue, we performed t-tests comparing the mean numbers of stimuli required to awaken the subject, the mean numbers of mental content-eliciting questions, and word count per report for the members of the 74 pairs elicited after sleep-utterance and silent sleep, respectively. We reasoned that if the values of the tests were well below the level of statistical significance, then it could be safely concluded that the procedural irregularities under consideration did not unduly bias the results.

The outcome was that all t values were well below the level of significance, and it was therefore concluded that no bias had been introduced from these sources (see Table 13.1).

TABLE 13.1
Stimuli, Questions, Word Counts, and Mentation-Absent Unscorable Reports

Factors Compared	After Sleep-Utterance	t(df = 73)	After Silent Sleep
Mean number of awakening stimuli	1.4	0.723 (n.s.)	1.5
Mean number of mentation-eliciting questions	2.0	0.743 (n.s.)	1.8
Mean word count per report	168.8	0.706 (n.s.)	211.3
Percent reports mentation-absent or unscorable	25.0	(n.s.)	22.3

CONTENT ANALYSIS OF MENTATION REPORTS

In our previous study (Arkin et al., 1972a), many of our content-analysis scales occasioned difficulty for the judges in their attempts to categorize the reports. For example, some of the subdivisions were based on over-elaborate subtleties concerning which consensus during training was not sufficiently well attained. Accordingly, our replication study, benefiting from lessons thus learned, utilized 13 relatively uncomplicated scales developed around the following categories:

1. Utterance—aural/verbal   (5 subcategories)
2. Visual experiences   (3 subcategories)
3. Action   (4 subcategories)
4. Number of characters   (4 subcategories)
5. Self-representation   (3 subcategories)
6. Bizarreness   (4 subcategories)
7. Interpersonal action   (2 subcategories)
8. Emotion   (3 subcategories)
9. Reference to the laboratory or experimental situation   (2 subcategories)
10. Reference to work and/or school   (2 subcategories)
11. Change of scene   (3 subcategories)
12. Narrative quality   (3 subcategories)
13. Presence of mentation   (3 subcategories)

The details of these scales may be found in Appendix 1. In contrast to the judges participating in the earlier study (Arkin et al., 1972a), the present work employed two graduate students who were more verbally sophisticated and more experienced in evaluation of the psychological content of mentation reports. They were "blind" to the experimental condition with which each report was associated, although they knew that the subjects were sleep-talkers. The order of the reports was randomized and each was judged independently. If any were scored differently, the two judges subsequently reconciled their evaluations and the reconciled scores were employed for the statistical computations assessing the hypotheses.

JUDGMENTS OF UTTERANCE:
AURAL-VERBAL CATEGORY

The utterance category was actually rather broad in scale and was comprised of five components. The judges were told that the experimenters were "interested in learning about the frequency with which vocalization, references to printed or written words and to nonvocal sounds occur in the mental experience of people while asleep."

Each report was edited to exclude references to any sounds and vocalization involved in arousing and querying the subjects. Only the *first substantive* report of mentation was supplied, omitting additional matter related by the subject as a result of further questioning by the experimenter in eliciting mental content.

The judges were asked to assign each report to one and only one category in accordance with the following scheme of priorities:

1. The subject recalled *himself* as vocalizing in the present or immediate past as part of a sleep experience, i.e., any expression indicating that the subject was in the midst of, or had just spoken or vocalized, during an experience imagined or dreamt prior to awakening.

2. The subject recalled someone else (human or animal) vocalizing *other* than the subject and not including the subject.

3. The mentation report contained only references to *unspoken* words or anticipated vocalization, but not actual utterances, as part of the sleep experience.

4. The mentation report contained references solely to nonvocal aural experience, i.e., sounds that were nonvocal and nonverbal in nature.

5. No vocal, verbal or sound reference whatsoever.

The judges were told further that if they had doubts about category 1 or 2, they were to place a question mark after the categorization and then use the next most appropriate alternate rating in parentheses. This instruction was introduced to maximize refinement of the judgments and it gave rise to two sets of scores: conservative and liberal. The former consisted of categorizations about which the judge had no doubt, and the latter included a few additional categorizations of reports containing an element of ambiguity.

Results: Utterance—Aural-Verbal Category Judgments

The results for each category are presented separately in Table 13.2. The interjudge reliability was high (r = .95). In accordance with the prediction, the proportion of NREM postsleep-utterance reports containing references to the subject vocalizing in a sleep-imagined experience was significantly greater than the proportion of such reports elicited from NREM silent sleep. Taking the conservative judgments as a basis for conclusions, the proportion of "subject-vocalizing" categorizations in postsleep-utterance reports was 27.0%, in comparison to 12.2% for the same category in silent sleep reports (p = .02, two-tailed test), and taking the more liberal judgments as a basis similarly resulted in 33.8% subject-vocalizing categorizations of mentation reports following sleep-utterance, in contrast to 14.9% in silent sleep reports (p = .005, two-tailed test). It is of interest that this latter result is almost identical to that obtained in the earlier study (Arkin et al., 1972a), in which the proportion of reports scored as subject vocalizing by both judges at that time was also 33.8% of the postutterance and 12.9% of the silent sleep reports. Furthermore, the specific reports so categorized in the entire sample by the judges in the earlier study (Arkin et al., 1972a) and those by the judges in the present report were virtually identical.

In view of this all but identical result, a special statistical analysis performed in the earlier work (Arkin et al., 1972a), but not in the present study, seems applicable. As indicated previously, some subjects vocalize in their sleep more than others and thus contributed more usable report pairs to the population sample than the less voluble subjects (see page 229). Therefore, in order to be able to generalize our observations to *sleep-talkers* rather than restrict our conclusions to our population of pairs of sleep-utterance versus silent sleep observations, a procedure had been carried out in which the contribution of each subject was appropriately weighted in the analysis. Accordingly, the data were cast in a split-plot analysis of variance design (Winer, 1962) in which pairs were nested within subjects. This procedure provided that the greater the number of report pairs contributed by a subject, the smaller the weight given to each pair. In this way, the contribution of each subject was equally represented in the analysis. The outcome was essentially unaffected. Reports categorized as subject vocalizing occurred significantly more frequently from post-utterance awakenings than those from silent sleep ($F_{1,16}$ = 1.418, $p \leq$ .01).

By contrast, the outcome of judgments in the remainder of the components of the utterance–aural-verbal category showed *no* significant differences between postutterance and silent sleep conditions. This was likewise so in the earlier study (Arkin et al., 1972a).

TABLE 13.2
Differential Frequencies of Utterance—Aural-Verbal Event Categorizations for Mentation Reports

Category	NREM Sleep-Utterance Reports	NREM Silent Sleep Reports	Significance Level
Subject vocalizing	Conservative judgments 20 (27.0%) Liberal judgments 25 (33.8%)	Conservative judgments 9(12.2%) Liberal judgments 11(14.9%)	$p = .02$ $p = .005$
Others vocalizing	5 (6.8%)	6(8.1%)	n.s.
Reference to unspoken words including anticipated utterance	2 (2.7%)	3(4.1%)	n.s.
Reference to nonvocal, nonverbal sound	3 (4.1%)	2(2.7%)	n.s.
Total vocalizing, aural, verbal event categorizations (all four preceding categories)	35 (47.3%)	22(29.7%)	—
No vocal or sound reference	39 (52.7%)	52(70.3%)	—

233

TABLE 13.3

Sign Test on Homogeneous Subsample of Report Pairs: NREM Sleep Utterance versus
NREM Silent Sleep

Mentation Reports	Number Postsleep Utterances	Number Silent Sleep	Number Report Pairs by Subject	Report Pairs by Sleep Stage	
Judged as subject vocalizing	11[a]	1[a]	4 subjects, 1 pair each	Stage 2	= 8
				Stage 3–4	= 3
			4 subjects, 2 pairs each	Stage 1 NREM =	1
			total = 12		= 12

[a]p = .006, 2-tailed test.

Analysis of Subsample of Mentation Report Pairs With Maximal Control of Extraneous Variance: Subject Vocalizing Categorizations.

The analyses described were carried out on a sample that was somewhat heterogeneous with respect to sleep stage. For example, Stage 3–4 reports were often paired with Stage 2 reports because they fulfilled the requirements of being closest together in time, as well as one following sleep-utterance and the other being associated with silent sleep. Of the entire population of reports in which *both* judges agreed that *either or both* members of a pair of reports were categorized as subject vocalizing, a subsample of 12 report pairs was available comprised as follows:

1. Both were from the same sleep stage (eight from Stage 2, three from Stage 3–4, and one from Stage one NREM).[1]
2. Both were from the same approximate time of night (range 11–140 min apart; mean = 47.5 min; SD = 35.9 min).
3. Both possessed recall of mentation prior to awakening.
4. Both judges agreed that either or both members of each report pair be categorized as subject vocalizing.

This subsample was processed by a sign test (Table 13.3). The same outcome was produced as for the previous analysis of the more heterogeneous population (page 232–233). After sleep-utterance with maximal control over

---

[1]It would be desirable to replicate this phase of the study with a larger sample, inasmuch as one of the members of one Stage 3 pair in this subsample barely fulfilled the respective sleep-stage criteria (20.2% delta-wave content). Reducing the size of this subsample from 12 to 11 pairs of reports accordingly, however, does not seriously reduce the statistical significance of the finding presented in Table 13.3. That is p = .006 with 12 pairs becomes p = .011 with 11 pairs.

extraneous sources of variance, mentation reports are much more likely to be categorized as subject vocalizing than after silent sleep (p = .006, two-tailed test). Again, virtually the same result was obtained in the earlier study (Arkin et al., 1972a).

JUDGMENTS OF MENTAL CONTENT OF REPORTS:
ALL REMAINING CATEGORIES

The results of these analyses are presented in Table 13.4. Interjudge reliability was uniformly high (r = .79–.98). Throughout, *no* significant differences were detected in the postsleep-utterance NREM content in comparison to that of silent NREM sleep, with the sole exception of the subject vocalizing category as previously described. Mentation reports after sleep-utterance were categorized as containing references to interpersonal action in 39.2% of the sample as opposed to 27.0% for silent sleep reports with mean ratings of ratings of .39 and .27 respectively. These differences approached significance at the .10 level and probably reflected the overlapping between the subject vocalizing and the interpersonal action categories.

DISCUSSION

The results described support the hypothesis that the content and quantity of sleep mentation following NREM sleep-utterance is essentially similar to that occurring during NREM silent sleep with one exception: After sleep-utterance, it is significantly more probable that the subject will remember mentation in which he was actively vocalizing in an imagined sleep experience. It is intriguing to recall at this point that sleep-utterance tends to occur *without* the subject being aware during wakefulness that he had just vocalized *overtly* and *aloud.*

The results also validate our criterion of third-order concordance in which the only discernible relation between the mentation report and the immediately preceding sleep-utterance was that the report contained a reference to active vocalization in some manner and possessed no other basis for concordance categorization.

Foulkes (1966) has provided convincing evidence that NREM mentation exists. Attempts made to correlate NREM mentation with various concomitant electrographic tonic states and phasic events have not resulted in the delineation of any clear or simple pattern. (See Pivik's 1978 review.) It is of interest, therefore, to present additional data that indicate a positive relationship between a common observable, objective event and a specific variety of mental experience during NREM sleep, that is, experimenter-

TABLE 13.4
Mental Content Analysis of NREM Mentation Reports Elicited from Postsleep-Utterance and Silent Sleep Conditions

Content Category	Proportions of Reports Assigned to Content Categories and Mean Ratings						Interjudge Reliability (r)
	Postsleep Utterance			Silent Sleep			
	Mean Ratings	Number Reports	%	Mean Ratings	Number Reports	%	
Visual imagery	.66	44	59.5	.70	46	62.2	.90
General action (overt behavior of human, animal, or inanimate object)	.84	40	54.1	.99	46	62.2	.90
Characters present	1.30	49	66.2	1.20	49	66.2	.93
Self-representation	1.20	51	68.9	1.00	46	62.2	.98
Bizarreness/incongruity	.16	9	12.2	.22	15	20.3	.89
Interpersonal action	.39	29	39.2	.27	20	27.0	.87
Emotion	.12	7	9.4	.16	10	13.5	.79
Reference to laboratory/experimental situation	.27	20	27.0	.22	16	21.6	.89
Work and/or school	.08	6	8.1	.08	6	8.1	.91
Changes of scene	.65	44	59.5	.74	47	63.5	.97
Narrative quality	.73	45	60.8	.66	42	56.7	.87
Utterance, aural and verbal	see Table 13.2	35	47.3	see Table 13.2	22	29.7	.95
No mention recalled	—	19	25.7	—	19	25.7	.95

observed vocalization is associated with the subject having an imagined experience of utterance during sleep. Hauri (1973) has remarked that the inability to determine specifically which sleep-utterance episodes arise from ongoing NREM mentation limits its usefulness in the study of this realm of observation. The same may be said of the usual NREM mentation report— we have no *certain* way of distinguishing between actual NREM mentation or hypnopompic mentation when such reports are elicited following NREM awakenings. Although this is true in an absolute sense, it is certainly possible to significantly reduce the error in this context by simply obtaining a mentation report immediately after sleep-utterance and assessing its content in relation to the preceding sleep-speech. Positive signs of concordance will suggest that the sleep-speech was indeed derived from previous sleep mentation, but the converse is not necessarily so; i.e., a lack of concordance need not rule out that the sleep-speech reflected sleep mentation—it may merely mean that recall processes were inefficient.

How might the results enlighten us about microdissociative sleep-utterance phenomena? The results do not lend themselves to a simple interpretation, and at least three alternative hypotheses accounting for sleep-utterance are worthy of consideration.

Alternative 1. Microdissociative NREM sleep-utterances result from poorly coordinated activation of neural circuits involved with vocalization and speech such that they occur without discernible relation to any ongoing subjective experiences of NREM mentation. Such an explanation seems applicable to *some* utterances, particularly those which are explosive in nature resembling ictal automatisms (Chase, Cullen, Niedermeyer, Start, & Blumer, 1967) and in association with which subjects are usually unable to recall any sleep mentation whatsoever (Arkin & Brown, 1972). But such a hypothesis would not account for the large proportion of occurrences in which sleep-speech content and associated NREM mentation reports are closely concordant (see Chapter 10).

Alternative 2. Inasmuch as most NREM utterances are concomitant with transitory movement-arousals (chapter 7), the sleep-utterance is only an additional manifestation of this brief increment of activation and reflects mentation related to this movement-arousal state rather than NREM sleep itself.

If this were true, however, one would expect that a content analysis of mentation reports, such as that just presented, would disclose significant *differences* between postsleep-utterance and silent sleep reports, corresponding to the differences in their concomitant electrographic pictures, as well as differences in the respective word counts of the two groups of reports, and the respective group frequencies of no-recall reports.

Alternative 3.   This is a restatement of the original working hypothesis that many NREM utterances are the outgrowth of *previous* streams of *ongoing* NREM mentation that, from time to time during movement-arousal intervals, are reflected by actual vocalization. This hypothesis is consistent with the present finding of essential similarity between mentation elicited from NREM silent sleep and after NREM sleep-utterance, with the sole exception of the significantly greater frequency of sleep experience in which the sleeper depicts himself or herself as vocalizing; and it also fits with our previous findings of frequent unambiguous concordance between NREM mentation reports and the immediately preceding sleep-utterance content.

It is noteworthy that sleep-imagined vocalization may occur in the silent NREM sleep of sleep-talking subjects but without concomitant overt vocalization (12.2–14.9% of NREM silent sleep reports). This indicates that conditions other than merely sleep-imagined vocalization must be fulfilled before overt sleep-utterance is emitted. It is possible, therefore, that some varieties of sleep-speech are most likely to occur when two or three conditions are simultaneously fulfilled:

1. the need to assert or express oneself or enhance the sense of self-existence; and/or
2. the presence of an emotion of proper intensity; and/or
3. a breach of motor outflow thresholds for vocalization due to diminution of threshold and/or increase of motor outflow intensities.

Any of these factors alone are apparently insufficient to result in sleep-utterance, but must act in concert.

The results reported in this chapter find support in MacNeilage's study (1971) described in Chapter 7. Mentation reports were elicited under three conditions: in association with sleep-talking, muscle activity of the vocal apparatus without sleep-talking, and a control devoid of both muscle activity and sleep-talking. The reports were scored for visual imagery, physical activity of the self, physical activity of others, coherence, relation to the experimental situation, and verbal content.

The awakening condition following sleep-utterance and the control without muscle activity and utterance most closely resemble the categories of "sleep-utterance" and "silent sleep" employed in the present chapter. Her findings comparing reports following sleep-talking to those from the control condition were that the proportion of dreams, coherent dreams, visual content, and physical activity were uniformly but only slightly higher (mean difference = 5.5%; range 1.1–9.7%) for the sleep-talking incidents. The level of statistical significance was not reported. By contrast, the percentage of sleep-talking reports categorized as possessing verbal content was 43.8 as opposed to 23.1 for the controls—a difference of 20.7%.

Correspondingly, if all categorizations of verbal content of the mentation reports described earlier in the chapter are combined (the sum of subject vocalizing, others vocalizing, anticipated speech, and references to words without imagined vocalization), we arrive at a proportion of 47.4% verbal content categorizations for the postsleep-utterance reports and 29.8% for the silent sleep reports—a difference of 17.6%. These figures are in rather close agreement, differing by only 3.1% (i.e. MacNeilage, 20.7% vs. Arkin, 17.6%).

It is of additional interest that MacNeilage's analysis of mentation reports obtained from her three abundant sleep-talkers in comparison to her two nonsleep-talkers showed, with minor differences, similar proportions in all content categories. This suggests that sleep mentation of sleep-talkers might be similar to that of a matched group of nonsleep-talkers. However, her subject population was much too small to evaluate this possibility. (In Arkin et al., 1972a, it was stated by mistake that MacNeilage compared her abundant sleep-talker subjects to five nonsleep-talkers instead of two, as stated here.)

In conclusion, it is evident that sleep-imagined vocalization occurs intermittently throughout the night in all stages of sleep and without actual overt vocalization. Snyder (1970) has reported that 86–100% of medium-length and long REM reports contain references to discussion or conversation. Might it be that inner dialogue of the sort described by Vygotsky (1962) is continued during sleep and serves some important functions such as aiding in the preservation of the sense of self, as well as maintenance of the integration of psycholinguistic systems?

14 Special Abilities Manifested During Sleep-Talking Episodes

CLINICAL-ANECDOTAL LITERATURE

Various observers have reported that during sleep-talking and/or somnambulism, functioning at a level superior to that of the waking state has been observed for certain abilities. These include improved ability to use a foreign tongue (Radestock, 1879), to orate, and recite essays and verse (Spitta, 1873), or other linguistic accomplishments (Maury, 1878); alleged telepathic and clairvoyant powers (Burrell, 1904); improved memory and recall of previously experienced items (Cook, 1937; Maury, 1878; Pinkerton, 1839); improved musicianship such as singing and mimicry of instruments (Pinkerton, 1839); improved literary creativity (McGregor, 1964); and improved mathematical ability (Hadamard, 1954).

According to Hadamard (1954), the following amusing event occurred in the life of the mother of L.E. Dickson, the eminent mathematician:

> His [Dickson's] mother and her sister, who, at school, were rivals in geometry, had spent a long and futile evening over a certain problem. During the night, his mother dreamed of it and began developing the solution in a loud and clear voice; her sister, hearing that, arose and took notes. On the following morning in class, she happened to have the right solution which Dickson's mother failed to know [p. 7].

Taken at face value, one might say that the cognitive state associated with this sleep-talking episode was compatible with complicated problem-solving mentation but that the amnesic tendency concurrent with somniloquy prevented retention and recall.

240

Similar wakeful phenomena have been described in some detail by Mühl (1963) in her book on automatic writing. One of her subjects, for example, was able to write smooth verse during wakeful automatic writing states. She was totally unaware of this process while it was going on and totally unable to do it at will in ordinary states of wakeful consciousness. This observation is reminiscent of descriptions by Goethe of his own creative "spells" in which he sometimes "awakened himself" by the noise of his quills on writing paper.

In a recent paper illustrating a possible relationship between somniloquy and creativity, Krippner and Stoller (1973) presented case material that would have been considerably more valuable if tape recordings of the sleep-speeches had been made rather than having relied on handwritten notes. In addition, it is unfortunate that attempts were not made to repeat the observations in a laboratory with standard electrographic recording. The material at hand is consistent with a macrodissociative state accompanied by a wakeful EEG tracing, similar to that of the female hypnotic subject described in Chapter 13, to Rice and Fisher's patient who was subject to fugues in association with sleep (Rice & Fisher, 1976), or to Batson's subject (Batson, 1977). At any rate, Stoller had been living with a young woman *(A)* for 18 months who, from "time to time.... would talk in her sleep, often holding lucid conversations with *L.S.* [Stoller]." For unspecified reasons, *L.S.* decided to read aloud and "discuss his poetry with *A*" while she was in a somniloqual state and "was surprised to find that her comments were very helpful, and much more discerning than most of her waking remarks." Typically, a dialogue would begin about 6:30 a.m., when *L.S.* would awake to the sound of *A*'s sleep-talking. At this point, *L.S.* would obtain a pen and paper, return to bed, and initiate a conversation. Not only would *A* respond to *L.S.*'s questions, she would also incorporate other sounds (e.g., birds, a distant train, the pen scratching on the sheet of paper) into her remarks. The conversation would terminate about 7:00 a.m., when *L.S.* had to awaken *A* "so that they could attend classes at the college they both attended." Stoller detailed several of their interchanges while she was "asleep"; among them were his recitation of a poem whereon she would respond with a mixture of loosely organized associations and imagery that appeared to be occasionally interwoven with hallucinatory experience, as follows:

    A: Careful. I just fell off a cliff and I didn't want to hit my head on any rocks.
    L.S.: Are you all right?
    A: Yes, I hit a piece of wood; I tried to grab it and got a splinter in my hand.

Over a period of several months, *L.S.* recorded *A*'s responses to his poetry. "Once she was awakened, she was unaware of the dialogue" and *L.S.* did not mention it to her. However, one day he read her several pages of the dialogue. *A* was surprised and said very little. The next morning, at 6:30 a.m., they had the following conversation:

L.S.: What did you think of your early morning responses to my poetry when I read them to you?

A: You didn't read them to me. You read them to her when she was awake. She doesn't remember anything when she is awake.

This last response strongly suggests the possibility that *A* had been experiencing psychical dissociative reactions. For example, her "sleep-talking self" deemed her waking personality as "not very imaginative." Following *L.S.*'s continued attempts to bring the "sleep dialogues" to *A*'s wakeful consciousness, she was alleged to have developed "more confidence in her original ideas" and became a more creative person.

In summary, the clinical–anecdotal literature contains a number of references in which the authors contend that creative abilities not available to wakeful consciousness may become manifested during sleep-talking episodes.

LABORATORY OBSERVATIONS

Creative or imaginative type phenomena of the sort described earlier have never been observed by me in my laboratory experience with sleep-talking. I know of no other investigator who has reported similar findings. It is my opinion that the clinical–anecdotal literature deals with rare macrodissociative psychical states that would be accompanied by a wakeful type of EEG, rather than being closely associated with electrographically defined sleep. As previously mentioned, this was the case with the female subject used in the posthypnotically stimulated sleep-talking work, Batson's subject (1977), and with the case of sleep-associated fugues described by Rice and Fisher (1976). An additional feature held in common by these three subjects and that of Krippner and Stoller was the clear tendency toward amnesia for the dissociated sleep-associated experience.

15 The Psychoanalytic Literature and Somniloquy

To the best of my knowledge, there is neither a general paper nor section of a book written from the psychoanalytic perspective that deals with sleep-talking. Like so much else in this area, small comments and references are dispersed in almost piecemeal fashion throughout. By contrast, there is a somewhat richer literature on speech in nocturnal dreams, and a review of this area seems useful by way of introduction.

HALLUCINATED SPEECH IN NOCTURNAL DREAMS

We begin by presenting Freud's statements and beliefs pertaining to this topic.

Phenomenology of Speech in Dreams
(Freud, 1900/1966)

In order for linguistic events to be classified by Freud as a dream speech, they must possess something of the sensory character of speech, with linguistic-motoric and acoustical accompaniments, and must be described by the dreamer as "speeches." Freud drew a careful distinction between "actual" speech occurring as part and parcel of dreamed events as opposed to speeches devoid of acoustic or motor accompaniments—those speeches which are not vividly felt or heard as spoken "aloud" in the dream experience. The latter might include dreamed implicit speech or mental references to speech, material that was being read in the dream, or thoughts of a speechlike nature similar to those that may occur during wakefulness. The dream-speech may be fragmentary and possess varying degrees of coherence ranging from those approximating speeches of wakefulness to apparently meaningless phrases and neologisms like "Auf Ungeseres [Freud, 1900/1966, p. 442]" or "Myops [p. 443]."

Dreamed conversations may vary along a similar continuum of reasonableness to complete irrationality.

Speeches in dreams often consist of relatively clear and compact segments and contiguous portions that serve to connect them and effect a kind of closure, or a facade, for gaps within and between such clear segments. Freud compared dream-speech structure to that of breccia in which variegated stones are held together by a binding, cement-like material.

The Sources of Manifestly Dreamed Speeches

Freud states that vividly dreamed spoken words are invariably copies and/or combinations of words and verbal utterances actually spoken or heard by the dreamer on the day preceding the dream. One exception to this rule is the dreamed reproduction of unconscious compulsive thoughts arising from within the psyche somewhat independently of day residua, such as the dreamed speeches produced by the "Rat Man" during his analysis (Freud, 1909/1955b). Obsessional thoughts in wakefulness are deemed to be incomplete and distorted versions of a more elaborate unconscious text. The latter may appear in dreams as spoken words to complete the whole.

The general rule just given, however, applies only to vividly experienced dreamed utterances that are described by the dreamer as actual speeches. Contrastingly, other sorts of speeches, which are those lacking in acoustic or linguistic-motor accompaniments, may be derived from day residual wakeful thought activity, often borne unmodified into the dream, or from verbal material that had been read by the dreamer previously.

Freud was not entirely consistent in applying the rule on which he was almost adamant. First, in most instances, he insisted that speeches vividly dreamt must have arisen from residuals of the previous day. Yet, in one example in a dream of Freud's own, a portion of the phrase "Auf Geseres" was traced to a speech that came to Freud's attention at a much earlier time in his life than the previous day (Freud, 1900/1953, p. 442–444). Indeed, in another place, Freud seems to recognize this implicitly when, discussing the sources of dreamed speech, he extends the time limit of day residua from the single preceding day to "the preceding *days* [1909/1955a, p. 21, italics added]. Actually, there has been a recent tendency in the psychoanalytic literature to liberalize the backward time interval limits of day residua in general; Altman (1975), for example, employs the more indefinite phrase "current events [p. 11]" to denote the day residuum.

Second, Freud again traces a vividly dreamed speech of his own—"Non vixit"—to something he had recently read rather than said or heard [1900/1953, p. 421–425]. As Fliess (1953) indicated, this is contrary to Freud's statement, "Whatever stands out markedly in dreams as a speech can be traced back to real speeches which have been spoken or heard by the dreamer [1900/1953, p. 420]."

Dreamed Speech, Dream Formation, Dream Work, and Dream Meaning

Wakeful utterances produced or heard by an individual may act as dream instigators (Freud, 1917/1963, vol. 15 S.E., p. 182). Baudry (1974) pointed out that whether this actually occurs in certain instances may be partly dependent on whether the daytime words had been endowed with significant cathectic intensity. In this regard, he cited a statement of Freud's who in describing a specific dream mentioned that the quasispoken thought, "'I can't bear the sight of it'... in the dream... failed to emerge as a speech in the strict sense....[1900/1953, pp. 420–421]."

Indeed, the role of emotional (i.e., cathectic) intensity in the production of speech in neuropathological syndromes such as aphasia, and vividly imagined speech in states of crisis in normals had been previously cited by Freud (1891/1953). In the former, the stereotyped utterances of two aphasic patients were directly related to conditions prevailing just before the moment of injury or illness preceding the onset of the brain affliction involved; and in the latter, Freud referred to two life-threatening personal experiences in which he implicitly heard the words "Now it's all up with you" as if they were being shouted in his ears.

In terms of dream-work mechanisms and unconscious meanings, Freud believed that the dream work cannot create new speeches, but, rather, in the most arbitrary manner, takes the day residua items and may dismember them into fragments, rearrange their order, select some, reject others, remove them from their daytime contexts, and put disparate terms together in a new pattern. In this fashion, a speech in a dream that appears to be a coherent whole may turn out in the course of analysis to be composed of three or four detached, unrelated, latent dream thought fragments. In producing this new version, the dream work will often disregard the meaning that the words originally possessed in the latent dream thoughts and endow them with a novel one in accordance with the requirements of the unconscious wish, dream-work parameters, and the censorship. Freud (1917/1963) enlarges on this in the following manner:

> Only where the word-presentations occurring in the day's residues are recent and current residues of *perceptions*, and not the expression of *thoughts*, are they themselves treated like thing-presentations, and subjected to the influence of

condensation and displacement. Hence, the rule laid down in *The Interpretation of Dreams,* and since confirmed beyond all doubt, that words and speeches in the dream content are not freshly formed, but are modelled on speeches from the day preceding the dream (or on some other recent impressions, such as something that has been read). It is very noteworthy how little the dream-work keeps to the word-presentations; it is always ready to exchange one word for another till it finds the expression which is most handy for plastic representation [Vol. 15, S.E., p. 228].

Finally, at times, dreamed spoken words function mainly as allusions to occasions during which the spoken words were uttered. The reader is referred to Freud's *Interpretation of Dreams* for many fascinating examples of the foregoing formulations.

Freud recommended that often one fruitful point of departure in the clinical interpretation of dreams is the selection of any dreamed speech followed by elicitation of associations and previous days' events, and demonstration of interconnections between them.

One cannot feel entirely sympathetic to Freud's views on the lack of creativity of the dream work. On the one hand, he insisted that the dream work does not create speeches anew, and on the other, he described the dream-work mechanisms involved as carrying out what other students consider to be a typical variety of creative work. Many artistic endeavors involve fragmentation, rearrangement, and a new synthesis of elements so obtained. An excellent example is provided by Lowes (1927) in his *The Road to Xanadu,* which convincingly describes the manner in which Coleridge used the imagery of the log of a marine captain in his creation of the *Rhyme of the Ancient Mariner.*

Several laboratory observations are worth citing in connection with Freud's ideas on spoken words in dreams.

First, the description of dismemberment, distortion, or transformation of verbal input, supposedly by dream-work mechanisms, has actually been observed by Berger (1963) and Lasaga and Lasaga (1973). Berger's subjects slept the night in the laboratory exposed to subawakening-threshold tape recordings of a set of four personal names. During REM sleep, these recordings were played, and the subjects were awakened for mentation reports a matter of seconds afterward. Significantly often, the mentation report, usually of a vivid visual dream, would contain an easily recognizable transformation of the stimulus name. For example, the name "Gillian" was followed by a dream with a manifest reference to "Chile" and to "linen"; the name "Andrew" was followed by manifest reference to "land" and to "hand"; and the name "Naomi" led to the content items "An aim to ski"—and later a friend who says "Ah, show me." The bulk of the outcomes of the experimental stimuli producing recognizable dream incorporations of the stimulus names contained transformations based on an assonance relation. That is, the acoustic features of certain phonemes and morphemes were lifted bodily out of the names containing them, and arbitrarily recombined and re-employed to suit the ongoing dream events of the moment, without apparent regard to the meanings of these names in reality. This seems to be very much in accord with Freud's description of dismemberment, distortion, and recombination of words spoken or heard during the day. That the stimulus names were not, strictly speaking, day residua but introduced concomitantly with the ongoing dream seems of little importance. The interval between the perception of the day residuum could be seen as merely shortened from the previous day to the previous few moments in the experiment between introduction of the stimulus during REM sleep and obtaining the dream report. The underlying mechanisms are probably not dissimilar. Indeed, Fisher's replicative studies of Poetzl's research indicates that dream work on day residua begins shortly after its daytime perception and need not wait until the prospective night's sleep (Fisher, 1957).

Second, exactly the same kinds of word dismemberment and production of incoherent and disorganized phrases and neologisms that Freud described in dreamed spoken words are also to be frequently observed in sleep-speeches. That is, the words often seem to have been subjected to primary process influences during the process of their emergence and final utterance. (See Chapter 19 for aphasiclike utterances.) With sleep-speeches as with dreamed spoken words, it is often possible to trace speech elements to day residua. For example, a Stage 4 sleep-speech uttered at 5:31 a.m. consisted of "Gundrum is the word for hundred in—hundred—in—hundred in hundred in S—Latin—Latin—to hundred." Although the subject recalled no related mentation on being awakened 8 sec afterward, he did say on hearing the playback of this sleep-speech the following morning that he was reminded of a linguistics lecture in which the teacher had compared the word "hundred" as it appears in several different but related languages. The subject had recalled being especially puzzled by the fact that "hund-" was related to 100 in Latin and "dog" in German. The instructor informed him that there was no relationship. It is possible that the G in the neologism Gundrum is derived partly from the G in German; and if so, would be illustrative of primary process manipulation of day residua manifested in a sleep-speech. Noteworthy is the fact that despite the subject's total amnesia for sleep experience associated with the sleep-speech, he recalled appropriately matching day-residual material after being primed by hearing a tape recording of his sleep-speech the following morning. This had been repeatedly observed in our laboratory. It suggests the possibility that certain daytime cognitions acquire "preconscious cathexis" of sufficient strength to participate in sleep-speech production but are nevertheless barred from short-term memory after sleep-utterance. It is a dramatic example of the sequestering of memory systems.

The psychoanalytic literature on speeches in dreams had little to add to Freud's comments until Isakower published two papers related to the topic

(1939, 1954). In the first (1939), he hypothesized that the human linguistic–auditory function is the nucleus of the superego. He provided three illustrative examples including:

1. a description of the evolution of auditory hallucinations starting from alarming auditory experience, and progressing from increasing sensitivity to what was heard and attributions of special meanings to the latter, through falsifications of auditory perception and finally to hallucinations;

2. a reference to a schizophrenic patient who felt compelled to repeat aloud, "I am Max Koch [his own name] from Alland [p. 346]" whenever he felt threatened (it was the speaking aloud that persuaded Isakower to classify the phenomenon as a regressive superego manifestation); and

3. quotation of the two danger experiences of Freud, cited earlier in this chapter, in which the thought "Now it's all up with you [p. 347]" struck Isakower as possessing a last-judgment sort of quality.

In the same paper, Isakower (1939) described sleep-onset and awakenings from sleep as involving traversals of speech barrier in which a flare-up of auditory–linguistic activity precedes both its temporary extinction in sleep and its re-arousal on awakening. On the occasion of sleep onset, Isakower was impressed not only by the content reflecting the stamp of the superego, but by the "tone and shape of a well-organized grammatical structure [p. 348]," which he ascribed to the superego. Similarly, on awakening, words or short sentences remained with the dreamer that, although shorter and more succinct than at sleep onset, nevertheless possessed a superego tinge that inspired in the subject an "inexplicable respect."

Grotjahn (1942) reported on his observations and speculations regarding the process of awakening from sleep. Many of his specimens are consistent with Isakower's contention that awakening is often associated with hearing spoken words of oneself or some phantasied person, and some even contain clear superego admonitory material. However, some of the hallucinated spoken words do not possess such qualities. Grotjahn, as contrasted to Isakower, believes that in the course of awakening, the first psychological task is the re-establishment of the body-ego (self-feeling) as distinct and separate from the external world together with self-orientation as to space, time, and causality. This is followed by the re-establishment of the ego function of both a sense and a capability of volition, and not until then does the influence of the superego become conscious; prior to this time it functions unconsciously as the dream censorship.

Mittelmann (1949) described the following dream of a homosexual patient: "He hears his mother's voice but spoken with the analyst's accent. 'John, get up.'" On the same night the patient had a second dream involving Negro men, running down staircases, control of a tense situation by means of magical gestures, and so forth. Mittelmann specifically asked the patient whether he had heard the words "John, get up" spoken during the previous day. The patient apparently could not recall such an event, although Mittelman did not say so unambiguously. Instead, he wrote that his question elicited recall of the patient's anticipation of his being called by a new homosexual friend who resembled the Negro in the dream. Mittelman's interpretation did not involve reference to superego function but rather that the "dream is the patient's attempt by magic omnipotence to master his fear of the relationship with this prospective partner [p. 437–438]."

In the second paper, Isakower (1954) offered the formulation that "speech elements in dreams are a direct contribution from the superego to the manifest content of the dream [p. 3]." It is curious that he provided only one clinical example, and an atypical one at that. A 30-year-old man who was partial to risky extramarital escapades and Wagnerian operas had attended a performance of Lohengrin on the night of the dream. In the early part, a direct speech occurred: "How much this Lohengrin is costing me already!"; and after waking, while recalling the dream, the subject half-heard half-said to himself, "Your swinish love life...shall yet come into the open." Both speeches were ascribed to superego influence—the guilt about his sexual life and fear of exposure. The first speech occurred within the matrix of the dream and seemed to exemplify the traversal of the barrier of speech from sleep to wakefulness, whereas the second is an after-comment possibly occurring in the hypnopompic state. In the latter instance, the self-reproachful superego component is unambiguous, whereas in the former, the self-critical meaning of the speech was disguised and affected by secondary revision.

In 1972, Isakower further commented on his thesis by way of final summary to F. Baudry (1974) in the course of personal discussion and made the following points:

1. The superego influences the dream ("affixes its stamp on the dream [Baudry, 1974, p. 583]" during the process of secondary revision and not before.

2. A manifestation of such influence is the dreamed spoken word that represents the traversal of the language barrier, entailing a partial awakening and re-establishment of the censorship.

3. The phenomenon was considered dynamically to be a first attempt at auto-interpretation of the dream instigated by the self-observing function of the superego.

4. Any spoken words, even those that do not manifestly indicate an evaluation of the dream, are considered as outcomes of superego function.

5. Inasmuch as the dream occurs in an optical matrix, the appearance of spoken words implies a shift from dreaming to wakeful consciousness.

6. Linguistic elements in dreams are viewed as solely originating in the superego. The principle of multiple function was deemed to not be involved in dreamed spoken words, inasmuch as drive and defense components of the final dreamed synthesis were considered to be extensions of superego activity. Manifest content of dream narratives with themes of punishment were considered to be fantasies utilized by the dream work but not created by it.

By way of preliminary criticism, the assertion that the auditory function is the nucleus of the superego seems arbitrary. There is a great deal of strong evidence that childhood visual experience of the parents' eyes, faces, and nonverbal behavior are powerful superego determinants (Riess, 1978). Secondly, the congenitally deaf are by no means conscienceless. Without an "auditory nucleus," how, then, do such unfortunates acquire a superego? Balkanyi's (1964) assertion of poor superego development in the congenitally deaf does not find support in the extensive observations of Furth (1973), who carefully documents his conclusions that although preschool congenitally deaf children do have poor impulse control, this is ascribable to accumulated frustration in learning to adapt to a world despite a cognitive handicap. By the time they arrive at adulthood, there is no unusual antisocial tendency or superego defect characteristic of them. Finally, Isakower's choice of words strongly suggests reification of the superego as a real entity rather than as a theoretical construct.

The next development in psychoanalytic thought regarding dreamed spoken words is contained in an essay by Fliess (1953) that anticipates some of Baudry's ideas, inasmuch as Fliess specifically describes contributions of the id and ego, as well as the superego, to dreamed speeches. His extended comments include points of similarity and difference, elaborations on, and emendations to, the empirical observations and formulations of both Freud and Isakower. The most significant contribution for the present purpose is summarized in the following quotations:

> To sum up: it is the ego that fantasies under the impulsion of the return of the repressed from a time when there had not yet been a super-ego; it is the super-ego that enters the fantasy in a speech expressing rejection. It is the ego that dreams and speaks in the dream; it is the super ego that, permanent and rudimentary as a censor, requires dream work on the speech and, temporarily re-established, enforces 'direct speech'.... [The dream speech] is allusive, simultaneously, to fantasy reproductive of an infantile trauma and thereby expressive of ego, and to an element in the fantasy reactive to it in terms of the conscience and thereby expressive of the super-ego. One could say that it is the ego that speaks and the super-ego that makes it speak and, in applying Freud's formulation, suppose that in the first instance content of the id penetrates into the ego directly, in the second, by way of the ego ideal [pp. 142–143].

Baudry undertook to evaluate Isakower's hypothesis that dreamed spoken words are "direct contributions from the superego to the manifest content of the dream [Isakower, 1954, p. 3]." Initially, he asked whether it was a testable hypothesis inasmuch as no established criteria are available to ascertain whether such a direct superego contribution has been made. He therefore sought to refine and isolate testable aspects of the problem and assess them in the light of clinical evidence. Baudry proposed the following: Manifest content in the dream portraying self-observation often appears in the dream because some component of the dream is perceived as threatening by the sleeping ego, thereby stimulating the censorship to react. Because self-observation is often associated with self-criticism and is sometimes a consequence of it, one might expect that a token of superego activity in a dream would be representation of some manifest conflict situation involving ego and superego. Self-observation was selected because dreamed spoken words often contain items suggestive of one part of the self commenting on another part. In addition, self-observation and self-evaluation are closely interwoven (Stein, 1966). Inasmuch as superego activity is often signaled by guilt feelings or betokened by defenses against them, Baudry asks specifically whether it is possible to detect in the manifest or latent content related to dreamed spoken words an important component of guilt-related conflicts. In this fashion, the problem is redefined from one requiring demonstration of an abstract entity (the superego) to one involving demonstration of derivatives deemed to reflect activity of the construct. Baudry's proposal implies, conversely, that a conflict situation capable of arousing the censor to impose self-observation on the ego is likely to be one involving guilt. Contrary to Isakower, who saw the superego affecting dreams only at the point of secondary revision, Baudry more correctly, in my opinion, sees the activity of the superego as continuous, though in altered form, throughout the process of dream formation involving excitement of the unconscious wish, dream work, secondary revision, and dream forgetting. Admittedly, Baudry stresses the prohibitive–punitive functions of the superego; he takes this position because other superego influences, such as those stemming from the ego-ideal, have, in his experience, infrequently participated in the dreams of his patients in which spoken words were reported by them.

Baudry recommends turning to Waelder's Principle of Multiple Function (1936) as an organizing perspective for dream-analytic data when clinical evidence fails to reveal conflicts involving the superego. Such a development was foreshadowed by Waelder himself in his discussion of over-determination, and by Fliess in the paper mentioned earlier (1953). This approach involves interpreting a particular element as the outcome of ego functioning with synthetic and defensive admixtures of active and passive modalities in relationship to influence stemming from the id, reality, superego and compulsion to repeat.

Among the important results of Baudry's investigation are the following:

1. Contrary to expectations, associations to the dreamed spoken words were either absent, sparse, or not easily relatable to the crucial theme of the dream.

2. In only one instance could the dream speech be traced back to a day-residual speech. (Unfortunately, the total number of dreams in the sample was not mentioned so that the proportion of such occurrences in the population under consideration cannot be given.) This lack of clear relationship to speeches of the previous day, upon which presence Freud insisted, could not be ascribed to intense resistance inasmuch as such predicted relationships were not descernible even where the dream as a whole could be understood.

3. Spoken words occurring in hypnagogic or hypnopompic states were found more likely to possess prohibitive–punitive connotations than those occurring at the beginning or in the middle of dreams.

4. Some patients who strongly resist regression (often those with obsessional features), and who tend to think without imagery have produced dreams consisting almost entirely of conversations. In the analysis of such dreams, the prohibitive–punitive influence of the superego seemed no more evident than in their other dreams lacking spoken words.

5. Certain dreams with spoken words were deemed to have a structure similar to waking fantasies or daydreams and thought to be the product of a mental apparatus insufficiently regressed to allow visual imagery. This latter circumstance may result from ego-defensive activity, external variables (nap dreams or sleep resumption dreams), or the continuation of a presleep preoccupation, spoken words of which do not reflect superego content directly.

6. Clinical vignettes of analyses of dreams with spoken words were presented demonstrating the following:

   a. application of the Principle of Multiple Function to a dreamed speech in which could be discerned components related to sexual and aggressive drives, superego (reproaches to self and analyst), the repetition compulsion (repetition of traumatic scenes and childhood failures), and defensive ego functioning indicated by spoken words reflecting condensation, displacement, and projection processes;

   b. the spoken word as an attempt at verbalized communication in one case and at manifest reproach in another; and

   c. an episode of sleep-talking overheard by a sleeping spouse and elicitation of a concomitant dream with first-order concordance between the two. This observation is discussed further when the psychoanalytic commentary on sleep-talking proper is presented.

Somewhat differently from Isakower, Baudry concluded that conflicts derived from guilt may be but are not always discernible in the analysis of dreamed spoken words and that important components of drive and defense also contribute to the meaning and form of dreams. The multiple meanings of the spoken words were fruitfully illuminated by application of the Principle of Multiple Function, again contrary to Isakower's beliefs.

Fisher (1976) expanded the discussion of the issue of dreamed spoken words. He agreed with Baudry's conclusions that the spoken word in dreams may be a manifestation of superego influence but that this is clearly not true of all spoken words, and that drive and defense factors may also make crucial contributions. Similarly, he confirmed Baudry's impression that the example of the dream speech cited by Isakower, tinged with the ominous, portentous, threatening, awesome, and oracular qualities, are extremely rare occurrences, and perhaps should not be classified as dream but as hypnopompic or hypnagogic phenomena. Fisher agreed with Isakower that the "crossing of the frontiers of speech" (Isakower, 1954) during awakening may well be the occasion for especially intense superego preponderance, inasmuch as the process of re-establishment of censorship functions may involve a momentary over-correction process in the psychic equilibrium. However, he cautions that this formulation may not be applicable to the spoken word in dreams, in which state the direct influence of the superego is contrastingly subtle in its manifestations. Accordingly, Fisher indicated his belief that Isakower mistakenly attempted to utilize the paradigm of crossing the speech frontier from sleep to awakening as the model for spoken words in dreams. Fisher further registered his disagreement with Isakower's insistence that dreams are exclusively optical phenomena and that spoken words necessarily imply a shift toward wakefulness, and even that spoken words are not part of the dream at all. Rather, Fisher correctly emphasized that dreaming involved hallucinatory processes in all sensory modalities including hallucinated linguistic events.

Baudry, following Fisher, Kahn, Edwards, and Davis (1975), thought that utterances associated with Stage 4 night-terrors were eruptive expressions of uncontrolled anxiety, not part of a manifest dream, and hence insusceptible to analysis. Fisher (1976), on the contrary, felt that this latter assertion regarding insusceptibility to analysis was not strictly true inasmuch as such verbal content is often related to central psychodynamic issues.

Fisher (1976), like Baudry, has only rarely observed that dreamed spoken words could be related to verbal day residua and has given thought to the disparity between their findings and those of Freud, which were of an opposite nature: Fisher attempted to account for this by Freud's almost unique cognitive talents—i.e., an eidetic memory and capacity for recovering subliminal and indifferent impressions possibly enabled Freud to more regularly track down the specific verbal day residua. A final decision concerning the validity of this explanation must be withheld until a controlled clinical study is carried out with a sufficiently large number of patients, each of whom contribute a sufficiently large number of dreams to a sufficiently large number of analysts who possess differing qualities of sensitivity to such clinical material. Many psychoanalysts, including Freud and Isakower, have drawn sweeping conclusions on the basis of clinical observations unspecified as to total number, number of patients, kinds of patients, setting of data collection, manner of selection of patients, etc. Such research is of great importance not only for clinical practice validation, but for basic scientific psychological research in dream formation processes. *One cannot look solely to standard laboratory study of dreams for a solution to many of these questions. Most laboratory data have been obtained from paid subjects, who are not attempting to gain relief from mental torment by adjunctive or even necessary employment of clinical dream analysis, who are not in the throes of intense, emotional transferences, who thereby and therefrom do not have understandable psychodynamic reasons for mobilizing hypernormal censorship and defensive activity, and who expect that once the experiment is over, they will return psychologically to the status quo ante, rather than be continuously striving for further self-understanding and psychological growth. It has been demonstrated in several laboratory studies that such factors as these may crucially influence the nature of experimental data— making for differences with those revealed by careful clinical study.* (For expanded commentary on this issue, see Arkin, Chapter 17 in Arkin, Antrobus, & Ellman, 1978.)

Second, some psychoanalytic clinicians like Isakower have been guilty, in my opinion, of excluding certain phenomena such as dreamed speech or actual sleep-talking from the very realm of dreams because they don't fit conveniently into Freud's theory of dream formation. This violates proper scientific procedure inasmuch as theory is here used to constrain and distort empirical observations rather than modify theory to accommodate objective findings.

Freud's aphorism to the effect that a dream is the disguised attempted fulfillment of a repressed wish, regardless of its brilliant terseness, neither fully defines nor delimits the scope of the dream, and slavish adherence to such formulations eventually serves to impair rather than further scientific understanding of dreams and related phenomena. A dream is more than the just-mentioned aphorism. For example, M. M. R. Kahn (1976) has written that "a person in his dreaming experience can actualize aspects of the self that perhaps never become overtly available to his introspection or his dreams, and yet it enriches his life and its lack can impoverish his experience of others, himself, and his sleep [p. 330]."

Suppose a sleeper utters a phrase aloud that on subsequent awakening bears a clear, first-order concordance with what the subject *himself* describes as an ongoing dream. One may not cavalierly dismiss the sleep-speech as not part of the dream merely because it is a vocal rather than an "optical phenomenon" or because it fails to fulfill Freudian dream formation theory criteria. Rather it is incumbent on theoreticians to appropriately emend and enlarge psychoanalytic dream formation theory to accommodate such phenomena as the rich audio-linguistic and motor concomitants of dreams that do not interrupt or perturb the dreaming process in any known way. Further details on motor concomitants of dreams are presented later on in the section on psychoanalytic aspects of somniloquy proper, as distinguished from and related to spoken words in dreams.

Freud's theoretical conceptions provided that dream formation regularly entails psychic regression to the chronologically earliest modes and memorial contents of mentation. Freud assumed that such early experience consisted of visual imagery and hence dreaming was largely an optical phenomenon. This assumption, however, is called into question by the cogent evidence presented by Piaget (1954), which strongly suggest that the earliest form of mentation is *sensorimotor* in nature, much of it involving inborn imitative tendencies; and after a certain proficiency at imitation of externally observed actions is acquired, the infant slowly develops the capacity for imagery despite the absence of the object—a phenomenon described by Piaget as resulting from deferred imitation. The important point is that sensorimotor modes of cognition are prior to the development of visual imagery.

Freud's emphasis of visual imagery at the expense of other modes of dream mentation may well have been influenced by his observational base consisting of dreams recalled in the morning by which time a great deal of dream experience, especially verbal detail, is no longer available for retrieval. By contrast, laboratory observation on large populations of subjects have repeatedly demonstrated the ubiquity of dreamed speech and dialogue (Arkin et al., 1972a; Cipolli, Dubois, & Salzarulo, 1974; Cipolli & Salzarulo, 1975; MacNeilage, 1971; McGuigan & Tanner, 1970, Salzarulo & Cipolli, 1974; Schnee, 1978; Snyder, 1970). Indeed, this finding had been reported much earlier by Calkins (1893) on the basis of repeated intranightly awakenings of two "normal" subjects.

The view advocated here that motor imagery is at least contemporaneous with visual imagery in the infant, or even prior to it in development, is consistent with the findings of Mahl (1977) obtained during psychoanalytic sessions. A typical sequence was frequently observed in which repetitive, pattern motor behaviors regularly preceded conscious imagery that could then be psychologically related to the preceding events. Mahl concluded that:

> *The essence of an unconscious wish or memory, of a thing-cathexis may be a potential for bodily innervation, or perhaps covert innervations and their*

sensory feedback. The frequency with which one can observe *the regular progression from a bodily expression to primitive ideation, to eventual verbalization* suggests that these are some of the transitional stages in the process of something becoming conscious. [Mahl hypothesized that] the nucleus of unconscious wishes and memories consists of excitatory potentials for very *concrete bodily excitations,* which are specific instances of the abstract categories termed "wish" or memory [p. 307—Mahl's italics].

Also, recently, regarding the issue of the primacy of regression to visual cognitive modes, Edelson (1972) has claimed that "Language as a symbolic system is, according to the rebus model [used by Freud to illustrate transformation of verbal to visual representations], logically prior and indispensable to dreaming as a symbolic system [p. 271]." Further commentary dealing with relationships between language and dreaming may be found in Jakobson (1956), Werner and Kaplan (1963), Edelheit (1969), and Litowitz (1976).

In the light of the foregoing, Arlow and Brenner's (1964) reformulation of psychoanalytic dream theory in terms of Freud's structural theory of the psyche is a distinct advance. It seems much more capable of providing for the new empirical research findings on dreams than Freud's classical topographic theory. The chief relevant considerations of their views are as follows:

1. The dreamwork is comprised of the interaction between psychic influences arising from the id, ego, and superego, which may be mutually enhancing, cooperative, acquiescent, or opposing in various combinations.

2. During sleep, various ego and superego processes are "regressively altered" resulting in the id playing a more unrestrained, inefficiently modulated role in fashioning sleep mentation. This combination of factors facilitates dream-work processes in the production of the dream as experienced.

3. Especially emphasized, in contradistinction to classical topographic theory, is the unevenness of the temporal and formal regression of ego and superego alterations—such formal regression deemed to be "both selective and variable [p. 128]." That is, some ego and superego processes may be relatively little changed from their wakeful manner of functioning, and others drastically so, in degrees of regression and efficiency. Furthermore, provision is made for fluctuations in the components of their functioning so that, for example, at one moment the bizarre events of a dream may feel real to the dreamer, and later on, the dreamer may realize "This is only a dream" but nevertheless continue dreaming; or else, the dream work may use regressive visual thinking and mature verbal thinking simultaneously, or in quick alternation during ongoing dreaming.

4. This principle of selective and variable alteration of ego and superego

function confers a much greater flexibility on Arlow and Brenner's reformulation of psychoanalytic dream formation theory, as compared to classical topographic theory. It enables one to draw distinctions between those alterations that are due to infantile regression and those that are a result of degrees of suspension of their activity and integration entailed by the states of sleep as psychophysiological processes. Thus, Arlow and Brenner (1964) speak of the *"nearly* complete suspension of motor activity" in sleep [p. 126—italics added]. This implies that in their view, overt sleep-speech need not be incompatible with ongoing dream mentation nor commit one to exclude such events from the realm of dreaming because they are not "pure" optical phenomena.

The reader is invited to turn to pp. 121–122 to review the REMP-associated sleep-speech and mentation report said to illustrate concordance based on psychoanalytic interpretation. In view of the role ascribed to disguise and symbolization in classical Freudian dream-formation theory, it is curious and inconsistent that the dreaming processes utilized symbols and disguise whereas the sleep-speech is direct and unambiguous. This subject was an actor and not at all bashful in his wakeful life; and yet he was not able to spontaneously retrieve the word "snatch" from his sleep-speech, preserving instead the short-term memory of his dream containing the disguised symbolic representation of the female genital. Perhaps the following account resolves the dilemma: Repressive tendencies were activated and selected "snatch" as their main target. Another possibility is that the homosexual component of the sleep-speech ("Cassius Clay's armpit") aroused even more anxiety, compelling the subject to repress the memory of the entire speech; and accordingly, the homosexual content in the manifest dream is even more intensely disguised than representation of the female genital. That repressive tendencies were indeed activated at some point in connection with this dream is suggested by the subject's omission of the recall of the entire manifest dream associated with this sleep-speech, when asked, as usual, to write down all dreams remembered from the previous night. He recalled six other dreams, most of which occurred earlier in the night than the one concomitant with the somniloquy. Because it was a more recent dream, it should have been remembered more easily than the earlier ones, were it not for the presumably activated repression. After being primed by hearing the tape recording of the first sentence of his mentation report, the entire remainder of the dream sprang to his mind in a somewhat shorter and slightly modified version.

By means of Arlow and Brenner's formulations (1964), one need not discount ad hoc activation of repression as a factor but nevertheless one experiences less puzzlement by the inconsistencies; that is, selective and variable regression of ego and superego functions are capable of permitting more or less mature *and* regressed derivatives to occur contemporaneously and thus accommodate more of the data satisfactorily.

SOMNILOQUY PROPER IN THE
PSYCHOANALYTIC LITERATURE

It is curious that Freud made no systematic or extensive comment on sleep-talking. It seems like such a natural point of departure for rich psychoanalytic theorizing in the area of dream-formation processes, cognition in general, psychoanalytic–linguistic mechanisms, and states of consciousness. As we see presently, he was certainly aware of the phenomenon and it *is* after all only a short step from dreamed spoken words to overt sleep-talking.

In 1966, I reviewed the psychoanalytic literature on sleep-talking and brought together whatever gleanings and snippets I could find; I attempted with these fragments to formulate a psychoanalytic interpretation of sleep-talking from the various metapsychological viewpoints as well as Waelder's Principle of Multiple Function (1936). This coverage included material from writers influenced by Freud but not strictly in the Freudian tradition. What follows is an updated and expanded version of this earlier review (Arkin, 1966).

In his discussion of children's dreams, Freud (1900/1953), quoted an episode of sleep-talking uttered by his daughter, Anna, then 19 months old, and tentatively classified it "under the heading of dreams." This occurrence impressed Freud. He referred to it in at least four places—in an earlier letter to Fliess (1897/1906), in the *Interpretation of Dreams* (1900/1953), in his shorter work *On Dreams* (1901/1952), and in his chapter on "Children's Dreams" in his *Introductory Lectures on Psychoanalysis* (1917/1963). His letter to Fliess contains the following paragraph topic sentence: "Do you think that children's speeches in their sleep count as dreams? If so, I can present you with the very youngest of wishful dreams [p. 267]." He then rendered the following background. The child had recently been deprived of food for a day because of a gastrointestinal upset attributed by her nurse to eating too many strawberries. Anna had been intensely fond of them. In her sleep that night, she was heard to have said, "Anna Fweud, Stwabewwies, wild stwabewwies, omblet, pudden! [p. 267]." Freud related that Anna had been in the habit of using her name to express the idea of taking possession of something she desired, and interpreted the dream speech as expressing retaliatory rebellion against being deprived of the much-loved treat.

An interesting companion to this observation is the account of Grotjahn (1938) on the sleep-speech and other dream indicators of a 28-month-old boy. The subject had visited the home of another baby whom he did not see, but in whose back yard dwelt a lovely rabbit that he tried to feed with stones. That night, "in his dream," he said, "Rabbit, stones, rabbit, stones, baby where? Baby bed! [p. 509]." Grotjahn concluded that the "most significant experience of the day was repeated in the dream, and the unsolved problem, 'Where is the baby?' found its answer in the dream [p. 509]." Additional specimens with the day residua are listed in Table 15.1.

TABLE 15.1
Day Residua and Sleep-Speech

Daytime Events	Sleep-Speech
Two puppies having a bitter fight over his mother's gloves in association with a car ride.	"Wow—wow, ran, gloves, ride, car! [said with excitement.]"
Being taught to be watchful about cars on the street.	"Watch out! Careful! Cars!"
Seing a monkey at the zoo grabbing his mother's gloves.	"Monkey!"
The dreamer refused to take his regular walk to his father's office to accompany the father home. He had indicated he preferred that his father remain alone at his office so that he could be alone with his mother. Grotjahn provided contextual material strongly suggestive of beginning Oedipal themes.	"Papa movie? Baby with mother alone!"
Events involving food.	"Food noch!" "Have flowers." [Flowers meant salad.] These sleep-speeches were uttered in a matter-of-fact tone much in contrast to his wakeful, apparently vociferous manner of making food requests.

Grotjahn concluded that besides direct expression of wish fulfillments, his subject's dreams, signaled by accompanying sleep-speech, indicated attempts to achieve mastery over intense, strange emotions that had been aroused during the days prior to the dream.

To return to Freud's comments regarding sleep-talking, he once discussed a paper of Sadger on somnambulism presented to the Vienna Psychoanalytic Society (1962, described in Nunberg & Federn). Sadger had asserted that there was a close relationship between somnambulism and dream life and that the overt actions performed in sleep stem only from sexual wishes of diverse sorts including exhibitionism, wishes for homosexual relations with parents, teachers, and the like. One of his patients was a young girl who besides sleep-walking also talked in her sleep, but did not betray any sexual secrets. Her somnambulism was interpreted as an expression of unconscious wishes to resume sleeping in her parents' bed after having been "evicted," and also to gratify homosexual longings for her mother. Sadger also referred to several fictional characters famous for their sleep-walking, including Lady Macbeth.

Freud stated that "Sadger is right in seeing a connection between somnambulism and dreams; but the puzzling question is: how is it that the paralysis of motility, which is characteristic of the dream, can be undone in sleepwalking while dream life nevertheless continues [p. 156]?" Although Freud did not include sleep-talking at this specific point, there is an implicit indication that he would not be averse to grouping them together as related phenomena. Freud then went on to say:

> The case of Lady Macbeth is not one of ordinary somnambulism, but something more like a nocturnal delirium. Case 1 [of Sadger's] is characteristic in that people who talk in their sleep never give away their secret on that occasion; what they say is only a substitution for what they are hiding (people who talk much have a secret). Yet Lady Macbeth, strangely enough, betrays the secret; but then, it is not her own secret, not that of the lady, for she plays everything in the role of her husband. She betrays only something which has some connection with her own secret [pp. 156–157].

In the *Metapsychological Supplement to the Theory of Dreams* (1917/1963 S.E. Vol. XIV), Freud once again referred to the same puzzle of somnambulism, but only in passing. He was concerned with large issues involving the metapsychology of sleep and dream formation and was considering the vicissitudes of a preconscious dream-wish formed from day residua in such a fashion as to provide a potential means of expression for repressed impulses. Generally, during wakefulness, such mental formations proceed from the system Pre-Conscious (PCS) to awareness; or they "may bypass the CS and find direct motor discharge," or they may proceed to dream formation. Regarding the possibility of motor discharge, he commented that "access to motility normally lies yet another step beyond the censorship of consciousness. But we do meet with exceptional instances in which this happens, in the form of somnambulism. We do not know what conditions make this possible, or why it does not happen more often [p. 227]."

The aforementioned citations appear to indicate that Freud regarded somnambulism as an anomaly with equivocal status in which dream consciousness and dream-work mechanisms (distortion and disguise) are capable of co-occurrence with motor discharge. In all of his writings, there is only one explicit reference known to me of a sleep-talking incident—that of the infant Anna Freud described earlier—and this he classified as dream-related. It seems reasonable to surmise that the relatively small scale of somniloquy as opposed to the larger scale somnambulism suggested to him that somniloquy is more easily compatible with dreaming in the usual sense.

In the *Project for a Scientific Psychology* (1895/1966), Freud drew a distinction between motor discharge and motor elements: "Dreams are devoid of motor discharge, and for the most part of motor elements [p. 338]." Second, he recognized transitions between states of dream and wakeful consciousness: "Dreams exhibit every degree of transition to the waking state [p. 338]." Third, he drew attention to slight motor manifestations of thinking: "As is well known indeed, what is called conscious thought takes place to the accompaniment of slight motor expenditure [p. 367]"; and a little later, he added: "the current of speech-innervations during thought is obviously very small. We do not really speak, any more than we really move when we imagine a motor image. But the idea and the movement only differ quantitatively.... If thought is intense, no doubt people speak out loud (p. 367)." These ideas later evolved into conceptualizing thinking as "essentially an experimental kind of acting, accompanied by relatively small amounts of cathexis together with less expenditure (discharge) of them [Freud, 1911/1958, S.E. Vol. XII, p. 221]."

Might Freud have considered somniloquy as a system-preconscious-mediated expression of motor speech *elements* (as mentioned earlier) as opposed to considering somnambulism as a motor *discharge* phenomenon? Such a notion seems compatible with a statement of Sandler, Holder, and Dare (1975) in their presentation of dream processes in the topographical frame of reference: "Motor activity is considerably restricted by the state of sleep, being limited to such phenomena as groaning, grinding of teeth, slight body movements ('restless sleep'), *talking or mumbling,* and occasionally sleep-walking [p. 164—italics added]." The same notion is apparently also very similar to the formulations of Landauer and Schilder, described later.

This entire line of thought seems more comprehensible if considered from perspectives in the *Metapsychological Supplement to the Theory of Dreams* (Freud, 1917/1963). At one extreme of a range of conditions, Freud postulated a state of absolute narcissism manifested by dreamless sleep. This state is disturbed by cathected day residua which, when linked up with and reinforced by unconscious repressed impulses, oppose the narcissistic, dreamless state from within the psyche. When unimpeded, such tendencies ultimately lead to an externalized projection of the internal process in the form of a dream permitting simultaneously the discharge of the cathexes and continuation of sleep—a compromise outcome. The preconscious day residua are formed into preconscious dream wishes, so fashioned as to provide a means of expression for those unconscious repressed impulses that find them suitable for the purpose. Normally, the drive-invested PCS process pursues a regressive course through the system UCS to the system Perception-Consciousness (PCPT-CS), exciting it from within to produce a dream. Although Freud did not specifically so indicate, it is conceivable, however, that the regressive course is attenuated or evaded in some atypical "short circuit" fashion; or else the drive-besieged system PCS does not relinquish all of its word-presentation cathexes to transformation into thing-presentation cathexes, leading eventually to fragmentary eruptions of speech-infused hallucinatory dreams—a kind of state intermediate between dream and somnambulism, yet experienced subjectively as a dream in many instances, and itself sharing the effects and resources of many dream-work mechanisms.

Ferenczi (1916) reports an instance of sleep-laughter which, in its particular context, he interpreted as the outcome of the reversal of latent dream thoughts of sexual impotence and impending death—i.e., the laughter was considered a reversal of the weeping and sobbing appropriate to the unconscious mentation. Here the implication is fairly clear that Ferenczi considered an episode of sleep-utterance to be a defensive reaction to unconscious processes related to an ongoing concomitant dream. Freud cited this specimen as an example of reversal of affect in his 1919 edition of The Interpretation of Dreams (p. 472). Grotjahn, in his 1945 paper on laughter in dreams, added to Freud's comment that the laughter here also expressed the hostility of the dreamer toward death.

Jones (1927) briefly relates an incident of somnambulism with somniloquy. A girl of 20 years, after hearing Jones' lecture, queried him as to the meaning of an episode that occurred when she was 12. While she was asleep in her parents' bedroom, she arose and walked. Her father asked her what she was going to do, and she replied, "to fetch a shawl to crack" (as in a nutcracker). Jones speculated that the phrase was derived from erotic and aggressive wishes toward the father's penis. The latter was symbolized by "shawl"—an example of mantle symbolism signifying the male genital.

It can thus been seen that Freud, Ferenczi, and Jones treated at least some sleep-speech occurrences as being the resultant of processes resembling dream work and dream formation.

Landauer (1918) wrote a long, complicated paper on the activities of the sleeper, including references to sleep-talking. Included among his initial considerations is the notion of sleep *intensity* (p. 338), as opposed to the depth of sleep, which he deems a not very useful concept. By intensity, he wished to indicate a parameter of sleep denoting a factor of how strongly sleep is desired by the subject and the tenacity with which it is maintained despite disturbing stimuli. Second, he represented various activities in sleep as the result of interaction between three more or less separate selves or egos: the sentinel *(Wache),* the remaining or remainder-self *(Rest-ich)* and the dreaming self, all of which cooperate or oppose one another in various combinations within the confines of the actual person.

In general, the remainder-self wishes only to sleep. The sentinel maintains alertness to external stimuli and protects the sleeping remainder-self by fending off or diluting unimportant but possibly disturbing external events. The sentinel is capable of awakening the remainder-self if the input from the environment so warrants, as in perception of danger to self or others. The dream-self, frequently subdivided, is normally obedient to the remainder-self. In the presence of daytime stress or unfinished business, it maintains quiet by permitting such residual effects or strivings to continue and be satisfied as hallucinated fantasy during sleep. However, such satisfaction is not always achieved, and the dream-self may take more or less complete possession of the actual person and carry out various dream activities, including sleep-talking.

Landauer believes that his views are entirely consonant with those of Freud (and indeed bear more than a slight family resemblance to them). He described instances of his own sleep-talking (as reported to him by his wife), and those of a fellow army officer whose somniloquy Landauer overheard and noted. With both, he viewed the content of the sleep-speech within the context of momentous current reality concerns, which had actively persisted during sleep, and hypothesized that the sleep-speeches were the outcome of a conflict between the "remainder ego" and the "dream ego"—the former wishing to remain asleep and the latter striving for expansive self-expression, to gain pleasure, or to deal further with daytime strivings in the medium of sleep fantasy.

Schilder and Kauders (1956) acknowledged being much influenced by Landauer (1918) and described the topography of the psyche during sleep as consisting of: (1) a sleep ego—the part that truly sleeps and wishes to remain asleep; (2) a waking ego—the part that maintains contact with the extrapsychic world and evaluates stimuli in accordance with whether they are a threat to the sleeper; and (3) the dream ego, further subdivided into a preconscious dream ego that merges with the waking ego (the boundaries being only vaguely defined) and an unconscious dream ego. Schilder writes that:

> Occasionally, dreams are encountered the structure of which resembles that of the mentation occurring in the psychic system preconscious, i.e., they demonstrate to a considerable extent the manner in which everyday thinking works, except that these trains [of thought] are cut off from consciousness. As a rule, the motility of the sleeping person is blocked. Yet occasionally, especially in dreams of the preconscious type, the motility may be accessible, and we are dealing with those persons who talk or carry out more or less complicated actions in their sleep [p. 69].

Schilder further mentions that conversation between a sleeper and a waking person with whom he is in rapport is possible and that when awakened, the sleeper has a complete amnesia for the event. The intensity of the sleep is said to diminish as the strength of the rapport increases. Concurrently, the sleeper's conversations become progressively more coherent as the waking process continues. Schilder ascribes this to the gradual replacement of unconscious elements by preconscious elements, the qualities of the latter bearing an increasing resemblance to those of the conscious state. This description appears entirely consonant with our laboratory findings (see Chap. 12).

Teplitz (1958) treats somnambulism and somniloquy as psychoanalytically equivalent phenomena—in the former, muscles of locomotion are activated; in the latter, muscles of speech. She bases her comments on clinical study of several people with somnambulism, some of whom also spoke or wept in their sleep. Her views are that the highly organized motor activities "partially replace visual projection and other sensory absorptions of the tension of the visual dreaming [p. 109]."

[The] patterned motility [is important] as a partial defense against sleep itself. Although sleep is partially given up, in the motor area, it is also partially preserved as a defense against perceptions, both internal and external. To the sleep-walking patients, sleep itself was frightening because it was associated with loss of voluntary muscular control generally, with loss of sphincter control, or with death or loss of identity. These patients had intense fear of loss of control over forbidden, hostile or sexual impulses—....Somnambulism served to decrease anxiety about loss of autonomy or about death....Aggression, independence, and differentiation from the parents are dramatically expressed in sleep-walking by patients in whose real life their expression is too threatening. These patients tended to be outwardly compliant in waking life. The feelings of autonomy and self-assertion were threatened in sleep by the withdrawal from external sensory (mainly visual and auditory) and proprioceptive stimulation, and by loss of voluntary muscular control. These feelings of autonomy typically first develop around the second year of life, when toilet-training and the development of motor skills are so prominent [p. 96].

As a symptom in which sleep is partially given up in terms of bodily motility, somnambulism also has a sleep-preservative function and *partially* maintains repression. Activation of the body's voluntary musculature replaces passive fears of loss of control or of death [p. 108].

Thus, sleep-walking, more dramatic and exhibitionistic than sleep-talking, is thought to permit flight from dangers associated with sleep in bed. (The role of exhibitionism is consistent with the history of one of my experimental sleep-talking subjects, who related that prior to spontaneous sleep-walking as a child, she would consciously *feign* sleep-walking to intimidate a younger sibling.) Teplitz goes on to cite Rapaport (1951), who believed that somnambulism, amnesia, and fugue act out unconscious wishes rather than express them in symbolic form in dreams. Gutheil (1960) believed that somnambulistic performances, including sleep-talking, are not dreams in the strict sense, but "dramatizations of dreams." Along similar lines, Marburg (1929) asserted that certain dreams that feature a feeling of omnipotence may lead to various actions in sleep, including sleep-talking.

A more recent psychoanalytic contribution to the literature on somniloquy is contained in the paper by Baudry (1974), reviewed earlier, on dreamed spoken words. A sleep-speech episode is described therein that he believes accords well with Isakower's formulations that speech in dreams is "associated with awakening phenomena and implies a clear self-critical judgment dealing with the latent content of the dream [p. 598]." Thus, a young married woman related the following about nine months after the birth of her son: "I dreamt of the baby falling out of the bed and I shouted, 'No! No!' as I grabbed onto his thigh. In reality, I had grabbed on X's thigh (husband). We both awoke suddenly. I said to X, 'I though you were E!' (child). He told me that he had been awakened by hearing the shout, 'No! No!' [p. 597]." The patient went on to relate that E, her son, is very strong, difficult to manage, and was felt by her to be capable of standing up and throwing himself out of his carriage. Her associations to "No! No!" were, "That's when I'm overwhelmed or found fault with...sometimes, X approaches me to make love and I don't want to [p. 597]." The patient added that she felt herself to be a very good mother and mentioned boasting about her children; she experienced annoyance about being tied down to nursing her baby and had recently toyed with thoughts of weaning him. Baudry stated that in the recent past, useful comparison had been made between making love, nursing, and the analytic situation, where as a function of the transference, she perceived herself as a child blissfully incorporating it, or the one who was incapable of satisfying her analyst's needs and always fell short of requirements no matter how much she gave. She also felt that all of her children's needs must be fulfilled lest she would classify herself as a bad mother. The "No! No!" was said by Baudry to express a prohibition on several levels and broke through into speech and motility "presumably because the content of the dream was too threatening and could no longer be tolerated by the sleeping ego. It also expressed a turning away from the husband and child: "I don't want to make love/nurse anymore [p. 598]." One may perhaps agree that the episode exemplifies Isakower's awakening phenomenon, but the episode also acquires much deeper meaning from the perspective of the Principle of Multiple Function. Certainly, the hypnopompic thought specimen of Isakower, "Your swinish love life...shall yet come into the open" is an unambiguous self-threat, superego derivative—it needs no interpretation to elucidate it. By contrast, Baudry's specimen is somewhat ambiguous. The "No! No!" in the manifest dream seems to express the dreamer's wish to prevent her son's being injured; the self-prohibitive–punitive superego element is arrived at only through inferences, cogent though they may be. Earlier in his paper, Baudry cited a comment of Freud's (1900/1953, p. 421) pertaining to a manifest dream component, that the dream contained the *thought*, "I can't bear the sight of it," which was said by Freud to have "failed to emerge as a speech." Baudry wondered whether this implied "some sort of threshold, an intensity of cathexis which if sufficient will allow the element to be experienced as a speech rather than as a thought [p. 585]." The underlying sense of the conjecture appears to be that as the psychic energy invested in a specific item increases, it is capable of transforming the inner experience from an unspoken, but nevertheless discrete thought, into implicit, hallucinatory speech. This is an intriguing thought and an intensity factor could well play a role in production of sleep-speech. However, sleep-speech is so variable, ranging from bland or humorous words to elaborate frenzied emissions, that cognitive and shifting dynamic equilibratory factors are likely to play a more important part. In this connection, it is worth recalling that many dreams with intense affect are not accompanied by speech, indicating that intense affect is not a sufficient condition for sleep-speech.

Fisher has made several important contributions to the psychoanalytic literature on sleep-speech. In his first commentary (Fisher, 1965), he postulated that instinctual drive discharge occurs in REM sleep but is quantitatively reduced in NREM sleep. He therefore expressed puzzlement that a number of sleep activities, including sleep-talking occurring during NREM sleep, may nevertheless be associated with instinctual drive discharge. Accordingly, he hypothesized that one reason sleep-talking occurs chiefly in NREM sleep may be that motor paralysis is not as marked as it is in REM sleep; but he then finds further difficulty in reconciling this with reports that some sleep-talking occurs in REM sleep as well. Actually, although motor activity is tonically suppressed in REM sleep, there is a great deal of phasic motor activity that manifests itself in brief twitches and body movements of varying magnitude. That sleep-utterance may accompany such REM motor episodes or even be their main manifestation need not, therefore, constitute any serious inconsistency. Second, Fisher's views at this time (1965) were in accord with the then prevalent notion that psychologically, REM and NREM sleep were sharply distinct. His most recent beliefs (Rice & Fisher, 1976) in this regard indicate greater appreciation for their underlying intersections and interrelationships besides their separateness. This paper deals with sleep-talking as a manifestation of fugue states in sleep, the main descriptive, clinical, and electrographic features of which were given in Chapter 11. Briefly, the patient was a 46-year-old male who had a propensity for episodes of sustained psychic dissociation. These became exacerbated and much more elaborate following the death of his father, to whom he was closely attached. The clinical picture was one of recurrent fugue states appearing in association with sleep, as well as by day. The patient was observed in the laboratory over 3 nights and produced sleep-talking episodes. Their content dealt with dramatic emotional utterances of an apparently hallucinatory nature, in which the patient spoke aloud concerning his father. At one moment, mournful recognition was given to the fact of his father's death with expressions of deepest despair, hopelessness, and helplessness, and at the next, his father was spoken of as if he were still alive, could be saved, was coming home from the hospital, giving rise to refusals to accept his father as dead, etc. These sleep-talking episodes were considered to be nocturnal equivalents of the patient's daytime fugue episodes, resembling them in mental content but being dissimilar in that they lacked motility.

In all, five episodes of vocalization in association with sleep occurred. During the first laboratory night, shortly after the first REMP while in Stage 2, the patient awoke moaning and crying. A few minutes later, he was yelling in his sleep; and during the third laboratory night, two episodes spontaneously occurred in the predormescent interval, and two others out of REM sleep immediately after the sounding of an awakening buzzer signal. The latter episodes seemed to possess more vivid, dreamlike hallucinatory qualities than those from predormescence, suggesting to the authors that a dreamlike psychological state related to the previous REMP was continued after arousal.

Rice and Fisher (1976) concluded that "the data suggest a continuity of, and reciprocity between the physiological substrates of psychological phenomena in the three organismic states of wakefulness, NREM and REM sleep. They do *not* appear to be *trichotomized in process or in function,* i.e. there may be overlapping or leakage. Similar interrelatedness and continuity are reflected in the psychological sphere [p. 86—italics added]." This passage is quoted at length and the foregoing phrase italicized to contrast it with Fisher's earlier comment on sleep-talking (1965) in which a dichotomous, mutually exclusive relationship between REM and NREM sleep seemed to be implied. If, accordingly, the boundaries between the two states may be thought of as semipermeable, the problems that seemed originally puzzling (Fisher, 1965) regarding the psychoeconomic aspects of sleep-talking in relation to state of consciousness seem less difficult of formulation. In other words, dreaming and instinctual drive discharge need not be restricted to REM sleep, because both occur in association with NREM sleep as well; and frequent sporadic motor discharges, especially in phasic form, are ubiquitous in REM sleep. Thus, somniloquy need not be excluded from, or considered as unrelated to, dreaming processes.

Finally, in a series of excellent psychophysiological studies on the NREM (mostly Stage 4) night-terror, Fisher et al. (1975) described sleep-speech in relation to these acute, nocturnal, hallucinatory panic states. Besides establishing such phenomena as different psychophysiologically from the REM nightmare and as a direct ego-disruptive breakthrough of anxiety, rather than an essentially dream-derived phenomenon, these studies have had no direct relationship to the general psychoanalytic theory of dream formation. Between the usual blander occurrences of often dream-associated, common NREM sleep-talking and the Stage 4 night-terror, a series of intermediate forms are observable so that they may be arranged on a gradual continuum, with transitional states between them (see Chapter 18.) Fisher's findings are consistent with the clinical formulations of Sperling (1958) on pavor nocturnus.

Turning now to comments of authorities who have not been identified as working within the mainstream of Freudian thought, but whose ideas are compatible with it, the following may be cited: As previously mentioned, Cameron (1952) collected observations on the omnipresent sleep-talking among U.S. troops in the Persian Gulf command in World War II. Impressed by the realistic vividness of his own accompanying dreams, he tentatively suggested that if one held to the wish-fulfillment hypothesis concerning dreams, it would appear that conscious rejection of a painful reality was coupled with, and was compensated by, a more realistically structured dream world, and carried to the point that the sleeping behavior (in this case, talking) became more and more like the normal waking behavior. That is, the inescapable horrible reality of war was replaced by a vivid psychic reality during sleep, fashioned in accordance with the sleeper's emotional needs rather than being reflective of external exigencies. De Sanctis (1899) mentions a similar phenomenon under stressful arctic conditions.

Adler (1964) asserted that the unity of psychic life persists in sleep. Sleep-talking, as well as other sleep phenomena such as bruxism, walking in sleep, dreaming, and the like, purportedly bear the indelible stamp of the lifestyle of the sleeper. He did not offer any specific example of this principle involving sleep-talking.

Sullivan (1956) apparently believed that when self-security is endangered by dream formation, and its wakeful remembrance interferes with successful maintenance of dissociation of a major system, dream recall may cease. This may leave disturbed sleep in its wake, accompanied by anguished sleep-vocalization.

> The person with a major system in dissociation may recall from his sleep very vivid and blatantly meaningful dreams as long as nothing provides a path between these dreams and his security. As long as this situation continues, it is all very simple; for one thing, dreams that can be remembered come a little nearer to satisfying the tendencies concerned than do dreams that have to be forgotten. But if, perhaps as a result of someone else's attempt at interpretation or of something read in a book, these dreams come to interfere with the self-system's suave function of keeping the dissociated tendency out of awareness, then the person will cease to recall any dreams whatsoever. He may have very disturbed sleep, his wife may report that he groans and yells in his sleep, and he may startle into full awareness over and over during the night, but he will have no trace of recollection of any dream. In other words, the self will be on the job from then on, and sleep will be maintained at a level at which primitive processes cannot intrude into awareness [p. 180].

In other words, if conscious memory of specific dream contents arouses anxiety for whatever reason, dream recall may be suppressed, leading to sleep disturbances including sleep-vocalization.

Psychoanalytic Formulation of Sleep-Talking

In my first review of sleep-talking (Arkin, 1966), I attempted to paraphrase and synthesize a preliminary psychoanalytic formulation of somniloquy based on the available material in the literature. This included a set of comments from the topographic, dynamic, economic, genetic, and adaptive viewpoints, including as well, perspectives offered by the Principle of Multiple Function (Waelder, 1936). Since that time, new laboratory data have emerged and new work has been published, both requiring that changes be made.

I wish to emphasize that my aim at this specific point has been to arrive at psychoanalytic formulations that take into account, as best as I am able, the writings of those authors who have worked in the psychoanalytic tradition. In so doing, I am not necessarily agreeing, disagreeing, or endorsing the scientific validity of such a synthesis. Second, the reader is reminded yet once more that throughout the book, I've repeatedly drawn attention to the great variability of the phenomena associated with somniloquy and so any formulations put forth must of necessity be complex and tentative.

Somniloquy in Relation to the Wakefulness–Sleep Continuum

Freud used the terms sleep and wakefulness in special ways (Freud, 1917/1963). In one sense, sleep is presented theoretically as a state of mentationless quiescence—"The narcissism of the state of sleep implies a withdrawal of cathexis from all ideas of objects, from both the unconscious and preconscious portions of these ideas [p. 224]." In another context, "dreams only show us the dreamer insofar as he is *not* sleeping [p. 223]," and this is the correlate of the fact that "the repressed portion of the system UCS does not comply with the wish to sleep that comes from the ego, that it retains its cathexis in whole or in part, and that in general . . . it has acquired a certain measure of independence from the ego [p. 223]." These comments suggest that for Freud, one essential criterion for sleep was quiescent inactivity and for wakefulness, by contrast, signs of activity. Freud clearly saw sleep as a nonunitary process with components that were "asleep" (inactive) and components that were "awake" (active). Thus, a person could be asleep (relatively inactive physically, with interest in, and alertness to, external real events drastically reduced) and could also be awake in part (forming dreams, censoring them while in process of formation, carrying out dream work and secondary revision). That is, part of the sleeper's mind could be awake while he is somatically asleep, and other parts be asleep. This contention accords reasonably well with laboratory data.

In the same way, sleep-utterance phenomena might be approached from an analogous perspective. The person who emits utterances in association with slumber may be considered as "asleep" for the following reasons:

1. He is unaware of, and uninterested in, the external world of the moment as such.

2. He tends to maintain a similar lack of awareness and/or amnesia for sleep-talking episodes as he does for most other sleep mentation.

3. He may emit utterances within the psychological context of dreaming sleep (both REM and NREM) as defined by behavioral and mentation report criteria. A review of the sleep-utterance–mentation-report concordance data should convince the reader that many sleep-utterances occur while the subject is deeply immersed in a sleep-associated dream experience and that the content of the report of such experience and the sleep-speech are often unambiguously interwoven and concordant; that is, they stem from the same psychological process.

4. He maintains the usual degree of paralysis of motility except for the act of utterance. As previously pointed out, the purported absence of motility during dreaming is a relative, not an absolute, phenomenon. Insistence on absolute lack of motor discharge as an essential criterion for "true dreaming" is not borne out by laboratory study. Even Lucretius knew this without laboratory measurement, but by behavioral observation (Lucretius, 1951).

And by contrast, the person who emits sleep-utterances may be considered "awake" for the following reasons:

1. The content and structure of many, but by no means a majority of, sleep-speeches may resemble preconscious mentation (less primary and more secondary process than is usual in silent, exclusively hallucinatory dreaming). That is, many sleep-utterances occur in the context of what Freud (1916/1925) described as "dreams from above." These were dreams that "correspond to thoughts or intentions of the day before which have contrived during the night to obtain reinforcement from repressed material that is debarred from the ego [p. 111]." Such dreams often seem to be a replay of daily events.

2. During sleep-utterances, the sleeper is often, but only in a minority of instances, able to cathect and respond to an external object as in dialogue between somniloquists and wakeful observers. However, in opposition to this if considered as evidence for wakefulness, it must be remembered that such dialogue occurs at least initially during a state in which the individual is subjectively asleep (he finally "awakens" after some interchanges), and that amnesia and perceptual distortions during the experience are common. To a less dramatic but not less definite degree, experimental evidence indicates that

the capacity for specific responsiveness and psychological transformation of external input is maintained throughout sleep (Berger, 1963; Lasaga & Lasaga, 1973; Williams, 1973).

3. The usual degree of paralysis of motility is partially overcome in that the musculature of speech is activated. Although this is true, Freud, it will be recalled, was willing to consider much grosser forms of activity as compatible with "dream life" during somnambulism.

Sleep-Utterance from a Dynamic Point of View

Sleep-talking incidents and their content appear to be influenced by dream formation tendencies and dream-work mechanisms such as displacement, condensation, secondary revision, and symbolization. This is clearly evident in occurrences with neologisms and fragmentation of words and word sequences. The content may reflect or/and represent attempts at wish-fulfillment, defenses against negative affects, memories, and drive-cathected fantasies. As the manifest dream unfolds with the mediation of varying amounts of secondary revision, the manifestly dreamed events may themselves secondarily elicit affective verbal responses that add further components of somniloquy; i.e., the subject may overtly react vocally to his own hallucinated productions.

Sleep-Utterance from the Economic Point of View

Sleep-utterance may occur after a certain cathectic intensity threshold is attained; the distribution of cathexes and countercathexes is altered so as to modify the drastic inhibition of motility during sleep and to increase the permeability of the psychic barriers involved. The net result may be the facilitation of more intense discharge of drive energies and affects.

Sleep-Utterance from the Genetic Viewpoint

Sleep-speech is the resultant of unresolved psychic conflict originating in the phase of development in which the main problem is the acquisition of mastery over sphincter control and motility.[1] In addition, conflicts deriving from childhood masturbation, voyeurism and exhibitionism, primal scene fantasies, and the Oedipal situation may contribute additional determinants

---

[1]Baudry (1974) apparently misunderstood this portion of my 1966 review and credited me with this point, when actually the credit for it belongs to Teplitz (1958).

in varying degrees. Attempts to achieve belated mastery over traumatic experiences must likewise frequently play a role in sleep-speech occurrences.

Sleep-Utterance from the Adaptive Viewpoint

The ego apparatus in using sleep-speech deals with the manifold problems outlined earlier, while maintaining repression and sleep. That is, despite overt expression of sleep-associated mentation under conditions of diminished ego controls, amnestic tendencies characteristic of sleep-talking episodes both facilitate and reflect the effects of repression. This aids fulfillment of the adaptive task of the moment—the securing of sleep.

Sleep-Utterance in Accordance with the Principle of Multiple Function

The ego apparatus of the sleeper copes with psychic pressures acting on it as follows:

1. Some id impulses are gratified—partial removal of the paralysis of motility may permit self-assertion, aggression, exhibitionistic satisfactions, and displaced discharge in fantasy of excretory products from below upward to the vocal apparatus, all of which may find expression in the act and content of a sleep-utterance. Also, inasmuch as many sleep-talking episodes are accompanied by distressing mentation, and being known as a chronic sleep-talker often exposes one to mild humiliation, one might presume that masochistic needs are fulfilled during such events. At the same time, if one assigns biopsychological tendencies to the id, an additional demand is satisfied—the need to sleep.

2. The claims of the superego may be partly fulfilled when something only *related* to a secret guilt-laden thought is confessed, i.e., the *form* of a confessional is enacted partly in response to a superego command to confess and expiate sins. For example, Isakower might say, if his hypothesis about hallucinated speech in dreams is extended to overt sleep-talking, that the act of somniloquy and its content were disguised derivatives or explicit expressions of superego reproaches and imperatives.

3. The stress of a painful reality may be partly reduced when florid sleep-speech lends more reality to a dream that "seeks" to reverse an undesired external situation.

4. With respect to the defensive functions of the ego, words uttered aloud (an organized active behavior) may diminish fears of passivity, loss of autonomy, fears of castration and death—all of which may be implied by personal meanings attached to yielding to sleep. That is, the self-assertion, motility, rebellious drive, and affect discharge and replacement of anxiety-

arousing visual imagery by spoken words may serve to combat the foregoing frightening ideas.

5. The mediating and synthetic capabilities of the ego are thus manifested by sleep-speech, insofar as defensive functioning and discharge of id energies are integrated within a single overt act. Furthermore, along similar lines, the same behavior that performs defense functions and facilitates id expression may bear the imprint of the superego. That is, the *trappings* of a confession may be "staged" in lieu of the revelation of the actual content of the guarded secret. Thus, the expression of a mere token of a secret may be a way of evading the full disclosure of the "real" secret; and the subject may hope thereby to obtain absolution without enduring the dreaded punishment felt by him to be appropriate to his "crime."

6. That many sleep-speeches seem to reflect ongoing distressing experience or attempts to avert fearful hallucinated occurrences suggests that the compulsion to repeat traumata plays a role in their genesis and content.

7. Sleep-utterance may serve to maintain and reinforce the ego when it evaluates the input of the moment as excessively threatening. Verbalization vitally assists in preserving ego integrity (Edelheit, 1969).

8. In summary, sleep-utterance, in accordance with the Principle of Multiple Function, serves to comply with, and integrate simultaneously, tendencies arising from the id, superego, the compulsion to repeat, and the reality of the moment—the state of slumber.

FURTHER CONSIDERATIONS

Further considerations regarding a psychoanalytic formulation of somniloquy occasioned by contemporary developments in sleep psychophysiology and psychoanalytic theory are discussed here.

It was urged earlier that the classical psychoanalytic theory of dreaming be refurbished to take full account of new phenomenological and electrographic findings of sleep research. In particular, it was contended that insistence on *total* inhibition of motor discharge during dreaming failed to accord with laboratory observations. The new sleep research has clearly demonstrated abundant phasic motor discharge during REM sleep of a variety of muscle groups as manifested by REMs (Dement & Kleitman, 1957) MEMAs (Pessah & Roffwarg, 1972) facial twitches, laryngeal muscles (McGuigan & Tanner, 1970), and small limb movements (Gardner & Grossman, 1976; Stoyva, 1965a,b; Wolpert, 1960).

Furthermore, there are positive correlations between certain parameters of these electrographic data and the phenomenology of dreamed events. The issue of the extent of correlations between specific directionality of REMs and dreamed events is currently a matter of incompletely settled controversy.

(See discussions of psychophysical parallelism in dreams in Arkin, Antrobus, & Ellman, 1978.) However, a new important finding not mentioned in this source is that of McGinty and Siegel (1977) in laboratory studies of cats with implanted electrodes. It was shown that in particular neurons associated with specific motor behavior such as head movement, the discharge patterns during REM sleep closely resembled those patterns occurring in wakefulness. This was taken to indicate "an expression during REMs of normal movement patterns [p. 154]." In whatever manner the controversy is finally resolved, it will be necessary to take this result into account, if replicated.

In sum, the statement in Freud's (1895/1966) *Project,* "Dreams are devoid of motor discharge . . . .We are paralyzed in dreams [p.338]", must be revised. That is, from the vantage point of empirical psychophysiological findings, the classic psychoanalytic tenet of absolute incompatibility of motor activity and dreaming must be modified to the less stringent statement that motor activity is tonically drastically reduced and phasically activated in irregular fashion during REM dreaming; and during NREM dreaming, motor activity, though reduced in comparison to wakefulness, is greater tonically than during REM dreaming. Although NREM sleep contains abundant phasic events including motor activity, their cognitive correlates, if any, have not yet been established for a randomly selected population.

As mentioned earlier, the reformulation of psychoanalytic dream formation theory from classical topographic terms to more recent structural theory terms (Arlow & Brenner, 1964) provides for uneven and variable psychic regression and *nearly* complete motor paralysis during dreaming. These changes seem capable of accommodating certain types of somniloquy as derivatives of dream-formation processes. I refer to micro- and some intermediate-dissociative sleep-talking episodes arising out of electro-graphically typical REM and NREM sleep, and if the current thrust toward reformulation of general psychoanalytic theory into cognitive-psychological information-processing conceptualizations prevails, it is likely that such newer motions would be equally capable of explaining these types of somniloquy as arising from dream-formation processes. In Chapter 17, a formulation of sleep-talking is presented in terms of Hilgard's Neodissociationist Cognitive Theory, which seems quite compatible with the new trends of psychoanalytic theorizing as exemplified by the writings of Rosenblatt and Thickstun (1977), Peterfreund & Schwartz (1971), and others.

16

Miscellaneous Psychological Theories of Sleep-Utterance

A variety of conceptualizations and commentary as to the nature of sleep-talking are to be found mostly in diffuse and dispersed fragments in the clinical–anecdotal literature. Many of them are quite cogent. They are couched in a range of perspectives including the more or less psychological, psychophysiological, and neurological. The psychoanalytic literature was large enough to warrant a separate chapter; and I devote a separate chapter as well to my own views on the subject, and those of other researchers who have worked with modern electrographic methods, in Chapter 17. Here we are concerned only with the less well-known clinicians and observers.

ORIGIN AND MEANING OF SLEEP-TALKING

The theory most widely held is that sleep-speech is the outcome of localized threshold activation of cerebral speech centers occuring against a background of generalized cerebral inhibition, which maintains behavioral sleep. One group of observers holds that such localized threshold activation occurs during a dream (Andriani, 1892); Cameron, 1952; Carpenter, 1849; Elder, 1927; Jung, 1957; Lipps, 1909; MacNish, 1838; Moreau, 1820; Pinkerton, 1839; Symonds, 1851; Walsh, 1920a,b; Winterstein, 1953), whereas a second group believes that this process occurs independently of dreaming (Ellis, 1926; Goecker, 1935; Pötzl, 1929a,b; Salmon, 1910; Trömner, 1911a,b).

Andriani (1892) is a leading exponent of the former viewpoint, and his ideas are worth quoting extensively, not only for their intrinsic interest, but because his paper, one of the few dealing exclusively with somniloquy, was published 8 years prior to Freud's *Traumdeutung* (1900) and contains many prophetic ideas that were most fully developed in the psychoanalytic theory of dreaming. Andriani's name does not appear in Freud's magnificent and thorough introductory review of the scientific literature on dreams and, to the best of my knowledge, was, therefore, unknown to Freud. For example, the following concepts are clearly contained in larval form in the following paragraphs: the residua of wakeful mentation persisting during sleep, their further intensification by more primitive deep unconscious psychic activity, the loss of logical coherence of the stream of sleep mentation, the relaxation of psychic censorship, the connection of mentation with somatic sources of innervation, the general importance of dynamic unconscious factors in the production of the dream, and the postulation of an unconscious mind. The following is a translation of passages from Andriani (1892) taken from the original Italian, and I beg the reader's indulgence for its stiffness:

> Sleep-talking is a spoken dream [*un soqno parlato*]. It reflects our internal state during a dream analogous to waking speech reflecting our waking consciousness of our waking selves and the external world. . . . During dreams, the activities of our senses are more or less suspended, consciousness dims, the will and ability to reflect are absent. The subject matter of sleep-speeches originates from the depth of our unconscious [*fondo dell'inconsciente*] either by spontaneous and natural activity of the brain centers, or by some unknown centripetal current coming from the sense organs. In further explanation of this, we are reminded that the subjects of many dreams and sleep-speeches are frequently inspired in the brain by certain sensitive or sensorial impressions which are not sufficiently strong to awaken the sleeper, but sufficient to activate unconscious cerebration [*cerebrazione psichica inconsciente*]. Therefore, we have no conscious choice or control of the subject matter of dreams or sleep-speech—this is imposed on us by the unconscious activity of the brain in the form of a psychophysiological innervation not strong enough to activate superior psychological functions (and awaken the sleeper) but nevertheless sufficient to activate speech centers.
>
> Furthermore, sleep-speech occurs whenever this psychophysical innervation is active independently of the conscious [*la coscienza*] and the will, and ceases when it becomes inactive. That is why it is ordinarily useless to look for a logical connection between words uttered in sleep-speech. Such words are as confused and fitful as the ideas of dreams. The unclear articulation of sleep-speech is likewise due to the intermittent and relatively weaker affect of this psychophysical innervation. By contrast, the innervation of waking speech is stronger and steadier. Wakefulness passes into sleep and vice versa by imperceptible degrees. There is a certain similarity between the automatic utterances of an awake but engrossed man who thinks aloud, and the utterances of a sleep-talker. People do not dream or sleep-talk unless something has been left awakened in their psychic activities during sleep, and the more that sleep approaches waking by imperceptible degrees, the more favorable are the

conditions under which dreams and sleep-talking will occur. Furthermore, the more sleep approaches wakefulness, the more likely will the utterances be clear, well articulated, logical and easier to remember....Sleep-speech is always the expression of our innermost feelings—the mind freed of restraints stemming from reality, conscience, education, and consciousness, reveals itself "in the nude." As the dream is the life of the unconscious, sleep-talking is its voice. In wakefulness, we can think without talking; in sleep, we can dream without talking. In order for speech to occur in either case, a stronger stimulus is required than for the production of a thought. Therefore, sleep-talking does not occur unless the dreamer is deeply touched....Often, the idea of a dream or of sleep-talking may be brought about by obscure currents that derive from the depth of organic life, from the skin, mucous, and serous membranes, blood vessels, the viscera, joints and tendons, etc. Such currents are continuously flowing, but under normal conditions such successions of sensations, ideas, feelings and actions of our psychic life are not felt. Sometimes, illness strengthens them and brings them to awareness; at other times, higher psychic activity is dimmed and lower forms, no longer held in check by the higher forms, take the upper hand.

Andriani goes on to say that there are many abnormal psychological conditions, a prominent symptom of which is impaired control of speech production together with some disturbance in consciousness. These include the sudden utterances of normally engrossed people, sleep-talking with or without somnambulism, nightmares and night-terrors with speech, chemical narcosis, hypnosis, postepileptic states, certain hysterical attacks, deliria secondary to fevers, toxic states and other organic brain disease, and functional psychoses. He believes that the underlying mechanism of this symptom is more or less the same in all of these states and presents observations (too detailed to quote here) to support this hypothesis.

Trömner (1911a,b) is the most representative of the second group of observers who believes that sleep-speech occurs independently of dreaming, and rarely, if ever, in association with it.

Sleep is a general, probably sub-cortically elicited inhibition of cortical functions with preservation of circumscribed, dissociated areas of diminished reactivity [1911a]....Dreams arise from focal excitation of such an area in the cortical sensory zone. When similar focal excitation involves the motor cortex, somniloquy and somnambulism may result. Somniloquy is an after-effect of daytime excitation arising from the circumscribed awakening of the motor component of language concepts. It is rarely based on dreams. Somniloquy is inhibited speech [1911b]....In most cases, sleep-talking occurs without accompanying dreams. It corresponds merely to a partial motor cortex excitation in that only *motor* components of speech–language concepts are activated. The reverse phenomenon (arousal of purely sensory elements of language concepts) may occur in those relatively rare dreams and hypnogogic states in which suddenly an internal voice sounds with hallucinatory clarity, and calls out some sentence to us [1911b].

Finally, many authorities, without committing themselves to a psychophysiological theory, believe or imply that sleep-talking is a manifestation or accompaniment of dreaming (Bañuelos, 1940; Erickson, 1941; Fischer, 1839; Fosgate, 1850; Freud, 1901/1952; Freud in Nunberg & Federn, 1962; Höche, 1928; Janet, 1925; Löwenfeld, 1907; Lucretius, 58 B.C./1951; Marburg, 1929; Massarotti, 1950; Maury, 1878; Moll, 1889/1958; Pai, 1946; Radestock, 1879; Schilder & Kauders, 1956; Spitta, 1873; Vaschide & Pieron, 1902; Vogl, 1964; Walsh, 1920a,b; Winterstein, 1953).

SLEEP-TALKING AND HYPNOTIC STATES

Estabrooks (1957) believes that the not uncommon phenomenon of conversing with a sleep-talker who responds more or less appropriately is really an instance of the sleeper's entering into an hypnotic state. In his opinion, sleep-talkers are generally good hypnotic subjects, and he describes a method of hypnotic induction used with sleeping subjects without their consent or conscious knowledge. The operator begins talking in a very low voice and suggests that the sleeper hears him and understands him with his "unconscious mind"; the sleeper is told that he will remain asleep and respond to questions by talking without awakening. About one-fifth of subjects are said to respond and can be led into "somnambulistic" hypnosis; the others merely awaken. Those who are susceptible to the procedure have amnesia for it on being awakened. Other observers (Fosgate, 1850; von Economo, 1926; Winterstein, 1953) report similar phenomena.

Related to this line of thought is the assertion that people who have talked in their sleep are likely to be capable of automatic writing (Mühl, 1963). One spontaneous case of this type is described in Chapter 20—an English-speaking patient who spoke Russian only in her sleep but was incapable of it while awake, and who also wrote a clinically significant passage of automatic writing.

Ferenczi (1909/1950) likens somnambulistic performance to the carrying out of posthypnotic suggestions; the somnambulistic act is said to be performed in obedience to an inner commanding voice.

The opinion that hypnotic and sleep-talking states are related is held by others (Cook, 1937; Gutheil, 1960; Schilder & Kauders, 1956). In this respect, it is interesting to note that in "somnambulistic" hypnotic trance, an observer can converse with a "self" of the subject that is different from the normal waking conscious "self" as one may do with sleep-talkers, and following such conversations, spontaneous amnesia is common. Furthermore, often the speech of people in deep hypnosis is thick and fragmentary, as it frequently is in sleep-speech. It may be possible to discover other points of similarity. Mühl (1963) describes phenomena in automatic writing states, which might also be analogous.

My own personal experience cautions me against accepting any generalization about relationships between hypnosis and sleep-talking. First of all, sleep-talkers as a group form a most heterogeneous population and, second, in repeatedly attempting to hypnotize eight adult sleep-talkers, only three were capable of achieving states of consciousness classically considered as evidence of deep hypnosis. I do not think that sleep-talkers are any worse or better hypnotic subjects than any persons randomly selected from the general population. Further, discussions about whether subjects are "really" in a hypnotic state are always awkward because of the lack of agreement concerning the scientific meaning of the phrase.

17

A Contemporary Theoretical Organizing Perspective for Sleep-Utterance

SLEEP-UTTERANCE AND PSYCHIC DISSOCIATION

In previous publications (Arkin, 1970; Arkin et al. 1972a; Arkin, 1974b), it was hypothesized that sleep-utterance could represent the output of an evanescent, spontaneously evolved psychoneural system in sleep, the activity of which deserves to be classified as a "miniature dissociative reaction." This phrase was selected because the phenomena of sleep-utterances seemed analogous in many respects to features of the classical dissociative syndromes described by Janet (1889, 1907). The term was introduced by him because of the prevailing theory of the time that memories were brought to awareness by a process of association with the mainstream of conscious ideas, and memories that existed but were not available to awareness were somehow "*dis*-associated." Janet utilized this concept in accounting for the clinical phenomena of somnambulism and fugues characterized by sustained behavioral episodes with rich psychological content related to deep personal concerns, and for which the patient had amnesia during his usual "normal" state.

WEST'S DEFINITION OF PSYCHIC DISSOCIATION

Although many other clinicians have written extensively on dissociation (see Hilgard, 1977, for a detailed discussion and bibliography, the best clinical review and psychiatric discussion known to me is that of West (1967). For the present purposes, West's essay contributes the following three items: (1) a contemporary multidimensional definition of psychic dissociation; (2) a comprehensive classification of psychic dissociative phenomena based on an expansion of the components of this definition; and (3) a demonstration of the ubiquity of psychic dissociation in everyday life.

West defines psychic dissociation in terms of a disturbance of integration of cognitive components involved in information processing. These components include neural organizations that simultaneously and continuously (1) scan and screen informational inputs; (2) process both new and old information in a manner facilitating modulation of the state and content of awareness; (3) integrate and associate new with previously stored information; and (4) control information output in the form of behavioral action so that mentation and action may be related. *Dissociation, then, is said to occur when incoming, stored, or outgoing information is actively prevented from undergoing integration with its normal network of associations.*

These considerations were used by West for the classification of dissociative reactions in Table 17.1.

Thus, West (1967) proposes to employ dissociation as the most general term to describe certain normal vicissitudes, aspects, and disorders of information processing in humans that entail relative and variable unavailability to normal wakeful consciousness of various mental contents. If this be allowed, a number of terms used by others to describe similar or related phenomena, such as unconsciously motivated repression (Freud), dissociation (Janet, 1925; Prince, 1906), and co-conscious (Prince, 1906) may be classified as subsets of a general psychophysiological adaptive mechanism for dealing with information.

West, (1967) concurs with distinctions drawn elsewhere (Arkin, 1966) between "normally occurring sleep-talking [p. 896]" on the one hand, and sleep-talking as part of a trance state emerging in relation to sleep, on the other. He classifies the latter as belonging to "somnambulistic trance states", so-called because they are "profound, self-limited and nocturnal [p. 896]." Such patients are deemed to actually awaken, spontaneously become entranced, though nevertheless remaining in bed, and emit elaborate sleep-speech, often of a conversational nature, for which they have subsequent amnesia. Similarly, a distinction is drawn between the relatively small-scale, NREM-associated somnambulistic episodes observed in the laboratory (Gastaut & Broughton, 1965; Jacobson & Kales, 1967; Kales & Jacobson, 1967) with apparently nonpurposive, nondramatic, noncommunicative wanderings and movement, versus the elaborate, personally expressive, dramatic, richly symbolic episodes epitomized by Lady Macbeth's sleepwalking. The latter type of syndrome deserves separate categorization as a somnambulistic trance state.

TABLE 17.1
Dissociative Reactions[a]

I. Dissociation of incoming information
   A. From part of the environment
      1. Selective inattention
      2. Hypnotic anesthesia
      3. Hysterical anesthesia (usually involving a limited area of the body or one sensory modality)
      4. Anesthesias in the psychoses (often associated with self-mutilation)
   B. From the environment as a whole
      1. Concentration, daydreaming, brown study, reverie
      2. Distraction or highly focused attention (for example, analgesia of injured athlete or wounded soldier while caught up in the excitement of the moment; pain threshold of normal subjects can be elevated 40% by simple distraction)
      3. Hypnotic trance (open channel or rapport with hypnotist is usually retained; if rapport is lost, hypnosis may become a dissociative trance state)
      *4. Dissociative trance states (psychogenic stupor, twilight state, dream state)
      *5. Other trancelike states (highway hypnosis, fixation or fascination in flyers, self-induced trances by mystics and fakirs, trances in religious ecstasy or frenzy)
      *6. Somnambulistic trance
II. Dissociation of certain portions of stored information (memory and/or sensibility) from the remainder
   A. Suppression (information is deliberately put out of awareness)
   B. Repression (stored information that should be possible to call to awareness cannot be recalled)
   C. Dreams and hallucinations (stored portions of information, being processed in a preconscious stream, emerge into awareness and are experienced as though they were incoming information)
   *D. Estrangements and paramnesias (feelings of unreality or estrangement, derealization, depersonalization, déjà fait, déjà pensé, cosmic consciousness, Weltschmerz, etc.)
   *E. Amnesia (psychogenic)
   *F. Multiple personality
III. Dissociation of output—actions or behavior (often accompanied by elements of I and II)
   A. Inhibition or blocking of output: briefly, under stress ("freezing"); of a motor function (conversion reactions of paralysis, aphonia, etc.); of the entire body (catatonia); in episodes (catalepsy); in attacks (cataplexy).
   *B. Parapraxes, psychogenic tics, motor automatisms
   *C. Automatic writing
   *D. Ganser syndrome
   *E. Dissociated experiences related to sleep (for example, sleep paralysis, sleep-talking, sleep-walking, enuresis in adults, somnolentia, sleep hallucinations)
   *F. Fugue
   *G. Frenzied or violent states of dissociated behavior (amok, berserk, latah, arctic hysteria, pathological intoxication, dissociative delirium, hysterical fit).

[a]From West, 1967, p. 890.

Note: The items marked with an asterisk have been traditionally described as clinical syndromes; the others are phemomena that range from benign, everyday occurrences to features of major psychiatric disorders.

Examples of sleep-speech occurring in somnambulistic trance states have been cited and described elsewhere in this book, e.g., the case of sleep-related fugue (Rice & Fisher, 1976), the extended sleep-speech of Batson's subject (1977), the sleep-restricted automatic writing in Russian (Chapter 20), the published tape recordings of the sleep-talking of MacGregor (1964), the observations on the female subject used in the pilot study of posthypnotically stimulated sleep-talking (Chapter 11), Burrell's case (1904), and other case histories (Cook, 1937; Goddard, 1926).

West remarks that certain physiological changes in brain function, such as those that occur in relation to the sleep cycle, may facilitate emergence of dissociative behavior.

Evans (1972) has speculated that certain subjects are prone to shifting from one state of consciousness to another with relative ease and may be capable more readily of dissociated behavior in sleep. Indeed, as previously mentioned, he has published striking experimental demonstrations of dissociated sleep behavior. Estabrooks (1957) has described means by which Braidian hypnosis can be induced by suggestions to sleeping subjects; and part of this implies that their minds must be available to process such input.

West (1967) has stated that dissociation as he defines it may occur even during organic deliria; many parallels are observable between behavior, experience, and cognition in deliria, sleep-utterance episodes, and the other more classical dissociation syndromes. Lipowski (1967) has written an excellent review of deliria—a syndrome characterized by global cognitive disturbances subsumed under the term *clouded consciousness.* He cites the frequent occurrence of such phenomena as hallucinations to which the subject responds, memory disturbances of varying degree (involving registration, retention, and recall with special impairment of recent memory), impaired perceptual discrimination, and so on. Of particular interest is his comment that "Speech may be affected to a varying extent. It may be slow and slurred, or under pressure to the point of incoherence. Perseveration ... of speech is common. There may be dysphasia or paraphasia. Incoherent muttering is usually a feature of severe delirium [p. 243]." Lipowski contends that delirium may be the "only psychiatric syndrome of universal susceptibility [p. 244]," although individual differences are given due weight. Clinical observation of deliria thus supports the notion of the ubiquitous human potential for psychic dissociation.

West's (1967) Classification of Dissociative Phenomena in Relation to Sleep-Utterance. In accordance with West's scheme (1967), the following phenomena are observable in connection with sleep-utterances that may be understood as the effects of dissociation of incoming information derived from within or outside of the body, dissociation of components of stored information from the main internal store, and dissociation of output: (Arkin-this volume)

1. Sleep-utterances express input from endogenous sources, i.e., they appear to arise spontaneously, requiring no external stimuli to initiate or sustain them.

2. They often accompany and/or reflect the content and the subject's imagined participation within streams of mentation associated with sleep. This is demonstrated by variable degrees of concordance with recalled mentation elicited during immediately subsequent wakefulness.

3. The content of the sleep-speech may be ample and yet bear *no* discernible relationship to the equally ample content of the immediately following mentation report. This suggests the possibility of multiple, dissociated concurrent streams of mentation.

4. There is a lack of simultaneous critical awareness of external reality at the moment of the occurrence. That is, when accompanied by awareness, the subject treats the sleep-imagined experience associated with the sleep-utterance as if it were real. Furthermore, when receiving a threshold arousal stimulus, he describes experiences and behaves in accordance with customarily expected characteristics of one who has been asleep and has just been awakened.

5. There is a strong tendency for amnesia, which is more marked for mentation accompanying NREM utterances than REMP utterances.

6. Lack of associated recalled mentation is often total; i.e., the subject may deny recall of any pre-awakening experience whatsoever. Inasmuch as this outcome is usual when sleep-utterances possess marked degrees of linguistic disorganization, the possibility exists that such speech emissions may occur in the absence of awareness.

7. The psycholinguistic integrity of the emitted speech tends to possess broadly varying degrees of disturbance.

An idealized model of a *non*dissociated sleep-speech would entail the concurrent full awareness of a more or less correctly organized utterance while it was in progress, and also the capacity to retain such awareness in short-term memory as betokened by the subjects' ability to give a mentation report possessing extensive first-order concordance with the speech. That is, the utterance, the awareness of it, the correctness of it, and its retrieval would be intimately interwoven instead of separated. Such an event involves the integration of the gamut of psycholinguistic functions and short-term memory; and accordingly, dissociation occurs to the extent to which these cognitive components function independently of one another.

Although no precise measures of the degrees of such dissociation have been developed, it seems at least conceptually useful to imagine a sort of spectrum of dissociation events in accordance with (1) how independently of one another cognitive components are functioning; and (2) for over how long an interval of time. Thus, on a more or less ad hoc basis, sleep-utterance episodes have been classified throughout this book as micro, intermediate, or macrodissociative episodes in accordance with combinations of these two considerations.

HILGARD'S NEODISSOCIATIONIST THEORY

More recently, Hilgard (1973, 1977) has proposed a neodissociationist theory, arising out of his experiences with hypnotic analgesia. Although suitable hypnotic subjects in trance at one "level" denied experiencing experimental pain stimuli and seemed impervious to them, awareness of the pain at "different levels" was indicated by mentation reports obtained by means of a special "hidden-observer" technique utilizing automatic talking and writing; and futhermore, perception of the pain at this different level was indicated by concomitant heart rate and blood pressure changes essentially the same as those occurring under similar circumstances during normal wakefulness. Hilgard explained these phenomena on the basis of psychic dissociation involving simultaneously operating, multiple cognitive (or dissociated) systems. The provisions of Hilgard's theory nicely encompass sleep-utterance phenomena, and actually, the observations on sleep-utterance support it and broaden its scope. Although, as previously indicated, sleep-utterance may be just as easily formulated in terms of West's perceptual release and dissociation theory of hallucinations (West, 1967, 1975), Hilgard's proposals seem to have the potential of greater generality and application. In view of its relevance to our theme, the main concepts of Hilgard's theory are summarized next in quotations and paraphrases from his 1973 article.

The "Executive Ego, Usually Identified by the Person as the Self that Plans and Manages His Affairs."

> The basic assumption of neodissociation theory proposes that the unity which exists in personal cognitive functioning is somewhat precarious and unstable. An executive ego provides a basis for self-perception and for conceiving the self as an agent. Its integrity is provided largely through the continuity of the personal memories, not through any unusual self-consistency either in awareness or behavior. This executive ego has many constraints upon it, both through internal conflicts and insufficiencies, and through environmental pressures, physical and social, including hypnotic interactions [p. 405].

Hierarchical Structure of Subsystems.

> There are many subordinate control systems that represent fractions of total cognitive functioning.... It is proposed that these substructures have at any one time a hierarchical arrangement, but their hierarchical positions can shift [p. 406].

Thus, a subsystem momentarily dominant in the control hierarchy can modulate, activate or inhibit the function of other momentarily subordinate systems.

> For example, the cognitive control system that produces dreams is more prominent than it is in waking, though it is doubtless present at a lower level in waking also, as in daydreams and fantasy production generally [p. 406].

Partial Autonomy of Subsystems.

> Once a system is activated, it may exert its controls autonomously, even though it is a subordinate system. [For example, one often whistles "mindlessly" when one works and it seems to start, stop, or go through a repertoire seemingly all of its own accord. Furthermore] each of the subordinate cognitive control structures is...related to a system of inputs and outputs, with feedback arrangements. As a control or monitoring system, the structure can seek or avoid inputs and enhance or inhibit outputs [p. 406].

The Partitions Separating Dissociated Systems May Possess Considerable Variability as to Their Potentials for Mutual Influence.

> The problem of separation, both in awareness and in behavior, is an empirical one and may be a matter of both dimensionality and degree. That is, cognitive and behavioral systems that are separated in one dimension may be interacting in another, and separation or interaction need not be sharp in order for some dissociative process to be demonstrated. Hence, there may be partial dissociations, according to various criteria, and these may tell us about important aspects of cognitive functioning [p. 404].

Although Hilgard made this comment in a specific discussion of hypnotic dissociation, it is nevertheless consistent with his description of his "general framework."

The Ubiquity of Dissociated Phenomena.   Dissociated phenomena are frequent daily occurrences. Human life as we know it has not been possible devoid of them. Examples include daydreaming, humming or doodling while carrying out a task bearing a higher priority in the hierarchy prevailing at the moment, selective inattention, reveries, "brown study," concentration, nocturnal dreams, and hypnagogic experience.

How might the foregoing formulations be applied to sleep-utterance phenomena? During slumber, the sleep executive ego acquires ascendancy over its wakeful counterpart. Its related subordinate semiautonomous cognitive systems include those mediating imagery, covert utterance, overt utterance, moral codes, and memory, which in turn is subdivided into echoic, short-term, and long-term components. Accordingly, our definition of somniloquy may now be reformulated as follows: *Somniloquy is the output of the overt utterance system during psychological sleep occurring in varying degrees of dissociation from the memory and imagery subsystems along a continuum from minimal to apparently complete dissociations, while, at the same time, having little or no dissociation from individual moral code subsystems.*

In his literature review, Hilgard drew attention to the ancestry of his theory in the writings of Janet (1889, 1907), Breuer and Freud (1895), Sidis (1898), and Prince (1909). These more or less strict forms of dissociation theory were discredited by White and Shevach (1942), but Hilgard asserts, correctly in my opinion, that with appropriate modifications, his neodissociationist theory can meet their objections.

In his literature review, Hilgard drew attention to the ancestry of his theory in the writings of Janet (1889, 1907), Breuer and Freud (1893), Sidis (1898), and Prince (1909). These more or less strict forms of dissociation theory were discredited by White and Shevach (1942), but Hilgard asserts, correctly in my opinion, that with appropriate modifications, his neodissociationist theory can meet their objections.

Hilgard went on to cite the root formulations and basic concepts of other psychologists whose ideas are related or similar to his own but may utilize different metaphors. These may be listed as follows:

1. cognitive structures (Lewin, 1935; Piaget, 1952; Tolman, 1932);
2. habit-family hierarchies (Berlyne, 1965; Hull, 1934);
3. images, plans, and TOTEs (test–operate–test–exit); (Miller, Galanter, & Pribram, 1960);
4. role enactments (Sarbin & Coe, 1972); and
5. psychoanalytic ego psychology—the idea of hierarchy in psychic structure (Rapaport, 1960).

Of particular interest to psychoanalytically oriented readers, he also cited the concept of separate ego structures subordinate to a dominant ego (Gill & Brenman, 1959), and to the concept of various ego apparatuses, especially those in the conflict-free ego sphere (Hartmann, 1964). To these, one might add earlier formulations by Glover (1930/1956, 1943/1956) in which, during the earliest phases of ego development, the primitive ego is described as a loose organization of relatively unrelated, unsynthesized elements, and that possibly "there are as many primary egos as there are combinations of erotogenic zones with reactive discharge systems [1930, p. 120]." With further development, these more or less separate ego elements or "ego nuclei" undergo a merging, integration process leading ultimately to more definitive ego synthesis in which its history and composition out of earlier fragmentary elements is always discernible in varying degrees. Certainly, a recent trend of psychoanalytic thought congenial to Hilgard's neodissociationist theory may be found in the work of Kernberg (1976), Kohut (1977), and Rosenblatt and Thickstun (1977). All of these ideas bear a certainly family resemblance, because the mind is conceptualized as being constructed of descriptively unconscious and conscious interactive components with widely varying degrees of independence, interrelatedness, and hierarchic organization in which the various components have subordinate and supraordinate relations to one another, in themselves subject to change over time; this is basic to Freudian psychology.

The hypothesis of somniloquy as the output of a sleep-associated cognitive subsystem, operating in varying degrees of dissociation from the "executive ego" of the subject, as well as the more general dissociation theory of Hilgard (1977), finds additional support from neurophysiological and clinical observations as described next.

Observations during Electrical Brain Stimulation

Several investigators have reported that electrical stimulation of selected areas in the brain during neurosurgery is capable of producing concomitant alterations in psycholinguistic functioning. Such effects may be observable within the context of normal operation of the other major cognitive systems or else be accompanied by varying amounts of change. Thus, Penfield and Roberts (1959) report that stimulation of selected areas of the exposed cerebral cortex may produce complete speech arrest, hesitation and slurring, distortion and repetition of words, confusion of numbers while counting, and inability to name objects with resumption of ability to speak on cessation of stimulation. In addition, following termination of the electrical stimulus and concomitant speech arrest, there is often an outburst of words as if a pressure to talk, in response to questions put to the patient by the surgeon, had accumulated during the interval arrest and had suddenly acquired release. Also, it was possible, by electrical stimulation, to elicit fractions of the motor speech act, such as involuntary sustained emissions of vowel sounds with preservation of awareness.

In another report, Schaltenbrand (1965) described the effects of stimulation of parts of thalamic nuclei. In contrast to the speech-arrest phenomena observed by Penfield and Roberts (1959) with cortical stimulation, involuntary small amounts of speech were often evoked and patients were unable to remain silent even when so commanded. Some examples from his first paper were:

"I see something, I hear something. Now I say thou to thee."
"Now one goes home."
"Thank you." [repeatedly]
"High."

One multilingual Polish lady would start to speak in her native tongue during the stimulation and would say afterwards that she had heard people talking in front of her, whom she answered. To quote Schaltenbrand further, *"Some patients have a dim memory of the happenings during the stimulation but are not able to repeat what they had been saying* [italics added]." This resembles some psychological-dissociative and also some sleep-utterance phenomena.

In a later paper, Schaltenbrand (1975) provided additional observations on the effects of electrical stimulation of certain thalamic nuclei. In 25% of his patients, short, involuntary sequences of words were uttered. Schaltenbrand referred to this phenomenon as "compulsory speech." In some cases, a specific sequence would occur with all stimulations, whereas in others, sequences were different with subsequent stimulations. The latter was especially the case when stimulating the caudal portion of the ventral thalamic nucleus. Thus, in one patient, a typical utterance with the initial stimulus was, "Left is at my side"; with the second stimulus, "Professor, I know exactly what people are talking about me"; and the third stimulus produced a repeated, "The, the, the, the." In another patient, a series of stimuli at a group of slightly differing thalamic loci produced a remark about "15 drops," followed by, "as fast as that I also would have" with the next stimulus; succeeding stimuli resulted in, "I had to cough," "Help yourself," "Knock me down," "I feel warm," and "I want to spit."

Most of the patients uttering such compulsory speech, as remarked in the previous Schaltenbrand paper, were unable to recall what they had said or even the fact of their having said anything at all, despite their being conscious immediately after stimulus termination. Occasionally, when asked to count before stimulation, some patients would resume counting spontaneously afterward but skip back to an earlier number. Such episodes resembled psychomotor epileptic attacks with hallucinations.

Statistical evaluation indicated that compulsory speech was more probable with "dominant" thalamus stimulation. When on occasion compulsory speech was evoked from the right thalamus, the patients were judged left-handed. A second type of speech phenomenon consisted of monosyllabic yells and exclamations of an emotional nature, and these could be elicited from stimulation of either side.

Schaltenbrand believes that the thalamus is not responsible for the synthesis of sentences and propositional, abstract expressions. Rather, he asserts that it is involved in releasing and termination of performed speech patterns.

The observations reported by Schaltenbrand are not only illustrative of possible verbal output cognitive subsystems, but interestingly, both their content and the apparent manner of utterance strongly resemble many sleep-utterances, suggesting the possibility that some sleep-speech involves selective thalamic activation. The findings of both Penfield and Roberts (1959) and

Schaltenbrand (1965, 1975) resemble other features of sleep-utterance phenomena, particularly with regard to memory disturbance in association with an immediately prior utterance. Furthermore, the capacity for experimental production of dissociated phenomena (in Hilgard's sense) by means of brain stimulation provides further support for the possibility of the physiological reality of the referents of the terms of his theory.

Observations during Seizures with Ictal Dysphasia and Speech Automatism

Another line of evidence for Hilgard's theory comes from studies of ictal dysphasia and speech automatisms (Chase, Cullen, Niedermeyer, Start, & Blumer, 1967; Driver, Falconer, & Serafetinedes, 1964; Falconer, 1967; Serafetinedes, 1966; Serafetinedes & Falconer, 1963).

On the basis of a large proportion of patients with temporal lobe epilepsy, ictal dysphasia is defined as an inability on the part of the patient to express himself by the correct words while he is still conscious and without impairment of articulation or hearing, leading to short outbursts of expressive or combined expressive–receptive dysphasias. Ictal speech automatisms, on the other hand, are utterances occurring at the onset of, or during, an epileptic seizure consisting of identifiable words or phrases that are linguistically correct but for which the patient has no subsequent recall. These automatisms are categorized into five subtypes as: (1) warnings; (2) recurrent utterances (repeated stereotyped, apparently meaningless phrases); (3) irrelevant utterances (seemingly conversational, lengthy but out of context); (4) emotional utterances (seemingly in response to and participation in emotionally intense hallucinatory experiences); and (5) perplexity utterances (thought to reflect attempts at self-orientation).

Comparison of these subtypes with our descriptions of sleep-utterances reveals striking similarities. Furthermore, inasmuch as ictal automatisms are deemed to be capable of arising from the *nondominant* hemisphere, the interesting possibility arises that much sleep-utterance reflects the activity of the nondominant hemisphere during sleep, when the coordinative efficiency of the dominant hemisphere is likely to be erratic.

A further interesting feature of ictal automatisms is the demonstration by Chase et al. (1967) that during paroxysms of temporal lobe epilepsy, automatic utterances and meaning were less subject to, or completely unreactive to, delayed auditory feedback, whereas in normal consciousness, the same patient displayed the usual speech impairments normally resulting from this procedure. These findings on ictal utterances provide a further line of evidence for the capabilities of the brain for formation of dissociated cognitive subsystems that may emit speech independent of the "executive ego."

Clinical Studies of Aphasia

The potentiality for more or less dissociated independent operation of components of cognition is well demonstrated by clinical phenomena of aphasic syndromes; and such dissociation is epitomized by data emerging during recovery from aphasia in polyglot individuals. On this point, Paradis (1977) states:

> Languages may be recovered in one or any combination of six basic patterns. Patients with little expressive difficulty in one language may be unable to utter or even repeat a word of another language even though they may retain comprehension of it. They may lose one or several languages entirely, including comprehension, as though they had never spoken such language(s) before, but at the same time regain a satisfactory degree of comprehension and expression in one or several others . . . .Comprehension and expression can be impaired not only selectively but differentially [p. 112–113].

Paradis (1977) speaks favorably of the hypothesis that the nonmanifested language is not lost but rather inhibited from expression by an inability to retrieve stored linguistic material. This view is borne out by the following observations: (1) Certain patients retain ability to comprehend words of a language despite total incapacity to utter a word belonging to it; (2) Loss of a specific language is frequently short-lived and may eventually return at a rate too rapid to result from a relearning mechanism; and (3) Psychoneurotic individuals without significant organic cerebral lesions show similar polyglot behaviors; and perhaps the most striking is the return of unavailable languages in special states of consciousness such as delirium ictal episodes or hypnosis. A vivid example of this phenomenon may be seen in Chapter 20 in which a person who could neither speak, write, nor comprehend Russian during wakefulness uttered Russian phrases in association with sleep and carried out acts of automatic writing during macrodissociative states entirely in Russian.

Experimental Studies on Divided Attention and Awareness

A host of recent investigations of cognition in normals has amply demonstrated the operation and some characteristics of dissociated cognitive subsystems (e.g., Broadbent, 1958; Cherry, 1953; Deutsch & Deutsch, 1963; Hirst, Neisser, & Spelke, 1978; Kahneman, 1973; Norman, 1976; Oswald, 1962; Spelke, Hirst, & Neisser, 1976).

In an interesting experimental paradigm, Antrobus, Singer, Goldstein, & Fortgang (1970) studied subjects who were under high pressure with strong incentives to accurately respond to rapidly changing experimental stimulus patterns. An integral part of the work was the assessment of spontaneous mentation unrelated to the experimental task—"stimulus-independent thought." Antrobus concluded that the tendency to daydream or produce stimulus-independent thought is extremely strong, difficult to suppress, and may be carried out concurrently with perceptual processing of unrelated sensory information. That is, humans seem obliged to engage in stimulus-independent streams of mentation that may occur "in parallel" with adaptive, critical interaction with input from external sources. These findings are in good accord with Hilgard's theory.

The Experience of Divided Consciousness
on the Part of the Subject during Sleep-Speech

The phenomena of lack of concordance between sleep-speech and the immediately following mentation report, commonly observed, lends itself reasonably to explanation in terms of an intrapsychic dissociation hypothesis. That is, when the sleep-speech content and the mentation report content are strikingly disparate, they are seemingly products of different or dissociated cognitive subsystems operating concurrently. But the supportive observations presented thus far have been presented chiefly from the vantage point of the experimenter.

By contrast, in this section, I would like to provide details of sleep-speech occurrences in which the subject's inner experience is quite clearly divided between a sleep state and a wakeful state of consciousness, as though for a brief interval he had been riding the two horses of divided consciousness in virtual simultaneity. It is my hope in this fashion to further substantiate the reality of psychic dissociation as a basic feature of many sleep-utterance episodes. All examples to follow will illustrate *divided consciousness* in association with sleep-speech as a subspecies of the broader category of intrapsychic dissociation.

First, as quoted in full on p. 214, Maury (1857) described an occurrence in which he was immersed in a dream about tobacco while asleep in a classroom. He was nevertheless somehow dimly aware of the teacher calling on him in external reality but responded aloud in terms of his dream experience, much to his own embarrassment.

Second, here are two accounts of sleep-speech in a home setting from my own experience:

a. At 7:15 a.m., I heard my sleeping wife whisper a syllable or two sounding like "Ah soo." Immediately I asked "You up?" and she replied affirmatively. I told her I heard her say something, whereupon she described a vivid dream with a kinesthetic experience:

A tallish, skinny young fellow dressed like a cowboy with cowboy boots was coming to the end of some chore involving the care of small children. He was something like a camp counselor and sort of lounging and relaxing against the wall, crossing one leg over the other, and sighing. In the dream this cowboy said, "*As soon* as I'm finished with all of this, I'm going to get away and be alone and be by myself—maybe Montana [italics added]." Thus, my wife had said a part of the cowboy's dreamed lines *for* him (or with him), "As soon as"—heard by me as "Ah soo." And while saying these words aloud, she reported feeling her tongue move against her teeth and hard palate. This was strictly coterminous with "as soon as" in her recollection; the remainder of the dreamed speech was solely thought and devoid of concurrent sensation arising from the linguistic apparatus or elsewhere. My wife stated specifically that "The words, both spoken and thought, were not said by me in the dream, but by the cowboy."

This incident is interesting for several reasons. First, it illustrates the rare variety of dissociation in which a sleep-talker says aloud the lines of a different dream character from oneself. The event is reminiscent of real-life occurrences in which one is raptly watching a theatrical performance and mentally speaks the lines of the actors during the course of vicarious experience. Second, it quite clearly exemplifies divided consciousness in which the sleeper is dwelling in two realms at once—that of dream and that of reality.

b. Some years ago, I had been in a hospital for an elective hernia repair. Three days after surgery, at about 4:00 a.m., I had the following experience that I wrote up several hours later while it was still fresh in my mind:

I had been in the midst of a vivid dream in which I was conversing animatedly with one or more persons. I could recall no other detail except that I was suddenly aware of a pressure on my hip that I quickly recognized "in my sleep" as the awakening hand of the nurse's aide who had come to take my temperature and pulse. This required that I interrupt my conversation with my dream companions whose visages were still before me; and so out of considerations of courtesy, I said to them spontaneously, aloud and distinctly, "Excuse me." I heard myself say these words and, like my wife in the previous example, I could feel momentary kinesthetic sensations as my lips moved. The entire incident seemed to occur in a state of consciousness in which the dream experience continued and was prolonged into the beginnings of wakefulness brought on by the aide's touch. The flavor of the dream was as if I had been having a pleasant, interesting social conversation, which I wished to continue, and had regrettably been "called away" to attend some dreary assignment.

The qualities of the incident were partly influenced by my familiarity with the meaning of the aide's touch. This had happened several times previously when I was awakened from sleep for the same reason; i.e., I had become conditioned to the touch, because I had been having my temperature and pulse taken every 4 hr around the clock.

As in the previous example, this experience illustrates a variety of divided consciousness in which a sleep-imagined world is reacted to as if it were real, and at the same time, awareness of reality is registered and responded to appropriately.

Third, the following occurrences took place in the laboratory:

a. REM sleep-speech #192 (Appendix 2) dealt with a vivid visual dream about a tree full of peacocks. The subject's immediately following mentation report began with "Uuh—oh—I was just sort of sleep-talking. I said something about this tree made up of birds, etc."

b. REM sleep-speech #49 (Appendix 2) dealt with an angry contretemps. It was the last REMP of the night and, shortly afterward, the subject recounted in his morning recall a first-order concordant dream concluding with "I think I talked here because I woke up and almost heard myself."

c. Stage 2 sleep-speech #503 (Appendix 2) consisted of 2 parts: The first was a section mentioning a sunny street as if the subject had been awakened and was giving a mentation report—a sort of laboratory dream with accompanying sleep-speech. It ended with a typical "and that's it." This was followed without interruption by a second section in which the subject said, "Oh sure, taking it in and creating great works." The experimenter, using the answering dialogue method (Chapter 10) then interposed, "Did you take it in?"; whereupon the fully awakened subject responded with astonished laughter and "Again I don't know what's going on—uh—no—uh—that's funny, I can't, I know you didn't say that and I s—, I mean, ooh, somebody said, 'taking it in' and 'taking it in no doubt'—some part of my mind, and I answered 'sure I'm taking it in and creating great works'; it's the strangest thing."

d. Stage 4 sleep-speech #558 (Appendix 2) dealt with a subject frantically shouting "Hold it!" repeatedly. During the course of the speech, he sat up in bed as part of the dreamed action. The lengthy mentation report referred to "getting" a lady in his dream who darted under his bed in an apparently disconcerting manner leading to his exhorting her to desist. The experimenter inquired as to why he had yelled at her, and the subject replied, "Because I guess she couldn't hear me or else she didn't want to, so I guess, you know, I just got up and started yelling at her."

e. Stage 2 sleep-speech #566 (Appendix 2)—The subject said "I just want to sleep." The mentation report included the statement, "I was dreaming about sleeping, 'n then I don't—remember anything. I don't think." The experimenter inquired whether the words "I just want to sleep" meant anything. The subject replied, "Yeah—I remember saying it—but I don't remember why—and you know, I don't remember if it was in response to something—I, it *saying that almost woke me up but not quite*—that's all [italics added].'

f. Perhaps the most extensive description of the divided consciousness phenomenon was provided by our subject *D.C.,* whose predilection for talking in REM sleep has been mentioned many times thus far.

I had asked her to describe as best as she could her inner experience when she became aware of her own sleep-talking. Her written response was:

> When I am aware of hearing myself talk in sleep, it is usually when I am awakened, or awaken. It is as if the sound of my voice were suspended in auditory memory and a period of time has intervened between the hearing and "rehearing." The sound would vanish from memory, I think, if I didn't awaken because there is no sort of willed postponement of recall [a postponement for the purpose of bringing it to mind at a later time]. It entails rather a startling ability to pull back the sounds at will rather than willing to keep them in memory.
>
> When I wake myself up by hearing my own sleep-speech is something else. Then the sound itself wakes me up with the initial feeling that any external sort of sound creates. Then I can or do pull it back in the manner discussed above.

Several days earlier, the subject had compared her inner experience of retrieval of sleep-speech to occasions in school when, lost in thought, she would be suddenly called on by the teacher. At first, she would not know what the teacher had asked but would then be able to "pull back" the sounds and rehear them.

The items of greatest interest are, first, that she perceives her own voice as an externally derived stimulus like any other external arousing event; and second, her description of the retrieval process involving hearing, rehearing, and an effortful "pulling back" of the words.

Chemically Produced State-Dependent Phenomena

Another demonstration of dissociated cognitive systems comes from clinical observation and research on state-dependent phenomena brought about by pharmacologic agents. In these investigations, it has been shown that while under the influence of certain drugs, particularly general anesthetics, humans are nevertheless capable of maintaining consciousness and critically interacting verbally with the experimenter and yet may be completely or partly amnestic for these experiences even when the drug effects are rapidly removed.

Fischer (1977) contends that

> [The] brain processes and stores information differently at each level of arousal. The same event is very different in our perception, depending on whether we are

calm, in a panic, or in between. Our memory of events, I believe, is distributed over a variety of arousal states. Each bit of knowledge is bound to, and most easily retrieved at, a particular level of arousal. The greater the difference between these states, the more difficult it is to recall in one state specifics learned in another [p. 68].

The best known clinical example is the alcoholic "blackout" in which an alcoholic individual while drunk converses and interacts more or less appropriately with persons and objects in his environment for sustained intervals, and for which events he has a complete loss of memory during subsequent sober states. Occasions have been reported in which events occurring during blacked-out intervals, such as hiding money or alcohol, were recalled in *subsequent* alcoholic bouts—an apparently genuine state-dependent effect (Mello, 1972; Overton, 1972). State-dependent learning has been demonstrable in experimental animals with a variety of drugs (Overton, 1972); that is, responses established under specific contingencies possess the lowest response threshold when the drug condition is repeated. Experimental state-dependent learning of verbal items during alcohol intoxication has been observed in normal college students (Goodwin, Powell, Bremer, Haine, & Stern, 1969). Subsequent administration of alcohol permitted retrieval of memories for this material, despite intervening amnesia in the undrugged state. Diethelm and Barr (1962) reported that alcoholic patients talked more openly and revealed more guilt, hostility, and other emotions while intoxicated than they did during soberness when such material was not volunteered. Usually, the contents of these alcoholic interviews were not recalled during subsequent sobriety. Additional material on state-dependent effects of alcohol may be found in Mello and Mendelson (1969), and Ryback (1970). Mazzia and Randt (1966) and Osborn et al. (1967) have demonstrated correct cognitive functioning during light intoxication with intravenous thiopental, for which events there was amnesia on recovery shortly afterward. Osborn, Bunker, Cooper, Frank, and Hilgard (1967) were unable to detect recall in a subsequent thiopental state, but good hypnotic subjects were able to show some slight recovery of memory for the thiopental events when they were subsequently hypnotized. Thus, individual differences appear to play a role. Mazzia and Randt (1966) did not carry out subsequent tests under thiopental conditions.

State-dependent phenomena have been observed during light stage administration or recovery from many other anesthetics. I am informed by a surgical recovery room nurse with many years of experience that spontaneous speech is both frequent and abundant, often accompanied by hallucinatory phenomena, during recovery from agents such as Ketamine, Innovar, and Fluethane. As a rule, the content, like sleep-speech, deals with mundane, everyday items. Typically, the productions are said to be consistent with the character of the patient during wakefulness; staid people speak of staid matters, and crude people speak of crude matters. Overt self-reproachful content and guilt are rare except in cases of elective abortion, in which instance they are more commonly observed. In all cases, amnesia is the rule following complete recovery from the anesthesia. These phenomena all deserve careful controlled study—a feasible possibility.

Laboratory Study of Sleep-Mentation

Further evidence of the existence and activity of cognitive subsystems in varying degrees of dissociation is provided by the huge literature on day and night dreaming and sleep mentation. (For comprehensive reviews, see Singer, 1975, on daydreaming; Goodenough, 1978, on memory of sleep mentation; Arkin & Antrobus, 1978, in Arkin, Antrobus, and Ellman, 1978 on the effects of external stimuli on sleep mentation; Williams, 1973 on information processing during sleep; and Aarons, 1976, on learning during sleep. Also see Evans, 1972, for a review of his work and that of his colleagues on verbally induced responses during sleep with intervening wakeful amnesia.)

Relevance of Studies on
Lateral Specialization of Cerebral Function

Additional evidence of neurophysiological organization capable of mediating dissociated cognitive systems is provided by accumulating observation and research on lateral specialization of cerebral function (Sperry, 1973). The findings vividly demonstrate specific, distinctive, complex, cognitive activities mediated by the nondominant hemisphere, that are conducted independently and outside of the domain of awareness of, and unavailable to verbal encoding by, the dominant hemisphere. For example, in a therapeutically commissurotomized patient in which the functional connections between cerebral hemispheres were destroyed, a pin-up picture was flashed to the visual flield subserved by the nondominant hemisphere. This elicited a grin, a chuckle, but paradoxically, a denial of having seen anything; and when the same picture was flashed to the visual field connected to the dominant hemisphere, the same grin was repeated and the percept was quickly described as a nude woman (Gazzaniga, 1970). This observation was in good accord with the well-established principle that the dominant hemisphere bears chief responsibility for verbal, linear, logical linguistic processes, especially propositional speech (Jackson, 1874–1879/1958), and that the nondominant hemisphere is essentially without capability of significant speech production. In a recent comprehensive review of right hemisphere linguistic capacities, however (Searleman, 1977), a large body of evidence is presented demonstrating that it is indeed capable of limited speech output. The findings were somewhat in accord with Jackson's early contention that the right hemisphere could produce nonpropositional, automatic, overlearned phrases (Jackson, 1874–1879/1958).

Moscovitch (1973), on the basis of investigation of the right hemisphere linguistic abilities of normals, has proposed that the left hemisphere normally inhibits or suppresses attempts of the right hemisphere to carry out linguistic processing, by means of inhibitory influences across the cerebral commissures; and following section of these commissures, the linguistic capabilities of the right hemisphere are disinhibited in some degree. Consistent with this "model of functional localization" (Moscovitch, 1973) is Kinsbourne's observation (1971) that the right hemisphere can often be the source of aphasic speech. Nebes (1974) also views the two hemispheres as competing for access to output channels over a broader range of cognitive processing.

With this briefest of backgrounds, let us now ask whether at least some sleep-utterance, especially the extremely disorganized variety, could reflect dysequilibria between the hemispheres or else arise directly out of physiologically disinhibited activity of the nondominant hemisphere during sleep.

Is evidence available indicating that the relative amounts of neural activity within the two hemispheres undergo periodic shifts in balance and/or incoordination under physiological conditions during sleep? Goldstein, Stolzfus, and Gardocki (1972) have shown that in seven right-handed humans, the amplitude of the EEG was higher over the right hemisphere than over the left during NREM sleep and that this relationship underwent reversal during stage REM. Thus, asymmetries in activation levels occur and reciprocally shift patterns during the sleep cycle. That such a finding is compatible with a hypothesized disturbance in major hemispherical dominance gains in credibility when viewed in the context of Berlucchi's (1964, 1966) report of activity levels in the corpus callosum of unrestrained, unanesthetized cats during Stages W, NREM, and REM. Tonic activity was observed throughout but was greatest in Stage W, intermediate in NREM, and least in Stage REM. At the same time, activation levels within the respective hemispheres tend to be least during NREM sleep and approach or exceed those of Stage W during REMPs.

Keeping in mind that the corpus callosum is the main neural channel by which one cortical hemisphere communicates with the other, these findings suggest a loosening of integration in sleep between intrahemispheric levels of activation and diminished commissural mediation of interhemispheric cortical dominance factors. Such a notion finds further support from Berlucchi's study on cats indicating that the normal bilateral synchrony of

EEG spindles and slow waves is permanently lost after section of the corpus callosum (1964, 1966). Similar findings were described by Greenberg (1967) for one commissurotomized human who had been ill with intractable epilepsy.

Thus, the available evidence is consistent with, and does not preclude, the suggestion that some sleep-utterance could represent the vocalized output of the minor hemisphere when it undergoes diminished or poorly coordinated dominance influences from the major hemisphere. This might account for those speeches that are chaotic eruptions of linguistic fragments. On the other hand, it is possible that inter- and intra-hemispheric imbalances may be all that are necessary to establish conditions for sleep-utterances that may always arise from the dominant hemisphere when it is appropriately active during sleep, rather than from the nondominant hemisphere. Evarts (1967), in his work on neuronal unit behavior, describes modifications in patterns and organization of activity during both REM and NREM sleep that are compatible with impairment and/or loosening of larger scale neural integration in sleep. Under such circumstances, activation and inhibition within the dominant hemisphere in sleep may operate by "fits and starts" rather than by relatively smooth coordination, resulting at such times in sleep-utterance.

After writing the first draft of this section with its speculation that some somniloquy may reflect disinhibited activity of the nondominant hemisphere, I had the pleasure of coming across Van Valen's short *Note on Dreams* (1973) in which he "would like to make the outlandish but testable suggestion that the nonverbal cerebral hemisphere controls the content of ordinary dreaming by a shift in dominance from the verbal hemisphere [p. 19]." Among the 11 supporting observations listed by him was "the incoherence of audible speech from a sleeping person," "the occurrence of somniloquy mostly in NREM sleep," and "the predominance of left-hand movement in dreams." This last, and fascinating, phenomenon is consistent with the notion of the nondominant hemisphere disinhibition playing some sort of role in sleep-utterance. Muller-Limmroth (1965) described an anecdotal observation that the nondominant hand possesses greater responsivity during sleep. Jovanovic (1971), in a systematic study of 20 subjects, found that when unilateral movements were made during sleep, the nondominant hand produced the movement 70% of the time. The range over the subjects reached from 55–92%. This tendency was observed in both REM and NREM sleep. And in a preliminary analysis of carefully collected data on motor behavior during sleep, Gardner and Grossman (1976) found in one right-handed subject a 2 to 1 preponderance of left-handed movements on each of six laboratory nights.

Certainly, with modern electrographic technology, it should be possible to test the prediction that a subgroup of subjects would show consistent differences in electrical activity recorded from dominant-speech-area electrode placements and corresponding nondominant hemisphere placements in association with sleep-speech as opposed to wakeful speech. Furthermore, it should be possible to test the prediction (Pessah & Roffwarg, 1972) that bursts of middle ear muscle activity (MEMAs) would occur with preferential intensity in association with sleep-utterance. These authors, on the basis of preliminary examination of mentation reports elicited in proximity to MEMAs suggested that the latter were tokens of auditory imagery in dreams. Inasmuch as mentation reports elicited following sleep-utterance often contain reference to audition and sleep-hallucinated speech, it seems reasonable to expect increased MEMA with somniloquy.

Complementary Perspectives on Sleep-Utterance

Sleep-utterance may also be viewed from a somewhat different but complementary perspective offered by the theory of microgenesis of thought, perception, and behavior. For a general review of this theory, the reader is referred to Flavell and Draguns (1957), who attribute the coinage of the term microgenesis to Werner (1956) in his attempt to approximately render into English the German word *Aktualgenese,* originally introduced in 1928 by Sander (see Undeutsch [1942] for the preferred account of Sander's work). Flavell and Draguns (1957) drew on the writings of Sander (op. cit.), Jung (1919), especially Schilder (1920/1951a, 1920/1951b, 1942), Freud (1900/1953), Werner (1948), and Rapaport (1951) in formulating a general statement of a model of microgenesis of thought, which may be paraphrased as follows:

1. The ongoing mental stream as it is experienced in normal wakefulness by humans is the emergent product of a continuous, rapid, developmental, evolutionary process arising from an elemental state and acquiring its "final" form in awareness in a matter of seconds or less.

2. Mentation in its most elemental form consists of more or less continuous sequences of global, diffuse, undifferentiated, fluctuating sets of psychological items without articulation, clearly defined interrelationships, or structures.

3. Under the dominating influence of primitive urges and affects, subsets of these items will compete for, or be driven toward, further expression and will preferentially enter into the microgenetic thought process. At this early stage, the principles governing combination and association of thoughts resemble those proposed by Freud (1900/1953) for primary process mentation, i.e., association by contiguity, by superficial external similarity, by possession of common personal predicates and a prevalence of condensation and displacement.

4. The evolving thought process tends first toward one, and then another

of premature forms of expression often framed in dichotomous fashion of me–not me, or good–bad, and similar varieties.

5. Subsequent evolution is characterized by further differentiation into components that acquire logical or intelligible interrelationships. Normally, in the "final," fully evolved phase, mentation is said to be reality-rather than drive-oriented, and the earlier nonlogical components have been aborted and deprived of significant influence over the experienced outcome. In most people, under normal circumstances, this rapid developmental process is absent or minimally present in awareness, and the thinker is conscious only of the completed thought. According to Schilder (1920/1951), however, various phases of the microgenetic process may enter into and remain in awareness after final completion of the thought.

Flavell and Draguns (1957) go on to propose that the microgenetic model is usefully applicable to cognition of pathological persons under normal conditions and of normal persons under atypical, abnormal conditions. Pathological or atypical cognition tends to "manifest formal characteristics similar to those already predicted for microgenetically incomplete cognition [p. 205]." For example, in Schilder's words (1920/1951), much schizophrenic verbalization consists of formations "which normally would be only transitory phases in thought development, appearing as the end results of thought processes [p. 514]." That is, pathological or atypical thought results from premature termination of the microgenetic evolution of thought prior to what would normally have emerged as the fully developed outcome, which produces instead the contents of a normally preliminary microgenetic phase in thought development as the final version—i.e., abnormal cognition is incomplete cognition. Even better, in Flavell and Dragun's words (1957), "Normal, logical cognition is seen as a microdevelopmental achievement of the organism and deviations therefrom as developmental arrests [p. 205]."

The principle of microgenesis has been usefully applied to abnormal cognition in schizophrenia and general paresis (Schilder, 1920/1951a; 1920/1951b), in aphasia (Brown, 1977; Werner, 1956), and in amnestic syndromes (Talland, 1960). Brown (1977) has recently developed a comprehensive neuropsychological model of cognition using microgenesis as a key organizing perspective.

Sleep-utterances in this scheme may thus be understood as microgenetically incomplete sets of verbal fragments vocalized prior to what would have been normal closure had they been spoken during wakefulness. If one may assign phases of microgenetic development to cognitive subsystems in varying degrees of dissociation and interrelationship, it seems reasonable to conclude that microgenetic and neodissociation theory are reconcilable and that sleep-utterance phenomena may be usefully described in terms of either, depending on scientific requirements.

Dissociationist Theory and Recent Theorizing in the Psychophysiology of Sleep

Dement and Mitler (1974) have proposed a "process view" in which sleep states are conceptualized as "the outward manifestation of a number of processes that are going on independently, simultaneously, in combination, at different times, with different relationships, and so on [p. 283]." This formulation with its emphasis on interacting, quasi-independent components resulting in an outward manifestation is structurally very similar to Hilgard's proposals. In fact, Dement and Mitler (1974) go on to describe in detail various data demonstrating that many sleep processes "can be experimentally dissociated from one another on a temporal basis [p. 288]." It was further suggested that a major reason for assuming that sleep states are stable and continuous, at least in adults, has been the arbitrary selection of the duration of epoch scores. Thus, in the standard 30-sec epoch, three or four clear-cut state changes may be observable. When sleep is scored in accordance with 3-sec epochs, a more valid, extremely dynamic and variable picture of sleep emerged with frequent transitions of state. A cat, for example, could be apparently deeply asleep, wake up, look around, and resume sound sleep, all within a few seconds.

Such a concept is in accord with ideas suggested by Cordeau (1970), who advocated that somnologists should no longer conceive of Stage W, NREM, and REM sleep as completely different states, each with its own system biochemically and anatomically clearly defined throughout the brainstem; rather, Cordeau recommends that sleep and wakefulness be considered as "mixed" states in which several neural systems participate in a variable manner, and at different brainstem levels.

Morgane and Stern (1974) offer the concept that "neural aggregates responsible for patterns of sleep or waking may be present at all levels of the brainstem in a sort of multitiered type of organization with several substations projecting both rostrally and caudally, each substation reciprocally linked and providing positive or, most probably, negative feedback loops responsible for the so-called 'reticular homeostasis' [p. 117–118]."

Similarly, Moruzzi's (1974) thinking is that the sleep–waking cycle is governed by two antagonistic ascending systems arising in the brainstem, which are the reticular activating system and the deactivating structures of the lower brainstem that modulate all cerebral processes, which in turn are also reciprocally organized. "Wakefulness" is deemed by Moruzzi not to be a physiological entity, but rather an "abstract term to indicate that the 'level of activation' must be within given ranges for the usual types of activity to be carried out [p. 29]." The cerebral mechanisms related to the sleep–wakefulness cycle are said to "simply register the outcome of a struggle [between these two systems] which is decided at the level of the brain stem [p. 29]."

In summary, the contemporary picture of sleep and wakefulness involves the conception of these behavioral manifestations as the outcome of the complex dynamic interaction of many psychoneural subsystems with frequent transitional events between different short-lived states. This formulation seems to be in good neurophysiological accord with the principles of Hilgard's neodissociationist theory, in that it calls for a scheme of interacting quasi-independent subsystems under the variable sway of some major executive system.

It is possible that the probability of sleep-utterance episodes is greatest when the antagonistically based equilibrium between sleep-waking systems becomes unstable. In such a case, one system thrusts toward wakefulness and encounters an inhibitory counterthrust, in the midst of which lively psychophysiological fracas, sleep-speech tends to be emitted reflecting, in many cases, ongoing sleep mentation.

CONCLUSION

A variety of lines of evidence derived from investigations and theoretical formulations of diverse types support the validity of, or are consistent with, Hilgard's concept of dissociated cognitive subsystems operating under broadly varying degrees of mutual integration, and all in relation to a wakeful "executive ego." Employing this concept facilitates the handling of certain dichotomous questions, such as whether a subject is asleep or awake at a given moment. That is, accepting Hilgard's hypothesis permits us to formulate the problem in the following manner: The psychophysiological corpus is composed of a more or less integrated organization of cognitive subsystems, each of which requires a certain minimal intrasystemic level of activation in order to maintain its momentary functional existence as a system—otherwise, it temporarily ceases to manifest itself in a manner detectable to the subject and/or an external observer. When the intrasystemic level of activation is adequate, the system may temporarily preempt awareness, utterance mechanisms, and/or autonomic response channels, etc., in sleep as well as in wakefulness. Thus, in the course of sleep-onset, the activation level of the "executive ego" diminishes to a point where subsystems ordinarily subordinate to it in wakefulness may manifest themselves, perhaps by being released from inhibition or by receiving added increments of activation. This may result in hypnagogic mentation, and even utterance, which may or may not be capable of retrieval if the subject is awakened at this point. If sleep is allowed to continue, the usual procession of psychophysiological events normally ensues and cognitive subsystems of different types eventually operate to produce dreams or sleep-utterances or muscular movements that are often endowed with meaning, maintain the capacity for perceiving external stimuli and alerting the "executive ego" into wakefulness, etc. The question now is not whether the subject is "asleep or awake" at a given moment, but rather which of his one or more cognitive subsystems possess adequate intrasystemic activation to manifest themselves in a manner detectable to the subject and/or the experimenter at a given time; and whether the experiential correlates of the activity of these subsystems are retrievable by the executive ego when awakened, or to what extent might such processes have been dissociated thus eluding retrieval, or have been occurring without participation of mechanisms that mediate retrieval. In effect, we have customarily described sleep-onset as the moment when the "executive ego" no longer possesses sufficient activation to maintain critical responsivity to external stimuli. The person was then said to be "asleep," but in fact many of his cognitive subsystems remained "awake," and/or many which had been relatively dormant during wakefulness "woke up during sleep." In addition, such a perspective permits us to ascribe more meaning to the concept that a person may be psychologically asleep but psychophysiologically aroused over short time intervals as previously indicated.

What specifications may be formulated about interactions between cognitive subsystems that are necessary conditions for the occurrence of microdissociative sleep-utterance? As noted in the course of discussion of the comparison between NREM mentation reports elicited from silent sleep and those following sleep-utterances, sleep-imagined vocalization, as part of a sleep-imagined experience such as a dream, may occur among sleep-talkers, but *without actual, overt* vocalization (12.2–14.9% of silent sleep reports). So an imagined scene of oneself vocalizing during sleep experience is by itself not sufficient to produce overt sleep-utterance.

Also, as previously described, the typical electrographic context of a sleep-utterance is that of a movement-arousal episode; yet only a small proportion of the movement-arousals of sleep-talkers are associated with sleep-talking. So movement-arousal by itself is not sufficient to produce sleep-utterance.

But as noted in Chapter 13, an aspect of mentation reports that seems to be more probably associated with sleep-utterance is an imagined sequence of sleep experience in which the subject himself is vocalizing (27.0–33.8% of our NREM reports), as opposed to others vocalizing or to nonacoustic content reports.

In view of these considerations, it seems reasonable to say that at least microdissociated NREM sleep-speech episodes are most likely to occur when two or three conditions are *simultaneously* fulfilled as follows:

1. The subject is motivated to assert himself vocally and/or enhance the sense of self-existence to the point of imagining himself vocalizing during a sleep experience.
2. The subject is aroused to a level of appropriate intensity and possibly an affect of appropriate quality.

3. Overt vocal output channels undergo a diminution of outflow thresholds and/or receive an increase of motor activation from neurolinguistic circuits responsible for speech.

Very likely, the same may be specified for REM sleep-utterance, but our data was insufficient to test the hypotheses in a manner similar to that carried out with our NREM reports.

18

Sleep-Talking in Relation to Cognitive Psychology: Memory, Psycholinguistics, and Aphasia

The scientific literature dealing with wakeful cognition is intimidatingly huge. Until 1953, when the new electrographic sleep research era was inaugurated by Aserinsky, Kleitman, and Dement, cognition in sleep was by contrast unexplored; and even now, only the surface has been lightly touched. Most of the leading and influential ideas arose in clinical settings, and Freud's theories of dream formation and psychic structure dominated the field and have by no means lost much of their usefulness nor influence. As stated elsewhere (Arkin, Antrobus, & Ellman, 1978a), the data base of theories of sleep cognition has been and will continue to be sleep mentation reports, including those of vivid dreams as a special subset. It naturally follows that sleep-utterance lends itself as both an independent and adjunctive source of empirical material to be included in such a data base. A study of the form, content, and correlates of sleep-utterance is rich territory. Three areas of cognitive psychology to which sleep-utterance seems relevant are the ontological status of sleep mentation, the study of memory mechanisms, and psycholinguistics, and we comment on some points of contact between them. But first we must deal with a fundamental issue—*in what senses may we say that when a person somniloquizes, he is in fact "talking in his sleep?"*

SLEEP-UTTERANCE AS UTTERANCE DURING SLEEP

It is necessary to state at once that a universally accepted unambiguous definition of sleep has not yet been formulated. Although polygraphic parameters, particularly those derived from the combined use of the EEG, submental EMG, and EOG, have been used by sleep researchers (providing the most pragmatic criteria yet available), there are, nevertheless, exceptions and transitional states that are not conveniently subsumed under them. Examples are the *"phases intermédiares"* of Lairy, Goldsteinas, and Guennoc (1968) and ambiguous REM sleep of Cartwright, Monroe, and Palmer (1967). For our purposes, it will suffice to quote two recent authoritative views. Dement and Mitler (1974) stated:

> The salient feature of wakefulness is the environmental engagement of the organism. He sees, hears, and responds to the world around him. The onset of sleep, which seems to be the onset of NREM sleep in most humans, entails the cessation of the above processes. There is a moment somewhere in the transition from wakefulness to sleep where the organism essentially, though not entirely, stops perceiving the environment [p. 286].
>
> The moment of sleep (i.e., the cessation of perception) is apparently quite abrupt. While there may be important predisposing changes leading up to it, and consequences of its occurrence leading away from it, the point of sleep onset itself seems relatively easy to determine within a second or two. For example, suppose we ask an individual to sit with his eyes taped open and to make a motor response when a light flash (S^d) is presented. At some point he will not respond to the S^d. The moment of sleep is best defined as the point of perceptual disengagement (i.e., failure to respond to the S^d). *Immediately after such a failure, the EEG patterns may still show waking patterns, such as alpha rhythms. Thus, we could conceivably abolish slow waves and spindles without abolishing the process of perceptual disengagement. Accordingly, we must acknowledge that it is not clear if slow waves and spindles are processes which really begin at the point of response inhibition and only build up enough to appear in the EEG a few minutes later, or are entirely separate and redundant processes* [italics added]. But until proven otherwise, we must think of slow waves and spindles as meaningful although often belated signs of a central inhibitory state [p. 287].
>
> At the present time, the best sign of the moment of sleep appears to be the breakdown of visual fixation and the appearance of slow eye movements [p. 287]."

These extended quotations appear in an essay advocating the "process view [p. 283]" of sleep as opposed to the old, pre-electrographic-era notion of sleep as a "single, totally uniform state [p. 272]"—a state in which one was either awake or asleep with a transitional zone between. The process view conceives of sleep as the "outward manifestation of a number of processes that are going on independently, simultaneously, in combination, at different times, with different relationships, and so on [p. 283]." In a further discussion, the authors described at length the extent to which the electrographic components used in defining the various sleep states may not be exclusive property of these sleep stages, and also stated that these components may be capable of isolation either under natural or experimental circumstances. For example, the drastic and sudden motor inhibition of REM sleep may occur independently in wakeful consciousness as the clinical symptom cataplexy.

Noteworthy in this essay of Dement and Mitler are (1) the high priority given to behavioral and psychological criteria of the central inhibitory state, rather than exclusive dependence or emphasis on electrographic indicators: and (2) the acknowledgment of dissociable components of sleep processes.

Likewise, Johnson (1970), in a comprehensive paper, evaluated the evidence for unique correspondences between physiological processes and mentally defined states. Reviewing the present state of the art in the electrographic assessment of sleep and varieties of awareness, he questioned "whether one can interpret or draw inferences from EEG or autonomic responses without prior knowledge as to the state of consciousness of the subject." And he concluded his paper by remarking that:

> The hope for a simple arousal continuum on which a subject's position could be clearly defined by his responses must be abandoned. Not only have our sympathetic responses failed to allow us to draw conclusions about level of sympathetic tone, but they, as well as the EEG, fail us in our efforts to draw conclusions as to the state of consciousness. Instead of using our autonomic and EEG measures to define state, the reverse appears more appropriate. We must first determine the state before we can interpret our physiological measure [p. 515].

Microdissociation and Sleep

Earlier in this book, it was established that typical microdissociative somniloquy occurs within the electrographic context of a movement-arousal episode. Rechtschaffen and Kales (1968) classify such events in a pragmatic but nevertheless somewhat arbitrary manner. If their durations exceed half of the interval of the epoch concerned, and simultaneously obscure the EEG and EOG tracings, they are categorized as MT (Movement Time).[1] In such cases,

---

[1]Rechtschaffen and Kales (1968) clearly distinguish between the following:

Bodily Movements—considered as discrete physiological events that may or may not be of sufficient duration to occur within an epoch scorable as MT, but that, nevertheless, do involve substantial displacement of the body or one of its larger parts.

Movement-Arousals—considered merely as an indication of some increase of muscle activity with minimal or no actual spatial charge of a body part, and, again, that may or may not be of sufficient duration to occur within an epoch scorable as MT.

Movement Time (MT)—a score assigned to epochs immediately preceding or following a sleep stage in which electrographic tracings of the EEG and EOG are unreadable for more than half of the epoch because of muscle tension and/or amplifier-blockng artifacts occasioned by movement of the subject.

In practice, the three conditions often overlap and co-occur, but it is possible for a body movement or a movement-arousal to occupy half or less of an epoch and not alter the sleep-stage score of the epoch under consideration.

they are counted neither as unambiguous sleep nor wakefulness because of currently insufficient knowledge of their behavioral and/or subjective correlates. If, on the other hand, half of the epoch or less is occupied by a movement-arousal incident, its sleep-state classification depends on the electrographic characteristics of the readable remainder of the record. The category "movement-arousal," therefore, is not necessarily considered incompatible with ongoing sleep but is recommended to the experimenter as a herald of some impending change in whatever sleep state has obtained before its occurrence.

Moreover, in many instances, (for example, see Fig. 7.3), the EEG is artifact-free at the exact moment of utterance and fulfills the criteria of unambiguous sleep. Similar findings have been reported by others during episodes of somnambulism; i.e. coordinated motor activity was maintained in the presence of electroencephalographically unambiguous slow-wave sleep (Broughton 1973; Jacobson & Kales 1967; Kales & Jacobson 1967). Finally, it is well known that during episodes of somnambulism outside the laboratory, the patient may be "awakened" by an observer and concurrently actually report a subjective experience of having been awakened or else report a sense of awakening from a vivid dream during a somnambulistic episode (such events are described in Chapter 10). Similarly, subjects awakened after microdissociative somniloquy behave as if they had been asleep and report subjective experiences of having first been awakened from sleep or dreaming (see Appendix 2).

The relevant point to be gleaned from these previous comments is that despite certain electrographic signs of increased arousal apparently signaling wakefulness, a subject may nevertheless be, or remain, *psychologically* asleep, especially if such occurrences are immediately preceded and rapidly followed by unambiguous electrographic correlates of sleep. This latter sequence actually describes the electrographic structure of a typical microdissociative sleep-utterance episode. In other words, *psychological and electrographic sleep may often be slightly out of phase.* The relationship between psychological and electrographic sleep is one of high positive correlation, but less than 1—a close relationship but flexible in nature, and the one state component may lag the other. Such a notion seems compatible with the process view of sleep as formulated by Dement and Mitler (1974, see p. 322).

Further support for this suggestion arises from the demonstration that when subjects are awakened there is a delay in the full recovery of wakeful critical reactivity, even though typical electrographic signs of wakefulness prevail. Thus, experimental results of others reviewed by Tebbs (1972) demonstrate that postawakening performance decrements may range from 25 to 360% below full wakeful levels, and that although the rate of recovery is most rapid during the few minutes following the awakening, complete recovery may require as long as 25 min. Findings consistent with these have been reported by Feltin and Broughton (1968) and Scott (1969). In addition,

Broughton (1968) has demonstrated the carryover of NREM sleep components of the occipital visual evoked potential, or increased latencies and decreased amplitudes of later components, into immediately following wakefulness.

Intermediate and Macrodissociation and Sleep

As the duration of the somniloquy increases, the electrographic tracings will contain progressively larger amounts or admixtures of wakefulness pattern components, with gradual parallel evolving development of psychological sleep into altered states of consciousness characteristic of intermediate or macrodissociated psychic states. Examples of electrographic recording of macrodissociations are provided by Rice and Fisher (1976) in the sleep-associated fugue patient, and the carrying out of posthypnotic suggestions in sleep by a subject of Schiff, Bunney, and Freedman (1961), by my female macrodissociative somniloquist (Experiment IX, Chapter 11), by some of the subjects participating in the exploratory work on dialogue between sleep-talkers and wakeful observers (Chapter 12), by Batson's subject (Batson, 1977; see also speech 572 in Appendix 2, and Fig. 7.5), by some extensive sleep-speeches in the terminal baseline series of one of the posthypnotically stimulated sleep-talking subjects (speeches 7–14), and by night-terror behavior (Fisher, Kahn, Edwards, & Davis, 1975; Gastaut & Broughton, 1965).

Examples of intermediate dissociation may be found in many REM and NREM speeches of middling length (e.g., speeches 56, 80, 183, 185, 192, 220, 455, 464, etc.) It should also be noted that just as with microdissociative episodes, awakenings after the larger scale dissociations produce mentation reports of having been dreaming or asleep, often with strong amnestic tendencies manifested. That is, subjects behave as if they had been *psychologically* asleep at such times, despite a wakeful EEG. Actually, Gastaut and Broughton (1965) described episodes of sustained alpha frequencies lasting 1 min or more in normal subjects as well as pathological subjects who were behaviorally and mentally asleep. Such epochs were classified as Stage 1^a3 and distinguished from sleep-onset 1 NREM. (See Chapter 19 for a full description.)

Conclusion

Tentatively, therefore, it seems reasonable to consider the relatively brief episodes of sleep-utterance as occurring within intervals of momentary variations, alterations, and/or interruptions of typical electrographic sleep, but within the context of preserved continuity of psychological sleep, or else with minimal or inessential qualitative change in it. This grouping would correspond to those sleep-utterance episodes previously referred to as *micro*dissociative; and in gradual progressive fashion, as the duration of the sleep-utterance increases and the electrographic tracings contain progressively larger admixtures of wakefulness components, the episode will be more validly categorized as a sleep-associated altered state of consciousness—a dissociated psychic state of intermediate duration, or what West (1967) might categorize as a minor somnambulistic trance state. Both types of sleep-utterance episodes with gradations in between have been observed within and across subjects in our basic subject pool. Let us turn now to the next question.

THE EXISTENCE OF SLEEP MENTATION

Does sleep mentation really exist? How do we know that it does? Investigations of sleep mentation have customarily employed a paradigm consisting of correlation of electrographic measurements with verbal reports of the recall of sleep experience described by the subject as having been in progress just prior to being experimentally awakened. Both Rechtschaffen (1967) and Stoyva and Kamiya (1968), in excellent papers, have considered the problems involved in relying on such an approach to scientific study of private experience in general.

According to Rechtschaffen (1967), the belief that a sleep mentation report is a valid indicator of sleep experience is based on faith in the orderliness of verbal communication and orderliness in relationships between reports and experience. Such faith, no matter how reasonable, cannot vitiate the fact that processes intervening between experience and verbalization of the report decrease the closeness of these relationships. Rechtschaffen classified such processes as those associated with wakeful recall of the previous dream experience and those involved with the verbalization of such recall, referred to as "translation." Translation entails three separate steps: (1) choice of words appropriate to the recalled experience; (2) the decision to utter such words; and (3) the actual motor acts involved in the utterance.

The path between the beginning of the recall and the completion of translation is thorny with occasion for distortion, and partial and selective amnesia and conscious omission. Sometimes a person's initial judgment of not having dreamt is followed by sudden detailed dream recall a few moments later; and during recall and translation, one often touches things up a bit.

As experimenters, we are nevertheless inclined to accept the mentation report as a more or less veridical account of sleep experience because such acceptance is the most parsimonious attitude (requires the fewest gratuitous assumptions); because the phenomena reported by the dreamer have a certain prevalence, in that similar perceptual experience occurs in other contexts;

because it is plausible to assume that subjects purportedly describing sleep experience are in fact doing so in accordance with their reasonable best and most sincere efforts rather than lying; and because the experimenter has had similar private dream experience. None of these guides to evaluation of sleep mentation reports, singly or in combination, provide us with certainty that they achieve their intended purposes. At best, they are built on probabilistic bases, and attempts at their systematic application often encounter difficulty.

Stoyva and Kamiya (1968) formulated a general approach to the validation of assertions concerning private experience. They propose that sleep experience (including dreaming) be considered a hypothetical construct that is indexed in an imperfect way by both typical electrographic and behavioral events on the one hand, and on the other, retrospective verbal mentation reports elicited on waking the subject in close association with such former events. The combined use of these three correlates of sleep experience is an instance of the principle of convergent operations as a means of validation of hypothetical processes not accessible to direct observation. Thus, the greater the degree of congruence between these three sets of observations, the more justified the investigator is in making the diagnosis of prior ongoing sleep experience. Accordingly, it seems reasonable to assert that confidence in such diagnoses may be still further enhanced if awakenings are made immediately following somniloquy and concordance between its content and that of the mentation report is demonstrable. Only the most flinty, unbending skeptic would persevere in his doubt about the existence of sleep mentation if a person, who is asleep by behavioral and electrographic criteria, spontaneously utters words that are unambiguously concordant with those words spoken as part of a dream in progress so described by the subject as occurring immediately prior to awakening; the same applies when the sleep-talking content clearly describes or is derived from sleep-imagined nonverbal events subsequently recalled as a dream during wakefulness. This is precisely what happens in the overwhelming majority of instances of REMP-associated—and often enough in NREM-associated—sleep-utterances, to establish that at least there are specific demonstrable occasions when the existence of sleep mentation can be shown. The impressive proportion of concordance between NREM utterance and the following mentation report is of special importance because it provides additional evidence of the existence of NREM mentation where reliable electrographic indices of NREM mentation have not yet been established (Pivik, 1978); i.e., these findings increase the sense of conviction that experience in NREM sleep is indeed there to be remembered.

The foregoing considerations have a bearing on a recent philosophical controversy dealing with the ontological status of dreaming. Malcolm (1964) challenges the belief that dreams are conscious experiences during sleep. He denies, even, that they are illusory or delusive experiences, because there is no way of proving them to be experiences at all. A key consideration to his argument is his literal application of Wittgenstein's dictum that an inner process stands in need of outward criteria as a necessary condition to establish its ontological reality. The only evidence we have of the existence of dreaming experience, according to Malcolm, is ultimately the retrospective report of a wakeful individual. Even the evidence correlating human REM sleep with dreaming is discounted as applying only to what an awakened subject says at the moment, and it is a mere assumption that reports given after awakening have any relation to what was experienced, if anything, during sleep. As Wittgenstein (1953) put it:

> Must I make some assumption about whether people are deceived by their memories or not? Whether they really had these images while they slept, or whether it merely seems so to them on waking? . . . Do we even ask ourselves this when someone is telling us his dream? And if not, is it because we are sure his memory won't have deceived him? (And suppose it were a man with a quite specially bad memory?) [p. 184].

Ayer (1960), in the course of refuting Malcolm's arguments, cites the possibility of sleep-talking incidents as fulfilling an outward criterion of verification. "People talk in their sleep . . . . Suppose, then, we found that his waking report . . . agreed with what we overheard him saying in his sleep, would this not be corroboration [p. 52]?" Surely, Malcolm has driven himself into an untenable position by a gratuitous assumption that sleep and consciousness are mutually exclusive.

SLEEP-UTTERANCE AND MEMORY VARIABLES

The amount of research and theorizing involving factors influencing dream recall is vast and has been excellently reviewed by Rechtschaffen (1973), Koulack and Goodenough (1976) and Goodenough (1978). Here I will merely draw attention to the ways in which laboratory data on sleep-utterance complement, differ with, or perhaps extend the findings and models which have emerged in this line of endeavor; and my remarks will mostly concern microdissociative phenomena.

First, it is of interest to point out that with few exceptions, the experimental psychology of memory as it currently stands has been developed largely on the basis of findings obtained during wakefulness, and by means of measurement of subjects' responses to carefully structured experimental tasks. The main yield, though of immense theoretical value, has been questioned as to how useful it is in answering Klatzky's (1975) question: "What is the nature of forgetting in the real world? [p. 169]." For example, what is one likely to remember if, during a spontaneous conversation, one is interrupted with the question, "What was going through your mind just before you were interrupted?" What would be the nature and proportion of concordance between the content of the subject's conversation words and his recall? What would he omit, distort, rearrange, or embellish? And why? It would be difficult to carry out such experiments more than once, if even that, because one's expectancy of interruption would doubtless affect one's stream of speech. Second, an important consideration is to what extent are the findings of research on memory during wakefulness comparable or in agreement with findings obtained in relation to sleep? Does one find phenomena in connection with sleep corresponding to wakeful memory phenomena or categories? Or, are they entirely different?

Sleep-utterance provides a possibly unique experimental situation in which the subject spontaneously emits an internally generated, idiosyncratic, personal, definable signal laden with psycholinguistic information in a sleep-related state of consciousness, with the potentiality for recall-recognition assessment afterward during a wakeful state of consciousness.

Sleep-Utterance and Multistage Memory Theory

Modern memory theory divides wakeful auditory memory processes into three stages (Keele, 1973):

1. Short-term sensory storage (STSS), referring to an evanescent process in which acoustic information is stored just long enough to permit adequate auditory perception. Attempts to measure this interval have yielded variable duration estimates, but the consensus appears to be that useful information may reside in STSS memory not much longer than about 10 sec.

2. Short-term memory (STM), referring to a stage in which information is processed further, involving forms of reorganization, thinking, recoding, and the like. Estimates of its duration vary with experimental conditions, but when information rehearsal is prevented, STM lasts about 10–20 sec.

3. Long-term memory (LTM): Information retrievable after about 20 sec is deemed to have entered LTM. Some theorists consider it useful to divide LTM into that prevailing shortly after STM has ended, and LTM covering longer intervals such as hours, days, weeks, or longer.

Corresponding categories of memory processes or stages are observable in association with sleep-utterance phenomena. Inasmuch as subjects were usually awakened for mentation reports 30–40 sec or less following NREM speech, it was possible to demonstrate the presence of STSS and STM memory stages during a situation in which rehearsal, distraction, and interference factors were all minimized. The combined concordance rate for all NREM pairs obtained by the standard awakening method of eliciting reports, 5–30 sec after the utterance, was 33.5%, whereas the comparable figure yielded by the "dialogue" method (see Chapter 10 on concordance) was 92.3% ($p < .001$). The important features of this latter method are that the experimenter usually intervened in less than 5 sec after the utterance, and also that he attempted to directly participate in the subject's experience of the moment, "catching it on the wing," rather than first waking the subject and then eliciting retrospective recall in wakefulness (see pairs 448 and 502 in Appendix 1 for examples of the dialogue method).

It is interesting to compare the concordance rate of Stage 2 sleep-utterance report pairs with the rate of correct recall of digits acoustically introduced to a different population of subjects in Stage 2 "silent sleep." Oltman, Goodenough, Koulack, Maclin, Schroeder, and Flannagan (1977) carried out the following experiment on 12 college students. Throughout the night, a tape recording of one-syllable, randomly selected digits was played every 30 sec, to which the subjects became quickly habituated. In accordance with a prearranged schedule, subjects were awakened after 1, 5, and 10 sec intervals and the accuracy of their recall for the digits tested. The mean proportion of correct recall was 25% ($p < .001$), and importantly, no drop in performance was observed with the longer time intervals between stimulus and test. Individual differences were marked and some subjects could achieve 50% accuracy even at 20 sec intervals. The habituation to the stimuli enabled the experimenters to assess the behavior of unattended STSS and STM traces. The mean duration of the persistence of these traces as indicated by the proportion of correct recall at the various intervals is longer than in similar experiments carried out in wakefulness. The authors concluded that some characteristics of STSS and STM differ in sleep as compared to wakefulness and hypothesized that STSS traces decay less rapidly in sleep because of less interference from other mentation.

The result on Stage 2 sleep-utterance–mentation-report concordance (Chapter 10) is more than twice as great correct recall as for the subjects of Oltman et al. (1977) on the basis of group comparisons (58% versus 25%); but the best subjects of Oltman et al. (1977) approximated this figure (i.e., 50% correct at 20 sec stimulus-tested intervals). Both studies are consistent with the hypothesized existence of STSS and STM in association with sleep; both studies indicate that STSS and STM function differently in sleep as compared to wakefulness. An additional difference between the studies was the considerable variation in degree of concordance, corresponding to the accuracy of digit recall, across different time interval conditions; i.e., the dialogue method of experimental intervention yielded a very high rate of concordance (92.3%), as opposed to the much lower rate in the 5–30 sec postsleep-utterance condition. By contrast, Oltman et al. (1977) found no drop in performance level with increasing time intervals between digit stimuli and recall test. These differences may be the result of differences in methodology—spontaneous verbal utterance versus passively received acoustic stimuli—and differences in sharpness of target (specific digits versus unpredictable words). Individual subject differences certainly played a role in both studies.

Efficiency of Retrieval in Relation to Sleep Stage

In an early paper, Rechtschaffen et al., (1963a) described NREM mentation as "more poorly recalled" than that of REM. This comment was based on the finding that NREM reports have significantly lower total word counts. Two or more possibilities exist, however: Either NREM mentation is equal to or even greater in amount than that of REM, but recall mechanisms after NREM awakenings operate less efficiently, thus accounting for the lower word counts; or NREM mentation is in fact less in amount than that of REM, and recall mechanisms following awakenings from both types of sleep do not differ significantly in efficiency. Other investigators have commented on this issue (Brazier, 1967; Goodenough, 1968; Kales & Jacobson, 1967; Pivik & Foulkes, 1968; Rechtschaffen, 1967; Stoyva & Kamiya, 1968). What might help further in evaluating this question are at least partly independent indicators of two separable factors: the presence versus absence of mentation, and the functional efficiency of recall mechanisms involved in retrieving such mentation.

It seems reasonable to assume that a sleep-speech occurrence signals the presence of endogenous sleep mentation and that the degree of its concordance with a subsequent mentation report provides an indication of the efficiency of STM at that moment. In considering this approach, we exclude no-content mentation reports that might result from totally nonfunctioning rather than inadequately functioning STM. That is, a mentation report containing at least one content item indicates that STM was at least *partly* functioning, otherwise no mentation at all would be recalled. Thus, given an adequate sample of mentation reports from the different sleep stages with at least one content item, a significantly greater proportion of *concordance* between sleep-utterance–mentation-report pairs derived from a specific sleep stage would be consistent with the hypothesis of greater efficiency of retrieval mechanisms in the sleep stage concerned. That is, mentation as betokened by the sleep-utterance would be present, and the question is, in which sleep stage do retrieval mechanisms produce the highest proportion of concordance?

The data tabulations on 28 sleep-talkers in Chapter 10 dealing with concordance findings may be partly recast in Table 18.1:

TABLE 18.1
Retrieval and Sleep Stage

Sleep Stage	Total Number of Reports	Percentage Reports with Some Recall	Percentage Reports with Concordance	Ratio of Percentage Concordance Between Utterance and Report Pairs to Percentage Reports with Recalled Mentation
REMP	24	95.8	79.2	.83
Stage 2	85	78.8	45.8	.58
Stage 3–4	52	61.5	21.1	.35

Note that 95.8% of 24 REMP, 78.8% of 85 Stage 2, and 61.5% of 52 Stage 3–4 awakenings contained at least one item of content. Correspondingly, some degree of concordance was found between 79.2% of REMP, 45.8% of Stage 2, and 21.1% of Stage 3–4 sleep-utterance mentation report pairs. The respective ratios of these percentages (% concordance/% reports with recall) are .83 for REMP, .58 for Stage 2, and .35 for Stage 3–4 (REMP versus 2: $t = 2.66, p < .006$; REMP versus Stage 3–4: $t = 2.70, p < .006$; Stage 2 versus Stage 3–4: $t = 2.70; p < .006$).

This result is consistent with the hypothesis that STM functions with greatest efficiency in association with REM sleep, intermediate efficiency with Stage 2 and least efficiency with Stage 3–4.

Several cautions must be raised regarding this tentative conclusion. First, one must consider whether the higher auditory arousal thresholds of Stage 3–4 and the fact that they come from an earlier time of the night may have played a more influential recall-hampering role than relative inefficiency of retrieval functions. There is no clear or easy answer to this objection with the available data. Inasmuch as the same two parameters are about equal between Stage REM and Stage 2, however, the conclusion that retrieval mechanisms following Stage 2 awakenings are less efficient than those following Stage REM is not vitiated by the foregoing consideration.

A second caution arises from the possibility that indeterminate differences between the amount of sleep mentation content and word counts of sleep-utterance and mentation reports may have artifactually influenced the results. For example, a sleep-speech with a higher word count has a greater chance of acquiring concordance with a subsequent mentation report than a sleep-speech of smaller length. Similarly, given equal functioning efficiency of sleep-stage-associated retrieval mechanisms, differing amounts of sleep mentation would have indeterminately differing likelihoods of attaining concordance with sleep-utterances. Again, I have no clear, facile answer to such awkward sources of confounding. I can say, however, that although not quantitatively studied, the relationships revealed by the data processing seemed to hold up even when speeches and mentation reports of approximately equal length were compared. Given a sufficiently larger data sample, this possibility seems capable of controlled assessment. A further observation in support of the conclusion of this post hoc study, crude as it is, may be found in the fact that long NREM mentation reports are often not concordant with their preceding speeches, and that equally often, NREM speeches are longer than those arising out of REM sleep. Thus, there are at least some occasions when the just-mentioned explanations do not apply.

Efficiency of Retrieval in Relation to Time of Night

Unless one has a suitably large data pool obtained by appropriate sampling methods, conclusions about time-of-night effects are subject to question on the grounds of being confounded with sleep-stage effects. For example, sleep-talking is rare in association with the first REMP, and there is much more Stage 3–4 than 2 in the first half of the night. With this caveat in mind, the following is based on pooled NREM speeches, i.e., combined Stages, 2, 3, and 4. Of 77 NREM speeches occurring *after* the first 3 hr of sleep, 43% showed either first- or second- order concordance; and by contrast, of 45 NREM speeches occurring *during* the first 3 hr, 22% showed combined concordance ($p = .04$). Taken at face value, these results suggest that NREM mentation retrieval mechanisms are more efficient after the first 3 hr of sleep than in the interval before. However, the issue cannot be decided until comparable samples of, say, Stage 2 sleep-utterance report pairs from the first 3 hr of sleep and afterward are assessed. The above findings are, nevertheless, consistent with those of Pivik and Foulkes (1968), who found that NREM sleep mentation was more readily recalled following awakenings during the second half of the night. Of special relevance to the problem of confounds, they also claimed that this difference could not be solely ascribed to the greater predominance of Stages 3–4 early in the night—i.e., the time-of-night effect in question was somewhat independent of sleep stage. Overall Stage 2 recall occurred in 71.6% of their awakenings, as compared to only 28.6% of awakenings from Stage 2 in the earliest part of the night prior to the first REMP.

Tracy and Tracy (1974), however, failed to confirm the time-of-night effects claimed by Pivik and Foulkes (1968), and further controlled research is needed. Perhaps determinations of sleep-speech–mentation-report concordance with adequate sampling may help elucidate a question that seems deceptively easy to answer.

Recognition Versus Recall

As in the study of wakeful memory, mechanisms involved in recognition as opposed to recall in association with NREM sleep were again found to differ in efficiency. Thus, on 36 occasions distributed over 12 subjects, the latter were presented with a distinctive word or phrase taken from the sleep-utterance and asked if it meant anything to them. (See discussion of methods in the concordance section of Chapter 10.) This resulted in a 25% increase in combined concordance (18.6% first-order plus 6.3% combined second- and third-order). Of equal importance is the lack of additional recall in 62.5% of the foregoing subset despite such cues. These results suggest that although previously uttered words may be out of reach of unassisted, spontaneous short-term memory, some may nevertheless be temporarily stored and retrievable by testing for recognition, whereas the majority quickly become inaccessible.

In one sense, the dialogue method of experimenter intervention may be looked on as utilizing key word presentation, involving as it did immediate experimenter verbalization of a portion of the subject's sleep-speech. If this is accepted as a variant of a recognition versus recall test, then combined concordance likelihood seems greater than with the usual awakening method (combined NREM concordance rate with dialogue method = 92.3%, versus 33.5% with the usual awakening technique).

Sleep-Utterance Phenomena in Relation to Dream Recall Theory

Goodenough in his review of the dream recall problem (1978) usefully organized the topic in terms of two types of hypotheses attempting to account for the tendency to forget dreams: sleep mentation content-centered explanations, and memory-process explanations. The former state that factors related to parameters of the dream experience itself are prepotent in producing dream recall failure; and the latter state that memory-process features, especially those relating to sleep conditions, are the most influential variables. I now list these variables and comment on possible relationships and points of similarity or difference with sleep-utterance phenomena. In so doing, I do not dwell on the specific evidence, pro or con, regarding these hypotheses. The reader is referred to the original reviews for details.

Content-Centered Factors

Dream Content Salience.   This hypothesizes that the greater the novelty, bizarreness, emotionality, or intensity of the experience—the more salient it appears to be—the greater the probability, other things being equal, that it will be recalled. The evidence in favor of this hypothesis was generally strong.

Most of the studies reviewed by Goodenough (1978) deal with recall of REM dreams, both on the occasion of laboratory awakenings during the night and also during attempts at morning recall. Not only was salience of the dream content considered, but relationships between psychological indices of arousal intensity and dream recall efficiency, and dream content salience were also studied. NREM mentation has been less thoroughly investigated in these respects.

What sorts of analogous observations are available in studies on sleep-utterance? With the material at hand, we are best able to compare sleep-utterance content with wakeful recall elicited shortly afterward, both in relationship to associated sleep stage and time of night. In principle, it would have been possible to correlate these observations and results with efficiency of morning recall and precise systematic measurement of physiological variables, but this was outside the scope of both the experimental plans and the apparatus available under the conditions of the original investigations. Therefore, only general impressionistic comments can be made at this time from the viewpoint of sleep-utterance work.

First, no definite assertions are possible as to whether sleep-speech content with greater salience is more likely to be concordant with associated mentation report content. The main reason for such difficulty is that we have no independent valid measure of salience. What may strike the experimenter as a novel, bizarre, or intense-affect-bearing item might be judged or perceived much differently by the subject, as relatively conventional or bland.

Second, it can be said that by everyday, common-sense standards, many specimens were observed in accordance with the salience hypothesis in which items in speeches uttered with intense, lively affect were indeed concordant with mentation reports (e.g., speeches 49, 192, 558 in Appendix 2); but on the other hand, the opposite was often observed. That is, speeches with intense affect were often nonconcordant with mentation reports or were associated with no-content reports (e.g., speeches 80, 445, 486 in Appendix 2). The findings of Fisher, Kahn, Edwards, Davis, and Fine (1974) on Stage 4 night-terrors are consistent with these observations. In all, 58% of mentation reports obtained after severe night-terrors (heart rate greater than 108 beats per min), possessed definite recall of mentation, 7% vague recall, and 35% no recall. With the milder night-terrors (heart rate less than 108 beats per min), the outcome was almost identical—57% definite recall, 6% vague, and 37% no recall. However, the authors state that concordance here was more frequent and striking than in the severe arousals, but quantitative evidence on this point was not provided.

Correspondingly, seemingly contrary to the salience hypothesis, many instances of what impressed the experimenter as bland, colorless speeches were observed to be concordant with mentation reports (e.g. speeches 195, 317, 448). As previously indicated, however, it is entirely possible that systematic ratings by subjects of the salience of components of their own sleep-speeches and mentation reports might disclose a pattern in agreement with the dream salience notion. It should be stressed that Koulack & Goodenough (1976) qualified their dream salience hypothesis as accounting mainly for retrieval from dreams with moderately low to moderately high arousal levels, indicating that repression may operate against dream salience to thwart retrieval from the highest affect-laden dreams, particularly on occasions of morning recall. To the factor of repression in such instances, one might add the cognition-impairing effects of input overload (Gottschalk, Haer, & Bates, 1972). Further, Koulack and Goodenough (1976) cite a great deal of impressive evidence that external distraction upon awakening impairs retrieval efficiency; it is possible that the highest arousal levels function as an "internal distraction" to likewise impair retrieval. Of possible relevance is the report of Talland (1960) who, in his work on a microgenetic approach to the amnestic syndrome, points out that in order to be capable of retrieval, experiences must initially become embedded in the appropriate cognitive system. In both normal subjects and patients afflicted with Korsakoff's syndrome, it has been demonstrated that clear perception is an insufficient condition for accurate or even approximately correct recall.

Effective remembering depends on cognitive system-embedding factors that develop subsequent to perception. In intact persons, completion of perceptual processes tends to include embedding as well, but in abnormal conditions these two processes may become divorced and perception itself may not attain full development. The incompletely structured percepts thus acquired will be registered incomplete in the cognitive system subserving retrieval. Some items of material perceived under conditions of intense affect, then, may not be capable of completed perceptual processing and cognitive system embedment and thus remain inaccessible to recall. A similar inadequate embedment mechanism may be a factor in the frequent amnesia for mentation associated with sleep-utterance as generally observed.

Dream Disorganization.   It seems reasonable to surmise that well-organized mentation will be retrieved more efficiently than that experienced as a mass of chaotic percepts. However, Goodenough (1978) cited Barber (1969) as having carried out a study in which no relationship was detected between dream disorganization and dream retrieval efficiency. Rough comparison with sleep-speeches and mentation reports suggested a somewhat different picture. There seemed to be a distinct tendency for grossly disorganized sleep-speeches, especially those resembling jargon aphasia, to be paired with no-content or nonconcordant mentation reports (see Table 18.2 and p. *470*. To be sure, exceptions were observed. It is equally plausible to ascribe this tendency to such speeches being more likely to occur in the first half of the night and also in association with Stage 4, when mentation retrieval is generally more difficult than from Stage REM. That is, the just-mentioned possible correlation might reflect sleep stage and time-of-night factors rather than psycholinguistic disorganization variables. A further consideration is that the most influential, even more basic common factor may be one that gives rise to a cognitive state that is characterized both by disorganized sleep-speech and also by inefficient retrieval of sleep mentation. On the other hand, although chaotically organized visual dream percepts might not pose special retrieval difficulties, as in Barber's study (1969), disorganized word sequences might be specifically burdensome.

The Role of Dream Kinesthesia in Recall Failure.   Rorschach (1942) hypothesized that actual body movement at the moment of awakening serves to inhibit recall of dreamed body movement. Lying still with eyes closed on awakening favors dream recall whereas concomitant muscular activity has a hampering effect. This accords well with observations of other investigators cited by Goodenough (1978). It raises the question of whether the movements of the vocal apparatus in sleep-speech, including tongue and lips with their rich nerve supply, serve to hamper dream imagery retrieval as well. It would be interesting to determine the comparative effects of vocalization without words, vocalization with words, and control finger movements without vocalization on *wakeful* imagery recall. In Chapter 17 dealing with the subjective experience of sleep-talking, I describe a personal experience with my own sleep-talking that is consistent with Rorschach's hypothesis.

Disinterest in Dream Content.   Goodenough (1978) reviews the literature inquiring into possible relationships between dream recall efficiency and level of interest in one's dreams. All things considered, he concludes that such factors can account for only a limited range of dream recall phenomena. Although no evidence from sleep-talking research is available enabling one to evaluate the level of interest in one's dreams, it seems reasonable to hypothesize that the act of overt verbalization already betokens more than mere indifference to what one says or what was going on during a sleep experience, and yet, the difficulty in recall of concordant mentation, particularly marked from NREM sleep, is apparent from inspection of the results on concordance presented in Chapter 10. Thus, it would seem that interest is no guarantee of recall—a conclusion suggested by several lines of evidence.

Repression as a Factor in Dream Recall Failure.   Goodenough (1978) is prepared to accept that though repression is often responsible for specific instances of dream recall failure, it cannot be held to be a major factor of general importance in accounting for the fact that most dream material is forgotten. The results on sleep-talking–mentation-report concordance bear this out. Sleep-speeches that are often associated with nonconcordant or no-content mentation reports are frequently so bland and innocuous that one is compelled to wonder what is so terrible in them as to require repression? This question is applicable only if we take the target of repression to be the sleep-speech itself. However, on the basis of psychoanalytic theory, one might properly infer that the sleep-speech, though innocent enough in itself, is associatively connected with deeply repressed contents such that the unconscious ego in an "all out" effort to maximize defensive efficiency overshoots the mark and represses "everything in the neighborhood"—an occurrence with which psychoanalytic clinicians are familiar. And it is indeed possible that if subjects were required to free associate in wakefulness following a sleep-utterance, or else free associate to specific key words in the sleep-speech content, warded off, repressed derivatives might become manifest.

Memory Process Factors

Under this category, Goodenough (1978) includes factors influencing the ability to recall any experience during sleep independent of the content of that sleep experience, and relating rather to memory processes in general without regard to the qualitative nature of the material to be retrieved.

It has been a commonplace of anecdotal and scientific observation that acquisition of new information during sleep is impaired. (Aarons 1976; Simon & Emmons 1956). This was traditionally explained on the basis of a belief that sleep involved de-afferentation from the sources of input. Deficiencies in retention of material perceived in association with sleep were then generally explained as inadequacy of stimulus registration. Recent investigation has revealed, however, that discrimination of auditory stimuli is possible during sleep and that they are capable of evoking responses related to that which was learned during wakefulness (reviewed by Aarons, 1976). It follows, then, that retention-failure of information received during sleep is at least partly the result of limitations of *sleep memory* processes. This notion is further supported by the finding that subjects who perform equally well on memory and intelligence tests during wakefulness may nevertheless show amongst themselves marked individual differences in the frequency with which they are able to report dreams. Thus, at least in some respects, memory processes appear to function differently in sleep than in wakefulness. In other respects, however, observations on sleep memory are quite in accord with the well-established memory phenomena observed in waking subjects. It is to these that we now turn.

Classical Memory Phenomena in Relation to Sleep.   Goodenough (1978) concluded, as a result of his review of the literature, that classical factors operative in wakeful recall, such as primacy, recency, and "length of list" (total number of dreams of the night to be recalled) all influenced the ability to correctly recall the material of dream reports elicited during the previous night. Parallel results were obtained on morning recall of tests of words shown to subjects during a series of brief awakenings during the preceding night (Goodenough, Sapan, Cohen, Portnoff, & Shapiro, 1971). In both types of item recall tested (for dreams or words), result patterns were similar to those obtained on the basis of studies of wakeful memory.

The data collected by us (Arkin et al., 1970a) on morning recall of somniloquy did not lend itself to a systematic study in which we could control for item salience, recognition memory of sleep-speech content versus its spontaneous recall, order effects, etc. We can say, however, that morning recall of dreams or any other mentation of the previous night unambiguously related in discernible ways to specific sleep-speeches (first-order concordance) was a great rarity with respect to NREM episodes but somewhat more common with respect to REM-associated somniloquy. A perusal of Appendix 2 will bear this out.

This is only what would be expected on the basis of studies of morning recall of REM versus NREM mentation occurring *without* concomitant sleep-speech, and this impression is also in accord with the general understanding that sleep-talkers do not remember their sleep-speeches of the previous night. The morning recall of special sleep-speech items is a somewhat different matter from that of morning recall of dreams, the content of which may show second- or third-order concordance with the previous night's somniloquy; but there again, the pattern of results follows that of the greater ability to recall in the morning REM mentation as opposed to NREM mentation. Further, there is greatly increased risk of false positive concordance scores when comparing sleep-speeches and morning recall content. (See introduction to Appendix 2 for discussion of this issue.)

State-Dependent Recall Factors.   Goodenough (1978) likewise reviewed literature relevant to the notion that wakeful retrieval of sleep mentation is hampered by difference in wakeful as opposed to sleep states of consciousness—an idea related to the demonstration of state-dependent learning (Overton, 1964). Only the studies of Evans, Gustafson, O'Connell, Orne, and Shor (1970), Evans (1972), and Perry, Evans, O'Connell, Orne, and Orne (1978) have provided evidence demonstrating the possibility of such factors being effective influences. These have involved the acquisition of simple motor responses during REM sleep with intervening wakeful amnesia but with capability of re-elicitation during subsequent REM sleep across nights. Only one clinical report known to me (Burrell, 1904) describes similar phenomena in a case of flamboyant sleep-talking and sleep-walking, in which articles hidden during somnambulism, their location "forgotten" during wakefulness, and then retrieval during subsequent somnambulism, was described.

It would be fascinating to attempt to engage a sleep-talker in a specific dialogue (see Chapter 12) and a test for comparative recall in subsequent wakefulness and sleep-talking states. Would memory for the sleep-talking episode content be better preferentially in subsequent sleep-utterance states as opposed to wakefulness? It seems more plausible to expect positive results with subjects whose sleep-speech arises in connection with sustained macrodissociative episodes rather than the more common microdissociative NREM sleep-speech episodes. Results of morning recall with subjects 1 and 3 in the posthypnotically stimulated sleep-talking work described in Chapter 11 are consistent with this expectation.

Impairment in Memory-Trace Consolidation. Koulack and Goodenough (1976) and Goodenough (1978) also examined considerations relating dream recall to memory-trace consolidation factors. The initial assumption of the family of explanations utilizing this factor is that consolidation of memory traces is impaired during sleep. Trace consolidation is said to occur, in Goodenough's view, when information is transferred from STM to LTM. Attention is called to the several ways in which consolidation processes have been conceptualized in the literature, and also the different modes of application of the concept to sleep-related phenomena. I refer here only to the very particular sense of this term employed by Goodenough in elaborating his model of dream recall—that of "rapid" consolidation in a matter of seconds. This is opposed, for example, to durations of consolidative processes involving much more time as conceptualized by others in discussion of memory consolidation (e.g., Fowler, Sullivan, & Ekstrand, 1973). Goodenough addresses the specific problem of why sleep experiences are generally so difficult to recall unless waking attention is focused on them during the interval immediately subsequent to their occurrence. His model accounting for this entails the following considerations:

1. The duration of information momentarily in sleep STM is assumed to be of the order of seconds rather than minutes or hours.

2. The effective transfer of information from sleep STM to LTM requires adequate rehearsal processes, i.e., such activities as repetition or recycling, recoding, and reorganization of information preparatory to insertion into LTM.

3. The effective transfer of information from STM to LTM is impaired at low levels of arousal, especially during sleep.

4. Consolidation processes are impaired by sleep itself, because sleep involves diminished capacity for rehearsal.

5. Consolidation processes are subject to interference by succeeding input during sleep and by distraction stimuli on awakening.

6. If awakening occurs during the life of an STM trace, then the contents of the immediately preceding sleep experience may be retrievable from STM directly; and given this entry into LTM, the subject may be able to recall some of the content of a preceding dream. But if the awakening is delayed until the

STM trace has expired, retrieval may be difficult or impossible. Thus, consolidation of sleep experience cannot be effectively carried out unless a distraction-free waking state occurs during the life of the STM trace.

7. Processing effectiveness is thus assumed to be a function of two factors: arousal level, and distraction–interference influences.

8. Neither recall nor processing of target material automatically follows when arousal occurs while the short-term trace is still active; rather, the target items are only a few of the many events, stimuli, and thoughts that compete for the limited resources of the cognitive system. Hence, it is assumed that only the items in such arrays that are most salient to the individual at the moment are likely to be processed and retrievable, and by virtue of such salience are more likely to win out in competition with interference-distraction influences at the time of awakening.

9. Effective processing of material at the time of its occurrence does not guarantee successful retrieval in the following morning. In this context, repression may be added to interference–distraction influences hampering recall.

Interference on morning awakening affects recall presumably in the same manner as it affects recall of other items during wakefulness; as indicated earlier, frequency of other dreams during the night, and ordinal position in the sequence of such dreams are examples of such factors. In addition, salience of dream items, as defined by their affective components, serves to protect dreams against interference. Thus, in the morning, dreams with moderate affect are more likely to be recalled than those with lowest affect, whereas some dreams with the highest affect may be repressed and less available to recall than many dreams of lower salience value.

Memory Trace Consolidation and Sleep-Utterance Phenomena

How well do sleep-utterance phenomena conform to the Goodenough-Koulack Model? Let us consider the question in terms of the main relevant points.

Rapid Trace Consolidation. The results on concordance between mentation report and sleep-utterance content are quite consistent with the notion of rapid trace consolidation. This is particularly striking with NREM utterances. Combined concordance for all NREM sleep stages was 92.3% using the dialogue method of content retrieval, which minimizes the time interval between utterance and report elicitation, versus 33.5% NREM combined concordance with the usual awakening technique, involving 5–30 sec intervals between utterance and report elicitation.

The data obtained from awakenings following REMP-associated utterances are somewhat less consistent at first glance with the rapid consolidation hypothesis. Concordance was detectable between utterance and report over elicitation time intervals far in excess of 30 sec. This may be explained without embarrassment to the remainder of Goodenough's model, however, by recourse to the fact that REMP sleep-speech entails a moment of extremely brief relatively increased arousal, even to the point of evanescent awakening—a condition in accordance with the model's proviso that increases in arousal usually favor consolidation and entry into LTM (see further discussion). Further, REM dreams are likely to possess more intense affect and therefore higher salience values than NREM, and retrieval from LTM is thus less likely to be hampered by interference factors (Koulack & Goodenough, 1976).

Consolidation and Rehearsal Processes.   Sleep-utterance and other concomitant mentation seemingly occur with minimal opportunities for rehearsal. The sleep-talking subject does not know in advance when he will be tested. In my work (Arkin et al., 1970a; 1972a) subjects were awakened during "silent sleep" even more often than after sleep-utterance. This fact confers an unique advantage on this experimental technique for study of items in STSS or STM with both rehearsal and interference influences minimized. As previously stated, it is difficult to find other similar situations wherein subjects emit a spontaneous utterance and are capable of having their retrieval ability tested unexpectedly under conditions where interference, distraction, and rehearsal factors are all held to a minimum. The experimental results with NREM utterances are quite in accord with Goodenough's rapid-consolidation model, as indicated by the high rates of no-content and no-discernible-concordance reports. Of added interest is that the event of overt utterance in itself appears to have no influence through interference–distraction or other factors on the rate of reports with recall; i.e., in one study (Arkin et al., 1972a), NREM silent sleep reports with recall constituted 77.7% of the sample, and NREM sleep utterance reports 75.0%; correspondingly, the mean total word counts of mentation reports were not significantly different (211.3 versus 168.8 words per report respectively). This suggests that utilizing cognitive resources in the production of sleep-utterance has no gross hampering effect on retrieval capacity for sleep mentation occurring in association with it.

Once more, at first glance, the REM sleep-utterance data are somewhat less consistent with Goodenough's proposal about the opportunity for rehearsal and greater likelihood of recall. Both NREM and REM utterances tend to occur in association with movement-arousal episodes, and presumably opportunities for rehearsal are not too dissimilar. However, as discussed,

REM mentation is likely to possess higher salience levels, and this, in accord with the related proviso of the Goodenough–Koulack model, could account for the greater concordance between REM utterances and reports than for NREM.

Retrieval and Arousal.   Eysenck (1976) has selectively reviewed the literature on relationships between arousal, learning, and memory in wakefulness and has suggested that, in general, memory studies should consider differential effects of at least four varieties of arousal: item arousal at input and item arousal at output (arousal occasioned by perception and performance with regard to specific items involved), and subject arousal at input and output (background arousal level of the subject during the intervals occupied by input and output). The model set forth by Koulack and Goodenough (1976) and Goodenough (1978) appears to take these variables into account. Eysenck (1976) proposes that "high arousal has the effect of biasing the subject's search process toward readily accessible stored information more than is the case with lower levels of arousal [p. 401]." The degree of ready accessibility of such stored information is an index of its functional dominance—a concept reminiscent of salience of dream content elements.

The level of subject arousal at input in Eysenck's scheme appears to correspond to the level of arousal during the interval in which the sleep mentation is being experienced. For example, the level of arousal during REM sleep is greater than during NREM, and this may increase the likelihood of successful retrieval subsequently. Similarly, during output after awakening, the competition between sleep mentation and interference–distraction influences is likely to be dominated by items with the greatest arousal potential; and increments of arousal to the point of brief awakening during the life of the STM trace of the sleep mentation item favor successful retrieval. These latter two considerations correspond to Eysenck's item and subject arousal at output variables, respectively.

Once more, in general, the concordance data on sleep-utterance and mentation report are roughly consistent with the formulations of Eysenck (1976), Koulack and Goodenough (1976), and Goodenough (1978), but as mentioned before, exceptions are observable. In Eysenck's terms, high item and high subject arousal levels at input have often been followed by poor retrieval (see speeches 80, 445, and 486, Appendix 2), and low item and low subject arousal levels by successful retrieval (e.g., speeches 195, 317, 448, Appendix 2). These exceptions are among the observations that have inclined me to select the concept of psychic dissociation (Hilgard, 1973) as the best perspective from which to view sleep-utterance phenomena. Thus, in terms of the model of sleep-utterance proposed in Chapter 17, during sleep-related states of consciousness, the efficiency of the executive ego is impaired with resulting functional incoordination. The cognitive subsystems, or components thereof, participating in the mediation and various memory storage stages of psychological items involved in experience of imagery, thought, and affect are subject to less overall integration, with a great deal of ensuing simultaneous, unharmonious release of inhibition, deficiency of organization, monitoring, and control. Maintenance of sustained goal-directedness of mentation is given up in varying degree and tends to be replaced by brief, abortive, incoordinated, often mutually opposed mental tendencies of subsystem components. The hands holding the reins of cognition begin to falter, or tug and relax unsystematically, with the result that the members of the cognitive team of horses each tend to go their own way in varying directions and in varying degrees. Thus, in one instance, level of arousal, STM efficiency, and degree of salience will be mutually supportive and enhance recall; whereas in other instances extremely high arousal may overwhelm STM and selective cognitive evaluation of item salience, and thereby impair recall.

SLEEP-UTTERANCE AND PSYCHOLINGUISTICS

Bruner (1969) has suggested that for analytic purposes, it is useful to draw a distinction between two major types of memory function: one that he refers to as memory with record, and a second called memory without record. In the former type, specific events are recoverable in attempts by the subject to recall or recognize stored items; in the latter type, memory without record, experiences are transformed into some process that changes the nature of an organism, alters its skills, or transmutes the rules that govern its behavior, and such experiences or encounters remain essentially inaccessible to subsequent recall as specific contents of awareness. Among the innumerable instances of memory storage without record are those rules and skills learned in order to make possible elaboration of thought sequences mediated by psycholinguistic processes, on which psycholinguistic competence depends. The reader will recognize a certain kinship between Bruner's "memory with record" and Tulving's (1972) "episodic memory," and "memory without record" and Tulving's "semantic memory," although Bruner's category is a broader concept of which semantic memory is a special subset.

Until now, we have been exploring sleep-related memory processes with record—that which governs what can be brought to mind after experimental awakenings. We now turn to an area of sleep-related memory without record, the ways in which such memory for linguistic skills is preserved or impaired in relation to sleep. With the possible and questionable exception of somnambulism—a relatively crude phenomenon—somniloquy provides the experimenter with an almost unique opportunity to study memory processes without record (Bruner, 1969) in relation to sleep.

Like the field of memory research, the burgeoning area of psycholinguistics has been developed largely on the basis of the study of linguistic behavior of normal subjects during wakefulness, and those with functional psychoses or organic brain pathology. The reader who has persevered until now could surely not evade the notion that sleep-utterance phenomena provide interested investigators with unique opportunities to observe psycholinguistic behavior during physiological, i.e., "normal," altered states of consciousness. Systematic research in this terrain might be expected not only to yield data relevant to the general psychology and neurology of wakeful language behavior, but also to illuminate the little-known topic of the psychoneural aspects of language during sleep.

Exposition of the subject is undertaken most conveniently by way of recent conceptualizations of models of *speech production* (Clark & Clark, 1977; Lashley, 1951; Laver, 1970; MacNeilage, 1970; MacNeilage & MacNeilage, 1973). For the purpose at hand, the most convenient expositional format is that of Laver (1970), according to whom speech production entails the more-or-less integrated sequential exercise of five separable functions:

1. ideational processes including intent, target, or goal of the anticipated utterance and its approximate semantic content;
2. utilization of the permanent storage of linguistic information;
3. planning processes aimed at the construction of a neurolinguistic program adequate for the expression of the speaker's idea;
4. execution of the neurolinguistic program by muscular systems involved in utterance production; and
5. monitoring of output including detection and correction of errors, i.e., discrepancies between ideational intent and nature of outputs during the several steps in the utterance sequence.

The remainder of this large section is devoted to brief expositions of authoritative contemporary perspectives in psycholinguistics in accordance with the topic headings of Laver's (1970), format to be followed in each instance by discussion and speculation relating such material to observations made during laboratory study of sleep-utterance.

Speech-Initiating Ideational Processes

What is the general thrust of contemporary, influential neuropsychological models of behavior instigation? And how is speech production, a special complex behavior, related to the more general models of motivation? A common basic concept underlying many contemporary models is that goal-directedness and implementation of psychoneural plans are essential in the elaboration of *all* behavior. Such plans and their components are considered as organized into complex hierarchies, and it is postulated that an overall, coordinative, controlling system normally operates to integrate subordinate components of plans leading to behavioral outputs (e.g., Brown, 1977; Gallistel, 1974; John, 1976; Luria, 1973; Pribram, 1976). Every complex form of behavior is a function of the combined interaction of different factors, the constituent elements of which are usually widely distributed over the various zones of the brain. A significant alteration of any one factor, such as that produced by a brain lesion, will disturb the effective performance of some psychological processes but leave others intact. When the functioning of components of neural systems is impaired, the patterns of interaction between the remaining, still active neural components undergo changes in response to these alterations of physiological conditions. As a result, according to Luria (1973), there is a "reorganization of the working parts of the brain, so that the disturbed function can be performed in a new way [p. 104]." This persistent attempt to carry out goal-directed behaviors with remaining intact system components influenced and modified by other dynamic pathological factors, such as reflex effects, shock, irritation, etc., largely fashion what the clinician characterizes as neuro-pathological syndromes.

Accordingly, most contemporary models of *speech production* postulate that verbal expressions are goal-directed or else the manifestations of goal-directed functioning and involve the implementation of hierarchically organized plans vulnerable to widely varying degrees and patterns of disruption, each in turn capable of resulting from a wide variety of factors (Brown, 1977; Clark & Clark, 1977; Luria, 1973; MacNeilage, 1970; Miller, Galanter, & Pribram, 1960; Vygotsky, 1962; Werner & Kaplan, 1963). Signs of persistent intentionality, goal-directedness, or functioning of psychoneural plans may be manifested in seriously abnormal as well as normal speech production. For example, even in the case of the crude utterances occurring in limbic epileptic automatisms, it is reasonable to ask why the patient utters just these words, even if they are primitive, recurrent, and apparently meaningless, and does not utter other specific words instead? And does not the employment of native-language–specific morphemes and phonemes betoken the operation of a sort of elementary, short-span, planfulness despite the nonsensical, inappropriate overall content?

Luria (1973) states that "narrative expressive speech or expression begins with an *intention* or *plan,* which subsequently must be recoded into a verbal form and moulded into a speech expression [p. 318]." Accordingly, it seems reasonable to postulate similarly that speech-initiating ideational processes actuated by goal-directed intentional and planful factors lead ultimately to somniloquy, just as they actuate wakeful utterance. What sorts of relationships might there be between such intentional initiating processes and the specific content of the overt sleep-utterance? The situation presents certain problems that are not usually troublesome in wakeful speech. If a wakeful person says "Dammit" when attempting to open a recalcitrant door, an observer has little difficulty in understanding the event and what led to utterance of the expletive. Similarly, if an observer was puzzled on hearing a wakeful person suddenly mutter "Thank God," he could ask the speaker what was going on within his mind to account for the utterance, and in most cases confidently expect a clarifying response. Matters are not so easy with sleep-utterance. The observer has not the benefit of contextual cues afforded by unambiguous wakeful behavior sequences, nor may he so readily expect clarifying responses to inquiries about the sleeper's experience or sleep-speech prior to awakening. Nevertheless, we approach the topic of speech-initiating ideation by reviewing data on sleep-mentation–somniloquy concordance (Chapter 10).

In the following section, we are guided by the principle that in the course of ongoing behavior, information may be emitted and processed by systems under the control of the nervous system, and that such activities may, in varying degree, or may not at all involve registration in or accessibility to the subject's awareness (e.g., John, 1976; Libet, 1966; Schiffrin & Schneider, 1977; Schneider & Schiffrin, 1977).

In this fashion, we have a scheme that provides for occurrences in which (1) specific sleep-ideational processes achieve unambiguous expression in sleep-speech; (2) such processes do *not* achieve unambiguous expression in sleep-speech as judged by a lack of discernible relationship between sleep-speech content and that of the associated mentation report; and (3) an ideational process can achieve overt verbal expression but without evidence of concomitant effective retrieval processes immediately afterward.

Be reminded of the experimental set-up. Subjects in the laboratory utter words in association with sleep, are awakened shortly afterward, and asked to report what had been passing through their minds (see Chapter 10).

Let us now review the kinds of concordance relationships observed between the content of sleep-speeches and that of mentation reports.

Sleep-Speech Is Emitted and Concordant Mentation Is Recalled in a Subsequent Awakening. (First-, second-, and third-order concordance combined.) The most reasonable interpretation of such occurrences is that an ideational process during sleep had initiated an overt utterance and that the pool of associated mentation involved was, in varying degrees, accessible to the retrieval mechanisms of the wakeful executive ego. Such a possibility seems more probable when presenting the subject with a key sleep-speech verbal item results in elicitation of additional recall clearly related to the sleep-speech. (See previous discussion of stimulated recall—Chapter 10.)

Example:

Sleep-Speech—Stage 4
Uh—[sighs] chicken her other ones—oh—all other ones—chickens.

Mentation Report
   E: Charlotte.
   S: Yes?
   E: What were you thinking?
   S: Um—oh—let's see—oh—first of all I was thinking about the Julia books, and how they were outside getting them—um—and then—.
   E: Yes? and then?
   S: Then they had, had a guy in green sweater, he kept disappearing after he comes to ours—.
   E: Do you remember anything else?
   S: Um—.
   E: Do you remember anything else, Charlotte?
   S: Um. No.
   E: Do you remember about chickens?
   S: Yes. Yes. In the first part, er, they was all about chickens—red chickens and then—yellow chickens and all kinds of mesu—mesuzah and chickens and chickens—.

Sleep-Speech Is Emitted, Mentation Is Indeed Recalled, but It Bears No Discernible Concordance with the Content of the Utterance. In such instances, it is reasonable to hypothesize, at least in some of the instances, that the speech was initiated by a specific ideational process that was dissociated from an entirely different ideational process and that the mental content of the latter only was retrieved by the awakened executive ego. This outcome suggests that two or more separate streams of ideation may be concurrent in sleep—one preempting the utterance apparatus or else preferentially selected by it, but operating beyond the reach of wakeful retrieval mechanisms; and another stream to which retrieval mechanisms may or may not have access but which nevertheless does not become verbalized in the sleep-speech. Such a possibility seems more probable when attempts to stimulate further recall are successful in achieving increased material despite the fact that none of these additional items so produced are discernibly concordant with the sleep-speech.

Example:

Sleep-Speech—Stage 4
   Mbls—a—mi—be—better—seems that six books home and I haven't even got them yet—i—ea—where—i—ea—what?—mbl—a *rag* in a *rags* bed, *rag!* I don't even have a *rag*—mm—*bag*—mm—*baggette*—okay.

Mentation Report
   S: Um—flowers and a boat—.
   E: Can you be more specific? What about the flowers and the boat?

S: Th'—Th'Th'—the boat was receding and I um—under a bridge and boat
and flowers are receding in opposite direction, and that—that direction's
away from me—.
E: Was there anything more?
S: No, thank you.
E: Do you remember anything about a rag and a bag?
S: No—nothing that I can remember.
E: Can you remember anything before the boat and the flowers?
S: To me it seems a blank.

[categorized as no discernible concordance]

The notion of multiple streams of mentation in parallel is included in
Hilgard's neodissociationist theory, but it is of further interest to cite a similar
concept from a different source (Schiffrin & Schneider, 1977; Schneider &
Schiffrin, 1977); this deals in part with automatic information processing of
nodes "without the necessity of active control or attention by the subject [p.
2]." Such "automatic processes often appear to act in parallel with one
another and sometimes appear to be independent of one another [p. 160]."

*Sleep-Speech Is Emitted and No Mentation Is Recalled Whatsoever,
Despite Attempts to Stimulate Recall.*   At least three interpretations are
compatible with our observations.

1. Ideational processes in sleep initiated somniloquy but the experimentally awakened executive ego could not retrieve ideation of any sort, not
even from an active pool dissociated from that which produced the utterance.
This interpretation seems most appropriate when the sleep-utterance was
reasonably well organized linguistically. That is, the utterance of a correctly
constructed, complex speech suggests that a correspondingly high level of
well-organized cognitive ideational activity was prior to, and associated with
it, even though the ideation was beyond retrieval.

Example:

Sleep-Speech—Stage 2
Mm—mm—hey—wait a minute, will ya? I'm not even there yet—mbl—
people—mbl—wait a minute—mbl—mm.

Mentation Report
E: Who did you want to wait, Al?
S: Mm?—excuse me?
E: Who do you want to wait a minute?
S: I can't—I don't understand.
E: Could you tell me what you were thinking about just now?
S: Uh—yes—let me see—it uh—I was not—I was not sleeping at the same
time—I was not you know—I was on the verge of falling asleep—uh—it

seemed as if several ideas going through my head sort of—you know—one—one tangled up with the other ones—I can't really pinpoint any—any one specific—a specific one—that's about all I can tell offhand—.

2. A certain proportion of speeches are structurally disorganized in degrees varying from slight abnormalities to chaotic sequences of linguistic fragments. This may result from a momentary sleep ideational-process disorder that overtaxes the capacities of the speech planning, articulation, and monitoring functions. Thus, if the stream of thought proceeds at an excessively rapid rate or shifts in topical content and affective intensity too frequently, the speech functions located later on in the "assembly line" may not be able to "keep up."

Example:

Sleep-Speech—Stage 4

Yes—yeh—don't get (?) excited [loud mbl] or he's away—I dunno know—mbls—away—shway—[many rapid mbls] try basement of grade school (?) [buzzer sounds briefly but *S* continues] to do my reduced—go—ahead—don't close yet—don't go—mbls—sneak—sneak—to go reek—you—reek—to steak—stoke—[then slower] she said to—uh—to find some theft [pause] uh with Burt (?)—will burn you—would burn things—burnt objects (?)—burn and you—at the same time—you there (?) at the same time.

Mentation Report

S: Valentine.
E: Can you tell me any more about it?
S: No, that's all.

[scored as no discernible concordance]

3. Speech may be emitted without impetus from or reflecting any ideational process whatsoever. For example, it is conceivable, particularly with utterances that are maximally disorganized, unintelligible, and followed by no-content mentation reports, that they arise from "noise-like" bursts of activation of the neuromuscular apparatus at a "subideational level," resembling some ictal process. It is also possible that individuals in general harbor a number of semi-autonomous low emission threshold utterance sequences, or else experience a lowering of such thresholds under conditions of special psychophysiological contexts of altered arousal levels. One or more of these sequences may compete for utterance channels in a chaotic way, or else the utterance channels may not be equal to the task of efficient selection and processing, with the net result of a markedly disorganized sleep-speech. Here the most influential factor in sleep-speech production would not be the initiating ideational process, but rather the altered arousal state facilitating the expression of "prepared" low emission threshold word sequences.

Example:

Sleep-Speech—Stage 4
> Wai, wai, ho, ho, ho, ho, ho gotta check the file, gotta check the file out on those, hah?—hey ol' boy?

Mentation Report
> No recall.

In Summary

In summary, the relationships between speech-initiating ideational processes during sleep and the actual somniloquy content are complex and do not lend themselves to simple formulation. The observed experimental outcomes of the paradigm of comparison of sleep-speech and mentation report content seem to be capable of expression in terms of the following sets of variables:

1. those belonging to the sleep mentation stream itself;
2. those belonging to interactions between concurrent more or less separate streams of mentation;
3. those relating to accessibility of the utterance channel;
4. those relating to accessibility of retrieval channels during experimental awakenings;
5. those having to do with the interactions between retrieval channels; and
6. those having to do with temporal factors such as the life-span of mentation in STM.

Thus, the most important possibilities among the experimental outcomes are:

1. One or more speech-initiating processes are activated in sleep and succeed in achieving unambiguous overt expression in a sleep-speech. Such a possibility would be suggested by some degree of concordance between sleep-speech and mentation report.

2. Although activated, the process does not achieve overt expression as indicated by a lack of discernible concordance between sleep-speech and report, despite recall of some sleep mentation. This possibility could result from:

a. competition from other activated speech-initiation processes that inhibit or take precedence over the sleep-speech related process under consideration and seize the utterance channel; or else the utterance channel has a lower reception threshold to the speech-initiating process concerned.

b. cognitive selection biases in recall that were incompatible with or antagonistic to the mentation expressed in the sleep-speech but accepting of an alternate parallel stream of mentation, the one actually retrieved. In this instance, the cognitive processing channel was in functional contact with *both* streams but "decided" to reject the one that had achieved utterance and retrieve another not overtly expressed. Here the accent is on a single processing channel favoring one stream of mentation over another, although in prior contact with both.

c. the cognitive processing channel itself, that although in functional relation with the stream of mentation expressed in the sleep-speech, and that normally would have been involved in its retrieval, loses its access or priority to awareness. Such an eventuality could be followed by its being superseded by a different processing channel in functional relation with a parallel, *separate* stream of mentation not involved in or related to the sleep-speech; and in this latter case, the separate, totally different stream is retrieved. Here the accent is on the replacement of one processing channel by another, each in prior contact with separate streams of mentation.

A second possible sequel to the loss of access to awareness on the part of a previously engaged processing channel is a massive inhibition of *all* retrieval operations giving rise to no-content mentation reports.

d. the stream of mentation overtly expressed in the sleep-speech abruptly ceasing and being followed in serial fashion by a new stream flowing in the same cognitive processing channel. Because of the short life of mentation in STM, the first stream that had been expressed in the sleep-speech is lost to retrieval on awakening, presumably being "resorbed" into LTM. Here the accent is on a temporal factor—the short life spans of mentation in STM.

The difficulty in critically testing these hypotheses makes any attempt impracticable. The foregoing was written for the purpose of providing an organizing perspective for the experimental outcomes observed when employing the sleep-speech-mentation report comparison paradigm. However, the various mechanisms suggested to account for the data correspond to similar mechanisms proposed by others investigating wakeful cognitive processes. Recently Pribram (1976) has proposed a model of self-consciousness and intentionality that appears to provide a conceptual scaffolding for many of the more speculative hypotheses suggested earlier.

The Permanent Storage of Linguistic Information

In this category, Laver (1970) distinguishes *what* is stored from *how* it is stored. In either case, storage is said to consist of "the neural correlates of potential linguistic behavior [p. 63]."

Basic Structural and Content Elements

Is the status of linguistic elements and contents in LTM during sleep essentially different from that of wakefulness? In most instances, wakeful, linguistically competent people can call on their linguistic resources to adequately express complex thought and participate in interpersonal communication. This fact implies, as Laver states, that the neural correlates of such behavior exist in potential form, more or less readily available when necessary for wakeful life goals. Do we have any data that provide us with some indication of the usual functional availability of such stored information during various states of consciousness?

It is known that transitional states between wakefulness and sleep are often the occasion of inner mentally experienced but nonvocalized speech remnants that display interesting abnormalities (Arkin & Brown, 1972; Froeschels, 1946; Luria, 1974; Mintz, 1948; Oswald, 1962). Many of these abnormalities resemble psycholinguistic phenomena often observed in clinical pathological states. The same may be said of speech in dreams (Freud, 1900/1953; Kraepelin, 1906; Werner & Kaplan, 1963). And even in *wakeful* speech, spontaneous, error-free fluent production is a rarity even among the well-educated (Goldman-Eisler, 1964).

However, the status of the permanent storage of linguistic information seems most reasonably assessed on the basis of the subject's best possible performance rather than his usual or worst. We are interested in the question of what is permanently stored and available if called on for the most efficient performance, rather than what is routinely, mundanely, or clumsily used in daily life, drowsiness, or sleep.

Accordingly, sleep-speech at its highest level of competence is not incompatible with correct syntax, especially in relatively short portions of utterances, with the use of extensive vocabulary resources and words from other than one's native language. Native language-specific phonemes, morphemes, syllables, words, phrases, clauses, and sentences appearing in wakeful speech—the whole panoply of contents available to wakeful articulatory programs in one's native tongue occur at one time or another in sleep-speech. Perusal of Appendix 2 will provide many examples. Whitaker (1974), in his essay "Is the Grammar in the Brain?" asks, "How is a linguistic grammar psychologically (and, by extension, neurologically) real, i.e., how does it relate to the mental grammar? What is the relationship of the mental grammar to language behavior, and thus, the relationship of the linguistic grammar to such language behavior? And how do any of these relate to neural mechanisms and functions [p. 76]." That the elements and forms contained in such grammar persist and manifest themselves in sleep-speech attests to the preservation of the neuro-psychological reality of these items in the psycholinguistic system during sleep. MacNeilage and MacNeilage (1973) make a similar point; one which is further dramatized by slips of the tongue and attempts at self-correction during sleep-speech, which is discussed further in the following section. Does the sleep-speech of multilingual individuals provide useful information about linguistic storage during sleep? Contrary to one statement in the literature (Gastaut & Broughton, 1965), sleep-speech in a multilingual individual need not be in his native tongue. We have had subjects speak at one time in Spanish or French and at others in English and combinations of both in the same speech. In our clinical material (see Chapter 20), we have an instance of the not unprecedented situation of an adult who spoke in her sleep in one language, Russian, in this case, to which she was thoroughly exposed as a child, but who could not speak this language in wakefulness. Another patient, a young adult psychologist, related a history of somniloquy in Roumanian, German, and English. The patient's first languages were German and Yiddish; the second was Roumanian. The third was English, which was learned subsequent to the age of 13 after arrival in the United States. There was no marked trace of a foreign accent in the patient's wakeful English unless drowsiness supervened.

On the other hand, as described in Chapters 8 and 9 on qualitative aspects of sleep utterance, we have observed all levels and intermediate varieties of linguistic fragmentation so that utterances may consist of what seem like mere "vocal detritus," and it is possible that one factor in such occurrences is a temporary disruption of linguistic memory stores during sleep; or else such phenomena could be a partial reflection of impaired function of mechanisms mediating access to an intact storage system. Nevertheless, our observations permit us to conclude that sleep per se or sleep-associated states are not incompatible with functional integrity of linguistic storage systems and may even permit access to linguistic stores unavailable to normal wakeful consciousness. This conclusion is consistent with that of Cipolli, DuBois, and Salzarulo (1975) to the effect that "subjects are capable of very complex linguistic expressions during sleep [p. 322]."

Lexical Storage Systems in Sleep

Lexical storage systems may be organized on the basis of different principles. For example, one may involve groupings of semantically disparate words together on the basis of assonance; another may involve groupings of words solely on the basis of related semantic content. Differences in features of somniloquy in relation to certain parameters may bring into selective relief the manifestations of such organizing principles.

Word Assonance and Lexical Storage in Sleep. Speeches from Stage 3–4, in the earlier parts of the night, and following which recalled mentation is sparse or absent are more likely to contain strings of clang associations.

Example:

Sleep-Speech—Stage 3
> (I don't know—lower fishes (?))—hellooo (?) fishes? mbl VERY FUNNY
> FISHES? flashes, mbl—FUNNY FLASHES—I JUST SAW I JUST SAW
> FUNNY, RED, yellow and bigger (?) and YELLOW—that's funny [p] I
> don't know why (?)

> [See also Table 18.1 for additional examples.]

REMP speeches, on the other hand, virtually never contain clang
associations. Stage 2 speeches are also not especially notable for clang
associations, although they do occur.

Example:

Sleep-Speech—Stage 2
> MMMM—what lustre! (?) [p] S'true—please (?) enjoy—your charm?—
> joy?—go ahead (?) don't even (?) mention—mbl—mention—gonna
> hoisted—get the rest, get the rest, of those oysters—m'not available
> anymore.

Semantic Relationships and Lexical Storage in Sleep.   The not infrequent
observation in both REM and NREM sleep mentation of report pairs
possessing concordance based on a shared concept or topic (i.e., second-order
concordance) suggests that during sleep, the lexical storage system utilizing a
semantic organizing principle is available to cognitive processing.

Example:

Sleep-Speech—Stage 2
> Oh—what d'you think a whale eats?

Mentation Report
> I was thinking that I didn't get to sleep but I know I went to sleep because—of
> a surprise, I was going out with the *boats* again, 'n I think it's because I don't
> understand, I don't know why they, the people on the *boats* are—are being
> chased and I don't know why—'n oh—I don't know what else—.

It is of interest that the proportion of second-order concordance arising from
REM sleep exceeds that of NREM (approximately 21% versus 8%
respectively). It is not possible with the data at hand to ascribe this to greater
availability of the semantically based lexical storage system, because it may
merely reflect more efficient retrieval of REM mentation. Efficient
information retrieval requires an efficient addressing system for the
information in storage. To what extent the observations reported here reflect

storage system characteristics versus addressing system efficiency in relation to sleep stage and time of night may be impossible to assess without further experiment. Interesting, also, is the roughly equal proportion of second-order concordance in both Stages 2 and 3–4 sleep (8.2% versus 7.7%), despite the greater first-order concordance in Stage 2 awakenings (17.6% versus 9.6%). It suggests that semantically based lexical storage is equally available to NREM sleep retrieval systems, regardless of NREM sleep stage.

Discussion

The organization and output of the lexical storage system during sleep, and relationships between modern psycholinguistic theory and dreams have recently received increasing attention (Cipolli & Salzarulo, 1975; Edelson, 1972; Goetzinger, 1973; Litowitz, 1976; Salzarulo & Cipolli, 1974). The reader is referred to the original sources inasmuch as a detailed review would take us too far afield. Instead, commentary is restricted to areas that may be illumined by sleep-speech phenomena.

First, the elicitation or production of associations based on assonance is a common phenomenon in many varying conditions and in wakefulness as well as sleep. Jung (1919) states that drowsiness and psychological distraction during word association tests favor the appearance of clang associations. Jung also cites Stransky's work (1905) on forced, rapid, wakeful speech in which subjects are prone to produce clang associations. Similarly, clang associations are usually experienced when single words or phrases are repeated or heard for sustained intervals, as in verbal transformation experiments dealing with reiterated input (Warren, 1968). Children love to produce clang associations during word games. They are also commonly observed in people ill with schizophrenia (Bleuler, 1923) or brain injury sequellae (Luria, 1974).

In sleep, associations based on word assonance were the predominant result of Berger's work on subwaking-threshold verbal stimulation of subjects during REM sleep (Berger, 1963). This finding has been confirmed by Castaldo and Holzman (1967, 1969) and Lasaga and Lasaga (1973) as a result of stimulation during REM sleep. With regard to similar experiments in NREM sleep, Castaldo and Shevrin (1970) found a tendency toward conceptual types of responses in Stage 2 (responses based on a semantic relation rather than assonance); but Lasaga and Lasaga (1973) detected many assonance-type responses in Stages 2, 3, and 4.

Because assonance-type associations are frequent in a variety of states of consciousness under normal and pathological conditions, it seems reasonable to seek explanations in terms of alterations of attention deployment patterns, cognitive regression, and/or cognitive immaturity, rather than on the predominant basis of lowered or increased arousal levels alone. Certainly cognitive processes and arousal levels are related, so that events in the one sphere continually interact with and influence those in the other.

The complexity of such interactions is increased when one evaluates experienced mentation as elicited in sleep mentation reports as opposed to sleep mentation reflected in verbalized overt sleep-speech. REM mentation reports are noted for the relatively higher amount of primary-process type thinking and bizarreness, and NREM mentation for the greater prevalence of secondary-process reality-oriented type thinking (Fisher, 1965). And in Berger's (1963) work with the effects of external stimulation by means of tape recordings of names, the predominant mode of dream incorporation of such stimuli was, as already mentioned, that of assonance—a classical manifestation of primary-process thinking (Freud, 1900/1953). These observations accord well with the frequent appearance of neologisms and verbal condensations in presumably REM dreams (Kraepelin, 1906) and in hypnagogic states (Froeschels, 1946; Mintz, 1948).

One factor common to all of the conditions just mentioned is the essentially passive attitude of the observing ego toward stimuli arising from internal or external sources. By contrast, when the sleeper *actively emits* word sequences, the foregoing relationships undergo a partial *reversal.* Thus, REM sleep speech virtually never contains strings of clang associations, neologisms, or severely internally disorganized sequences, and Stage 3–4 is the usual context in which clang associations and severely disorganized speech occurs. This observation accords well with the expectation that the usual coordinated wakeful integration between speech perception, linguistic mentation, and speech production undergoes a degree of dissociation and loosening in sleep and certain altered states of consciousness.

Actually, the structural aspects of REM sleep-speech conform more closely to the recent laboratory findings suggesting that speech in REM mentation reports resembles the subjects' everyday wakeful language, rather than the traditional notion that dream speech is incoherent, distorted, syntactically incorrect, condensed, and neologistic (Salzarulo & Cipolli, 1974; Snyder, 1970). Replications of these findings are needed as they seem counter to traditional views. Indeed, along possibly related lines, Lenneberg (1970) specifically discussed the issue of the clinical dissociability of speaking from other cognitive functions. That is, the capacity to say whatever one wishes to say, the capacity to understand what is being said, and to communicate coherently by writing can be each affected adversely independently of one another; one capacity may be intact in the presence of impairment of the other and vice versa—a phenomenon labeled as "double dissociation [p. 364]." Such sleep-speech phenomena seem to provide possible interesting models for varieties of aphasia (about which more will be said later).

The Planning Process of Neurolinguistic Programs for the Expression of an Idea, as Revealed by its Articulated Output, and the Monitoring Processes Involved

Although these are conceptually distinct considerations, they are most conveniently treated here under one heading. To begin with, Laver (1970) states that "program planning involves the selection and eventual temporal organization of the neural correlates of lexical items and their morphological and syntactic arrangement, together with their associated phonology—the criterion for each lexical, morphological, or syntactical choice being that it should be semantically relevant to the expression of the speaker's initial idea [p. 66]." It is clearly implied in his exposition that the effectiveness of utterances in these respects may be assessed only by study of the actual articulatory output, i.e., what is overtly uttered.

The evidence is compelling that in wakeful speech the preparation and articulation of a speech program is *not* carried out on an unit-by-unit basis, such as syllable-by-syllable or even word-by-word. It is much more likely that neural elements corresponding to considerably longer sequences of speech are assembled prior to utterance, and then articulated as a single, continuous program (Fromkin, 1973a; Laver, 1970).

The linguistic unit in English that is recommended by Laver for designation as a typical preassembled sequence of words primed for utterance is called the "tone group"—a speech sequence that lasts, on the average, for about seven or eight syllables, and that contains only one emphasized syllable, receiving a major change of pitch or intonation; this syllable is usually placed at or near the end of the tone-group, as in "tonight we shall have the pleasure of hearing *cha*mber music." That the tone-group is the usual unit of neuro-linguistic prepreparation is indicated by the finding that intonational and occasionally syntactic choices made in the initial part of the tone-group are generally functions of choices made for the latter part, and are, therefore, logically anticipatory of such later choices. Support for this idea comes from structural analysis of slips of the tongue and hesitation pauses (Boomer, 1965; Boomer & Laver, 1968); Fromkin (1973a,b) has carried out extensive studies of spontaneous linguistic errors on a much broader scope that demonstrate the operation of neuro-linguistic programs in production of speech sequences—programs that operate in accordance with "morphophonemic rules [p. 115, 1973a]."

A most important stage in efficient speech-program implementation is the temporary storage of the organized word assembly sequence in a short-term buffer memory system prior to their actual articulation, and even prior to their being subject to disordering influences ultimately leading to speech errors (Fromkin, 1973a). Perhaps much of the disorder in many sleep-speeches arises from physiological transitory impairment of this buffer memory system in states of diminished vigilance such as sleep. Both linguistic programming and monitoring mechanisms are said by Laver (1970) to normally operate automatically outside of awareness and maintain almost constant surveillance over psycholinguistic processes with potential for overt utterance. This assertion certainly corresponds with everyday experience. Programming and monitoring functions are best conceptualized in a two-fold manner as (1) the detection of inappropriate neuro-linguistic programs; and (2) their editorial revision by the "brain–mind." The detection system must determine the neuro-linguistic characteristics of a program under consideration by means of sensory and neural reports and then evaluate the extent to which the program is an appropriate semantic expression of the speaker's mentation. Should errors be detected *prior* to utterance, implicit editorial revision processes are initiated to bring about suitable emendations; and if errors are detected *after* utterance, the monitoring function will be manifested in the correction of the overt error. Thus, the brain's revisionary capabilities may find application prior to or subsequent to speech program articulation.

Laver (1970) considers a program as incorrect if it distorts in some respect the communication of the speakers' idea. This may occur in at least two ways: (1) The utterance may contain a form not found in the language (as in the slip: "He performed the trick with true magishnical art"); (2) The utterance may consist entirely of linguistically correct forms but is an incorrect expression of the speaker's semantic intentions (as in the sentence and self-correction: "he used his knife—er—fork to cut the meat"). Although Laver does not specifically comment about the following possibility, it seems to reasonably follow from his formulations that an utterance may be considered partly correct if, despite some grammatical error, it nevertheless effectively communicates the speaker's ideas. For example, "that don't make no difference" or "a difference, it don't make" will communicate "that doesn't make any difference" more reliably than "a difference make it don't." We introduce this commonplace observation here to cover instances in somniloquy in which the gist of an utterance is understood although it is incorrect linguistically.

How might sleep-utterance phenomena be related to these considerations derived from the psycholinguistics of wakefulness?

First, we may note that the state of sleep per se, regardless of sleep stage, is not inherently incompatible with effective psycholinguistic program-planning. That is, we have numerous examples of sleep-utterances possessing first- or second-order concordance with associated mentation reports, which clearly indicate that the subject's initiating ideational process was adequately expressed by this sleep-speech (e.g., speeches 192, 195, 448, 515, 550). Furthermore, although a sleep-utterance may possess defective psycholinguistic structure, it may nevertheless be capable of expressing or reflecting in a recognizable way a retrievable, albeit chaotic, ideational process occurring in sleep.

Example:

Sleep-Speech—Stage 2

Um, uh, uh, mm—mm—that's because the wood is much rougher than we thought—but that she had to have Lorna there we had to have her—uh, huh—hm, mm.

Mentation Report

E: Gordon?—What was going through your mind?

S: That—the bed was rather large—and I was sleeping and a lot was starting to happen—because of—they could only put me at one place at one time, it was impossible to cover everything that was going on—and—and being on this *wooden* track, *this rough wooden track, this rough* hewn track that very much wobbled and it was very much—it was very much tight and—was not a foolish or very steady thing to do but—if they were to get the information that's all they could do, cause they weren't paying them enough to put another one in, and no one knew or no one cared not to, to do this and—.

Second, sleep per se is not incompatible with articulation of "correct" phonemic, morphemic and syllabic components of wakeful speech during the sleep-utterances; nor is it incompatible with preservation of correct or intelligible syntax, tone-group structure, and semantic expression during sleep. Support for this assertion may be found in the course of general perusal of the speeches in Appendix 2 and in the examples cited throughout the book.

Both of the foregoing observations seem sufficient to establish that implicit linguistic pre-utterance editorial revisionary processes operate with varying degrees of efficiency during sleep. The availability of *postutterance* monitoring processes is indicated by two additional sets of observations:

1. The not infrequent occurrence of the subject uttering in sleep a self-correction of an overt error, or an apparently "unintended" sequence.

Example:

Sleep-Speech—Stage 4

I wannt take a net—a—note—a—note—pa—duh—uh—duh—shit! I mean—you know—I'd like a nice pillow, you know with a nice trim (?) blanket—a pillow—that came up over my shoulders—that was tucked in a little bit—away some of the steam (?), you know (living in) (?) the drudgery, you know—she was never—uh—mbl—hot stuff but uh—mbl.

[See Table 18.2 for additional examples.]

2. A variant of the foregoing consisting of occurrences in which the subject emits an utterance with a sequence of preliminary unidentifiable fragmentary, verbal sounds spoken with a characteristic difficulty. It is as if the speaker were groping for an utterance that correctly matched his preformed program and was "dissatisfied" with each initial attempt quite early in the course of the utterance. The subject nevertheless persists, tries again, and eventually there emerges one or more recognizable words that are phonically related to the initial set of fragments. With emergence of the "sought for" word, the listener has an impression of a log jam being broken followed by a fluent segment.

Example:

Sleep-Speech—Stage 2

I bet uh—hmm [P] have to think about that, anyway—mbl—just come out of the woodwork and I can't really remember what except that I well we were looking in the la—it seemed rather expensive type things—mbl—that's what the university normally uses, and the fullest—mbl—was on the left and that was the youngest of the *leak leak after leaft—least* active hum—They threw that on then they, the appointments became less and less possible less and less well spaced or at any rate they began to compete with the rest—of the office for sovereignty.

[See Table 18.2 for additional examples.]

Such observations suggest that the embedded of the utterance provided unsatisfactory feedback to the monitoring function, which then undertook to institute corrective measures until the match between output and feedback was appropriate.

Third, despite the previous statements to the effect that sleep per se is not incompatible with a broad range of "normal" psycholinguistic performance, the more typical findings are, nevertheless, variable degrees of impairment. But lest we be hasty and unfairly depreciate typical linguistic performance in sleep-speech, it is well to be reminded of Goldman-Eisler's (1964) comment regarding her studies of wakeful spontaneous speech: "The sentences which I submitted to analysis had to be grammatically correct sentences and these are very difficult to find in spontaneous speech. I went through heaps of recorded speech uttered by highly educated academic people and I found only seven sentences! [p. 113]" Is it sleep-speech, then, that is impaired primarily or *spontaneous* speech in sleep and in wakefulness? However this question is finally answered, the most frequent manifestations of sleep-utterance linguistic malfunction are described in the following three sections.

Disturbances of Sustained Temporal Sequential Coherence. This is more likely to be observed in proportion to the length of the utterances. Thus, although the internal linguistic structure of component small sequence units may be intact, logical relationship between the sequences comprising the entire utterance manifests variable degrees of impairment. This may tend to obfuscate the overall semantic content of the speech.

Examples:

Sleep-Speech—Stage 2

> Hm—a fact—thassa fact— I was bd—yeah—this was over at Medical Center—uh—mm—I don't remember this well—it just sort of occurred to me while you mentioned City College—mbl open and I was tired and I just sort of wanted—and these things are just sort of wanted—and these things are just sort of handy—to have—because I hadn't remembered where everything was—like—I don't know—priests—priests for teaching and all this rot (?)—it's a CATHOLIC school—and I just went up and sort of relaxed compared to what I imagined it would be on a regular college where you sort of had to pound like Sammy Glick to get registered—.

[Also see speeches 11, 13, 14, 285, 328.]

The most likely sorts of factors involved in these phenomena include those related to the following:

1. Salzinger's immediacy hypothesis (1971) accounting for schizophrenic behavior patterns states that schizophrenics' behavior is excessively governed by stimuli that are immediate in their spatial and temporal environments. Among such controlling stimuli are those comprised of a subject's immediately prior responses, including his own speech. Because a schizophrenic individual is unable to respond adequately to his relatively remote self-produced prior words, his speech tends to make sense only for short segments unduly influenced by the brief segment uttered just immediately before. Similar conditions and findings prevail during sleep-speech; i.e., any currently uttered segment tends to be most influenced by the immediately prior verbal segment rather than a remotely prior one.

2. Fromkin (1973a), in her model of speech production, postulated a buffer zone that stores verbal segments in STM during the preparation of an utterance and retains them until released at the chosen moment of utterance. We have seen earlier that in sleep, particularly in NREM sleep, the contents of STM are particularly evanescent and recall processes are inefficient. Further, the ability to deploy sufficiently sustained and properly patterned attention is impaired at such times. The result is decreased ability to maintain an adequate hierarchy between the main, dominant thematic component of the utterance and suppressively contain competing, less relevant segments. The outcome is in accord with Salzinger's immediacy hypothesis—the currently uttered segment is under the greater influence of immediately prior rather than

remotely prior segments that rapidly disappear from STM. Thus, longer sleep speeches often lack an overall thematic coherence because of loss of continuity with remotely earlier segments, and the impaired ability to contain competing less relevant, less intended segments in a state of silence. Despite possible disturbances of linguistic sequential coherence, however, long REMP speeches are more likely to possess a clearly discernible topic or theme than long NREM speeches.

Example:

Sleep-Speech—Stage REM
"Mm—hm—mother—you gotta get some eggs 'cause seeing all these people all know that I like eggs too, so get a dozen eggs. Please put this in a soft bag, thank you.

Mentation Report
OK—I just came in and I wanted to know (?) where (?) it's at counter (?)—mbl—eggs—mbl—eggs [p] for a fine (?) trip.

Intra-utterance Pauses, Hesitations, Omissions, and Unclarity of Words or Phrases. A word or phrase may fail to reach the threshold of clear articulation, and critically affect the intelligibility of the utterance. Such occurrences seem equally likely with REMP and NREM speeches and may eventuate in one or more of the following ways:

1. In an otherwise clearly enunciated sequence, a word or phrase may lack crystal clarity in articulations and sound "fuzzy" in varying degrees. Much of the time, this defect is not so marked as to prevent identification of the verbal material, even without assistance from the context. On the other hand, it is often necessary to have contextual aids provided by clear preceding and following words, affective tone, and also a mentation report for such purposes.

Example:

Sleep Speech—Stage REM
Mbl goes down mbl bubbles but as it goes to the top the bubbles break and mbl back down.

Mentation Report
Yah?—I was dreaming that—something—mbl—miniature golf perpetual motion machine in which it was a sort of bear in a pond and as it went up to the top—well—it collected bubbles on the bottom and as it went up to the top, bubbles broke and since air is lighter than the mass of the body, the body fell back down to the bottom and there it picked up bubbles again.

2. Despite a few identifiable words, an utterance may contain an inordinate number of mumbled words or phrases, or else the entire utterance

may be mumbled. In either case, understanding of semantic content is precluded unless the affective tone is distinctive. That is, an utterance may consist of unrecognizable wordlike or nonverbal emotional sounds uttered with a tone of anger or fear. This might enable the experimenter to infer only a sleep-ideational process of a frightening or hostile nature.

3. A word or phrase may be omitted entirely from a sequence, creating variable difficulty in grasping the semantic content. Such an omission is inferred when well-articulated but more or less semantically unrelated sequences precede and follow a brief intervening silence.

On the other hand, such silences may represent sleep-speech analogies to the pauses and hesitations studied in wakeful, *spontaneous* speech by Goldman-Eisler (1968). Analysis of tape recordings of such wakeful speech indicated that normal adults tend to utter brief strings of words of five words or less and that pausing between them occupies an average of 40–50% of utterance time. These sequences are not related to syntactical units, and a large proportion of them have no systematic linguistic explanation, nor do they appear to usefully serve communication. Some pauses were observed to occur at clause junctures or else at the ends of sentences, but many more were located within syntactic unit boundaries and served to fragment context rather than ease comprehension. Goldman-Eisler concluded that pausing is as much a component of spontaneous speech as the words themselves and that pausing may even be essential in the production of spontaneous utterance. Fascinating experimental results were reported, strongly suggesting that pauses were reliable behavioral signs of brain processes involved with utterance planning and word selection, in contrast to continuous, rapid speech that was the result of well-learned, more or less automatic verbal sequences. That is, the speaker during a pause is enmeshed in planning the next utterance; and he "fires when ready," at which time the utterance emerges in a group as a string of words.

Returning to apparent omissions of words, sometimes within a sleep-utterance and without intervening pause, there are abrupt changes of semantic content—a change in midstream without discernible transitional bridging material.

Example:

Sleep-Speech—Stage 4
    Hm—hm—that's all there is—there is no—more to—there's no more
    voice—so—to—there's no more you know—pushing.

One could surmise that the sleeper "had in mind" appropriate bridging words and failed to utter them because of planning, editorial revision, or monitoring failure. On the other hand, such occurrences could represent the sudden inhibition of an ongoing word sequence by a differing, competing sequence with higher priority semantic importance for whatever reason—greater intrinsic interest, psychological defense, and the like. Regardless of the nature of the underlying psychoneural process, such abrupt intra-utterance changes verge descriptively on the next variety of linguistic abnormality.

Disturbances of Linguistic Organization on Brief and Intermediate Temporal Scales. Many utterances have been observed that strikingly resemble varieties of disordered psycholinguistic manifestations of organic brain disease, such as aphasias of many types (Arkin & Brown, 1972; Brown, 1972); epileptic automatisms (Chase et al. 1967; Serafetinedes, 1966); and results of electrical stimulation of the brain (Schaltenbrand, 1965, 1975; Serafetinedes & Falconer, 1963). In certain instances, similarities to schizophrenic jargon and flights of ideas may be seen. As stated earlier, this entire class of occurrences is much more likely to occur in NREM rather than REMP speeches, Stage 3–4 rather than 2, in the first 3 hr of sleep, and with little or no recall of mentation following experimental awakenings after utterances.

As we have seen earlier (p. 339–340), a common noteworthy feature of many sleep-speeches is the repetition of words that have phonemes and morphemes in common but are not semantically related (e.g., Speeches 67, 80, 464). Often, such repetitions continue almost indefinitely until superseded by another repeated sequence of words based on a different phonemic or morphemic "root" and without increased clarification of the semantic content or goal of the utterance. At other times, an utterance contains a repetitive section that "self-terminates" and is followed by more or less intelligible, more linguistically "correct" material with some discernible semantic content, however rudimentary it may be. This latter portion may or may not seem to bear some understandable relationship to the repetitive section, particularly the word that terminates it, as well as the sequence preceding the repetitions; also, as previously stated, such speeches impress the listener as an attempt at labored groping toward a psycholinguistic target. Other miscellaneous illustrations of disordered psycholinguistic functioning in sleep-speech include anomalies of word order, nonsensical sequences, and possible neologisms (e.g., Speeches 39, 46, 49, 80, 551).

Discussion

Another useful perspective from which to view the foregoing material is provided by modern control theory. It has become customary in contemporary neurophysiology to regard neural structures as complex information-processing systems (Pribram, 1976). Lindsay and Norman (1977) describe a typical information-processing system as being comprised of three components: a memory, a processor, and an input–output mechanism.

The memory is regarded as a storage system for information. Such information may consist of data used by the processor in carrying out its operations, or else consist of programs—i.e., hierarchical sets of instruction sequences that guide the processor.

The processor is responsible for the actual performance of operations. In so doing, it (1) interprets and evaluates information; (2) compares data sets; (3) makes selections and decisions regarding specific program utilization; (4) monitors output; and (5) modifies programs and ongoing performances on the occasion of mismatching between performance parameters and goals or end-points at any stage of the process, whether intermediate or terminal.

The input–output mechanisms are means by which information enters and leaves the system. Input may be derived from sources internal or external to the organism, and similarly, output may be directed to internal or external locations.

The direction of flow or information from input, through the processor, to output is called a *feedforward (open-loop)* path. *Feedback (closed-loop)* paths are involved when information consisting of ongoing evaluation and measurement of preliminary and intermediate stages of information processing, as well as performance at the moment of terminal output, is then relayed backward to the processor for performance evaluation, monitoring, modification, or correction (Mulholland, 1977). Thus, feedback may be produced at any stage of the generation of behavior; it may be termed *internal* feedback if it arises at some stage prior to the terminal output, and *external* feedback if it is produced by monitoring mechanisms at the completion of performances, cognitive acts in general, and speech production in particular.

Under normal conditions, processes involved in speech-initiating ideation, utilization of the contents of lexical memory storage, planning and preparation of a speech-utterance program, and its final utterance appear to make preponderant use of feedforward paths; and feedback paths acquire special importance during the process of pre-utterance editorial revision and postutterance monitoring.

Information Processing and Output under Variable Feedback Conditions

The efficiency of information-processing mechanisms in regularly producing linguistically correct utterances during normal wakefulness is very far from perfect (Goldman-Eisler, 1964). It is, therefore, of considerable interest to observe that sleep-speech provides the investigator with a broad spectrum of variability in the efficiency of information-processing, feedforward, and feedback mechanisms during sleep. That is, one can find many instances at one extreme of such disorganization of speech such as to force one to conclude that editorial revision and monitoring feedback mechanisms are virtually inoperative; intermediate disturbed forms in which the effects of feedback can be observed in situ (instances of self-correction and quasi-repetitive groping toward an apparent linguistic goal); and forms at the other extreme in which correct, fluent articulations are observed. Such observations suggest the feasiblility of a research program correlating indices of feedback efficiency and other information-processing effectiveness with sleep stages, time of night, postsleep-utterance mentation reports, contingent phasic event density, and specific experimental variables already demonstrated as capable of influencing sleep-utterance.

For expository purposes, I should like to invite the reader to consider sleep-talking (typically a phenomenon occurring under physiological circumstances) in relation to certain other pathological and experimental conditions in which inner implicit or external overt speech frequently occurs, and which speech bears the imprint of preponderantly internal cognitive–affective influences and/or impairments, rather than being relatively simple, direct, easily understandable responses to external stimuli.

The following outline is meant to be a representative rather than an exhaustive list of conditions in which implicit and/or explicit speech is prone to occur. The bibliographical citations are given purely as a source of information to readers desiring additional material relating to such matters; they are not offered in support of any assertions of mine. The list contains, therefore, references describing clinical and experimental studies, as well as naturalistic observation, carried out in the three major states of consciousness (wakefulness, transitional states, and sleep) during which psycholinguistic phenomena are typically observed.

I. Wakefulness
   A. Excessive deviation from optimum arousal levels (Eysenck, 1976; Hebb, 1972)
   B. Daydreaming and reveries (Singer, 1975)
   C. Pathological conditions occurring in temporal relation to wakefulness
      1. 1. Aphasia (Lenneberg, 1970)
      2. Ictal automatism and ictal dysphasia (Chase, Cullen, Niedermeyer, Start, & Blumer, 1967; Serafetinedes & Falconer, 1963)
      3. Emotive speech (Jackson, 1874, 1878, 1879/1958)
      4. Gilles de la Tourette's Syndrome (Ascher, 1974)
      5. Schizophrenic states (Bleuler, 1911/1952; Gerson et al., 1977)
      6. Drug effects (Bowers & Freedman, 1975; Mello & Mendelson, 1975)
      7. Dissociated states (West, 1967)
   D. Experimental studies
      1. Experimental alteration of auditory feedback (Klein, 1965; Lee 1950; Mahl, 1972)

2. Sensory overload (Gottschalk et al., 1972)
3. Relaxed wakefulness (Foulkes & Fleisher, 1975)
4. Electrical brain stimulation (Schaltenbrand, 1965, 1975; Serafetinedes & Falconer, 1963).
5. Spontaneous wakeful speech (Goldman-Eisler, 1968)

II. Transitional states
   A. Hypnagogic states (Froeschels, 1946; Horowitz, 1978; Luria, 1974; Mintz, 1948; Schacter, 1976; Vogel, 1978)
   B. Hypnopomic states (Horowitz, 1978)
   C. Pathological conditions
      1. Daytime sleepiness states with automatic speech (Guilleminault, Billard, Montplaisir, & Dement, 1975a; Guilleminault, Phillips, & Dement, 1975b)
      2. Drug effects (Bowers & Freedman, 1975; Viscott, 1968)
      3. Deliria (Lipowski, 1967)
   D. Experimental sleep deprivation (Berger & Oswald, 1962; Morris, Williams, & Lubin, 1960)

III. Sleep
   A. REM and NREM mentation including morning-recall dreams containing speech segments (Freud, 1900/1953; Foulkes, 1966; Kraepelin, 1906; Snyder, 1970; Werner & Kaplan, 1963)
   B. Common sleep-talking (Arkin, this volume)
   C. Pathological conditions
      1. Sleep-talking produced by psychic conflict (Arkin, this volume)
      2. Night-terrors (Fisher et al., 1974)
      3. Drug effects (Arkin, Antrobus, Toth, & Baker, 1968; Arkin & Steiner, 1978)

The foregoing conditions lend themselves to a classification scheme based on information-processing principles. All have in common the utilization of feedforward paths in the course of their traverse through the information-processing system, to the final output consisting of implicit and explicit speech. *The differences between them may be imagined to result in part from the points in the system at which feedback paths are introduced and the various patterns of their deployment.* For example, a speech-initiating idea may receive adequate processing and speech-program planning, but during the actual utterance, a slip of the tongue occurs that is corrected by feedback produced by speech monitoring mechanisms. This would be an instance in which feedback would be recruited at the terminal output phase of the action concerned. In some instances, slips are either unnoticed or allowed to remain uncorrected, in which case feedback at that point of the action will be designated as momentarily and slightly impaired. In certain extreme cases of jargon aphasia, feedback paths may be considered to be almost totally ineffective and a word salad is emitted without correction, or even without evident realization on the part of the patient that his verbal output is defective.

In other cases, such as "pure" posterior aphasia (Gerson, Benson, & Frazier, 1977), the patient is unable to utilize internal, pre-utterance feedback in the elaboration of correct syntactic and semantic speech programs to appropriately express his "normal" speech-initiating ideation; and following defective utterance, feedback may be provided by monitoring mechanisms, as evidenced by signs of the patient's awareness and distress over his defective performance. However, because of the internal linguistic programming defect, such feedback remains ineffective in bringing about post-utterance remediation. Curiously, Birch and Lee (1955) found that masking the speech of patients with expressive aphasia resulted in striking improvement of their speech performance, presumably as an effect of reducing the influence of postutterance auditory feedback.

By contrast, in certain cases of schizophrenia, the language function may be intact; the patient is able to construct more or less correct syntactic and semantic speech programs that appropriately express his speech-initiating ideation, but in many instances, the utterance strikes the audience as abnormal because it reflects a disorder of prespeech-programming thought processes; i.e., speech-initiating ideation itself is faulty, having received defective information processing with impaired internal feedback at a quite early stage in the course of utterance production. I do not insist on the scientific validity of the foregoing, rather crude, notions; they are a heuristic device. But what does it all have to do with sleep-speech phenomena? What is desired is some scheme that can accommodate those sleep-speeches that are chaotic versus the well-organized, and those that show self-correction, groping for the correct-next-word phenomenon, and virtually total disorganization. Presumably, competent information processing entails at almost every step of the way detection and correction of mismatches between each successive input–output subordinate microstage of the total sequence, ultimately leading to the terminal output—and presumably this is mediated through internal feedback mechanisms (Pribram, 1976).

Accordingly, variations in the spatial and temporal patterning of feedback at different loci in the pathways from speech-initiating ideation to overt utterance could be invoked to partially explain not only sleep-speech phenomena but other observations as well. One of the clearest demonstrations of the importance of post-utterance feedback or speech monitoring in the elaboration of normal speech is provided by experimental alteration of feedback contingencies (Klein, 1965; Lee, 1950; Mahl, 1972). For example, Mahl observed 17 college students under conditions in which they could not hear themselves talk as a result of experimental voice-masking techniques. Among his findings were increased verbal productivity, verbal spontaneity, disordered syntax, loss of the thread of one's own comments, fragmentation and disorganization of verbal sequences, intrusion of irrelevant thoughts, and *"thinking out loud" without awareness of either the event as such or its mental content.* These findings strongly resemble many sleep-speech phenomena.

Chase et al. (1967) hypothesized that ictal speech automatisms uttered in profoundly altered states of consciousness provide examples of speech output activity functioning predominantly in an open-loop, feedforward mode without feedback. In this respect, ictal speech conditions resemble those of many sleep-speeches, particularly those followed by postutterance no-content mentation reports. Because delayed auditory feedback (DAF) produces characteristic adverse effects on wakeful speech, it was thought useful to observe the results of DAF on ongoing speech during an ictal automatic episode, with the hope of critically testing whether ictal speech is generated in the absence of feedback. If DAF did not produce alteration of ictal speech, it would indicate that natural feedback was not operative at such times.

Accordingly, focal seizures were instigated in two trials with one adult patient with ictal automatisms, and DAF was introduced during and after the seizures. Speech uttered during the seizure either did not show effects of DAF or else showed them to a lesser extent than during the postseizure interval. Chase et al. (1967) concluded that the speech motor system is capable of operating in an open loop with respect to air-conducted auditory feedback. Because only one subject was employed and only a small number of observations made, this work needs replication; and it would naturally be of great interest to employ DAF systematically with active sleep-talkers at various times of the night and different stages of sleep. The technique would provide an objective correlate of sleep-speech under varying conditions and thus assist in greater understanding of speech mechanisms in sleep.

Turning now to the issue of possible relationships between sleep-speech and aphasic speech, a set of sleep-speeches characterized by moderate to severe disorganization are presented in Table 18.2. The following are a number of excerpts from various sleep-speeches with "aphasiological diagnoses" made by Dr. Jason Brown (Arkin & Brown, 1972; Brown, 1972). These excerpts exemplify striking correspondences between certain forms of aphasia and sleep-speeches, especially those associated with NREM sleep.

1. Phonemic (literal) paraphasia
    a. "David, I day David that *you*... that day dated day dravid Dave dravid about 25 or 30 noked, naked day dreams..." [*S*'s name is David.]
    b. "Sneak to go—reek—you—reek to, steak, stoke... She said to find some theft..."
2. Semantic (verbal aphasia) paraphasia
    a. "Very funny fishes? flashes... I just saw funny, red, yellow and bigger (?) and yellow..."
    b. "...Six books home..."

TABLE 18.2
Utterances Demonstrating Profound Disorganization, Clang Associations, and/or
Repetitiveness

Sleep Stage	Sleep-Speech	Mentation Report
Stage 4 (#472)[a]	Wai, wai, ho, ho, ho, ho, ho gotta check the file, gotta check the file out on those, hah?—hey ol' boy?	No recall
Stage 4 (#493)	[Sounds, garbled words, calling out in a questioning, anxious, and disappointed intonation] Eh?—All Ri—Molly! Maia— Ma—eh—bah—ma—ma.	No recall
Stage 3 (#37)	(I don't know—lower *fishes* (?))— hellooo (?) *fishes?* mbl VERY *FUNNY FISHES? flashes,* mbl— *FUNNY FLASHES—I JUST SAW— I JUST SAW FUNNY,* RED, *yellow,* and bigger (?) and *YELLOW*—that's *funny.* [p] I don't know why (?)	Not awakened
Stage 4 (#39)	[Moans] Mm—mm—the *only*—mbl—it *might break* is the *only one* the *old one?* It looks like it *might break* but it *zasbreak?* [sic]	Not awakened
NREM (#46) [subject's name is "David"]	*David*—I *day David* that *you— you—that's you* that *day— dated—day—dravide dave dravid* about 25 or 30 *noked naked day dreams*—the second dream tie it all up—*you kep bouncing them on—you kept bouncing them on and on as if you had a regular meter—* and *as if you had a regular* dream in, look *on and on as if you* were con- tinuing on to the next paragraph— then *you* knew at last—.	Not awakened
Stage 4 (#80)	Yes—yeh—don't get (?) excited [loud mbl] or he's *away*— I dunno know-mbls-*away—shway*— [many rapid mbls] try *base*ment of *grade* school (?) [buzzer sounds briefly but S continues] to do my reduced—go— ahead—don't close yet—don't go—mbls— *sneak—sneak*— to go *reek—you— reek* to *steak—stoke*— [then slower] she said to—uh—to find some theft [p] uh *with Burt* (?)—*will burn* you—*would burn* things—*burnt* objects	S: Valentine. E: Can you tell me any more about it? S: No, that's all. [Scored as no discernible concordance]

TABLE 18.2 *(continued)*

Sleep Stage	Sleep-Speech	Mentation Report
	(?)—*burn* and *you—at the same time—you* there (?) *at the same time.*	
Stage 4 (#45)	*Gundrum* is the word for *hundred* in—*hundred*—in *hundred* in a *hundred* in s—Latin—Latin—*Hundred.*	*S:* Um—I don't know, I wasn't paying attention—I—was kind of listening to what you had to say there, that's strange—. *E:* Can't you recall anything else? *S:* No—I can't—nothing else. [categorized as no recall]
Stage 4 (#546)	Mbls—a—mi—be—better—seems that six books home and I haven't even got them yet—i—ea—where—i—ea—what?—mbl—a *rag* in a *rags* bed, *rag!* I don't even have a *rag*—mm—bag—*baggette—okay.*	*S:* Um—flowers and a boat—. *E:* Can you be more specific? What about the flowers and the boat? *S:* Th—Th'Th'—the boat was receding and I um—under a bridge and boat and flowers are receding in opposite direction, and that—that direction's away from me—. *E:* Was there anything more? *S:* No, thank you. *E:* Do you remember anything about a rag and a bag? *S:* No—nothing that I can remember. *E:* Can you remember anything before the boat and the flowers? *S:* To me it seems a blank. [categorized as no discernible concordance]

(continued)

TABLE 18.2 *(continued)*

Sleep Stage	Sleep-Speech	Mentation Report
Stage 2 (#83)	Mm*mm*—what *lustre!* (?) [p] *S-true*—please (?) enjoy—your charm?—joy?—go ahead (?) don't even (?) *mention*—mbl—*mention*—gonna hoisted—*get the rest, get the rest,* of those *oysters*—m-not available anymore.	Mbl—pearls but it kinds of fades—and mbl—59th (?)—no idea at all" [scored as no discernible concordance]
Stage 4 (#100)	Just that—play by ear—get some kill of the—the ideas.	No—Jesus Christ—uh I really can't remember. [scored as no recall]
Stage 2 (#298)	Hm—hm—that's all *there is—there is no more to—there's no more voice*—so—to—*there's no more you know*—pushing.	[scored as no discernible concordance]

[a]The numbers in parentheses refer to the number of the speech or mentation report–speech pair in Appendix 1.

3. Neologistic paraphasia
   a. "Gundrum is the word for hundred..."
   b. "It goes *drench* more about Bonnie..."
4. Semantic jargon
   "you kept bouncing them on and on as if you had a regular meter...and as if you had a regular dream in...as if you were continuing on to the next paragraph..."
5. Mixed jargon
   "she shad hero sher...sher sheril S—H—A—W [spelled out aloud by S] takes part—loses but lost—invincible is u—as—usual..."

A possible kinship between aphasic and sleep-speech is not a new idea. Kraepelin (1906), Trömner (1911a,b) and Marburg (1929) each remarked on the similarities between sleep-speech or dream speech, and aphasic speech. Is it possible that many sleep-speeches provide physiological models of aphasia? Luria and Hutton (1977) indicate that inner speech phenomena occurring in normals at sleep onset resembles observations made during full wakefulness on patients afflicted with amnestic aphasia. Ey (1950) points to the commonly occurring paraphasic forms in hypnagogic and hypnopompic states. Inasmuch as masking of auditory feedback has been reported to produce *improvement* in the speech of aphasics (Birch, 1956; Birch & Lee, 1955), one is tempted to ask whether the sleep-speech of aphasics would be more correct than their wakeful speech. That wakeful neurological impairments may undergo amelioration during sleep is not without precedent (Arkin, Lutzky, & Toth,

TABLE 18.3
Speeches Demonstrating Self-Monitoring and Self-Corrections

Sleep-Stage	Sleep-Speech	Mentation Report
Stage 2 (#464)	I bet uh—hmm—have to think about that, anyway—mbl—just come out of the woodwork and I can't really remember what except that I well we were looking in the la— it seemed rather expensive things—mbl— that's what the university normally uses, and the fullest—mbl—was on the left and that was the youngest of the *leak leak after left—least* active hum— they threw that on then they, the appoint- ments became less and less possible less and less well spaced or at any rate they began to compete with the rest—of the office for sovereignty.	[not awakened]
Stage 4 (#43)	Mm—uh—duh—*she shad hero sher uh sher sheril S—H—A—W* [spelled out by subject] takes part—loses but lost—uh invin- cible is u as usual-mbl.	*E:* David. *S:* What did you say? I didn't hear you. *E:* What's going through your mind? *S:* Nothing esp- ecially—wasn't more than that— *E:* You say you can't recall anything? *S:* Nothing more than what I've said. *E:* What did you say? *S:* Hmph—about uh— that the gangster um—the uneasiness of feeling that there were gangsters— so on— [scored as no discernible concordance]
Stage 4 (#46)	*I wanna take a net—a—note—a note—pa— duh—uh—duh—shit!* I mean—you know—I'd like a nice pillow, you know with a	[not awakened]

(continued

TABLE 18.3 *(continued)*

Sleep-Stage	Sleep-Speech	Mentation Report
	nice trim (?) blanket—a pillow—that came up over my shoulders—that was tucked in a little bit—away some of the stem (?), you know (living in (?)) the drudgery, you know—she was never-uh—mbl—hot stuff but uh—mbl.	
Stage 4 (#555)	(Make a big trick about (?))—make a racket mbl is it do they flap—ap—they visit—just—they figured—just figured mbl a dreamer and did he dream—and what he dreamed the *second—the—er—first time—like—uh—s' about* all	S: The—uh— nothing really special—I imagine at the time I was think-ing about the job itself. [categorized as no recall]
Stage 2 (#312)	uh, huh, *helda, heldi, see,* uuh the most interesting and certain*ly* the most respect and was the most revered of all the *ladies who poured tea,* simp*ly* because it, she was *older* and quieter—and had more time to pour *tea*—mm—.	[no recall]
Stage 4 (#508)	Mbls [sounding like announcements at an air terminal-plane announcements] Airway R—E—V—I—S—E—D [spelled out by subject] Mbl—flight mbl—secure.	E: Does reciting the letters some-thing like A—S—D—U—C mean any-thing to you? S: No. [categorized as no recall]

1972; Nielsen, 1936). Indeed, Jason Brown has related to me an anecdotal observation of a ward nurse that a patient afflicted by day with severe aphasia spoke communicably in her sleep.

In Summary

In summary, although sleep is compatible with brief intervals of psycholinguistic functioning comparable to wakeful levels, the strong tendency is toward varying degrees of impairment and disorganization. Such impairment tends to resemble those observable in organic and functional psychopathological syndromes rather than errors characteristic of wakeful speech. As such, they may possibly provide physiological models of these psycholinguistic disorders. Is there any way in which we might relate these psycholinguistic observations to the hypothesis of dissociated cognitive subsystems? Current psycholinguistic theory is based is based largely on data obtained from wakeful subjects in which Hilgard's (1973, 1977) "executive ego" plays a dominant role in all cognitive behavior. A fundamental postulate of psycholinguistic theory was formulated by Lashley (1951) to the effect that prior to internal or overt articulation, an *aggregate* of word units is partially activated or primed. One can imagine that this process normally entails secondary activation (with possibly less intensity) of related, but less appropriate linguistic components stored in contiguous or intersecting fashion to those components whose emission threshold has experienced the most drastic decrease—specifically, those words that are about to be overtly uttered. To be sure, tokens of secondary activation of such related components are the various speech errors. In wakefulness, implicit editing and monitoring by the executive ego more or less efficiently modulates, guides, and constrains psycholinguistic processes, usually leading to verbal output characterized by acceptable form and communicability. The verbal components secondarily and more weakly activated are generally held in check and not permitted access to utterance channels; and if they elude such constraints, corrective processes tend to be initiated. By contrast, in sleep, the components of dissociated psycholinguistic processes ultimately leading to overt utterance are relatively less well-integrated. Linguistic components that are secondarily activated (but that are nevertheless inappropriate in varying degree) are no longer held in check or efficiently modulated by implicit editing processes and acquire access to overt utterance channels. This results in a relatively high proportion of outputs containing errors of diverse sorts. The less efficient monitoring results in most of these errors remaining uncorrected.

Several authors have formulated neuro-psychological accounts of aphasic and schizophrenic language phenomena that seem equally applicable to sleep-speech and quite compatible with Hilgard's neodissociationist theory (1973, 1977).

Maher (1972) asserts that normal more or less coherent speech requires the effective, instantaneous inhibition of associations related to each element of the utterance and that such inhibitory skills become impaired in much schizophrenia resulting in characteristic language disturbances.

Stevens (1973) proposed a subcortical neural substrate for schizophrenic thought disorder. The basic concept involves a hypothetical gating mechanism consisting of "filtering structures" within the neostriatal and limbic striatal matrices located between cortical mantle and afferent fiber tracts of the motor, sensory, and visceral systems. In schizophrenic states, the gating structures become overwhelmed and normal inhibition becomes impaired and unequal to its physiological task. The patient then loses ability to prevent competing mentation and associations from emerging into consciousness, with resulting disruption of coherence of thought.

Brown (1977) suggests that sleep-speech represents meaningful, nonrandom action at a limbic–presentational level intermediate between nonpurposive behavior characteristic of the lower sensorimotor level and directed purposeful behavior of the next higher neocortical level, in terms of his microgenetic analysis.

Geschwind (1969) views posterior aphasia as the result of a "disconnection" between the auditory association cortex (Wernicke's area) and the motor association are a (Broca's area). Normally, the auditory association area is said to exert control over the motor association area by means of neural activity carried through the arcuate fasciculus. The motor association area is said to contain the learned rules of language, encoding, and overlearned verbal sequences. When disconnection occurs for whatever pathological reason, Broca's area devoid of Wernicke's area control is thought capable of "running on in isolation," yielding fluent but aphasic speech. One wonders, then, whether slow-wave sleep tends to bring about a "functional dissociation" syndrome rapidly reversed by wakefulness or other sleep stages such as Stages 2 or REM.

Luria (1974) and Luria and Hutton (1977) offer a Pavlovian scheme to account for both certain types of aphasic phenomena and linguistic anomalies during sleep-onset mentation and dreaming sleep. His departure is taken from Pavlov's "rule of force," which states that all normal, cortical, neurodynamic processes are governed by the principle that strong or significant stimuli produce strong responses, and weak or insignificant stimuli elicit weak responses. This principle is said to provide for the high selectivity of neurodynamic processes. However, higher neural activity requires capacities to quickly and effectively inhibit patterns currently active and execute fluent transitions from one excitation pattern to the next. This capacity is termed neural plasticity, and normal linguistic mentation requires integrity and coordination of processes subserving both the rule of force and plasticity; in pathological states involving the cerebral cortex, both capacities may be disturbed.

Pathological cortical states are associated with alterations in the manner of function of the rule of force. First, according to Luria (1974), an inhibitory or "phase" state of cortical activity produces a condition in which occurs an *"equalization* of excitation evoked by stimuli of different strength [p. 8]"; i.e., strong or significant stimuli evoke responses equal to those produced by weak or insignificant ones or their traces. Second, a paradoxical stage follows in which weak or insignificant stimuli evoke even more intense responses than those resulting from strong or significant stimuli (or their respective traces). The important consequent is that the selectivity of mental processes undergoes impairment such that secondary, insignificant associations are elicited with the same probability as that of the primary, significant ones. And with the loss of plasticity, excitations become pathologically inert, and fluent transition from one pattern to successors is made difficult. The ultimate outcome is disorganization of mentation. The most relevant aspect of this description is Luria's assertion that similar states are normally observable in sleep-onset states, dreams, and during deep exhaustion. Luria claims that the foregoing principles are superior to those of Freud in accounting for dream processes.

Of equal interest is Luria's (1974) description of the psycholinguistic defects associated with specific types of brain damage. Thus, circumscribed damage to the convex parts of the left temporal zones of the cortex disrupts the highly selective system of phonematic opposition: "Secondary phonemic cues are evoked with the same probability as basic ones, and a breakdown of the paradigmatic organization of the *phonematic* level of linguistic codes is observed [p. 9]"; and if pathology is "limited by the tertiary zones of the *temporo-parieto-occipital* cortex, similar disturbances of selectivity can be observed on a *higher, semantic level* [p. 9]." The former condition is marked by confusion of similar phonemes and "literal paraphasia" typical for sensory or acoustic aphasic syndromes; and the latter condition is associated with syndromes of "amnestic aphasia" with verbal paraphasia, in which a whole network of words is elicited with equal probability. A portion of such a verbal network has phonematic resemblance with the sought-for word, and another portion possesses a semantic similarity with it. Luria states that rather than by true forgetting of words, the results are accounted for by evocation of whole assemblies of similar or related words with equal probability. These clinical observations strongly resemble the recurrent, assonantial-type, sleep-utterances, as well as the groping-for-a-target-word phenomenon repeatedly observed in sleep-speech. It seems reasonable to suggest once more that sleep, particularly slow-wave sleep, may be accompanied by physiological, transitory, reversible neural patterns similar to those maintained indefinitely under cortical pathological conditions; and both may be associated with aphasic speech.

Thus, one of the most remarkable aspects of somniloquy is its demonstration that under physiological conditions, the psycholinguistic system of the executive ego (a system of mind-boggling complexity) is capable of undergoing varying degrees of dismantlement in sleep and relatively rapid functional reintegration when the subject is awakened. It is this very tendency of the psycholinguistic system to display variability during sleep and transitional, related states that provides a fertile field for future investigation into sleep mentation, related areas of psychophysiology, and cognitive psychology.

We have had frequent occasion to notice that wakeful mentation report-content elicited immediately after sleep-utterance may possess concordances of varying degree on a continuum ranging from unmistakable, through indirect, to nondiscernible concordances, and no recall of mentation, as well. Such sleep speech mentation report pairs as numbers 47, 315, 316, and 511 suggest the possibility that if subjects initially gave rise to nonconcordant pairs, but were then asked to free-associate immediately after rendering their mentation reports, the free-association content might increasingly possess content items that would clearly be seen as related to or derived from the same sphere of cognitive activity that gave rise to the original sleep-speech. Such an array of data systematically collected in close sequence (sleep-speech, mentation report, and free-association) might provide further fascinating, unique opportunities to investigate the germination of deep psycholinguistic structures (Chomsky, 1972) in sleep, their interactions with other activated deep structures, and their subsequent transformations into surface structure as reflected in wakeful recall and association networks. Such experiments could be carried out under various conditions such as spontaneous sleep-speech and sleep-speech influenced by the various experimental techniques described earlier. In such fashion, a true experimental psycholinguistics of sleep could be developed.

19 Pathological and Experimental States Related to Somniloquy

A typical feature of night terror and daytime hypersomnia episodes, sequellae of experimental sleep deprivation, and frequently of REM narcolepsy-cataplexy events is the occurrence of spontaneous vocalization with and without speech, which appears to reflect internal experience rather than external stimuli, and for which there are strong amnestic tendencies. It is therefore of interest to relate such phenomena to the typical somniloquy of more or less normal people under normal circumstances.

In exploring this issue, a useful organizing perspective is afforded by the concept of anomalous state of consciousness manifestation in the otherwise prevailing state of the moment. That is, during the four conditions under discussion, the prevailing state, whether it is wakefulness or Stage 4 sleep, is perturbed by the sudden appearance of behavioral, subjective, and electrographic components of some other state of consciousness; and depending on how small the time scale one uses, such manifestation may temporarily preempt the previously prevailing condition, or else blend or interact with it, concurrently producing a complex of multiple components. This concept of anomalous state of consciousness manifestation has been utilized by Dement and Rechtschaffen (1968), Guilleminault, Billard, Montplaisir, and Dement, (1975a), Guilleminault, Phillips, and Dement (1975b), Vogel (1976), and others.

THE NIGHT-TERROR AND SLEEP-UTTERANCE

Broughton (1968), Fisher, Kahn, Edwards, and Davis (1974, 1975), and Gastaut and Broughton (1965) have carried out extensive laboratory studies on night-terror syndromes, the episodes of which have a special predilection for occurring in association with Stage 3–4 sleep prior to the first REMP of the night, or else afterward but nevertheless during the early hours of sleep. These episodes are typically distinguishable from REM nightmares and the less common Stage 2 night-terror.

Stage 3–4 episodes are the most severe. Behaviorally, the attack begins suddenly with loud, intense screams infused with the utmost abject terror, cries for help, and other vocalizations including speech, moans, groans, sighs, curses, etc. The accompanying measures of autonomic activity quickly and strikingly increase so that the heart rate may double or nearly triple the pre-attack level. Frequently, gross body movements occur to the point of actual somnambulism with overt fight–flight behavior. Subjects are disoriented, confused, delusional, immersed in vivid, monothematic, terrifying hallucinatory experience, produce extensive automatic behavior, and are relatively nonreactive to external stimuli (and hence respond poorly to efforts to bring about full wakefulness). The attack in adults generally lasts 1–2 min, often with immediate return to sleep. There is a tendency for partial to complete amnesia for the experience.

The EEG accompanying attacks is one of sustained alpha rhythm described by Gastaut and Broughton (1965) as phase Ia^3 [p. 211]." Gastaut and Broughton note that episodes of behavioral and subjective sleep accompanied by wakeful EEG patterns are not rarities in sleep research with *normal* subjects. Under such circumstances, the subject is motorically quiet, and heart rate and respiration are regular. Investigative eye movements and blinking often occur without producing blocking of the sustained, continuous alpha frequencies. "If this rhythm continues long enough (1 minute or more), it constitutes a *veritable phase of sleep,* which we propose to call phase Ia^3 to distinguish it from those other phases of sleep, Ia^1 and Ia^2, which contain some alpha activity and are seen chiefly during falling asleep [p. 211; italics added]." When phase Ia^3 follows Stage 3–4, tendon reflex activity is either attenuated or abolished. Further, the awakening threshold to experimenter stimulation is greatly increased and the subject is partially or completely amnestic for preceding events. (The similarity of this description of phase Ia^3 to that presented for many intermediate and macrodissociative episodes is striking, and there is probably considerable overlap between the two. For example, see the sleep-speech of Batson's subject (# 572—Appendix 2) and my female posthypnotically stimulated sleep-talking subject.)

By contrast to the Stage 3–4 night-terror episodes, the REM nightmare occurs during an ongoing REMP and continues for several minutes, followed by full wakefulness behaviorally, subjectively, and electrographically. As is typical of REM sleep, there is tonic inhibition of muscle tone. Vocalization and screaming are rare. Autonomic changes are mild to moderate or else may not be detectable. The subject is in good contact on awakening, the anxiety quickly dissipates, and variable degrees of recall of a previous vivid, anxiety-infused dream are common, and certainly more abundant than after Stage 3–4 night-terrors. The contents of such dreams are generally more elaborate and narrativelike, in which the subject is threatened with harm or destruction after a possibly prolonged previous dream scenario of a blander nature.

Finally, Fisher et al. (1975) describe less common subjects who are prone to both Stage 2 and Stage 3–4 night-terrors, and REM nightmares as well.

Fisher et al. (1974, 1975) differ somewhat from Gastaut and Broughton (1965) and Broughton (1968, 1973), in that the latter claim that only nonelaborated vague frightening items of mentation are retrievable in a small proportion of awakenings and that amnesia for inner experience during night-terrors is striking. Fisher et al. (1974) demonstrated that some distinct mental content was recalled in a mean of 58% of post-night-terror awakenings, many of which yielded mentation reports clearly concordant with the night-terror speeches. This figure approaches content recall rates obtained from routine NREM awakenings of normal subjects (Arkin, Toth, Baker, & Hastey, 1970a; Foulkes, 1966). More recently, Kales, Davis, Russek, Martin, Kuhn, and Kales (1978a) found that 43.8% of 32 adult subjects had vague recall, and 34.4% had specific recall on being awakened after night-terror episodes, which, although somewhat lower than found by Fisher et al. (1974), is still substantial.

Broughton (1968) has characterized Stage 4 night-terrors, along with enuresis and somnambulism, as "disorders of arousal." He has demonstrated that individuals so afflicted have high and unstable baseline autonomic activity levels, and that when nocturnal arousal episodes occur, acute hyperintense activation accompanies them; especially in the case of night terrors, temporarily impaired cognitive organizations respond to the experience generated by such hyperaugmented activation by production of terrifying imagery, which feels quite real to the disoriented and confused subject, and further enhances the terror. Broughton noted that similarly impaired cognition may occur with nonsleep-disorder subjects under conditions of precipitate intense stress, which generates sudden huge increments of arousal. He does not attempt a rigorous definition of the concept "disorder of arousal," but judging from his contextual usages, he implies that such disorders are best explained on the basis of physiological factors. Broughton's (1973) research convinced him that nocturnal enuresis, sleep-walking, nightmares, and night-terrors

should in fact be considered as *arousal disorders* [Broughton's italics]. This does not imply that psychological factors play no important role in their genesis, but rather that the prevalent belief that the attacks are precipitated by co-existent mental activity is questionable. First, their symptomatology is largely explicable by a combination of physiological changes predisposing to the particular attack type. Second, there is no direct evidence that recurrent mental activity actually triggers the attacks [p. 113].

In other words, Broughton's view is that physiological factors and predispositions are the most influential variables in the causation of the syndromes under consideration and that psychological factors play a secondary role;—hence, disorders of arousal;—and night-terrors are analogous to excessive startle reactions in predisposed individuals. Broughton believes, however, that physiological predisposition is influenced by chronic underlying nonspecific psychic conflicts that interact with the precariously balanced physiological equilibrium.

Fisher et al. (1975), taking a different position, subscribe to a more "holistic approach and that both views [recurrent anxious mentation versus psychophysiological arousal disorder as equally important causal factors] are correct and not irreconcilable [p. 381]." Fisher et al. (1975) suggest that the night-terror is not a dream in the usual sense but a symptom, a pathological process erupting during NREM sleep that both betokens, and is the resultant of, ego weakness—an impairment of its capacity to control anxiety; and the disposition to such sleep "diastrophism" may be related to past traumata and precipitated by psychological as well as by nonpsychological factors.

Setting aside the issue of the relative importance of psychological and physiological trigger events in the production of night terrors, Broughton (1968, 1973) and Fisher et al. (1975) are in accord in viewing the phenomenon as an outbreak of panic during episodes of arousal from slow-wave sleep in which excessive physiological activation and psychological variables play interactive roles.

More recently, Dement and Mitler (1975) advanced a fascinating speculation to the effect that night-terrors are "precipitated by a burst of phasic activity arising in NREM sleep [p. 176]," and about the same time Benoit and Adrien (1975), in commenting on the sleep of children, stated:

> The large number of missed REM periods, the long transitional phase preceding the first REM period (which reflects the "difficulty" in the establishment of paradoxical sleep) and the great sensitivity of the 1st cycle, which can be disrupted by psychological factors like anxiety, should be related to the paroxystic episodes of sleep in children (night terrors, nightmares, sleepwalking, sleep-talking); it is probably not only coincidental that such episodes occur at the beginning of the night [pp. 28–29].

It is unfortunate that neither of these collaborative authors enlarged on these related thoughts. But, inasmuch as phasic activity and REM sleep are intimately related, a possible hypothetical extension suggests itself.

Might it be that a night-terror results from manifestation of out-of-normal-context REM sleep components into slow-wave sleep, much as narcolepsy and cataplexy result from anomalous manifestation of separable REM components into wakefulness (Arkin, 1978). That is, if such "intrusions" may occur in wakefulness, why not into NREM sleep as well? And if this were indeed possible, presumably the details of such anomalous episodes would reflect the influence of time of night and NREM sleep variables.

One cannot hope to experimentally test this hypothesis easily in humans, but short of this, one may inquire to what extent it would be in accord with observations obtained in animal research and with the results of clinical studies with psychoactive drugs in humans. Certainly such a hypothesis would not be incompatible with the views of Broughton (1968, 1973) and Fisher et al. (1975), but rather constitute a complementary extension of them.

One might begin by asking whether any experimental animal syndromes have been described that resemble night-terrrors in some important respects and may therefore provide a partial analogue. Jouvet (1975), referring to his earlier research, states that the bilateral ablation of the caudal portion of the locus coeruleus selectively suppresses the massive tonic inhibition of overt motoric behave during REM sleep. Cats with such a lesion behave normally when awake or during slow-wave sleep but enter an intensely dramatic stereotyped "pseudo-hallucinatory" behavioral state when a REMP onset would normally occur. "They suddenly stand up, leap, and either display some aggressive behavior or play with their front paws as they might play with a mouse or show a rage behavior or a defense reaction against a larger predator.... During these episodes, the animals do not react to visual stimuli and they often collide with the walls of the observation cage [pp. 511–512]." Such occurrences, even at their most frenzied, are accompanied by relaxed nictitating membranes virtually covering the pupils that are themselves constricted, i.e., by vegetative ocular behavior of deep sleep despite intense motor-affective expression. Usually these episodes last for 4–5 min, at the end of which interval the animals return to NREM sleep or suddenly awaken. In short, the phenomena described suggested an occurrence of "REM dreaming experience" without the normal tonic motor inhibition.

One may note the following points of similarity between the cat episodes and human night-terrors: (1) intense, emotional, dramatic fight–flight behavior; (2) vivid hallucinatory quality of experience; and (3) apparent loss of critical reactivity to stimuli originating from the surroundings.

The hypothesis that Stage 3–4 night-terrors result from anomalous manifestation of REM sleep components into Stage 3–4 sleep would predict that drugs that ameliorate night-terrors would also tend to reduce one or more REM sleep parameters, that psychoactive drugs that do not influence REM sleep directly or indirectly would be without effect on night-terrors, and that drugs that increase REM sleep parameters would exacerbate night-terrors. In these respects, drug effects on narcolepsy would parallel those on Stage 3–4 night-terrors inasmuch as common etiologic factors are being postulated— anomalous manifestation of REM sleep components in a different previously prevailing state of consciousness. Furthermore, analogous drug effects should be observed on the periodic motoric-dream phenomena occurring in Jouvet's (1975) locus coeruleus lesioned cats.

How well does this hypothesis accord with pharmacological research findings? Drugs of several classes have been shown to ameliorate night terrors. These include diazepam—a benzodiazepine (Fisher, Kahn, Edwards, Davis, 1973b); imipramine—a dibenzazepine (Pesikoff & Davis, 1971; Tec, 1974); and various barbiturates (Bakwin & Bakwin, 1972; McGraw & Oliven, 1959; Nielsen, 1941). And conversely, certain drugs either were found to be without beneficial effect, such as chlorpromazine in some cases (a phenothiazine), and diphenylhydantoin—a hydantoin anticonvulsant, (Fisher et al, 1973b); or else exacerbated the condition, as did chlorpromazine in some cases (Fisher et al, 1973b; Flemenbaum, 1976; MacLeod & Fisher, 1978).

How these drugs, whether ameliorative, noneffective, or exacerbative, affect REM sleep parameters is the crucial question. In attempting to deal with this question, I rely chiefly on the most recent exhaustive and critical review known to me of drug effects on sleep by Kay, Blackburn, Buckingham, and Karacan (1976). These authors rightly distinguish between pilot, tentative, and preliminary studies on the one hand and definitive studies on the other. Only the latter, in their assessment, were sufficiently well designed, used a subject population greater than four, were adequately controlled, and had data properly statistically analyzed, to permit solid conclusions to be drawn.

Thus, findings of nondefinitive studies, although valuable as confirmation of definitive studies, were not used in arriving at relevant conclusions regarding the drug classes in the discussion to follow and in Table 19.1. Furthermore, the conclusions relate to drug *classes* rather than specific drugs. With these stipulations in mind, Table 19.1 presents the specific drugs that have received some sort of test in the treatment of night-terrors and the drug classes of which they are members. They are grouped in accordance with whether such drug class members generally suppress, enhance, or do not affect REM sleep parameters in ordinary clinical dosage.

It therefore appears consistent with the hypothesis advanced that members of those drug classes that tend to reduce REM sleep parameters also ameliorate night-terrors; and that a member of a drug class that does not affect or else increases REM parameters either does not benefit night-terror patients or exacerbates their condition.

Two additional observations made by Fisher et al. (1975) may be viewed from the perspective of night-terror as REM sleep-component intrusion. First: Prior to the severest night-terror attacks, Fisher et al. found unusually prolonged Stages 3–4 and unusually low indices of sympathetic activity.

TABLE 19.1
Drug Effects on REM Sleep and Night-Terrors

Clinically Used Specific Drugs	Drug Class	Effect on Night-Terrors	Effect of Drug Class on REM Sleep Parameters
Diazepam	Benzodiazepine	Ameliorative (Fisher et al., 1973)	Reduction (Kay et al., 1976)
Imipramine	Dibenzazepine (tricyclic antidepressant)	Ameliorative (Pesikoff et al., 1971; Tec, 1974	Reduction (Kay et al., 1976)
Phenobarbital and other	Barbiturates	Ameliorative (Nielsen, 1941; McGraw & Oliven, 1959; Bakwin & Bakwin, 1972	Reduction (Kay et al., 1976)
Chlorpromazine	Phenothiazine	No change or else exacerbative (Fischer et al., 1973; Flemenbaum, 1976; MacLeod & Fisher, 1978)	Increase initially followed by development of tolerance
Diphenylhydantoin	Hydantoin anticonvulsant	No change	No significant effect on REM or NREM parameters (Hartmann, 1970)

Might the striking bradycardia prevailing before the worst attacks reflect parasympathetic dominance? Sitaram, Wyatt, Dawson, and Gillin (1976) have shown that intravenous infusions of physostigmine (an anticholinesterase) are capable of initiation of REMPs prior to their normally scheduled appearance. From this and ancillary findings, it was suggested that cholinergic systems are involved in REMP instigation; and the effect of physostigmine, then, would lead to accumulation of acetylcholine with shortened first REMP latency. This might partly explain that the bulk of night-terrors occur relatively soon after sleep onset—the mean latency of night-terrors was 44.5 min after sleep onset (Fisher et al., 1975). Briefly, the hypothesized abnormally high blood acetylcholine level involved in producing the striking bradycardia would also serve to prematurely trigger the REM sleep components showing themselves in the night-terror phenomenon.

Second: Fisher et al. (1975) reported that the mere sound of the awakening buzzer was often sufficient to initiate a typical night-terror. Now if it is so that night-terrors are slow-wave sleep analogues to narcoleptic–cataplectic attacks in wakefulness, the sound of the awakening buzzer as reported by Fisher et al. (1975) may be analogous to an "emotion provoking event" typically capable of producing a wakeful cataplectic attack. That is, the buzzer sound during sleep may well startle the subject, and the emotion thus produced could instigate a night-terror episode by a neural process similar to that involved in wakeful cataplexy, except that it occurs within the matrix of Stage 4 sleep.

In conclusion, inasmuch as REM suppressants like imipramine appear to benefit other parasomniac disorders such as somnambulism (Tec, 1974) and nocturnal enuresis (Fraser, 1972), perhaps the disorders of arousal (Broughton, 1968; 1973) may also be classified along with night-terrors as subsets of anomalous REM sleep-component manifestation (ARCM), along with REM narcolepsy-cataplexy syndromes.[1]

EXCESSIVE DAYTIME SLEEPINESS
SYNDROMES AND SLEEP-UTTERANCE

Guilleminault et al. (1975a, b) have described signs of altered states of consciousness during episodes of excessive daytime sleepiness. Examination of the clinical records at the Sleep Disorders Clinic of the Stanford University School of Medicine revealed a recurrent automatic behavior syndrome among 75 narcoleptic–cataplectic patients, 20 sleep-apneic patients, and seven others with nonspecific hypersomnia. An episode lasting from a few seconds to hours appeared almost daily with each patient. During such occurrences, more or less accurate and appropriate performance of simple tasks and utterance of simple linguistic responses is possible; but if the demands in either area become complex, errors and inappropriate verbalization—some trivial and some fatefully gross in proportion and costliness to life and property—are commonplace. Episodes may occur anywhere—while driving and in ongoing social interactions.

According to Guilleminault et al. (1975a, b):

> During these episodes simple questions are answered appropriately, but if the conversation requires complex answers, the inappropriate or meaningless sentences the patient makes in response are quite evident. A common feature is a sudden burst of words sometimes without any meaning, and always without any

---

[1] Fisher et al. (1973b) tentatively concluded that diazepam ameliorated night-terror syndromes by reducing Stage 4 sleep—the "somatic matrix" of the night-terror. However, on this basis, Stage 4 suppression could not account for the positive therapeutic effects of tricyclic antidepressants that either do not significantly affect slow-wave sleep or may even increase it—especially Stage 3 (Kay et al., 1976). By contrast, the ARCM hypothesis is able to accommodate this finding.

> relation to what the patient might have just been saying. All of our patients
> expressed embarrassment and concern about these abrupt and meaningless
> intrusions in their conversation [p. 379].

Varying degrees of amnesia for such episodes were very frequent. Although
memory for their content may be absent or impaired, there were also
instances of residues of imagery as in a "broken movie." Similar phenomena
were observable during writing. For example, one patient while filling out a
questionnaire wrote "on or about 85," which was completely unrelated to the
task at hand, nor could the patient explain the meaning or why he wrote it.
The description of these episodes, with accompanying memory disturbance,
is very similar to that offered by Tharp (1976) in his account of speech
disorder during narcoleptic attacks.

In cataplectic attacks of brief duration not exceeding one min, wakeful
consciousness and memory appear undisturbed. But if the attack persists, a
novel situation supervenes in which admixtures of both dream sequences and
reality perception coexist. The patient is aware of his surroundings,
attempts—often successfully—to carry out simple commands of the
physician, correctly processes information, and yet lives in a dream scenario
he knows is unreal but that may be sufficiently intense to result in his calling
out the name of a dream character or attempting flight from a scary scene.
Similar characteristics and modes of mentation occurring during narcoleptic
episodes have been reported by Vogel (1976).

What are the characteristics of the electrographic records accompanying
the various altered states of consciousness? These may be of several types,
each of very short duration:

Microsleep Episodes Typical of Hypersomnia Patients.   These may be (1)
a sudden, brief burst of typical Stage 1 NREM, and/or (2) a brief burst of
synchronous theta frequencies from central monopolar leads ($C_3/A_2, C_4/A_1,$
O_2/A_1). Usually such incidents are repetitive and occur in clusters.

MicroREM Episodes Typical of Narcoleptic Patients.   This is a short
interval of EMG suppression with one or more REMs.

Typical of Cataplectic Patients.   Tracings reveal no striking differences
from records of wakefulness; however for intervals usually not exceeding 10
sec, tracings during attacks and the same subjects' REM sleep are
indistinguishable.

Typical of Sleep-Apneic Patients.   Sleep stages of sleep-apneic episodes
are often difficult to classify. Common occurrences are high-amplitude slow
waves concurrent with chin EMG suppression, together with agitated,
frequent abnormal limb and body movements. With resumption of

respiration, Stage 1 NREM-like tracings or "brief alpha arousals" tend to occur. Although the electrographic picture resembles one characteristic of low arousal-threshold conditions,patients are usually most difficult to "awaken" at such times. Thus, in the case of sleep-apnea patients, the altered state of consciousness is manifested most dramatically in association with sleep rather than wakefulness.

On the whole then, altered states of consciousness of a spontaneous pathological nature have been exemplified in Stage 3–4 night-terrors, narcolepsy, cataplexy, nonspecific hypersomnia, and sleep-apnea attacks. With the exception of the latter, the resemblance of these phenomena to many occurrences detailed in Chapters 7, 8, 9, 11, and 18 concerning various types of sleep-talking episodes is striking. In one form or another, they illustrate psychic dissociative processes over a broad range from micro- and intermediate through macroscales of magnitude, as well as demonstrating the reality of anomalous state of consciousness manifestation.

Let us turn now to similar alterations of consciousness and "intrusion" phenomena produced in normals by the relatively uncomplicated expedient of experimental sleep deprivation.

EXPERIMENTAL SLEEP DEPRIVATION AND SLEEP-UTTERANCE

Morris, Williams, and Lubin (1960) and Berger and Oswald (1962) made extensive observations on the effects of experimental sleep deprivation with normal subjects. A total of 37 experimental and 37 control subjects participated in two separate studies of Morris et al. (1960). They were all young adult men in the armed forces. Experimental subjects were kept awake for 72–98 hr continuously and were periodically observed and tested. Behavior was recorded but not electrographically monitored. The outstanding relevant findings were progressive tendencies to visual misperception, temporal disorientation, and cognitive disorganization, with increasing sleep loss. The most striking subjective phenomena occurred during short intermittent pauses in ongoing behavior accompanied by intense drowsiness termed "lapses." The most severe of them ended in sleep. They were usually self-limited, lasted for several seconds, and most likely would have been classified as "microsleeps" if electrographically monitored. Actually, Johnson, Slye, and Dement (1965) and Naitoh, Kales, Kollar, Smith, and Jacobson (1969), in the course of specific electrographic study of sleep deprivation, identified such lapses as microsleep episodes.

Those lapses in the Morris et al. (1960) study falling in the middle range between sleep and wakefulness were characterized by a fascinating inner state in which the subject was dimly aware that people were talking, but not of the content of what they were saying. Confusion between external and internal events was typical, with intrusive thoughts or dreams blended with real occurrences to produce distorted perception, behavior, and speech. Amnesia for these experiences set in rapidly. Among the commonly observed anomalies in speech were tendencies to ramble, vagueness, repetition, abrupt shifts in topics, intrusive thoughts, unfinished statements, mispronounciation, omission of syllables, fusion of words, neologisms, diminished self-correction of speech errors, and production of jargon.

Berger and Oswald (1962) studied six normal male medical students under conditions of four continuous nights of experimental sleep deprivation. The descriptive findings regarding behavior, speech, and inner experience were virtually identical to those of Morris et al. (1960).

On the whole, the results of both experiments show that behavioral and subjective phenomena of sleep can be coaxed to manifestation in wakefulness, and/or blend with wakeful consciousness, by means of experimental sleep deprivation with normal subjects. The features of such manifestations bear strong resemblances to those reported by Guilleminault et al. (1975a, b) as occurring spontaneously in episodes of sleep in REM narcolepsy–cataplexy as well as in nonspecific hypersomnia syndromes; and both the sleep deprivation and pathological syndromes resemble many sleep-utterance incidents occurring spontaneously in normal subjects. It seems reasonable, then, to view the phenomena of spontaneous and experimental production of sleep-utterance in normals (Arkin et al., 1970a; Farber, Arkin, Ellman, Antrobus, & Nelson, 1973), experimentally produced manifestations of sleep in wakefulness (Berger & Oswald, 1962; Morris et al., 1960), the pathologic sleep-speeches accompanying night-terrors (Broughton, 1968; Fisher et al., 1974; Gastaut & Broughton, 1965), the pathologic "intrusions" of sleep into wakefulness with altered states of consciousness (Guilleminault et al., 1975a, b), the immersion of oneself in vivid daydreaming (Singer, 1975), and other similar phenomena, as illustrative of the propensity for psychic and psychophysiological dissociation in humans, and the possibility of more or less independent manifestation of components of cognitive subsystem processes (Hilgard, 1977). In short, it is suggested that the ARCM phenomena discussed in this chapter be viewed as examples of complex dissociated cognitive subsystem activity.

20 Clinical Uses of Sleep-Talking

A prevailing opinion among depth psychologists is that emotionally charged mentation unavailable to wakeful consciousness is typically a pathogenic factor in psychologic suffering. It is surprising, therefore, that so few references have appeared in the literature describing possible therapeutic uses of sleep-talking. Certainly this is not a novel thought.

CLINICAL USES OF SLEEP-TALKING

Perhaps the earliest such mention is that of Esquirol(1832), who believed that the underlying basis of a "delirium" (i.e., psychosis) is often revealed in words spoken by patients out of dreams rather than in their wakeful productions. The next related comment known to me is that of Andriani (1892), who advised physicians that dreams and somniloquy provide very useful information with which to investigate the diseases of the nervous system and, specifically, those of the brain. Although, as previously mentioned, material involving sleep-talking appeared sporadically, and mostly in dribs and drabs, no clinician known to me described utilizing sleep-talking in some specific technical manner until Janet (1925). In his comprehensive treatise on psychotherapeutics, he stated that:

> Madame D's traumatic memories were mainly brought to light, to begin with at any rate, by a study of her dreams. In all these cases, we were careful to write down the actual words used by the subject during the state of sleep, to record them without any modification. Madame D was kept under observation while

asleep, and a record was taken of whatever she murmured. In other cases, I had the subject wakened suddenly, in order that a note might be made of what she said the instant after being awakened. These words were only recorded if they had a definite meaning and were related to some specific happening [p. 594–595].

The most detailed of all case histories in which sleep-talking served as a technical adjunct appears in a paper devoted to the clinical psychological problem of pain (Engel, 1959). The patient was a 27-year-old married woman who had suffered chronically from three different types of severe pain in her face and head since the age of 11.

During the period of therapy, there occurred a number of experiences during sleep which her husband wrote down and brought in for discussion. The patient had complete amnesia for these experiences but was able to bring important associations. Two such episodes were particularly revealing.

1. One night she said, while asleep, "He hit me in the face with a buckle. I was a naughty girl!" This recalled an incident at age four. She had been naughty and mother insisted that father punish her. He was undressing. As he pulled his belt from his pants, he suddenly struck her violently in the face with the buckle end. [This was one determinant of the face as a location of the pain.]

2. The most dramatic episode concerned the auto accident to which she had briefly alluded in the first interview. At the time, she merely said that she had been in an auto accident at age eleven, and that she suffered a fractured kneecap and was in a cast for a year. She did not mention any injury suffered by mother. (First face pain began when patient was 11 or 12.)

While asleep, the patient tossed restlessly and began talking (reliving a traumatic episode). "I know he didn't have any lights on. He turned them on after he got to the middle of the street. We never start to cross the street without looking." She cried out in pain, "My knee, my knee! That morphine makes me see the lights all over again. That car is rolling mother down the street and it isn't going to stop. I can't stand that car rollering her. I see her face full of blood. The eye is cut. She is dead. My face, my face, my face hurts." (Injury to mother's face as determinant of site of pain.) The patient beat on the bed. She awakened and appeared terrified. "I have to get up and see if I can walk!" She struggled with her husband to get up, but was unable to. Her teeth chattered violently and she had a shaking chill at this point. "I am cold like I was sitting in the snow that night." The husband observed, "She was breathing rapidly and her legs were icy cold. There was decided swelling of the right cheek which was red and hot over the area of the pain. I sensed this temperature change by contrasting the two sides of the face. She writhed, clutched and gasped, so intense was the pain." The patient was then able to describe the accident in more detail. It was a cold, wintry night, 13°F below zero, with snow on the ground. Mother and daughter stepped from the streetcar and started to cross the street. Suddenly, they realized a car without lights was bearing down on them. Just before striking, the headlights were turned on and glared in their eyes. Mother raised her hand to protect her face. She was struck by the car and dragged a half a block. The patient was knocked to her knees and found herself alone in the dark sitting in the snow. She screamed; she felt alone and deserted. She shivered with the cold and it seemed endless before anyone picked her up. When she saw her mother, her face looked "like someone had beaten it with a hammer . . . ." The patient was brought to a hospital where she . . . had repetitive frightening dreams of the accident [p. 914].

It seems clear from both the Janet and the Engel references that the sleep-talking content reflected repressed traumatic memories and that recording them and eliciting associations appeared to be helpful in reconstructing more complete details of the actual occurrences previously unavailable to wakeful consciousness.

Turning now to a pediatric population, Vogl (1964) commented as follows:

The clear pearl-like laughter in the midst of sleep, bright shouts as if the child were at play, a smile when the mother tucks the child in more securely, none of this is unhealthy. It does, however indicate that even the positive experiences of the day were of such intensity that the child requires the additional time of night to encompass them. Since unpleasant experiences are generally far more disturbing, it is to be feared that such a child will be unable to work out the difficulties during the day. He will relive them in his sleep but in a more sleep disturbing manner—and with this we have arrived at the neurotic symptom.

The brief statements above should be sufficient indication that talking in one's sleep, *per se,* is insufficient evidence of anxiety or fear, as the medical term of *pavor nocturnus* would otherwise seem to indicate. Since fear is one of the most impressive infantile experiences, it is actually very often the root of such symptoms. But since this need not be the case, it is necessary to obtain an exact description of the nature of the sleep-talking and sudden startled awakenings.

Under clinical conditions, one may provoke such nocturnal actions in order to become oneself an eye and ear witness: such observation starts with the turning out of the light, continues with the covering of the child, and soon, to the careful attempts to waken the child, etc., all with the purpose of personal observation of the entire process for a precise evaluation of sounds and words in context. One may converse with some children as they sleep without awakening them. Another similarity between this situation and hypnosis is not to be overlooked; for this reason one is repeatedly tempted to include some suggestive therapy. Here more extensive experience with a great many children could perhaps lead to new therapeutic methods.

It seems obvious to regard sleep-talking as somewhat comparable to psychologically significant dreams and treat the sleep-talking with the same weight as dreams. When this is done, it is not only possible to gain therapy material from these talks, but also to ascribe to them the possible onset of self-healing. Also obvious is the interpretation that the only difference between dreams and such talks is a matter of degree. And finally one may interpret the patient's over-extended and over-intense review of the day's experiences as a neuropathological sign. Missing here, however, are the necessary conclusive investigations.

At all times, though, one must consider: that when the sleep-talking is charged with negative feelings and groans, the child is probably in a state of violent conflict and at the limit of his strength. Under such circumstances, the physician is no longer conscience-bound to make an exact diagnosis, even if from the somatic point of view there seems to be no indication for it. (No matter how extensive the sleep-talking may be, the child most of the time wakes up rested.) If, however, the child is tired and listless on waking, or if this talk results in startled awakening, or loud shrieking, this is already enough indication for symptomatic treatment. Especially is this true if such night activity is followed by anxiety, accompanied by pounding of the heart, drenching sweat or interrupted sleep.

Manifestations of sleep disturbances may be of even greater intensity. They may take such form as the child suddenly jumping out of bed and without awakening running through the inhabited rooms of the apartment. There are some children who can be only brought back to bed after they have been awakened and quieted.

It is often difficult to differentiate whether a child while running through the apartment is still asleep, drowsy or awake. Only the drowsy child would actually hurt himself—the awake as well as the sleep-walking child avoids all obstacles. But even the half asleep child is unlikely to hurt himself, since he knows his home even in his sleep. The child's facial expression as well is not indicative: stark fear produces the same expression whether the child is awake or asleep. Even without fear, the sleep-walking child will have wide open eyes. Closed, especially tightly closed eyes, are more likely to indicate that the child is not asleep. True sleep-walking can be determined through a knowledgeable evaluation of the child's reaction or action to such stimuli as being washed with cold water. Such knowledgeability is not the sole province of the physician who has witnessed one sleep-walking episode on the part of the child. The one who lives with the child and has been a repeated witness of such episodes may arrive at a more exact evaluation. By washing the child in cold water, one may witness the process of gradual recovery from his state of anxiety. Once awake, the child may have no recollection of his fear and, in fact, be astonished. If one leaves him in peace, he creeps quietly back to bed. Sometimes, he will talk or dream, but usually he quiets down quickly and goes to sleep, preferably in the presence of a grown-up. [p. 128–130].

Using a more direct approach to utilization of sleep-talking as an adjunct in therapy, Cahen (1965) instructed his patients to keep a tape recorder at their bedside during the night. The sound of the patient's voice actuates a relay switch that results in a permanent tape recording of whatever is said at "threshold" intensity. Patients are then able to relate their dreams aloud on awakening during the night and have them recorded immediately for subsequent analysis during the day. Cahen believes that the procedure presents greater and more accurate recall of the dream as experienced, in comparison to that possible under conditions of morning recall. When subjects hear their nightly mentation reports during wakefulness, recall and recognition is evoked and useful comparisons between morning recall and the recorded material are possible. Be that as it may, the relevant point is Cahen's frequent observation of another sort of recorded verbal material of which the patient has no retrievable memory whatsoever. Some of this material seems comparable in every respect to ordinary dreaming, whereas another variety consists of disorganized word-salad type sequences. From our present vantage point, the first kind may have been a wakeful mentation report following which the patient fell asleep and, by morning, the material was beyond retrieval; or, it may have been a sleep-speech. The second kind, however, does indeed sound like the not uncommon type of disorganized sleep-talking often heard in the laboratory (see Chapters 7 and 18) and reported in the clinical literature. Although Cahen has not found the latter type of recorded material therapeutically useful (he considers it to be more a physiological than a psychological product—that is, not a "dream"), he suggested that it might have interesting potential for future study.

Finally, Bertini, Gregolini, and Vitali (1972) and Bertini, Ruggeri, and Torre (1974a,b) have described a technique by which they claim to experimentally produce REM sleep-talking. Although their primary interest is in the area of research, they have indicated their future plans to explore the therapeutic possibilities offered by their approach. The details of their technique were given in Chapter 11 of this book. In brief, 11 subjects had been trained to free-associate aloud by day in response to a white noise stimulus. After the task was well-learned, when the stimulus was introduced during REM and NREM sleep, subjects emitted sustained dream-like verbalizations.

Frequently, in the next morning, subjects had no spontaneous recall of their previous night's verbalizations, and sometimes they did not recognize them even after hearing the tape recording. Nocturnal recordings contained items not found in the morning recall and often provided a point of departure for psychological association to new material. There was often a striking contrast between the emotionally infused quality of the night records and the detached quality of the morning reports. In one case, such contrast was said to occasion intense surprise and subsequent deep psychological insight. Certainly, whether such mentation truly represents a verbalized dream occurring during sleep is a separate issue from whether the procedure has therapeutic usefulness.

In my personal experience, I know of only one instance where sleep-talking and sleep-associated automatic writing appeared to play a useful therapeutic role. A talented, middle-aged American woman whom I knew well socially had been emotionally troubled and agitated most of her life. She had received prolonged psychotherapy. Among her symptoms was a chronic tendency to talk in her sleep in Russian—a language she knew nothing of by day; she could neither read, write, nor speak it in wakeful consciousness. Knowledge of her somniloquy came through her husband's observations—the patient had no recall of repeated episodes or their content. Her husband also did not know Russian but described the sleep-speeches as having either an angry or pleading quality. When angry, she often uttered, "Davai!" or "Shtatakoi!", and when pleading, something that sounded like "Plauaritzkou." On a number of occasions, her excitement became so intense that her husband, in alarm, awakened her by slapping her face, whereupon she asked whether *he* was having some trouble or emergency of his own.

The patient spent 1 year in Russia from age 10 to 11 with her father, visiting his relatives. Her father was a tyrannical individual and on one climactic occasion beat and humiliated her in front of the family in a fruitless attempt to induce her to give her best party shoes to a younger female cousin. Even this harsh treatment did not coerce the patient to yielding to his request. After her return to the United States, she consciously forgot whatever Russian she knew. She was aware that from time to time she would be caught off guard when her gaze would fall on a Russian newspaper. At such times, she had the impression that she recognized a common word, but this would be a fleeting, anxiety-arousing experience that was quickly terminated by the abrupt loss of this sense of recognition—as though knowing some Russian words would provoke swift and awesome punishment (her speculation).

It is of significance that the incident of the beating was not itself completely repressed. Actually, the patient wrote about it in her adult life in a vivid, moving, dramatic short story, which she connected with the beating incident.

One day, she was dozing in bed at about 4:00 p.m. She had long been in the habit of keeping a pad and pen at her bedside as a way of collecting useful phrases and poetic expressions. She was awakened by her husband, who was standing by her bed. She thought she had been dreaming that she was writing about something to do with writing. She felt terribly depressed and believed that her husband was angry with her (which in fact he was not). At this point, she arose and the pad she had alongside her fell to the floor. She experienced intense anxiety on seeing that she had written something in Russian on it. She examined it carefully and knew none of the meanings of any of the words except the equivalents for "yes" and "no." When I informed her subsequently that the phrase her husband reported she often used, "Shtatakoi" meant "What is it?", she again suddenly experienced intense anxiety, terminating a sustained feeling of well-being. I then arranged for the entire written text to be translated by Robert Dempsey, a librarian of the New York Academy of Medicine, who is fluent in Russian and English. The patient was ambivalent about learning the meaning of what she had written—intensely curious, yes, but also very anxious. Nevertheless, she persevered in her wish to be "enlightened." The written text is reproduced in Fig. 20.1, with the English

AUTOMATIC WRITING OF A PATIENT WITH
A DISSOCIATION SYNDROME AND SLEEP-TALKING

	ENGLISH TRANSLATION *
(handwritten)	No, very much. Let me have it.
	I, understand yes. Who was that riding by (?)
	you. Go away. listen
	Let me have my shoes
	Give it to me, cook.
	Yes, faster. this is urgent
	I, no. I'm eating. Go away.
(handwritten)	(undecipherable) whatever these are. Let me have it.
(handwritten)	Listen to me.
	please
(handwritten)	Give it to me
(handwritten)	I am lost. yes. I **
	am/lost **
(handwritten)	No (?) no. Thank you
	What is it.

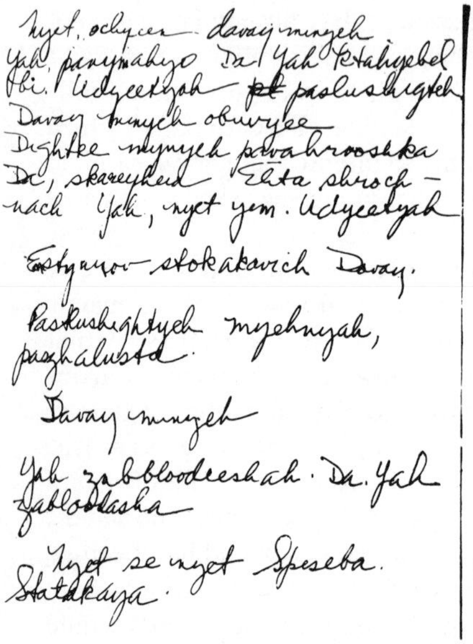

*Translated by Robert Dempsey, Librarian, New York Academy of Medicine.

**These are impossible verb forms in modern Russian; it could be a child's rhyme.

FIG. 20.1. Automatic writing of a patient with a dissociation syndrome and sleep-talking.

translation alongside. While hearing this translation, the patient was fiercely anxious but much relieved afterward. She dreaded the notion that she might have expressed a great deal of anger—an emotion of which she was most fearful—and felt reassured because what had been written seemed "not so bad." Over a 3-year period, I questioned the patient intermittently about her psychological state. One month after hearing the English translation, she completely forgot it, although she retained a general notion that it had to do with asking for something. Most important, she has experienced a new sense of sustained calm not previously known to her. She had always felt disturbed about not knowing. Her husband reported that following her hearing the translation, all sleep-talking in Russian ceased and the overall frequency of somniloquy appreciably diminished. In other words, a therapeutic effect had apparently been achieved.

There are several noteworthy features:

1. In the automatic writing, the previous sleep-speeches heard by her husband, and in the childhood trauma-related short story written by her,

21

Addendum: New Studies of Sleep-Talking (Heynick, 1980a, b)

While the present volume was in the process of final editing, two new articles on somniloquy written by F. Heynick (1980a, 1980b) came to my attention. Space limitations permit me to write only of the highlights of his work and the reader is referred to the original papers for details when they appear.

Subjects and Data Collection

Heynick (1980a, 1980b) based his paper on 86 sleep talking episodes uttered by 15 native Dutch-speaking subjects sleeping at home. They were all *unpaid* volunteers chosen from over 150 people responding to radio and newspaper advertisements for "chronic sleep-talkers." They ranged in age from 12-83; 10 were female and 5 male. The research was carried out under the auspices of the Technische Hogeschool of Eindhoven in The Netherlands. No indication was given regarding the total population reached by the advertisements, nor the total geographic area surveyed, so we cannot use the data to hazard quantitative estimates about the prevalence of sleep-talking. The data do suggest, however, in conformity with findings described earlier in the book, that sleep-talking is indeed common.

Electro-encephalographic monitoring was not feasible. Subjects were supplied with cassette-tape recorders equipped with a voice-triggered microphone. About 2 weeks after home recording, subjects were asked, while awake, a series of 25 questions about their verbalizations. Heynick sought to compare sleep-speech with wakeful speech along a number of psycho-linguistic dimensions, and to elicit subjects' comments about aspects of their somniloquy.

Results

In his paper on Verbal Aggression (1980b) Heynick found that of his total of 86 sleep-speeches, only 5 (5.9%) were found to contain maledictions (hostile utterances). These 5 speeches were uttered by 4 female subjects. None were uttered by males. Neither sexual nor scatological profanities were observed, although sexual ones are very common in wakeful Dutch speech. Heynick concludes that this infrequency of malediction in sleep-speech indicates that sleep mentation does not reflect a welling-up of aggressive or sexual feelings, and is, therefore, more continuous rather than complementary with respect to waking mentation.

Both the findings and conclusion accord well with those presented earlier here, as well as with considerations suggesting that intra-psychic censorship remains unexpectedly vigilant during sleep-speech episodes (see p. 105 this volume).

In his paper on linguistic aspects of Freud's model (1980a), Heynick primarily reviewed Freud's model of linguistic phenomena in dream formation, and secondarily explored its applicability to overt sleep-speech. I will select for comment only those points that have bearing on aspects of sleep-speech and recommend to the reader that he consult Heynick's paper for detailed discussion of psychoanalytic linguistic phenomena in dreaming.

Firstly, Heynick states that both hallucinated dream-speech and overt sleep-speech are notable for their correct syntactic grammaticality. The laboratory work of Goetzinger (1973) and Salzarulo and Cipolli (1974) on hallucinated dreamed speech is cited as arriving at similar conclusions. This claim does not accord well with the reports based on self recording at home published by E. Kraepelin, I. Kurz and A. Höche on this topic, as described by Werner and Kaplan (1963). According to the latters' account of the work of these observers (in their chapter "Handling of linguistic forms in Dreams" p. 240–252), hallucinated dreamed-speech *commonly* contains grammatical errors. Is it possible that the specimens collected under conditions of laboratory awakenings are different from those obtained by self-recording at home?

Heynick extended his claim of typical correct grammaticality to include sleep-speech as well. Whereas this is true of many sleep-speeches, incorrect grammaticality is so extremely common in sleep-speech, I do not believe one may validly assert that correct grammaticality is typical (see chapter 18 this volume for details).

Heynick's (1980b) sleep-speech sample of 86 closely resemble most of those contained in the appendix of this volume and those reported by Sewitch (1976) who recorded sleep-speeches in a similar manner i.e., without electrographic monitoring and under home conditions. Mean total word count, mental content and apparent affective tone were all similar. Several of his specimens possess features that I should like to quote in full because they have bearing on some of the matters discussed in earlier chapters here.

One of the speeches was "Th...there he comes. Yeah, there he comes...uh...what! he's riding past!...bah...to...to...Come, 1...let's walk it. Idiot!" The speaker recalled an associated dream and claimed that although in the dream scenario, it was she who produced most of the utterance it was her sister, and not herself who said "Idiot!" (In the dream they had been waiting at a bus-stop, and the driver passed them by without stopping.) This account adds to the small series of occurrences described on p. 292 (this volume) in which the sleep-talker speaks aloud words uttered by a different character in the dream. Such observations lend support to the dissociation hypothesis put forward in Chapter 17.

In Table 18.1 of this volume, a group of sleep-speeches are presented illustrating a variety of psycholinguistic pathologies. Heynick's sample contains 3 good examples of an undue repetition tendency:

1–"I want to decorate a tree, and then I'm going to decorate another tree, and then I'm going to decorate another tree and then I'm going to see how that tree is being decorated, and how it's being maintained."

2–"You...you...you...can'oot' (sic) them. Be quiet for a change. be...be...quiet...quiet for a change. No, not those...those...those...things."

3–And...and...the...those...those...those *feeperkins* (sic) that your cooping downstairs, those...those f...those *feeperkins,* that's it...that's something else again...what kind of stuff is that?...that, that, the...," (Note the interesting neologism "feeperkins").

Examples of ongoing self-monitoring during sleep-speech production are offered in Table 18.2. To these may be added the following from Heynick's sample: "Keep your hands off the vinyl, and keep your hands off *that...uh...those (?) tiles.* What are you, completely crazy? Vermin!"

The self-monitoring operation is denoted by the pause after "that" and the change to "those."

On p. 216 of this volume several sleep-speeches are presented which suggest that an hallucinated dialogue was in process. This common phenomenon in sleep-speech is also supportive of the dissociation perspective discussed in chapter 17. Here are 3 specimens from Heynick's sample:

1. "Before you go to that other side, you'll have finished this side before the ride. Right? (pause) No, I'm right! Huh?"

2. "It's always that way. Oh. Then we used to call it a shaving-brush."

3. "Wait a second, I hear something all of a sudden. Yeah,...(it was*) action and reaction."

It is valuable to have additional external corroboration or mutually consistent findings from several different laboratories studying the same area.

Heynick is planning more extensive sleep-talking research in the future and one may look forward to it with keen anticipation.

---

*These words "it was" were inferred by Heynick as having been excluded by the time lag of the voice trigger of the tape recorder.

APPENDIX 1

Content analysis scales for comparisons of NREM
mentation following sleep-speech and silent sleep.

CATEGORY SCALES—NREM MENTATION

I. Indications of visual experience.
   0 = No indications of visual experience present, e.g., "I was aware of a
   sweet taste and some rumbling sounds."
   1 = Possible visual imagery, i.e., a report *suggestive* of visual experience
   without specific mention of words clearly denoting visual processes,
   e.g., "I guess I was in a room—I think there was a rug on the floor and
   there may have been a chair."
   2 = Specific use of words unequivocably denoting visual processes, i.e.,
   reports mentioning seeing, watching, looking, in connection with one
   or two scenes, images, panoramas, pictures, etc; color, darkness, light,
   dimness.

II. Action: Mention of overt behavior of a human, animal, or object.
   0 = No act or specified behavior of any sort, e.g., "a rag."
   1 = Indication of a *passive* or *sessile* action: "A man was sitting at a desk,";
   "A cat was perched on a pedestal gazing attentively."

2 = Clearly indicated activity involving *movement* or change of position. "A monkey was walking on the grass."

3 = Maximal activity: "Children were rushing about in all directions, jumping all around, and climbing in and out of windows."

III. Characters.
   0 = No characters mentioned or implied.
   1 = *One* character clearly mentioned or strongly implied.
   2 = More than one character mentioned or strongly implied.
   3 = A group, party, gathering, crowd, etc.

IV. Self-Representation.
   0 = Self not mentioned—no specific mention of "I."
   1 = Specific mention of "I" but as an observer only.
   2 = Specific mention of self as participant, as actor, or object of action.

V. Bizarreness and incongruity (vs. the normal and usual).
   0 = Only everyday normal events or components.
   1 = Two or more normal components in unlikely combinations, e.g., "A tea kettle in the bathroom."
   2 = Unusual elements in unlikely combinations, e.g., "An oil painting of Popeye the Sailor in a neon light frame."
   3 = Fantastic thoughts and/or distorted images. "He had a waxed moustache with green scales and layers of rust on his hands—each finger was like a whistle and melodies issued from them."

VI. Interpersonal action.
   0 = No interpersonal action.
   1 = Some kind of interpersonal interaction.

VII. Emotion.
   0 = None mentioned.
   1 = Presence of mild or moderate emotion mentioned or implied.
   2 = Presence of strong emotion mentioned or implied.

VIII. Reference to laboratory or experimental situation.
   0 = Absence of any such reference.
   1 = Any direct or indirect reference to a laboratory or experimental situation.

IX. Work and/or school.
   0 = Absence of reference to work and/or school.
   1 = Any direct or indirect reference to work or school.

X. Changes of scene.
   0 = No clear scene.
   1 = One clear scene.
   2 = More than one clear scene.

XI. Elaborateness of narrative or story quality.
   0 = No elaboration.
   1 = Slight narrative or story quality.
   2 = Elaborate story-like narration.

XII. No mentation.
   0 = No ongoing mentation.
   1 = Ongoing mentation sensed but forgotten.
   2 = Strong sense of ongoing mentation but forgotten.

UTTERANCE—AURAL—VERBAL CONTENT SCALE

TO THE RATERS: We are interested in learning about the *frequency with which vocalization, references to printed or written words, and to nonvocal sounds occur in the mental experience of people while asleep.* You are being furnished with two collections of items:

1. A set of mentation reports elicited by awakening subjects who were asleep in the laboratory. These consist of what subjects recalled of what was going through their minds prior to being awakened.
2. A set of scoring categories and rules by which you are to classify each report. Each report is given *one and only one* score; and reports are scored in accordance with the following system of priorities:
   a. If a report qualifies for score ①, use score ① regardless of whether *it also* qualifies for the score categories ②, ③, ④, or ⑤.
   b. If a report does *not* qualify for score ① but *does* for score ②, use score ② regardless of whether it *also* qualifies for other score categories.
   c. Continue with same principle for other score categories.

These rules may not cover all cases. We are, after all, interested in determining how often do sleepers have experiences of themselves or others vocalizing, referring to words without vocalization and of other non-vocal sounds. Therefore, if you come across a report which contains a clear indication of actual vocalization or of an *act, verb* or *idiom usually associated with or implemented by vocalization,* use score ① or ② accordingly, even though we have not covered this in our examples. If you have doubts, use a "?"

after score ① or ② only, e.g. ① "?", or ② "?" and then place one alternate rating in parentheses.

Categories for Classifying Mentation Reports with Respect to Content Pertaining to Vocalization, Speech, Words, or Sounds

① Subject vocalizing in present or immediate past, i.e. any expression denoting that subject was in the midst of or had just finished talking or vocalizing during his sleep experience.

    a. "I was 'talking to'-, 'saying that'-, 'demanding', 'discussing', 'singing', 'laughing', 'asking', 'requesting', 'crying'" or *"We* were 'talking', 'jabbering', 'arguing', 'discussing', etc."; "He and I were saying'; 'We said that'-, I told him-'," etc.

    b. Use score ① even though the personal pronoun is omitted, e.g. the subject might say merely "talking to '*X*', or 'saying that', etc.

    c. Use score ① whenever the mentation report contains an *idiom* or synonym that denotes the subject to be thinking, daydreaming, or musing *audibly* in the present or immediate past.

    d. Use score ② whenever idioms are used that *usually* imply the use of spoken words such as "I was harsh with X" or *any other activity usually implemented or accompanied by vocalization.*

② Vocalization on the part of someone (human or animal) *other than the subject and not including the subject.* (If anything suggests tha the *subject* was vocalizing along with someone else, use score ①, e.g. "They were 'saying', 'talking to me', etc." (but no specific mention of or clear implication of the *subject vocalizing* as a participant). Use score ② whenever the report contains idioms which usually imply vocalization (or speech), e.g. "She was rude to him" or "they were sharp with me", etc.

③ Use score ③ whenever a reference to anticipated vocalization or *unspoken* words appears in the report, e.g. "The book title was Jehovah's Honeymoon," "The headlines said the moon contained signs of life," "I was just about to say yes."

④ Use score ④ whenever a reference to nonvocal and nonverbal sound appears in the report, e.g. "The bells rang," "The neighborhood was clangorous."

⑤ No vocal or sound reference.

Please read the *entire* report *carefully* before entering the category number. Use subscript *a* whenever rating 3 is based on anticipated vocalization, e.g., 3_a.

APPENDIX 2

A comprehensive presentation of known laboratory specimens of sleep-speech, related mentation reports and morning dream recall.

ORIENTATION

As stated in the introductory chapter, the goal of this book is the comprehensive assemblage of potentially useful scholarly material pertaining to sleep-utterance. It seems basic to the proper achievement of this goal to provide the interested student with a full presentation of the data base out of which most of the book grew. Accordingly, Appendix 2 contains almost all of the verbatim sleep-speeches recorded in the course of my own investigations, together with those of other researchers, as long as the sleep-speech had been recorded electrically or mechanically on the occasion of its utterance, and the concomitant electrographic events were known. The sole exclusions from my own data were numerous sleep-speeches uttered after posthypnotic suggestions by hypnosis subjects 1 and 2 as described in Chapter 11. These speeches were excluded because I felt that this was a specialized topic and the reader had been provided in the text with a sufficient number of sleep-speeches uttered under conditions of *effective* posthypnotic or ordinary nonhypnotic suggestion. Otherwise, *all* sleep-speeches from my own data pool were included, provided that at least *one* word was intelligible and that the associated type of sleep—NREM or REM—had been ascertained.

In addition, all sleep-speeches recorded by other investigators known to me were included. Thus, the sleep-speeches published by Fisher, Kahn, Edwards,

Davis, and Fine (1974), MacNeilage (1971), and Rechtschaffen, Goodenough, and Shapiro (1962) were included with the courteous permission of the authors. The macrodissociative speeches uttered by a patient during fugue states in sleep (Rice & Fisher, 1976) appear in the body of the text (Chapter 11). Finally, Horace Batson kindly permitted me to reproduce the macrodissociative speech of one of his subjects (speech 572).

GUIDE TO CONSTRUCTION, TERMINOLOGY, AND ABBREVIATIONS USED IN TABLE A.2

Column 1. Column 1, on the left, contains:

1. the coded initials serving as identification of the subject for reference purposes;

2. a number in the upper left-hand corner denoting the index number of the sleep-speech—thus, when in the text, reference is made to speech 32, it may be found by locating it in accordance with this number;

3. the type of sleep with which the utterance was associated, i.e., REM or NREM, and specific NREM sleep stages (1, 2, 3, or 4) where possible;

4. denotation as to whether the sleep-speech occurred during the first 3 hr of sleep, in which case the expression "1st 3 hours" will appear; otherwise it may be assumed that the utterance occurred afterward;

5. the experimental condition during which the sleep-speech was uttered:

a. B.L. = baseline night of sleep undisturbed by experimental intervention other than presleep application of electrodes. Thus, 1st B.L. = the first baseline night, 3rd B.L. = the third baseline night, and so on.

b. T.B.L. = in several instances, studies were conducted in which the experimental schedule called for an additional baseline series at the end of the study for purposes of assessing the effects of experimental variables; i.e., they were terminal baseline nights or T.B.L., e.g. 2nd T.B.L. = the second night of a T.B.L. series.

c. W.U. = wake-up nights, i.e., nights in which the subject was awakened for experimental purposes, such as obtaining mentation reports.

d. B.L. + W.U. = baseline nights during which the sole experimental intervention was awakening the subject for mentation reports. Thus, 2nd B.L. + W.U. = the 2nd night of a series in which the subject was requested to sleep as normally as possible with the sole addition of a variable number of wake-ups for mentation reports.

e. U-HYP = unsuccessful attempts at inducing presleep hypnosis. As indicated in Chapter 11, the greater proportion of subjects in the work on posthypnotically stimulated sleep-talking appeared truly refractory to attempts to induce a hypnotic trance. These subjects, nevertheless, often uttered sleep-speech. It seemed reasonable and useful to include these sleep-speeches in the appendix labeled accordingly, for they seemed indistinguishable both electrographically and phenomenologically from "normal" spontaneous sleep-speech. Thus, 3rd B.L. + U-HYP = the third in a series of nights following the initial B.L. series in which presleep induction of a hypnotic trance was attempted without success, and during which night the subject's sleep was otherwise undisturbed.

   f. PHS = a night in which a presleep posthypnotic suggestion had been given. In all instances included in Appendix 2, there was no convincing evidence of presleep hypnotic trance induction or effectiveness of any posthypnotic suggestion. Thus, all sleep-speeches so denoted in Appendix 2 should be distinguished from those sleep-speeches following PHS presented in Chapter 11 as examples of successful use of PHS or nonhypnotic suggestion in stimulating sleep-speech production.

   g. Recovery night = nights *without* presleep administration of drugs on laboratory nights but following one to three previous consecutive nights at home with presleep ingestion of a *d*-amphetamine–barbiturate mixture for REM deprivation (see chapter 11).

Column 2.   Column 2, second from the left, contains what could be discerned of the actual sleep-speech on the tape recording. In reproducing these, the following conventions were used:

1. A question mark in parentheses indicates that the preceding word was not enunciated or recorded with crystal clarity but was nevertheless intelligible. Sometimes the question mark is preceded by more than one word and the entire group is contained in a larger set of parentheses. This indicates that the entire larger enclosed group was "fuzzy" but still intelligible. Thus, in the speech "(That was (?)) really beautiful", the two words, "that was," though not sharply enunciated, were intelligible.

2. A question mark *not* contained within parentheses indicates, as in standard prose, an interrogative expression.

3. "Mbl" denotes speech that is mumbled and hence completely unintelligible.

4. [p] indicates a long pause; — indicates a short pause.

5. Italics in a verbal expression in the sleep speech and/or mentation report column denote a special feature to which the reader's attention is drawn, such as the words on which a concordance categorization was based in the event that such basis was not obvious, or clang associations, repetitions, etc. By contrast, material spelled out entirely in capital letters denotes an occasion of the *subject's* spontaneous inflectional emphasis in the expression. In the event that a special feature receives such inflectional emphasis, it is spelled in capitals and italicized as well.

Column 3.   Column 3, third from the left, contains either the subject's mentation reports obtained on awakening the subjects shortly after sleep-utterance, or else the subject's morning recall of his or her dreams. As in Column 2, italics indicate a feature of special interest and the conventions set forth are similarly followed here.

Column 4.   Column 4, fourth from the left, draws attention to noteworthy items such as relevant personal information about the subject (serving to provide a background for some of the sleep-speech content), the concordance categorization of the sleep-speech–mentation-report pair, the rationale of such categorization in each case, and the other items of interest.[1]

When postsleep-speech mentation reports are obtained immediately after sleep-utterance, categorizations of concordance in accordance with the scheme presented in Chapter 10 are obviously useful. However, such categorizations were not routinely employed when assessing sleep-speeches in relation to morning dream recall data because of the greater likelihood of temporal misattribution of a specific sleep-speech to a specific dream retrieved in morning recall. It has been shown that mentation reports collected over the course of a single night often possess commonalities both as to theme and specific content items (Rechtschaffen, 1963a). This finding suggests the possibility that a sleep-speech–*morning*-recall pair, appearing clearly susceptible to categorization as first-order concordance, could in fact have resulted from persistence of a nocturnal preoccupation throughout the night rather than from a close temporal relationship between a sleep-speech and a dream. Therefore, concordance between a sleep-speech and morning recall was scored occasionally only if there was unambiguous first-order concordance, and it seemed of interest to bring such occurrences to the attention of the interested reader. Thus, attempts to systematically categorize sleep-speech and morning recall were not carried out.

---

[1]When Appendix 2 was prepared, these categorizations were rescored anew. Therefore, there are possibly slight but trivial differences between these categorizations and those as tabulated in Chapter 10, which reproduce the tabulations from my original publication on this topic, (Arkin, Toth, Baker, & Hastey, 1970a).

TABLE A.2

Catalogue of Sleep Speeches and Associated Features
Collected Under Laboratory Conditions

Sleep Speech No., Associated Sleep Stage Occurence during 1st 3 hrs. of Sleep, and Laboratory Night Specifications	Sleep-Speech	Mentation Report or Morning Recall of Dreams	Noteworthy Features and Comments
1. Subject: S.R.			*S was a former U.S. paratrooper and a film and literature major.*
1 Stage 2 1st 3 hrs. 1st B.L.	"Air parade. . .(no-um-deelat (?) [bland, low intensity, slow rate] ."	Morning recall: "A dream in which I was talking with someone."	
2 Stage REM 1st 3 hrs. 1st T.B.L. after PHS series	"Le langue Francais mais non— je vous en pris—voila."	Morning recall: "One dream, I'm sure took place in *France* because I can remember speaking *French*." A second dream was about the experiment.	Subject was studying and practicing elementary French by day. First-order concordance.
3 Stage REM 1st 3 hrs. 1st T.B.L.	"C'est vrai—[P]—I don't call you anything—[P]—oh, shut up."	Morning recall: as in speech 2.	
4 Stage NREM 1st T.B.L.	"Gathering around (?) Mrs. Johnson."	Morning recall: as in speech 2.	

5
Stage REM
1st T.B.L.

"Mm—hmm—baseball high (?) hit two in the infield."

Morning recall: as in speech 2.

6
Stage REM
2nd T.B.L.

"I wonder if, he's going to attempt to sit down there—mbl."

Morning recall: an elaborate dream about his mother visiting him in the Vietnam combat zone to bring him cookies.

7
Stage NREM
1st 3 hrs
3rd T.B.L.

"Mbls—all the rest went to me —I'm NOT glubb (?) [3 moans] poor little bugger—I'd do anything to lick (?) a *film* class tch, tch, tch well—hm—Dear Bob, it was interesting—mm— [P] — wierd (?) [P] —mm—hm—that, of course, is a TV viewer's discount book (?) and that's just as easy as HELL to refute—if you want me to—don't you want to be my *buddy*—hm? mbl—looks good— that's the way of the philosopher —mm but like all good things— came to an end—that's not a bad line—[yawn]—if I knew just when

Although speeches 7–14 were all preceded by typical NREM sleep, the electrographic concomitants of these vocalizations were not typical. There was a great deal of muscle-tension artifact and the subject was a poor wakeful alpha producer, making valid assessment of sleep stage versus wakefulness impossible. The psychophysiological context, extended duration of

Morning recall: "One dream (I think it was about a trip to *France*—actually not a trip to *France*. It took place on a barge traveling down the Seine— a barge quite similar to the one in L'Atlante, a *French film* of the early '30s. Some of the passengers were Michele Simon, my roommate Tony, Duke Christie (an old *buddy* from the Airborne), and a girl I've seen somewhere before but cannot place, I don't remember most of what transpired but one image was rather clear—I was sitting on the fantail

As indicated earlier, strict application of our rules for scoring concordance would require that this pair be categorized as first order concordance, because of the words "buddy" and "film" appearing in the texts of both; further evidence of concordance is found in the French words at the end of the speech, and the references to France in the dream. Yet, because of the long interval between sleepspeech and morning recall, other explanations of the results are possible, such as the speech and a remotely subsequent dream being derived inde-

sleepspeeches, and morning amnesia for the occurrences qualify them for the category of sleep-related macrodissociative episodes.

8
Stage NREM
1st 3 hrs
3rd T.B.L.

—assessezasseiez vous, *mais vous etes bien sur tour.*"

"Mm—after a while, hard to tell —mm—I just wondered if my snow job was getting to be just a little bit less than my—know job [P] don't get carried away now, cause—tch—tch—it's only out there you know with the cover out for you—I got a philosophy at home that's BIGGER—oh! Myah!— so look (?) [P]—well—what kind of proof would you like? Heh, heh! O.K. [yawn]—yah—that can be quite cute—little fight— O.K.—we'll figure out something

with my feet in the water (an impossibility on anything larger than a skiff), eating Hershey's chocolate kisses, and flipping the tinfoil into the Seine. I also feel *I talked* in my sleep during this dream.

"I only remember that the other dream was very sad. This is only a feeling—the dream itself remains a mystery to me."

The subject, after hearing the huge amount of sleepspeech on the tapes later on, was visibly surprised and taken aback by the quantity.

Morning recall:
as in speech 7.

pendently from the same preoccupation or theme. Notice also the relative incoherence of the speech as a whole, the yawn toward the end suggestive of a macrodissociative episode, and the frequent silliness. The subsequent speeches uttered on this night are mostly similar in these respects.

Note the many similarities between speeches 7-14 and the recurrent reference to philosophy and the general silliness and incoherence of the speeches as a whole, as well as their vivid "lived-in" quality. All of these exemplify macrodissociation.

9
Stage NREM
1st 3 hrs
3rd T.B.L.

–anything you'd like me to tell her?–O.K.–let's see–well–I guess I'd better do some–some of the old pattern? pat (?) in the optimistic things like never determine anything before you put your enemy at least uncon-scious–uh–at LEAST mm–mm – [yawn]."

"Mm–hm–and [P] and I mbls –mbl–it was try–that is the trouble with philosophy–and uh you can smash them up too– that–that's show biz or phil-osophy biz is however you want to call it–it's fun–at any rate– aah–the boys know a little more –wrapped it all up and said, "That's YOU" and they pointed this kind of head and I said "Oh, well," uh–tch– crazy–but you got to take her to Sunday School–and you know the word is YES–it said

Morning recall: as in speech 7.

See previous comments of speeches 7-9. Note the italicized phrase "ooarico ungarico–some-thing or other." It is suggestive of the operation of speech-monitor-ing mechanisms during this episode; i.e., the subject gave evidence of "dissatisfaction" with his speech output and provided a spontaneous indication of it.

it's an all inclusive–all pliable
HEAD–just–you know put it in
your pocket–be careful when
you come to adhesives and it
worked out just fine and uh–
except the weather changed on
me and you know [whistles and
prolonged yawns] mbl–the part
about–*aa–ee–ooarico–ungarico–
something or other*, it's a pity
my brains isn't working in the
old channels–tch–tch–tch–
switch at least to channel 4–
unh."

10
Stage NREM
1st 3 hrs.
3rd T.B.L.

"Mm–mm [said many times] |–
there he is at **Pete Kellar**'s–oh!
sure wish I'd mbl–oh–mbl–
pahsing fahncy [English accent]
mbl spessing fency [Yiddish
accent] mbl from philosophy we
never, never know–it's a chuckle
in my mandorin sleeve–however,
I'm not chucking–except
physically–aw–let's see–I think
I'm too tired to even get a–
mbl–even if I just shut one eye
–tch, tch, tch,–looks beauti-
fully–anyway–be a man to do
that, otherwise I'm going to
conk out [3-4 phrases in French]
mn–hm [P] mbls."

Morning recall:
as in speech 7.

11
Stage NREM
1st 3 hrs
3rd T.B.L.

"False—mbl—false—falsely made and checks there (?) falsely made (?) doctrine—which, of course, like philosophy—to be written and changed and put in a little book or piece of paper—professed and changed within a matter of hours—changed like the ideology of a book—but—uh—Descartes did a refutation—of perhaps the even the possibility—the adding knowledge for our (?) possibility of completing a real act of philosophy—in toto and uninterrupted—made him put up his hands and say 'Well, all right'—aah! looks at dramatos (?) might even read his way through James Agee—but I'm saving—I'll give it to the other White Knight when [yawn] we have to because—uh—Suds (?) and all the other scholars."

Morning recall: as in speech 7.

12
Stage NREM
1st 3 hrs.
3rd T.B.L.

"Whatever it is, I dood it but I'm not sorry—mm—mm—hm— yeah, don't worry about it—mbls —mbls—mbls—your little attitude out there—ah!—it might be mbl— ah! [P] mbl—hm—mbl—ah!"

Morning recall: as in speech 7.

13
Stage NREM
1st 3 hrs.
3rd T.B.L.

"Ah—yes! [P] —mm—disproving a philosophic theory with my head— [makes spitting noise and whistle to make a sound resemb- ling a gun shooting and a bullet whine] —to mbl—Victor's— Borge's style and eh—and it can also be done holding a [whistle 3 times] mbl—machine's fit— only after proper discernation— and disability—mbl—it goes kind of like [same gun and bullet whine noise as above] and you take that and bury it—oh! I have a question from the back row—Mr. Ike (?)—Dr. I.Q.—Dr. I.Q. and what is the question?— looks like a world destroyer— vision? Vision you dunt gat [spoken in a Jewish accent] — now it's just one of those things you have to take on faith—no Virginia—very nice—mbl [P] mm—hm."

Morning recall: as in speech 7.

14
Stage NREM
1st 3 hrs.
3rd T.B.L.

"Mbl—I don't know—lousy—mbl which is long, as its going (?) [laughter] damn convenient—I think I'll look behind it—mbl— a very handy thing it looks like a mother—if you stretch things a bit and you're some kind of mother anyway right now—ah! I had made a progression (?) after the regression—stuff up to stuffing back—not bad, eh?— anyway—if you pardon that bit of self-regarding—there's a lot of books in there that'll teach you how—to do absolutely nothing— to teach you how to do it—got a Machiavelli and uh—know about Machiavelli and all I can say is that there's only one Prince and Machiavelli created him and that's just the half of it—with luck, you'll never find out the whole of it—O.K.—so I think we've gotten to the sweet role—Sweden (?)—well—let's see—mm [scratch-

Morning recall: as in speech 7.

404

15
Stage NREM
1st 3 hrs.
3rd T.B.L.

noise] –I just can't think of any-thing more earth shattering than– [yawn–sounds of movement] [P] mbl."

"Mbl–cat (?)–mbl–tch,–tch–hm–hm–not until he's hatched (?) [P] mbls [P] mbl–he had to fight for it–read (?) them there books to use the vernacular– from which I never had to pro-ceed (?) hm."

Morning recall: as in speech 7.

16
Stage NREM
1st 3 hrs.
3rd T.B.L.

"Smoosch! (?)–hm–hm–mm–mere! tout est majestre (?) commes les autres–ah!–sous tour, sans vie (?) sans tu (?)– ah!–que vous le *Seine* (?) [P] Part 2–The Agony and the Ecstasy scene 1–the opening of the play–mm–".

Morning recall: as in speech 7.

Note the clear reference to a French film, reference to the Seine, and French words in both sleep-speech and morning recall.

17
Stage NREM
1st 3 hrs.
3rd T.B.L.

"Thursday–you take the subway (?) ?"

Morning recall: as in speech 7.

For the remainder of this night, the speeches were more typically microdissociative in scale.

18
Stage NREM
3rd T.B.L.

"Mbl–I heard that–I believe it too–it'll be (?) the one time of the year I was in sometime (?) Scandinavians–ohh!–mbl– work came from."

Morning recall: as in speech 7.

19
Stage NREM
3rd T.B.L.

"Voici (?)–vous est intelligent (?)–plus intelligent voici–tout tel–mbl."

Morning recall: as in speech 7.

20
Stage NREM
3rd T.B.L.

"Hm–the Odyssey it's a good name for a shop–mbl–I arrived only for the Odyssey phase, however."

Morning recall: as in speech 7.

21
Stage NREM
3rd T.B.L.

"Mbl–that's the way it's gotta be blocked– right smack in front (?). Kenneth."

Morning recall: as in speech 7.

22
Stage NREM
3rd T.B.L.

"Hm?–hm–thank you."

Morning recall: as in speech 7.

23
Stage NREM
3rd T.B.L.

"I'll buy that–mbl."

Morning recall: as in speech 7.

24
Stage NREM
3rd T.B.L.

"(Believe me (?)– I don't ask."

Morning recall: as in speech 7.

406

25 Stage REM 3rd T.B.L.	"Bobby Benson— B bar B."	Morning recall: as in speech 7.
26 Stage NREM 1st 3 hrs. 4th T.B.L.	"Mbl–be careful it's a conspiracy (?)–not just yet–mbl."	Morning recall: "In one of the dreams I can recall discussing the pain threshold of Lawrence of Arabia with someone. Another dream had something to do with driving around in Los Angeles."
27 Stage NREM 1st 3 hrs 4th T.B.L.	"Mm [P] yeah [the latter word was whispered]."	Morning recall: as in speech 26.
28 Stage NREM 1st 3 hrs. 4th T.B.L.	"Whose?"	As in speech 26.
29 Stage NREM 1st 3 hrs. 4 T.B.L.	"Mbl much better (?)."	As in speech 26.
30 Stage NREM 1st 3 hrs. 4th T.B.L.	"Why? (?)–mm–MM [as though objecting to something]."	As in speech 26.

407

31
Stage NREM
4th T.B.L.

"This WAY (?)—not you—mbl."

As in speech 26.

32
Stage NREM
4th T.B.L.

"Tear up (?)—right?"

As in speech 26.

33
Stage NREM
4th T.B.L.

"I don't want it."

As in speech 26.

34
Stage NREM
1st 3 hrs.
5th T.B.L.

"Mbls—Mr. Worzen—perhaps put some—mbls—but—mbls—when the papers are down and the chips are in, you are my favorite—uh! [changed position and grunted] — whatever you call."

Morning recall: "Tony, my roommate and C. Judson, my ex-roommate, and D. Christie, a friend from the Army, were up at Vassar for some kind of dance —and I didn't seem to stay at the dance long—I went wandering around and I'm not exactly certain what happened—I just remember one thing—I got a package somebody said, 'Package for Mr. R,' and it was full of cookies, and candies and things and it was

408

from Mary Jane Shlook or something—I don't know—some weird
last name—very German and very
long—and she happened to be
there at the dance and she also
asked me if I wanted a ride home
and when I said—uh—Oh, I have
to ask oh, yeah—I guess Mac was
there, too and Tom—and I said
I have to ask Mac, Tom and
Tony if they would all want to
go home—I did and they said,
'Well, not now,' and so she said,
'Why don't I cook you a nice
home-cooked dinner,' and I said,
'Here at Vassar? What are you
going to use for food?' and she
said 'use the food in the package
you haven't finished it.' and so
we did."

| 35
Stage NREM
1st 3 hrs.
5th T.B.L. | "[coughs twice] Mbl—time and all that—[P] I was sittin' waitin' for you to go—I [P] Ooh!—how long can you DO it?" | Morning recall:
as in speech 34. |
| 36
Stage NREM
5th T.B.L. | "[coughs] Mbls—a great big book." | Morning recall:
as in speech 34. |

2. *Subject: N.D.*

S was a college
English student.

37 Stage 3 1st 3 hrs. 1st B.L.	"(I don't know lower fishes (?))–hellooo! (?)–fishes?–mbl VERY FUNNY fishes?–FLASHES–*nadjes* (?)–FUNNY FLASHES–I JUST SAW–I JUST SAW–SAW FUNNY, RED YELLOW and bigger (?) and YELLOW that's FUNNY [P] I don't know why (?) [spoken in an excited, rapid, poorly controlled, somewhat explosive manner]."	Morning recall: "I was dreaming this morning when I awoke but I can't remember what.–However, just an aura of it remains, like a frame without a picture–."	Noteworthy in the sleep-speech itself is the alliterative perseveration, references to visual images with color, severe linguistic disorganization, and a possible neologism "nadjes (?)."
38 Stage 4 1st 3 hrs. 1st B.L.	"Mbls–everybody (?) [spoken rapidly and unclearly]."	Morning recall: as in speech 37.	
39 Stage 4 1st 3 hrs. 2nd B.L.	"[moans] Mm–mm–the only–mbl–it might break is the only one the old one?–it looks like it might break but it *zasbreak*."	Morning recall: "I had a very clear dream of which I can only remember it taking place in or around a theater and the word 'entertainment' seems uppermost."	Noteworthy once more is the tendency to alliterative perseveration, linguistic disorganization, and the neologism "zasbreak."

40 Stage 4 1st 3 hrs. 1st B.L. + W.U.	"Oh—Joe (?) mm—I had it— I had it—oh, I had it—mm."	Mentation report: "Yes—um—*I had it* all arranged for to tell you uh—ohh—um—at a party—I was gonna be a host and, and Alex was coming to a party and J was getting ready to invite him, and I spent a lot of time making sure that, that (?) surroundings would be pleasant."	First order concordance on the basis of "I had it" appearing in both sleep-speech and mentation report. It is difficult to say whether the repetition of "I had it" should be considered as perseveration or the sort of repetition that frequently accompanies enthusiasm.
41 Stage 2 1st B.L. + W.U.	"Mm—(Mike Fallan (?)) all (covered by the (?)) statement [P] yessir."	Mentation report: 'Dream—about—what um—Wilson no—Woodrow Wierdo [sic] Wheelson um—some poet, I don't know exactly who—and *I are arguing* about a woman."	Third order concordance on the basis of subject describing himself as "arguing" in the mentation report
42 Stage 2 2nd B.L. + W.U.	"Generally (?) speaking— generally speaking the—the um CAR is better."	Mentation report elicited by "dialogue method": *E*: "Better than what Dave?" *S*: "What?" *E*: "The car is better than what?" *S*: "Oh—than anything else I guess—can't think of what else—it's very good." *E*: "What was going through your mind?" *S*: "Um—some kind of a *discussion*—um—and I had, I was sitting in an armchair or something, and I reached a conclusion or it was—I felt as if—	First order concordance based on "car" and "better" appearing in both sleep speech and mentation report. Noteworthy also is the visual imagery of hallucinatory intensity implied by the experience of the girls' presence and participation in a dialogue in a living-room setting.

I was certain about this— and I *very calmly and very perfunctorily said*—that *the car*, whatever I said before, *is better* and there was a girl present, sitting near me, in this living-room setting—mmm and I had a feeling she —she—er—was not of my opinion at first—but that I was convincing her somehow."

43
Stage 4
2nd B.L. + W.U.

"Mm—uh—duh—she—shad—hero sher—uh—sher—sheril—S—H—A—W [spelled out aloud by *S*] takes part—loses but lost—uh—invincible as u as usual—mbl."

Mentation report:

E: "What's going through your mind?"

S: "Nothing especially more than that."

E: "You say you can't recall anything?"

S: "Nothing more than what I've said."

E: "What did you say?"

S: "Um—about uh—that the gangster um—the uneasiness of the feeling that there were gangsters [P] and so on."

No discernible concordance. Noteworthy are the apparent repeated attempts to utter the final target word without success. In "desperation," the subject spelled it out S—H—A—W. Also striking is the linguistic disorganization and the suggestion that the subject believed that he had already given a mentation report when in fact he hadn't.

44 Stage 4 1st 3 hrs. 3rd B.L. + W.U.	"Oh—mbl—what was it?"	Mentation report: "Nothing in particular—all sorts of things um —books—all kinds of scattered things— nothing special.	No discernible concordance.
45 Stage 4 3rd B.L. + W.U.	"Gundrum [sic] is the word for HUNdred in—hundred—in hundred in—s—hundred in s—Latin— Latin—to HUNdred."	Mentation report: "Um—I don't know, I wasn't paying attention—I—was kind of listening to what you had to say there—that's strange."	(1) the neologism GUNDRUM; (2) the perseveration and linguistic disorganization; and (3) the subject was awakened 8 seconds after the last word of the sleep-speech; a speech in which there was a labored repeated attempt to say aloud a simple sentence. Yet the subject reports paradoxically that he "wasn't paying attention" and "listening to what [*E*] had to say." Such observations are in accord with the dissociation perspective set forth in Chapter 17.
46 Stage NREM 1st 3 hrs. Recovery night following one previous night on a *d*-amphetamine-pentobarbital combination.	"*David*—I *day* David that *you*— that's *you* that *day—dated—day —dravid—dave dravid* about 25 or 30 *noked naked day dreams*— the second dream tie it all up— *you kept bouncing them on— you kept bouncing them on and on as if you had a regular meter.*"	Not awakened.	Note the striking perseverative tendencies with clang associations, and severe linguistic disorganization.
47 Stage 2 Recovery night as in speech 46.	"Together with the usual number of *parts*, joints that is, where bones fit together."	Mentation report: "Mm—um— not very clearly, I'm not thinking clearly at all. [P] All my	First order concordance. Noteworthy is the appearance of "part" in the sleep-speech and the same sound

thoughts are *fragmented*—
which is not usually the case
but I'm very tired—um—I was
thinking in *part* about my
roommate and his girl friend, and
she's always over the *apart*—at
the, the *apart*ment; she's always
there, so much so that he
doesn't even have time to do
his work—mm."

element in three separate places in
the mentation report as well as in 3
separate semantic contexts— a portion, i.e., "part"; a group of pieces,
i.e. "fragmented"; and as a syllable
in a related word, i.e. "apartment."

3. Subject: M.R.

S was a college student.

48
Stage 3
1st 3 hrs.
1st B.L.

"Not THAT ballroom—mbl
[spoken intensely]."

Morning recall: "There were a
lot of people having a coffee
break. It had to do with this
experiment. There were more
than us three. I was talking to a
man. You came in with sheets
with names of future people in
the experiment. You asked somebody if you thought they would
fit the requirements of this
experiment. Then all the people
filed out of the room except me
and this man. I had a vague feeling there was one woman in the
group I didn't like."

49
Stage REM
1st B.L.

"You'll have to—you're gonna have tuss [sic]—(if you don't (?))—I'll lay a *chair* over your *head*—mbl—leave them up—you leave them up!—I'll bust your BUTT!—mbl [uttered with great intensity and angry tone]."

Morning recall equivalent to a mentation report because the associated sleep-speech was uttered at the end of the fourth and last REMP of the night: "In a repeat performance of 'Merry Wives of Windsor,' as I was putting on my costume, I met J.K. (a figure from my prep school days). He said he had been in the Reserves and that's why he had the utilities on. That made sense. He invited me down about nine flights of stairs to a subbasement in the theatre to get some new piece of costume. When I got back, the curtain was up, and not remembering at one moment all my entrances and exits, I panicked. I had an intricate make-up job and just couldn't do anything right. I could hear Falstaff up on the stage bellowing away and I was shot through with fear that I wouldn't be there in time. I decided to take my make-up off, as it started caking and cracking, and blobbed a gigantic blob of alboline on my face. Then some big, powerful guy whom I

First-order concordance based on obvious detailed correspondence of incident in sleep-speech and dream, as well as the words "chair" and "head" in common. Noteworthy also is the correct surmise of having actually talked in his sleep, and his description of his experience as "almost" hearing himself. This is of further interest because his speech was quite loud.

knew was a Mormon was trying
to help me keep my sleeves up
and out of the water. I told him
I'd bash him one in the head—
with *a chair. I think I talked
here because I woke up and almost heard myself.*

50
Stage REM
3rd B.L.

"In from (?) enemy's silence (?)
—mbl—enemy's SILENCE."

Morning recall: "One dream was
about war. I was crawling in the
desert among tanks. They
weren't firing; in fact, I didn't
even know if they were occupied.
I finally reached my lines only to
have them all open up. [P] Also
dreamed of swimming in ocean
with D. Lots of surf; some boat-
ing; some diving; I think I may
have talked here but I may have
dreamed it."

Second-order concordance based on
items pertaining to war appearing in
both sleep-speech and mentation report.

51
Stage NREM
1st B.L. + W.U.

"God almighty [this was
whispered]."

The subject was not awakened
after this speech. His morning
recall included: "I don't think I
talked last night although I had a
stentorian dream and I should

have. Halfway through the dream I wondered if I was talking. I was trumpeting to the world what a fine fellow I was."

52
Stage REM
2nd B.L. + W.U.

"Hmph—mbls—let it grow (?)."

Mentation report elicited 1 min. after sleep-speech: "Oh—hello—right before you woke me, I was thinking about athletics. I was thinking about particularly track and field—there were five sort of all time champions practicing track and various weight throws—strange different weights—not real things. I was out watching them—and uh—one of the things was you threw this weight—kinda like a hammer throw except as soon as it hit the ground—he started pulling it back—then he'd scream 'Gee!' and flip it to the right, or 'Haw' and flip it to the left; and just before that happened, I was standing on shore with C—looking at an incapacitated windjammer—and then *we both said*, 'How about the Captain's ship—he must be back by now.' "

Third-order concordance based on subject's describing self as saying "We both said [etc.]"

53
Stage 2
2nd B.L. + W.U.

"Mm!!! Over there:—a terrifying experience—mbls—dog Scotty—[spoken with tense excitement]."

Mentation report 15 sec. after sleep-speech: "Yah! kind of a wild thing. I opened my eyes exactly as you hit that buzzer—

No discernible concordance.

which is sort of interesting—uh—
this time, I was thinking about
sort of buildings here in New
York City—how some of them
are pretty and some are ugly—
and that whole thing I just did—
that bit [a play] at one of the
museums here in New York City
—about feeling ugly, and New
York being sort of a bland, hide-
ous place there."

54
Stage REM
2nd B.L. + W.U.

"Tar (?) smells sort of like
Cassius Clay's armpit and
old Prein's snatch."

Mentation report elicited 1 min.
after sleep-speech: "Oh boy—
yah—I was going through a
turnstile in a subway and put 35
cents in for a hamburger—well,
it was kind of silly of me but I
didn't realize you couldn't get a
hamburger from a turnstile, so I
went to the lady in the booth
who I told my problem; and she
said I'd have to sign a whole
bunch of papers and I'd get my
15 or 20 cent back in the mail—
big deal so I watched them come

No discernible concordance. However, see Chapters 10 and 15 for a
discussion of concordance based on
psychoanalytic considerations. That
is, the lady in the subway booth
may be a derivative of an unconscious cloaca fantasy also signified
in the sleep-speech by "old Prein's
snatch."

through—then someone else popped into my group—an age difference—sort of funny—2 years, 12 years, 1 month, no years, 26 days."

55 Stage REM 2nd B.L. + W.U.	"Wait a minute."	Subject was not awakened after this speech. Morning recall included the following dream: I thought it was time to get up before it was and I took all the tape and electrodes off my face. I awoke in panic for a moment fearing reprisal but the electrodes were still in place."	No discernible concordance. However, the reference to time in both speech and report suggests a second-order concordance. The sleep-speech was uttered during the fourth and last REMP of the night.
56 Stage 3-4 1st 3 hrs. 4th B.L. + W.U.	"How much money——mbls—mbls."	Mentation report: "I don't think I can remember."	No recall.
57 Stage REM 4th B.L. + W.U.	"Mm—hmm [P] (I have it; Here again (?)), you find many startling similarities."	Mentation report: "I remember distinctly in my sleep, *I was speaking* about just one guy—one guy—sort of over and over again. I was just thinking about my mother's bed at home, which is a single, and being in bed with Maria D.—and oh God, I remember taking some of this nonsense I've got on me—some of the electrodes off, because I had the electrodes on there too, but they	Third-order concordance based on "I was speaking" in the mentation report.

were evil somehow, I had to un-
do the last electrode which was
sealed on to my head like with
bishop's sealing wax, and I broke
that."

*S was a premedical student
employed part-time in a
department store.*

5. Subject: L.H.

58 Stage NREM 1st 3 hrs. 1st B.L.	"We said to each other—mbl— have time—dinner—mbls."	Morning recall: no dreams remembered.	
59 Stage NREM 1st B.L.	"Don't worry—don't worry— mbl."	Same as speech 58.	
60 Stage NREM 1st B.L.	"I wish I had some water (?)."	Same as speech 58.	
61 1st 3 hrs 2nd B.L.	"[moans]—Can't stand her!— cran't stand her!—crank stand her!—cran't stand it! [sic]—	Morning recall: "Dreamt that I was eating in a restaurant when a group of people came in led	Of interest is the expression of hos- tility toward a girl in the sleep- speech and toward a girl he "dis-

I'm tired (?)" [said with an agitated driven quality]"

by a *girl who I knew and disliked.* They insisted on sitting at my table and they were terrible company. They told me about their party that their friends gave for them to which I didn't come because I did not receive an invitation sent to me on time. Their friends turned out to be very good friends of mine and I was annoyed that my friends didn't give me the invitation."

liked" in the morning recall. Note the perseveration, intense anger, and verbal errors, e.g. "cran't" and "crank" for can't.

"Mbls—(I can't change without a *credit slip*—mbls (?))."

Morning recall:
1. "One very long dream that continued through awakenings—starts out as myself and two friends are driving through the snow to get to a ski resort. We finally arrive at Killington, Vermont, and we go to the only hotel in town. We obtain lodging and sit around the lobby for a while. I have forgotten my draft card and so we can't go drinking. Instead, we go to the indoor pool where we swim. We can't remember which room is ours and, indeed, we never really find out. We meet some girls skiing and there there is a controversy as to how long we should

Of interest are the references to money in both sleep-speech and morning recall in three of the four dreams recalled.

stay and *a settling of accounts
as to who owes what to whom.*
The continuity is broken when I
awaken.

2. "Same characters, but we are
back in New York and all are
working together. The friend I
went swimming with (the pool
was full of people and resembled
the Columbia pool) told me that
he got me a date for *$5.* I was
angry, feeling that if he brought
her around without a *price tag*
and I liked her, nothing would
stop me from taking her out,
while if I didn't like her, nothing
would induce me to take her out.
I woke up again.

3. "This friend and I are looking
for someplace in Manhattan to
have a quick lunch. We decide
on a hot dog place. My other
friend is waiting outside. It
seems I have been neglecting him
for the one I am with. I woke
up."

4. "The next day we eat lunch in a very busy sandwich place and *walk out without paying the bill.* As we walk off, I casually, my friend a little nervous, we decide to eat there more often. I woke up."

63 Stage 4 1st 3 hrs. 3rd B.L.	"Mbl—*oh, come on now*—boy! Jesus Christ! You guys are special—mbl—mbl [spoken with irritation]."	Morning recall: as in speech 62	Of interest is the sleep-speech expression of vigorous sentiment toward companions and to a *controversy* in the morning recall.
64 Stage 4 3rd B.L.	"[moans]—"I'm happy (?) to start—mbls—just take one off (?)—mbls."	Morning recall: as in speech 62	
65 Stage 4 3rd B.L.	"Mbls—(how much does (?))—what do you want to travel for—*how much does he want to sell them for*and as much as you can get [groan] exASPERATING—mbl."	Morning recall: as in speech 62.	Of interest are the references to money in sleep-speech and morning recall.
66 Stage 2 3rd B.L.	"Mbl—forty years—mmm."	Morning recall: as in speech 62.	
67 Stage 4 1st 3 hrs. 4th B.L.	*"I wanna take a net—a note—a note—a note-pa duh—uh—duh—shit!—I mean—you know*—I'd like a nice pillow, you know—with a	Morning recall: "I was outside typing an essay for a medical school application on an electrical typewriter. I was combin-	Noteworthy is the perseverative tendency toward an apparent linguistic target with an exasperated self-correction in the first part of

424

nice trim (?) blanket—a pillow, that came up over my shoulders— that was tucked in a little bit— that would be very nice—take away some of the steam (?), you know (living in (?)) the drudgery, you know—she was never—uh— mbl—hot stuff but uh—mbl."

ing two different rough drafts in- to one finished paper. A wo- man waiting for a bus kept push- ing the foot pedal of the type- writer and became annoying. I told her to stop and we argued. I insulted her and she stopped. We then argued for a while. I was never heated or very serious at any time. I just wanted her to go away."

the speech, as indicated by the words italicized.

68
Stage NREM
1st 3 hrs
4th B.L.

"All right."

Morning recall:
as in speech 67.

69
Stage NREM
1st 3 hrs.
4th B.L.

"Mbl—yes—go ahead!"

Morning recall:
as in speech 67.

70
Stage NREM
1st 3 hrs.
4th B.L.

"Mbls—I—I—piece—mbl."

Morning recall:
as in speech 67.

71 Stage NREM 4th B.L.	"Mm—Mbls—say (?)—uh—mbl—yeah—that's it."	Morning recall: as in speech 67.
72 Stage NREM 4th B.L.	"Mm—also—mbl."	Morning recall: as in speech 67.
73 Stage NREM 4th B.L.	"Mbl—it's strange—to describe (?) that—ah, come on guys—you embarrass me—mbl."	Morning recall: as in speech 67.
74 Stage NREM 4th B.L.	"It was not male (?)—no!—but it's not one but it's kind of better."	Morning recall: as in speech 67.
75 Stage NREM 4th B.L.	"What was that (?)—it was (?) was really—[spoken slowly and softly]."	Morning recall: as in speech 67.
76 Stage NREM 5th B.L.	"Mbl—mbl—mbl—can't sink [P] you look (?)."	Morning recall: "It was the last day of school. Instead of a school building, it was a movie house. I was carrying two books with me. I was talking to someone and when I went back, a third book was there. It was the works of Shakespeare. I showed it to the woman at the ticket window. I started to walk home, met a friend and we talked about the prospects of Columbia's team for next year.

77 Stage 2 1st 3 hrs. 1st B.L. + W.U.	"Mbl–oh yeah–I didn't think you were. So?–mm."	Mentation report: "I remember 255. I don't know whether it's 2 colon 55 like the time, or 255 number, or what but it's got kind of stuck in my mind for some reason. [*E*: "Anything else?"] I also have a kind of feeling that–I'd also been thinking about files and invoices–much as the same kind of work every day at Bloomingdale's Department store–but I don't have anything really definite on that."	No discernible concordance. Note the divergent streams of mentation in the sleep-speech as compared to the mentation.
78 Stage 2 1st B.L. + W.U.	"Mbls–in due course–yes–mbl–441–451–mbl–mm."	Mentation report: "I can't remember anything–nothing special–nothing at all."	No recall. Note the numbers in the sleep-speech and the reference to 255 in the previous mentation report suggestive of persisting mental tendencies.
79 Stage 4 1st 3 hrs. 2nd B.L. + W.U.	Subject was emitting a garbled speech with repetitions of the word "moving." The first awakening stimulus was succeeded by the following speech. "Yeah, it's all that time–it's all that paper,	Mentation report: "Nothing in particular. I don't know."	No recall. Apparently the subject continued talking in his sleep following two awakening stimuli, and lacked recall on definitive awakenings.

boy," and a second awakening
stimulus succeeded by, "Yeah,
I say, I've got all of you—mbl—
paper—mbl."

80
Stage 4
1st 3 hrs.
2nd B.L. + W.U.

"Yes—yeh—don't get (?) excited
[loud mbl] or he's *away*—I dunno know—mbls—*away—shway*—
[many rapid mbls] try *basement*
of *grade* school (?) [buzzer
sounds briefly but *S* continues]
to do my reduced—go—ahead—
don't close yet—don't go—mbls—
sneak—to go *reek—you—reek* to
steak—stoke—[then slower] she
said to—uh—to find some theft
[P] uh *with Burt* (?)—*will burn*
you—*would burn* things—*burnt*
objects (?)—*burn* and *you at the
same time—you* there (?) *at the
same time.*"

Mentation report:
S: "Valentine."
E: "Can you tell me any more
about it?"
S: "No, that's all."

No discernible concordance. Note
the perseverative clang associations,
jargonistic disorganization, and
continuation of sleep-talking through
the awakening stimulus as in speech
79.

81
Stage 3
1st 3 hrs.
2nd B.L. + W.U.

"Mbl—take an—mbl—keep it
mbl."

S not awakened.

82
Stage 2
1st 3 hrs.
2nd B.L. + W.U.

"Mbl—blowing of the horn—
mm mm."

Mentation report: "Well, I was
just thinking of what we were
talking about before and, uh—you
know—can't—well—I was thinking
about—position—me—involved as

No discernible concordance.

assistant buyer and having, on the one hand—and having to do the job on the other, and how they might interact through personal connections uh—contacts etc., etc.—uh—I don't know if this stuff is going to come out all right—that's about it."

83 Stage 2 1st 3 hrs. 2nd B.L. + W.U.	"MmMMM—what lustre (?)—[P]—(s'true—please (?)) enjoy—your charm?—joy?—go ahead (?) don't even (?) mention—mbl—mention—gonna *hoisted*—get the *rest* of those *oysters*—m'not available anymore."	Mentation report: "Mbl—pearls (?)—[E inquires further] "It kind of fades—mbls—59th (?)—no idea at all."	No recall. Note the perseveration in the sleep-speech as italicized and the disorganization.
84 Stage 2 1st 3 hrs. 2nd B.L. + W.U.	"Mbl—alright!—alright!—mbls—psychology experiments—you better not."	Not awakened.	
85 Stage 2 2nd B.L. + W.U.	"Could I—could—I—touch the top (?)?—mbl."	Not awakened.	

86 Stage 2 2nd B.L. + W.U.	"Mbls–yɛh–mbls–Teddy Roosevelt (?) [P] mbls–mbls [P] [moans]."	Not awakened.	
87 Stage 2 1st U-HYP + W.U.	"Mbls [P] oh–boy–[whistles]."	Not awakened.	
88 Stage 4 1st U-HYP + W.U.	"Mbls–worry, worry, worry."	Mentation report: "I don't know–nothing."	No recall.
89 Stage 2 1st 3 hrs. 2nd U-HYP + W.U.	"Right [P] –aah! mbl–mm– mm–hm."	Mentation report: "A kind of overall thing–I was thinking about blouses–red ones and white ones–cotton ones and rayon ones–like that."	No discernible concordance. However, preoccupation with women's clothes was manifest throughout the night (see following), and probably relates to department store employment.
90 Stage 3 1st 3 hrs. 2nd U–HYP + W.U.	"Umph–yeah–it was more conducive to dress shopping–mm–hm–hm."	Mentation report: "I was thinking of actually three or four of the same blouse (?) in the same column or pattern–uh–actually that these would be arranged by style and color, rather than either by style or as I would find them."	Second-order concordance based on items pertaining to clothing in both sleep-speech and mentation report.
91 Stage 2 1st 3 hrs. 2nd U–HYP + W.U.	"Mbl–prospector (?)– here and now (?)–mbl."	Mentation report: "I've been kind of working and and doing the same thing in the same department–mbl–kind of continu-	No discernible concordance.

ous and uh—a changeover from—
suits to blouses, you know, it's
[P] makes it discontinuous
[chuckles] actually but there's
really no problem I can think of—
it's going along OK. [*E:* "You
mean this was a continuation of
what you were thinking before I
woke you up?"] Yeah—yeah—
that's what I was trying to say
before this—that's good."

92 Stage 2 1st 3 hrs. 2nd U-HYP + W.U.	"Mbls—yeah—right!—oh?—any other shirts (?)—mbls."	Not awakened.	
93 Stage 2 1st 3 hrs. 2nd U-HYP + W.U.	"Mbl—private (?) paid by the (?)."	Not awakened.	
94 Stage 3 2nd U-HYP + W.U.	"Mbl—and uh—hmmm [P] uh— that's what I need— a (manual thing—you can imagine wha	Mentation report: "Nothing actually—not that I recall."	No recall.

the (?)) other side tape was (?)
—mmmm."

95
Stage 3
2nd U-HYP + W.U.

"Hm— [burst of rapid incomprehensible speech] —uh (it is even WHAT is (?))—mm—hm [P] mbls [P] yeah [P] mm—mm—mm."

Not awakened.

Note the striking disorganization.

96
Stage 2
2nd U-HYP + W.U.

"Hm—hm—hm—hm—hm [P] hmph!—nothing [P] hm."

Not awakened.

97
Stage REM
2nd U-HYP + W.U.

"Into (?) the new territory."

Morning recall: "It starts off in Bloomingdale's where I'm with two friends and *we were discussing* what we were going to do and for some reason or other we decided we were *going to Puerto Rico*—uh—we go through a whole lot of planning and everything and we have to call it off—then later that night, I got a message left for me—I was supposed to call someone immediately, and I do, and it turns out that plans for going to Puerto Rico are back on and this brings up a lot of problems for me—leave of absence or quitting my job—a place to stay—how we were going to get there—I never got there in my dream."

Second-degree concordance based on references to travel in both speech and morning recall. In this instance, one may be more confident in surmising that the sleep-speech and morning recall are related, inasmuch as the speech occurred during the last REMP of the night and fairly proximate to elicitation of the morning recall.

432

98
Stage NREM
1st 3 hrs.
3rd U-HYP + W.U.

"Mbls—(none of that (?))—
No—No."

Not awakened.

99
Stage NREM
1st 3 hrs.
3rd U-HYP + W.U.

"[chuckles] —Seventeen and (?)
play—a spotted man (?)—it's
wholly (?) for me—remember
(?)—mm—mm."

Not awakened.

100
Stage 4
1st 3 hrs.
3rd U-HYP + W.U.

"Just that—play by ear—get
some kill off the the ideas."

"Mentation report: "No—Jesus
Christ—uh—I really can't remember."

No recall.

101
Stage NREM
1st 3 hrs.
3rd U-HYP + W.U.

"(Ooh my (?))—shoot."

Not awakened. However, the
morning recall contained an unambiguous reference to a des-
perate proposal to *shoot* two
women. "I was a soldier in a
World War I setting and for some
reason or other was hiding out
in an old barn. When it was
light, I discovered that an allied
soldier and his wife and daughter
were hiding out there too. We

First-order concordance based on
the word "shoot" in both sleep-
speech and morning recall. However, see cautionary comment in the
introduction to the appendix and
also the comment relating to speech
7, both with regard to concordance
between sleep-speech and morning
recall.

were going to sit tight and just hide as long as we can, but we discovered that enemy arms and munitions were hidden there. I suggested we wait till they return, *shoot* both women and fight to the death. They suggested we flee—can't remember more."

102 Stage NREM 1st 3 hrs. 3rd U-HYP + W.U.	"Oh dad."	Not awakened.
103 Stage NREM 3rd U-HYP + W.U.	"Mbls—mbls—I—just-just [P] [chuckle] —attach—rough (?) box."	Not awakened.
104 Stage NREM 3rd U-HYP + W.U.	"Mbls—never (?) saw a clown."	Not awakened.
105 Stage NREM 3rd U-HYP + W.U.	"Mbls—mbls—(birch tree (?))—just—mbls—to appear."	Not awakened.
106 Stage NREM 3rd U-HYP + W.U.	"[chuckles] —catch 'em both says [P] (this was promised—wasn't known— (?))."	Not awakened.
107 Stage NREM 3rd U-HYP + W.U.	"Mbls—lights."	Not awakened.

108
Stage NREM
1st 3 hrs.
4th U-HYP + W.U.

"I don't know (?) seem to be able to get the—uh—the goddam snow balls (?)—mbl."

Not awakened.
Morning recall: "I do remember riding on a train with someone."

109
Stage NREM
1st 3 hrs.
4th U-HYP + W.U.

"Mbl—this—this [P] I'm talking about—hm—hm—hm."

Not awakened.

110
Stage NREM
1st 3 hrs.
4th U-HYP + W.U.

"Mbls—really (?) big!-mbl."

Not awakened.

111
Stage 3
1st 3 hrs.
4th U-HYP + W.U.

"Mbl—(I think we ought to (?))—mbls."

Mentation report: "I really don't have anything to say."

No recall.

112
Stage NREM
4th U-HYP + W.U.

"All right! [sighs]—mbl [said angrily]."

Not awakened.

113
Stage NREM
4th U-HYP + W.U.

"Mbl—this—this [P] I'm talking about—hm—hm—hm."

Not awakened.

114 Stage 3 4th U-HYP + W.U.	"Mbls—(you're not seeing—are seeing—mbl—all can see the problem—the problem (?))—mbls."	Not awakened.	No recall. Note the perseveration of "see" and "problem."
115 Stage NREM 4th U-HYP + W.U.	"[sigh]—mbl—DO it [P] mm."	Not awakened.	
116 Stage NREM 4th U-HYP + W.U.	"Mbls—here! [P] mm."	Not awakened.	
117 Stage NREM 1st 3 hrs. 5th U-HYP + W.U.	"Yeah?—yeah? [P] that's a little better—[following is whispered] (it's too warm (?))."	Not awakened. Morning recall: none.	
118 Stage NREM 1st 3 hrs. 5th U-HYP + W.U.	"Mbl—that's the [P] mbl."	Not awakened.	
119 Stage NREM 5th U-HYP + W.U.	"[moans and grunts]—Really has—has a great meaning [petulant sounds]."	Not awakened.	
120 Stage NREM 1st 3 hrs. 7th U-HYP + W.U.	"Mbl—press—mbl."	Not awakened.	

121 Stage 3 1st 3 hrs. 7th U-HYP + W.U.	"I got a problem—most people do."	Mentation report: "I was just trying to—thinking in general—on —uh—uh—thinking in general on things and knowledge and what can be known and what can't— and reflection on the possibilities of knowing things that can be known—so you CAN go ahead with your investigation. [E inquires further.] That's all."	No discernible concordance. A case for second-order concordance might be made, however, because both speech and mentation report reflect careful cogitation. Subject may have lapsed back into sleep-talking at the end of the mentation report.
122 Stage 4 7th U-HYP + W.U.	"I'm confused (?)."	Mentation report: "I was think-ing—mbl—I was thinking—on—mbl —a scholar in quest of some sort of idea or information and there's a man his quest of the same type leading to entirely different paths —two paths that never cross."	No discernible concordance: See commentary on speech 121, however.
123 Stage 3 7th U-HYP + W.U.	"Tell her it makes a monkey sneeze—mbl."	Mentation report: "Things kind of just began to fade out— back into a kind of a sleep-cov-ered world and—nothing's been going through my mind and yet everything—that's all."	No recall.

124 Stage 3 7th U-HYP + W.U.	"[chuckles]—Last night I."	Mentation report: "I kind of forget."	No recall.

6. *Subject: D.C.*

S was a college architecture major.

125 Stage REM 1st B.L.	"Mbl—exam—Friday(?)—mbl."	Not awakened; no morning recall.
126 Stage REM 1st B.L.	"Would (wood?) in the box if it were a box would (?) it become a house and not a box?"	As in speech 125.
127 Stage REM 1st B.L.	"Sure—mbl—I'll never tell him."	As in speech 125.
128 Stage REM 1st B.L.	"Why didn't someone—mbl—turn to the laboratory [P] (oh yeah (?))."	As in speech 125.
129 Stage REM 1st 3 hrs. 2nd B.L.	"Oh, dad."	Morning recall: 1. "Girl in social work and I were being tested and she was in this big 'test house' and had nothing to do so she got drunk and was sick so she couldn't be tested. 2. "Had parties with old high school friends and L. had B. in. Then New Year's Eve party—her

family and we all brought one
guest.

3. "Mother was being silly; we
all laughed as she tried on an old
coat. Then we saw the animals
that the neighbors were raising.
Some were beavers that they had
cut the tails off of."

130 Stage REM 2nd B.L.	"I don't know what you call those quimballs (?) mbls [P] Tomorrow afternoon (?)—I woke myself from talking that time [P] so what?"	Morning recall: as in speech 129.	Note the rarely occurring self-awakening resulting from sleep-talking. This has been observed almost solely in REM sleep-speech episodes.
131 Stage REM 2nd B.L.	"Oh—I understand—let's just mbl [P] mmph! [P] aach!	Morning recall: as in speech 129.	
132 Stage REM 3rd B.L.	"Mbl—mbl—shorts and jacket and socks—shirts (?)—mm."	Morning recall: no dreams recalled.	
133 Stage REM 3rd B.L.	"Tell him that we're here—mbls."	As in speech 132.	

134 Stage REM 3rd B.L.	"[laughter] —Where? [P] mbl."	As in speech 132.
135 Stage REM 1st 3 hrs. 4th B.L.	"Mbl—the whole thing is—mbl."	Morning recall: 1. "I was polishing my shoes. 2. "Joyce was sick and I took some sort of penance thing from the Catholic church and brought them to Mrs. N. who was in the hospital—then at home. She said her *doctor* was out of town but was a good one—Donnie O. 3. "I was singing in the choir. 4. "We were at a cocktail party discussing what we wanted to become. I discussed carving. A nun was there."
136 Stage REM 4th B.L.	"Didn't you hear about collections?—oh."	Morning recall: as in speech 135.
137 Stage REM 4th B.L.	"Mother, mother, mother, mother, mbls—mbls—mbls [said as if humorously chiding mother]."	Morning recall: as in speech 135.
138 Stage REM 4th B.L.	"Oh dear— [chuckles] —I can't work."	Morning recall: as in speech 135.

139
Stage REM
4th B.L.

"Oh yeah—there was something else I was s'posed to talk about [P] hey, *doctor*, aren't you mbl — [giggles]."

Morning recall:
as in speech 135.

140
Stage REM
4th B.L.

"Oh—that's worth it."

Morning recall:
as in speech 135.

141
Stage 2
4th B.L.

"Mbls—oh—what happened?"

Morning recall:
as in speech 135.

142
Stage REM
1st 3 hrs.
5th B.L.

"[giggles] —Touched your face— [giggle] —no *mother*, I'm just kidding [P] —well— [sings] —me— mbl."

Morning recall:
1. "Dreamt all about antiquity.

2. "L. and I were playing cards at Christmas and creating different things. We lived in an apartment and kept asking people in to see what we and our children (!?) had made.

3. "*Mother's* hat was on wrong when we went to leave after seeing Barbara Streisand.

First-order concordance based on reference to "mother" in both speech and morning recall.

4. "Dreamt K. came for Christmas and we talked. There was strain but we got along fine. She borrowed my long underwear for the ski trip we went on."

143 Stage REM 5th B.L.	"I don't know (?) mbl— [sounds reminiscent of weeping]."	Morning recall: as in speech 142.	
144 Stage REM 5th B.L.	"Everything's (?) fine—mbl."	Morning recall: as in speech 142.	
145 Stage REM 5th B.L.	"Mbl—(really I felt so important like this (?)) nope— [giggle]."	Morning recall: as in speech 142.	
146 Stage REM 5th B.L.	"Oh—(I like (?)) to have your hands back at your side."	Morning recall: as in speech 142.	
147 Stage REM 5th B.L.	"(I'd hate to see a couple more drawers I don't know about (?)) —[chuckle] that was a low blow, wasn't it?"	Morning recall: as in speech 142.	
148 Stage REM 5th B.L.	"*K'S (?) brother* mbl—pity (?)"	Morning recall: as in speech 142.	First-order concordance based on proper name *"K."* and *"brother"* appearing in both sleep-speech and morning recall.

149
Stage REM
5th B.L.

"K?—I'm on the ends now."

Morning recall:
as in speech 142.

First-order concordance based on proper name "*K.*" appearing in both sleep-speech and morning recall.

150
Stage REM
5th B.L.

"Mbl—experts."

Morning recall:
as in speech 142.

151
Stage REM
1st 3 hrs.
6th B.L.

"[chuckle] —That's funny."

Morning recall:
1. "Dreamt I was going to be picked up in Brooklyn and that Mrs. H. knew the car license number. I asked her how and she said she knew the plate from different cities.

2. "Dreamt I was out with Dick and Flo.

3. "Japanese girl had a huge piece of cake and asked him to take her to a bar. He was really surprised and told her he was.

4. "Was taking care of some children or at least doing so with *my own and other mother* on a vacation and they all got sick.

The one that got sick first hardly
ever had any exercise but looked
healthy enough."

152
Stage REM
90 sec after onset
6th B.L.

"You can tell how beautiful it
was—mbl—pretty [spoken
quite loudly]."

Morning recall:
as in speech 151.

153
Stage REM
6th B.L.

"Mbls—please."

Morning recall:
as in speech 151.

154
Stage REM
6th B.L.

"Oh [P] I think I'm gonna fin-
ish THIS one, you know, but
I don't think anything anymore—
mbl."

Morning recall:
as in speech 151.

155
Stage 3-4
6th B.L.

"Oh!—oh—*mom*! [chuckle]—
mbl."

Morning recall:
as in speech 151.

First-order concordance based on
reference to own mother in sleep-
speech and morning recall.

156
Stage 3-4
6th B.L.

Mbls [P]—definitely tied [P]
t'isn't good."

Morning recall:
as in speech 151.

157
Stage REM
6th B.L.

"Alice—mbls.—I was told to."

Morning recall:
as in speech 151.

158
Stage REM
6th B.L.

"Careful—move this one over (?)
mbl—that's all for now [P]
huh."

Morning recall:
as in speech 151.

444

159 Stage REM 6th B.L.	"So therefore I'm excused."	Morning recall: as in speech 151.	
160 Stage REM 6th B.L.	"You know who called me C. last? [P] mbl–a stuh–ra–a–nge person–ugh [P] truly weird– [chuckle]."	Morning recall: as in speech 151.	
161 Stage 4 1st 3 hrs. 1st B.L. + W.U.	"Mmph–I'll just sit down– mbls."	Not awakened; no morning recall.	
162 Stage 2 1st B.L. + W.U.	"Nyeah–you're facing one way –mbl–talk (?)."	Not awakened; no morning recall.	
163 Stage REM 1st B.L. + W.U.	"Telling her how I can tell [P] that really likes."	Mentation report: "I was thinking *how I can tell* philoso- pher better than the other–how much more I *liked* them–and how there was this girl sitting in my class–oh–who got up to leave or something and I was saying I	First-order concordance based on words or phrases in both sleep- speech and mentation report: "like," "how I can tell," and "telling her."

liked her better than somebody else because I was really more *like* the philosopher Wheeler and uh—I was *telling her* (?) about Robert Anderson and [mbl] that we read the textbooks of the philosophers we *liked* and the others we sort of skimmed over."

164 Stage REM 1st B.L. + W.U.	"Oh yeah—a restaurant—down Broadway [P] mm—hm—mbl—too."	Mentation report: "I dreamt I was walking along *down Broadway* and somebody just—one of my friends had just read the same paper—the same newspaper I had and it said this *restaurant*—the Boardman (?), had just gotten government funds to make it a better *restaurant* aaand [P] I had been taking part in some kind of exam where they woke you up [laughs] and they were gonna wake me up and I was supposed to tell them about this Boardman thing."	First-order concordance based on same words and phrases in both sleep-speech and mentation report: "down Broadway," and "restaurant."
165 Stage 2 1st B.L. + W.U.	"(Looks like some box (?)) to oval shaped thing—I—mbl."	Mentation report: "Yeah?—we started playing this—mbl—*box*—mbl—and—mbl—like everybody else—and I had the same idea. It was on Broadway—mbl—that's all I can remember.	First-order concordance based on the word "box" in both sleep-speech and mentation report.

166
Stage REM
1st B.L. + W.U.

"Oh–let me explain to you the answer to my question–mbl–we talked about."

Not awakened.

167
Stage REM
1st 3 hrs.
2nd B.L. + W.U.

"What is that mbl."

Not awakened. Morning recall: "I remember seeing two blobs that had something to do with medicine."

168
Stage 2
2nd B.L. + W.U.

"Oh–my arm feels as though it's asleep."

Mentation report: "Oh–gee –supposed to remember what I've been dreaming about [P] I don't remember anything [P] all I seem to remember are the–uh– images of school and–mbl– school and things I have to re- member [P] I'm standing in front of a hall–year–and some- body–um–called on the tele- phone and *I told him* to get off and they had this book ready for me–mbls."

Third-order concordance based on the subject saying "I told him" in the mentation report.

169
Stage 2
2nd B.L. + W.U.

"No–mbls."

Not awakened; morning recall as in speech 167.

170 Stage 2 2nd B.L. + W.U.	"This girl more–mbl–all the time–hoogh!"	Not awakened; morning recall as in speech 167.	
171 Stage REM 2nd B.L. + W.U.	"I was just reading about that I think."	Mentation report: "Oh, I just dreamed that these people were picketing Eisenhower and there was an (expression in his face (?)) –said–uh–only I didn't quite get to finish my dream about this, and I started late and it was recognition that it was not my own but someone else's idea and –uh–was interrupted from finishing the thing about the robbery of the bank by that horrible buzzer in the elevator."	No discernible concordance. This categorization is conservative. That is, the word "said" in the mentation report could well imply "I said," which would warrant a third-order concordance score.
172 Stage REM 2nd B.L. + W.U.	"(That last (?)) fish was rotten [P] please don't look inside any more–or if you do just don't give me the rotten ones, huh?"	Not awakened; morning recall as in speech 167.	
173 Stage 2 2nd B.L. + W.U.	"Mbl and dance–oh– [sung]."	Not awakened; morning recall as in speech 167.	
174 Stage REM 2nd B.L. + W.U.	"(Shall I wake her up (?)) and find out what it is? [P] all right–sleep [P] uh–huh–(tell her to (?)) squeeze the buzzer."	Not awakened; morning recall as in speech 167.	The sleep-speech suggests that the *S* had reversed roles and is playing the *E*.

175
Stage REM
2nd B.L. + W.U.

"What's that—and I know it [P] uh—huh—I DO feel (?)—but when (?) I'm having corn and Nancy has to have half an ear of corn."

Not awakened; morning recall as in speech 167.

176
Stage REM
2nd B.L. + W.U.

"Mbl—orchestra (?) food, it might make ya sick—say—oogh! —I don't like this [P] [chuckle] —mbl—I told ya this morning about not—not eating like all the people—mbl—you know— that's one of the reasons."

Not awakened; morning recall as in speech 167.

177
Stage REM
1st 3 hrs.
3rd B.L. + W.U.

"Wait!—no don't scratch (more holes (?)) [said with anxious tone]."

Not awakened. Morning recall:
1. "I dreamed I was playing a guitar in Van Cortland Park and Debbie was teaching me.

2. "We re-did our house in red brick and brown paint.

3. "My friends visited me on my birthday and we sat on the porch. I picked up things in the garden. Larry had been home alone on the porch.

4. "Jane, Gretchen (?) and Irene going to do something and she would drive her car."

178
Stage REM
3rd B.L. + W.U.

"Smiling pulstat (?) [sic]."

Not awakened; morning recall as in speech 177.

179
Stage REM
3rd B.L. + W.U.

"Huh?—I don't know."

Not awakened; morning recall as in speech 177.

180
Stage REM
3rd B.L. + W.U.

"Oh—yeah, it's for you—mbls— pretty soon I'll eat (?) some— (so Spanish it's (?)) supposed to go."

Mentation report: "Yeah?—I was thinking—uh—that my brother was in this accident a long time ago and he, uh, got cut somewhere (?) that was very, very long, and he hadn't worn some kind of brace for it because he hadn't learned how to and so he buzzed the doctor, actually the minister, to show him how; and before this, this minister and I, and somebody else stayed over at my house because we were having a convention of sorts. We had like 26 or 27 guests, and filled all the beds and—uh, I could only find one bed that was free and uh—then either my brother, or my best friend, or somebody spent the

No discernible concordance.

450

whole day to a week and they crowded (?) us."

181
Stage 1 NREM after previous wake-up from REM sleep-speech. It may have been a kind of continuation of the previous REMP. The same applies to speeches 182 and 183.

Another possibility is that these speeches were uttered during ambiguous REM sleep (Cartwright et al., 1967) or, *Phase Intermediare* (Goldsteinas et al, 1966; Lairy et al., 1968)

3rd B.L. + W.U.

"Thanks (?)—mbls."

Not awakened; morning recall: as in speech 177.

182
Stage 1 NREM (proximate to previous REMP)
3rd B.L. + W.U.

"This has a very nice feel to it, you know?—it does."

Not awakened; morning recall: as in speech 177.

183
Stage 1 NREM (proximate to
previous REMP)
3rd B.L. + W.U.

"You know (?), sometime during the night, the kids (?) would
come in and I'd had two or
three pieces of cake (?) which
were wider (?)—mbl about 8
inches wide apiece on top of the
coffee, uh, can in abstract arrangement and light was falling on it—
really nice and I saw it was beautiful but then when I was awakened in the morning, I sort of
mbl—mbl—and so I'd have to
smell the sauce left, mbl."

Not awakened; morning recall: as
in speech 177.

184
Stage REM
3rd B.L. + W.U.

"(Every individual (?)) in the
family has a plan. How is
that?"

Mentation report: "God—my
own mind is worse than the
buzzer—as far as what I was
dreaming is concerned, it's
[subject resumes sleep and repeated stimulus does not awaken
her]."

No recall.

185
Stage REM
3rd B.L. + W.U.

"And I said, mbl—you know,
would you like to dance, or
something? and [P] school thing
and uh, (what's that? (?))—
yeah—telling him about my
Minnesotans (?) damned silly
[titters] mbl times that—[speech
interrupted by buzzer]."

Mentation report: "Oh—I heard
myself talking in my sleep and I
was talking about how I was off
somewhere on a trip and these
people and all—I was a *dance*—
at a *dance* and the people would
say, you know, something about
the dumb *Minnesotans* and so
then I would say, 'Well, you're
looking at one,' and then they

452

would spend all evening saying
how I wasn't like a *Minnesotan*
at all [titters] and uh [P]
(somehow or other (?)) that's all
on my mind—and then I was
standing in some corridor with
J.H. from B—mbl— rater and
then my brother (?) came and he
and I (took a view (?)) of the
same room and he kept tossing
me around and calling me a
dumb Swede, although I'm not
Swedish—and— [P] that's all."

186
Stage REM
3rd B.L. + W.U.

"Mbl goes down mbl bubbles
but as it goes to the top the
bubbles break and mbl back
down."

Mentation report: "Yah?—I was
dreaming that—something—mbl—
miniature golf perpetual motion machine in which it was a
sort of bear in a pond and as it
went up *to the top*—well—it
collected *bubbles* on the bottom
and as it went up *to the top,*
bubbles broke and since air is
lighter than the mass of the body,
the body fell *back down* to the
bottom and there it picked up
bubbles again."

First-order concordance based on
words and phrases shared by both
sleep-speech and mentation report:
"to the top," "bubbles," and back
down."

187
Stage REM
3rd B.L. + W.U.

"Mbl—weirdest (?) thing on the back porch."

Not awakened; morning recall: as in speech 177.

First-order concordance based on the word "porch" appearing in both sleep-speech and morning recall; sleep-speech from the last REMP of the night and shortly before final morning awakening.

188
Stage REM
4th B.L. + W.U.

"No, I really can't see what (I'm waiting for (?))— yeah (that's what I'm waiting for (?)) —I don't know—(nothing in use (?))—what to make of it?—uh."

Not awakened. Morning recall:

1. "We were building a house with mathematical proportions with birds. In this sleep experiment something was done mathematically, too.

2. "I saw a peacock tree which was really also a butterfly tree and called someone to come and see it—it shined.

3. "My mother and I were going on a trip (to Europe?) but first I had to have a series of tests on my back for allergies. The doctor turned into a minister and I wouldn't let him scratch me. Then another friend came to stay with him and delayed us more. Besides, our dog was new. We had forgotten to pack a lot of things—namely camera equipment.

4. "We went swimming."

453

189
Stage REM
4th B.L. + W.U.

"(And there (?)) I saw hers (?) in New York a long time—mbl—bright."

Mentation report: "Yeah?—oh I dreamt I was looking at a sky-scraper and *there wasn't any fog around* and were (?) *magnificently colored* buildings—just—oh—*hundreds of lights on* (?)—sky-scraper supposedly doing the mbl experiment except I was running up *watching* this and my brother came in and telling us about past dreams (?) that we'd had and then mbl came in to find out this one [P] I forgot to tell you we took lots and lots of pictures—*there wasn't any fog.*"

Second-order concordance based on commonality of references to brightness and seeing.

190
Stage REM
4th B.L. + W.U.

"Isn't (?) that two things going—which one's gonna be first—which one will keep?"

Not awakened; Morning recall as in speech 188.

191
Stage REM
4th B.L. + W.U.

"Hey—what's wrong with your little kid? THIS one."

Not awakened; morning recall as in speech 188.

This sleep-speech occurred 5 min prior to the next (192). The mentation report elicited *then* contains the phrase "what's wrong with"? hence first-order concordance.

192 Stage REM 4th B.L. + W.U.	"Peacock tree!? there's a tree full of peacocks and swallows and other colorations (?) aabsolutely, aaaabsolutely, go-o-or-geous—get my camera, Larry, and don't forget to turn the film or I'll have fits when it gets back—come *on*! God!—you should *see* it." [This was uttered with an air of brisk alert enthusiasm.]	Mentation report: "Uuh [uttered sleepily]—*oh—I was just sort of sleep talking.* I think—I said something about this *tree* made up of *birds* and the feathers all stuck out and it was *very beautiful* and *I woke up my family and told them to come look at it—* and—before that mbl I noticed a sort of butterfly tree—I was on a horse with somebody else and, I couldn't figure out what our two horses—*what's wrong with* them until he told me that my horse had mbl full of butterflies —and."	First-order concordance based on references to tree and birds in both sleep-speech and mentation report. Reference is made in the second part of the mentation report to an earlier dream in which the words "what's wrong" also appear in the sleep-speech 5 min prior. Also note the rare spontaneous awareness of having been sleep-talking.
193 Stage 1 NREM (proximate to previous REMP awakening) 4th B.L. + W.U.	"Umh—I got a pain in my back."	Not awakened; morning recall as in speech 188.	
194 Stage 1 NREM (proximate to previous REMP) 4th B.L. + W.U.	"Mbl—oh—boy—does my back hurt—huh."	Not awakened; morning recall as in speech 188.	
195 Stage 2 4th B.L. + W.U.	"Nyeh—who wants to be told —we ought (?) to look for ourselves."	Mentation report: "Oh, I dreamt I was in with the class or some other people and *we wanted to look* at some art history that mbl one of classes mbl—	First-order concordance based on the words "we" and "look" in both sleep-speech and mentation report.

		inside one of the buildings around here."	
196 Stage REM 4th B.L. + W.U.	"Oh—I don't think so—not on the sides, and on the top I don't like it either. [P] That's an old one—what do I want that for?"	Not awakened; morning recall as in speech 188.	
197 Stage REM 4th B.L. + W.U.	"I haven't (golf pussy (?)) [sounds of scratching] hmm— I gotta get busy."	Not awakened; morning recall as in speech 188.	
198 Stage REM 4th B.L. + W.U.	"Oh, God! [P] (It's to eat with (?))—mbls—a two inch saw."	Not awakened; morning recall as in speech 188.	
199 Stage REM 4th B.L. + W.U.	"Mm-hm—mother—you gotta get some eggs 'cause seeing all these people all know that I like eggs too, so get a dozen eggs. Please put this in a soft bag, thank you."	Mentation report: "O.K.—I just came in and I wanted to know (?) where (?) its at counter (?) —mbl—*eggs*—mbl—*eggs* [P] for a fine (?) trip."	First-order concordance based on the word "eggs" in both sleep-speech and mentation report.
200 Stage 3 4th B.L. + W.U.	"[whispered speech] Mbl—check (?)—it's not very much."	Mentation report: "I'm awake and I told you everything about the dream. [*E*: "Is that all?"] Yes."	No recall.

201 Stage REM 4th B.L. + W.U.	"Oh—no! Did you step in it?—mbl."	Not awakened; morning recall as in speech 188.
202 Stage NREM 1st 3 hrs. 1st B.L.—U-HYP	"Mbl—expected him— my gosh."	Morning recall: 1. "Only vaguely remember dreaming about a baby. 2. "Was at a political rally somewhere—at a fair grounds. Was working as a soda jerk in one of the booths. Kids came up and said Johnson and Humphrey were sitting outside waiting to be waited upon. I spoke to them for quite a while (mentioning that I was from Minnesota and Dad's name to Humphrey). It came time to do the dishes but as everyone filed by to put them in the sink, I was aware that it was mbl and all should be doing their own dishes. I became angry and quit.
203 Stage NREM 1st 3 hrs. 1st B.L.—U-HYP	"Oh?—yeah—it's still the same—yeah."	Morning recall: as in speech 202.
204 Stage REM 1st 3 hrs. 1st B.L.—U-HYP	"He makes me feel so badly—hmph."	Morning recall: as in speech 202.

205
Stage 2
1st 3 hrs.
1st B.L.—U-HYP

"I don't understand."

Morning recall:
as in speech 202.

206
Stage REM
1st B.L.—U-HYP

"Ooh—mbls—today."

Morning recall:
as in speech 202.

207
Stage REM
1st B.L.—U-HYP

"M—mother."

Morning recall:
as in speech 202.

208
Stage REM
1st B.L.—U-HYP

"All I did was that one section—
mbls—and then there's usually a
gap—mbls."

Morning recall:
as in speech 202.

209
Stage REM
1st B.L.—U-HYP

"I wanna buy it, Rima (?)—
mbls."

Morning recall:
as in speech 202.

210
Stage REM
1st B.L.—U-HYP

"Calling—what pills? (?) [P]
(spring clarinets (?)) like, you
know, mbls."

Morning recall:
as in speech 202.

211
Stage REM
1st B.L.—U-HYP

"Mbl—the hour [P] mbl—go along (?)."

Morning recall:
as in speech 202.

212
Stage REM
1st 3 hrs.
2nd B.L.—U-HYP

"Mbl—stand in the—the idea of seeing Patty—mbl."

Morning recall:

1. "Dreamt I was running a concession and all my money was stolen and I left so when I came back I just demanded all the money of the nearby bums and they gave it, so I had lots more than before.

2. "Kathy M. and I shared an apartment and a monkey called up and said he was hurt and in a box-car on 3rd Avenue. She said too bad, etc., and hung up on him and I was angry.

3. "Had a lovely view over a lake—a mountain top. It was roped off. I used to wander there lots. I was told to move my tent (with K.) so we could get a good view on our canoe trip.

4. "Mom and I talked about Pinky L. and Peggy L. being married. I had seen them years before. They had since been divorced and remarried.

5. "This boy in my art class
came to stay with us overnight as
a youth hosteler. He was very
dirty and unshaven. Next morning I gave him shaving cream and
it turned out that he had to be
in a wedding at Riverside Church
but I said the hole in your black
sweater showing your pink shirt
are OK because they're liberal."

213
Stage 2
1st 3 hrs.
2nd B.L.–U-HYP

"Why do they have to be in
that position?–they don't."

Morning recall:
as in speech 212.

214
Stage REM
2nd B.L.–U-HYP

"I talked this afternoon with the
doctors and I found that I have
mbl architectural support–mbl."

Morning recall:
as in speech 212.

215
Stage REM
2nd B.L.–U-HYP

"I always think you know, that
mbl–but (I didn't want to say
anything (?)) but its been a long
time after my exam with mbl–
[chuckles]."

Morning recall:
as in speech 212.

216 Stage REM 2nd B.L.–U-HYP	"[laughter] –Uh–maybe it's worth it–let's try it again– [laughter]."	Morning recall: as in speech 212.
217 Stage REM 2nd B.L.–U-HYP	"(I think that's (?)) the best mbl that I've seen in a long, long time."	Morning recall: as in speech 212.
218 Stage REM 2nd B.L.–U-HYP	"Why then just go to mbl and tell her what you want done. Remember how stuffed your closet gets and how it's impossible not only to wash it but to dry clothes; not only that but to iron them, so just remind him [said with vigor and irritation]."	Morning recall: as in speech 212.
219 Stage REM 2nd B.L.–U-HYP	"Collect (after some fun (?))."	Morning recall: as in speech 212.
220 Stage REM 2nd B.L.–U-HYP	"That colonel, you know, that Iva (?), that's here with our group–so she wanted to go to talk to him [P] that's–he lives in the town that she'll be in next year [P]. What kind of people do you go to talk to? Harbor (?) people? Classless (?) people? Hunters? (?) Anybody? Fisherman?–what."	Morning recall: as in speech 212.

221
Stage REM
1st 3 hrs.
3rd B.L.–U-HYP

"Mbl my brother when he comes."

Morning recall:
1. "This boy was doing something like selling things.

2. "Larry [*S*'s brother] was home and we kept meeting his friends. Bob L. came with us to see Tebaldi in some operatic work. Mike was to meet with me but I had to meet Larry instead. We went into the restaurant that sold corn flakes only."

First-order concordance based on reference to "brother" in the sleep-speech, and Larry, the subject's brother, in the morning recall.

222
Stage REM
3rd B.L.–U-HYP

"Oh–what's in that?"

Morning recall:
as in speech 221.

223
Stage REM
3rd B.L.–U-HYP

"Now with (?) what colors are mbl all I can think of ideas no mbl ideas certainly."

Morning recall:
as in speech 221.

224
Stage REM
3rd B.L.–U-HYP

"I smell mbl (pepper–peppermint (?)) mbl– [laughs] –it's so FUNNY."

Morning recall:
as in speech 221.

225 Stage REM 3rd B.L.–U-HYP	"Mm–my lip's bleeding."	Morning recall: as in speech 221.
226 Stage REM 3rd B.L.–U-HYP	"Mm–mm–tell (?) someone else."	Morning recall: as in speech 221.
227 Stage REM 3rd B.L.–U-HYP	"You been golfing lately? [P] in the backyard–you tell me whether it counts."	Morning recall: as in speech 221.
228 Stage REM 1st 3 hrs. 4th B.L.–U-HYP	"(After I get through (?))– mbls–now–but, er?"	Morning recall: "Dreamt that I was at a farm house and some cattle were stolen by neighbors. We (John M) took a flash picture of them stealing and they came looking for the film. But we had given it to a neighbor. I was hiding under a table. I slept in a sort of hotel rooming-house, only I was where the shower was so that at 6 each a.m. I was awak- ened and all the clothes hanging in my closet became damp with the shower spray. I planned to change a sleeping bag on the wall and sleep in it."
229 Stage REM 4th B.L.–U-HYP	"(What was it for? [P] well, what happens there (?)) [P] what's the symbol of the day?"	Morning recall: as in speech 228.

230
Stage REM
4th B.L.–U-HYP

"I don't know—mbls tell you something."

Morning recall:
as in speech 228.

231
Stage REM
4th B.L.–U-HYP

"That parasol—look!—L-O-O-K! [P] wow—weighs 190 pounds—I don't care."

Morning recall:
as in speech 228.

232
Stage REM
4th B.L.–U-HYP

"Oh—I thought—that was excellent—oh!—we were both—you know—I was concerned that I was really upset when you started to fly, low (?) oh (the only was I couldn't figure out (?)) what the HELL was going on."

Morning recall:
as in speech 228.

233
Stage REM
4th B.L.–U-HYP

"For you and no one else—and—it exists in imagination—but in imagination means—it exists [P] uh!"

Morning recall:
as in speech 228.

234
Stage NREM
4th B.L.–U-HYP

"Mbl?—OK [P] because I don't wanna get him out—mbl in cold water mbl."

Morning recall:
as in speech 228.

235
Stage REM
4th B.L.–U-HYP

"Mbls–cashier (?) suitcase and you see there's an awful lot of [titters] [P] platform–mbls."

Morning recall: as in speech 228.

236
Stage REM
4th B.L.–U-HYP

"I think so–yeh."

Morning recall: as in speech 228.

237
Stage REM
4th B.L.–U-HYP

"See if I could devise a way so that–they don't have to blame (?) you [whispered speech]."

Morning recall: as in speech 228.

238
Stage NREM
1st 3 hrs.
1st U-HYP–PHS

"Yeah–I know that [sigh] – it's –it's a wild place–36 colors."

Morning recall: "I don't remember any dreams, but when I initially fell asleep I was thinking of tarantula spiders."

239
Stage NREM
1st 3 hrs.
1st U-HYP–PHS

"I got a pain in my choke (?)– oh."

Morning recall: as in speech 238.

240
Stage REM
1st 3 hrs.
1st U-HYP–PHS

"Funny–tone (?)–I think it'll be better tonight expecially since we (put you (?)) mbl will be (my, my, my (?)) mbl."

Morning recall: as in speech 238.

241
Stage REM
1st 3 hrs.
1st U-HYP–PHS

"[laughter] –Hey, that's funny– [laughter] [P] how mbl–yeah, I'm not going this mbl–very much."

Morning recall: as in speech 238.

242
Stage REM
1st U-HYP—PHS

"Oh—mbl—I'm not sure—oh."

Morning recall:
as in speech 238.

243
Stage NREM
1st U-HYP—PHS

"Mbl—about a plane or a level (?)."

Morning recall:
as in speech 238.

244
Stage NREM
1st U-HYP—PHS

"Mbl—guy wants to look he knows the—the concept and all he knows is the feeling and the people."

Morning recall:
as in speech 238.

245
Stage REM
1st 3 hrs.
2nd U-HYP—PHS

"Oh—that's what, huh (?) [P] oh!—that's a good term—that's horrible."

Morning recall: "I dreamt that Picasso was working and a couple of us were studying with him. He made me throw my favorite pen away and my best stone carving."

246
Stage REM
2nd U-HYP—PHS

"[laughter] I don't think my, uh."

Morning recall:
as in speech 245.

247
Stage NREM
2nd U-HYP—PHS

"Oh—I'm sorry I didn't hear what you said— [chuckle]."

Morning recall:
as in speech 245.

248
Stage REM
1st 3 hrs.
3rd U-HYP—PHS

"Mbls your fingers—soon you'll eat your fingers and you'll mbl into anything."

Morning recall: "I dreamt we had gone to dinner with Sandy M. and the Pope's. As we left I noticed all the windows above the street were filled with people watching."

249
Stage REM
3rd U-HYP—PHS

"(I don't (?)) think so."

Morning recall:
as in speech 248.

250
Stage NREM
3rd U-HYP—PHS

"Och! [P] mbl—belongs here [P] mbl—oh—boy."

Morning recall: .
as in speech 248.

251
Stage REM
3rd U-HYP—PHS

"No! I don't want anybody to (read (?)) no, no, no, no, no!"

Morning recall:
as in speech 248.

252
Stage NREM
4th U-HYP—PHS

"[scratching noise] Mbl—I find very expressive."

Morning recall: "I was dreaming when awakened but I forgot the contents."

253
Stage NREM
4th U-HYP—PHS

"[scratching noise] Mm— it's funny how—lost things just (?) as a furniture store."

Morning recall:
as in speech 252.

254
Stage NREM
4th U-HYP—PHS

"It's that—mbls—mbl [P] well, you know—mbls."

Morning recall:
as in speech 252.

255 Stage REM 4th U-HYP–PHS	"[whispers] –Ma–a–n."	Morning recall: as in speech 252.
256 Stage REM 4th U-HYP–PHS	"Do you like (Cameron Garland)?"	Morning recall: as in speech 252.
257 Stage REM 4th U-HYP–PHS	"Mbl–I wanna get out of here, sort of [P] mbl–can get back [P] mbl–goodbye (?)."	Morning recall: as in speech 252.
258 Stage REM 4th U-HYP–PHS	"Physiologically somebody's on the verge of being drunk–I do not recommend that they get drunk and sleep it off if they don't get drunk and have a goddam awful head of–headache and hangover (?) anyhow."	Morning recall: as in speech 252.
259 Stage REM 4th U-HYP–PHS	"Help me!"	Morning recall: as in speech 252.

260
Stage REM
4th U-HYP—PHS

"(Oh—God—it's been going on around here since (?)) oh—look at all those funny people—mbl—mm—HM—all 15?—mbls—this man downstairs—mbls."

Morning recall: as in speech 252.

261
Stage REM
4th U-HYP—PHS

"What is that (?)"

Morning recall: as in speech 252.

262
Stage REM
4th U-HYP—PHS

"I wanna tell you about something—tell you about something (?) funny."

Morning recall: as in speech 252.

263
Stage REM
4th U-HYP—PHS

"Mbl—public mbl—down the street, you know?"

Morning recall: as in speech 252.

264
Stage NREM
4th U-HYP—PHS

"[laughter] —Mbls—if you ask ME."

Morning recall: as in speech 252.

265
Stage REM
1st 3 hrs.
5th U-HYP—PHS

"Hold this—girl."

Morning recall:
1. "There was a large gathering of people and I was talking about and examining a chair."

2. "We were camping out and I was cooking. Something happened definitely to the lady and on the way back to camp after a few days stay over (and I left

Carleton pamphlets), I convinced this boy to eat the
scrambled eggs I made."

266 Stage REM 1st 3 hrs. 5th U-HYP–PHS	"Is that YOUR (restaurant, dear(?))"	Morning recall: as in speech 265.
267 Stage NREM 1st 3 hrs. 5th U-HYP–PHS	"I can't do it—mbls—spine and (with the (?)) legs."	Morning recall: as in speech 265.
268 Stage NREM 5th U-HYP–PHS	"Interior space."	Morning recall: as in speech 265.
269 Stage REM 5th U-HYP–PHS	"Well—that's why I went out—I thought you'd understand that."	Morning recall: as in speech 265.
270 Stage REM 5th U-HYP–PHS	"Daddy?"	Morning recall: as in speech 265.

271
Stage REM
5th U-HYP—PHS

"That's (?) a friend of Kathy (?)
Mr. C. and Kenneth O'K."

Morning recall:
as in speech 265.

272
Stage REM
5th &-HYP—PHS

"I felt (?) one those all night
mbls."

Morning recall:
as in speech 265.

273
Stage REM
5th U-HYP—PHS

"[laughter] Don't you get it,
mother?—Sounds like it's got
like bubble gum (?) only it's
ballroom and stand [P] Listen
now—you can't call that op art."

Morning recall:
as in speech 265.

274
Stage REM
5th U-HYP—PHS

"(You wouldn't believe I was
wide awake (?)) mbl [P] I think
it before sleep I was thinking
that, however—ANYhow mbl—
talk to Chicago."

Morning recall:
as in speech 265.

275
Stage REM
5th U-HYP—PHS

"Mbl [whistle] (now it's all
alone (?) mbl—stay."

Morning recall:
as in speech 265.

276
Stage REM
5th U-HYP—PHS

"What do you think of this
mbl?"

Morning recall:
as in speech 265.

277
Stage REM
5th U-HYP—PHS

"Well—I sort of doubt if I
know where too but uh—you
know I was supposed to get an

Morning recall:
as in speech 265.

eye—EYE lamp uh—uh (lens prescription (?))—dark!"

278 Stage REM 1st 3 hrs. 1st T.B.L.	"Oh, I was in the cutest trailer yesterday—ohh—mbl."	Morning recall: "Dreamt I was going to a Russian school. It seemed made up of doors arranged in a quadrangle. Lots of older men and I spent much time trying to find ways through those doors."
279 Stage 2 1st 3 hrs. 1st T.B.L.	"Shh!—mbl to drink beer with mbl—[all whispered] [P] [snicker]."	Morning recall: as in speech 278.
280 Stage 2 1st T.B.L.	"[moan]—I don't know [P] oh, God."	Morning recall: as in speech 278.
281 Stage 3 1st T.B.L.	"Did she find the clock before she left; or (did she (?)) mbl happened the clock rang—mbl."	Morning recall: as in speech 278.

| 282 Stage REM 1st T.B.L. | "Mother—today you must be sure at all times—(I bet (?)) that room is filled with people [P] every—place has been filled —mbls by now there should be someone to mbl [P] mbl—15 or 20 minutes." | Morning recall: as in speech 278. |

282
Stage REM
1st T.B.L.

"Mother—today you must be sure at all times—(I bet (?)) that room is filled with people [P] every—place has been filled —mbls by now there should be someone to mbl [P] mbl—15 or 20 minutes."

Morning recall:
as in speech 278.

283
Stage REM
1st T.B.L.

"Oh yeah mbls—at's pretty smart—as a matter of fact, that's what it me meant to ME [P] when I just read that I mbl I thought, you know, a combination move of something."

Morning recall:
as in speech 278.

284
Stage REM
1st 3 hrs.
2nd T.B.L.

"Mbl—m—yeah."

Morning recall:
1. "Dreamt I was singing spirituals in a candlelight church service with Nancy O—really Natalie B. I was explaining as we went along—then some man took our solo—the man next to me asked if I were an O.

2. "Had dreamt earlier that a *falcon's claws* were grasping me by the mouth."

285
Stage NREM
1st 3 hrs.
2nd T.B.L.

"[scratching noise] Mm—hm—I get different—different feelings mbl—you know, you sort of a trembling (?), you know, rushing

Morning recall:
as in speech 284.

forward [P] if that were the
case one plate should be higher
than the other but it isn't."

286
Stage REM
1st 3 hrs.
2nd T.B.L.

"That's not fair, you don't move
(?) that."

Morning recall:
as in speech 284.

287
Stage REM
1st 3 hrs.
2nd T.B.L.

"Oh, it was so funny, I ran into
both of them—mbl (kind of
assumptions (?)) [P], first of all
mbl that, uh psychiatrists should
be different (?) [P] that was
wonderful, wasn't it?"

Morning recall:
as in speech 284.

288
Stage REM
2nd T.B.L.

"Goodnight."

Morning recall:
as in speech 284.

289
Stage REM
2nd T.B.L.

"Did he (write them (?))—I
hadn't thought about the (Lone-
ly Wolf (?)) [P] why did you
say that's his?"

Morning recall:
as in speech 284.

290
Stage REM
2nd T.B.L.

"Mbls—I'm dreaming that I was mbls—mouth [P] or genitals (?) [P] open mouth wide and (bump your head (?)) falcon's beaks—falcon's claws—mbls."

Morning recall:
as in speech 284.

First order concordance based on references to "falcon's" claws and "mouth" in both sleep-speeches and morning recall.

291
Stage 4
1st 3 hrs.
3rd T.B.L.

"(Eat me (?) up—give me mbl."

Morning recall:
1. "In doing my paper for ancient art, I had done research into four "kinds" of art. One was a column, one a head, one a head with torso. Of course, the art world would be so much the richer for my discoveries.

2. "There were about six of us sight-seeing in some foreign country. This one boy reminded me of Frank. Dottie B. always wanted to know when and if I had seen her friend at the park. This boy reminded me of Frank [who] finally gave up his old girl-friend because we were such good friends."

292
REMP onset
1st 3 hrs.
3rd T.B.L.

"Close your eyes tighter [laughter]."

Morning recall:
as in speech 291.

293
Stage REM
1st 3 hrs.
3rd T.B.L.

"Hey, look!"

Morning recall:
as in speech 291.

294
Stage REM
1st 3 hrs.
3rd T.B.L.

"Uh—why doesn't he (wear it in
two ties (?)) [P] not in the living room, huh? [laughter]"

Morning recall:
as in speech 291.

295
Stage REM
1st 3 hrs.
3rd T.B.L.

"(I'm tired of evening games (?)
—I'm tired of these mbls—[P] of
what I was going to mbl—he sent
me those Indian things. The
Indians at home ARE [P] mbl—
what that had to do with the
transmission of television."

Morning recall:
as in speech 291.

296
Stage REM
3rd T.B.L.

"Mbls get to the end."

Morning recall:
as in speech 291.

297
Stage REM
3rd T.B.L.

"How (?) healthy, love (?) him,
you're cute, you're (?) wunner-
ful (sic) [P] mbls."

Morning recall:
as in speech 291.

298 Stage 2 2nd B.L. + W.U.	"Hm—hm—that's all there is—there is no more to—there's no more voice—so to—there's no more you know—pushing."	Mentation report: "I was apparently going to take—take my friends to for—to lunch because we were trying to put this very fine veneer on it at the store for them and apparently right there we were going to have them for lunch—I don't know what happened but all of a sudden *people became terribly busy running around* and doing things and—because a lady from the Bourbon happened to *call me*—me and get my attention and that's why I tried to find out what was going on and why the place was moving and she reacted as everyone else had as to what was wrong you know—but uh—and for a while the store looked as though it would close completely—there would be no one there—but then—uh—mbls—hm—hm—yes [P] OK—and that's it."	Second order concordance based on the reference to "voice," "pushing," and general suggestion of a crowd scene in the sleep-speech, and the words "call me," "moving," and a crowd scene in the mentation report."
299 Stage NREM 2nd B.L. + W.U.	"Hm?—hm—and then—later—mm."	Mentation report: no recall.	No recall.

300
Stage 2
2nd B.L. + W.U.

"Hm, OK."

Mentation report—
stimulated recall—
dialogue method:
E: "Are you awake?"
S: "MM–mm."
E: "What's OK?"
S: "It was like the end of a
dream where everything was
all over with—where all of the
action was over with and all
of the speaking parts were
over with and they were just
sort of you know doing the
end—the closing credits—just
the nice part—and a couple
were sitting at this round table
and—uh—on a dance floor—it
was a bare dance floor in a
huge room and it was as
though you were watching
them close up and then you
were slowly watching them
farther and farther away and
then they got up and started
dancing round and round and—

First order concordance based on
"OK" appearing in both sleep-speech
and mentation report. Noteworthy
is the rich and elaborate visual imagery with movement of people, color,
thematic content, and unambiguous
labelling of the experience by the
subject as a dream, although it occurred in association with Stage 2.

I had to give the signal to *O.K.*
them—to start the spot lights
and the things just at the
right moment—mbl—again
there was no music and yet
there was music because the
people would—who were dancing like there was no visible
music—there were just people,
you know—and everything was
done in blue and and it was
just sort of like the end of a
dream—like this was the symbolic part that they—whoever
they were—had finally gotten
together—this man and this
woman and I know that I was
dreaming it—I had been looking forward to this particular
part."

301
Stage 2
1st 3 hrs.
3rd B.L. + W.U.

"(And did I (?))—I feel as
though I've told you this before
but I know I haven't—it's a very
sunny day and an Irish girl Mary
M. was participating in the dream
and she was sort of mbl—it's a
nice day—it was beautiful—it
was outside and wh—not too cold
—just pleasant and uh."

Mentation report: The subject
was called 15 sec later and responded with a hesitant "uh-uh"
and silence.
E then entered the room and
asked, "Were you awake just
a few minutes ago and talking?"
S denied he had been awake.
E then asked, "Just tell what-

No recall. This was an equivocal instance. The content of the utterance suggests that *S* had awakened
spontaneously and provided a mentation report. However, his comment that he had been asleep, dreaming, and awakened by *E*'s entrance
indicates a sleep-speech.

ever has been passing through your mind."

S "Uh—I felt when you first came in as though sort of like I'd just woken suddenly—there was a a dream going on, I can't remember the details to tell it, though I remember there was something happening."

302
Stage 3-4
1st 3 hrs.
3rd B.L. + W.U.

"Duh—I was uh—there was— there were a lot of people involved and (heck of a lot (?))—a lot of them—the top (?) to the arees (?) but just the bottoms to them that—at first and then they didn't stay long—they were mbl and make out and they didn't talk about it but it just mean you had it [sighs]."

Mentation report: "Mm?—uh—I was looking forward to the buzzer this time—because I had something to say [P]. [E: "Anything else?"] "MM— mm—at Paramount—it was a picture for Paramount—mbl—that was nothing."

No discernible concordance. Note the disorganization of the sleep-speech.

303
Stage NREM
1st 3 hrs.
3rd B.L. + W.U.

"Wait a minute—mm—HM."

Not awakened.

304 Stage NREM 3rd B.L. + W.U.	"Boston—mbl [P] mm?"	Not awakened.	
305 Stage 3-4 3rd B.L. + W.U.	"Mm [P] I don't know."	Mentation report: no recall—unable to completely awaken.	No recall.
306 Stage REM 3rd B.L. + W.U.	"MM—ooh! mm—HM."	Mentation report: "I was—I think I've had this dream before since I've been sleeping at—I'd just finished playing checkers and I was coming to the sidewalk from the door when suddenly I sort of called Oliver (?) you know."	Third-order concordance based on "I called" in the mentation report.
307 Stage 2 3rd B.L. + W.U.	"Umph—OK."	Mentation report: "Mm—I had been looking at the catalogue of one of the furniture show rooms listed (?) in the paper—and there was a desk in there—18th century desk that we had wanted for the house but they didn't have it for us to come by and look at it so after calling them they did have it by (?)—I went along with two friends to look at the desk and up at a place called Baker and told them I'd take the desk and they asked if they could deliver it and *I said, 'Yes, they could'—that was fine!*"	Second-order concordance based on verbal indication of assent in sleep-speech and "I said, 'yes they could—that was fine' " in the mentation report.

308
Stage 2
4th B.L. + W.U.

"MM—mm—that's GOOD."

Mentation report: "That some-how this table was still interre-lated into our little—the subject of my dream—though no one was talking about it specifically, it was obvious that it was part of it and suddenly it changed from outside to inside and it was cool and I was entertaining a young lady in the office or at the office and we had just received an O.K. on the washing machine that we had just put in—wha? [P] uh—gay—yes-gay, gay something about a *good* whispering glaze because the people were silent or they didn't care or something like that."

First-order concordance based on the word "good" appearing in both sleep-speech and mentation report. Note the disorganized quality of the mentation report as though *S* were not fully awake.

309
Stage 3-4
4th B.L. + W.U.

"Um—mm—hm [chuckle] that's what SHE thinks."

Mentation report—stimulated recall—dialogue method:
E: "What did you say?"
S: "That's what she thinks."
E: "What who thinks?"

First-order concordance based on repetition of "That's what she thinks" in mentation report.

S: "Vivian."

E: "Are you awake now?"

S: "Mm–hm–yeah–no this Vivian I started–a girl I would call Vivian that I dreamed about before."

310
Stage 2
4th B.L. + W.U.

"(Take a taxi (?)) mbl–and I was to send a ticket (?) in New Orlean."

Mentation report–
stimulated recall:

E: "Are you awake?"

S: "Mm–hm."

E: "What were you saying?"

S: "*I was tell* ya (?) about who had set first choice in picking up a table [P] I THINK."

Third-order concordance based on "I tell" in the mentation report.

311
Stage 3-4
4th B.L. + W.U.

"Tit for tat? mm–how interesting."

Mentation report: "About an electric chef that we were going to put out."

No discernible concordance.

312
Stage 2
1st 3 hrs.
Recovery night after one previous night on *d*-amphetamine-pentobarbital presleep + W.U.

"Uh-huh–helda–heldi–dee–[grunt] the most interesting and certainly the most respecting was the most revered of all the ladies who poured tea, simply because it, she was older and quieter–and had more time to pour tea–mm."

Mentation report–
stimulated recall–
attempt at dialogue method.

E: "Gordon?" [*S*'s name]

S: "Um?"

E: "What was that you were telling me?"

S: "Nn–m–just happened."

E: "Is there anything else?"

S: "I felt very funny when I thought about, not comfortable any more but [grunt] I think that's all."

No discernible concordance. The speech is a noteworthy example of a groping for a linguistic target with preliminary perseveration, i.e. "helda–heldi–dee–" finally becomes "ladies" and "tea."

483

313 Stage 2 1st 3 hrs. Recovery night as in speech 312	"[grunt] —**It**'s a high shot."	Mentation report: "Um?—um—whatever it was, it's gone."	No recall.
314 Stage 3-4 Recovery night as in speech 312	"Mm—mm—it isn't that way at all—one doesn't slash, one just simply offers—that's the way it's done."	Mentation report: "That—this fireplace that—apparently—my wife had been able to buy—2 fireplaces—though we could only use one—and—however she bought them, and when she got them back home and got them here, every time she looked in the fire, they didn't look like the ones she had bought, they looked like the old ones that we didn't care for—then of course we were constantly changing the table in order to get rid of these diapers that came on the 16th of the month."	No discernible concordance.
315 Stage 2 Recovery night as in speech 312	"Um—chestnut tree."	Mentation report: "I was thinking that there was so much snow and everything, it was difficult	No discernible concordance.

to get to the antique dealer's but nevertheless I was able to make it and we kept one big cauldron on the fire just bubbling even though we didn't need it because—we just thought it looked nice and—then—there was the—um [S drifts back to sleep]."

316
Sleep-Onset NREM
(after wake-up from speech 315, 4:19, and stimulus by E)
Recovery night as in speech 312.

E: "Anything else?"
S: "Um—mm—he's going to be pleased—mm."

Mentation report: "I was just thinking like a little boy thinks, of all the things you could do if you had—a lot of paper hats and paper airplanes and paper kites. [E: "Anything else?"] That our—that the antique dealer, and there was one man and there were two women and I said to him 'I would like to have this *chest*—it was very nice—but I thought the stain on it was just too unattractive."

No discernible concordance. Noteworthy is the continuation of the content of the mentation report from speech 315 through speech 316 and the interesting emergence of a word component of speech 315 in the mentation report of speech 316; i.e., "chestnut tree" in the sleep-speech 315 and the word "chest" in the mentation report of 316. It is also possible that the latent category "wood" is exemplified by "chestnut tree," "paper," and "chest."

317
Stage 2
1st 3 hrs.
Recovery night following two previous nights on a *d*-amphetamine-pentobarbital combination + W.U.

"Um—uh—uh—mm—mm [humming] that's because the wood is much rougher that we thought—but that she had to have Lorna there we had to have her uh—huh—[hum]—mm."

Mentation report: "That—the bed was rather large—and I was sleeping and a lot started to happen—because of—they could only put me at one place at one time, it was impossible to cover everything that was going on—and—and being on this *wooden* track, this *rough wooden* track,

First-order concordance based on the words "wood" and "rough" appearing in both sleep-speech and mentation report.

this *rough*-hewn track that very
much ˙ wobbled and it was very
much—it was very much tight
and—was not a foolish or very
steady thing to do but—if they
were to get the information that's
all they could do, 'cause they
weren't paying them enough to
put another one in, and no one
knew or no one cared not to, to
do this and."

318 Stage NREM 1st 3 hrs. Recovery night as in speech 317	"[sounds of surprise and distaste] Um—um—strange—huh—oh, it's cold—um—um."	Not awakened.
319 Stage NREM 1st 3 hrs. Recovery night as in speech 317	"Mm—mm—uh—huh—it's a book, it's under there."	Not awakened.
320 Stage NREM 1st 3 hrs. Recovery night as in speech 317.	"Mm—mh—mh—mm—seems to be going down—hill—one wants it so they hold on and the trains."	Not awakened.

321 Stage NREM 1st 3 hrs. Recovery night as in speech 317.	"Mm—um—um—one can assume—little conscious after—uh—huh—uh."	Not awakened.	
322 Stage REM Recovery night as in speech 317.	"Um—bitch, bitch—ooh."	Mentation report: "I was just thinking about the—the run of events and what have you and things to do—the promotion that we're doing that goes hand and hand with our film. The mbl become unsuccessful—it's releasing—this film area neighborhood groups."	No discernible concordance.
323 Stage REM Recovery night as in speech 317.	"Now how much?"	Mentation report: "Um—just a moment—Jack—er—Jack Warner has made—er mbl—F. March last starred in the Who Plants the Star in the film version of This Heart for mbl—movie *offers* from Italy and for Sandra Dee."	Second-order concordance based on the topic of prices on finances in sleep-speech and mentation report.
324 Stage 2 2nd B.L. series (night 1)	"My neck is really."	Not awakened throughout night. Morning recall too voluminous—does not warrant detailed account. In general, the content dealt with train and travel arrangements and the advertising business.	
325 Stage 2 2nd B.L. series (night 3)	"Oh crap."	Not awakened; as in speech 324.	

326
Stage 2
2nd B.L. series (night 3)

"[sigh] ooh—oh, shit—mm
[sigh]."

Not awakened; morning recall
as in speech 324.

327
Stage 1 NREM
2nd B.L. series (night 3)

"Oh—oh—um—hm—a hundred
percent for that—oh."

Not awakened; morning recall
as in speech 324.

328
Stage 2
2nd B.L. series (night 3)

"Mm—hm—mm—mm—Oh—Jesus
Christ—feeling great—ooh—huh
—huh—mm—mm—[tch]—oh—
just great [sighs]—uh—hm—
yeah—uh—oh—ooh damn [tch]
oh gotta see the proof of the
play, you know [sigh] uh—
such a major thing—we should
always say that proofs are actually pending we decide what we
want to do based on that but
anyway it's a 24 hour thing
and uh."

Not awakened; morning recall
as in speech 324.

329
Stage 2
2nd B.L. series (night 3)

"Oh—chr—let cri—oh [moan]—
oh—[moan]—mm—very
aggressive."

Not awakened; morning recall
as in speech 324.

330 Stage 1 NREM 3rd B.L. series (night 2)	"MM—and it must be the president because my wife and I are taking a tour with Melanie."	Not awakened; morning recall: "Something about scientists and doctors—there's this scientist who was doing some research but he didn't do a very good job; etc."	Possible reference to the author?
331 Stage 2 3rd B.L. series (night 2)	"[whispered mbls] Students paid for a dull piece of furniture—so dull I was getting mbl eight, sixteen mbl—good night."	Not awakened; morning recall as in speech 330.	
332 Stage 4 1st 3 hrs. 3rd B.L. series (night 3)	"Not it's mbls."	Not awakened; morning recall as in speech 330.	
333 Stage 2 1st 3 hrs. 3rd B.L. series (night 3)	"It's—so—typical."	Not awakened; morning recall as in speech 330.	
334 Stage REM 3rd B.L. series (night 3)	"It's—uh—like a Quaker boarding house with a Quaker office. He's going in to apply for a job—to an interview."	Not awakened; morning recall as in speech 330.	
335 Stage REM 3rd B.L. series (night 3)	"Uhm—oh—I think there's something wrong with my pastor—a house devoted to love—there's a swimming pool—which is mbls—we're going round and round.	Not awakened; morning recall as in speech 330.	

336
Stage 1 NREM
3rd B.L. series (night 3)

8. *Subject: H.E.*

"Mbls—how'd it even get there?—I told her not to put her presents in the church, or rather I didn't mbl—hm."

Not awakened; morning recall as in speech 330.

S was a liberal arts college student.

337
Stage 3
1st 3 hrs.
3rd B.L.

"What's the matter?—mm—you can talk to me [P] did you mbl."

Morning recall: none.

338
Stage 4
1st 3 hrs.
3rd B.L. + W.U.

"Ooh!"

Mentation report: "I was thinking—Dr. Arkin and— *we were talking* about—something not too sure—I'm not too sure what—something doctrinal—I was looking and let's see I was looking—I was eying in bed as I am and I was looking under my arm with my elbow up in the air at him and then I suddenly realized I was concentrating on his look—a little more than usually—and I had a strange sensation then about that."

Third-order concordance based on "we were talking."

339 Stage 2 3rd B.L. + W.U.	MM—NO—oo."	Mentation report: "You and I were talking about the significance of something—I don't remember what it was—it had something to do with Islam—or something like that—religion—and you supposed something I didn't agree with—you quoted a sentence obviously from religion—something written and accepted. I said that the sentence didn't state what you implied; it just sort of hinted at it."	Second-order concordance based on indications of disagreement in sleep-speech and mentation report.
340 Stage REM 3rd B.L. + W.U.	"(That was (?)) really beautiful."	Mentation report: "I was looking at a hillside and they were plowing it and mbl it patchwork and they were plowing it and as the plow went across the hill and down and the across and everything—weaving and pattern and just seeing the plow—changing—changing of space—the plow and pattern on the back of the hillside—*it was really pretty.*"	Second-order concordance based on expression of aesthetic admiration in both sleep-speech and mentation report.
341 Stage NREM 1st 3 hrs. 3rd B.L.—U-HYP	"That's (?) different."	Not awakened; morning recall too voluminous and does not warrant detailed account.	

342
Stage NREM
2nd U-HYP + PHS

"Ssss—mm—it's too (?) fine?"

Not awakened; morning recall
as in speech 341.

343
Stage NREM
5th U-HYP + PHS

"I did too [or two]."

Not awakened; morning recall
as in speech 341.

344
Stage NREM
1st 3 hrs.
6th U-HYP + PHS

"Hm—that must be mbl—hey,
Pop."

Not awakened; morning recall
as in speech 341.

345
At stage REM onset
1st 3 hrs.
1st T.B.L.

"[whispers and a moan] [P]
Help—help—mbls—help—help me,
God, help me—oh."

Not awakened; but stated on
the following morning that she
believed she talked in her sleep—
she remembered awakening after
talking but recalled no associated
dream. She was then told that
she had whimpered but this information triggered no recognition. She was then told that
she may have had a nightmare
and had implored God's help.
This resulted in instant recogni-

First-order concordance based on
stimulated recall in following morning. This is an interesting rare specimen of morning recall of sleep-talking episode, brought to mind by
stimulated recall technique.

tion with appropriate affect, and listening to the tape reinforced this recognition. The word "God" was the trigger—she remembered she "was in process of awakening and was saying, 'help me, God help me' at the end and I remember awakening after talking in sleep but do not recall dream or words."

346
Stage NREM
3rd T.B.L.

"What's the matter?"

Morning recall: "Walking into a very pleasant sunny hotel lobby in Puerto Rico—and meeting my friend Emily Yellin and other people and holding superficial cheerful conversation. Then she is no longer present and a group standing around eating some kind of sandwich. An important, desired person, leader-sort, young man, says we should always bring lunch when we come here."

9. Subject: O.A.

347
Stage 4
1st 3 hrs.
1st B.L.

"What? What?"

Morning recall: not available.

348
Stage 2
1st 3 hrs.
1st B.L.

"I don't know what—what the."

As in speech 347.

349
Stage 3
1st 3 hrs.
2nd B.L.

"Ren, den, den [singing] —I'm sorry—I talk too much."

Morning recall: "I remember something more or less happening to me. I remember talking with someone—maybe friends."

350
Stage 4
1st 3 hrs.
2nd B.L.

"Hey wait a minute [P] stop everything."

Morning recall: as in speech 349.

351
Stage 3
1st 3 hrs.
2nd B.L.

"No, no."

Morning recall: as in speech 349.

352
Stage REM
2nd B.L.

"No, not a sphere—I'm sorry."

Morning recall: as in speech 349.

353
Stage 3
2nd B.L.

"Hey, what are we playing, Bill? What are we playing for?"

Morning recall:
as in speech 349.

354
Stage 4
1st 3 hrs.
3rd B.L.

"Was he mbl fixed up inside?"

Morning recall:
1. "I went out with a few other couples in my car. We went to an affair and to eat—I don't remember who the people were."

2. "I remember talking to mother and aunt and my cousin in California. I asked them where something was and they misunderstood me and then I said, 'Where's the location— where's it located?' The dream took place in my house. We were all in the bedroom, father, mother, aunt and mother, and there was a girl trying on a dress. My aunt and mother are dressmakers."

355
Stage 3
1st 3 hrs.
3rd B.L.

"Mbl—why?"

Morning recall:
as in speech 354.

356
Stage 4
1st 3 hrs.
3rd B.L.

"What do you mean it's wrong: it's confidence, confidence. Oh, cut it out, mbls."

Morning recall:
as in speech 354.

357
Stage 3
1st 3 hrs.
3rd B.L.

"Yeah—yeah—yeah—mbl."

Morning recall:
as in speech 354.

358
Stage 3
3rd B.L.

"How come you say—I'm sorry—my mistake."

Morning recall:
as in speech 354.

359
Stage 2
3rd B.L.

"That's exactly it."

Morning recall:
as in speech 354.

360
Stage 3
3rd B.L.

"Mostly mbl—I notice that mbl."

Morning recall:
as in speech 354.

361
Stage 1 NREM
3rd B.L.

"Good."

Morning recall:
as in speech 354.

362
Stage 4
1st 3 hrs.
4th B.L.

"All the Japanese you want, but not me that's all."

Morning recall:
1. "I woke up and you gave me a melon. Then I went back to sleep."

2. "I don't know whether I saw it in the movies or read it: It was a western. There were two or three principal characters. I believe there was a fight, possibly with a knife. I wasn't frightened. It was a knife or a gun.

3. "I was checking meters. I couldn't read the numbers."

4. "A girl had told me she came to you. I said, 'Whatever happened to Joanne? Is she coming here any more? You said, 'No.' She had said she came here."

363 Stage 4 4th B.L.	"Did you hurt yourself? mbl."	Morning recall: as in speech 362.	
364 Stage 2 4th B.L.	"No, no mbl—because it doesn't make sense."	Morning recall: as in speech 362.	
365 Stage 2 4th B.L.	"Mbl—isn't that enough? [moans]."	Morning recall: as in speech 362.	
366 Stage 4 4th B.L.	"No, no, no, no please. Heh, heh. Can I stop them? What do you want to stop them or what? I don't know	Morning recall: as in speech 362.	It is tempting to relate this sleep-speech to the "fight" dream.

how they're going to come
down. I'm going to try to make
it. Nice and easy now [spoken
with an air of excited panic]."

367
Stage 2
4th B.L.

"Mbl the solution—the graph
of the equation gives you (?)
you know that also—well."

Morning recall:
as in speech 362.

368
Stage REM
4th B.L.

"OK (?) Charlie, I'm sorry.
Excuse me S—."

Morning recall:
as in speech 362.

369
Stage 4
1st 3 hrs.
5th B.L.

"It's following me. It's following you—not bad [laughter]."

Morning recall: "It took
place in California. We had a
house there. My father and I
went somewhere. I don't know
whether to buy something or see
someone. We were driving around
and I noticed an old fence ended
in some woman's house. We (?)
jumped over the fence. There
were lots of flowers there. Before
we left, my father was telling her
—my friend. Before we left, I
woke up."

370	"What—what—what."	Morning recall:
Stage 3		as in speech 369.
1st 3 hrs.		
5th B.L.		

370
Stage 3
1st 3 hrs.
5th B.L.

"What—what—what."

Morning recall:
as in speech 369.

371
Stage 2
1st 3 hrs.
5th B.L.

"I don't know mbl. I'm not sure."

Morning recall:
as in speech 369.

372
Stage REM
1st 3 hrs.
5th B.L.

"Oh, oh, oh—Don't."

Morning recall:
as in speech 369.

373
Stage 3
1st 3 hrs.
5th B.L.

"Aw, come on; stop the C— (?)."

Morning recall:
as in speech 369.

374
Stage 2
1st 3 hrs.
5th B.L.

"Going back to school."

Morning recall:
as in speech 369.

375
Stage 4
1st 3 hrs.
6th B.L.

"In here now."

Morning recall:
1. "I was in the house with my mother. She had gotten a call. My father must have called up. She must have been talking to me—before my father—something about getting results or something.

2. "I don't know if it started
with me actually taking part or if
I was reading this as a play—but
it ended—I was playing this part.
I don't know what it was—it started out with a girl coming from a
town to the city to this particular place—Someone—not myself—
and this girl had planned something so they taken some money.
I said to him, 'You're very clever,
very smart.' And as we were
leaving we saw the girls and we
knocked on the door and they
said they weren't staying there—
they were staying at another
room."

3. In another dream, *the subject recalled saying "Wait a minute"* in connection with someone leaving.

376
Stage 4
1st 3 hrs.
6th B.L.

"Fum, fum, fum, mbl—forget
it."

Morning recall:
as in speech 375.

377
Stage REM
6th B.L.

"Yes."

Morning recall:
as in speech 375.

378
Stage 2
6th B.L.

"I don't know mbl."

Morning recall:
as in speech 375.

379
Stage REM
6th B.L.

"Hey, wait a minute."

Morning recall:
as in speech 375.

First-order concordance based on the words "Wait a minute" appearing in both sleep-speech and mentation report.

380
Stage 4
1st 3 hrs.
1st B.L.–U-HYP

"No, no."

Morning recall: "We were in a room—just talking, talking around—nothing special."

381
Stage 2
1st 3 hrs.
1st B.L.–U-HYP

"Oh, my God! That's really amazing."

Morning recall:
as in speech 380.

382
Stage 2
1st B.L.–U-HYP

"I'm so (?) hot."

Morning recall:
as in speech 380.

383
Stage 4
1st 3 hrs.
2nd B.L.–U-HYP

"Aw, come on now [affect seemed fearful]."

Morning recall:
1. "I was downstairs in my aunt's house; we had quite a few people—company over there. I was sitting by the window. I

It is tempting to categorize speeches 383, 384, and 386 as possessing second-order concordance with dream 1; and speech 385 with dream 2; but see cautionary comments earlier.

noticed some—boys, much shorter
than usual—walking around with
bows. One had a big stick and
broke a window. Then they
started downstairs to where the
people lived. I went outside and
blocked the entrance. Then the
super came. They broke into his
house and came out with beer
cans and sandwiches—all of a sudden they multiplied and became
smaller and many more of them.
I think I started stepping on
them. As part of the same
dream, some friend of mine came.
He was figuring something out.
I think he was writing a paper.
Then someone else I know came
into the picture and showed him
how to solve what he was solving
for. [The subject felt that he
said the word "No!" during this
dream.]

2. "It involved [my] cousin.
Something happened to her. I

remember counting six. SHe had some kind of holes in her feet. I remember laughing at her. There was some other woman around."

384
Stage 3-4
1st 3 hrs.
2nd B.L.–U-HYP

"It seemed none of us watched over this."

Morning recall:
as in speech 383.

385
Stage 3
2nd B.L.–U-HYP

"Check the temperature."

Morning recall:
as in speech 383.

386
Stage 4
2nd B.L.–U-HYP

"HOLD IT! HOLD IT! HOLD IT! [as if in panic] [P] Too tight."

Morning recall:
as in speech 383.

387
Stage 2
2nd B.L.–U-HYP

"Mbls–but (?) my fault."

Morning recall:
as in speech 383.

388
Stage 4
1st 3 hrs.
3rd B.L.–U-HYP

"Oh, no, no, no."

Morning recall: "Someone gave me a test tube of something. I don't know what. They asked me to find out what was in it. Later on I recall going to a building and there was someone's office with a few friends of mine. It seemed to be like a doctor's place or a medical building. I was going in for something and

they were going to wait for me
till I came out. I don't know if
I had the test tube."

389
Stage 4
1st 3 hrs.
3rd B.L.–U-HYP

"Hey, wait a minute. You don't
throw it—mbl. And you don't
throw it—mbl. So don't
throw it."

Morning recall:
as in speech 388.

390
Stage 2
3rd B.L.–HYP

"No—mbl—Yes, I did [as if
defending himself]."

Morning recall:
as in speech 388.

391
Stage 4
1st 3 hrs.
4th B.L.–U-HYP

"Hey, wait a minute, wait a
minute, wait a minute [P]
eh."

Morning recall:
no dreams recalled.

392
Stage 4
1st 3 hrs.
4th B.L.–U-HYP

"Mbls—officer. No, no (?).
I'll be leaving five."

As in speech 391.

393
Stage 3
4th B.L.–U-HYP

"Mbl—wait a minute now. Help
me. No, no, no [P] I'm sorry
my mistake [P] mbl."

As in speech 391.

394	"No, no? We'll see mbl."	As in speech 391.
Stage 2		
4th B.L.–U-HYP		

395	"What are you talking about;"	As in speech 391.
Stage REM		
4th B.L.–U-HYP		

396
Stage 3
1st 3 hrs.
5th B.L.–U-HYP

"One more decimal—wait a second—particular mbl."

Morning recall:

1. "I remember—did you ever see those rockets where part of it detaches and glides to the ground? Me and two other people were detached from a mother rocket and we were just sort of gliding. We wanted to get to a specific place but we came short and ended up on a beach. It was myself, another fella and a girl. I'm not sure. At first we were trying to get a hitch, to get a ride to where we were going; but then that wasn't important anymore, and we just stayed on the beach.

2. "I hardly remember anything from it. It seemed as if I helped this woman. Wait a minute. I was with my little cousin. It took place in front of the house. This woman came along with a

carriage. There was a little baby in there and she was loaded. I helped her with something. I can't remember."

397
Stage 4
5th B.L.–U-HYP

"Pour quoi–what's the matter? What's the matter? What? Probably order some of it pretty soon [laughter]. What else?"

Morning recall:
as in speech 396.

398
Stage 3
5th B.L.–U-HYP

"Hmm–ask us–mbl. Don't worry–it [P] too slow."

Morning recall:
as in speech 396.

399
Stage 4
5th B.L.–U-HYP

"I'm sorry. Excuse me–what– Yes, sir. What did I say? Ha, ha. It's (?) jumping. What's the matter?"

Morning recall:
as in speech 396.

400
Stage REM
5th B.L.–U-HYP

"Oh, what."

Morning recall:
as in speech 396.

401
Stage 3
1st PHY–U-HYP

"What–what have you got in your hand there?"

Morning recall:
1. "I went to a soccer game with this girl I know. When we went

to the stadium, there was a fight between two groups of people with rifles. One group had red shirts on—they came out losing—they were disarmed and the arena of the stadium they let out. I was holding a rifle.

2. "I had another dream before number one. It seemed to have taken place in California. I remember being there with some relatives and their children. It was like in a huge park part of it—where people were—it was a sunny day—just grass on the ground. People were sliding like ice skates on skiis. There were a lot of people there, like a big amusement park. I remember this woman. She was feeding some kind of animal in some peculiar way.

3. "I went somewhere to fill out some type of application and I find some friend of mine working there. It took me a very long time to fill out the application. I made a few mistakes. I had to fill out separate sheets with all the courses and grades I've gotten also.

4. "I remember walking through somewheres where there are a lot of tables—a cafeteria or library. There was some people reading, some talking, some studying. I remember going to the library twice during the dream. Only once did I actually sit down to do anything."

402
Stage 4
1st 3 hrs.
1st PHS—U-HYP

"I don't know."

Morning recall:
as in speech 401.

403
Stage 4
1st 3 hrs.
1st PHS—U-HYP

"Huh—what—you mean a transducer mbl—walkie-talkie."

Morning recall:
as in speech 401

404
Stage 3
1st 3 hrs.
1st PHS—U-HYP

"Mbls—oww—well, whatever it is, it's supposed to work on me. —I'm pretty sure. How are you doing anyway?"

Morning recall:
as in speech 401.

405
Stage 3
1st 3 hrs.
1st PHS—U-HYP

"Wait a minute, wait a minute, wait a minute—whoa."

Morning recall: as in speech 401.

406
Stage 2
1st 3 hrs.
1st PHS—U-HYP

"Wow! mbl—I don't know—the usual crap and all that. How are the others—you know."

Morning recall: as in speech 401.

407
Stage 3
1st 3 hrs.
1st PHS—U-HYP

"[sounds of agreement] Yeah."

Morning recall: as in speech 401.

408
Stage 4
1st PHS—U-HYP

"Which one? [P] Which one?"

Morning recall: as in speech 401.

409
Stage 2
1st PHS—U-HYP

"Oh, oh, oh—well, yeah—mbl."

Morning recall: as in speech 401.

410
Stage 2
1st PHS—U-HYP

"Mbl—I don't know what it is."

Morning recall: as in speech 401.

411
Stage 2
1st PHS—U-HYP

"Mbl—it's, it's."

Morning recall. as in speech 401.

412
Stage 2
1st PHS—U-HYP

"[groan] Oh, Oh [P] what?" [as if listening, questioning and responding] uh-huh."

Morning recall:
as in speech 401.

413
Stage 3-4
1st 3 hrs.
3rd PHS—U-HYP

"I've got (a composition (?))—I don't know. Is there (another bedroom (?))?"

Morning recall:

1. The subject was going to his aunt's house, where his father and a cousin were expecting company. We drove with a friend in his car. The top was down. It began to rain. They looked for a parking space stopping in one spot and then moving on to another.

2. A class in school was being held outside, maybe in the street. A friend was making wisecracks.

3. The subject believed he had talked in his sleep saying, "If you want to save *money*, don't drink." He felt he awoke momentarily and uttered these words [see speech 419].

414
Stage 3
1st 3 hrs.
3rd PHS–U-HYP

"(Take it (easy)) easy!"

Morning recall:
as in speech 413.

415
Stage 2
1st 3 hrs.
3rd PHS–U-HYP

"Mm, hm—yes, yes!"

Morning recall:
as in speech 413.

416
Stage 2
3rd PHS–U-HYP

"Her eyes are blue?"

Morning recall:
as in speech 413.

417
Stage 2
3rd PHS–U-HYP

"Oh, nothing to say (?)—mbl."

Morning recall:
as in speech 413.

418
Stage 3
3rd PHS–U-HYP

"Oh, brother, oh [laughter]—
ho, ho, ho."

Morning recall:
as in speech 413.

No discernible concordance.

419
Stage REM
3rd PHS–U-HYP

"You're (looking for (?) some
money [P] don't you—(fur
coat (?))."

Morning recall:
as in speech 413.

First-order concordance based on
"money" in both sleep-speech and
morning recall.

420
Stage 4
1st 3 hrs.
4th PHS–U-HYP

"Hey; wait a minute; wait a minute; hold it [P] (tell me (?)) mbl
—Don't bet on me again. Don't
bet on me now!"

"Morning recall:
1. "The first one took place in
Manhattan. I was riding along
with one of my friends. My top
was down. Somebody was blocking the car. He said, 'Watch out

No discernible concordance.

for the water.' (somebody was washing his car.) I swerved around.

2. "The dream took place at home and there were many people there.

3. "Went back to a store to retrieve a package he had left there shopping. It was still there."

421
Stage 2
1st 3 hrs.
4th PHS−U-HYP

"Oh, boy."

Morning recall:
as in speech 420.

No discernible concordance.

422
Stage 2
1st 3 hrs.
4th PHS−U-HYP

"Homework, homework, homework—what homework? [P] mbl."

Morning recall:
as in speech 420.

423
Stage 4
1st 3 hrs.
4th PHS−U-HYP

"Mbl [laughter] very, very odd. I like that—that's very cute."

Morning recall:
as in speech 420.

424 Stage 2 1st 3 hrs. 4th PHS—U-HYP	"Yeah."	Morning recall: as in speech 420.
425 Stage 3 1st 3 hrs. 4th PHS—U-HYP	"Ma, ma."	Morning recall: as in speech 420.
426 Stage 3 4th PHS—U-HYP	"No—mbl—a little."	Morning recall: as in speech 420.
427 Stage REM 4th PHS—U-HYP	"Quiet down, will you?"	Morning recall: as in speech 420.
428 Stage 3 1st 3 hrs. 5th PHS—U-HYP	"Hello?—Hello?—mbl."	Morning recall: "I'm talking with my mother and she told me that I didn't talk in my sleep last night. She also said that A., a friend of the family, also said I hadn't talked. When I asked my mother how A. knew, she replied I talked to her on the phone."
429 Stage 4 1st 3 hrs. 6th PHS—U-HYP	"Hold it—hold it—hold it—it's no good. Where is he now? [P] So? So?"	Morning recall elicited during attempted hypnosis: 1. "I recall street numbers 73 and 74th St. There was a big parking lot where I parked my

car—*my parents* and cousin and myself were there. Many other people were there. We went to look around inside. We were just walking around. I'm not sure. Then I came back to the car and it was missing. I saw the *policeman*. The *police* car was driving away. I ran and tried to catch it to tell them but I couldn't catch them. I tried to look for other *policeman*—didn't see any. Finally, when I got back to the same place, someone told me the car was in a different parking lot. After that everything was all right.

2. "It took place in school. I had a class—I was supposed to go to class and the teacher was the instructor I had a year ago. It was in school. I wasn't going in the class. If I remember correctly, it was 10-15 minutes after the hour. I told a friend of

mine I didn't know what the hell was going on in there anyway. Finally, this friend of mine came. He convinced me to go to class. There was some kind of stupid reason for going in which it was 'warm' in there. I recall using that word, before we walked into class. There were some cookies outside the class— a kind my mother makes. I had two or three before walking in. I don't recall being in the class. It wasn't really conducted as a class. The teacher and a few of the students were there just talking around not really doing anything. A student was talking about the teacher. H said something that didn't make sense. He said this instructor changed his mark and gave him a grade, and he went from probation to an honor student."

430
Stage 2
1st 3 hrs.
6th PHS–U-HYP

"All right."

Morning recall:
as in speech 429.

431 Stage 3 1st 3 hrs. 6th PHS–U-HYP	"No! Please! No! No! No! No!—they were separated—his mother—policeman said that—please?"	Morning recall: as in speech 429.	First-order concordance based on reference to "policeman" in both sleep-speech and morning recall.
432 Stage 2 1st 3 hrs. 6th PHS–U-HYP	"Mbls—all right."	Morning recall: as in speech 429.	
433 Stage 2 6th PHS–U-HYP	"Oh—I'm sorry."	Morning recall: as in speech 429.	
434 Stage 2 6th PHS–U-HYP	"No, no, no, no [P] apartment mbls."	Morning recall: as in speech 429.	
435 Stage 2 6th PHS–U-HYP	"Oh, come on—no, no, no—I know."	Morning recall: as in speech 429.	
436 Stage 2 6th PHS–U-HYP	"Am I queer (?) or something?"	Morning recall: as in speech 429.	

437 Stage 2 6th PHS—U-HYP	"I was born mbl."	Morning recall: as in speech 429.	
438 Stage 2 6th PHS—U-HYP	"I know—mbls."	Morning recall: as in speech 429.	
439 Stage REM 6th PHS—U-HYP	"No—mbls."	Morning recall: as in speech 429.	
440 Stage 2 6th PHS—U-HYP	"No—no."	Morning recall: as in speech 429.	
441 Stage 2 6th PHS—U-HYP	"[mbls and moans] What shall I do?"	Morning recall: as in speech 429.	
442 Stage 2 6th PHS—U-HYP	"[laughter] I'll be damned—mbls —I don't know that—that's mbl."	Morning recall: as in speech 429.	
443 Stage 4 1st 3 hrs. 1st B.L. + W.U.	"Yeah—mm—it's high enough— yeah—it's not (tied to that thing (?))—mbl—right."	Mentation report [elicited 5 sec after sleep-speech: "No—no—it's still—actually I was thinking about having the subject sleep that's—getting uh—getting the subject to sleep."	No discernible concordance.

444
Stage REM
1st 3 hrs.
1st B.L. + W.U.

"No—no—why it's not—mbl."

Not awakened.

445
Stage 2
1st 3 hrs.
1st B.L. + W.U.

"Mm—mm—hey—wait a minute
will ya? I'm not even there yet—
mbl people mbl—wait a minute—
mbl—mm."

Mentation report [stimulated
recall—dialogue method]:
E: "Who did you want to wait,
   Al?"
S: "Mm?—excuse me?
E: "Who do you want to wait
   for a minute?
S: "I can't—I don't understand."
E: "Could you tell me what you
   were thinking about just now?"
S: "Uh—yes—let me see—it's—uh
   —I was not—I was not sleeping
   at the same time—I was not,
   you know—I was on the verge
   of falling asleep—uh—it seemed
   as if I had several ideas going
   through my head—sort of—
   you know—one—one tangled
   up with the other ones—I can't
   really pinpoint any—any one

No recall.

specific—a specific ONE—
that's about all I can tell offhand."

446 Stage 2 1st B.L. + W.U.	"Mm—mm—mm—mm—mm?— what was that?—yuh—what was that?—mm? [P] mm—hm."	Not awakened.	The sense of reality of an hallucin- ated experience is suggested by two requests for repetition in the sleep- speech, "What was that?"
447 Stage 1 1st B.L. + W.U.	"Oh—no—oh."	Not awakened.	
448 Stage 3 1st B.L. + W.U.	"What is this?"	Mentation report— stimulated recall— dialogue method: *E*: "What is what, Al?" *S*: "Oh—oh—I—uh—I was handed a—well—let me see— let me describe it—I was handed something—a math- ematical expression to give to someone or other. I was just looking at it and I said, 'What is this?' and that's all I meant by it—I was dreaming."	First-order concordance based on "What is this?" appearing in both sleep-speech and mentation report. Note the spontaneous description by the subject that the experience was a dream.
449 Stage 4 1st 3 hrs. 2nd B.L. + W.U.	"Mm—rape! (?) mbl—of course— of course—mbl—16—16 [P] mm."	Mentation report: "No— I [chuckles] it's odd but I just— seriously, I thought, you know, mbl hair flopping back and forth —nothing, specific—nothing special but it was hair just waving back and forth—in the air."	No discernible concordance.

450
Stage 2
2nd B.L. + W.U.

"Hm−mm−mm−charming (?)."
[After eliciting the mentation report I listened to this speech again and the slightly unclear word "charming" seemed in fact clearly discernible as "kill me"− but this may have been the effects of the suggestion.]

Mentation report: "Mm−oh− wait a˙minute−I−something like 'kill me'−or something like that− it was a−I guess−part of a dream or sort of a question that was posed−not by any particular person−as to what would happen you had too much of something− some−you know−something of that sort−and I said 'Kill me,' I guess."

First-order concordance based not on a word held in common, but the identifying feature of a two syllable, sonically similar expression in sleep-speech and mentation report−"charming (?)" and "kill me," respectively. The subject himself was uncertain.

451
Stage 3
2nd B.L. + W.U.

"Wha?−What?−Who?−I didn't hear."

Mentation report−stimulated recall elicited by dialogue meth-od:
E: "What didn't you hear?"
S: "That last one."
E: "What last one?"
S: "Ahm−something (place right (?)) by January−mbl−(don't know (?))."
E: "What was that?"
S: "(I don't know (?))−I don't know−I THOUGHT I did."

First-order concordance based on the word "hear" in the sleep-speech and the word "heard" in the men-tation report. Another possibility is third-order concordance based on reference to subject's talking− "−mention it−".

E: "Thought you who?" [Until now, the subject spoke in a soft voice—slightly trance-like and child-like with a slight whine; his next comments were spoken louder, more adult-like, definite and "awake."]

S: "I thought I did—thought I *heard* something (place right (?)) by January mbl."

E: "Thought you heard WHAT?"

S: "Hah!—by January."

E: "What about January?"

S: "Nothing—I just thought in my dream that I was asked, you know, I don't know, for some reason to *mention it* or get papers OR SOMETHING from that time. I don't KNOW—it just came up."

452
Stage 2
2nd B.L' + W.U.

"Yeah—yeah—yeah—OBviously."

Mentation report—
stimulated recall—
dialogue method:

E: "Obviously what?"

S: "Uh—someone—uh someone had come up with—it was a saying which followed directly from a title or something, you know—they started—they started to say it and I said, 'Obviously' you know, it followed."

First-order concordance based on the word "obviously" appearing in both sleep-speech and mentation report.

| 453
Stage 2
2nd B.L. + W.U. | "No–no (?)–mm–mm–mm–
[spoken rapidly as if communi-
cating negation]." | Mentation report–
stimulated recall–
dialogue method:
E: "What did you say?"
S: "I don't know–did I say
anything?"
E: "What was in your mind?"
S: *I was just discussing with*
someone or talking with
someone about–it was about
New York City, I believe." | Third-order concordance based on
reference to self "discussing" and
"talking" in the mentation report. |

10. Subject: A.T.   *S was a liberal arts student.*

| 454
Stage 2
1st 3 hrs.
1st B.L. + W.U. | "Aah–mm–hm–it's cannassert
[sic]." | Mentation report: "I can't re-
member anything. Uh–that's it–
–except it was just quiet" [This
report was elicited 98 sec after
the sleep-speech because he was
difficult to arouse.] | No recall. Note the possible neo-
logism "cannasert." |

| 455
Stage 2
1st 3 hrs.
1st B.L. + W.U. | "Hm–a fact–thassa fact–I was
mbl–yeah–this was over at the
Medical Center. Uh–mm–I don't
remember this well. It just sort | Mentation report: "Yeah–make–
uh–what was I thinking of just
then?–uh–*I was just discussing*
something with you–*I was just* | Third-order concordance based on
the reference to self-talking in men-
tation report: "I was just discuss-
ing." Note the disorganization of |

of occurred to me while you mentioned City College. Mbl-open and I was tired and I just sort of wanted—and these things are just sort of wanted—and these things are just sort of handy to have—because I hadn't remembered where everything was—like—I don't know. Priests—priests for teaching and all this rot (?). It's a CATHOLIC school—and I just went up and sort of relaxed now I went up and—mm—it was relaxing compared to what I imagined it would be on a regular college where you sort of had to pound like Sammy Glick to get registered—mm."

discussion my—just was dreaming before then, wasn't I? uh—MM—there's nothing important—I was just—I was just—I was just—I'd just fallen asleep for a second from what you'd said a few minutes before—or from what I'd said a few minutes before and that's it."

the speech despite the prevailing theme of academic life.

456
Stage 2
1st 3 hrs.
2nd B.L. + W.U.

"Hey Bill."

Mentation report: no recall.

No recall.

457
Stage 2
2nd B.L. + W.U.

"I'd say that was [whispered]."

Mentation report: "Um?—uh—I had a cocktail party or something and somebody's talking to me, talking to somebody but nothing important—um—uh—uh—no I can't remember anything about what was going on—no—no—no—no—no—can't recall all—I can't

Third-order concordance based on references to self-talking in the mentation report: "We were talking" and "I was preaching."

recall what was going on—there was somebody talking to me—yeah—Paul W.—a friend was talking to me and *we were talking* about something. *I think I was sort of preaching* or something and he—that was it. You know *we talked* for a few minutes, not very much."

458
Stage 2
1st 3 hrs.
Recovery night after two nights on *d*-amphetamine and pentabarbital.

"That's interesting."

Mentation report: no recall.

459
Stage 2
1st 3 hrs.
Recovery night as in speech 458.

"Mbl—mm—I wouldn't turn it on, don't know anything about the electronic makeup of the thing—what? (dixie cup lock-ups (?))."

Mentation report: "What was going through my mind? Um—nothing much really—uh—just the search for somebody who's suitably compatible that's the one thing, uh—I don't know, just curiosity this is another—uh-huh."

No discernible concordance.

460
Stage NREM
1st 3 hrs.
Recovery night as in speech 458.

"Huh—I don't know, gee, I don't know—uh [P] um—um—I don't know [P] huh [P] huh."

Not awakened.

461
Stage 2
1st 3 hrs.
Recovery night as in speech 458.

"Yeah uh—huh—mm—don't know whether I have—Wow—what'd you do?"

Mentation report: "Apparently it was the movement or the fact that you and Dr. Arkin are moving your office somewhere else—um—because over cross the street, he has a desk open, about 25 capacity, 25% capacity and there's all sorts of things, all sorts of very fine, very rich things on the desk top and I had this dream that I was with somebody this time it was a girl, wh—so—and—and she looked at the, well we both sort of looked at them and one of us or the wind or somebody shut the door so we couldn't look at them anymore, and that's it."

No discernible concordance.

462
Stage 2
1st 3 hrs.
Recovery night as in speech 458.

"Um—yes—mm—started, yeah—um—yeah—huh—what are you short of places for people to sleep—um."

Mentation report: "Yes, oh, I just woke up uh—uh—I would work from four to two whenever I had to go to work which was sometime it's not—um—who's in charge—um—well, a girl with a soft face, not so hard and not so castrating was enchanting it or at least in charge—um."

No discernible concordance.

463
Stage 2
1st 3 hrs.
Recovery night as in speech 458.

"I, I, I—wh—wh—wh—are you dragging something down? I have this feeling something's about to fall—it was near the table and I just—mbl—I'm sorry, I'm very sorry, uh, huh."

Mentation report: "Yes? Uh, uh well, I'm at this party with a couple of friends from Columbia who are very mbl—very, very nice friends—I well—we sort of played around, look at things that we don't know how to fix or any thing mbl."

No discernible concordance.

464
Stage NREM
1st 3 hrs.
Recovery night as in speech 458.

"I bet—uh—hum—have to think about that—anyway mbl just come out of the woodwork and I can't really remember what happened except that I well, we were looking in the la—it seemed the rather expensive type things—that's what the university normally uses, and the fullest mbl was on the left and that was the youngest of the *leak, leakafter, leaft*—[sic] *least* active hum— they threw that, on their they, the appointments became less and less well spaced, or at any rate they began to compete with the rest of—the office for sovereignty."

Not awakened.

Note the perseveration and groping for the target word "least" (italicized). Such phenomena suggests concurrent operation of speech-monitoring mechanisms during some sleep-speech states.

465 Stage NREM 1st 3 hrs. Recovery night as in speech 458.	"Um–[grunts]–and that's about all I can remember really."	Not awakened.	
466 Stage NREM 1st 3 hrs. Recovery night as in speech 458.	"Somebody called me–um–doing to her–um–uh–huh–huh."	Not awakened.	
467 Stage NREM 1st 3 hrs. Recovery night as in speech 458.	"Um–[grunts] great–[grunts]."	Not awakened.	
468 Stage 2 Recovery night as in speech 458.	"Yeah."	Mentation report: no recall.	
469 Stage NREM Recovery night as in speech 458.	"Umm–um–see–uh [P] umm, it's easy."	Mentation report: *"I was talking* to somebody in an office um."	Third-order concordance based on reference to self talking in the mentation report.
470 Stage NREM Recovery night as in speech 458.	"Yeah–um–I know what you mean, though–(very much (?))."	Mentation report: no recall.	
471 Stage 2 Recovery night as in speech 458.	"Uh–what was that? Hey, what happened here?–um."	Mentation report: "Um? Yes, uh well, I was just, just dozed off and I'm looking at the facilities in the Fullman Auditorium for–well–for ladies rooms	No discernible concordance.

and refreshments and things and I can't remember anything specifically and I can't remember anything even generally, beyond the pile of paper work that's necessary."

472 Stage 3-4 1st 3 hrs. T.B.L. + W.U.	"Wai—wai—ho—ho—ho—oho [sigh] gotta check the file, gotta check the file out on those, hah?—hey ol' boy?"	Mentation report: no recall.
473 Stage 3-4 1st 3 hrs. T.B.L. + W.U.	"Sure—mbl."	Mentation report: no recall.
474 Stage NREM 1st 3 hrs. T.B.L. + W.U.	"[moan] What was that? What was that? [whispered]"	Not awakened.
475 Stage 2 T.B.L. + W.U.	"Mm—sorry."	Mentation report: no recall.

476	"Sounds okay?"	Mentation report: no recall.
Stage 3-4		
T.B.L. + W.U.		

11. Subject: A.M.

S a college student; Canadian

477	"There seems to be some concern about whether I wear a short or a long dress."	Mentation report with stimulated recall:	No recall. This categorization is based on the first response of no recall of the sleep experience together with the stimulated recall referring to a concordant surmise related to daytime events rather than immediately prior, vividly recalled sleep experience.
Stage 2			
B.L. + W.U.			

S: "Um, oh, um—I don't know 'cause you, I was startled—forgot what I was thinking."

E: "Do these words mean anything to you—'it seems to be a question of whether I'll wear a short dress or a long dress.' "

S: "Oh, yeah—my roommate was going to a dance Friday night and so we were, we spent all week trying to find a long dress and stayed up, you know, later than usual, but I stayed up late last night —um—fixing a dress for her, taking it in and stuff, and then she found out today that she has to wear a short dress, so all the work was done in vain, and she had to, you know, change all her accessories and everything so I was probably thinking about that."

| 478
Stage 2
1st 3 hrs.
Recovery night—two prior
nights on *d*-amphetamine-pento-
barbital | "Wanta try it? [P] probably
yeah but it's kind of cold." | Mentation report:
E: "What were you thinking."
S: "about going to sleep." | No discernible concordance. |

12. Subject: B.L.   *S was a married college student*

| 479
Stage 2
1st 3 hrs.
1st B.L. + W.U. | "Mbl—jealous." | Mentation report—stimulated
recall:
E: "What was going through
your mind?"
S: "Oh, I was sort of well—think-
ing of sitting on benches at
the little park that's by the
um—the exit at mm—CCNY—
the little part where all the
neighbors sit around and just
look at the people walking by,
and it's dusty and not much
grass—and hot and dry and
pretty noisy—I can't remem-
ber going asleep from last
time." | No discernible concordance. No
additional recall. |

E: "Do you feel you were dreaming?"

S: "Yeah, but I don't remember being asleep."

E: "Were any of the people talking?"

S: "No—I wasn't up close to them—it was just, you know, that's how it was around, they had nothing to do with anything—nothing was going on."

480
Stage 2
1st 3 hrs.
1st B.L. + W.U.

"Uh huh—uh huh—uh huh."

Mentation report—stimulated recall:

E: "What was going through your mind?"

S: "Oh, I was thinking of walking a dog along the sidewalk there —that's about all."

E: "Were you speaking with anyone?"

S: "No—I don't think so. I don't remember being close to anyone at all."

E: "Do you remember saying "Uh huh"?"

S: "No—did I say that?"

E: "Yes."

S: [laughs] "No—I don't remember."

E: Can you connect it with anything?"

No discernible concordance. Stimulated recall results in no additional recall related to the sleep-speech.

481
Stage 2
1st B.L. + W.U.

"Well—a little sore—sit on my other side, huh?"

S: "Maybe I was buying something in a little store?"
E: "Do you remember that going through your mind?"
S: "Oh, I was shopping—maybe I had just bought something."
E: "Do you remember anything else?"
S: "No."

Mentation report: stimulated recall:
E: "What was going through your mind?"
S: "I was just falling asleep again."
E: "Were you thinking about anything?"
S: "Latin words."
E: "Do you remember what words?"
S: "Ohh—sort of price tag sort of words—that's how they seemed."

Third-order concordance based on reference to "I was just trying to say" in the mentation report.

E: "Do the words I'll turn over on my other side mean anything?"

S: "Um—I might have said that when I was awake, but I don't remember."

E: "Can you remember anything more of what was going through your mind?"

S: "I was at a meat market and um, I don't know cuts of meat very well, and they weren't labeled, ans so *I was just trying to say* the names of the meats to myself just then."

E: "Do you feel you were dreaming or thinking?"

S: "I don't know, it was just one of those little lapses, I guess I was dreaming."

482
Stage 2
1st B.L. + W.U.

"Ohh, yeah—mm—remember the, wanting to look inside the CCNY bookstore but not having the time, uh—oh."

Mentation report—stimulated recall:

E: "What was going through your mind?"

S: "Oh, something was going through my mind—oh—it was sort of an immediate thing too—oh—it was in a *store* and

First-order concordance based on reference to "store" in the mentation report and "bookstore" in the sleep-speech. Despite the first-order concordance, however, it is interesting in the light of the dissociation hypothesis, that the presentation of the specific complete sleep-speech

it was on a hot summer day
and it was something that was
out on the counters [P] but
beside from that I don't remember."

E: "Were you talking to someone?"

S: "I don't know—I might have
been talking to the sales clerk
asking what it was, or how
much it cost, or something
like that."

E: "Were you at the store, or
wanting to be at the store?"

S: "Oh, I was at it—I was I was
standing in the aisle."

E: "Do these words mean anything to you— 'wanting to
look inside the CCNY bookstore'?"

S: "No, but that's what I've
wanted to do for awhile."

elicited no sense of immediate recall
of just having uttered these words.

483 Stage 4 1st 3 hrs. 2nd B.L. + W.U.	"Mm—mm—hm—that's a problem —to you that you'll (?) peroxide [sigh] —ah—I have no idea—a—hm —[sigh] oh, I may feature something on the eyelids—hm."	Mentation report: "Well, I wasn't entirely asleep. I don't think—um —I thought I heard a—well, I'm not sure whether I was awake or not—um—at any rate I—mm—hm— hm—anyhow, it's a pretty good idea just to find out whether I could close my eyes for a little while, open them or turn my head—um—I was thinking of something—I knew that in my mind I was sort of humming a little song that I don't know the name of—that I heard on the radio earlier today."	No discernible concordance.

13. Subject: S.R.   *S was a college student.*

484 Stage 4 1st 3 hrs. Recovery night—2 nights *d*-amphetamine-pentobarbital	"Oh, that machine [whispered]."	Mentation report: "It's hard to say—I don't think there was anything special I was thinking at that moment."	No discernible concordance.

14. Subject: B.J.   *S was a college student.*

485 Stage 2 1st B.L. + W.U.	"No—no [moan]."	Mentation report: "Yes—I'm in a garden—purple flowers and black grass and at midnight the flowers start *singing lullabies*, and a pink moon comes out—there's a great big, black wall to this garden—	Third-order concordance based on a reference to vocalization "singing lullabies": Note the rich visual imagery from Stage 2.

and a great big wrought iron gate
and at the gate—the entrance way
is guarded by a golden peacock—
that's all."

---

15. Subject: G.R.   *S was a college student.*

486	"No! No! No! wait, no Sam	Mentation report—stimulated	No recall. Note the amnesia despite
Stage 3-4	—wait—No Sam—s—s—s—Sam—	recall:	intense affect.
1st 3 hrs.	No, no, I, I, I was, I was,	*E*: "Tell me everything that was	
1st B.L. + W.U.	awakened—mm hm [agitatedly]."	going through your mind."	
		S: "No, not exactly—Na, I don't	
		remember."	
		E: "Were you perhaps fighting	
		with somebody?"	
		S: "N—n—no."	
		E: "What emotions were you	
		aware of?"	
		S: "Nothing."	

---

16. Subject: D.J.   *S was a college student.*

487	"Um—yeah."	Mentation report: "Oh, I had	Third-order concordance based on
Stage 2		something to do with—I don't	reference to subject's "telling some-
1st B.L. + W.U.		remember, it just had something	body" in the mentation report.
		to do with *me telling somebody*	

something—like they were waiting
for my opinion and I had gave—
I gave it to them in about a word,
and I don't have anything from
before that."

488
Stage REM
Recovery night—2 nights
d-amphetamine-pentobarbital.

"Unh—that's it."

Mentation report: [The first part
of this mentation report was not
recorded.] "And *she was
describing* in a kind of humorous
way, what men were, what men
were like—*she was giving an un-
favorable description* in a kind of
humorous way and then er—which
was quite long; in fact, the whole
dream consisted of *that* and just a
sort of pause at the end to see if
that was the whole story."

Third-order concordance based on
reference to a person speaking at
length in the mentation report;
apparently, the sleep-speech occurred
during the pause at the end mentioned by the subject.

489
Stage 2
Recovery night as in speech 488.

"Uh—party politics."

Mentation report: "I was listening, uhm—I was in some big new
theater—it had just opened—it's
first time it had been used—and
I was listening to this girl describe
what was wrong with it to me in
a humorous way, and er—*I was
sort of taking it in and answering
it* and trying to observe where
she might be right—where she
didn't seem to be—and then at
the very end of the thing there
was sort of a scene like away

Third-order concordance based on
references to a dream character and
the subject verbalizing.

from this, as if I was putting my
hands on her in a, as if to em-
brace her or pull her to me. I
sup—well, it's like I put one of
my hands on her and she flinched
violently, because it was extremely cold, my hand was like ice."

17. Subject: G.P.   *S was a college student.*

490 Stage 4 1st 3 hrs. 1st B.L. + W.U.	"[sounds of distress] Jesus Christ."	Mentation report: no recall.	
491 Stage 3-4 1st 3 hrs. 2nd B.L. + W.U.	"Eeh—fantastic (?)—yes."	Mentation report: "There was —something about me *teaching*. I was in a room—it was some-thing to do with me *teaching*—I just had a student come up to me and *ask* me a question."	Third-order concordance based on reference to verbalizing in the mentation report.
492 Stage 3-4 2nd B.L. + W.U.	"[whisper] (What y'say (?))"	Mentation report: "This was about—someone—*we were talking* about—the—er—experiment again,	Third-order concordance based on reference to verbalizing in the men-tation report.

		about um—how the—we go, come here, and sleep and you listen in and then, er—I can't remember."	
493 Stage 4 1st 3 hrs. Recovery night—two nights *d*-amphetamine-pentobarbital.	"[sounds, garbled, calling out, questioning, anxious, disappointed] Eh?—alri' Molly! Maia—Ma—eh—bah—ma—ma."	Mentation report: no recall.	
494 Stage 2 1st 3 hrs. Recovery night as in speech 492.	"Yes—yes."	Mentation report: no recall.	
495 Stage 2 3rd B.L. + W.U.	"Mbls—a perfect grand (?)."	Mentation report: "I was thinking about—this experiment—something to do with different degrees of consciousness but—*I was asking* Dr. Arkin you know—oh what was I—oh—I don't know, it just seemed that I was on a different level, on one time that I woke up than I had been on another, and that er—this had merited looking into and *I just—we were just talking it over.*"	Third-order concordance based on references to verbalization in the mentation report.

18. Subject: G.C.   *S was an office worker.*

496 Stage 2 1st B.L. + W.U.	"Mm—no—that's all I remember—[sigh]."	Mentation report: "I was thinking about this experiment—I was that you were giving me in-	Second-order concordance based on reference to the experiment situation suggested by the stereotyped

structions—do something else—I got on the floor [P] [drifting back to sleep] —seems to some [P] maybe it's just a scratch of some sort [P] I feel as though there's a scratch on glass [P] it was a field."

E: "Do you remember anything else?"

S: "No, I don't."

sentence, "that's all I remember" in the sleep-speech.

| 497
Stage 3
1st B.L. + W.U. | "Mm—blue—blue and turquoise—mm." | Mentation report: "Something to do with a form paper." | No discernible concordance. |

19. Subject: K.L. .... *S was a college student.*

| 498
Stage 2
1st 3 hrs.
1st B.L. + W.U. | "Well um." | Mentation report: "I just started to—tell you without asking but I woke myself up—it was something, somewhat of *an explanation* about what I was doing to somebody, *I think explaining* this whole experiment, and it was, whoever it was, was wearing | Third-order concordance based on references to verbalization in the mentation report. |

something with polka dots; it was a girl with very long hair, um— and *then I started to speak and woke up.*"

499 Stage 2 1st B.L. + W.U.	"Sometimes I think I got the whole world on my mbl—you know crumble away into dust."	Mentation report: "Thinking that it was in front of the hospital, was a guy from Columbia, was collecting these things, the pa— you know, whatever there'd be to show of this, and my, um."	No discernible concordance.
500 Stage 2 3rd B.L. + W.U.	"Um—gee, I don't remember again; I'm sorry, nothing important."	Mentation report—stimulated recall: *E*: "What were you thinking?" *S*: "Um—well, I was, I was awake —um—I just think I was thinking about this *experiment*— and um—something like that— I don't know." *E*: "Do the words 'nothing important' mean anything?" *S*: "Um—um—no, they don't."	Second-order concordance based on the suggestive relationship between the stereotyped sentence in the experiment 'I don't remember again' and reference to the experiment in the mentation report.

20. Subject: L.E.   *S was a college student.*

501 Stage 2 1st B.L. + W.U.	"[sigh] [P] No I—I can't—yeah, it's so [slight chuckle]."	Mentation report: "Oh, um— I was thinking about um— heavens, I was hardly went to sleep I don't think—oh—good God—Terry again—*I was talking to him* um—was standing up—	Third-order concordance based on references to verbalization in the mentation report.

talking to him on the street—and
then in my house—about um—oh,
I think it was about his family
and how horrible they are, just
sort idly talking about it. Not
really serious. I think that's what
we were talking about I can't
remember anything else."
E: "Do you remember sighing?"
S: "No [chuckle]."

502
Stage 2
1st 3 hrs.
2nd B.L. + W.U.

"Um—um—um—the main press
(?) I have is, sounds so silly, a
sunny street, I don't know why,
or where, or anything, just a sunny street [laughs] and that's it—
oh sure, taking it in and creating
great works."

Mentation report—stimulated
recall—dialogue methos:
E: "Did you take it in?"
S: "[laughs] Again I don't know
what's going on—uh—no—uh—
that's funny, I can't, I knew
you didn't say that and Is—I
mean ooh, somebody said,
'taking it in and *taking it in*
no doubt'—some part of my
mind, and I answered, 'sure
I'm taking it in and creating
great works', it's the strangest
thing—uh—and I was referring

First-order concordance based on
identical words and phrases held in
common by sleep-speech and mentation report. Noteworthy is the unusual report of intrapsychic dissociative experience.

		to the fact that on this *sunny street*, there are people sometimes, sort of student types kind of strolling, all guys, I think, in suits and ties with sort of, I think it's sort of graduate student level, 'cause they're neat [laughs]."	
503 Stage 4 2nd B.L. + W.U.	"Umm—I don't care."	Mentation report: stimulated recall: *S*: "I can remember a church but I don't know whether that's from a dream or from what it really looks like." *E*: "Do the words 'I don't care' mean anything?" *S*: "Not in any particular dream tonight—no."	No discernible concordance.
504 Stage 2 Recovery night—*d*-amphetamine-pentobarbital combination	"How gloppy I am basically."	Mentation report: "Gosh, I can't remember—very busy about something—I think it was school or that kind of thing—friends were there."	No discernible concordance
			S a married college student and mother.
21. Subject: H.C.			
505 Stage 3 1st 3 hrs. 1st B.L. + W.U.	"Hi."	Mentation report—stimulated recall: "I was thinking about boots, I guess, about how we'd have to keep boots on or else they would get all wet."	No discernible concordance.

E: "Were you speaking to any-
body?"
S: "No."
E: "Does the word 'Hi' mean
anything?"
S: "No."

506 Stage 2 1st B.L. + W.U.	"No, I don't want to."	Mentation report: "I was going for a walk and you said to un-plug th–, the wires and I said, *'No, I don't need to:'* and that's all."	First-order concordance based on identical words and similar sentence in both sleep-speech and mentation report.
507 Stage 2 1st B.L. + W.U.	"No–o."	Mentation report: "I was think-ing that–you told me–to stop dreaming and take a walk, and I said, *'No'* because I was hooked up to the bed–and then there were about six people in the room, unhooking me."	First-order concordance based on an identical word in sleep-speech and mentation report.
508 Stage 4 2nd B.L. + W.U.	"Mbls [sounding like announce-ments at an air terminal–plane announcements] Airway–	Mentation report–stimulated recall: No recall following initial query.	No recall. The spelling of words suggests activity of speech self-monitoring.

	R–E–V–I–S–E–D [spelled out] mbl–flight mbl–secure."	*E*: "Does reciting letters someing like A–S–D–U–C mean anything to you?" *S*: "No."	
509 Stage 2 2nd B.L. + W.U.	"Uh–excuse me–mbl."	Mentation report–stimulated recall: *E*: "Can you remember anything that was going through your mind?" *S*: "No." *E*: "Do the words 'excuse me' mean anything?" *S*: "No. Nothing more than just excuse me."	No recall.
510 Stage 2 1st 3 hrs. Recovery night *d*-amphetamine-pentobarbital.	"Ohh!"	Mentation report: "Oh, first, I was thinking about the, the pines'n, in southern California, and we were walking along, and we went by these pines and we got, they all got out of the box'n you came down and you went riding on your bike."	No discernible concordance.
511 Stage 2 1st 3 hrs. Recovery night as in speech 510.	"Uh–[sigh] chicken her, other ones–oh–all–other ones–chickens."	Mentation report–stimulated recall: *E*: "What were you thinking?" *S*: "M–oh–let's see–oh first of all I was thinking about the Julia books, and how they were outside getting them–um–and."	No discernible concordance with initial mentation report; first-order concordance with stimulated recall based on reference to "chickens" in both sleep-speech and stimulated recall content.

E: "And then?"

S: "Then they had—had a guy in green sweater, he kept dis-appearing."

E: "Do you remember anything else?"

S: "Um—no."

E: "Do you remember about chickens?"

S: "Yes. Yes. In the first part, er, they was all about *chickens* —red *chickens* and then— yellow *chickens* 'n all kinds of mesu—mesuzah and *chickens* and *chickens.*"

512
Stage 2
Recovery night as in speech 510.

"Ohh—what d'you think a whale eats?"

Mention report: "I was think-ing that I didn't get to sleep but I know I went to sleep—because of a surprise I was goin' out with the *boats* again, 'n I think it's because I don't understand. I don't know wh' they, the people on the *boats* are, are being chased and I don't know why, 'n oh—I don't know what else."

Second-order concordance based on reference to a nautical topic in both sleep-speech and mentation report— "whales" and "boats".

513
Stage 2
Recovery night as in speech 510.

"O—oh—o—okay."

Mentation report—stimulated recall: "I was thinking that, we were in, in this, building and they were, they were writing down all the things that are the matter with it, with the place. We were dreaming about it—and uhm—I just remember that Batman and Robin were chasing them, the other man with the cape last week—"
E: "Do you remember saying 'Okay'?"
S: "I don't know."

No discernible concordance.

514
Stage 2
Recovery night as in speech 510.

"You realize it's dirty [sigh]."

Mentation report—stimulated recall:
"I was thinking about Carol D's husband, I think he was in, let's see, we were back in Connecticut, and I think *she said* he was New York going to school, but I think he was going to be a bartender or something like that—that's all."
E: "Do the words 'do you realize it's dirty' mean anything?"
S: "I remember that *I mentioned* to her that Doug and I were planning to go to New York and she may have said, 'Do you realize it's dirty?'—, it's the only thing I can think of."

No discernible concordance for mentation report; possible first-order concordance for stimulated recall content; however, because the subject was tentative, this cannot be concluded definitely.

S was a married college student.

515 Stage 3-4 1st 3 hrs. 1st B.L. + W.U.	"Mm—a cloud of dust—whinny."	Mentation report: "Was thinking of a mighty cloud of dust, a cloud of dust and mighty Hi Ho Silver, describing the actions of uh—um—mm, um—um—I don't have the name—the action—the institutor of a psychological study is—just the institutor and nothing else—more of a disadvantage after that—an organization man, that's what he actually is, that's about it."	First-order concordance based on the phrase "cloud of dust" in both sleep-speech and mentation report.
516 Stage 2 1st B.L. + W.U.	"That's her—mmm—mmm—mmm —mmm."	Mentation report: "Getting back to the same things again—getting squared away—further—dreaming —mbls—oh, hey—that's all."	No discernible concordance.
517 Stage 2 1st B.L. + W.U.	"One of us."	Mentation report: "We were thinking about what is—mbl—I think it was home, how they are, string of things—if then, if then,	No discernible concordance.

518
Stage NREM
1st B.L. + W.U.

"That's all now?"

Not awakened.

519
Stage 3
2nd B.L. + W.U.

"Mbl—no good as a drydock."

Mentation report: "This—one passage where it says—the hull of a ship, single mast, single boom, for a cutway (?) sail—probably (?)."

Second-order concordance based on the sleep-speech and mentation report referring to a nautical topic.

520
Stage 2
2nd B.L. + W.U.

"(What is that (?))—problem in your hand, huh?"

Mentation report: "The—er—gimmick we see there is something completely new to me. I never saw it before, before this, this evening—er—the relationship of—er—the characters to each other is something new too; I don't think I've been in that situation before—I know I've never seen anything like this character—that's all."

No discernible concordance.

521
Stage 1
1st 3 hrs.
3rd B.L. + W.U.

"M—yeah—how many actions (?) do you have?"

Mentation report: "Oh, it was—thinking about myself and my—my group's position at these things. Once again it's—wasn't asleep, was awake with the newspaper, definitely a newspaper and a *discussion* of what I had—

First-order concordance based on the same words or phrases appearing in sleep-speech and mentation report—"action," "how many."

before any troops, before any *action* was made—and then—the question of *how many* more could be brought in, *how many* we needed, what they were doing, who was gonna be in charge of that—uh, let's see—the main concern which we had so much trouble with was myself— was the lawyer who was out- ranked by the visiting general who demanded certain things being done without really con- sulting his subordinates or listen- ing to them—that's it."

522
Stage 2
3rd B.L. + W.U.

"Mbls—(if you know (?)) you're doing this, it's all right."

Mentation report: "Right now I'm not—dreaming of anything special at all—just reviewing the various dreams and various infor- mation about the dream that we have, but I wasn't thinking of any particular dream at all, *talk- ing* about the—dreams on the whole, doctors—one of the doc-

Third-order concordance based on reference to "talking" in the menta- tion report.

tors here, that's all in that dream."

523
Stage 2
3rd B.L. + W.U.

"So? (?)–didn't mbl–was annoyed mbl doing that scale either."

Mentation report: "Still thinking about the same problem— some kind of problem coming up after—money has been collected, uh—some mbl, research, whatever you want to call it and— money is being collected from— to further it in various ways and someone—some girl in the office gets money—bunch of money and she doesn't know what to do with it—she's got a hatful of money and really no place to go— the situation has come up in the dream, that's it."

No discernible concordance.

524
Stage REM
3rd B.L. + W.U.

"How much (is this last one (?)) you know?–I see."

Mentation report: "Yeah—I was dreaming of a—what I was doing in Princeton—I went down there to look up some books on a report on Jersey—a New Jersey report—a report that was written in New Jersey; I fugured they had it in the library mbl finding it—and met some girl—was walking along with her to the library, and just as—walking by a set-up on top of a temple that was on display with a—rocks, no not

Third—order concordance based on reference to the subject's asking a question in the mentation report. It might be argued that this pair be classified as first-order concordance because the sleep-speech also involved a question.

rocks—figures, you know, weathered figures and the half destroyed box which was the top of the center—last th'—last thing I remember was *asking the question* what it was for—that's about all."

525
Stage 2
3rd B.L. + W.U.

"Oooh—[P] (my stomach— stomach aches (?)) mbls."

Mentation report: "Yes? Oh uh, —a strange problem about availability of—money dealing with the—with the problem of how valuable certain money is, you know, because it's not, not being used—it's not around the need for a pound note, a new pound note—because the old ones are being used more and more and aren't available—being taken up by industry or something as a common problem which they— also the character of the guy who robbed this place—they know, er —I don't know where he lives—I haven't seen him but *I was talk-*

Third-order concordance based on references to the subject "talking" in the mentation report.

ing to some friends about him
and—was just a dream about
talking about him, that's it."

526
Stage 2
Recovery night—two nights on
d-amphetamine-pentobarbital
combination.

"Vase, mater [sic] —mm—nice—
nice."

Mentation report: "Yeah, oh the
—switch over to some kind of a
deal involving the—present
officialdom again—with officialdom we have the problems of—
so-called little people and the
problem of, one little person is—
mass (?) as I say and he's happy,
he gets it done in spite of the
opposition and the big boss, and
mean from the big boss, and
winds up helpin' the big boss
again and everybody's happy in
the end—mm—that's about what
I can remember of it."

No discernible concordance.

527
Stage 2
Recovery night as in speech 526.

"I don'want to know anything,
don' wanna know nothing."

Mentation report: "I wasn't actually sleeping at this time—thinking about the—thinking about the
—possibility of working in con-
junction with the—the work that
they're doing in the History department of General Studies dividing up—mbl—little pieces in the
cloak rooms into little pieces, ah—
the reproduction service is more
or less my job and—I was thinking about the fact that the only
thing that really interests me

No discernible concordance.

about it is the reproduction of
the original which I'm not
doing."

528 Stage 2 Recovery night as in speech 526.	"Mm quite a while mbl till (?) 11 to 12—mm."	Mentation report: no recall.	
529 Stage 2 Recovery night—three nights on *d*-amphetamine-pentobarbital combination.	"Mm—ah—that's why they want us to be the first marker, right Ma?—not supposed to know— mbl—you don't know what we are—you don't know anything about us—mmm—mmm.	Mentation report: "*I was telling* of mbl practicing—she was dulling it up. I'd like to do it myself mbl—we got run pick up couple o'people. I had dream; it doesn't mean anything but it was defin- itely a dream as far as having mbl and all mbl."	Third-order concordance based on reference to subject verbalizing in the mentation report.
530 Stage 2 Recovery night as in speech 529.	"Mbl that's—I can get some luck though too [moan]."	Mentation report: no recall.	
531 Stage 4 1st 3 hrs. 4th B.L. + W.U.	"Mbl—dull colors (?) cho— [groan] mmm."	Mentation report: "I was sort of —sort of stretched tight like— drum skin. You know—some- thing like that—tall room—very tall room—high ceiling."	No discernible concordance.

532 Stage 2 1st 3 hrs. 1st B.L. + W.U.	"Mbl—talk (?) 2, 3, 4, 6, [P] mbl."	Not awakened.	
533 Stage 1st 3 hrs. 1st B.L. + W.U.	"Mbl—very good (?) skill and (I get a lot (?)) from the ends and just mbl."	Mentation report: "I was just thinking—oh—how nice it would be to—to go to sleep again and how tired I was and how I wanted to sleep very badly, and that I hoped the buzzer wouldn't interrupt—and I was just like drifting off into sleep, and I was also like, also slipping into a dream, too but I don't know which one it was—and that's all."	No discernible concordance. It is of interest to note that although the sleep stage just prior to the speech was Stage 2, the subject describes the concomitant state of consciousness as "drifting off" and "slipping into a dream" all without awareness of speech.
534 Stage 4 1st 3 hrs. 1st B.L. + W.U.	"Who's (?) not doing this for money—mbl—I'm (?) NOT doing this for money—I'm doing this—just like that because I happen to be talking (to you (?))."	Mentation report: "Oh—I wasn't really thinking—I was kind of drifting—you know—I was just about to think to think—that's about all."	No discernible concordance.
535 Stage 1 NREM 1st B.L. + W.U.	"I'm not SURE—exactly what values go away I—I'll have to find out."	Mentation report: "I was think-uh—something to the effect that there was a study going on—this situation, kind of but not really I was thinking of someone—somebody else was going to do this	Third-order concordance based on references to "explaining" and "talking" in the mentation report.

too; a guy—it may have been George, and *I was explaining* about the buzzer and uh—*we were talking* about money—where the money was going to be allotted to pay for it—it was kind of mixed in with information about my new job. *We were talking* about taking money from different research grants to pay for it. It was taking place on a park bench outdoors and uh—my sleep is less deep now so I'll probably be able to remember more dreams —that's all."

Not awakened.

536
Stage 2
1st B.L. + W.U.

"You know, it's one thing to KNOW about something and then you start (living it (?)) it's very different—(I dunno home (?))."

537
Stage 2
1st B.L. + W.U.

"Oh—I'm getting confused between whether or not I was talking out loud to myself."

Mentation report: "I was thinking that I was *getting confused*— I didn't know whether I was

First-order concordance based on identical words in both sleep-speech and mentation report. Note that

talking out loud or to myself just now—I was thinking about things —the buzzers are coming awfully close together or what—I mean REALLY asleep but I think or I was, you know—I was slightly asl— I don't know—*I'm* very *confused*, and that's all."

although the subject had actually spoken aloud, she was not sure, and initially described herself as having been "thinking."

538 Stage 2 1st B.L. + W.U.	"Which is a white cat."	Apparent spontaneous awakening with spontaneous mentation report: "Which I somehow associate with a dream and wh—and telling of a dream. I don't know if there's a *white cat* around here or something—it seems to be connected with this place [P] [sighs] —and that's all [P]."	First-order concordance based on reference to "white cat" in both sleep-speech and mentation report.
539 Stage 2 1st B.L. + W.U.	"See, you ARE confusing me 'cause (?) it's Spanish [P] kind of—mm—mbl—it's confidante in (?) style."	Not awakened.	
540 Stage 2 1st B.L. + W.U.	"Mbl—showing the old stuff. I was thinking they're showing the old stuff—and so."	Mentation report: "Yes—*I was* still *thinking* about it all—didn't you just ring the buzzer?—what's happening here?"	First-order concordance based on identical words in sleep-speech and mentation report—"I was thinking."
541 Stage 2 1st B.L. + W.U.	"It's like you're reading the menu—for a restaurant—hm."	Not awakened.	

24. *Subject: M.J.*   *S was a college student.*

| 542
Stage 3
1st B.L. + W.U. | "Mm—but er—children." | Mentation report: "Yes—er—huh—again—just about the same things I was going over last time I was called—haven't really dropped off—or been asleep—since last call—in a state of—somebody who's asleep or who wasn't really—my mind just wandering, thinking of nothing in particular—getting no real observations on it just—about anything just—don't know just observations—wall anything from the size of the room and what's in the room—to—well—type of wall—room's a little warm—or anything like that." | No discernible concordance. |
| 543
Stage 2
1st B.L. + W.U. | "No—well—er—I'm sorry no—no really—was finished—I guess I almost went to sleep there—eh." | Mentation report: "Yes—oh—I think you just called me. Let me see—I think I was just—I thought I just—don't know—you just called me and *I was—hhhh—talking* about—or thinking about—*what I was saying*—at the time | Second-order concordance based on sleep-speech and mentation report having the experimental situation in common; or else third-order concordance. |

		when you called me again—when you called me."	
544 Stage 1 NREM 3rd B.L. + W.U.	"Haven't."	Mentation report: "I–I was thinking that—more or less out loud for a second that I *hadn't* been, that I *hadn't* been completely asleep 'n—that I more or less knew what was going on—while it was going on."	First-order concordance based on word "haven't" in the sleep-speech and "hadn't" in the mentation report.

25. Subject: S.J. *S was a college student.*

545 Stage 4 1st 3 hrs. 2nd B.L. + W.U.	"Ohh–oh–uh huh."	Mentation report—stimulated recall: S: "Um–uh–I just don't remember at all—I just–don't remember." E: "Do you feel something was going through your mind?—even though you can't remember?" S: "Uh–um–maybe something was, think something must have been—something must have been." E: "Do you remember saying: 'Ohh'– or 'uh huh.?" S: "No."	No recall.

560

546
Stage 4
1st 3 hrs.
Recovery night—one night on
d-amphetamine-pentobarbital
combination.

"A mi—be—better—seems that six books home and I haven't even got them yet—i—e—where—i—ea— what?—a rag in a rag's bed, rag! I don't even have a rag—bag—bag- gette—okay."

Mentation report—stimulated recall:
E: "What was going through your mind?"
S: "Um—flowers and a boat."
E: "Can you be more specific?"
S: "The—th'—th' boat was reced- ing and I um—under a bridge and boat; and flowers are re- ceding in opposite direction, and that—that direction's away from me."
E: "Do you remember anything about a rag and a bag?"

S: "No—nothing that I can remember."

No discernible concordance. Note the disorganization and apparent groping for a target with clang associations and perseveration.

547
Stage 2
Recovery night—two prior nights on *d*-amphetamine-pentobarbital combination

"Oh—uhh—yes."

Mentation report—stimulated recall:
E: "What was going through your mind?"
S: "Nothing—um."
E: "Do you remember saying yes?"

No recall.

S: "No, I don't. When did I say
that?—seems as if I always say
yes."

548
Stage 2
1st 3 hrs.
3rd B.L. + W.U.

"I think I have the first mbl all
wrong—seems like a very long
time uh—uh—uh—when we went
to bed and when we went to
sleep."

Mentation report—stimulated
recall:
"Um—I was standing on a large
lawn *talking* to Charlie who's
my brother and my stepfather
was behind me and Ronnie also.
Ronnie was playing with some
other children. I can't remember
much but that was the—that was
what I was thinking—my, I was
just, uh—I had been thinking that
Ronnie—Ronnie's uh ideas for
his baby-sitters which I was,
that's what my classification was,
was always, um—I don't know
what to call 'um."
E: "Do the words 'when we went
to sleep' mean anything?"
S: "No—they don't seem to
mean much to me."

Third-order concordance based on
reference to the subject talking to
someone in the mentation report.

549
Stage 4
3rd B.L. + W.U.

"Uh—No-o-oo-o-o! [cry—like
shudder]."

Mentation report—stimulated
recall:
"I was thinking that we better
get, that um Charlie 'n—Ronnie,
'n me and everybody, m—w—w—
we better hurry 'n get ready,
otherwise we'll be late."

No discernible concordance.

E: "Was there any reason to
make a frightened cry?"
S: "Not that I can think of."

550
Stage 2
3rd B.L. + W.U.

"Thank you very much. You
were, very nice to have along—
was a big help."

Mentation report: "Uh—uh—I
don't know what I was thinking—
I was thinking about er—some
thing I think. I was thinking
about getting back to Ronnie
and er—getting ready to go. I
think I don't remember. That
was the kind of thing I was thinking about—think *I was saying* to
somebody that, let's see—I
brought Charlie with me and um—
he was, seems like he was coming
across the street and *I said to
somebody* that um—he was, he's
been very *helpful* and I was glad
that he came."

First-order concordance based on
reference to "help" in both sleep-
speech and mentation report in an
apparently similar situation.

551
Stage 2
3rd B.L. + W.U.

"Uh—yes fro—yes, was crossing
yes, it was crossing, we were
crossing an intersection, it was
one which I'd mbl many times

Mentation report—stimulated
recall: "I remember *we went to
some place* which was er, I don't
know, had more *names* in it any-

Second-order concordance based on
references to travel in both sleep-
speech and mentation report; also
the specification of names in the

before crossing the intersection I expressed (?) some doubts that I did ordinarily when I was driving, it goes drench [sic] more about Ronnie and Charlie than I thought—that I thought."

way; I mean it had more *names* in its own *name*—that's all I remember its *name* about, but now I can't remember it."
E: "Would there be any reason for talking about crossing an intersection?—as you had done many times before?"
S: "I can't think of any reason."

sleep-speech (Ronnie and Charlie) and reference to "names" in the mentation report.

26: Subject: T.D.   *S was a rabbinical student.*

552
Stage 4
1st B.L. + W.U.

"What makes me a baby? I don't know."

Mentation report: "I can't, I'm trying to think—I can't remember what it was—I don't know—I guess—it wasn't anything important—I just can't remember what it was."

No recall.

553
Stage 2
Recovery night—two prior nights
d-amphetamine-pentobarbital combination

"It's a bad June—hah."

Mentation report: "Let me see—I was more or less just thinking of how actually *what I was going to say*—I don't think I was really asleep, or else my mind was just working in a different way and—my mind seemed to be just thinking about *what to say* right now in this case, uh—otherwise, that's all."

Third-order concordance based on reference to anticipated verbalization in this mentation report.

554 Stage 4 1st 3 hrs. Inadvertent concurrent use of *d*-amphetamine for weight control by day + W.U.	"Also, making a mess, a mess again."	Mentation report: "What was on my mind basically was—was as compared to the other box, compared to the other money, well this money was the money I got from—I guess a book—Dr. Arkin's, will this money be on duty, will it be uh, will I be able to share it, uh?"	No discernible concordance.
555 Stage 4 Drug use as in speech 554. This speech occurred only slightly in excess of the first 3 hrs. of sleep.	"Make a big trick about, make a racket and—is it do they flap, ap [sic] they visit they figured, they figure just a dream or and ah did he dream and what did he dream the second—er—the first time like uh—'s about all."	Mentation report: "Um—uh—the—nothing really special—the—I imagine at the time I was thinking about my job itself—uh."	No discernible concordance. Note the occurrence of a self-correction—"the second—er—the first time etc." Of additional interest is the perseverative tendency.
556 Stage 4 1st 3 hrs. 3rd B.L. + W.U.	"Mbls—that sort of forces it—this is the way—this is it."	Mentation report with initial provoked sleep-speech: *E*: "Danny." *S*: "Yeah—yeah—uh huh—I see the problem involved, sort of a minor catastrophe—?" *E*: "What's been going through your mind?"	No discernible concordance.

S: "Uh—don't know—uh—something—mbl—something had to
do with—with a something I
quote built—uh—bell water—
it was as if you were a—a
builder friend of mine or
something um—he seems to
be some kind of um—although,
other than the clothes themselves—uh—um—son't know
what's going on."

27. Subject: H.B.

*S was a 16-year-old
high school student.*

557 Stage 2 2nd B.L. + W.U.	"Yeah, still— [sigh]."	Mentation report—stimulated recall: "I'm wide-awake. I wasn't even dreaming then—I was goin' back to sleep. I wasn't dreaming anything special except go to bed; *I was telling myself*." E: "You said something like "yeah"." S: "You're kidding. I didn't hear it if I did—I don't know I said it."	Third-order concordance based on reference to self verbalizing in the mentation report.
558 Stage 4 1st 3 hrs. 3rd B.L. + W.U.	"Stop. Hold it! Hold it! Hold it! Just a minute. Hold it! Just a minute! Hold a minute—just a minute. Hold—no."	Mentation report—stimulated recall: S: "I was just going, you know— I was dreaming about getting this one person, this one lady.	Third-order concordance based on reference to the subject verbalizing in the mentation report. Equally appropriate would be a second-order concordance rating.

I got up and hair's stuck to
the electrodes. They won't
come off.

E: "What else made you get up?"

S: "That was it. I was dreaming
about her, except I wasn't
planning to sit up.

E: What about her?"

S: "Well, I think she was the
fourth one. Fourth person I
dreamed about and—think she
seemed to be the first one,
the first dog, the rest were all
cats, something like that, so it
would be the first time in my
life to use a certain thing and—
and then some—she went under the bed—you know—too
fast, so I sat up to *yell at her*
and then I hit the thing—

E: "Why were you telling her to
stop it?"

S: "Because I guess she couldn't
hear me, or else she didn't
want to, so I guess, you know,
*I just got up and started yell-
ing at her.*"

559 Stage REM 2nd B.L. + W.U.	"Argentina's a long way away—6000 miles."	Mentation report: "Uh—I was dreaming about this girl I used to go out with last summer—and uh—she's from *Argentina*—and uh—I uh—I don't know, see I—can't remember exactly what I was thinking but I—told her I'd go down there and see her but' I don't know, I can't remember exactly what I was thinking. So, that seems to be on my mind."	First-order concordance based on the word "Argentina" appearing in both sleep-speech and mentation report.
560 Stage 2 2nd B.L. + W.U.	"Oh—have to go to practice now—it's almost four o'clock."	Mentation report—stimulated recall: "Well, I was thinkin' about football season—eh, just thinkin' about football season in general—*practice*, stuff like that. *E*: "Does the word 'practice' mean anything to you?" *S*: "Yeah—well, quite a lot. I mean, uh—it used to be, take a large part of every day from about 3 to 8—take a *three o'clock bus*, get up there and get dressed by four—to on the field and uh—ya know, ya kinda—see yourself *have to* stop right in the middle o'stuff and go up ta, get up to the field fer practice."	First-order concordance based on references to "practice," the time, and the phrase 'have to' in the mentation report and sleep-speech.

29. Subject: D.P.M.

S was a college student and
former psychiatric patient.

561 Stage REM 1st B.L. + W.U.	[*S* chuckled spontaneously.]	Mentation report: difficult to decide whether the subject awakened herself spontaneously and attempted to provide a mentation report with *E*'s request; or whether the following is a continuation of sleep-speech. An experimental awakening was not carried out at this point. "Funny —I forget right away [P] mbl— throwing chairs—mbl—every time I was at a party like that mbls— politicians or mbls—extort money from the people. I was *laughing* because I could see through his character—mbls [P] mbls college— mbls."	Second-order concordance based on reference to laughter in the possibly spontaneous mentation report, and the spontaneous initial laughter emitted by the subject in association with REM sleep.
562 Stage 2 2nd B.L. + W.U.	"Mike—Mike [P] from the window [P] I don't want to get up, I don't want to."	Mentation report— stimulated recall— dialogue method: *E*: "Why don't you want to get up?"	First-order concordance based on identical words and similar sentences in both sleep-speech and mentation report—"I don't want to."

S: "*I don't want to* face them."

E: "What don't you want to face?"

S: I don't want to face another day."

E: "Why?"

S: "I'm tired."

E: "What are you tired of?"

S: "I'm tired of having to face the same problems, never achieving anything."

E: "What do you think you'd like to achieve and what problems to solve?"

[The subject did not respond at this point and was called by her first name five times before she was definitively awake and responded.]

E: "What has been going through your mind?"

S: "Yes, I uh—I was in the doctor's office and he wanted me to leave and uh, *I didn't want to*, leave—and um—and huh, uh, it was morning—and *I didn't want to get up* [P] I kept telling the doctor that I didn't want the same kind of problems that I have all the time."

E: "Anything else?"

S: "Uh—I seem to have been walking up a hill 'n—'n I was very tired and I didn't want to go on—and people were urging me to—come up. There was a whole group of people climbing—It was a hill and they kept urging me to go on and I didn't want to. I wanted to stop and sit down— [sigh] I was tired."

E: "Was it a dream, thought, or image?"

S: "It was a dream—extremely clear."

563
Stage REM
2nd B.L. + W.U.

"You don't have to."

Mentation report— stimulated recall— dialogue method:

E: "You don't have to what?"

S: "Um, *you don't have*, *I'm telling* the girl uh—oh, it was still at the hospital and this nurse came over and believed this girl. She took my rice

First-order concordance based on an identical sentence appearing in both sleep-speech and mentation report.

and uh—and she said that I
had stolen hers so—uh, the
nurse came over and took her
side and said uh—uh—Oh, she
says, 'I have—*I don't have to*
have anyone stick up for me
anymore because I feel like
something' so—I don't know
I answered, '*You don't have
to*'—oh—'*you don't have to*
feel like anyone' or something
like that, I don't remember—
'*you don't have to*' I said—Oh,
she she said, '*I don't have to*
fight for myself anymore, I
have someone else sticking up
for me' uh, I don't know, I
just—remember answering '*You
don't have to!*' ''

E: "Are you awake?"
S: "Uh, yes, now I am. I was
asleep when—when you—
talked to me. I was dreaming."
E: "Was my voice in the dream
at all?"
S: "Uh, no—no—no, I had turned
around and gone to leave the
place where I was talking to
this girl and then your voice
came in."
E: "Did my voice wake you up
with the first question?"
S: "I think so."

| 564
Stage REM
2nd B.L. + W.U. | "I don't know why you can't be honest—it's not right." | Mentation report—
stimulated recall—
dialogue method:
E: "Right about what?"
S: "Uh—it would seem that I find fault with my mother's cooking—and someone made the statement, 'Well, she's very hostile towards her mother so she'll find fault with everything' —so I said, 'No, usually I'm *right*.' " | First-order concordance based on the word "right" in both sleep-speech and mentation report. |

30. Subject: A.E.   *S was a college student.*

| 565
Stage 4
1st 3 hrs.
2nd B.L. + W.U. | "What the hell is going on?" | Mentation report: "I don't know—I don't remember—I'm—I don't know—all that I remember is—I don't know why I had this one image for a second of being in a auditorium and the whole front of it like for the screen and all was blue but that's all!" | No discernible concordance. |

566 Stage 2 1st 3 hrs. 2nd B.L. + W.U.	"I just want to sleep."	Mentation report— stimulated recall: *E*: "What has been going through your mind?" *S*: "Uh—oh, I don't know—I was dreaming about *sleeping* 'n then I don't—remember any- thing I don't think." *E*: "Do the words 'I just want to sleep' mean anything?" *S*: "Yeah—I remember saying it— but I don't remember why— but I don't remember why— and, you know, I don't remem- ber if it was in response to something—I, it saying that almost woke me up but not quite—that's all."	First-order concordance based on the word "sleep" in both sleep- speech and mentation report.
567 Stage 3 2nd B.L. + W.U.	"It's a dream—fuck—fuck— uh—oh—eee."	Mentation report— stimulated recall: *E*: "What was going through your mind?" *S*: "Hm—mm—nothing—I don't think—oh, I don't know why." *E*: "Does the word 'fuck' mean anything?" *S*: "[laughter] Yeah, lots but nothing immediate [laughter]."	No recall.

568 Stage 2 2nd B.L. + W.U.	"Oh—oh—tch God—I, I don't know what they're talking about."	Mentation report: "Um—I don't remember anything—I'm sorry, I just really don't."	No recall.
569 Stage 2 2nd B.L. + W.U.	"Something about a cowboy."	Mentation report—stimulated recall: *E*: "What was going through your mind?" *S*: "Oh—well, I'm very tired so it's **nice** to sleep and—I don't know. I wanna stay asleep, I think." *E*: "Does the word 'cowboy' mean anything?" *S*: "Yeah—this movie 'Midnight Cowboy' with Dustin Hoffman opened and I'm supposed to go see it Thursday night after I have dinner with these people. I'm supposed to go see the movie with them."	No recall initially. Possible first-order concordance with stimulated recall.
570 Stage 2 2nd B.L. + W.U.	"Oh—[sigh] [whispered mbl] nothing."	Mentation report—stimulated recall: *E*: "What has been going through your mind?"	No recall.

S: "Oh—I don't know—like—I guess, you know, it's just nice to be [laugh] able to sleep—some enjoyment."

E: "Does the word 'nothing' mean anything to you?"

S: "Um—I don't know. I was probably describing the state of my consciousness."

571
Stage 3
2nd B.L. + W.U.

"Heh—is that light?—guess so."

Mentation report: "I just wanted to know if the big square patch of *light* on the wall was connected with like, you know, Pepsi-Cola or Coca Cola or something—hm? I don't know what I'm talking about. Well, that's not unusual."

First-order concordance based on the word "light" in both sleep-speech and mentation report.

31. S was a "normal" adult male tobacco addict.

Courtesy of Dr. H. Batson

572
Preceded by 45 min. of Stage 2
1st B.L. + W.U.
3:09 (courtesy of Horace Batson)

"How terrible. . .so awful. . . terrible. . .terrible. . .Why did they do it, all those people. . . Why. . . suffering. . .so terrible. . . Why . . . Why didn't they listen. . . Why did they do it. . .who thought of this. . .It's so terrible . . .so terrible. . . If they were told. . .why didn't they listen. . . Why should they (lie to (?)) you.

"If they were told of the catastrophe. . .if they elected him. . . Why did they do it. . .They just ruined the whole city. Didn't they

Batson's comments: "since sleep-utterance is not part of my objective, I waited for S to awaken before any inquiry about the sleep-speech.

"I told S that he was talking in his sleep and he asked what he said. S appeared surprised that he did sleep talk.

"I told S about the content of the speech and his only association was about his prediction of the death of President Kennedy. To this day he is not aware that he spoke at the lab."

know. . . Why didn't they listen. . .
so terrible. . . It's all my fault. . .
I can't stand to look at it. . . How
could a whole city destroy itself
like that. Why did they elect him
. . . When he said if they elected
him he would destroy them and
then they said it was a terrible
sight. It was like a treacherous
(downpour (?) here.

"Why did they elect the wrong
man. . . why did it have to be such
a disaster. . . why didn't they
listen. . . twice. . . Why did they
elect him. Why were they so foolish. . . Why did they do it. . . it was
so terrible. . . they were told—
twice. . . and they would not listen
. . . a whole city in ruins. . . decay
and these hungry people. . . The
people dying. . . but why. . . Why
do they have to kill him now. . .
have to kill him to save the city. . .
why must they kill him. . . twice

S was a "normal" adult male tobacco
addict.

. . .Why can't they hold a new
election? Why must they kill him?
Why have they elected him. . .
Why can't they do some solution
—mbl—Why must they kill him?
The whole thing's falling down. . .
The chaos. . . one man caused all
that. . . Why can one man destroy
the whole city. . . they did it. . .
they elected him. . . But they
always elect him his body always
was they must have known that
would happen. . . [knocks head]
. . .They wanted it that way. . .
they were told. . . they knew. . .
Why would they kill him. . .
[knocks head again on microphone] "

NREM Speeches with Mentation Reports		
Speech	*Report*	*Categorization According to Arkin's Scale*
1 "It suddenly refers somehow to dream number one."	"I'm quite sure that somehow I dreamt something but I somehow can't recall a single thing. It may have been a conceptual *dream*. I think, if I remember correctly, I had been thinking about the *general experimental situation* here—the *laboratory*."	First- or second-order concordance.
2 "If I knew what I was doing mbls—perfect."	"The last thing I remember before the buzzer was *talking* to somebody about an experiment. I can't remember anything else."	Third-order concordance.
3 "Um, I'd say it was moderately poor; don't remember what I was reaching for, I remember dimly."	Garbled incoherent report beginning with: "There was something with this *left hand*.	Second-order concordance based on "reaching" in speech and "hand" in report.
4 "I don't think it will hurt too much."	"I've just been putting things together. I suppose in a kind of semi-poetical or musical fashion—some idea I was thinking of, just before I came over here I was thinking of writing a poem for Valentine to give to someone, but I had forgotten to do it early enough, so I didn't get it done. I sort of feel in that sort of mood." [Stimulated recall contained references to a concordant childhood memory about pain and surgery but nothing pertaining immediately to the sleep mentation.]	No discernible concordance. However, the content of the stimulated recall contained references to pain suggestive of second-order concordance.
5 "Am I dreaming? [P] color perry boy is more effective than color perry two."	"I think I was just thinking about those alpha particles." (The subject was a physics student who occasionally gave reports of having been thinking about physics problems during NREM periods.) "I think they were supposedly a half a wave length different from each	No discernible concordance with the initial spontaneous recall; but, first-order concordance with the stimulated recall—"counter parry"

other somehow. I think they're supposed to cancel, and I was thinking about this process, I guess; I'm not sure. And then the thought hit me, you know, I was supposed to be awake. And so I woke up and asked you if I was supposed to be recalling this or what, because I think I was really dreaming or asleep again, kind of, or going back into it. Didn't recall how I woke up." Following this report, the experimenter asked "Can you tell me what the words 'color perry' mean?" The subject responded in amazement, "My heavens! I was dreaming about fencing too. . . Did I say *counter parry*?" The experimenter indicated that the subject had said something during her sleep. The subject continued: "Oh, gee whiz! I don't recall, but it's very clear that I must have been doing something about fencing. . . I think I said two things. . . one thing and immediately something else. . . sort of one topic, one paragraph. . . that was pretty far back. . . I bet you I was dreaming about fencing, and somehow I switched to alpha particles again. . . Say, when I was dreaming about fencing, did I say *'counter parry one, counter parry two'*?. . . No, no! Couldn't have been that! Are you sure I said something about fencing and not something about these alpha particles or something else?"

related to the sleep-speech component "color parry."

REM Speech with Mentation Report

6

"Take it off. Let me do it myself. I could do it myself."

"Gee, what a dream. I had a date. It seems like I was a boy in the dream—or was I? No, I couldn't have been because someone was putting make-up on me—lipstick and doing my eyebrows. And I didn't like it. I thought it looked awful and wanted to *take it off and they wouldn't let me* and I was mad. My mother was there. *I wanted to take it off* and put it back myself. They wouldn't let me, I guess. That's all I remember."

First-order concordance based on references to "taking it off" in both sleep-speech and mentation report.

Sleep Speech No.	Sleep Stage	Sleep Speech	Mentation Report	Categorization
Subject No. 1				
1.	2	"What?"	Not awakened or not available.	—
2.	2	"Mbl–craft, craft."	Not awakened or not available.	—
3.	2	"Turn 'em up, Rue,"	Not awakened or not available.	—
4.	2	"Oh, Boy."	Not awakened or not available.	—
5.	2	"I feel like I'm going to–sleep-ing."	Not awakened or not available.	—
6	REM	"Oh–the last one."	Not awakened or not available.	—
7	2	"Uh huh, how long ya gonna be?"	Not awakened or not available.	—
Subject No. 2				
8	2	"Yeah."	Not awakened or not available.	—
9	3	"Oh, yeah, oh."	Not awakened or not available.	—
10	2	"Looks bad."	Not awakened or not available.	—
11	Alpha (REM interruption)	"Nurse, prepare the patient in room 24A for immediate surgery, brain point, lower lumbar, immediate surgery–3.8'–count lumbar."	Subject reported dreaming about a *brain operation* although he had no recollection of having talked	First-order concordance based on reference to brain surgery in sleep-speech and mentation report.
12	Alpha	"Get out of here, dammit, get out of here right now!"	No recall.	No recall.
Subject No. 3				
13	2	"No! no, I don't [in an emotional manner]"	Subject reported remembering only that he was washing a patient in a hospital where he worked.	No discernible concordance.

581

Sleep-Speeches Reported by
Fisher et al. (1974) Emitted by
Patients with Night-Terror Syndromes

Examples with concordance between sleep-speech and recall.

Heart rate/stage	Verbalization	Recall
Heart rate from 80 to 160/Min. Stage 4	"AOH! AAH!–HEY HEY, WATCH–WATCH–WATCH–WATCH–watch!! What's with me? Hold it. . . Hold it. . . Hold. . . It wasn't me now! IT'S NOT ME ANYMORE!! Oh, shit, you are *stepping on me now*, Dummy!! Hey, I switched. . . I'm here now. I'm here now. I'm in the middle position now. There you go. OK?" (Cleared throat.)	"In the room, you know, and, like someone was going to step on me. . . It was like–just like–It was a mixup like, you were doing–You weren't doing me harm purposely, you know what I mean? You follow me? . . . Well, someone was coming in. I didn't know who was coming to fix something up here and, I was like in the wrong slot. And you didn't realize I was in this wrong spot and *you were stepping on–you were step-ping on me*, or something like this, and then I'm trying to tell you like I'm here. I'm over here. I'm over here, or something like this, I don't know. But it was violent there for a couple of seconds, yes. It was. Because I had a burst of energy. . ."
Heart rate from 50 to 128/Min. Stage 3–4	(Screams) "Help! Hey! Help! Hey get! It's near my throat! Things choking me! *Something is stuck in my throat!*"	*"Something is choking in my throat. . .* It is choking in my throat, whatever the fuck is in there. . . I just want to know why, I'd like to know what the hell is in my throat. *It just woke me up that's all!*" (Any idea what was choking you?) "No. . . a piece of wire."
Heart rate from 60 to 120/Min. Stage 3	(Muffled scream) "Frank, where the fuck are we? You have a match? Anybody with a match?. . . Has anybody a match around?"	"One of the people here asked to have the light on and I think in one department here. So I said it was OK. There was a hard time finding it. It was very dark. I thought they wanted to. . . And that's where I got

panicky. . . I don't know what it was that really frightened me, the boxes themselves in front of me. . ."

There were several quite anxious arousals that did not reach night terror proportions by the heart rate criterion, but which vividly illustrate concordance:

Heart rate from 48 to 92/Min. Stage 3	"Lights! I got a snake or something here!! Get the lights on, please, can you get the lights on? *Can you get the fucking lights on,* goddamnit. Are you awake?"	"I felt like I was going to have a nightmare. . . I had sensations there was something on the bed like a snake . . . it was damned low and moving up towards me, moving up the bed. . . The potential fear. . . might be the most interesting thing, namely, you build up a certain panic about *not being able to turn the lights on*; that seems to be one of the most important goals in a situation like that. Otherwise I thought I was with Mary Liz because I was actually talking to her, telling her to turn on the lights."

Heart rate from 60 to 104/Min. Stage 4	"Christ, Christ, P-l-e-a-s-e! Please, please what are you doing to me? P-l-e-a-s-e! He's killing me! Aren't you? P-l-e-a-s-e! Help!"	"I remember thinking that there was somebody in the room who was doing. . . I don't think I expected to be, uh, rescued from it, you know?"

There were several examples of total lack of concordance.

Heart rate from 69 to 140/Min. Stage 4	"Oh, oh, I can't, I can't, I love you, I love you. . .please mommy, please, mommy, I love you. Oh please I love you, please, please."	(What was just going on?) "I don't know. I have no idea. . . I heard a click. I think I did dream. . . All I remember having is Coke to drink, and I took a pill, I took a sleeping pill in the dream and I remember going to sleep, the first time I had a good night's sleep, and all these other people were in the same place. It wasn't even a hospital and people were just waiting there."
Heart rate from 52 to 84/Min. Stage 4	"Hey Goddamnit! Yechh! Goddamnit! This is pro-This is too hard or something. What the hell is this? Look, hey look. . . Now look. . . Now you're putting this goddamn thing on a hundred watts or some goddamn thing! You know, it's not—I'm not built to be electrocuted."	"I was just thinking that I couldn't sleep and I was waiting for some tea that never came or something. . . The tea belonged to the East India Tea Company."

Examples of what have been classified in this book as macrodissociation episodes.

Verbatim Transcript of Tape Recording

EPISODE A

Patient: He's in the hospital today. That's right. I have to wait for my father to come home. Yes, I'm going to wait for my father. No, he's not dead. He can't be dead. He's home. Yes, he's home; yes, he's home.

EPISODE B

Patient: I wish I knew myself or. . . my father (mumbling–sighs). I wish my father were still here. Uh, I'll wait for him. Yes, I will wait for him. I will wait for him (pause–sighs). I did everything I could to keep him alive. I couldn't do any more. I spent every penny I had on nurses and doctors. I just couldn't. . . (pause). Well (sigh), he'll be back–one day. There's nobody really that can help me, maybe, except myself. My father. I wish he were here to help me. I wish my father was here to help me–(pause–sighs). Oh well. . . it's just not so (mumbling) . . . what's the. . . anything going on. I don't know any more. Oh well, I don't know any more. It's just terrible, terrible, it's just terrible.

EPISODE C

[Buzzer sounds]

Patient: (Mumbling). . . well, I think I see. . . (shouting) what's my father doing here? My father. Hello. Here's my father, my father wants me now. My father wants me. Yes, I'm waiting for my father. Yes, I'm waiting for my father. . . Do you hear that noise? That's the ambulance bringing my father home. That's the ambulance bringing my father home. I guess he fooled me. Everybody keeps telling me my father is dead. Do you hear that noise? That's the ambulance. . . it says whoop . . . whoop (he imitates the ambulance's sound). Help me. I guess it's not true, it's not true. I'm going to wait right here, I know. Don't take me to the doctors any more. Don't take me to the doctors. They can't help me. They can't help me. Nobody can help me any more. Nobody can help me any more. Nobody. . . No. I'm going to wait here for my father. Wait here for my father . . . they . . . everybody keeps saying that he's dead and I know he *isn't* dead. He's the only one that can help me. The doctors don't seem to know. Nobody, nobody, nobody (pause). How I wish I were dead again. Oh, well . . . no, no . . . oh . . . (pause). Oh, I can't stand it. I can't stand life any more. There's nobody any more. Nobody. Nobody (sobbing, he bangs the bed, more softly slaps his body).

EPISODE D

[E calls patient by name.]
Patient: What the . . . who's calling him . . . what . . . (buzzer sounds) yeah . . . well, yeah, who's making that noise, who's making that noise?
E: What was going through your mind just now?
Patient: Well, uh. I don't know what you mean. Who? Who's that? I don't know. Who's talking? I'm going to sit right here (with increasing crecendo and banging) because I want my father home. (He resumes in a more normal voice.) He's not dead I tell you. He's home . . . yes. I need him. What? What is it? Huh? Oh (sighs), what's going on . . . oh, God.

References

Aarons, L. *Conditioned sleep vocalization.* Paper presented at the annual meeting of the Association for the Psychophysiological Study of Sleep, Boston, 1969.

Aarons, L. Evoked sleep-talking. *Perceptual and Motor Skills,* 1970, *31,* 27–40.

Aarons, L. Sleep-assisted instruction. *Psychological Bulletin,* 1976, *83,* 1–40.

Abe, K., & Shimakawa, M. Genetic and developmental aspects of sleep-talking and teeth-grinding. *Acta Paedopsychiatrica* (Basel), 1966, 339–344. (a)

Abe, K., & Shimakawa, M. Predisposition to sleepwalking. *Psychiat. Neurol.* (Basel), 1966, *152,* 306–312. (b)

Abercrombie, J. *Inquiries concerning the intellectual powers* (16th ed.) London: Murray, 1860.

Adler, A. *Social interest: A challenge to mankind.* New York: Capricorn, 1964. (Originally published, 1939.)

Agnew, H. W., Jr., Webb, W. B., & Williams, R. L. Comparison of stage 4 and REM sleep deprivation. *Perceptual and Motor Skills,* 1967, *24,* 851–858.

Aird, R. B., Venturini, A. M., & Spielman, P. M. Antecedents of temporal lobe epilepsy. *Archives of Neurology,* 1967, *16,* 67–73.

Altman, L. L. *The dream in psychoanalysis, rev. ed.* New York: International Universities Press, 1975.

Andriani, G. Fisiologia psicologica del sonniloquio. *Ann. di Neurol.* (Torino), 1892, *10,* 299–308.

Antrobus, J. S., Antrobus, J. S., & Fisher, C. Discrimination of dreaming and non-dreaming sleep. *Archives of General Psychiatry,* 1965, *12,* 395–401.

Antrobus, J. S., Singer, J. L., Goldstein, S., & Fortgang, M. Mind-wandering and cognitive structure. *Transactions of the New York Academy of Science,* 1970, *32,* 242–252.

Aristotle. On dreams. In R. M. Hutchins (Ed.), *Great books of the western world* (Vol. 1). Chicago: Encyclopaedia Britannica, 1952.

Arkin, A. M. Post-hypnotically stimulated sleep-talking. Report of a pilot study. Unpublished observations, 1960.

Arkin, A. M. Sleep talking: A review. *Journal of Nervous and Mental Disease,* 1966, *143,* 101–122.

590 REFERENCES

Arkin, A. M. The degree of concordance between sleep-talking and mentation recalled in wakefulness. (Paper presented at the meeting of the Association for the Psychophysiological Study of Sleep, Santa Monica, April 1967.) *Psychophysiology*, 1968, *4*, 396. (Abstract)

Arkin, A. M. Qualitative observations on sleep utterance in the laboratory. M. Bertini (Ed.), *The atti del Simposio Internazionale sulla psicofisiologia del sonno e del sogno. Proceedings of an International Symposium*, Rome, 1967. Milan: Editrice Vita a Pensiero, 1970.

Arkin, A. M. Review of MacNeilage, P. F. & MacNeilage, L. A., Central processes controlling speech production during sleeping and waking. *Sleep Research*, 1974, *3*, 331–333. (a)

Arkin, A. M. *Somniloquy as the ouput of dissociated cognitive subsystems.* Paper presented at the meeting of the Association for the Psychophysiological Study of Sleep, Jackson Hole, May 1974. (b)

Arkin, A. M. Night-terrors as anomalous REM sleep component manifestation in slow-wave sleep. *Waking and Sleeping*, 1978, *2*, 143–147.

Arkin, A. M., Antrobus, J. S., & Ellman, S. J. (Eds.), *The mind in sleep: Psychology and psychophysiology.* Hillsdale, N.J.: Lawrence Erlbaum Associates, 1978. (a)

Arkin, A. M., Antrobus, J. S., Toth, M. F., & Baker, J. The effects of chemically induced REMP deprivation on sleep vocalization and NREM mentation—An initial exploration. *Psychophysiology*, 1968, *5*, 217. (Abstract)

Arkin, A. M., Antrobus, J. S., Toth, M. F., Baker, J., & Jackler, F. A comparison of the content of mentation reports elicited after non-rapid eye movement (NREM) associated sleep-utterance and NREM "silent" sleep. *Journal of Nervous and Mental Disease*, 1972, *115*, 422–435. (a)

Arkin, A. M., Batson, H. W., & Ellman, S. J. *Heart rate preceding movement arousal with and without accompanying sleep-speech in tobacco addicts.* Paper presented at the meeting of the Association for the Psychophysiological Study of Sleep, Palo Alto, 1978. (b)

Arkin, A. M., & Brown, J. W. Resemblances between NREM associated sleep-speech, drowsy speech, and aphasic and schizophrenic speech. *Psychophysiology*, 1972, *9*, 140. (Abstract)

Arkin, A. M., Farber, J., Antrobus, J. S., Ellman, S. J., & Nelson, W. T. The effects of repeated sleep interruption and elicited verbalization on sleep-speech frequency of chronic sleep-talkers: Preliminary observations. *Sleep Research*, 1973. Brain Information Service, University of California, Los Angeles.

Arkin, A. M., Hastey, J. M., & Reiser, M. F. *Dialogue between sleeptalkers and the experimenter.* Paper presented at the meeting of the Association for the Psychophysiological Study of Sleep, Gainesville: Florida, March 1966. (a)

Arkin, A. M., Hastey, J. M., & Reiser, M. F. Post-hypnotically stimulated sleep-talking. *Journal of Nervous and Mental Disease*, 1966, *142*, 293–309. (b)

Arkin, A. M., Lutzky, H., & Toth, M. F. Congenital nystagmus and sleep: A replication. *Psychophysiology*, 1972, *9*, 210–217.

Arkin, A. M., Sanders, K. I., Ellman, S. J., Antrobus, J. S., Farber, J., & Nelson, W. T. *The rarity of pain sensation in sleep mentation reports.* 2nd International Sleep Research Congress, Edinburgh, Scotland, June 1975.

Arkin, A. M., & Steiner, S. S. Drugs and dreams. In A. M. Arkin, J. S. Antrobus, & S. J. Ellman (Eds.), *The mind in sleep: Psychology and psychophysiology.* Hillsdale, N.J.: Lawrence Erlbaum Associates, 1978.

Arkin, A. M., & Toth, M. F. Unpublished observations. 1970.

Arkin, A. M., Toth, M. F., & Baker, J. *A comparison between the content of mentation reports elicited after NREM-associated sleep-utterance and NREM "silent" sleep.* Paper presented at the annual meeting of the Association for the Psychophysiological Study of Sleep, Boston, 1969.

Arkin, A. M., Toth, M. F., Baker, J., & Hastey, J. M. The degree of concordance between the content of sleep-talking and mentation recalled in wakefulness. *Journal of Nervous and Mental Disease*, 1970, *151*, 375–393. (a)

Arkin, A. M., Toth, M., Baker, J., & Hastey, J. M. The frequency of sleep-talking in the laboratory among chronic sleep-talkers and good dream recallers. *Journal of Nervous and Mental Disease*, 1970, *157*, 369–374. (b)

Arkin, A. M., Toth, M. F., & Esrachi, O. Electrographic aspects of sleep-talking. (Paper presented at the meeting of the Association for the Psychophysiological Study of Sleep, Santa Fe, March 1970.) *Psychophysiology*, 1970, *7*, 354. (Abstract) (c)

Arlow, J. A., & Brenner, C. *Psychoanalytic concepts and structural theory*. New York: International Universities Press, 1964.

Ascher, E. Motor syndromes of functional or undetermined origin. In S. Arieti & E. B. Brody (Eds.), *The American handbook of psychiatry* (2nd ed.). New York: Basic Books, 1974.

Ayer, A. J. Professor Malcolm on dreams. *Journal of Philosophy*, 1960, *LVII, 16*, 517–535.

Baekeland, F. Pentobarbital and dextroamphetamine sulphate: Effects on the sleep cycle in man. *Psychopharmacologia*, 1967, *11*, 388–396.

Bakwin, H., & Bakwin, R. M. *Behavior disorders in children* (4th ed.). Philadelphia: W. B. Saunders, 1972.

Balkanyi, C. On verbalization. *International Journal of Psychoanalysis*, 1964, *45*, 64–74.

Bañuelos, M. *Patología y clínica del sueño y estados afines*. Barcelona, Madrid: Editorial Cientifico Medica, 1940.

Barber, B. Factors underlying individual differences in rate of dream reporting. *Psychophysiology*, 1969, *6*, 247–248.

Barros-Ferreira, M. de, Chodkiewicz, J. P., Lairy, G. C., & Salzarulo, P. Disorganized relations of tonic and phasic events of REM sleep in a case of brain-stem tumor. *Electroencephalography and Clinical Neurophysiology*, 1975, *38*, 203–207.

Batson, H. W. Unpublished observations, 1977.

Batson, H. W., Arkin, A. M., & Ellman, S. J. *Sleep-talking in tobacco addicts under baseline and deprivation conditions*. Paper presented at the meeting of the Association for the Psychophysiological Study of Sleep, Palo Alto, 1978.

Baudry, F. Remarks on spoken words in the dream. *Psychoanalytic Quarterly*, 1974, *XLIII, 4*, 581–605.

Benoit, O. & Adrien, J. PGO activity as a criterion of paradoxical sleep. A critical review. In G. C. Lairy & P. Salzarulo, (Eds.), *The experimental study of human sleep: Methodological problems*. Proceedings of International Symposium, Bardolino, Italy, April 3–5, 1974. (New Jersey: Elsevier Scientific Publishing Co.) 1975.

Berdie, R. F., & Wallen, R. Some psychological aspects of enuresis in adult males. *American Journal of Orthopsychiatry*, 1945, *15*, 153–159.

Berger, R. J., & Oswald, I. Effects of sleep deprivation on behavior, subsequent sleep, and dreaming. *Journal of Mental Science*, 1962, *108*, 457–465.

Berger, R. J. Experimental modification of dream content by meaningful verbal stimuli. *British Journal of Psychiatry*, 1963, *109*, 722–740.

Berlucchi, G. Callosal activity in unrestrained, unanesthetized cats. *Archives of Italian Biology*, 1964, *103*, 623–624.

Berlucchi, G. Electroencephalographic studies in "split-brain" cats. *Electroencephalography and Clinical Neurophysiology*, 1966, *20*, 348–356.

Berlyne, D. E. *Structure and direction in thinking*. New York: John Wiley, 1965.

Bertini, M., Gregolini, H., & Vitali, S. Dream research: A new experimental tool. *Psychophysiology*, 1972, *9*, 115. (a) (Abstract)

Bertini, M., & Pontalti, C. Clinical perspectives of a new technique in dreaming research. *Psychophysiology*, 1972, *9*, 140. (b) (Abstract)

Bertini, M., Ruggeri, G., & Torre, A. *Induced verbalizations during awake, REM and NREM*. Paper presented at the Second European Congress on Sleep Research, Rome, April 8–11, 1974. (a)

Bertini, M., Ruggeri, G., & Torre, A. Induced verbalizations during awake, REM, and NREM states. In P. Levin & W. P. Koella (Eds.), *Sleep*, 1974. (Proceedings of the Second European Congress on Sleep Research, Rome, 1974.) Basel: S. Karger, 1975. (b)

Birch, H. G. Experimental investigations in expressive aphasia. *New York State Journal of Medicine*, 1956, *56*, 3849–3852.

Birch, H. G., & Lee, J. H. Cortical inhibition in expressive aphasia. *Archives of Neurology and Psychiatry*, 1955, *74*, 514–517.

Bleuler, E. *Lehrbuch der psychiatrie* (4th ed.) Berlin: Springer, 1923.

Bleuler, E. *Dementia praecox, or the group of schizophrenias* [J. Zinkin, trans.]. New York: International Universities Press, 1952. (Originally published, 1911.)

Bone, R. N., Hopkins, D. C., Buttermore, G., Jr., Belcher, M. O., McIntyre, C. L., Calef, R. S., & Cowling, L. W. *Sixteen personality correlates of sleeptalkers*. Paper presented at the meeting of the Association for the Psychophysiological Study of Sleep, San Diego, 1973.

Boomer, D. S. Hesitation and grammatical encoding. *Language and Speech*, 1965, *8*, 148–158.

Boomer, D. S., & Laver, J. D. M. Slips of the tongue. *British Journal of Communication*, 1968, *3*, 2–12.

Bossard, R. *Psychologie des traumbewusstseins* Zurich: Rascher, 1951.

Bowers, M. B., & Freedman, D. X. Psychoses associated with drug use. In S. Arieti (Ed.), *American handbook of psychiatry* (Vol. 4). New York: Basic Books, Inc., 1975.

Bixler, E. O., Kales, A., Soldatos, C. R., Kales, J. D., & Healey, S. Prevalence of sleep disorders in the Los Angeles Metropolitan area. *American Journal of Psychiatry*, 1979, *36*, 10, 1257–1262.

Brazier, M. A. B. Absence of dreaming or failure to recall? *Experimental Neurology*, 1967, *19* (Supplement 4), 91–98.

Bregman, L. E. *Die schlafsiörungen und ihre behandlung*. Berlin: S. Karger, 1910.

Breuer, J., & Freud, S. Studies in hysteria. In J. Strachey (Ed.), *Complete psychological works of S. Freud* (Vol. II of the Standard Edition). London: Hogarth Press, 1895/1955.

Broadbent, D. E. *Perception and communication*. London: Pergamon Press, 1958.

Brock, S., & Wiesel, B. The narcoleptic-cataplectic syndrome—An excessive and dissociated reaction of the sleep mechanism and its accompanying mental states. *Journal of Nervous and Mental Disease*, 1941, *94*, 700–712.

Broughton, R. Sleep disorders: Disorders of arousal? *Science*, 1968, *159*, 1070–1078.

Broughton, R. Confusional sleep disorders: Interrelationship with memory consolidation and retrieval in sleep. In P. D. MacLean (Ed.), *A triune concept of the brain and behavior*. Toronto: University of Toronto Press, 1973.

Broughton, R. Aggression during sleepwalking: A case report. *Sleep Research*, 1978, *7*, 215.

Brown, H. *Sleep and sleeplessness*. London: Hutchinson, 1910.

Brown, J. *Aphasia, apraxia and agnosia: Clinical and theoretical aspects*. Springfield, Ill.: Charles C Thomas, 1972.

Brown, J. *Mind, brain, and consciousness: The neuropsychology of cognition*. New York: Academic Press, 1977.

Brown, J., & Cartwright, R. D. Subjective indications of NREM dreaming. *Sleep Research*, 1976, *5*, 114. (Abstract)

Brown, J. N., & Cartwright, R. D. Subject versus experimenter elicited dream reports: Who knows best? *Sleep Research*, 1977, *6*, 199. (Brain Information Service, Brain Research Institute, University of California, Los Angeles.)

Brown, J. N., & Cartwright, R. D. Locating NREM dreaming through instrumental responses. *Psychophysiology*, 1978, *15*, 35–39.

Bruner, J. S. Modalities of memory. In G. A. Talland & N. C. Waugh (Eds.), *The pathology of memory*. New York: Academic Press, 1969.

Burrell, D. R. A case of sleep-talking. *Proceedings of the American Medico-Psychological Association*, St. Louis, 1904.

Cahen, R. *Traitement analytique et magnetophone*. Revue due la Société de Recherche Psychotherapeutique de Langue Francaise, Paris, 1965.

Calkins, M. W. Statistics of dreams. *American Journal of Psychology*, 1893, *5*, 311–343.

Cameron, A. W. B. Some observations and a hypothesis concerning sleep-talking. *Psychiatry*, 1952, *15*, 95–96.

Carpenter, W. N. On sleep. In *Cyclopedia of Anatomy and Physiology*, 1849, *4*, 691. (Sherwood, Gilbert & Piper, London.)

Carpenter, W. N. *Principles of mental physiology*. New York: Appleton, 1886.

Cartwright, R. D. *Night life: Explorations in dreaming*. Englewood Cliffs, N.J.: Prentice-Hall, 1977.

Cartwright, R. D., Monroe, L. J., & Palmer, C. Individual differences in response to REM deprivation. *Archives of General Psychiatry*, 1967, *16*, 297–303.

Cartwright, R. D., Weiner, L., & Wicklund, J. *Effects of lab training in dream recall on psychotherapy behavior*. Paper presented at the meeting of the Association for the Psychophysiological Study of Sleep, Edinburgh, 1975.

Castaldo, V., & Holzman, P. The effect of hearing one's voice on sleep mentation. *Journal of Nervous and Mental Disease*, 1967, *144*, 2–13.

Castaldo, V., & Holzman, P. The effects of hearing one's own voice on dreaming content: A replication. *Journal of Nervous and Mental Disease*, 1969, *148*, 74–82.

Castaldo, V., & Shevrin, H. Different effect of auditory stimulus as a function of rapid eye movement and non-rapid eye movement sleep. *Journal of Nervous and Mental Disease*, 1970, *150*, 195–200.

Chase, R. A., Cullen, J. K., Niedermeyer, E. F. L., Start, R., & Blumer, D. P. Ictal speech automatisms and swearing: Studies on the auditory feedback control of speech. *Journal of Nervous and Mental Disease*, 1967, *144*, 5, 406–420.

Cherry, C. Some experiments on the recognition of speech with one and two ears. *Journal of the Acoustical Society of America*, 1953, *25*, 975–979.

Child, C. M. Statistics of "unconscious cerebration." *American Journal of Psychology*, 1892, *5*, 249–269.

Chomsky, N. *Language and mind*. New York: Harcourt, Brace, Jovanovich, Inc., 1972.

Cipolli, C., Dubois, D., & Salzarulo, P. Framework for a psycholinguistic approach to the experimental study of verbal behavior related to sleep. In G. C. Lairy & P. Salzarulo (Eds.), *The experimental study of human sleep: Methodological problems*. Proceedings of International Symposium, Bardolino, Italy, April 3–5, 1974. (Elsevier Scientific Publishing Co., New Jersey.)

Cipolli, C., & Salzarulo, P. Effect of a memory retrieval task on recall of verbal material obtained after awakening from sleep. *Biological Psychology*, 1975, *3*, 321–326.

Clardy, E. R., & Hill, B. C. Sleep disorders in institutionalized and disturbed children and delinquent boys. *Nervous Child*, 1949, *8*, 1, 5.

Clark, H. H., & Clark, E. V. *Psychology and language: An introduction to psycholinguistics*. New York: Harcourt, Brace, Jovanovich, Inc., 1977.

Coe, W. C., Basden, B., Basden, D., & Graham, C. Post-hypnotic amnesia: Suggestions of an active process in dissociative phenomena. *Journal of Abnormal Psychology*, 1976, *85*, 5, 455–458.

Cohen, H. D., Shapiro, A., Goodenough, D. R., & Saunders, D. *The EEG during stage IV sleep-talking*. Paper presented at the meeting of the Association for the Psychophysiological Study of Sleep, Washington, D.C., March 1965.

Cook, T. W. A case of abnormal reproduction during sleep. *Journal of Abnormal Social Psychology*, 1937, *39*, 465–470.

Cordeau, J. P. Monoamines and the physiology of sleep and waking. In A. Barbeau & F. H. McDonell (Eds.), *L-dopa and parkinsonism*. Philadelphia: F. A. Davis, 1970.

Crile, G. W. *A mechanistic view of war and peace*. Cited by W. S. Walsh. New York: American University Press, 1920.

Darwin, E. *Zoonomia or the laws of organic life* (Vol. 1). Dublin: Dugdae, 1800.

DeBartolo, A. E. Personal communication, 1977.

Deese, J. Thought into speech. *American Scientist*, 1978, *66*, 314–321.

Dement, W. C. Eye movements during sleep. In M. B. Bender (Ed.), *The oculomotor system*. New York: Hoeber, 1964.

Dement, W. C. An essay on dreams: The role of physiology in understanding their nature. In *New directions in psychology* (Vol. 2). New York: Rinehart & Winston, 1965.

Dement, W. C. *Some must watch while some must sleep*. San Francisco: W. H. Freeman, 1972.

Dement, W. C., & Kleitman, N. Cyclic variations in EEG during sleep and their relation to eye movements, bodily motility and dreaming. *Electroencephalography and Clinical Neurophysiology*, 1957, *9*, 673–690. (a)

Dement, W. C., & Kleitman, N. The relation of eye movements during sleep to dream activity: An objective method for the study of dreaming. *Journal of Experimental Psychology*, 1957, *53*, 339–346. (b)

Dement, W. C., & Mitler, M. M. An introduction to sleep. In O. Petre-Quadens, & J. D. Schlag (Eds.), *Basic sleep mechanisms*. New York: Academic Press, 1974.

Dement, W. C., & Mitler, M. M. An overview of sleep research: Past, present and future. In S. E. Arieti, D. A. Hamburg & K. H. Brodie (Eds.), *American handbook of psychiatry* (2nd ed.). New York: Basic Books, 1975.

Dement, W. C., & Rechtschaffen, A. Narcolepsy: Polygraphic aspects, experimental and theoretical considerations. In H. Gastaut, E. Lugaresi, G. Berti-Ceroni & G. Coccagna (Eds.), *Proceedings of the 15th European Meeting on Electroencephalography*, Bologna, 1967. Bologna, Italy: Gaggi, 1968.

Dement, A., Karacan, I., Ware, J. C., & Williams, R. L. Somnambulism: A case report. *Sleep Research*, 1978, *7*, 220.

DeSanctis, S. *I sogni*. Torino: Bocca, 1899.

Deutsch, J. A., & Deutsch, D. Attention: Some theoretical considerations. *Psychological Review*, 1963, *70*, 80–90.

Diatkine, R. Les troubles du sommeil chez l'enfant. *Les entretiens de Bichat*. Paris: Medicine, 1963.

Diethelm, O., & Barr, R. M. Psychotherapeutic interviews and alcohol intoxication. *Quarterly Journal for the Study of Alcohol*, 1962, *23*, 243–251.

Driver, N. W. Falconer, M. A., & Serafetinedes, E. A. Ictal speech automatism reproduced by activation procedure. *Neurology*, 1964, *14*, 455–463.

Economo, von, C. Die pathologie des schlafes. In Handbuch der normalen und pathologischen physiologie (Vol. 17), 1926.

Edelheit, H. Speech and psychic structure. *Journal of the American Psychoanalytic Association*, 1969, *17*, 381–412.

Edelson, M. Language and dreams: The interpretation of dreams revisited. *Psychoanalytic Study of the Child*, 1972, *27*, 203–282.

Edmonds, C. Severe somnambulism: A case study. *Journal of Clinical Psychology*, 1967, *23*, 237–239.

Elder, W. *Studies in psychology*. London: Heineman, 1927.

Ellis, H. *The world of dreams*. New York: Houghton Mifflin, 1926.

Engel, G. I. "Psychogenic" pain and the pain-prone patient. *American Journal of Medicine*, 1959, *XXVI*, 6, 899–918.

Erickson, M. H. Occurrence of a dream in an eight-month-old infant. *Psychoanalytical Quarterly*, 1941, *10*, 393.

Esquirol, J. *Des maladies mentales*. Cited by Andriani, 1892.

Estabrooks, G. H. *Hypnotism*. New York: Dutton, 1957.

Evans, C. Sleep experience survey. London Sunday Times, November 30, 1969.

Evans, F. J., Gustafson, L. A., O'Connell, D. N., Orne, M. T., & Shor, R. E. Verbally induced behavioral responses during sleep. *Journal of Nervous and Mental Disease*, 1970, *150*, 171–187.

Evans, F. J. Hypnosis and sleep: Techniques for exploring cognitive activity during sleep. In E. Fromm & R. E. Shor (Eds.), *Hypnosis: Research developments and perspectives*. Chicago: Aldine, 1972.

Evans, J. Rocking at night. *Journal of Child Psychology and Psychiatry*, 1961, *2*, 71–85.

Evarts, E. V. Unit activity in sleep and wakefulness. In G. C. Quarton, T. Melnechuk & F. O. Schmitt (Eds.), *The neurosciences*. New York: Rockefeller University Press, 1967.

Ey, H. *Etudes psychiatriques* (Vol. 1) Paris: Desclée de Brouwer, 1950.

Eysenck, M. W. Arousal, learning and memory. *Psychological Bulletin*, 1976, *83*, 389–404.

Falconer, M. A. Brain mechanisms suggested by neurophysiological studies. In C. H. Milliken & F. L. Dailey (Eds.), *Brain mechanisms, speech and language*. New York: Grune & Stratton, 1967.

Farber, J., Arkin, A. M., Ellman, S. J., Antrobus, J. S., & Nelson, W. T. The effects of sleep interruption, deprivation and elicited verbalizations on sleep-speech parameters. *Sleep Research*, 1973. (Brain Information Service, University of California, Los Angeles.)

Farber, J., Arkin, A. M., Ellman, S. J., Antrobus, J. S., & Nelson, W. T. Experimentally produced sleep-talking: A new technique. *Waking and Sleeping*, 1978, *2*, 175–179.

Feltin, M., & Broughton, R. J. Differential effects of arousal from slow wave sleep versus REM sleep. *Psychophysiology*, 1968, *5*, 231. (Abstract)

Ferenczi, S. *Interchange of affect in dreams: Theory and technique of psychoanalysis*. London: Intl. Psychoanalytic Library, 1916.

Ferenczi, S. *Sex in psychoanalysis*. New York: Brunner, 1950. (Originally published, 1909.)

Fischer, F. *Der somnambulismus*. Basel: Schweighauser, 1839.

Fischer, R. State-bound knowledge: "I can't remember what I said last night, but it must have been good". *Psychology Today*, 1977, *10*, 68–72.

Fisher, C. Psychoanalytic implications of recent research on sleep and dreaming. *Journal of the American Psychoanalytic Association*, 1965, *13*, 290.

Fisher, C. Spoken words in dreams: A critique of the views of Otto Isakower. *Psychoanalytic Quarterly*, 1976, *XLV*, 1, 100–109.

Fisher, C. A study of the preliminary stages of the construction of dreams and images. *Journal of the American Psychoanalytic Association*, 1957, *5*, 5–60.

Fisher, C., Kahn, E., Edwards, A., & Davis, D. A psychophysiological study of nightmares and night terrors. I. Physiological aspects of the stage 4 night terror. *Journal of Nervous and Mental Disease*, 1973, *157*, 75–98. (a)

Fisher, C., Kahn, E., Edwards, A., & Davis, D. M. A psychophysiological study of nightmares and night terrors. II. The suppression of stage 4 night terrors with diazepam. *Archives of General Psychiatry*, 1973, *28*, 252–259. (b)

Fisher, C., Kahn, E., Edwards, A., Davis, D. M., & Fine, J. A psychophysiological study of nightmares and night terrors. III. Mental content and recall of stage 4 night terrors. *Journal of Nervous and Mental Disease*, 1974, *158*, 174–188.

Fisher, C., Kahn, E., Edwards, A., & Davis, D. M. A psychophysiological study of nightmares and night terrors. I. Physiological aspects of the stage 4 night terror. In L. Goldberger & V. H. Rosen (Eds.), *Psychoanalysis and contemporary science* (Vol. III). New York: International Universities Press, 1975.

Fiss, H., Klein, G. S., & Bokert, E. Waking fantasies following interruption of two types of sleep. *Archives of General Psychiatry*, 1966, *14*, 543–551.

Flavell, J. H., & Draguns, J. A microgenetic approach to perception and thought. *Psychological Bulletin*, 1957, *54*, 197–215.

Flemenbaum, A. Pavor nocturnus: A complication of single tricyclic or neuroleptic dosage. *American Journal of Psychiatry*, 1976, *133*, 570–572.

Fliess, R. On the "spoken word" in the dream. In R. Fliess (Ed.), *The revival of interest in the dream*. New York: International Universities Press, 1953.

Fosgate, B. *Sleep psychologically considered with reference to sensation and memory*. New York: Putnam, 1850.

Foulkes, D. *The psychology of sleep*. New York: Charles Scribners & Sons, 1966.

Foulkes, D., & Fleisher, S. Mental activity in relaxed wakefulness. *Journal of Abnormal Psychology*, 1975, *84*, 66–75.

Fowler, M. J., Sullivan, M. J., & Ekstrand, B. R. Sleep and memory. *Science*, 1973, *179*, 302–304.

Fraser, M. S. Nocturnal enuresis. *Practitioner*, 1972, *208*, 203.

Freemon, F. R., McNew, J. J., & Adey, W. R. Sleep of unrestrained chimpanzee: Cortical and subcortical recordings. *Experimental Neurology*, 1969, *25*, 129–137.

Freemon, F. R., & Walter, R. D. Electrical activity of human limbic system during sleep. *Comprehensive Psychiatry*, 1970, *11*, 544–551.

Freud, S. Metapsychological supplement to the theory of dreams. In *Collected papers*. London: Hogarth Press, 1925. (Originally published, 1916.)

Freud, S. Interpretation of dreams. In *The standard edition of the complete psychological works of Sigmund Freud* (Vol. 4). London: Hogarth, 1953. (a)

Freud, S. *On aphasia*. New York: International Universities Press, 1953. (Originally published, 1891.) (b)

Freud, S. *On dreams*. J. Strachey (Trans.) New York: W. W. Norton & Co., 1952. (Originally published, 1901)

Freud, S. Analysis of a phobia in a five-year-old boy. In *The standard edition of the complete works of Sigmund Freud* (Vol. 10). London: Hogarth Press, 1955. (Originally published, 1909.) (a)

Freud, S. Notes upon a case of obsessional neurosis. In *The standard edition of the complete works of Sigmund Freud* (Vol. 10). London: Hogarth Press, 1955. (Originally published, 1909.) (b)

Freud, S. Formulations on the two principles of mental functioning. In *The standard edition of the complete works of Sigmund Freud* (Vol. 12). London: Hogarth Press, 1958. (Originally published 1911.)

Freud, S. In H. Nunberg & E. Federn (Eds.), *Minutes of the Vienna Psychoanalytic Society* (Vol. 1). New York: International Universities Press, 1962.

Freud, S. Introductory lectures on psychoanalysis. In *The standard edition of the complete psychological works of Sigmund Freud* (Vol. 14, 15, 16). London: Hogarth Press, 1963. (Originally published, 1917.)

Freud, S. Letter to Wilhelm Fliess #73. Pre-psychoanalytic publications and unpublished drafts (Vol. I). In J. Strachey (Ed.). *The standard edition of the complete psychological works of Sigmund Freud.* London: Hogarth Press, 1966. (Originally published, 1897.) (a)

Freud, S. Project for a scientific psychology. In *The standard edition of the complete psychological works of Sigmund Freud* (Vol. I). London: Hogarth Press, 1966. (Originally published, 1895.) (b)

Froeschels, E. A peculiar intermediary state between waking and sleep. *Journal of Clinical Psychopathology*, 1946, *7*, 825–833.

Fromkin, V. A. Slips of the tongue. *Scientific American*, 1973, *6*, 110–117. (a)

Fromkin, V. A. (Ed.) *Speech errors as linguistic evidence.* The Hague: Mouton, 1973. (b)

Furth, H. G. *Deafness and learning: A psychosocial approach.* Belmont, Calif.: Wadsworth, 1973.

Gahagan, L. Sex differences in recall of stereotyped dreams, sleep-talking and sleep-walking. *Journal of Genetic Psychology*, 1936, *48*, 227–236.

Gallistel, C. R. Motivation as central organizing process: The psychophysical approach to its functional and neurophysiological analysis. In J. K. Cole & R. B. Sanderegger (Eds.), *Nebraska Symposium on Motivation*, 1974. Lincoln: University of Nebraska Press, 1975.

Gambi, D., Torrioli, M. G., Stefanini, M. C., Torre, A., & Santalucia, A. Nightmares: Heart rate and body movements in pre-adolescent periods. In W. P. Koella & P. Levin (Eds.), *Sleep* (Third European Congress on Sleep Research, Montpellier, 1976.) Basel: S. Karger, 1977.

Gardner, R., Jr., & Grossman, W. I. Normal motor patterns in sleep in man. In E. D. Weitzman (Ed.), *Advances in sleep research* (Vol. 2) New York: Spectrum Publications, John Wiley & Sons, 1976.

Gastaut, H. Les composantes actives de la fonction hypnique (enurisie, somnambulisme, cauchemar, etc.); leurs relations avec l'activité mentale, onirique et non-onirique, au cours du sommeil. In H. Gastaut, G. Lugaresi, G. Cerone, & G. Coccagna (Eds.), *Proceedings of the XVth European Meeting on Electroencephalography*, Bologna, 1967.

Gastaut, H., & Broughton, R. A clinical and polygraphic study of episodic phenomena during sleep—Academic address. In J. Wortis (Ed.), *Recent advances in biological psychiatry* (Vol. 7). New York: Plenum Press, 1965.

Gastaut, H., Dongier, M., Broughton, R., & Tassinari, C. A. Etude EEG graphique et clinique des crises d'angoisse diurnes et nocturnes. *Revue Neurologique*, 1963, *109*, 333–335.

Gazzaniga, M. S. *The bisected brain.* New York: Appleton-Century-Crofts, 1970.

Gerson, S. N., Benson, D. F., & Frazier, S. H. Diagnosis: Schizophrenia versus posterior aphasia. *American Journal of Psychiatry*, 1977, *134*, 9, 966–969.

Geschwind, N. Problems in the anatomical understanding of the aphasias. In A. L. Benton (Ed.), *Contributions to clinical neuropsychology*. Chicago: Aldine, 1969.

Gill, M., & Brenman, M. *Hypnosis and related states.* New York: International Universities Press, 1959.

Glover, E. The concept of dissociation. In *On the early development of the mind.* New York: International Universities Press, 1956. (Originally published, 1943.) (a)

Glover, E. Grades of ego-differentiation. In *On the early development of mind.* New York: International Universities Press, 1956. (Originally published, 1930.) (b)

Goddard, H. H. A case of dual personality. *Journal of Abnormal Social Psychology*, 1926, *21*, 1976.

Goecker, J. *Somnambulismus und verwandte bewusstseinstörungen in ihrer gerichtarzlichen bedeutung.* Unpublished dissertation, University of Düsseldorf, 1935.

Goetzinger, E. The problem of dream speech (an experimental investigation). In U. J. Jovanovic (Ed.), *The Nature of Sleep, International Symposium*, Wurzburg, 1971. Stuttgart: Gustav Fischer Verlag, 1973.

Goldman-Eisler, F. Hesitation, information, and levels of speech production. In A. V. S. deReuck & M. O'Connor (Eds.), Ciba Foundation Symposium, *Disorders of Language*. Boston: Little, Brown & Co., 1964.

Goldman-Eisler, F. *Psycholinguistics: Experiments in spontaneous speech.* New York: Academic Press, 1968.

Goldstein, L., Stolzfus, N. W., & Gardocki, J. F. Changes in interhemispheric amplitude relationships in the EEG during sleep. *Physiology and Behavior*, 1972, *8*, 811–815. (Brain Research Publications.)

Goldstein, L., Guennoc, A., & Vidal, J. C. Nouvelles données cliniques sur le vécu des phases intermédiares du sommeil. *Revue Neurologie*, 1966, *115*, 507–511.

Goode, G. B. Sleep paralysis. *Archives of Neurology*, 1962, *6*, 228–234.

Goodenough, D. R. The phenomena of dream recall. In L. E. Abt & B. F. Riess, (Eds.), *Progress in clinical psychology*. New York: Stratton, 1968.

Goodenough, D. R. Dream recall-History and current status of the field. In A. M. Arkin, J. S. Antrobus & S. J. Ellman (Eds.), *The mind in sleep*. Hillsdale, N.J.: Lawrence Erlbaum Associates, 1978.

Goodenough, D. R., Lewis, H. B., Shapiro, A., & Sleser, I. Some correlates of dream reporting following laboratory awakenings. *Journal of Nervous and Mental Disease*, 1965, *140*, 365–373.

Goodenough, D. R., Sapan, J., Cohen, H., Portnoff, G., & Shapiro, A. Some experiments concerning the effects of sleep on memory. *Psychophysiology*, 1971, *8*, 749–762.

598 REFERENCES

Goodwin, O. W., Powell, B., Bremer, D., Haine, H., & Stern, J. Alcohol and recall: State dependent effects in man. *Science,* 1969, *163,* 1358-1360.

Gottschalk, L. A., Haer, J. C., & Bates, D. E. Effect of sensory overload on psychological state. *Archives of General Psychiatry,* 1972, *27,* 451-457.

Gowers, W. R. *The borderland of epilepsy.* Philadelphia: Blakiston, 1907.

Gradess, R. S., Stone, J., Steiner, S. S. & Ellman, S. J. *Coordinated motor responding in sleeping human subjects.* Paper presented at the meeting of the Association for the Psychophysiological Study of Sleep, Bruges, Belgium, 1971.

Granda, A. M., & Hammack, J. T. Operant behavior during sleep. *Science,* 1961, *133,* 1485-1486.

Green, S. A. Single case study. A case of functional sleep seizures. *Journal of Nervous and Mental Disease,* 1977, *164,* 223-227.

Green, W. J. The effect of LSD on the sleep-dream cycle. *Journal of Nervous and Mental Disease,* 1965, *140,* 417-426.

Greenberg, R. *Sleep patterns with a split-brain.* Paper presented at the Association for the Psychophysiological Study of Sleep. Santa Monica, Calif., 1967.

Greenberg, R., & Pearlman, C. Delirium tremens and dreaming. *American Journal of Psychiatry,* 1967, *124,* 133-142.

Griesinger, W. *Mental pathology and therapeutics* (2nd ed.) London: New Sydenham Society, 1867.

Gross, M. M., Goodenough, D., Tobin, M., Halpert, E., Lepore, D., Perlstein, A., Sirota, M., Dibianco, J., Fuller, R., & Kishner, I. Sleep disturbances and hallucinations in the acute alcoholic psychoses. *Journal of Nervous and Mental Disease,* 1966, *142,* 493-514.

Grotjahn, M. Dream observations in a two-year four-months old baby. *Psychoanalytic Quarterly,* 1938, *7,* 507-513.

Grotjahn, M. The process of awakening. *Psychoanalytic Review,* 1942, *29,* 1-19.

Grotjahn, M. Laughter in dreams. *Psychoanalytic Quarterly,* 1945, *14,* 221-227.

Guilleminault, C., Billard, M., Montplaisir, J., & Dement, W. C. Altered states of consciousness in disorders of daytime sleepiness. *Journal of the Neurological Sciences,* 1975, *26,* 377-393. (a)

Guilleminault, C., & Brusset, B. Sleep and schizophrenia: Nightmares, insomnia, and autonomic discharges (study on a young chronic schizophrenic). In U.J. Jovanovic (Ed.), *The Nature of Sleep,* Stuttgart: Gustav Fischer Verlag, 1973.

Guilleminault, C., Pedley, T., & Dement, W. C. Sleep-walking and epilepsy. *Sleep Research,* 1977, *6,* 1970. (Brain Information Service, Brain Research Institute, University of California, Los Angeles.)

Guilleminault, C., Phillips, R., & Dement, W. C. A syndrome of hypersomnia with automatic behavior. *Electroencephalography and Clinical Neurophysiology,* 1975, *38,* 403-413. (b)

Gutheil, E. A. *Handbook of dream analysis.* New York: Grove Press, 1960.

Guthrie, E. R. *The psychology of human conflict.* New York: Harper, 1938.

Greenberg, R., & Pearlman, C. Delirium tremens and dreaming. *American Journal of Psychiatry,* 1967, *124,* 133-142.

Greenberg, R. *Sleep patterns with a split-brain.* Paper presented at the Association for the Psychophysiological Study of Sleep, Santa Monica, Calif., 1967.

Hadamard, J. *The psychology of invention in the mathematical field.* New York: Dover, 1954.

Halasz, P., Rajna, P., Pal, I., Kundra, O., Vargha, M., Balogh, A., & Kemeny, A. K-complexes and micro-arousals as functions of the sleep process. In W. P. Koella & P. Levin (Eds.), *Sleep, 1976* (Third European Congress on Sleep Research, Montpellier, 1976.) Basel: S. Karger, 1977.

Hammond, W. A. *Sleep and its derangements.* Philadelphia: Lippincott, 1883.

Hartmann, E. The effects of diphenylhydantoin (DPH) on sleep in man. *Psychophysiology,* 1970, *7,* 316.

Hartmann, H. *Essays on ego psychology.* New York: International Universities Press, 1964.

Hauri, P. White noise and dream reporting. *Sleep Research,* 1972 (Vol. 1). (Brain Information Service, Brain Research Institute, Los Angeles.)

Hauri, P. Review of Arkin, A. M., Antrobus, J. S., Toth, M. F., Baker, J., & Jackler, F. A comparison of the content of mention reports elicited after NREM-associated sleep-utterance and NREM silent sleep. *Sleep Reviews,* 1973, *73,* 66.

Hebb, D. O. *Textbook of psychology* (3rd ed.). Philadelphia: Saunders, 1972.

Henning, H. *Der Traum als assoziativer kurzschluss.* Wiesbaden: Bergmann, 1914.

Heynick, F. Linguistic aspects of Freud's dream model. Presented at 5th Congress of European Sleep Research Society, Sept. Amsterdam. 1980, (a)

Heynick, F. Verbal aggression (or the lack of it) in sleep-talking. *Maledicta: The International Journal of Verbal Aggression,* 1980, (b)

Hilgard, E. R. A neodissociationist interpretation of pain reduction in hypnosis. *Psychological Review,* 1973, *80,* 396–411.

Hilgard, E. R. Hypnosis. *Annual Review of Psychology,* 1975, *26,* 19–44. (Annual Reviews, Inc., Palo Alto, Calif.)

Hilgard, E. R. *Divided consciousness: Multiple controls in human thought and action.* New York: Wiley, 1977.

Hirst, W., Neisser, U., & Spelke, E. Divided attention. *Human Nature,* 1978, *1,* 54–61.

Höche, A. H. *Schlaf und traum.* Berlin: Ulstein, 1928.

Holzman, P. S., & Rousey, C. Monitoring, activation and disinhibition: Effects of white noise masking on spoken thought. *Journal of Abnormal Psychology,* 1970, *75, 3,* 227–241.

Horowitz, M. *Image formation and cognition* (2nd ed.). New York: Appleton-Century-Crofts, 1978.

Hobson, J. A., Goldfrank, F., & Snyder, R. Respiration and mental activity in sleep. *Journal of Psychiatric Research,* 1965, *3,* 79–90.

Hull, C. L. The concept of the habit-family hierarchy and maze learning. *Psychological Review,* 1934, *41,* 33–54.

Isakower, O. The exceptional position of the auditory sphere. *International Journal of Psychoanalysis,* 1939, *20,* 340–348.

Isakower, O. Spoken words in dreams. A preliminary communication. *Psychoanalytic Quarterly,* 1954, *23,* 1–6.

Isakower, O. *Personal communication to Baudry, F.,* 1972. Cited in Baudry, F., 1974.

Jackson, J. H. *Selected writings of John Hughlings Jackson.* New York: Basic Books, 1958. (a. On the nature of the duality of the brain, 1874. b. On affections of speech from disease of the brain, 1878, 1879.)

Jackson, M. M. Anticipatory cardiac acceleration during sleep. *Science,* 1942, *96,* 564–565.

Jacobson, E. & Kales, A. Somnambulism: All night EEG and related studies. In S. S. Kety, E. V. Evarts & H. L. Williams (Eds.), *Sleep and altered states of consciousness.* Baltimore: Williams & Wilkins, 1967.

Jacobson, A., Kales, J. D., & Kales, A. Clinical and electrophysiological correlates of sleep disorders in children. In A. Kales (Ed.), *Sleep: Physiology and pathology.* Philadelphia: J. B. Lippincott, 1969.

Jacobson, A., Kales, A., Lehmann, D., & Zweizig, J. R. Somnambulism: All-night electroencephalographic studies. *Science,* 1965, *148,* 975–977.

Jacobson, E. *Progressive relaxation* (2nd ed.). Chicago: University of Chicago Press, 1938.

Jakobson, R. Two aspects of language and two types of aphasia disturbances. In R. Jakobson & M. Halle (Eds.), *Fundamentals of language.* The Hague: Mouton, 1956.

Janet, P. *L'automatism e psychologique.* Paris: Felix Alcan, 1889.

Janet, P. *The major symptoms of hysteria.* New York: MacMillan, 1907.

Janet, P. *Psychological healing.* London: Allen & Unwin, 1925.

Janis, I. L., Mahl, G. F., Hagan, J., & Holt, R. R. *Personality development and assessment.* New York: Harcourt, Brace & World, 1969.

John, E. R. A model of consciousness. In G. E. Schwartz & D. Shapiro (Eds.), *Consciousness and self-regulation*. New York: Plenum Press, 1976.

Johnson, L. C., Burdick, J. A., & Smith, J. Sleep during alcohol intake and withdrawal in the chronic alcoholic. *Archives of General Psychiatry*, 1970, 22, 406–418.

Johnson, L. C., Slye, E. S., & Dement, W. C. Electroencephalographic and autonomic activity during and after prolonged sleep deprivation. *Psychosomatic Medicine*, 1965, 27, 415–423.

Johnson, L. C. A psychophysiology for all states. *Psychophysiology*, 1970, 6, 501–516.

Jones, E. The mantle symbol. *International Journal of Psychoanalysis*, 1927, 8, 64.

Jouvet, M. The function of dreaming: A neurophysiologist's point of view. In M. S. Gazzaniga & C. Blakemore (Eds.), *Handbook of Psychobiology*. New York: Academic Press, 1975.

Jovanovic, U. J. *Normal sleep in man*. Stuttgart: Hippokrates Verlag, 1971.

Jovanovic, U. J. *Psychomotor epilepsy*. Springfield, Ill.: Charles C Thomas, 1974.

Jovanovic, U. J. Sleep disturbances in neuropsychiatric patients. *Waking and Sleeping*, 1976, 1, 67–88.

Jung, C. G. *Studies in word association* (M. D. Eder, Ed. and trans.). New York: Moffat, 1919.

Jung, C. G. *Psychiatric studies*. New York: Pantheon Books, 1957.

Kahn, M. M. R. The changing use of dreams in psychoanalytic practice. In search of the dreaming experience. *International Journal of Psychoanalysis*, 1976, 57, 325–330.

Kahneman, D. *Attention and effort*. Englewood Cliffs, N.J.: Prentice–Hall, 1973.

Kales, A., Jacobson, A., Paulson, M. J., Kales, J. D., & Walter, R. D. Somnambulism: Psychophysiological correlates. I. All night EEG studies. *Archives of General Psychiatry*, 1966, 14, 586–596.

Kales, A., & Jacobson, A. Mental activity during sleep: Recall studies, somnambulism, and effects of rapid eye movement deprivation and drugs. *Experimental Neurology*, 1967, 19 (Supplement 4), 81–91.

Kales, A., & Kales, J. D. Sleep disorders. *New England Journal of Medicine*, 1974, 290, 487–499.

Kales, A., Kales, J. D., Humphrey, F. J., Kuhn, W., Tan, T. L., & Soldatos, C. R. Clinical characteristics of patients with sleepwalking. *Sleep Research*, 1977, 6, 171. (Brain Information Service, Brain Research Institute, University of California, Los Angeles.)

Kales, J. D., Davis, R., Russek, E., Martin, E. D., Kuhn, W., & Kales, A. Clinical characteristics of patients with night terrors: Further studies. *Sleep Research*, 1978, 7, 191. (a)

Kales, J. D., Humphrey, F. J., Martin, E. D., Russek, E., Kuhn, W., Pelicci, L., & Kales, A. Clinical characteristics of patients with sleepwalking: Further studies. *Sleep Research*, 1978, 7, 192. (b)

Kamiya, J. Behavioral, subjective and physiological aspects of drowsiness and sleep. In D. W. Fiske & S. R. Maddi (Eds.), *Functions of varied experience*. Homewood, Ill.: Dorsey Press, 1961.

Kanner, L. *Child psychiatry* (3rd ed.). Springfield, Ill.: Charles C. Thomas, 1957.

Kay, D. C. Personal communication, November 14, 1974.

Kay, D. C. Human sleep and EEG through a cycle of methadone dependence. *Electroencephalography and clinical neurophysiology*, 1975, 38, 35–43.

Kay, D. C., Blackburn, A. B., Buckingham, J. A., & Karacan, I. Human pharmacology of sleep. In R. L. Williams & I. Karacan (Eds.), *Pharmacology of sleep*. New York: Wiley, 1976.

Keele, S. W. *Attention and human performance*. Santa Monica, Calif.: Goodyear Publishing Co., 1973.

Kernberg, O. *Object relations theory and clinical psychoanalysis*. New York: Aronson, 1976.

Kinsbourne, M. The minor hemisphere as a source of aphasic speech. *Transactions of the American Neurological Association*, 1971, 96, 141–145.

Klatzky, R. L. *Human memory: Structures and processes*. San Francisco: W. H. Freeman, 1975.

Klein, G. S. On hearing one's own voice: An aspect of cognitive control in spoken thought. In N. S. Greenfield & W. C. Lewis (Eds.), *Psychoanalysis and current biological thought*. Madison: University of Wisconsin Press, 1965.

Kleitman, N. The nature of dreaming. In G. E. W. Wolstenholme, & M. O'Connor (Eds.), *The nature of sleep*. (Ciba Foundation Symposium.) Boston: Little, Brown, 1960. (a)

Kleitman, N. Patterns of dreaming. *Scientific American*, 1960, *203*, 82–88. (b)

Kleitman, N. *Sleep and wakefulness* (2nd ed.). Chicago: University of Chicago Press, 1963.

Kohut, H. *The restoration of the self*. New York: International Universities Press, 1977.

Koulack, D., & Goodenough, D. R. Dream recall and dream recall failure: An arousal-retrieval model. *Psychological Bulletin*, 1976, *83*, 975–984.

Kraepelin, E. Über sprachstörungen im traume. *Psychologische Arbeiten*, 5, 1. (Leipzig, 1906.)

Kratochvíl, S., & MacDonald, H. Sleep in hypnosis: An EEG study. *American Journal of Clinical Hypnosis*, 1972, *15*, 29–37.

Krippner, S., & Stoller, L. Sleeptalking and creativity. A case study. *Journal of the American Society of Psychosomatic Dentistry and Medicine*, 1973, *20*, 107–114.

Lairy, G. C., Goldsteinas, L., & Guennoc, A. Phases intermédiaires du sommeil de nuit des malades mentaux. In *Rève et conscience*. Paris: P.U.F, 1968.

Landauer, K. Handlungen des schlafenden. *Z. Ges. Neurol. Psychiat. Originalien*, 1918, *39*, 329–351.

Lasaga, J. I., & Lasaga, A. M. Sleep learning and progressive blurring of perception during sleep. *Perceptual and Motor Skills*, 1973, *37*, 51–62.

Lashley, K. S. The problem of serial order in behavior. In L. A. Jeffries (Ed.), *Cerebral mechanisms in behavior*. New York: Wiley, 1951.

Laver, J. The production of speech. In J. Lyon (Ed.), *New horizons in linguistics*. Harmondsworth, Middlesex, England: Penguin Books, 1970.

LeBoeuf, A. A behavioral treatment of chronic sleeptalking. *Journal of Behavior Therapy and Experimental Psychiatry*, 1979, *10*, 83–84.

Lechner, K. *Die klinischen formen der schlaflosigkeit*. Deuticke–Leipzig und Wien, 1909.

Lee, B. S. Effects of delayed speech feedback. *Journal of the Acoustical Society of America*, 1950, *22*, 823–826.

Lenneberg, E. H. Brain correlates of language. In F. O. Schmitt (Ed.), *The neurosciences 2nd study program*. New York: Rockefeller University Press, 1970.

Lewin, K. *A dynamic theory of personality*. New York: McGraw-Hill, 1935.

Libet, B. Brain stimulation and conscious experience. In J. C. Eccles (Ed.), *Brain and conscious experience*. New York: Springer Verlag, 1966.

Lichter, I., & Muir, R. C. The pattern of swallowing during sleep. *Electroencephalography and Clinical Neurophysiology*, 1975, *38*, 427–432.

Lindner, R. M. Hypnoanalysis in a case of hysterical somnambulism. *Psychoanalytic Review*, 1945, *32*, 325–339.

Lindsay, P. H., & Norman, D. A. *Human information processing: An introduction to psychology* (2nd ed.). New York: Academic Press, 1977.

Lipowski, Z. J. Delirium, clouding of consciousness and confusion. *Journal of Nervous and Mental Disease*, 1967, *145*, 227–255.

Lipps, T. *Leitfaden der psychologie* (Vol. 3). Leipzig: Engelman, 1909.

Litowitz, B. E. Language: Waking and sleeping. In *Psychoanalysis and contemporary science* 1975 (Vol. IV). New York: International Universities Press, 1976.

Löwenfeld, J. *Somnambulismus und spiritismus* (2nd ed.). Wiesbaden: Bergmann, 1907.

Lowes, J. L. *The Road to Xanadu*. Boston: Houghton Mifflin, 1927.

Lucretius. The nature of the universe. London: Penguin Classics, 1951. (Originally 58 B.C.)

Luria, A. R. *The waking brain*. New York: Basic Books, 1973.

Luria, A. R. Language and brain. *Brain and Language*, 1974, *1*, 14.

Luria, A. R., & Hutton, T. J. A modern assessment of the basic forms of aphasia. *Brain and Language*, 1977, *4*, 129–151.

MacLeod, M. N., & Fisher, P. Pavor nocturnus in a schizophrenic patient: A review and case study. *American Journal of Psychiatry*, 1978, *135*, 235–236.

MacNeilage, L. A. *Activity of the speech apparatus during sleep and its relation to dream reports*. Unpublished doctoral dissertation, Columbia University, 1971.

MacNeilage, P. F. Motor control of serial ordering of speech. *Psychological Review*, 1970, 77, 182–196.

MacNeilage, P. F., Cohen, D. B., & MacNeilage, L. A. Subjects' estimates of sleeptalking propensity and dream recall frequency are positively related. *Sleep Research*, 1972, 1, 113. (Brain Information Service, University of California, Los Angeles.)

MacNeilage, P. F., & MacNeilage, L. A. Central processes controlling speech production. In F. J. McGuigan & R. A. Schoonover (Eds.), *The psychophysiology of thinking*. New York: Academic Press, 1973.

MacNish, R. *The philosophy of sleep*. Glasgow: M'Phun, 1838.

Maher, B. The language of schizophrenia: a review and interpretation. *British Journal of Psychiatry*, 1972, 120, 3–17.

Mahl, G. Body movement, ideation, and verbalization during psychoanalysis. In N. Freedman & S. Grand (Eds.), *Communicative structures and psychic structures*. New York: Plenum Press, 1977.

Mahl, G. People talking when they can't hear their voices. In A. W. Siegman & B. Pope (Eds.), *Studies in dyadic communication*. New York: Pergamon, 1972.

Malcolm, N. The concept of dreaming. In D. F. Gustafson (Ed.), *Essays in philosophical psychology*. New York: Anchor, 1964.

Marburg, O. Der schlaf, seine störungen und deren behandlung. In *Bücher der ärztlichen praxis*. Wien/Berlin: Springer, 1929.

Martin, W. R., Jasinksi, D. R., Haertzen, C. A., Kay, D. C., Jones, B. E., Mansky, P. A., & Carpenter, R. W. Methadone—A re-evaluation. *Archives of General Psychiatry*, 1973, 28, 286–295.

Massarotti, V. *Sonno e insomnia*. Milan: Edizioni Giovanni Bolla, 1950.

Maury, A. De certain faits observés dans les rêves et dans l'état intermediare entre le sommeil et la veille. *Annales Médico-Psychologiques*, 1857 sev. 3, tome 3, 157–176.

Maury, L. F. A. *Le sommeil et les rêves* (4th ed.). Paris: Didier, 1878.

Mazzia, V. D. B., & Randt, C. Amnesia and eye movements in first stage anesthesia. *Archives of Neurology*, 1966, 14, 522–525.

McDonald, D. G., Schicht, W. W., Frazier, R. E., Shallenberger, H. D., & Edwards, D. J. Studies of information processing during sleep. *Psychophysiology*, 1975, 12, 624–629.

McGinty, D. J., & Siegel, J. M. Neuronal activity patterns during rapid-eye movement sleep: Relation to waking patterns. In R. R. Drucker-Colin & J. L. McGaugh (Eds.), *Neurobiology of sleep and memory*. New York: Academic Press, 1977.

McGraw, R. B., & Oliven, J. F. Miscellaneous therapies. In S. Arieti (Ed.), *American handbook of psychiatry* (1st ed.). New York: Basic Books, 1959.

McGregor, D. *The dream world of Dion McGregor*. New York: Geis, 1964.

McGuigan, F. J., & Tanner, R. *Covert oral behavior during conversational and visual dreams*. Paper presented at the annual meeting of the Association for the Psychophysiological Study of Sleep, Sante Fe, 1970.

Mello, N. K. Behavioral studies of alcoholism. In B. Kissin & H. Begleiter (Eds.), *The biology of alcoholism* (Vol. 2). *Physiology and Behavior*. New York: Plenum Press, 1972.

Mello, N. K., & Mendelson, J. K. Alcoholism: A bio-behavioral disorder. In S. Arieti (Ed.), *American handbook of psychiatry* (Vol. 4). New York: Basic Books, 1975.

Mick, B. A. Headaches and sleepwalking (a letter to the editor). *Journal of the American Medical Association*, 1974, 229, 393.

Miller, C. F. *Psychophathologie des bewusstseins*. Leipzig: Abel, 1889.

Miller, G. A., Galanter, E., & Pribram, K. *Plans and the structure of behavior*. New York: Holt, Rinehart & Winston, 1960.

Miller, N. Learning of visceral and glandular responses. *Science*, 1969, 163, 434–445.

Mintz, A. Schizophrenic speech and sleepy speech. *Journal of Abnormal and Social Psychology*, 1948, *43*, 548–549.

Mittelmann, B. Ego functions and dreams. *Psychoanalytic Quarterly*, 1949, *18*, 434–448.

Moll, A. *The study of hypnosis*. New York: Julian Press, 1958. (Originally published, 1889.)

Montplaisir, J., & Lester, E. *A case of nocturnal rocking*. Paper presented at the meeting of the Association for the Psychophysiological Study of Sleep, Houston, Texas, 1977.

Moreau, de la Sarthe. *Rêves*. In *Société de medicins et de chirurgiens*. Dictionnaire des sciences médicales (Vol. 48). Paris: Pancouke, 1820.

Morgane, P. J., & Stern, W. C. Chemical anatomy of brain circuits in relation to sleep and wakefulness. In E. D. Weitzman (Ed.), *Advances in sleep research* (Vol. 1). New York: Spectrum Publications, 1974.

Morris, G. O., Williams, H. L., & Lubin, A. Misperception and disorientation during sleep deprivation. *A.M.A. Archives of General Psychiatry*, 1960, *2*, 247–254.

Moruzzi, G. Neural mechanisms of the sleep-waking cycle. In O. Petre-Quadens & J. D. Schlag (Eds.), *Basic sleep mechanisms*. New York: Academic Press, 1974.

Moscovich, M. Language and the cerebral hemispheres: Reaction time studies and their implications for models of cerebral dominance. In P. Pliner, L. Krames & T. Alloway (Eds.), *Communication and affect: Language and thought*. New York: Academic Press, 1973.

Mot, F. *The psychology of soldiers' dreams*. Cited by W. S. Walsh, 1920.

Mühl, A. *Automatic writing: An approach to the unconscious* (2nd ed.). New York: Helix Press, 1963.

Mulholland, T. B. Biofeedback as scientific method. In G. E. Schwartz, & J. Beatty (Eds.), *Biofeedback: Theory and research*. New York: Academic Press, 1977.

Muller, C. *Sleepwalking and sleep talking*. Praxis, 1970.

Muller-Limmroth, W. *Der schlaf des menschen*. Konstanz: K-Guden-Lomberg, 1965.

Murray, H. A. et al. *Explorations in personality*. New York: Oxford University Press, 1938.

Muzet, A., & Michel, C. Heart rate preceding short activation phases in sleep. *Waking and Sleeping*, 1977, *1*, 175–180.

Myslobodsky, M. S., Ben-Mayor, V., Yedid-Levy, B., & Mintz, M. Hemispheric asymmetry of EEG and averaged visual evoked potentials during non-REM sleep. In W. P. Koella & P. Levin (Eds.), *Sleep, 1976*. (Third European Congress on Sleep Research, Montpellier, 1976). Basel: S. Karger, 1977.

Naitoh, P., Kales, A., Kollar, E. J., Smith, J. C., & Jacobson, A. Electroencephalographic activity after prolonged sleep loss. *Electroencephalography and Clinical Neurophysiology*, 1969, *27*, 2–11.

Naitoh, P., Muzet, A., Johnson, L. C., & Mosse, J. Body movements during sleep after sleep loss. *Psychophysiology*, 1973, *10*, 4, 363–368.

Nebes, R. D. Hemispheric specialization in commissurotomized man. *Psychological Bulletin*, 1974, *81*, 1, 1–14.

Neisser, U. *Cognitive psychology*. New York: Appleton-Century-Crofts, 1967.

Neufeld, W. Relaxation methods in U.S. Navy air schools. *American Journal of Psychiatry*, 1951, *108*, 132–137.

The New Yorker. The talk of the town, June 17, 1974, p. 25.

Nielsen, J. M. Extreme encephalitic Parkinsonism with contractures which relax during somnambulistic states. *Bulletin of Los Angeles Neurological Society*, 1936, *1*, 28–30.

Nielsen, J. M. *A textbook of clinical neurology*. New York: Paul B. Hoeber, 1941.

Norman, D. A. *Memory and attention: An introduction to human information processing* (2nd ed.). New York: Wiley, 1976.

Ogilvie, R., Hunt, H., Sawicki, C., & McGowan, K. Searching for lucid dreams. *Sleep research*, 1978, *7*, 165.

Oltman, R. K., Goodenough, D. R., Koulack, D., Maclin, E., Schroeder, H. R., & Flannagan, M. Short-term memory during Stage 2 sleep. *Psychophysiology*, 1977, *14*, 5, 439–444.

Orr, W. J., Dozier, J. E., Green L., and Cromwell, R. I. Self-induced waking: Changes in dreams and sleep patterns. Comprehensive Psychiatry, 1968, 499–506.

Osborn, A. G., Bunker, J. P., Cooper, L. M., Frank, G. S., & Hilgard, E. R. Effects of thiopental sedation on learning and memory. Science, 1967, 157, 574–576.

Oswald, I. Sleeping and waking: Physiology and psychology. New York: Elsevier, 1962.

Oswald, I. Physiology of sleep accompanying dreaming. In The scientific basis of medicine. London: Annual Reviews, 1964.

Oswald, I. Sleep and dependence on amphetamine and other drugs. In A. Kales (Ed.), Sleep: Physiology and pathology. Philadelphia: J. B. Lippincott Co., 1969.

Oswald, I. Drug research and human sleep. In H. W. Elliott, R. Okun & R. George (Eds.), Annual review of pharmacology (Vol. 13). Palo Alto, Calif.: Annual Reviews, Inc., 1973.

Oswald, I. Pharmacology of sleep. In P. O. Petre-Quadens & J. D. Schlag (Eds.), Basic sleep mechanisms. New York: Academic Press, 1974.

Oswald, I., Taylor, A. M., & Treisman, M. Discriminative responses to stimulation during human sleep. Brain, 1960, 83, 440–453.

Overton, D. A. State-dependent or dissociated learning produced with pentobarbital. Journal of Comparative and Physiological Psychology, 1964, 57, 3–12.

Overton, D. A. State-dependent learning produced by alcohol and its relevance to alcoholism. In B. Kissin & H. Begleiter (Eds.), The biology of alcoholism (Vol. 2). Physiology and Behavior. New York: Plenum Press, 1972.

Overton, D. A. State-dependent retention of learned responses produced by drugs. Its relevance to sleep-learning and recall. In W. P. Koella, & P. Levin (Eds.), Sleep: Physiology, biochemistry, psychology, pharmacology, clinical implications. Basel: S. Karger, 1973.

Pai, M. N. Sleep-walking and sleep activities. Journal of Mental Science, 1946, 92, 756.

Paradis, M. Bilingualism and aphasia. In H. Whitaker & H. A. Whitaker (Eds.), Studies in neurolinguistics (Vol. 3). New York: Academic Press, 1977.

Pascal, G. R., & Salzberg, H. E. A systematic approach to inducing hypnotic behavior. International Journal of Clinical and Experimental Hypnosis, 1959, 7, 161–167.

Passouant, P. Problemes physiopathologiques de la narcolepsie et periodicité du "sommeil rapide" au cours de nythemes. In H. Gastaut, G. Lugaresi, G. Cerone & G. Coccagna (Eds.), Proceedings of the 15th European Meeting on Electroencephalography. Bologna, Italy, 1967.

Passouant, P. Episodic phenomena during REM sleep. In W. P. Koella & P. Levin (Eds.), Sleep 1974. Second European Congress on Sleep Research, Rome, 1974.

Pears, D. F. Dreaming. In D. F. Gustafson (Ed.), Essays in philosophical psychology. New York: Anchor, 1964.

Penfield, W., & Roberts, L. Speech and brain mechanisms. Princeton, N.J.: Princeton University Press, 1959.

Perry, C. W., Evans, F. J., O'Connell, N. D., Orne, E. C., & Orne, M. T. Behavioral response to verbal stimuli administered and tested during REM sleep: A further investigation. Waking and Sleeping, 1978, 2, 1, 35–42.

Pesikoff, R. B., & Davis, P. C. Treatment of pavor nocturnus and somnambulism in children. American Journal of Psychiatry, 1971, 128, 778.

Pessah, M. A., & Roffwarg, H. P. Spontaneous middle ear muscle activity in man: A rapid eye movement sleep phenomenon. Science, 1972, 178, 773–778.

Peterfreund, E., & Schwartz, J. T. Information, systems and psychoanalysis. Psychological Issues, 1971, 7.

Piaget, J. The construction of reality in the child. New York: International Universities Press, 1952.

Piaget, J. The origins of intelligence in children. New York: Basic Books, 1954.

Pierce, C. M., Pilcon, H. H., McLary, J. H., & Noble, H. G. Enuresis: Clinical laboratory and EEG studies. U.S. Armed Forces Medical Journal, 1956, 7, 208.

Pinkerton, J. N. Sleep and its phenomena. London: Fry, 1839.

Pivik, T., & Foulkes, D. NREM mentation: Relation to personality, orientation time, and time of night. *Journal of Consulting and Clinical Psychology*, 1968, *37*, 144–151.

Pivik, R. T. Tonic states and phasic events in relation to sleep mentation. In A. M. Arkin, J. S. Antrobus & S. J. Ellman (Eds.), *The mind in sleep*. Hillsdale, N.J.: Lawrence Erlbaum, 1978.

Popoviciu, L., Asgian, B., Corfariu, O., & Szabó, L. Contribution to the knowledge of polygraphic polymorphism of paradoxical sleep. In W. P. Koella & P. Levin (Eds.), *Sleep: Physiology, biochemistry, psychology, pharmacology, clinical implications. Proceedings of the First European Congress on Sleep Research*. Basel: S. Karger, 1973.

Popoviciu, L., & Szabó, L. Clinical, electroencephalographic and polygraphic studies of sleep in non-convulsive nocturnal manifestations. In U. J. Jovanovic (Ed.), *The nature of sleep*. Stuttgart: Gustav Fischer Verlag, 1973.

Popoviciu, T. Frontier states between sleep incidents and nocturnal epileptic attacks. In W. P. Koella & P. Levin (Eds.), *Sleep 1976*. (Third European Congress on Sleep Research, Montpellier). Basel: S. Karger, 1977.

Pötzl, O. Der schlaf. *Jahreskurse für ärztliche Forbildung*, 1929, *5*, 62. (a)

Pötzl, O. Der schlaf als behandlungs-problem. In *Der schlaf: Mitteilungen und stellungnahme zum derzeitigen stände des schlafproblems*. Herausgegeben von Sarason, Munchen: J. F. Lehmann's Verlag, 1929. (b)

Pribram, K. H. Self-consciousness and intentionality. In G. E. Schwartz & D. Shapiro (Eds.), *Consciousness and self-regulation* (Vol. 1). New York: Plenum Press, 1976.

Prince, M. *Dissociation of a personality*. New York: Longmans, Green, 1909.

Radestock, P. *Schlaf und traum*. Leipzig: Breitkopf u. Härtel, 1879.

Rapaport, D. Consciousness: A psychopathological and psychodynamic view. In *Transactions of the 2nd Conference on Problems of Consciousness*. New York: Josiah Macy, Jr. Foundation, 1951.

Rapaport, D. The structure of psychoanalytic theory: A systematizing attempt. *Psychological Issues*, 1960, *6*. (International Universities Press, New York)

Rechtschaffen, A. Dream reports and dream experiences. *Experimental Neurology*, Supplement 4, 1967, 4–15.

Rechtschaffen, A. The psychophysiology of mental activity during sleep. In F. J. McGuigan & R. A. Schoonover (Eds.), *The psychophysiology of thinking*. New York: Academic Press, 1973.

Rechtschaffen, A., Goodenough, D. R., & Shapiro, A. Patterns of sleep-talking. *Archives of General Psychiatry* (Chicago), 1962, *7*, 418–426.

Rechtschaffen, A., Hauri, P., & Zeitlin, M. Auditory awakening thresholds in REM and NREM sleep stages. *Perceptual and Motor Skills*, 1966, *22*, 927–942.

Rechtschaffen, A., & Kales, A. (Eds.) *A manual of standardized terminology, techniques and scoring system for sleep stages of human subjects*. (National Institute of Health Publication No. 204) Washington, D.C.: United States Government Printing Office, 1968.

Rechtschaffen, A., & Maron, L. The effect of amphetamine on the sleep cycle. *Electroencephalography and Clinical Neurophysiology*, 1964, *16*, 438–445.

Rechtschaffen, A., Verdone, P., & Wheaton, J. Reports of mental activity during sleep. *Canadian Psychiatric Association Journal*, 1963, *8*, 409–414. (a)

Rechtschaffen, A., Vogel, G., & Shaikun, G. Interrelatedness of mental activity during sleep. *Archives of General Psychiatry*, 1963, *9*, 536–547. (b)

Reding, G. R., Rubright, W. C., & Zimmerman, S. O. Incidence of bruxism. *Journal of Dental Research*, 1966, *45*, 1198–1204.

Reding, G. R., Zepelin, H., Robinson, J. E., Zimmerman, S. O., & Smith, V. H. Nocturnal teeth-grinding: All night psychophysiological studies. *Journal of Dental Research*, 1968, *47*, 786–797.

Rice, E., & Fisher, C. Fugue states in sleep and wakefulness: A psychophysiological study. *Journal of Nervous and Mental Disease*, 1976, *163*, 2, 79–87.

Riess, A. The mother's eye for better and for worse. *Psychoanalytic Study of the Child*, New Haven: Yale University Press, 1978, *33*, 381-409.

Rorschach, H. *Psychodiagnostics: A diagnostic test based on perception*. Berne: Hans Huber, 1942.

Rosenblatt, A. D., & Thickstun, J. T. Modern psychoanalytic concepts in a general psychology, *Psychological Issues*, 1977, 11, 2, 3, Monograph 42, 43. (International Universities Press, New York.)

Ryback, R. S. Alcohol amnesia. *Quarterly Journal of Studies on Alcohol*, 1970, *31*, 3, 616-632.

Sadger, J. Sleep-walking and moon-walking. *Journal of Nervous and Mental Disease* (Supplement), 1920, *31*, 6-7, 33.

Sadger, J. Cited by S. Freud. In H. Nunberg & E. Federn (Eds.), *Minutes of the Vienna Psychoanalytic Society*. New York: International Universities Press.

Salamy, J. Instrumental responding to internal cues associated with REM sleep. *Psychonomic Science*, 1970, *18*, 342-343.

Salmon, A. *La fonction du sommeil*. Paris: Vigot, 1910.

Salzarulo, P., & Cipolli, C. Spontaneously recalled verbal material and its linguistic organization in relation to different stages of sleep. *Biological Psychology*, 1974, *2*, 47-57.

Salzinger, K. An hypothesis about schizophrenic behavior. *American Journal of Psychotherapy*, 1971, *25*, 601-614.

Sander, F. Experimentelle ergebnisse der gestalt - psychologie. In *Exp. Psychologie*. Jena, Germany: Fischer, 1928.

Sandler, J., Holder, A., & Dare, C. Frames of reference in psychoanalytic psychology IX: Dream processes in the topographical frame of reference. *British Journal of Medical Psychology*, 1975, *48*, 161-174.

Sarbin, T. R., & Coe, W. C. *Hypnosis: A social psychological analysis of influence communication*. New York: Holt, Rinehart & Winston, 1972.

Sassin, J. F., & Johnson, L. C. Body mobility during sleep and its relation to the K-complex. *Experimental Neurology*, 1968, *22*, 1, 133-144.

Satoh, T., & Harada, Y. Tooth-grinding during sleep as an arousal reaction. *Experientia* (Basel), 1971, *27*, 785-786.

Schachter, D. L. The hypnagogic state: A critical review of its literature. *Psychological Bulletin*, 1976, *83*, 452-481.

Schafer, R. A study of thought processes in a word association test. *Character and Personality*, 1945, *13*, 212-227.

Schaltenbrand, G. The effects of stereotactical stimulation in the depth of the brain. *Brain*, 1965, *88*, 835-840.

Schaltenbrand, G. The effects on speech and language of stereotactical stimulation in thalamus and corpus callosum. *Brain and Language*, 1975, *2*, 1, 70-77.

Schiff, S. K., Bunney, W. E., Jr., & Freedman, D. X. A study of ocular movements in hypnotically induced dreams. *The Journal of Nervous and Mental Disease*, 1961, *133*, 1, 59-68.

Schiffrin, R. M., & Schneider, W. Controlled and automatic human information processing: II. Perceptual learning, automatic attending and a general theory. *Psychological Review*, 1977, *84*, 2, 127-190.

Schilder, P. *Mind, perception and thought*. New York: Columbia University Press, 1942.

Schilder, P. On the development of thoughts. In D. Rapaport (Ed.), *Organization and pathology of thought*. New York: Columbia University Press, 1951. (Originally published, 1920.) (a)

Schilder, P. Studies concerning the psychology and symptomatology of general paresis. In D. Rapaport (Ed.), *Organization and pathology of thought*. New York: Columbia University Press, 1951. (Originally published, 1920.) (b)

Schilder, P., & Kauders, O. *The nature of hypnosis*. New York: International Universities Press, 1956.

Schnee, R. *Verbal communication between information processing sub-systems during sleep.* Unpublished doctoral dissertation, CUNY, 1978.

Schneider, W., & Schiffrin, R. M. Controlled and automatic human information processing. I. Detection, search and attention. *Psychological Review*, 1977, *84*, 1–66.

Schwartz, B. A. Discussion of N. Kleitman's paper, "The nature of dreaming." In G. E. W. Wolstenholme & M. O'Connor (Eds.), *The nature of sleep.* (Ciba Foundation Symposium.) Boston: Little, Brown, 1960.

Schwartz, D. *Unpublished paper,* 1976. Dept. of Psychology, CUNY.

Scott, J. Performance after abrupt arousal from sleep: Comparison of a simple motor, a visual-perceptual, and a cognitive task. *Proceedings of the 77th Annual Convention of the American Psychological Association*, 1969. (Summary)

Searleman, A. A review of right hemisphere linguistic capabilities. *Psychological Bulletin*, 1977, *84*, 503–528.

Seashore, G. E. The frequency of dreams. *Scientific Monthly*, 1916, *2*, 467.

Sechenov, I. *Reflexes of the brain.* Cambridge: MIT Press, 1965. (Originally published, 1863.)

Segal, S. J. Processing of the stimulus imagery and perception. In S. J. Segal (Ed.), *Imagery: Current cognitive approaches.* New York: Academic Press, 1971.

Serafetinedes, E. A. Speech findings in epilepsy and electrocortical stimulation: An overview. *Cortex*, 1966, *2*, 463–473.

Serafetinedes, E. A., & Falconer, M. A. Speech disturbances in temporal lobe seizures: A study in 100 epileptic patients submitted to anterior temporal lobectomy. *Brain*, 1963, *86*, 333–346.

Sewitch, D. *Relationship between the onset of somniloquy and time of night.* Unpublished baccalaureate thesis, Duke University, Department of Psychology, 1976.

Shapiro, A. Observations on some periodic and non-periodic phenomena in normal human sleep. *Annuals of the New York Academy of Science*, 1962, *98*, 1132–1143.

Sharf, B., Moskovitz, C., Lupton, M. D., & Klawans, H. L. Dream phenomena induced by chronic levodopa therapy. *Journal of Neural Transmission*, 1978, *43*, 143–151.

Sidis, B. The Psychology of Suggestion, New York: Appleton-Century 1898.

Silberer, H. *Der traum.* Stuttgart: Enke, 1919.

Simon, C. W., & Emmons, W. H. Responses to material presented during various levels of sleep. *Journal of Experimental Psychology*, 1956, *51*, 89–97.

Singer, J. L. *The inner world of daydreaming.* New York: Harper & Row, 1975.

Sitaram, N., Wyatt, R. J., Dawson, S., & Gillin, J. C. REM sleep induction by physostigmine infusion during sleep in normal volunteers. *Science*, 1976, *191*, 1281–1283.

Skinner, B. F. *Verbal behavior.* New York: Appleton-Century-Crofts, 1957.

Slater, E. In P. Laslett (Ed.), *The physical basis of mind.* Oxford: Blackwell, 1957.

Snyder, F. The phenomenology of dreaming. In L. Madow & L. H. Snow (Eds.), *The psychodynamic implications of the physiological studies on dreams.* Springfield, Ill.: Charles C Thomas, 1970.

Sours, J. A., Frumkin, P., & Indermill, R. R. Somnambulism. *Archives of General Psychiatry* (Chicago), 1963, *9*, 400–413.

Spelke, E., Hirst, W., & Neisser, U. Skills of divided attention. *Cognition*, 1976, *4*, 215–230.

Sperling, M. Pavor nocturnus. *Journal of the American Psychoanalytic Association*, 1958, *VI*, 1, 79–94.

Sperry, R. W. Lateral specialization of cerebral function in the surgically separated hemispheres. In F. J. McGuigan & R. A. Schoonover (Eds.), *The psychophysiology of thinking: Studies of covert processes.* New York: Academic Press, 1973.

Spitta, H. *Die traumzustande der menschlichen seele.* Doctoral dissertation, Tubingen, 1873.

Stein, M. Self observation, reality, and the super-ego. In R. Loewenstein, L. Newman, M. Schur & A. Solnit (Eds.), *Psychoanalysis: A general psychology: Essays in honor of Heinz Hartmann.* New York: Universities Press, Inc., 1966.

Stekel, W. *Der willie zum schlaf.* Wiesbaden: Bergmann, 1915.

Stevens, J. R. An anatomy of schizophrenia. *Archives of General Psychiatry*, 1973, *29*, 177–189.

Stevenson, J. H. Effect of posthypnotic dissociation on the performance of interfering tasks. *Journal of Abnormal Psychology*, 1976, *85*, 398–407.

Stoyva, J. M. Finger electromyographic activity during sleep: Its relation to dreaming in deaf and normal subjects. *Journal of Abnormal Psychology*, 1965, *70*, 343–349. (a)

Stoyva, J. M. Posthypnotically suggested dreams and the sleep cycle. *Archives of General Psychiatry*, 1965, *12*, 287–294. (b)

Stoyva, J. M., & Kamiya, J. Electrophysiological studies of dreaming as the prototype of a new strategy in the study of consciousness. *Psychological Review*, 1968, *75*, 192–205.

Stransky, E. *Uber sprachverwirtheit.* Marhold: Halle, 1905.

Sullivan, H. S. *Clinical studies in psychiatry.* New York: Norton, 1956.

Symonds, J. A. *Sleep and dreams.* London: Murray, 1851.

Szabó, L., & Waitsuk, P. Society proceedings, sectia de EEG si neurofiziologie clinica a uniunii societatilor de stiinte medicale din Republica Socialista Romania. In *Electroencephalogy and Clinical Neurophysiology*, 1971, *31*, 5, 522.

Tachibana, M., Tanaka, K., Hishikawa, Y., & Kaneko, Z. A sleep study of acute psychotic states due to alcohol and meprobamate addiction. In E. D. Weitzman (Ed.), *Advances in sleep research* (Vol. 2). New York: Spectrum Publications, 1976.

Talland, G. A. A microgenetic approach to the amnestic syndrome. *Journal of Abnormal Psychology*, 1960, *61*, 255–262.

Tani, K., Yoshu, N., Yoshino, I., & Kobayashi, E. Electroencephalographic study of parasomnia: Sleep-talking, enuresis and bruxism. *Physiology and Behavior*, 1966, *1*, 241–243.

Tart, C. *Personal communication*, July 15, 1974.

Tebbs, R. B. *Post-awakening visualization performances as a function of anxiety level, REM or NREM sleep, and time of night.* U.S. Air Force Academy, Colorado, 1972. SRL-TR-72-0005 AD-738-630.

Tec, L. Imipramine for nightmares. *Journal of the American Medical Association*, 1974, *228*, 978.

Teplitz, S. The ego and motility in sleep-walking. *Journal of the American Psychoanalytical Association*, 1958, *6*, 95–110.

Tharp, B. R. *Narcolepsy and epilepsy.* In C. Guilleminault, P. Passaunt & W. C. Dement (Eds.), *Narcolepsy.* New York: Spectrum, 1976.

Thomas, C. B., & Pederson, L. A. Psychobiological studies. II. Sleep habits of healthy young adults with observations on levels of cholesterol and circulating eosinophils. *Journal of Chronic Disease*, 1963, *16*, 1099–1114.

Tissie, P. *Les rêves.* Paris: Alcan, 1898.

Tolman, E. C. *Purposive behavior in animals and men.* New York: Appleton-Century-Crofts, 1932.

Townsend, U. E., Johnson, L. C., Naitoh, P., & Muzet, A. F. Heart rate preceding motility in sleep. *Psychophysiology*, 1975, *12*, 217–219.

Tracy, R. L., & Tracy, L. N. Reports of mental activity from sleep stages 2 and 4. *Perceptual and Motor Skills*, 1974, *38*, 647–648.

Treisman, A. M. Strategies and models of selective attention. *Psychological Review*, 1969, *76*, 282–299.

Trömner, E. Motorische schlafstörungen. *Deutsch. Z. Nervenhelk*, 1911, *41*, 257. (a)

Trömner, E. Über motorische schlafstörungen. *Z. Ges. Neurol. Psychiat. Originalien*, 1911, *4*, 228. (b)

Tuke, D. H. *Sleep-walking and hypnotism.* London: Churchill, 1884.

Tuke, D. H. (Ed.). *Dictionary of psychological medicine* (2 Vols.). Philadelphia: Balkiston, 1892.

Tulving, E. Episodic and semantic memory. In E. Tulving & W. Donaldson (Eds.), *Organization of memory.* New York: Academic Press, 1972.

Undeutsch, U. Die actualgenese in ihrer algemeinpsychologischen und ihrer charakterlogischen bedeutung. *Scientia*, 1942, 72, 37–42, 95–98.

Valian, V. V. Talk, talk, talk: A selective critical review of theories of speech production. In R. Freedle (Ed.), *Discourse production and comprehension. 1.* Norwood, N.J.: Ablex, 1977.

Van Valen, L. A note on dreams. *Journal of Biological Psychiatry*, 1973, 15, 19.

Vaschide, N., & Pieron, H. *La psychologie du rêve au point de vue medical.* Paris: Bailliere, 1902.

Verdone, P. Temporal reference of manifest dream content. *Perceptual and Motor Skills*, 1965, 20, 1253–1268.

Viscott, D. S. Chlordiazepoxide and hallucinations. *Archives of General Psychiatry*, 1968, 19, 370–376.

Vogel, G., Barrowclough, B., & Giesler, D. Limited discriminability of REM and sleep onset reports and its psychiatric implications. *Archives of General Psychiatry*, 1972, 26, 449–455.

Vogel, G. W. Mentation reported from naps of narcoleptics. In C. Guilleminault, P. Passouant, & W. C. Dement (Eds.), *Narcolepsy.* New York: Spectrum, 1976.

Vogel, G. W. Sleep-onset mentation. In A. M. Arkin, J. S. Antrobus & S. J. Ellman (Eds.), *The mind in sleep.* Hillsdale, N.J.: Lawrence Erlbaum Associates, 1978.

Vogl, M. Sleep disturbances of neurotic children. In E. Harms (Ed.), *Problems of sleep and dream in children.* New York: Pergamon Press-MacMillan, 1964.

Vygotsky, L. S. *Thought and language.* Cambridge: MIT Press, 1962.

Waelder, J. Analyse eines falles von pavor nocturnus. *Z. Psychoanal. Padagojik*, 1935, 9, 5.

Waelder, R. The principle of multiple function. *Psychoanalytic Quarterly*, 1936, 5, 45–62.

Wallis, H. *Masked epilepsy.* Edinburgh: Linginstone, 1956.

Walsh, W. S. Dreams of the feebleminded. *Med. Rec. Ann.* (Houston), 1920, 97, 395–398. (a)

Walsh, W. S. *The psychology of dreams.* New York: American University, 1920. (b)

Warren, R. M. Verbal transformation effect and auditory perceptual mechanisms. *Psychological Bulletin*, 1968, 70, 261–270.

Watt, H. J. *The common sense of dreams.* Worcester, Mass.: Clark University Press, 1929.

Werner, H. *Comparative psychology of mental development* (2nd ed.). Chicago: Follett, 1948.

Werner, H. Microgenesis and aphasia. *Journal of Abnormal Psychology*, 1956, 52, 347–353.

Werner, H., & Kaplan, B. *Symbol formation: An organismic developmental approach to language and the expression of thought.* New York: Wiley, 1963.

West, L. J. The dissociative reaction. In A. M. Freedman & H. J. Kaplan (Eds.), *Comprehensive textbook of psychiatry.* Baltimore: Williams & Wilkins, 1967.

West, L. J. A clinical and theoretical overview of hallucinatory phenomena. In R. K. Siegel & L. J. West (Eds.), *Hallucinations: Behavior, experience and theory.* New York: Wiley, 1975.

Whitaker, H. A. Is the grammar in the brain?: In D. Cohen (Ed.), *Explaining linguistic phenomena.* New York: Halsted Press, Wiley, 1974.

White, R. W., & Shevach, B. J. Hypnosis and the concept of dissociation. *Journal of Abnormal Psychology*, 1942, 37, 309–329.

Wile, I. S. Auto-suggested dreams as a factor in therapy. *American Journal of Orthopsychiatry*, 1934, 4, 449–463.

Williams, H. L. Cited by W. C. Dement (1965).

Williams, H. L. Information processing during sleep. In W. P. Koella & P. Levin (Eds.), *Sleep: Physiology, biochemistry, psychology, pharmacology, clinical implications.* Basel: S. Karger, 1973.

Williams, H. L., Morlock, H. C., Jr., & Morlock, J. V. Instrumental behavior during sleep. *Psychophysiology*, 1966, 2, 208–216.

Williams, R. L., Karacan, I., & Hursch, C. J. *Electroencephalography (EEG) of human sleep: Clinical applications.* New York: Wiley, 1974.

Williams, R., & Karacan, I. Sleep disorders and disordered sleep. In S. Arieti & M. F. Reiser (Eds.), *American handbook of psychiatry* (Vol. 4). New York: Basic Books, 1975.

Winer, B. J. *Statistical principles in experimental design*. New York: McGraw-Hill, 1962.

Winterstein, H. *Schlaf und traum* (2nd Aufl.). Berlin: Springer, 1953.

Wittgenstein, L. *Philosophical investigations*. Oxford: Blackwell; New York: MacMillan, 1953.

Wolpert, E. A. Studies in the psychophysiology of dreaming. II. An electromyographic study. *Archives of General Psychiatry*, 1960, 2, 231–241.

Zetlin, V. W. In preface to D. McGregor, *The dream world of Dion McGregor*. New York: Geis, 1964.

Ziehen, T. *Die geisteskrankheiten in kindes alter*. Berlin: Reuther & Reichard, 1926.

Zorick, F., Roth, T., Kramer, M., & Flessa, H. Intensification of daytime sleepiness by lymphoma. *Sleep Research*, 1977. (Brain Information Service, Brain Research Institute, University of California, Los Angeles.)

Author Index

Italics denote pages with bibliographic information.

A

Aarons, L., 197, 199, 200, 208, 209, 297, 323, *589*
Abe, K., 13, 23, 27, 33, 46, *589*
Adey, W. R., 84, *596*
Adler, A., 268, *589*
Adrien, J., 368, *591*
Agnew, H. W., Jr., 208, *589*
Aird, R. B., 14, 20, 21, 27, *589*
Altman, L. L., 244, *589*
Andriani, G., 12, 13, 14, 33, 90, 92, 99, 103, 107, 275, 276, 376, *589*
Antrobus, J. S., 9, 24, 53, 55, 100, 112, 158, 191, 193, 203, 226, 254, 274, 291, 297, 306, 353, 375, *589*, *590*, *595*
Arkin, A. M., 9, 12, 24, 25, 40, 47, 48, 52, 53, 58, 59, 61, 62, 63, 65, 66, 67, 71, 87, 93, 97, 100, 112, 114, 115, 130, 131, 141, 154, 156, 191, 192, 193, 196, 200, 205, 208, 216, 226, 227, 228, 230, 232, 235, 237, 239, 254, 255, 258, 269, 274, 280, 281, 297, 306, 324, 327, 338, 350, 353, 355, 358, 367, 368, 375, *589*, *590*, *591*, *595*
Arlow, J. A., 256, 257, 274, *591*
Ascher, E., 352, *591*
Asgian, B., 53, *605*
Ayer, A. J., 313, *591*

B

Baekeland, F., 195, 208, *591*
Baker, J., 47, 114, 193, 226, 227, 353, 367, *590*, *591*
Bakwin, H., 370, *591*
Bakwin, R. M., 370, *591*
Balkanyi, C., 250, *591*
Balogh, A., 57, *598*
Bañuelos, M., 12, 14, 33, 90, 213, 278, *591*
Barber, B., 321, 322, *591*
Barr, R. M., 296, *594*
Barros-Ferreira, M. de, 14, *591*
Barrowclough, B., 126, *609*
Basden, B., 145, *593*
Basden, D., 145, *593*
Bates, D. E., 321, *598*
Batson, H. W., 25, 67, 87, 95, 190, 191, 241, 242, 283, 310, *590*, *591*
Baudry, F., 107, 108, 245, 249, 251, 264, *591*
Belcher, M. O., 34, *592*
Benoit, O., 368, *591*
Benson, D. F., 354, *597*

Subject Index